Goren's Bridge Complete

BY Charles H. Goren

GOREN'S BRIDGE COMPLETE

GOREN'S NEW CONTRACT BRIDGE COMPLETE

CONTRACT BRIDGE COMPLETE

CONTRACT BRIDGE MADE EASY: A SELF-TEACHER

CONTRACT BRIDGE IN A NUTSHELL

THE STANDARD BOOK OF BIDDING

BETTER BRIDGE FOR BETTER PLAYERS

Goren's
Bridge Complete

A major revision of the standard
work for all bridge players

Charles H. Goren

BARRIE & JENKINS
London

GOREN'S BRIDGE COMPLETE © 1963, BY *Chancellor Hall Ltd.*
Copyright © 1942, 1944, 1947, 1951, 1957 by Charles H. Goren
All Rights Reserved
Printed in the United States of America

First published in Great Britain 1964
by Barrie & Jenkins Ltd.
2 Clement's Inn, London, WC2
Reprinted 1967, 1971
ISBN 0 214 15603 6

Printed in Great Britain by
Lowe & Brydone (Printers) Ltd.,
London, N.W.10

Contents

Contents

Contents

A*

Contents

Goren's Bridge Complete

1.

Opening bids

IN DEVOTING a considerable amount of time to the subject of opening bids, an author runs the risk of displeasing his reader, who may feel that a patronizing attitude is being adopted toward him. Students sometimes think that nothing more is required than to count up the hand and look for a biddable suit. But it is not as simple as all that, for the opening bid sometimes presents interesting problems even to the more experienced players.

The first question to dispose of is what scale of valuation to employ in these discussions. For many years the Honor Trick Table had been given top billing. But it will be seen that time marches on, and the honor trick, after twenty years of service, was at long last forced out of business. Valuation by point count has captured the fancy of bridge players throughout the world. The ease with which it can be applied and the greater accuracy that can be achieved in this manner account for its unprecedented popularity.

Various point counts have from time to time been offered to the public by the prophets of bridge. It is significant that the only one which survived is the

4–3–2–1

and it is the one upon which this system is based. The reason for its survival is to be found in its simplicity (there are 10 points in each suit), and the use of fractions, a mental hazard to most students, has been avoided.

THE POINT COUNT TABLE
(Table of High Cards)

Ace . . . . 4 points
King . . . . 3 points
Queen . . . . 2 points
Jack . . . . 1 point

The pack contains **40 points**.   An average hand contains **10 points**.

Unguarded Honors: Singleton honors other than the Ace lose a considerable part of their value by reason of being unprotected. In valuing your hand for the opening bid, therefore, if you have a singleton King, reduce it in value from 3 to 2. If you have a singleton Queen, reduce it in value from 2 to 1, and if you have a singleton Jack, treat it as a singleton spot card.

The Queen and the Jack when accompanied by only one small card should also be reduced in valuation by a point. This applies only to opening suit bids. Observe, however, that J x x receives its full value.

Deduct 1 point for an aceless hand.

Add 1 point for possession of all four aces.

26 points will normally produce game. (For a minor-suit game 29 points will be required.)

33 points will normally produce a small slam.

37 points will normally produce a grand slam.

The value of any hand for the purpose of making an opening bid is ascertained by adding the high-card point count to the points assigned for distribution.

Distribution points are as follows:[1]

Add 3 points for a void

Add 2 points for each singleton

Add 1 point for each doubleton

A quick or defensive trick is one which will probably win even though the opponents play the hand. In order to qualify as quick it must be able to win on the first two rounds. Here is the table of quick tricks:

2 QUICK TRICKS	1½ QUICK TRICKS	1 QUICK TRICK	½ QUICK TRICK
A K	A Q	A	K x
		K Q	

Requirements for opening suit Bids of 1

If your hand is worth 13 points, it rates as an optional opening. Whether or not you should open depends upon the ease with which you will be able to make your second bid, if necessary.

With hands of the 13-point class, be sure you have two quick (defensive) tricks.

If your hand is worth 14 points, it *must* be opened.

[1] This is the distributional count for declarer's hand; that is, when you are naming your own suit. Do not confuse it with the distributional count for "dummy hands" when you are raising partner. See page 41.

Biddable Suits

A four-card major suit is biddable if it contains 4 high-card points. Greater liberties may be taken in opening with a minor suit. Any five-card suit is biddable.

For example, these are biddable suits:

A x x x   K J x x   Q J 10 x [2]   10 x x x x

Rebiddable Suits

A rebiddable suit is one which may be bid a second time without partner's having supported it. The first requirement is that it must contain at least five cards. A four-card suit should not be rebid if partner has not raised it. If partner supports your four-card suit, you may rebid it as many times as your hand warrants. Not all five-card suits are rebiddable. Even a five-card suit should have solidity in order to be rebid. The following suits are rebiddable:

A K x x x[2]   A J x x x   K Q x x x
K J 9 x x   Q J 9 x x   x x x x x x

It will be noted that any six-card suit, regardless of its top strength, is rebiddable.

Deciding when to open the bidding

The table for opening bids has been offered above for your use. However, it is expected that you will regard it as your servant, not your master.

It is to be borne in mind that an opening bid is not an isolated event. It is the first step in a campaign and it is imperative to look one step ahead and contemplate what your partner is most likely to bid in response. You must then have a clear idea of what your second bid will be. If that second bid is going to cause you embarrassment, you have made an error. Either you should not have opened or you opened the bidding with the wrong suit. This, in plain language, sums up the principle of preparedness.

It is appropriate at this time to refer to the universally accepted convention known as the New-Suit-Forcing Principle, which is:

If you open the bidding with one of a suit and partner responds with some other suit, you are obliged to speak once more.

[2] A mild exception is to be noted in the case of Q J 10 x.

This is an obligation that rests only on the person who *opens* the bidding. It does not apply to anyone else at the table. (Nor does it apply when partner has previously passed.) This principle applies only to the showing of a new suit. If the opener bids 1 Spade, for example, and partner responds with 1 No Trump, the opener need not bid again, nor need the opener bid again if partner makes a simple raise from 1 to 2 in the same suit.

It has many times been suggested that no opening bid should be made unless the hand contains a rebid. That is essentially true, but let us see if we can clarify this rule by examining a few cases.

You deal and hold:

♠ A K J x   ♡ x x x   ◇ A x x   ♣ x x x

Our Pilgrim Fathers, assaying this hand, would have found that it contained three-plus honor tricks and a biddable suit. The impulse to bid would therefore have been irresistible. When partner responded to the Spade bid with 2 Hearts, the fun was over. No rebid was available that made a grain of sense. They couldn't rebid the four-card Spade suit; they couldn't raise the Hearts, and they couldn't, without complete disregard of sound economy, bid 2 No Trump, and to pass would be in violation of a sacred commitment. This situation should have been foreseen, and the solution would have been found in an original pass.

Observe how the point count would have done their thinking for them. This hand is worth only 12 points, and such hands must not be opened.

Permit me to change this hand slightly, retaining exactly the same high-card count:

♠ A K x x   ♡ A J 10 x   ◇ x x   ♣ x x x

Let us assume that you open with 1 Spade and your partner responds with 2 Diamonds. You are in a position to rebid by calling 2 Hearts. This permits partner to return to 2 Spades if he chooses. If partner's response happens to be 2 Hearts, you may pull yourself together and offer him a single raise. In any case, you have not been called upon to perform a painful task, yet you have discharged your obligation to rebid. Examine this hand in the light of point count. It has the value of 13 points, 12 in high cards and 1 for distribution. This renders it an optional opening, an option which one may exercise, if he regards himself as reasonably competent. This hand offers the convenience of a rebid in the second suit.

♠ K 10 x x x   ♡ A K J x   ◇ x x   ♣ x x

This hand may be opened because it is worth 13 points and has a convenient rebid of 2 Hearts when partner names a new suit.

Some players make a distinction between the requirements for vulnerable and non-vulnerable openings. Except in cases of pre-empts, I do not subscribe to that practice. If you think a hand calls for an opening bid, vulnerability ought not to deter you from opening.

♠ K Q 10 x x x   ♡ A x   ◇ Q x x   ♣ x x

This hand should be opened. It is worth 13 points and has a good convenient rebid. Note that all minimum opening bids must contain two defensive tricks. This hand meets with the requirement.

♠ A 10 9 x x   ♡ K Q 10 x   ◇ Q 10 x   ♣ x

This hand is valued at 13 points, contains two defensive tricks, and, since it contains nine cards in the major suits, we would prefer not to pass. It has a convenient rebid of 2 Hearts.

♠ K J x x   ♡ K 10 x x   ◇ x   ♣ A J x x

This hand is worth 14 points and is a mandatory opening of 1 Club.

Third-hand bidding

If a hand meets with the requirements of an opening bid, it may be opened in any position at the table. In fact, when you contemplate opening in third position, you may do so with a little less if you have a fairly good suit. The requirements are lower by 2 points, so that you may open in this position with 11 points, or sometimes even 10 if you have a very good suit. The following hand, which is worth 11 points, should be opened with 1 Heart in third position:

♠ Q x x   ♡ A K J x x   ◇ x x   ♣ x x x

When partner responds, there is no obligation to rebid.

Bids of this type have splendid defensive value, for if partner happens to have the opening lead, surely the best line of defense would have been indicated to him. However, some hands worth even more than 11 points should not be opened for lack of a good suit.

With the following hand I would prefer a pass:

♠ A x x x   ♡ A x x   ◇ A x x   ♣ x x x

The Short Club bid

This is not a system. It is a convenience. I make this point because so many players are heard to inquire, "Partner, do you play the Short Club?" as though referring to some special convention. They explain that they open with a Club to show three tricks. And what, pray, do you bid with

♠ K x x   ♡ x x   ◇ x x   ♣ A K Q 10 x x

Of course the answer is 1 Club.

The point of the Short Club is this: There are certain hands which must be opened because they contain more high cards than we are inclined to pass. Some of these hands offer no convenient opening because they would present a difficult rebidding problem. In such cases an opening bid of 1 Club is recommended on a three-card suit if it is headed by at least a Queen. For example:

♠ A K J x   ♡ J 10 x   ◇ x x x   ♣ A J x

This hand contains somewhat more than 14 points and therefore must not be passed. However, if you should make the normal opening bid of 1 Spade, it is evident that you will have no convenient rebid should partner respond with 2 Diamonds. For your own personal convenience this hand should be opened with 1 Club. If partner's response is 1 Spade, you raise to 2. If the response is 1 No Trump, you pass, and if his response is 2 Clubs, you should also pass.

This bid of 1 Club is made not *because* your Club holding is short, but *in spite of it*. It is a practice devised strictly for the convenience of the opener and it should be no concern of partner. He should treat all Club bids as though they were natural bids, being careful, however, not to raise Clubs without four good trumps. This subjects him to no hardship, since it is so easy to find some other bid at the level of 1.

There is another type of hand which should be opened with 1 Club:

♠ Q 10 x x   ♡ K x x x   ◇ 10 x   ♣ A K x

This meets the minimum requirements. However, it must not be opened with 1 of a major, because neither suit is biddable. A Club opening may be conveniently employed in this case. If partner responds with a major, that suit is raised. If partner responds with 1 Diamond, a rebid is available in one of the major suits.

When there is no occasion to worry about a rebid, a hand like this one, previously shown:

♠ A K J x   ♡ J 10 x   ◇ x x x   ♣ A J x

need not be opened with 1 Club.

When is there no occasion to worry about a rebid? When your partner has previously passed and, for that reason, you are persuaded that there is no more than a part score in the hand. In third position, for example, the proper opening with the above hand is 1 Spade, since you are trying for a part score and intend to pass any bid that partner makes.

Bidding more than one suit

When a hand contains more than one biddable suit, there is often a question as to the sequence in which they should be shown. While general principles may be laid down to cover the vast majority of hands, nevertheless there remains a considerable number of cases in which the exercise of sound judgment will be required. As is usual in such cases, the decision involves looking one step ahead in the bidding. Let us examine a few of the basic principles.

Length of suit is one of the prime considerations. When you hold two five-card suits, the higher-ranking (not necessarily the stronger) should be bid first.

♠ Q 10 x x x   ♡ A K x x x   ◇ K x   ♣ x

The proper opening bid is 1 Spade, not 1 Heart, although the Heart suit is stronger. When Hearts are shown on the next round, partner will have the option of returning to the first suit without increasing the contract.

As a general rule, with two suits of unequal length the longer is bid first.

♠ A K Q x   ♡ A J x x x   ◇ K x x   ♣ x

The proper opening bid is 1 Heart. When you bid Spades on the next round, partner will recognize that you have only four of them. There are certain exceptions to this principle which will be discussed later. (See pp. 13–14.)

Similarly, holding a 6-5 distribution, the six-card suit is shown first regardless of rank, but the subsequent bidding is developed in a somewhat different manner:

♠ x   ♡ A K x x x   ◇ A Q J x x x   ♣ x

You open the bidding with 1 Diamond, partner responds with 1 Spade. You next bid 2 Hearts. At this point, partner is under the impression that you have five Diamonds and four Hearts, but that impression will soon be corrected. Over your 2 Heart bid, let us assume that responder rebids his Spades. Now there may be a temptation to bid 3 Diamonds, but this should be stifled. The proper call is 3 Hearts. This will indicate that you have a five-card Heart suit, inasmuch as you have rebid it without support from partner. When your partner learns that you have five Hearts, he will realize that you must have six Diamonds, since with two five-card suits you would have shown the higher-ranking first.

Choice between two four-card suits

It is the hands that contain more than one four-card suit that seem to cause most concern.

Perhaps the simplest and most effective guide is the following: Look for the shortest suit in your hand (either singleton or doubleton) and bid first that suit which ranks below your singleton or doubleton. If the suit below is not biddable, select the next below that. To illustrate:

1. ♠ x x x   ♡ x x   ◇ A K J x   ♣ A Q J x

Here the shortest suit is Hearts. The suit ranking next below Hearts is Diamonds. The correct bid is 1 Diamond.

2. ♠ A K x x   ♡ x x x   ◇ x x   ♣ A Q J x

In this hand the shortest suit is Diamonds. The suit ranking next below is Clubs. The proper opening bid is 1 Club.

3. ♠ A K x x   ♡ A Q J x   ◇ x x x   ♣ x x

In this hand the shortest suit is Clubs. We must bid first the suit that ranks "next below" Clubs. Since there is no such suit, we start over, and the correct bid is 1 Spade.

4. ♠ x x x   ♡ A K x x   ◇ A Q J x   ♣ x x

In this hand the shortest suit is Clubs. The next suit below (for the purpose of this rule) is Spades, but since Spades are not biddable, we go to the next suit below that, and the proper bid is 1 Heart.

Let us take these four examples and see how conveniently this rule works out in practice.

In NO. 1 the opening bid is 1 Diamond. If partner responds with 1 Heart or 1 Spade, your rebid is 2 Clubs, permitting partner to return to 2 Diamonds. If partner responds with 2 Clubs, you are in a position to raise that suit.

In NO. 2 you open with 1 Club. If partner responds with either 1 Diamond or 1 Heart, your rebid is 1 Spade.

In NO. 3 the opening bid is 1 Spade. If partner bids 2 Hearts, you raise. If partner bids 2 Diamonds or 2 Clubs, you bid 2 Hearts, permitting partner to return to 2 Spades.

In NO. 4 the opening bid is 1 Heart. If partner bids either 1 Spade or 2 Clubs, your rebid is 2 Diamonds, permitting partner to return to 2 Hearts.

It will be seen, therefore, that in each case the rebid was very convenient, inasmuch as the second suit could be shown at a reasonable level and partner was permitted to return to the first suit at a level no higher than 2. That is the test.

Observe that if the wrong suit had been selected for the opening in any of these cases, it would have been impossible for partner to return to your original suit at the level of 2, and in case No. 2 it is quite apparent that if you open with 1 Spade, partner will be obliged to bid 2 of a red suit, which will force you immediately into the 3 zone if you choose to show your second suit.

The choice when holding three four-card suits

The same principle is followed when you have three four-card suits. Start with the suit immediately below your singleton.

The practical reason behind the rule is this: The probabilities favor partner's responding in your shortest suit, and this method renders your second bid more convenient.

♠ A K x x   ♡ A J 10 x   ◊ x   ♣ K J x x

The correct opening bid is 1 Club, the suit below the singleton. If partner responds with 1 Diamond, you rebid 1 Spade. If he then bids 2 Diamonds, you may bid 2 Hearts.

♠ A J x x   ♡ A Q x x   ◊ A J x x   ♣ x

The proper opening bid is 1 Spade. (Spades are considered to rank immediately below Clubs for the purpose of this rule.) If your partner responds with 2 Clubs, your next bid will be 2 Hearts, and if necessary or convenient, you may show the Diamonds later.

♠ A K J x   ♡ 10 x x   ◇ A Q J x   ♣ x x

Here the recommended bid is 1 Spade. Partner's most probable response is 2 Clubs, and your rebid will be 2 Diamonds, which will permit partner to return to 2 Spades if he chooses.

♠ A K J x   ♡ x x   ◇ A Q J x   ♣ 10 x x

With this hand the recommended bid is 1 Diamond. Partner is most likely to respond with 1 Heart, and you have the convenient rebid of 1 Spade, whereas had you opened with 1 Spade and partner responded with 2 Hearts, you would have been in an awkward position.

What happens, you will naturally ask, when partner does not act according to specifications and responds in an unexpected suit?

I agree that an awkward situation may develop, and you must extricate yourself in the cheapest possible manner, even though it involves a little tampering with the truth.

Look at the last hand again. You open with 1 Diamond, and partner responds, rudely enough, with 2 Clubs. You are sorry now that you did not open with 1 Spade, but it's too late to worry about that. What is the cheapest way to get out? Not by a bid of 2 Spades, because that makes it impossible for partner to return to 2 Diamonds. A raise to 3 Clubs is not desirable. The most practical solution is to tell a white lie about your Diamond suit. Rebid 2 Diamonds. At least partner will realize that you have not a strong opening bid. But, you will contend, a four-card suit is not rebiddable when unsupported by partner. You are quite right, and if you have a partner who is a stickler for technicalities, do not admit that you rebid the four-card suit. Slyly place a little Heart among your Diamonds and blame it on the bad lighting in the room. "I was almost sure I had five Diamonds." It's better to lie about a suit than about the strength of your hand as a whole.

With the hand before that, you opened with 1 Spade. Suppose partner responds with 2 Hearts. You are faced with a similar embarrassment. You may, if you choose, stretch a point and bid 3 Hearts; or you may engage in the same type of chicanery suggested above—misread your hand to see five Spades and rebid the suit.

In the majority of cases the recommended rule will work. One slight exception is suggested. Holding four Clubs and four Hearts, best results will, as a rule, be obtained by opening with 1 Club.

1. ♠ x x x   ♡ A Q x x   ◇ x x   ♣ A K x x

2. ♠ x x   ♡ A Q x x   ◇ x x x   ♣ A K x x

With NO. 1 the rule applies. Open 1 Club, the suit below the doubleton.

With NO. 2 the exception applies. The suit below the doubleton is Hearts, but it is better to open with 1 Club. If partner responds with 1 Diamond, the rebid is 1 Heart. If partner responds with 1 Spade, a slightly unnatural rebid of 1 No Trump should be resorted to, for a rebid of 2 Hearts, which makes it impossible for partner to return to 2 Clubs, would require a stronger hand than this. The objection to opening with 1 Heart is that partner might respond with 2 Diamonds, which would leave you in an awkward position.

Some exceptions

We come now to a few cases which are handled somewhat exceptionally:

OPENER	RESPONDER
♠ A K x x	♠ x x
♡ A Q x x	♡ K J x x x
◇ K Q 10 x	◇ J x x
♣ x	♣ x x x

The recommended rule for hands containing three four-card suits is to begin with that suit which ranks below the singleton. Under this rule, the opener's bid should be 1 Spade. But with a hand so rich in high cards, there is a slight risk involved in opening with 1 Spade, since partner may find it difficult to keep the bidding open. He may fear to show his suit at the level of 2. Observe how this works in the example shown. If the opening bid is 1 Spade, responder is obliged to pass; whereas had the opening bid been 1 Diamond, responder would have chanced a 1 Heart bid, whereupon the partnership would straightway have proceeded to game.

The exception to the rule may therefore be stated as follows: With 4-4-4-1 hands worth 20 points or more, where the normal opening should be 1 Spade, it is sound strategy to open with a minor suit to afford partner the opportunity to respond at the level of 1, since he probably has not a good hand.

Another type of hand which is managed exceptionally is the following:

♠ K x x x x   ♡ x   ◇ x x   ♣ A K J x x

The accepted rule is: With two five-card suits, bid first the higher-ranking. Following the rule would lead to discomfort with this hand. If you open with 1 Spade, partner will very likely respond with 2 in a red suit. Quite obviously you cannot afford to bid 3 Clubs. Your hand is not good enough. You are therefore forced to rebid the rather feeble Spade suit, which places you in a rather uncomfortable position.

The recommended procedure, therefore, is to open the bidding with 1 Club, as though your Spade suit were only four cards long. (For practical purposes, the Spade suit is not much better than a decent four-card suit.) When partner responds with one of the red suits, your rebid will be 1 Spade.

It is a good general policy to *treat any weak five-card suit as though it were a four-card suit,* for the purpose of arranging your sequence of bids.

A slightly different example:

♠ A K J x x ♡ x ◇ x x ♣ K x x x x

On hands of this type there is divided opinion. Some experts open this hand with 1 Club, so that both suits may be shown. Others prefer to open with 1 Spade, and over a response of 2 Diamonds or 2 Hearts, they rebid 2 Spades. The latter group, it will be seen, favors opening with the Spade suit if it is soundly rebiddable. They feel that it is no hardship to conceal the five-card Club suit. My own preference is for the latter view.

However, with hands of great strength, containing five Spades and five Clubs, a different type of problem arises. Where the hand is worth 20 points, partner may find it difficult to respond to a Spade bid (see pages 11 and 12). In such case it may be better tactics to open with 1 Club to facilitate partner's response. Spades should then be bid and rebid.

Reversing

It has been observed that with suits of unequal length you bid the longer first, regardless of rank. To this rule there are several exceptions, based entirely on expediency.

♠ A K J x ♡ K J x x x ◇ x x x ♣ x

How should you open this hand? Some players would bid 1 Heart, following the orthodox rule. But suppose partner's response is 2 Clubs. What then? If you wish to show your other suit, you must bid

2 Spades. This makes it impossible for your partner to return to 2 Hearts, and if he is forced to return to 3 Hearts, you may well be a little too high. The alternative—to rebid this questionable Heart suit, deliberately suppressing the Spades—is almost equally undesirable. Expediency therefore dictates that you deliberately misdescribe your hand for the sake of safety. You will originally treat the Hearts as though they were a four-card suit. In that case the proper opening would be 1 Spade. If partner responds with 2 Clubs, your rebid is 2 Hearts, which permits partner to return to 2 Spades if he chooses.

Let us examine a stronger hand:

♠ A Q 10 x   ♡ A K J x x   ◇ K x   ♣ x x

This is a very fine hand, and naturally your opening bid is 1 Heart. There is no necessity to misdescribe this hand. If partner bids 2 Diamonds, your rebid will be 2 Spades. It is true that this makes it impossible for your partner to return to 2 Hearts, but if partner is obliged to return to 3 Hearts, you are well prepared to play there. Your hand is sufficiently strong; it is worth 19 points, which is the requirement for a so-called reverse bid.

This sequence of bids—that is, Hearts first and then Spades (always showing more Hearts than Spades)—is technically known as a "reverse." This is a confusing term and is really a misnomer. Actually it is better to avoid the use of the expression. You will frequently hear people say, "Partner, you reversed. You showed a powerful hand." A better way to put it is this: Whenever you make it impossible for partner to return to 2 of your original suit, you should have a very good hand. Similarly, whenever you reach the level of 3 at your second bid, you should have a very good hand. That's all there is to it. There isn't any more!

♠ A J x x   ♡ A K J x x   ◇ x x x   ♣ x

The recommended opening bid with this hand is 1 Heart. If partner responds with 2 Clubs, you must not bid 2 Spades. That would make it impossible for partner to return to 2 Hearts, and might drive him to 3, for which you are not prepared. However, this is no hardship upon you, because you are in a position to make a very comfortable rebid of 2 Hearts.

Some players make it a practice to open hands like this with 1 Spade, in order to be able to show both suits. I do not approve of such practice. If you open with 1 Heart, there is only slight danger that the Spade suit will be lost, because if partner has four fairly good

Spades, he will be willing to show that suit. Another objection to opening with 1 Spade and later showing the Hearts is that partner will be under the impression that he is asked to choose between two more or less equal suits, in which case he may prefer Spades with approximately equal strength in Hearts.

To put the exception into the form of a rule: On hands of moderate strength with a five-card suit and a four-card suit which are next-door neighbors (Spades and Hearts, Hearts and Diamonds, Diamonds and Clubs), if the high-ranking suit is a *good* four-card suit, treat the second suit as though it were of equal length with the other. A few more illustrations:

♠ A K x x   ♡ Q J 10 x x   ◇ Q x   ♣ Q x

Bid 1 Spade, reserving 2 Hearts as a rebid.

♠ x x   ♡ A Q J x   ◇ K 10 9 x x   ♣ K x

Bid 1 Heart, reserving 2 Diamonds as a rebid.

♠ x x   ♡ x x   ◇ A K Q x   ♣ A 10 x x x

Bid 1 Diamond, reserving 2 Clubs as a rebid.

Players who have learned the above exception sometimes apply it improperly to a case such as this:

♠ A Q 10 x   ♡ x x   ◇ A Q J x x   ♣ x x

I have seen them open this hand with 1 Spade. This is highly improper. If they get a 2 Heart response, they are cornered. It is necessary for them to bid 3 Diamonds, and the hand is not good enough to rebid at that level. Such a bid should be based on a hand that is worth at least 19 points. The proper opening bid is 1 Diamond. If partner responds with 1 Heart, the rebid will be 1 Spade. If partner instead responds with 2 Clubs, it is not permissible to bid 2 Spades, because that makes it impossible for partner to return to 2 Diamonds; but the opener is not embarrassed, for he may conveniently rebid 2 Diamonds.

Let us take one or two more cases which involve looking ahead:

♠ A K x x   ♡ K J x   ◇ K 10 x x x   ♣ x

The orthodox opening bid is 1 Diamond. However, a brief glance into the future will warn of a possible 2 Club response. What would then be the rebid? Surely not 2 No Trump; and a rebid of 2 Spades would make it impossible for partner to return to 2 Diamonds. This hand is not strong enough to warrant such action. An exception should therefore be made in the interest of convenience, and the recommended opening bid is 1 Spade, which will take care of all responses. If partner bids 2 Hearts or 2 Diamonds, you have a good raise. If partner bids 2 Clubs, you will bid 2 Diamonds, permitting a return to 2 Spades if necessary.

If we transpose the Hearts and Clubs in the above hand:

♠ A K x x   ♡ x   ◇ K 10 x x x   ♣ K J x

Here again it is desirable to look into the future. We must not open with 1 Spade, because we will have no convenient rebid over 2 Hearts. The orthodox opening bid of 1 Diamond is therefore proper. If partner responds 1 Heart, we naturally rebid 1 Spade; if he responds 2 Clubs, our Club support gives us some assurance against immediate trouble whether we choose to raise the Clubs or stretch a point and bid 2 Spades.

As indicated above, the term "reverse" has been responsible for a great deal of confusion. A certain number of players make it a practice to go deliberately out of their way to "reverse" in order to show a good hand. I have seen the following strange phenomenon:

♠ K Q J 10 x   ♡ A K J x x   ◇ K x   ♣ x

Players holding this hand have actually been known to open with 1 Heart so that they could bid Spades later and "by reversing indicate a good hand." This borders on the absurd. There is no occasion to distort this hand. The opening bid should be 1 Spade, and on the next round a jump is made in Hearts to show the overpowering strength.

To summarize: A poor hand must sometimes be bid abnormally to avoid reaching a dangerously high level. With good hands we need not fear high levels, and such hands should be bid normally.

To repeat: All good hands should be bid naturally.

Opening 2 bids (in a suit)

Occasionally a player will hold a hand so powerful that game can be scored even though partner has little or nothing. He cannot afford to open with a game bid because he may desire partner's co-operation in an effort to discover the hand's possibilities, yet he cannot risk opening with a bid of 1, lest partner pass the hand out. The opening bid of 2 in a suit is employed in these cases to demand an eventual game contract. Partner is forced to respond and to *keep responding* until a game contract has been reached, no matter how empty a hand he may hold.

If the point count had accomplished nothing else, it would have justified its existence by reason of having simplified the problem of what constitutes an opening demand bid. The 5½ honor trick superstition which was born in the darkness of the early thirties has persisted for almost a generation, and despite the evil that it is known to have wrought, some players will carry it with them to the tomb.

Inasmuch as an opening 2 bid demands a game even with a trickless partner, the opener must *all but* have that game in his own hand. We used to say, "within a trick of game-in-hand," provided the hand contained at least four quick tricks.

Let us try it with point count. It takes 26 points to make a major-suit game. The opening 2 bidder with a normal hand (that is, one containing a five-card suit) should have 25 of those points in his own hand.

Let us examine a few illustrations:

A. ♠ A K Q J x x x   ♡ A x x   ♢ A x   ♣ x

Bid 2 Spades. You have nine certain winners. In other words, you have within a trick of a lay-down game in your own hand. Partner might not respond to a bid of 1 Spade, and yet an odd King or even an odd Queen might produce your tenth trick.

B. ♠ A K J   ♡ A K J x x   ♢ A   ♣ K Q 10 x

Bid 2 Hearts. Unless you run into extremely hard luck, you should not lose more than four tricks on this hand, which places you within a trick of game-in-hand.

C. ♠ A K x x   ♡ A K x x   ♢ x   ♣ A K x x

Bid 1 Club. This hand contains 23 points but is nowhere near an opening 2 bid. There are too many losing tricks. The correct opening is 1 Club. If partner is unable to respond, then be quite sure that no game will be missed.

Here is the formula:

> With a good five-card suit—25 points.
> With a good six-card suit—23 points.
> With a good seven-card suit—21 points.
> With a second good five-card suit, 1 point less is needed.
> If the game is to be in a minor suit, 2 points more will be needed.

HAND A, shown above, has a seven-card suit and is worth 21 points, 18 in high cards and 3 for distribution (2 for the singleton and 1 for the doubleton).

HAND B is worth 27 points, 25 in high cards and 2 for distribution.

HAND C is worth only 23 points and does not qualify for a demand bid.

In valuing your hand for the purpose of making an opening demand bid, you should assume that partner's hand is worthless. Unguarded honors should therefore not be relied upon. Holdings of Q x or J x should not be included among your assets for the purpose of the opening 2 bid.

Responses to 2 bids (suit)

The opening bid of 2 in a suit is unconditionally forcing to game. Responder must bid even with a blank hand and must keep on bidding, no matter how many calls it takes, until a final game contract is reached (or the opponents have been doubled).

With a weak hand the conventional response is 2 No Trump, regardless of distribution. Here is a 2 No Trump response to an opening 2 Diamond bid:

♠ 10 x x x x x   ♡ x   ◇ x x x   ♣ 10 x x

But where responder has definite values, he makes what is known as a positive response. *My policy is to make a good, old-fashioned natural response first,* and then show Aces and Kings individually at a later stage in the bidding, after the eventual trump suit has been determined.

The trump suit becomes established if responder raises it. It also becomes established if the opening 2 bidder rebids his suit. In that case it should be accepted as trump, and responder should not thereafter experiment with some new suit of his own.

The natural response may take the form of a simple raise, a simple take-out into a good biddable suit, or a response of 3 No Trump (this is to distinguish it from the negative response of 2 No Trump).

How much does responder need to make a positive response? The minimum requirement is 7 points (including high cards and distribution) if responder's hand contains one quick trick. But if the hand contains only ½ quick trick, then responder should have 8 points to justify a positive response. If the hand contains less than ½ quick trick, responder must make the negative response of 2 No Trump first, and on a later round he may show his suit if he deems it expedient to do so.

The preferable response, when adequate trump support is held, is the single raise. It establishes the trump suit, sets opener's mind at ease on that score, and is the signal to start showing Aces and Kings.

Responder ought not to show weak suits in response to a 2 demand bid. His suit should be headed by at least the Queen Jack.

For example:

OPENER	RESPONDER
♠ A Q J	♠ K 10 x x x
♡ A K Q J 10 x	♡ x x x
◇ x x	◇ A x
♣ A x	♣ x x x

The bidding:

OPENER	RESPONDER
2 Hearts	2 Spades (1)
3 Hearts (2)	4 Diamonds (3)
7 Hearts (4) or 7 No Trump	

1. I have a hand containing at least 7 points and one quick trick, or 8 points and ½ quick trick. My suit is at least as good as five to the Queen Jack.

2. It is my purpose to establish Hearts as the agreed suit. I do not require trump support from you. You may now show any Aces you are fortunate enough to have.

3. I cannot deny that I have the Ace of Diamonds.

4. You've said enough. Thirteen tricks are in sight, thanks to the information that you have a biddable Spade suit which I know to be headed by the King.

OPENER	RESPONDER
♠ A K Q J x x	♠ 10 x x
♡ A x	♡ K 10 x x
◇ A K Q 10	◇ J x x
♣ x	♣ x x x

The bidding:

OPENER	RESPONDER
2 Spades	2 No Trump
3 Diamonds	3 Spades
4 Hearts	5 Hearts
6 Spades	

The double raise

The double raise is a special bid. It denies a strong hand. It describes one that contains good trump support, either Q x x x or five small, but no Ace, no King, and no singleton. It warns partner not to bid a slam unless all he needs is plenty of trump support. For example:

♠ J x x x x   ♡ x x   ◊ Q x x   ♣ x x x

Raise partner's 2 Spades to 4 Spades.

Partner opens 2 Hearts; you hold:

1. ♠ K J x x x	♡ x x	◊ K x x	♣ x x x
2. ♠ x x	♡ Q 10 x	◊ K Q x	♣ 10 9 x x x
3. ♠ Q x x	♡ x x	◊ A Q x	♣ J x x x x
4. ♠ A Q x x	♡ x x x	◊ K J x x	♣ x x

1. Bid 2 Spades. Your hand is worth 8 points and contains one quick trick.

2. Bid 3 Hearts. You have normal trump support and 8 points in support of Hearts. Your hand contains one quick trick.

3. Bid 3 No Trump. Your hand contains 9 high-card points. The Club suit is too weak to show.

4. Bid 2 Spades. You will eventually play at a slam, but there is no hurry. Get ready for an exchange of information.

Opening No Trump bids

Ace	4 points
King	3 points
Queen	2 points
Jack	1 point

The pack contains 40 points.

Add 1 point for any hand containing all the Aces.

> 26 points will normally produce 3 No Trump
> 33 points will normally produce 6 No Trump
> 37 points will normally produce 7 No Trump

In No Trump bidding, only high cards are assigned numerical value; no points are allowed for distribution, though it is recognized that a long suit is a decided asset and that games may be made with a point or two less when a good suit is held.[3] It is desirable, however, to keep the figure 40 as a constant, so that when you reach the conclusion that your side has 37 points, you know that it is mathematically impossible for the opposition to hold an Ace, inasmuch as their combined assets cannot amount to more than 3 points.

This is one of the principal reasons why the 10 is not included in the above table of valuation. When I originally presented this method to the public in 1935, I assigned the value of ½ to a 10, but in recent years I have reached the conclusion that it is better practice to avoid these fractions and to permit the 10s to sway you one way or the other on close hands. This has proved highly acceptable to the public, to whom fractions are a mental hazard.

The 1 No Trump opening bid

Requirements for an opening bid of 1 No Trump are:
1. The hand must contain a point count of 16, 17, or 18.[4]
2. The hand must be of balanced distribution, that is:

$$4–3–3–3$$
$$4–4–3–2$$
$$5–3–3–2$$

with the proviso that the doubleton should be headed by a high honor. The fact that the five-card suit happens to be a major is no bar to the No Trump bid.

3. At least three suits must be protected. The following holdings constitute protection in this sense:

A x   K x   Q x x   J x x x

Hands counting 19–21 are too strong for an opening 1 No Trump, and since they are not quite big enough for a 2 No Trump bid, they should be opened with one of a suit with the intention to jump in No Trump if partner responds.

---

[3] The requirement for raises to 2 and 3 No Trump are lowered by 1 point where responder has a good five-card suit.
[4] This makes it an easy design to memorize. Each category contains exactly 3 counts —16–17–18 (1 No Trump), 19–20–21 (too big for 1 No Trump), 22–23–24 (2 No Trump), 25–26–27 (3 No Trump).

The 2 No Trump opening bid

An opening bid of 2 No Trump must not be confused with an opening bid of 2 of a suit. The 2 No Trump bid is not forcing. If partner has nothing, he may pass.

The requirements are:
1. The point count must be 22, 23, or 24.
2. The hand must be of balanced distribution.
3. All four suits must be protected.

The 3 No Trump opening bid

The requirements are:
1. The point count must be 25, 26, or 27.
2. The hand must be of balanced distribution.
3. All four suits must be protected.

Examples:

1. ♠ Q J 10	♡ K x x	◊ A x x	♣ A K J x
2. ♠ K x x	♡ K Q x	◊ A x x	♣ A K J x
3. ♠ K x x	♡ A K x	◊ 10 9 x x	♣ A x x
4. ♠ A K J	♡ K Q x	◊ A J x	♣ K Q x x
5. ♠ A Q J x x	♡ A Q 10	◊ A J	♣ K J x
6. ♠ A K J	♡ K Q x	◊ A K J	♣ K Q J x

HAND 1. This is a maximum 1 No Trump bid. A balanced hand, containing 18 points.

HAND 2. This hand is too big for 1 No Trump. It contains 20 points and should be opened with 1 Club with the intention of jumping to 2 No Trump if partner responds with a one-over-one.

HAND 3. This hand should be opened with 1 Club. Though it has the proper distribution and has three suits protected, it contains only 14 points.

HAND 4. This balanced hand, with all suits protected and 23 points, should be opened with 2 No Trump.

HAND 5. Open 2 No Trump. The hand contains 22 points in high cards with four suits well protected. Possession of a five-card major suit does not bar an opening No Trump bid.

HAND 6. Open 3 No Trump. This is a maximum, containing 27 points. Hands that are any stronger than this should be opened either

B

with a 2 bid or with an opening bid of 4 No Trump, which announces a holding of 28 or 29 points and has no relationship to the Blackwood Convention.

Responses to opening No Trump bids

When partner opens with 1 No Trump you need not strain a point to keep the bidding open. There is no real danger of missing anything if you are able to perform the simple function of counting, for partner's hand is limited to 18 points. (Even an extra 10 or a fifth card in some suit might render an 18-point hand too big for 1 No Trump), so that if you have less than 8 points, don't concern yourself too deeply with the hand.

Responder must not lose sight of the fact that it takes approximately 26 points to produce game at No Trump. When a five-card suit is held, the chances for game are reasonable with 25 points.

When the partnership assets amount to 33 or 34 points, you have enough to warrant the undertaking of a slam contract. (In these cases no checking for Aces is necessary, since the enemy cannot have two Aces inasmuch as their high-card holding is limited to 6 or 7 points.)

A combined holding of 37 or 38 should yield a grand slam (the opposition cannot have an Ace inasmuch as they hold at most 2 or 3 points).

Responses to opening bids of 1 No Trump

Responses differ, depending upon the type of hand held by responder. It may be balanced or unbalanced. Let us first take up responses:

With balanced hands

Where responder holds a hand which is distributed 5-3-3-2, there is no advantage in showing the five-card suit if it is a minor. (With a major suit, responder has some options.) It is better to raise the No Trump if the required count is held. Here are the requirements.

With a balanced hand and less than 8 points, pass.

Raise to 2 No Trump with 8 or 9 points. (You may raise with 7 points if you have a good five-card minor suit.)

Raise to 3 No Trump with 10 to 14 points.

Raise to 4 No Trump with 15 or 16 points.

Raise to 6 No Trump with 17 or 18 points.

If you hold 19 or 20 points, a bid of 6 No Trump is not quite adequate. First make a jump shift to 3 of some suit and then follow up with 6 No Trump. Showing a suit and jumping to 6 No Trump is a little stronger action than just jumping to 6 No Trump.

Raise to 7 No Trump with 21 or more, for then your partnership is assured of at least 37 points.

The 2 Club convention (Stayman Convention)

In the early days of contract, the opening No Trump bid had become branded with a scarlet letter which it little deserved. "Approach" bidders had made a social outcast of this call by decreeing that no hand should be opened with 1 No Trump where an opening suit bid was available. They were somewhat reminiscent of the ascetic who chose to recline on a bed of nails. But there was some little method to their madness, for they found that by opening with No Trumps they were on numerous hands passing up the opportunity to play at a sound major-suit contract where each partner had the required number of trumps. They considered it expedient therefore to explore the suit possibilities of a hand first. The No Trump contract they contended, could wait, while suits might be lost in the rush. In adopting this policy, they lost many advantages to be derived from an opening bid of 1 No Trump. Not until late in the day did it dawn on some explorers that with proper management one could have the penny and the cake as well. They could retain the advantage of opening with 1 No Trump and yet hold the door open to an investigation of the major-suit possibilities.

This was accomplished in various ways. One was by the major-suit check-back. When responder raised to 2 No Trump, opener was expected to bid 3 Hearts or 3 Spades if his opening contained a four-card major suit. But this opportunity was lost where responder raised directly to 3 No Trump. Then came various types of probing responses, and it was found that the most effective manner of uncovering the required information was by the use of a 2 Club response, as an asking bid. Conventions of this type put in their appearances under assorted names, each with variations of its own. In the resulting confusion, one frequently couldn't see the forest for the trees.

The merits of such a device cannot be denied, but we are convinced that only when the convention is distilled down to its elements does it serve an over-all useful purpose. So here it is in basic English.

You open with 1 No Trump and partner responds 2 Clubs. This is an artificial bid and has no relationship to the Club suit itself. If partner happens to have Clubs, it is a mere coincidence. But the bid is forcing, and the opening No Trump bidder, if he has a four-card major suit, shows it at once. However, the four-card suit must be headed by at least the Queen. If the opening No Trumper has no four-card major, he makes the routine rebid of 2 Diamonds. This bid is artificial and has no relationship to the suit itself. If the opening bidder happens to have two four-card majors, he first shows the Spades, and if it is expedient to do so, he shows the Hearts later. Consequently if the opener's first rebid is 2 Hearts, he denies possession of a biddable Spade holding. But if his rebid is 2 Spades, it does not rule out a biddable Heart suit.

Therefore the use of this convention (also known as the "Stayman Convention") changes the nature of the responses, so that when the No Trump bidder's partner calls 2 Spades, 2 Hearts or 2 Diamonds, it is a sign of relative weakness (responder definitely holds less than 8 points in high cards) and requests the No Trump bidder to withdraw from the auction. There is an exception to be noted, when opener holds 18 points plus strong support for his partner's take-out, in which case he may offer a single raise. But in no circumstances may he take any other form of action.

This convention should have no effect upon the normal jump-shift responses to the opening bid. Holding:

$$\spadesuit \text{ A Q 10 x x} \qquad \heartsuit \text{ x} \qquad \diamondsuit \text{ A Q 10 x} \qquad \clubsuit \text{ x x x}$$

it is still proper for responder to bid 3 Spades, forcing to game. With this hand there is nothing to be gained by use of the convention. However, where responder has a hand of moderate strength which contains a reasonably good five-card major suit, he may be faced with a choice of trying for game in a major suit or at No Trump. Since a response of 2 Hearts or 2 Spades would announce weakness, he must first bid 2 Clubs, and, assuming opener's response to be 2 Diamonds, he then shows his five-card major. For example responder holds:

$$\spadesuit \text{ K J x x x} \qquad \heartsuit \text{ A x x} \qquad \diamondsuit \text{ x x x} \qquad \clubsuit \text{ 10 x}$$

After partner opens 1 No Trump, responder cannot be sure of the best final contract. It may be in No Trump or it could be in Spades. Responder therefore bids 2 Clubs, which forces partner to speak. If partner rebids 2 Diamonds (denying a four-card major), responder now bids 2 Spades. Note that this bid is not forcing. If opener has a bare 16 points with no special support for Spades, a pass is in order. However, the opening No Trump bidder should strive to make a further call with even the slightest excess value; leaning perhaps somewhat in favor of a raise. However, where a raise is not available and opener has anything above the minimum requirements, he may try 2 No Trump. Observe that where responder's hand is strong enough to insist upon a game, he should jump to 3 of his major suit, though he has previously made a 2 Club response.

Where responder has inquired for a four-card major by bidding 2 Clubs and has been met by the 2 Diamond rebid, he must not bid a four-card major of his own. In this sequence such a bid unconditionally promises a five-card suit. Holding four-card suits, he must, therefore, return to No Trump.

Let us examine a few illustrative cases. In each of the following you are South and the bidding has proceeded as indicated.

1. ♠ A J x   ♡ K Q x x   ◇ A Q 10   ♣ x x x

EAST	SOUTH	WEST	NORTH
1 Diamond	1 No Trump	Pass	2 Clubs
Pass	?		

Pass. Partner is showing a Club suit and a weak hand. The 2 Club Convention does not apply when your partner makes an overcall of 1 No Trump. The inference is that if partner were interested in either major he would have made a take-out double.

2. ♠ A Q x x   ♡ Q J x   ◇ A x x   ♣ K x x

SOUTH	WEST	NORTH	EAST
1 No Trump	Pass	2 Clubs	Pass
2 Spades	Pass	3 Spades	Pass
?			

Pass. You have a bare minimum and partner's raise is not forcing. With 10 points or more, he would have jumped to game himself.

3. ♠ A J x x   ♡ K x   ◇ K Q 10 x   ♣ K J x

SOUTH	WEST	NORTH	EAST
1 No Trump	Pass	2 Clubs	Pass
2 Spades	Pass	2 No Trump	Pass
?			

Bid 3 No Trump. Partner has indicated possession of 8 or 9 points. Your 17 points insures a minimum of 25 for the partnership. In situations of this type it is advisable to speculate on the other point.

4. ♠ A x x x   ♡ Q x   ♢ x   ♣ K J 10 x x x

NORTH	EAST	SOUTH
1 No Trump	Pass	?

Bid 3 Clubs. You have a very fine Club suit and sufficient high-card points to insist upon a game. There is no need to employ the 2 Club Convention. If partner has a Spade suit, he will be in position to show it voluntarily over your 3 Club bid.

5. ♠ Q J 10 x x x   ♡ x   ♢ A J 10 x   ♣ x x

NORTH	EAST	SOUTH
1 No Trump	Pass	?

Bid 4 Spades. The jump to game in a major shows a good six-card suit with less than 10 points in high cards.

6. ♠ K Q x x   ♡ A x x   ♢ x x x   ♣ J x x

NORTH	EAST	SOUTH
1 No Trump	Pass	?

Bid 3 No Trump. The 2 Club Convention should not be employed on 4-3-3-3 hands. Such holdings will usually produce as many tricks in No Trump as in a suit.

7. ♠ 10 x x x   ♡ A Q J x   ♢ A Q   ♣ K 10 x

SOUTH	WEST	NORTH	EAST
1 No Trump	Pass	2 Clubs	Pass
?			

Bid 2 Hearts. With both majors, normal procedure is to show Spades first. However, in the present instance, the Spade holding is not biddable. The opener, therefore, must bid 2 Hearts. To be biddable according to the provisions of this convention, the texture of the suit should be at least Q x x x. In rare instances J x x x may be shown.

8. ♠ x x x x x   ♡ x x x x   ♢ J x x   ♣ J

NORTH	EAST	SOUTH
1 No Trump	Pass	?

Pass. On hands this weak it is better to leave well enough alone. No situation is desperate if partner has not been doubled.

9. ♠ x x   ♡ J 10 x x   ♢ x x   ♣ A K 10 x x

NORTH	EAST	SOUTH
1 No Trump	2 Diamonds	?

Bid 2 No Trump. East's overcall prevents you from employing the 2 Club Convention. You have no recourse, therefore, but to offer the No Trump raise. When partner has opened with 1 No Trump you may raise without a stopper in the adverse suit, and should strain to do so in the circumstances. Partner is still in position to show a biddable Heart suit if he has one.

10. ♠ A Q x x   ♡ K x x x   ◊ x   ♣ Q x x x

NORTH	EAST	SOUTH
1 No Trump	2 Diamonds	?

Bid 3 Diamonds. On hands of game-going potential where the opponents have deprived you of the 2 Club bid, it is still possible to check back for a major-suit fit by means of a cue bid in the opponent's suit. If partner bids either 3 Hearts or 3 Spades you will raise to 4. If he bids 3 No Trump, you will accept that contract.

Responses to 2 No Trump opening bids

With balanced hands

With less than 4 points, pass.

With 4 to 8 points, raise to 3 No Trump. You know there is no slam, since the most partner can have is 24 points $(24 + 8 = 32)$.

With 9 points raise to 4 No Trump. There may be a slam if partner has a maximum of 24 points $(24 + 9 = 33)$.

With 10 points there will be a slam unless partner has a minimum (22) points. Therefore first bid a suit and then raise to 4 No Trump. Bidding a suit and raising to 4 No Trump is stronger than just bidding 4 No Trump.

With 11 or 12 points bid 6 No Trump. You have at least 33 points if partner has a minimum of 22 $(22 + 11 = 33)$, and at most you have 36 if partner has a maximum of 24 $(24 + 12 = 36)$.

With 13 or 14 points first bid a suit and then bid 6 No Trump. This is stronger than just bidding 6 No Trump directly. It asks partner to bid 7 if he has a maximum.

With 15 points you may bid 7 No Trump. No checking for Aces is necessary, for opponents cannot have one if partner has bid correctly $(22 + 15 = 37)$. Opponents have at most 3 points.

With unbalanced hands

1. Bid any good six-card major suit regardless of the high-card content of your hand.

2. Bid any five-card major suit if your hand contains at least 4 points in high cards. (This may be shaded to 3 points with a highly unbalanced hand.)

3. Jump to 4 in a major suit with a good six-card suit and a hand containing about 8 points in high cards.

4. Where responder has a hand containing a four-card holding in either or both major suits, a 3 Club response (similar in nature to the 2 Club response to a 1 No Trump opening) may be employed, asking partner to show a biddable four-card major suit. With no major, opener rebids 3 Diamonds.

Examples: Partner opens with 2 No Trump. You hold:

♠ J x x x   ♡ x x x   ◇ x x x   ♣ J x x

Pass. The opening bid of 2 No Trump is not forcing. With a balanced hand it normally takes 4 points to justify a raise, though a raise may be given with 3 points if responder has a five-card suit headed by an honor.

♠ x x   ♡ x x x   ◇ K J x x x   ♣ x x x

Bid 3 No Trump. Nothing is to be gained by showing the Diamonds.

♠ Q x x   ♡ K x x   ◇ A x x x   ♣ Q x x

Bid 6 No Trump. You have 11 points and partner has at least 22, so you have at least 33 points and at most 35.

♠ x x   ♡ K Q x x x   ◇ K x x   ♣ J x x

Bid 3 Hearts, and if partner rebids 3 No Trump, raise to 4 No Trump. If you had one less Heart you would raise directly from 2 No Trump to 4 No Trump, which shows exactly 9 points. Bidding a suit and then raising to 4 No Trump shows a hand worth 10 points (or 9 points and a good five-card suit). If opener has 24 points, the slam should be a cinch, and even if opener has 23 points, there should be a reasonable play for it. Of course, if opener has only 22 points, he will pass the 4 No Trump bid.

♠ Q 10 x x   ♡ K x x x   ◇ 10 x x x   ♣ x

Bid 3 Clubs, asking partner to show a major suit. If he rebids either 3 Hearts or 3 Spades, you will raise to 4. If he rebids 3 Diamonds, you will return to 3 No Trump.

Responses to 3 No Trump opening bids

Bear in mind that opener has 25, 26, or 27 points. Try to ascertain whether your partnership has enough assets to reach 33 for a small slam or 37 for a grand slam.

With 7 points and no five-card suit bid 4 No Trump.

With 8 or 9 points bid 6 No Trump. Your team will have at least 33 and at most 36.

With 10 or 11 points bid 4 Diamonds[5] and then rebid 6 No Trump on the next round. Partner should bid 7 with a maximum opening. Showing a suit and then bidding 6 No Trump is stronger than a direct leap to 6 No Trump.

With 12 points bid 7 No Trump. No checking for Aces is necessary. The opposition cannot have one, since partner has at least 25 points and your total of 37 is assured.

Rebids by opening No Trump bidder

The opening No Trump bidder should bear in mind that his opening call almost fully describes his hand. Responder therefore knows within 2 points what opener has when he bids 1, 2, or 3 No Trump. Therefore a No Trump bidder should not subsequently take drastic action unless invited to do so by responder.

In fact, there are several situations in which it is incumbent upon the opener to pass:

1. When responder bids 3 No Trump.
2. When responder bids 4 Hearts or 4 Spades.
3. When responder raises to 2 No Trump and opener has just 16 points.
4. When responder bids 2 Diamonds, 2 Hearts or 2 Spades and opener has 16 or 17 points. However, with 18 points and a good major-suit fit, opener may raise.

Rebid by No Trump bidder after a response of 2 Diamonds

When responder bids 2 Diamonds, opener knows that he is facing a hand which contains less than 7 high-card points. He should therefore take no further action unless his No Trump is of

---

[5] The 4 Diamond bid is artificial. Four of a major may not conveniently be employed in this situation, because opener is permitted to pass, and the 4 Club bid in this case is employed as a conventional asking bid. (See page 136 for the Gerber Convention.)

B*

the maximum type. Where opener has a near maximum, which includes two high honors in responder's minor suit (Ace King x, Ace Queen x, or King Queen x), he should raise partner's suit to 3. Responder may, of course, pass, but sometimes he will be able to take a chance on 3 No Trump if he has a long minor suit that he knows will run.

NORTH:	♠ x	♡ K x x	◊ Q 10 x x x	♣ x x x
SOUTH:	♠ Q J x	♡ A x x	◊ A K x	♣ K J x x

South opens 1 No Trump; North responds 2 Diamonds, describing his hand, which is unbalanced and has insufficient high-card strength for a raise to 2 No Trump. South has a good 1 No Trump, containing 18 points, including two of the top honors in Diamonds. He therefore raises to 3 Diamonds. North is permitted to pass, but when he learns that partner has the Ace King and another Diamond, he knows he can probably run six tricks in that suit, with a good prospect of cashing the King of Hearts. He therefore takes a chance on 3 No Trump.

Opening pre-emptive bids

A pre-emptive bid is an opening of 3, 4, or 5 in a suit. Such bids denote hands that are relatively weak in high cards. They are made in fear that the opponents have a better holding and in an effort to destroy their lines of communication. They are naturally based on a very long trump suit.

A hand should not be opened with a pre-emptive bid merely because it has a long suit. Where adequate defensive strength is held, an orthodox opening bid of 1 in a suit is preferred. A pre-emptive bid should never be made with a hand which contains more than 9 points in high cards when not vulnerable and 10 points when vulnerable.

To put it in another way: Experienced players never pre-empt unless the future of the hand appears to be hopeless.

In making a pre-emptive bid you must have a reasonable amount of safety. You should be prepared, if you are doubled, to lose no more than 500 points. That is to say, if you are not vulnerable, you may overbid by three tricks. If you are vulnerable, you should restrict the overbid to only two tricks. For example:

♠ K Q J x x x x x   ♡ x   ◊ x x   ♣ x x

If not vulnerable, you may bid 4 Spades. This is an overbid of three tricks. Even if doubled, you will be down no more than 500 points. If you are set that many tricks, the opponents unquestionably have a game and conceivably even a slam. But if you are vulnerable, you may chance a bid of only 3 Spades, an overbid of two tricks, which, if doubled, will risk a set of 500 points.

Since pre-emptive bids are not made with good hands, if your partner pre-empts, you should not raise unless you have an unusual amount of strength. You can expect your partner to have overbid by three tricks if you are not vulnerable, and by two tricks if you are, so you know how many tricks he can win. You must provide the rest.

A pre-emptive bid of 4 in a major suit may sometimes be made on a good hand for strategic purposes when partner has already passed. For example:

$$\spadesuit \text{x} \qquad \heartsuit \text{A K Q 10 x x x} \qquad \diamondsuit \text{A J 10 x} \qquad \clubsuit \text{x}$$

If partner has previously passed, the chances of reaching a slam are so remote that they may, for practical purposes, be dismissed. A pre-emptive bid of 4 Hearts may therefore be good strategy. First of all, you expect to make it. Secondly, it minimizes the danger of the disquieting competition in Spades that may be expected from the opposition.

I have seen players make the pre-emptive bid of 3 Spades on a hand like the following:

$$\spadesuit \text{A K Q J 10 x} \qquad \heartsuit \text{x x} \qquad \diamondsuit \text{Q x x} \qquad \clubsuit \text{x x}$$

I heartily disapprove of this practice. The hand is too good for a pre-emptive bid. It is by no means hopeless. In fact, it has distinct possibilities. I prefer an opening bid of 1 Spade, despite the questionable defensive strength. If you do not choose to open with 1 Spade, it is better to pass and enter the bidding later.

OPENING BID QUIZ

You are the dealer. What do you bid with the following hands?

1. $\spadesuit$ x x x   2. $\spadesuit$ K Q 10 4   3. $\spadesuit$ x x
   $\heartsuit$ Q J x x $\heartsuit$ A 9 3 $\heartsuit$ A J 10 x
   $\diamondsuit$ A Q J x $\diamondsuit$ K 7 5 $\diamondsuit$ K Q 10 4
   $\clubsuit$ A x $\clubsuit$ Q 6 4 $\clubsuit$ K x x

4. ♠ A K 10 4
   ♡ K Q 10 6 x
   ◊ x x
   ♣ x x

5. ♠ A x
   ♡ Q x x
   ◊ K Q 10 9 x x
   ♣ x x

6. ♠ x
   ♡ Q x x
   ◊ K Q 9 x x
   ♣ A 10 x x

7. ♠ K Q 10
   ♡ A J 10
   ◊ K Q 9 x
   ♣ A K x

8. ♠ K Q J 10 9 x
   ♡ A
   ◊ A J 10 x x
   ♣ x

9. ♠ A K 10 9 8 x x
   ♡ x
   ◊ A K Q x
   ♣ A

10. ♠ Q 9 6 4
    ♡ A J x x
    ◊ x x
    ♣ A Q 3

11. ♠ A K J 10
    ♡ A K 5
    ◊ A Q
    ♣ A 10 x x

12. ♠ None
    ♡ A x x x x
    ◊ A x x x
    ♣ Q x x x

Partner opens the bidding with 2 Spades. What is your response?

13. ♠ x x x x x
    ♡ x x
    ◊ Q x
    ♣ x x x x

14. ♠ x x
    ♡ A J 10 9 x
    ◊ K x x
    ♣ x x x

15. ♠ K x x x
    ♡ x
    ◊ A K x x
    ♣ x x x x

16. ♠ K x
    ♡ A 10 x x
    ◊ x x x
    ♣ Q x x x

On the following hands, partner has opened with 1 No Trump. What is your response?

17. ♠ K x x
    ♡ A K x x
    ◊ x x x x
    ♣ x x

18. ♠ A 10 9 x x
    ♡ x x
    ◊ A 10 x
    ♣ x x x

19. ♠ A J x
    ♡ K Q 10 x
    ◊ x x x
    ♣ x x x

20. ♠ K 10 9 x x
    ♡ x x
    ◊ J 9 x x x
    ♣ x

21. ♠ K J 10 x x
    ♡ x x
    ◊ A K x
    ♣ x x x

22. ♠ x x
    ♡ K x x x x x
    ◊ x
    ♣ A x x x

On the following hands, the bidding has gone:

YOU	PARTNER
1 No Trump	2 Clubs

What is your rebid?

23. ♠ Q 10 x
    ♡ 10 x x x
    ◊ A K x
    ♣ A K x

24. ♠ A 10 x
    ♡ K x
    ◊ A Q x
    ♣ K J 10 8 x

25. ♠ A J 10 x
    ♡ K Q x x
    ◊ K x
    ♣ K 10 x

26. ♠ A J x
    ♡ Q 10 x x x
    ◊ K x
    ♣ A Q x

In the following hands, you are South and the bidding has proceeded as indicated. What is your bid?

27.

NORTH	EAST	SOUTH	WEST	♠ x x
1 No Trump	Pass	2 Clubs	Pass	♡ K x x x x
2 Spades	Pass	?		◇ A J x
				♣ x x x

28. ♠ A K J x
♡ K x
◇ J 10 x
♣ A J x x

SOUTH	WEST	NORTH	EAST
1 No Trump	Pass	3 Clubs	Pass
?			

29. ♠ K J x
♡ A J 9 5
◇ A x x
♣ K 10 x

SOUTH	WEST	NORTH	EAST
1 No Trump	Pass	2 Clubs	Pass
2 Hearts	Pass	3 Hearts	Pass
?			

30. ♠ K Q 10 x
♡ A J 9 x
◇ K x
♣ A 10 x

SOUTH	WEST	NORTH	EAST
1 No Trump	Pass	2 Clubs	Pass
2 Spades	Pass	2 No Trump	Pass
?			

31. ♠ x
♡ A 10 9 x
◇ K 10 9 x x
♣ K x x

NORTH	EAST	SOUTH
2 No Trump	Pass	?

32. ♠ A Q 10 9 x
♡ A J 10 x x
◇ x
♣ x x

NORTH	EAST	SOUTH
1 No Trump	Pass	?

33. ♠ K x x
♡ x
◇ K Q J 10 x x x
♣ A x

NORTH	EAST	SOUTH
1 No Trump	Pass	?

ANSWERS TO OPENING BID QUIZ

1. One Diamond.
While hearts is your suit below the doubleton, it does not measure up to our standards for a biddable major suit. (Q J 10 x is the minimum requirement.)

2. One Club.
This hand contains 14 points and is therefore a mandatory opening. However, 1 Club is preferred to 1 Spade because it establishes a convenient rebid. If partner responds 1 Heart or 1 Diamond, you will bid 1 Spade.

If he responds with 1 Spade you will raise. If partner responds with 2 Clubs or 1 No Trump, you may pass.

3. One Heart.
With two four-card biddable suits, the correct procedure is to bid the suit which ranks next below the doubleton.

4. One Spade.
In order to show both suits conveniently, it is better to treat them as though they were of equal length and

open 1 Spade in preference to 1 Heart. This leaves the Heart suit as a rebid if partner responds 2 Clubs or 2 Diamonds.

5. One Diamond.
You have 13 points which qualifies the hand for an optional opening. Since you have a convenient rebid, the hand should be opened. Note that all minimum openings must contain two defensive tricks.

6. Pass.
Despite the fact that you have the necessary prerequisites for an optional opening, with nine cards in the minor suits, it is considered better practice to pass. Alternatively, if your suits were the majors, you should lean in favor of opening the bidding.

7. Two No Trump.
You have the textbook requirements for this call, 22 high-card points, a balanced hand, and protection in all the suits.

8. One Spade.
While it is true that game is quite likely, this hand falls short of the basic requirements of an opening 2 demand bid. Naturally, when next it is your turn to speak you will make some bid which would drive the partnership to game.

9. Two Spades.
You have a good seven-card suit and 24 points, and expect to make a game opposite even the most barren holding partner might have.

10. One Club.
Since our Spade suit is not biddable, we treat the hand as if it contained only one four-card suit. By opening 1 Club, we have an answer to any response partner might make. If he responds with either major, we will raise. If he bids 1 Diamond, we will bid 1 Heart. If he responds with 1 No Trump or 2 Clubs, we will pass.

11. Three No Trump.
You have 25 high-card points to which you will add 1 point for possession of all the Aces, a balanced hand, with every suit guarded.

12. Pass.
Although your hand has the point count for an optional opening, repeated Spade responses from partner might prove embarrassing for want of a safe place to alight. All in all therefore, it is better to postpone action with this holding.

13. Four Spades.
You have five trumps with neither an Ace, a King, or a singleton. Unless partner's hand needs only trump support, he should avoid bidding a slam.

14. Three Hearts.
This is perfectly normal. You have 9 points and a good five-card suit, which is a very impressive holding opposite an opening Diamond bid.

15. Three Spades.
There is no necessity to hasten matters, for admittedly, you intend to reach slam on the hand. However, it is good policy to fix the trump suit at once, and thereafter show your side controls. Partner will then be in a strategic position in the matter of naming the final contract.

16. Three Spades.
Since partner has shown a good suit, your K-x is considered adequate trump support and you have the required high-card strength necessary for an immediate raise.

17. Two Clubs.
If partner bids 2 Hearts, we will carry on to 4 Hearts. If his rebid is either 2 Spades or 2 Diamonds, we propose to jump to 3 No Trump.

18. Two Clubs.
With hands containing a five-card major and 8 or 9 points, the recommended procedure is to employ the

2 Club Convention. If partner rebids either 2 Diamonds or 2 Hearts you can bid 2 Spades. If he rebids 2 Spades you may gamble on 4 Spades since your hand is worth 9 plus points.

19. Three No Trump.
There is no point in employing the 2 Club Convention when you have no distributional values favorable to suit play.

20. Two Spades.
While there are some holdings which may produce game opposite your hand, it is more discreet to announce an indifferent hand by bidding 2 Spades rather than employing the 2 Club Convention, which announces an 8-point hand.

21. Three Spades.
You have a good five-card suit and enough to insist on game. You will, of course, pass 3 No Trump.

22. Four Hearts.
With a good six-card major and an unbalanced hand, you have the values to insist on game. You should leap right to it.

23. Two Diamonds.
We do not consider the heart suit biddable, and rebid accordingly.

24. Two Diamonds, not
Two No Trump.
We must rebid 2 Diamonds when we do not have a biddable 4-card major. Of course, if partner rebids 2 No Trump, we fully intend to carry on to game.

25. Two Spades.
With two four-card majors, it is our practice to show the Spades first and then call Hearts on the next round, if expedient.

26. Two Hearts.
Do not jump the bidding in response to the 2 Club Convention because you happen to have a five-card major

suit. You may show it later on in the auction if it is convenient for you to do so.

27. Two No Trump.
A bid of 3 Hearts would be unduly aggressive, for this call shows a minimum of 10 points and is forcing to game.

28. Three Spades.
There is no reason to by-pass a good Spade holding when partner has insisted on game. His jump in Clubs does not preclude the possession of a four-card major suit holding.

29. Pass.
You have a minimum 1 No Trump opening with no distributional features. Since partner needs a maximum from you, game will probably be an uphill struggle.

30. Four Hearts.
While it is true that you have only 16 points, the quality of your points is very high. Furthermore, your partner has displayed strong interest in game.

31. Three Diamonds.
To use the Club Convention here would make it extremely difficult to arrive at a Diamond slam. Partner is expected to show a biddable Heart suit if he has one.

32. Three Spades.
If partner rebids 3 No Trump your next call will be 4 Hearts, forcing him to take a preference. Holding five-card suits of your own and a good hand, there is no reason to initiate the 2 Club Convention.

33. Four Clubs.
This hand is ideal for the Gerber Convention which is discussed at length on page 136 of this book. If partner shows 2 Aces, you will of course contract for a slam in Diamonds. If he shows 1 Ace, you can stop at 5 Diamonds.

2.

RESPONDER'S PROBLEMS will be simplified if he will bear constantly in mind the principle that *an opening bid facing an opening bid will produce game.*

The responder is frequently the first one of the partnership to recognize that his side possesses the sum total of two opening bids. When he ascertains this fact he should make a distinct effort to get to game if a convenient contract can be found.

Translated into points, the principle may be stated as follows: When a partnership possesses about 26 points, game should be reached. Why 26? The minimum opening bid normally contains about 13 points. Two opening bids, therefore, will equal 26 points.

Inasmuch as an opening bid of 1 of a suit is very indefinite in character and covers a wide range of hands, it is the duty of responder to keep the 1 bid open with some relatively weak holdings. If responder raises his partner's suit or bids any number of No Trump, his response contains the precise information as to his strength, for raises and No Trump bids are kept within strict limits. If the response is in a new suit, however, it may be ambiguous. Particularly if the response is made at a low level, a suit response may range from a hand of very mediocre strength (6 points) up to a hand of great power (18 points). Because a suit take-out is so ambiguous, it is made forcing for one round, so that responder will have an opportunity to rebid and describe the limits of his hand more exactly.

Responding to bids of 1 in a suit

Keeping the bidding open with weak hands

When your partner has opened the bidding with 1 of a suit and your hand contains some slight trick-taking power, you should strive to keep the bidding alive. This provides the opener with another chance to bid should he have another suit at which the hand might play better, or should he have a very powerful opening, one that is just short of a demand bid.

If you have little or nothing, of course, you must pass. The bidding may be kept open with a moderate hand in one of three ways:

I. By bidding 1 No Trump (1 Heart by partner, 1 No Trump by you).

II. By raising your partner from 1 to 2 in his suit (1 Heart by partner, 2 Hearts by you).

III. By bidding some other suit *at the level of 1* (1 Heart by partner, 1 Spade by you).

I. KEEPING THE BIDDING OPEN BY A BID OF I NO TRUMP

This is regarded as one of the milder responses. When you desire to keep the bidding alive with a moderate hand but are unable to give partner a raise and have no suit that you can show at the level of 1, the practice is to respond with 1 No Trump. Such a response must contain at least 6 points in high cards and may contain as many as 10 points. Note that distributional points are not counted in making No Trump responses.

In each of the following cases, partner has opened with 1 Spade and you hold:

♠ x x x   ♡ A x x x   ◇ x x x   ♣ x x x

Pass. You have only 4 points.

♠ x x x   ♡ K 10 x x   ◇ Q 10 x   ♣ J x x

Bid 1 No Trump. You have the required 6 points in high cards.

♠ x x   ♡ Q x x   ◇ K J x x x   ♣ x x x

Bid 1 No Trump. You have 6 points in high cards and are not able to show your suit at the level of 1.

♠ x x x   ♡ A x x   ◇ K x x   ♣ K x x x

Bid 1 No Trump. You have 10 points, which is maximum for such a response.

The response of 1 No Trump to partner's 1 Club

When the opening bid is 1 Club, the response of 1 No Trump is very rare. If responder decides to keep the bidding open on a light hand, he has available to him a choice of 1 Diamond, 1 Heart, or 1 Spade, even though the suit may be very weak.

Therefore, a response of 1 No Trump to partner's 1 Club indicates a rather fair hand, one that is evenly balanced and has a high-card content of 9, 10, or 11 points. For example:

♠ K x x   ♡ K x x   ◇ A x x x   ♣ x x x

Partner opens with 1 Club. If you respond with 1 Diamond and his rebid is 1 No Trump, you are a little reluctant to pass and yet have not sufficient values to raise to 2 No Trump. The dilemma is solved in this case by responding with 1 No Trump. This hand contains 10 high-card points. The 1 No Trump response to 1 Club is not made whenever the responder holds any four-card major suit.

For example:

♠ K x x   ♡ J x x x   ◇ A J x x   ♣ J x

In response to a 1 Club bid, the proper procedure is to bid 1 Diamond, not 1 No Trump, because partner may have a four-card Heart suit which he can show at the level of 1 and which you can very readily support.

The reader is cautioned, however, that this is a specialized bid and should not be tried on a strange partner though it may be adopted as part of your tactics in one of the trained partnerships.

Free Bids of 1 No Trump: When partner opens with 1 of a suit and the next opponent inserts a bid (known as an overcall), you are no longer under pressure to keep the bidding alive; the opposition has already done so, and partner is automatically afforded another chance to speak. Any action you may take at this point is purely voluntary and shows a desire to bid, which naturally must be supported by a good hand. For example:

♠ K 10 x   ♡ x x x   ◇ A x x   ♣ J x x x
(8 points)

Partner opens with 1 Heart. If the next hand passes, you respond with 1 No Trump to give your partner another chance. But if the adversary ahead of you overcalls with 1 Spade, it would be improper for you to bid 1 No Trump merely to show that you have a Spade stopper. That would denote a good hand and a desire to go places. You should pass it around to partner.

But holding:

♠ K 10 x   ♡ x x x   ◇ A Q x   ♣ J x x x
(10 points)

on the same sequence of bids, you may make a free bid of 1 No Trump. This is the minimum strength on which such action may be based. In other words, a free bid of 1 No Trump indicates a hand that is only slightly short of an ordinary 2 No Trump response. Such a bid should be supported by a point count of approximately 10, 11, or 12.

II. THE RAISE TO 2 IN THE SAME SUIT

This response is, generally speaking, a little more encouraging than the response of 1 No Trump. The first requirement is that you be mildly satisfied with partner's suit, which means that you must have what is considered normal trump support; that is, at least x x x x or Q x x or J 10 x. Until you learn otherwise, you must act on the assumption that your partner holds a four-card suit. If you determine, on subsequent rounds of bidding, that your partner holds a rebiddable (a good five-card) suit, then you may be satisfied with that suit as trump with less than normal support. If the hand is satisfactory in other respects, you may now raise with three small trumps or Q x. And if your partner has bid the suit a third time without support from you in that suit, you may presume that he has six and may raise with two small trumps.

In other words, if partner bids a suit once, assume a four-card suit. If he bids twice, assume a five-card suit. If he bids it a third time, assume a six-card suit. Generally speaking, for the trump suit to be acceptable, the partnership should possess eight cards of the suit.

In addition to trump support, your hand must possess certain trick-taking qualities to justify a raise. These trick-taking qualities can best be represented by assigning certain points. However, for purposes of raising, we must consider

"Dummy Points": In raising partner's suit bid, the value of the hand is determined by adding the points assigned for

A. High cards.
B. Short suits.

A. High cards are taken at their face value. But there is a slight adjustment in the trump suit. The King of partner's suit becomes promoted to an Ace and is considered to be worth 4 points. The Queen of partner's suit is promoted to the value of a King and is considered to be worth 3 points. The Jack of trumps becomes promoted to the rank of a Queen and becomes worth 2 points. However, there is a limit to the promotion, and if 4 points have already been counted in the trump suit alone, no promotion takes place. For example, if you hold Queen Jack x in partner's trumps, you promote the holding from 3 points to 4. Note that only 1 point is allowed for promotion. But if you hold in trumps King Jack x, you have already counted 4 points in that suit and therefore no promotion takes place.

B. Short suits in the dummy are valued as follows:

> **Add 1 point for each doubleton.**
> **Add 3 points for each singleton.**
> **Add 5 points for a void.**

It will be observed that the distributional count in the dummy hand is slightly different from the distributional count in the opener's hand. A more liberal allowance is made for short suits. Deductions must be made when the dummy hand contains defects. The most common defects are the following:

1. Possession of only 3 trumps.
2. Possession of a 4-3-3-3 distribution.
3. Possession of a short suit which contains an insufficiently guarded honor.

Wherever the dummy hand contains a flaw a point must be deducted. The limits of a single raise of partner's suit are 7 to 10 points inclusive. These points naturally include both high cards and distribution. Let us observe a few examples.

Your partner opens with 1 Spade and you hold:

> ♠ 10 x x x ♡ x x ◇ K Q J x ♣ x x x
> (7 points)

You have enough to justify keeping the bidding open by a raise to 2 Spades. The hand is worth 7 points, 6 in high cards and 1 for the doubleton. If the small Diamond were a Heart, the correct response would be 1 No Trump.

> ♠ Q x x x ♡ x ◇ Q 10 x x ♣ x x x x
> (8 points)

With this hand you may raise to 2 Spades. The hand is worth 8 points in support of partner, 3 for the Queen of trumps, which is promoted, 2 for the Queen of Diamonds, and 3 for the singleton Heart.

In some cases you may offer partner a single raise with slightly less than trump support if no other suitable bid is available. Suppose partner opens with 1 Spade and you hold:

♠ 10 9 x   ♡ x   ◇ K x x x x   ♣ Q x x x

you should bid 2 Spades. This hand is worth 7 points in support of
Spades, 5 in high cards and 3 for the singleton Heart, but a deduction
of 1 point is made because the hand possesses the defect of having
only three trumps. A No Trump response would be improper; first,
because the hand does not contain the necessary 6 points in high cards,
and secondly, because the singleton Heart renders such a response
highly undesirable.

The free raise

The raises discussed above had assumed cases in which the
opponent on your right has passed. When the adversary on your
right inserts a bid, you should not raise with any of the hands previously shown. In such a position you do not strain a point to act,
because the bidding is already kept open for your partner. Any action
by you at this time denotes a sound raise.

The question arises: What strength is required to justify a free
raise? In this position one should not have less than 9 points. Perhaps
it might be easy to commit the requirement to memory by viewing
the raise in this manner.

7 and 8 points represent a weak raise.

9 and 10 points represent a good raise.

Of course the free raise may be given with hands of considerably
more strength. It may range in value all the way to the point where a
hand would be worth a double raise. In other words, the free raise
might contain as many as 11 or 12 points.

Observe the following illustrations:

Your partner opens with 1 Spade and the next hand bids 2 Clubs.

1. ♠ J 10 x x   ♡ x   ◇ Q 10 x x   ♣ x x x x
2. ♠ J 10 x x   ♡ x   ◇ A 10 x x   ♣ x x x x
3. ♠ J 10 x x   ♡ x x   ◇ A Q x x   ♣ x x x

With HAND 1 you should not raise to 2 Spades although you
would have kept the bidding alive had second hand passed. The hand
is worth only 7 points in support of Spades.

With HAND 2 you may make a free raise. The hand possesses 9
points.

With HAND 3 you may make a free raise. It too is worth 9 points.

Note: A bid made after partner's opening bid has been doubled is
not considered a free bid in the strict sense of the term.

III. KEEPING THE BIDDING OPEN BY A BID OF 1 IN A SUIT

When your partner opens with 1 of a suit, you may keep the bidding alive on certain mediocre hands by naming a new suit, provided you are able to do so at the level of 1. Such a response does not promise any more strength than does the response of 1 No Trump. This is an important observation. A 1 No Trump response ranges from 6 to 10 points, all in high cards. A one-over-one response may be made with as little as 6 points, but since some of these points may be distributional, the one-over-one response may contain as little as 4 points in high cards.

Of course where it becomes necessary to increase the contract to show your suit, more strength is required. In order to respond at the level of 2 with a new suit, your hand must be of at least average strength (an average hand is worth 10 points). With weak hands, the wisest procedure is to make the cheapest response, and 1 of a suit is cheaper than 1 No Trump.

♠ J x x   ♡ K J x x   ◇ x x   ♣ Q 10 x x

Partner opens with 1 Diamond. You have the necessary high-card strength and should keep the bidding open. It is the practice of many players to respond with 1 No Trump. This is unsound. Your proper response is 1 Heart. Remember that a bid of 1 Heart does not promise any more strength than does a bid of 1 No Trump. Furthermore, the one-over-one response makes partner's rebid easier in any case in which his second suit happens to be Spades. By bidding 1 Heart you permit him to rebid by showing his Spade suit at the level of 1, whereas a 1 No Trump response would have forced him to the level of 2 in order to show the suit. This he may fear to do.

Avoid responding 1 No Trump when you can bid 1 of a suit.

The above principle may be demonstrated with the following example:

♠ x x   ♡ K J x x x   ◇ J x x   ♣ x x x

If partner opens the bidding with 1 Spade, you should pass. Holding 5 points, you have not sufficient high-card strength to respond with 1 No Trump. But if partner opens with 1 Club or 1 Diamond, you may respond with 1 Heart. Valued at Hearts, the hand is worth 6 points, 5 in high cards and 1 for the doubleton. It will be seen, therefore, that this hand was not strong enough for a response of 1 No Trump, yet it was strong enough for a response of 1 Heart.

Free one-over-one bids

The foregoing discussion has contemplated an opening bid by partner and a pass by second hand. When second hand bids, you are no longer under pressure to keep the bidding alive and should not speak, even at the level of 1, unless you have definite values. Let us take an example:

♠ K x x x x   ♡ x x x   ◇ Q x x   ♣ x x

Your partner opens with 1 Club. If the next hand passes, you should respond with 1 Spade; but if the opponent overcalls partner's Club bid with 1 Heart, for example, you must not make a free bid of 1 Spade. You should pass. Partner will have another opportunity, and your hand is too weak for a free bid. Your hand is worth only 6 points. A free bid, even at the level of 1, should denote a fairly good hand and should not be made with less than 9 or 10 points.

The following represents the minimum on which a free bid should be made at the level of 1:
Partner opens with 1 Club, next hand bids 1 Heart, you hold:

♠ A Q x x x   ♡ x x x   ◇ Q x x   ♣ x x

This hand is worth 9 points, 8 in high cards and 1 for distribution.

Needless to say, if your free bid must be made at the level of 2, even greater strength will be required. In that case your hand should be worth about 12 points.

IN A NUTSHELL

With a mediocre hand you may keep your partner's bid alive
A. By bidding 1 No Trump (6 to 10 points).
B. By bidding 1 of a suit. This requires 6 points, but the 6 points need not be made up entirely of high cards, for distributional points are allowed.
C. By raising to 2 of your partner's suit if your hand contains 7 to 10 "dummy points."

Responses of 2 in a suit

When it is necessary for you to increase the level to name your suit, more strength will be required. To respond at the level of 2, your hand must be of at least average strength. An average hand is worth 10 points. Wherever you have a choice between responding with 2 of a suit and 1 No Trump in borderline cases, you should choose the No Trump response, because it does not force partner to speak again with a minimum hand. Wherever you have no more than 9 points in high cards, assuming the hand is of a balanced nature, you are within the limits of a 1 No Trump response and should favor that bid. But where your hand is unbalanced and it is worth 10 points, you should then favor the response in a suit.

♠ 10 x x   ♡ x x   ◊ K x x   ♣ A J x x x

Partner has opened with 1 Heart. It is mandatory for you to keep the bidding alive, but your hand is not strong enough to justify a 2 Club response. You must therefore respond with 1 No Trump. Your hand contains 8 high-card points.

Free responses of 2 in a suit

Generally speaking, you may make a free response of 2 in a suit on about the same strength you would require for the bid if second hand had passed, provided your suit is lower-ranking than partner's suit.

♠ x x x   ♡ x x   ◊ A Q 10 x x   ♣ K J x

Partner has opened with 1 Heart, second hand overcalls with 1 Spade. Your hand is worth 11 points, 10 in high cards and 1 for distribution. You may therefore bid 2 Diamonds freely. Note that your suit is lower in rank than your partner's and permits him to rebid at the level of 2. But if as South you hold:

♠ x x x   ♡ A K x x x   ◊ x x   ♣ K x x

and the bidding has proceeded:

NORTH	EAST	SOUTH
1 Diamond	1 Spade	?

On this sequence of bids you should not make a free bid of 2 Hearts. Your hand has a total value of 11 points, 10 in high cards and 1 for distribution, but is not strong enough to force partner to bid at the level of 3. You should pass and hope for another chance.

Great caution is indicated when a free bid is made by responder in a suit higher in rank than his partner's suit.

♠ x x x   ♡ K Q 10 x x   ◊ Q J x x   ♣ x

Your partner opens with 1 Club and an opponent overcalls with 1 Spade. It would be extremely impolitic for you to bid 2 Hearts. Such action forces partner to speak again, and if his rebid is 3 Clubs, which is not at all unlikely, you will find yourself in a mess brought on by your own conduct. Had your partner's opening bid been 1 Spade and the overcall been 2 Clubs, a 2 Heart bid by you would not be attended by nearly so much danger, since it permits partner to rebid his suit, if necessary, at the level of 2. Similarly:

♠ K Q x x x   ♡ 10 x x   ◇ A x x   ♣ x x

Partner opens with 1 Heart and an opponent overcalls with 2 Clubs. You cannot afford to bid 2 Spades, for your partner may not be prepared to rebid safely at the level of 3, and unless he happens to have strength in Clubs, he cannot safely bid No Trump. In this case, however, you may stretch a point and raise your partner to 2 Hearts even though you have slightly less than normal trump support. Your hand is worth 9 points in support of Hearts and is therefore worth a free raise, which is not forcing. But if you had only two small Hearts, you would not be in a position to raise without any kind of trump support and it would be more discreet for you to pass.

Another illustration: As South you hold:

♠ x x x   ♡ A 10 x x x x   ◇ Q x x   ♣ x

The bidding has proceeded:

NORTH	EAST	SOUTH
1 Club	1 Spade	?

Despite the six-card suit, you dare not bid 2 Hearts, since this may force your partner to bid 3 Clubs, or possibly 2 No Trump, neither of which you will find very comfortable. You should pass. Actually it should require no great restraint to pass, for this hand is not the least bit impressive. If you value it, you will note that it is worth only 8 points, 6 in high cards and 2 for distribution.

Again as South you hold:

♠ K J x   ♡ A Q x x x   ◇ x x x   ♣ x x

The bidding has proceeded:

NORTH	EAST	SOUTH
1 Club	1 Spade	?

There may be contemplation on your part to bid 2 Hearts, but this is not good strategy. If partner is obliged to bid 3 Clubs, you will hardly know what to do; to try 3 No Trump over 3 Clubs may prove disastrous, because you have not yet learned whether your partner has a good hand. However, some action by you must be taken, and the recommended call is a free bid of 1 No Trump. This will denote a good hand but will give partner the option of passing if he has a minimum. If he rebids 2 Clubs or 2 Diamonds, you will have the opportunity to bid Hearts on the next round.

IN A NUTSHELL

Don't make a free response of 2 in a suit unless you are prepared to bid again over partner's forced rebid.

Responding with good hands

The jump raise from 1 to 3

When the responder jumps from 1 to 3 in the opener's suit, it is a demand for game.

The opener is obligated to go to game regardless of the fact that he may have opened an absolute minimum. There is one exception: if the responder has previously passed, the opener need not go on if he does not choose to.

The requirements for the double raise are specific.

1. Responder must have more than just normal trump support. The minimum requirement is x x x x. A raise from 1 to 3 should not be made with only three trumps. In such cases some temporizing bid in another suit is usually better.

2. To justify a double raise the responder, in addition to adequate trump support, must have, roughly speaking, the equivalent of a normal opening bid, that is to say 13 to 16 points. However, these points include both high cards and distribution. In other words, the double raise requires 13 to 16 "dummy points."[1]

Partner opens with 1 Spade and you hold:

1. ♠ K J 10 9	♡ x	◇ J x x x	♣ A Q 10
2. ♠ K Q x x	♡ x x	◇ A x x x	♣ K x x
3. ♠ K J x x	♡ x x x	◇ A K x	♣ K 10 x

With **HAND 1** respond 3 Spades. The hand is worth 14 points, 11 in high cards and 3 for the singleton.

[1] Refer to page 41 for "dummy points."

HAND 2. Bid 3 Spades. This hand is worth 13 points, 12 in high cards and 1 for doubleton.

HAND 3. Bid 3 Spades. This hand is worth 13 points. It has a face value of 14, but 1 point must be deducted because of the defect of the 4-3-3-3 distribution.

There are many players who when they hold strong trump support for partner make it a practice to respond with a double raise on almost all big hands, regardless of their strength. This is not approved in our methods.

It must be pointed out that a hand on which we offer a double raise in a major suit (1 Spade — 3 Spades) is not a hand of unlimited strength. In point of fact, it must be kept within specific limits. At its lower range the hand must be the equivalent in strength of an opening bid (13 points); at its top it must not exceed 16 points.

If a hand is worth 19 "dummy points," then the partnership is on the verge of a slam and a jump shift is in order. But hands that are valued at 17 and 18 points in support of partner require delicate treatment. While they are not strong enough for a jump shift, they are nevertheless too strong for the double raise and their strength must be described in a series of bids. Best results will usually be obtained by bidding two suits before supporting partner's bid. For example, as South you hold:

$$\spadesuit \text{ A x x x} \qquad \heartsuit \text{ x} \qquad \diamondsuit \text{ K Q 9 x} \qquad \clubsuit \text{ A J x x}$$

North has opened with 1 Spade. Your hand is worth 17 points and is therefore too strong for a double raise. Yet it lacks the 19 points which should form the basis for a jump shift. You therefore temporize with a bid of 2 Diamonds. When partner rebids 2 Spades, a jump to 4 would be inadequate. That might be done with many 14- or 15-point hands. Proper procedure is to temporize again with a bid of 3 Clubs, and if North returns to 3 Diamonds, you complete the description of your values by a jump to 4 Spades.

The jump from 1 to 4 in a major suit

The raise from 1 to 4 in a major suit is a specialized bid. It describes a hand that is very rich in trump support and in distribution (it must contain a singleton or void), but it is not rich in high cards. It is made on hands on which responder believes he has a fairly good chance to fulfill the contract and also is desirous of preventing any adverse bid.

Expressed in points, the pre-emptive raise from 1 to 4 should never contain more than 9 points in high cards.

To summarize: A jump from 1 to 3 indicates good trump support and good high-card strength. A jump from 1 to 4 indicates better trump support but less high-card strength.

| ♠ K J x x x | ♡ x | ◇ Q J 10 x x | ♣ x x |
| ♠ A x x x x x | ♡ x | ◇ x x | ♣ Q J x x |

Partner has opened with 1 Spade. Holding either of these hands, you should bid 4 Spades. Each of these hands is worth 11 points in support of Spades. Note that all the conditions are met with: five trumps, a singleton, and less than 9 points in high cards.

This pre-emptive raise is frequently referred to as a "shut-out" bid, an expression which does not sit well with this department. It has led to the belief that when the responder jumps to 4 Spades, the opener is obliged to pass willy-nilly and that under no circumstances should he reach for a slam.

There is no sound basis for such a theory, for if the opener happens to have most of the high-card strength and if it appears that all he needs is great trump support and distribution to produce a slam, there is no reason why he cannot gird up his loins and bid the slam. It is better to avoid the term "shut-out" bid. The triple raise is simply a descriptive bid.

The jump from 1 to 4 is handled somewhat differently when the player making such a raise has previously passed. A jump from 1 Spade to 4 Spades or from 1 Heart to 4 Hearts then becomes stronger than a jump from 1 to 3. The reason is this: After a previous pass, the jump from 1 to 3 is not forcing, and if responder finds that he has a hand which is worth, let us say, 15 points in support of Hearts, though it was not worth that much as an opening bid, he may jump to 4 Hearts, trusting that the third-hand bid contained at least 11 points.

The jump take-out in No Trump

A jump response of 2 No Trump is forcing to game, just as is a jump from 1 to 3 in a suit. In fact, it may be broadly stated that whenever a responder (who has not previously passed) makes a single jump, the partnership is committed to a game contract.

As in all cases where responder guarantees game, *his hand must at least equal an opening bid for him to jump to 2 No Trump* (13 points). Many players have formed the habit of regarding the 2 No

Trump response as a hand containing 2½ quick tricks. This is an unsound practice.

In addition to the high-card requirements, a 2 No Trump responder should have at least two cards of his partner's suit, and all other suits protected. In other words, this response describes not only the high-card strength of the hand but also indicates its type.

Examples: Partner having opened with 1 Spade:

♠ 10 x   ♡ K J x x   ◇ K J 10   ♣ A J x x

Respond with 2 No Trump. Your hand is just about the equal of an opening bid. The hand contains two cards in partner's suit and protection in all the unbid suits (point count 13).

♠ x x   ♡ A x x x   ◇ A x x   ♣ K x x x

It would be improper to respond with 2 No Trump, because you are not strong enough to insist upon a game contract. The hand contains 2½ quick tricks but is not equal to an opening bid. The hand contains only 11 points and is therefore 2 points short of the requirement. With this type of hand one must make haste slowly by making a temporary response, preferably in Clubs. Now if partner rebids 2 Spades, the responder may try 2 No Trump. This invites partner to proceed but does not force him to game, as would be the case had responder chosen to make a jump to 2 No Trump.

♠ Q x x   ♡ x x x   ◇ K J x x   ♣ A K x

This hand contains the equivalent of an opening bid and has the proper distribution, but a 2 No Trump response is not recommended because an unbid suit, Hearts, is not protected. A temporary bid of 2 Diamonds is the proper procedure, and whether or not No Trump will be tried later will depend upon developments.

Occasionally a 2 No Trump response is better than revealing a good minor suit. For example, your partner has opened the bidding with 1 Spade, and you hold:

♠ x x x   ♡ A Q x   ◇ K x   ♣ K J 10 x x

Your response is 2 No Trump rather than 2 Clubs. It is quite apparent that you desire to become declarer on this hand, to gain the advantage of having the lead come up to you in Diamonds and Hearts. Had your partner's opening bid been 1 Diamond, the 2 No Trump response should not be regarded as proper, because of the unguarded Spade suit.

For example, partner opens 1 Club. You hold:

♠ A Q x x   ♡ K J x   ◇ A x x   ♣ x x x

Where responder has a choice between a 2 No Trump response and a response of 1 in a good four-card major suit, preference should be given to the major.

Though you have a balanced hand containing 14 points, a 1 Spade response is to be preferred.

One more thought in connection with the 2 No Trump response. It is a precise bid and is definitely limited in strength. In other words, it must have precisely 13, 14, or 15 high-card points. If the hand contains more than 15 points and is of the No Trump type, the proper response is 3 No Trump.

The jump take-out to 3 No Trump

It has been seen above that the take-out of an opening bid of 1 of a suit to 2 No Trump requires 13, 14, or 15 points, but no more. With greater strength it is obligatory to make a stronger bid. Holding 16, 17, or 18 points and a 4-3-3-3 distribution, responder should bid 3 No Trump. This gives an exact picture of his hand and enables the opener to judge immediately the probable trick-taking capacity of the partnership. To put it in another way, in order to make a jump response of 3 No Trump, your hand must be equal to an opening 1 No Trump bid.

An illustration: Partner opened with 1 Spade. You should respond 3 No Trump on this hand.

♠ Q x x   ♡ A Q x   ◇ K x x x   ♣ A Q x

When the responder holds more than 18 points, his hand is too strong even for a 3 No Trump response, and he must make a more positive slam try in the form of a jump in a new suit.

IN A NUTSHELL

A jump to 2 No Trump by responder shows approximately the strength of an ordinary opening bid (13 to 15 points).

A jump to 3 No Trump by responder shows approximately the strength of an opening 1 No Trump bid (16 to 18 points).

Where responder's hand is worth 19 points, he should make a jump shift.

The jump take-out in a new suit

In the early days of contract bridge, the textbook requirement for a jump shift was stated to be about 3½ honor tricks and a good suit. However, possession of even more high-card strength than that does not necessarily justify a jump shift. The hand should be so composed that a slam can be visualized at once, else the big guns should be held up till the next round. Responder, too, should have a fairly good idea of where the hand can safely play.

A more specific idea of what constitutes a jump shift can be obtained by reference to point count. Where the responder holds a hand worth 19 points, including high cards and distribution, he may suggest a slam by the jump shift, for he knows that the partnership possesses, at the very least, within 1 point of the slam figures. Assuming the opener to have a minimum bid of 13 points, where responder has 19, the partnership is assured of 32.

There is a popular misconception to the effect that you are not permitted to make a jump take-out in a new suit unless you have support for your partner's suit. Where there is danger of a misfit, naturally one must proceed with caution, but responder may jump-shift if his hand is self-sustaining; that is, if he holds a solid suit of his own that requires no support, or where partner's suit is not relied upon. Responder does promise by his jump shift that there is a contract at which the hand can play conveniently.

♠ A K Q 10 x   ♡ x   ◇ A K J x x   ♣ x x

Partner opens with 1 Heart. You have no support in partner's suit, but this has all the earmarks of a slam in one of your two suits. You should therefore respond with 2 Spades, a jump shift. This hand is worth 20 points valued at responder's suit, 17 in high cards and 3 for distribution.

♠ x   ♡ A Q 10 x   ◇ A K J x x   ♣ x x x

Partner opens with 1 Spade. You have 14 points in high cards alone (or, as the old-timers would have said, 3½ high-card tricks), but it would be unwise to bid 3 Diamonds. You can hardly say that you are interested in a slam at this point. You are not even sure as to where the hand will play. You must proceed slowly until you determine the best contract. There is no question that you will eventually reach game. Your proper response is 2 Diamonds. If partner rebids his

Spades, you have plenty of bidding space in which to bid 3 Hearts, leaving the door open to any of a number of different contracts. Observe that this hand is worth only 16 points valued at your own suit.

♠ x   ♡ A K 10 x   ◇ A Q x x   ♣ Q 10 9 x

Partner opens with 1 Club. A 2 Heart response is acceptable, since the strong trump support makes slam prospects bright. This hand is worth 19 points in support of Clubs.

♠ A Q 10 x   ♡ x   ◇ A K J x   ♣ Q 10 x x

Partner opens with 1 Spade. Respond 3 Diamonds. There is a slam aroma about this hand. It is far too strong for a jump raise. This hand is worth 19 points in support of Spades.

♠ A K x x x   ♡ A Q x   ◇ Q J   ♣ K x x

Partner opens with 1 Diamond. Respond 2 Spades, though you have neither a powerful suit of your own nor strong support for partner's suit. If partner has no long trump suit, then his opening bid values, like yours, must be general and you can safely play in No Trump. Note that this hand is worth 19 points in high cards.

IN A NUTSHELL

A raise from 1 to 3 shows trump support and high-card tricks.

A jump from 1 to 4 shows plenty of trumps but not much in high cards.

A jump from 1 of a suit to 2 No Trump shows a balanced hand with about the equal of an opening bid (13 to 15 points).

A jump from 1 of a suit to 3 No Trump shows that the responder's hand is the equivalent of an opening 1 No Trump bid (16 to 18 points).

A jump take-out in a new suit is made only on hands that look like a slam (19 points). If only game is in prospect, the mere naming of a new suit by the responder is sufficient.

Choice of responses

On a great many hands there is a choice of response; that is, any of several bids may be technically correct. It is incumbent upon the responder in those cases to make the best of the choices.

Choice between a single raise and a 1 No Trump response

Some players regard this as a choice of rotten apples, inasmuch as these two responses are the less favored children. Where there is a close choice between raising your partner to 2 of his suit and 1 No Trump, the distribution of the hand will frequently determine the choice. Where you have a 4-3-3-3 distribution with normal trump support, our practice is to respond with 1 No Trump if the raise is of a minimum character (7 or 8 points); but we offer the raise in preference to the No Trump bid when the hand is worth 9 or 10 points in support of partner's major suit.

But where the hand contains a short suit, even a doubleton, the raise is preferred to the 1 No Trump response.

For example:

♠ A x x   ♡ 10 x x   ◇ K J x x   ♣ x x x

Partner opens with 1 Spade. You have a choice of responding with 1 No Trump or 2 Spades. Note that the hand is completely balanced, and in support of Spades we have 7 points. There are 8 high-card points, but inasmuch as the dummy contains a flaw, we must subtract a point and the hand is therefore worth only 7. Consequently, the 1 No Trump response is preferred. If one of the Hearts were transferred to the Clubs, we would prefer the raise to 2 Spades. Note that this would increase the "dummy points" by 1, for the hand would then be worth 8 points.

Even with a balanced hand a single raise should occasionally be preferred to a 1 No Trump response.

♠ K x x   ♡ Q x x x   ◇ A x x   ♣ J x x

Partner opens with 1 Spade. This hand contains 10 high-card points and would come within the limits of a 1 No Trump response. However with this hand we prefer the somewhat more favorable-sounding call of 2 Spades.

Choice between raising your partner and bidding your own suit

THE RULE OF FOUR-PLUS

This phase of bidding provides a stumbling block to even the more experienced players. One frequently is presented with a choice between giving partner a single raise in his major suit and

c

naming some other suit. Since it is usually more important to support your partner's major suit than to show your own, the question first to be answered is: "Can I afford to do both?"

If your hand is good enough to justify two bids, you should show your suit first and support partner's suit later. If you feel that your hand is not strong enough to do both, you should confine yourself to a single raise of partner's suit, hoping he can take further action.

The question arises: "How is one to determine whether or not the hand is worth two bids?"

One test is to be found in the table of playing tricks. If the responder's hand is worth four playing tricks or less in support of partner, the hand should be regarded as worth only one bid, in which case a single raise is given. However, if the responder's hand is worth more than four playing tricks, the hand can support two bids, and in that case the responder's suit is first shown.

Stated in terms of point count, *if responder's hand is above average strength (11 or 12 points), it is worth two bids and is therefore too strong for a single raise.* For example:

♠ A x x   ♡ x x   ◇ A J x x x   ♣ x x x

Your partner opens with 1 Spade. The question is whether to raise to 2 Spades or to bid 2 Diamonds. Is this hand worth two bids? If your instinct tells you that it is not, you are right. The hand counts up to a little over 3½ playing tricks. Since more than four are required to justify making two bids, the proper response is 2 Spades and not 2 Diamonds. The hand is worth 9 points in support of Spades and is well within the limits of a single raise.

Observe the following example:

♠ A x x x   ♡ x   ◇ A 10 x x x   ♣ x x x

Again the question is whether to raise the Spades or to show the Diamonds. Is this hand worth two bids? According to the old-time playing trick table this hand contains 5½ tricks. Therefore the hand is worth more than one bid, yet it is not strong enough in high cards for a jump to 3 Spades. In other words, this is the type of hand on which the most comfortable bid would be a response of 2½ Spades. In all such cases you make a temporizing bid first (2 Diamonds in this case), intending to raise partner's suit on the next round. You are sure to have another chance, because the 2 Diamond bid is a one-round force on the opener. This hand is worth 11 points in support of Spades and is therefore too big for a single raise.

In applying this principle you will frequently find it necessary to bid 2 in a very weak suit, as a waiting bid. For example:

♠ Q x x x   ♡ x x   ◇ K 10 x x   ♣ A x x

Your partner opens with 1 Spade. This hand is too good for a single raise but not good enough for a jump raise. It is worth 11 points (4½ playing tricks). This is another one of those hands which might best be described by a raise to 2½ Spades, a bid unfortunately not permitted by the lawmakers. You must therefore arrange to bid twice by first calling some other suit. There is no objection to a take-out to 2 Diamonds, since it is your full intention to raise Spades on the next round. Sometimes, it may be expedient to make this temporizing bid with a three-card minor suit. For example:

Partner opens with 1 Spade and you hold:

♠ Q x x x x   ♡ x x   ◇ K x x   ♣ A 10 x

This hand is worth 11 points in support of Spades. It is therefore obviously too good for a single raise, yet it is not strong enough for a jump to 3 Spades, which would insist upon game and which would promise a hand equal to an opening bid in strength (at least 13 points). Responder must arrange to bid twice, and the suggested response is first 2 Clubs. This should not shock even the most squeamish, for there is not the remotest danger that the hand will ever play in Clubs.

In cases such as are illustrated by the four previous examples, the responder's task is simplified if the opponent overcalls the opening bid. In each of these cases the responder should bid 2 Spades, a free bid, denoting a good hand. It is not now necessary to make indirect bids in the side suits, since the voluntary action on the part of responder indicates a good hand (about 9 to 12 points).

Choice between giving a double raise and naming a new suit

Here you have a choice between two good bids, either of which may be correct. Tactics may suggest that one is to be preferred on certain types of hands. Observe the following case:

♠ J x x x x   ♡ x   ◇ A Q x x   ♣ K x x

Partner opens with 1 Spade. This hand qualifies as a jump to 3 Spades (14 "dummy points").

The responder, if he chooses, may make a temporary bid of 2 Diamonds, intending to raise Spades later. I do not regard this as the best strategy, however, since little is to be gained by making an indirect bid in this case. *Where there is a direct bid which precisely describes your hand, such a bid is much preferable to indirect action.* A jump to 3 Spades exactly fits this hand and is a direct bid. An indirect bid in such a case may lead to confusion on subsequent rounds of bidding.

Sometimes a temporizing bid must be made where the responder's hand contains sufficient strength for a double raise but unfortunately does not possess the necessary four trumps.

Responding with two-suiters

When the responder has two suits, both of which he intends to show, they should usually be bid in the orthodox sequence. That is, with suits of equal length, he bids the higher-ranking first, whether they are four-carders or five-carders; with suits of unequal length, he bids the longer first. But remember the proviso, that *he intends to show both.*

Your hand must be strong to allow such action. If your hand is not of sufficient strength to justify the naming of both suits, common sense and economy will dictate the choice. Here is an illustration.

♠ A K J x   ♡ x x   ◊ x x   ♣ K 10 x x x

Partner opens with 1 Heart. With this hand you are prepared to show both suits, and you should bid them in the normal sequence; that is, the Clubs first. The proper response is 2 Clubs. If partner rebids 2 Hearts, you intend to bid 2 Spades, and partner will have a photographic description of your hand.

Some players engage in the unsound practice of responding with 1 Spade on the foregoing hand, explaining that they wish to keep the bidding low. But there is no necessity for keeping the bidding low with a hand that has game prospects. You have the equal of an opening bid yourself, so that the outlook for game is bright. It will be observed that responding with 1 Spade actually has the effect of getting the bidding to a higher stage than is necessary. If opener rebids 2 Hearts, responder no doubt intends to bid 3 Clubs, reaching the nine-trick level unnecessarily. Furthermore, opener will not have a description of responder's distribution.

Let us reduce the hand slightly:

♠ A J x x   ♡ x x   ◊ x x   ♣ K x x x x

Partner opens with 1 Heart. At first blush the natural response would be 2 Clubs. But your hand is not quite strong enough to justify a take-out to the 2 level. Rather than respond with 1 No Trump, bid 1 Spade. If partner rebids 2 Hearts, we recognize that there is no game and we pass. We had no intention of bidding both suits.

Another exception:

♠ A J x x   ♡ K 10 x x   ◊ x x x   ♣ x x

Partner opens with 1 Club. You can afford to make only one response (unless partner subsequently gets very excited). The orthodox response would be 1 Spade, but there is a certain practical objection to this bid. If partner happens to have a hand of moderate strength, containing a four-card Heart suit, he will now be unable to show his suit at the level of 1, and may be too weak to show it at the level of 2, and the Heart suit may be lost. The best practice, therefore, is to respond with 1 Heart. If partner has Hearts, he will have a pleasant raise. If partner's second suit is Spades, he is able to show it at the level of 1.

Observe how this hand works if opener's hand happens to be the following:

♠ x x   ♡ Q J x x   ◊ K Q x   ♣ A K x x

But if the hand is strong enough to warrant the showing of both suits, the normal sequence is followed.

♠ A Q 10 x   ♡ K Q J x   ◊ x x   ♣ x x x

Partner opens with 1 Club. This hand has fairly good game-going prospects. You can afford to show both suits. The proper response is 1 Spade, with the intention of bidding Hearts on the next round. This hand is worth 13 points, 12 in high cards and 1 for distribution. Therefore a distinct effort should be made to reach a game contract.

Responding when you have previously passed

It is of paramount importance to bear in mind that almost any response made by you under these conditions can be dropped by the opener. He recalls your previous pass and may have said to himself as he opened the bidding, "I know, from my partner's pass, that we have no game in this hand, but I am opening simply for a part score and I am going to drop any response he makes." It follows, therefore, that a player who has previously passed cannot make a temporary bid because it might turn out to be permanent. He must be prepared to play the hand at anything he bids.

♠ K x x x   ♡ x x   ◇ K 10 x x   ♣ A x x

Assume that your partner has dealt and bids 1 Spade. Your hand
is worth 12 "dummy points." It is therefore too good for a single
raise but just a shade short of the requirement for a jump to 3. It
is therefore necessary to temporize by bidding 2 Diamonds, intending to support Spades later. But if you have previously passed and
your partner opens with 1 Spade in third or fourth position, you
dare not bid 2 Diamonds, for partner might pass. Remember that
the naming of a new suit by a player who has previously passed is
not forcing. Under these conditions you should jump to 3 Spades.
If partner has shaded his third-hand opening, he need not proceed.
You are merely announcing that your hand is just short of a regula-
tion jump to 3 Spades.

What if, after passing, you feel convinced there is a game in the
hand? You ought to bid it. You have:

♠ K Q x x   ♡ Q 10 x x   ◇ K Q x x   ♣ x

On this hand you dealt and passed. Your partner in third position
opens with 1 Spade. What would you respond? In support of Spades
your hand is worth 15 "dummy points." Even if partner has made
a shaded third-hand bid consisting of only 11 points, you will have
the necessary values for game and should bid 4 Spades directly. In
view of your previous pass, a jump to 3 Spades would not be forcing
upon partner.

Observe that the above hand, when valued from the standpoint of
the bidder, is worth 13 points—14 on the surface, less the point a
prospective opener should deduct on all Aceless hands. Thirteen-point
hands are optional openings, an option which in this case we would
not prefer to exercise.

A jump in a new suit, after a previous pass, we regard as forcing
for one round at least. As dealer you hold:

♠ J x x x x   ♡ x   ◇ A K J 10 x x   ♣ x

You choose to pass and partner opens in third position with 1 Spade.
Obviously you will settle for no less than a game in Spades. A jump
to 3 Spades would be inadequate, for, in view of your previous pass,
it is not forcing. A raise to 4 Spades would almost surely be passed
by partner. The 3 Diamond bid serves as a one-round force and after
partner's next call you may be in better position to make a decision.

RESPONSES QUIZ

Your partner opens the bidding with 1 Diamond and the next hand passes. What do you bid on each of the following hands?

1. ♠ x x
♡ K Q x x
◊ K Q x x x
♣ x x

2. ♠ K 10 x
♡ A J 4
◊ K J 10 6
♠ Q 10 9

3. ♠ Q x x x
♡ K x x x
◊ x
♣ x x x x

4. ♠ A K Q x x x
♡ x
◊ A x
♣ K Q x x

5. ♠ Q x x x
♡ x x
◊ x
♣ K Q 10 x x x

6. ♠ A Q 10 x
♡ K Q x x
◊ x x
♣ K x x

7. ♠ Q x x
♡ x x
◊ x x x
♣ A Q 10 x x

Your partner opens with 1 Heart. Next hand passes. What is your response with each of the following?

8. ♠ x x x
♡ K Q x x x
◊ x x
♣ K x x

9. ♠ K Q x
♡ J 10 9 x
◊ x x x
♣ x x x

10. ♠ A J 9 x x
♡ K 10 x
◊ x x
♣ x x x

11. ♠ x
♡ x x
◊ K J 9 x x
♣ Q 10 9 x x

12. ♠ x
♡ Q J x
◊ x x x x
♣ A 10 9 x x

13. ♠ K Q x
♡ A 10 x
◊ K Q x x
♣ Q J x

14. ♠ A J x x x
♡ Q 10 x x
◊ x
♣ A x x

In the following hands, your partner opens with 1 Heart, and next hand bids one spade. What action do you take?

15. ♠ K J x
♡ x x
◊ K Q 10 x x
♣ J x x

16. ♠ x x x
♡ A K x x
◊ x x x
♣ x x x

You are South in the following examples, and the bidding has proceeded as indicated.

17. ♠ K 10 x
♡ J x
◊ Q 10 x
♣ A Q 10 x x

SOUTH	WEST	NORTH	EAST
Pass	Pass	1 Heart	Pass
?			

18.	♠ A x x	NORTH	EAST	SOUTH	
	♡ Q x x x	1 Club	Pass	?	
	◇ x x x x				
	♣ x x				

19.	♠ A x x x	NORTH	EAST	SOUTH	
	♡ K Q J x x	1 Spade	Pass	?	
	◇ x				
	♣ A x x				

20.	♠ K x x x	NORTH	EAST	SOUTH	
	♡ Q 10 x x x	1 Diamond	2 Clubs	?	
	◇ x x				
	♣ K x				

21.	♠ x x	SOUTH	WEST	NORTH	EAST
	♡ Q x x x	Pass	Pass	1 Heart	Pass
	◇ A K 10 x x	?			
	♣ J x				

22.	♠ A K 10 9 x x	SOUTH	WEST	NORTH	EAST
	♡ x	Pass	Pass	1 Diamond	Pass
	◇ Q x x x	?			
	♣ x x				

ANSWERS TO RESPONSES QUIZ

1. One Heart.
Do not overlook the opportunity to show a biddable major suit at the level of 1. If, instead, you raise Diamonds, partner may not have sufficient values to bid Hearts himself.

2. Two No Trump.
There is nothing to be gained by a jump raise in Diamonds when your hand is balanced. Your hand falls within the limits of the 2 No Trump response (13-15 high-card points).

3. One Heart.
Partner may have the necessary values to justify a jump to game in Hearts if you mention the suit. This should not be at all disagreeable; and if partner should choose to name some other suit, that would be acceptable to you. Note that your hand is worth 7 points, 5 in high cards, and 2 for distribution.

4. Two Spades.
The jump shift response flashes the potential slam signal. With 21 points, it is your duty to alert partner of this fact so that you can bide your time in search for the impending slam effort.

5. One Spade.
This hand does not measure up to the requirements for a 2-level response. Hence the Club suit must be suppressed. The Spade bid is preferable to a response of 1 No Trump.

6. One Spade.
The combined assets of the partnership demand that a game be reached. It is your intention to show the Heart suit next if partner's rebid is 2 Diamonds, which will force another bid from the opener.

7. One No Trump.
Your hand lacks the values for a 2-level response, and since you have no other biddable suit, a 1 No Trump response is obligatory.

8. Two Hearts.
The fact that you have five trumps for partner should not elevate your

hopes as to game prospects. Unless partner is prepared to bid over your single raise, game is highly unlikely. Your hand is worth only 9 points, which places it well within the limits of a single raise.

9. One No Trump.
Despite the four trumps, you are 1 point short of the values required for a single raise (7-10 points), and should keep the bidding alive with the only response available, that of 1 No Trump.

10. Two Hearts.
When your hand is worth only one progressive bid, it is wiser to raise partner's major suit with adequate trump support rather than branch off into a new suit of your own. In other words, your hand is not strong enough to justify showing both Spades and Hearts, and therefore you must make your election at this point. In all these cases, the single raise of partner's major suit is to be preferred to any other call.

11. One No Trump.
Of course, you will loathe this contract if partner chooses to pass, but since you are decidedly short on the values required for the 2-level response, you must respond with 1 No Trump rather than obscure partner's picture of the strength of your hand.

12. Two Hearts.
This hand is a tip-top raise counting 10 points in support of Hearts. It is not good enough to combine a 2 Club response with a subsequent Heart raise. When faced with a choice between bidding your own suit and raising partner, the simple raise is preferred with a mediocre hand.

13. Three No Trump.
This call shows a balanced hand with 16 to 18 high-card points and all unbid suits stopped. In order for slam to be possible, your partner must be able to carry on himself.

C*

14. Three Hearts.
Avoid bidding a mediocre suit when you have a perfect limit bid to describe the strength of your hand. The jump raise shows four-card trump support and from 13 to 16 points.

15. One No Trump.
This bid is not forcing upon partner. It simply promises a balanced hand with 9 to 11 high-card points and a stopper in the adverse suit.

16. Pass.
Despite your splendid trump support, the values for a free raise should rarely be based on less than 9 points.

17. Two No Trump.
After the original pass, this bid shows a balanced hand containing 11 to 12 points in high cards. Do not bid 2 Clubs. In view of the fact that you have previously passed this bid is not forcing, and you might find yourself playing the hand in that denomination.

18. One Heart.
Although the quality of the suit makes it unbiddable for purposes of opening the bidding, you are quite justified in responding with a Queen-high suit. Do not make the mistake of bidding 1 No Trump.

19. Two Hearts.
This is a temporizing bid, and, of course, forcing for one round. This hand is worth 17 points in support of Spades making it too strong for a mere double raise, but not quite strong enough for a jump-shift response which requires 19 points.

20. Pass.
You are definitely not strong enough to make a free bid of 2 Hearts, which would require partner to make his next bid at the level of 3. Remember, a pass does not amount to a surrender.

21. Three Hearts.
When you have passed originally, the limits of the jump raise are lowered. Your hand has splendid trump support together with 12 points in support of Hearts. Do not make the mistake of temporizing with 2 Diamonds. Partner is privileged to pass this bid and a game in Hearts might be missed.

22. Two Spades.
The jump-shift response is the only call that can force opener when one has passed originally. If partner raises your Spades, you will, of course, carry on to game. If, on the other hand, he bids another suit, you will be happy to support his Diamonds.

3.   Rebids

IF I WERE COERCED into making a statement as to which of the bids, in a normal auction, I believe to be the most important, I would choose the *second bid made by the opener*. Opening bids of 1 in a suit are necessarily ambiguous. They do not pretend to give a precise account of the strength of the hand or of its type. They may range from as little as 13 points to as many as 22 or 23 in some cases. In this respect they differ from opening bids of 1, 2, and 3 No Trump, which are completely descriptive.

It is on the second turn around that the opener will be called upon to narrow down the range of his holding, both as to strength and as to type. He will not always be able to do so. Some hands require a series of bids before an adequate picture can be painted.

The second bid will usually announce to which class of openings the particular hand belongs. Roughly speaking, the opener's hand will fall within four classifications:

A. *The Minimum Range.*

B. *The Good Hand.* This is just above minimum range.

C. *The Very Good Hand.* This is the type of hand on which opener makes a jump rebid. He wishes to reach game unless partner has made a shaded response.

D. *The Rock Crusher.* This hand is just below a 2 bid in strength, and now that partner has responded, you will insist upon reaching game willy-nilly.

Let us examine his appropriate form of action in each case.

A. *The Minimum Range.* This covers hands of the value of 13, 14, and 15 points, but may sometimes include 16-point hands.

With hands of this strength, if opener does not have the urge to bid again, he should not do so, unless his partner's response was forcing. If partner offers a single raise, naturally he should pass. If partner responds with 1 No Trump, opener should not bid again, unless his hand is unsuitable for No Trump play.

Where responder names a new suit, of course, opener must speak again, but he should do so at the lowest convenient level. How does opener indicate that his hand is in the minimum range? He may do so in several ways:

1. By a rebid of 1 No Trump (not 2 No Trump).
2. By a simple rebid of his own suit.
3. Where he has support for partner's major-suit take-out, he may give a single raise with hands in this class, if it is the most convenient bid.

B. *The Good Hand.* This includes hands of the value of 16, 17, and 18 points, but may sometimes include 19-point hands. On this type of holding, opener should make a constructive rebid of some kind. He should avoid making any rebid which will induce partner to believe that the hand is in the minimum range. In other words, he should not make a simple rebid of his own suit, he should not rebid 1 No Trump, he should not offer his partner a mere single raise.

C. *The Very Good Hand.* This covers hands of the value of 19, 20, and 21 points. Game will be there unless something is wrong with partner's response. A jump rebid of some kind is therefore indicated.

D. *The Rock Crusher.* This describes hands of the value of 22 points or more. On this type of hand, opener makes a jump-shift rebid in an effort to describe the strength of his hand.

Rebid by opener when partner has given a single raise

When you open with 1 of a suit, next hand passes, and partner raises to 2 of the same suit, you are not expected to feel encouraged. Responder may have kept the bidding open on very moderate values, ranging from 7 to 10 "dummy points." Unless you have considerably more than an opening bid, there will be no chance for game, and you should pass even though your hand contains another suit.

But if you have definite excess values, there is a chance for game, provided partner's raise was a fairly good one and not a questionable or "courtesy" raise. In such cases you test the nature of your partner's response. This you may do in one of several ways. The usual method is to bid 3 of your suit, which states, in effect, "Partner, I cannot tell how good your raise was. If you had a sketchy raise and were just keeping the bidding open for me, I'll expect you to pass, but if your raise was good, please go on to game. In other words, if your raise was based on 7 or 8 points, I wish you to pass, but if you had 9 or more, I would like you to go on to 4."

It is important for the opener to assess his values accurately when partner gives a single raise, before he decides whether to pass, to bid again, or to contract for game. When the responder raises the opening bid from 1 to 2, opener must revalue his hand if it contains a long trump suit. In addition to all the points he counted for high cards and distribution when he opened the hand, he must make the following adjustment:

Add 1 additional point for the fifth trump
Add 2 additional points for the sixth and each subsequent trump

After making this calculation, try to determine whether it is possible that the partnership has 26 points. If you find that the combined assets cannot reach this figure, by all means pass. In other words, if you had only 15 points, you know that the partnership cannot possibly have 26 when partner offers a single raise.

If you find that your hand upon revaluation is worth 18 points or more, then you may take a chance and contract for game, because partner has promised at least 7. But if you have less—let us say, 16 or 17 points—there may or may not be a game, depending upon how good partner's raise happened to be. In such a case you proceed to 3, asking him to go on if he had a representative raise.

Let us examine a few cases, in each of which you have opened with 1 Spade and partner has responded 2 Spades, both opponents passing.

♠ A K x x x　　♡ A x x　　◊ Q x x　　♣ x x

Pass. Your hand was originally worth 14 points, 13 in high cards and 1 for distribution. Now that Spades have been supported, you may add 1 point for the fifth Spade, giving your hand an adjusted value of 15 points. Even if partner has a maximum raise, you will not have the necessary 26 and should pass.

♠ A K 10 x x　　♡ A 10 x　　◊ K J x　　♣ x x

This hand had an original valuation of 16 points. Now that Spades have been supported, you add 1 point for the fifth Spade, bringing it up to 17 points. If partner had only 7 or 8, you do not wish to reach game, but if he had as many as 9 or 10, you would like to go on. Your proper procedure is to bid 3 Spades, and if partner has 9 or more points, he should carry on to 4.

♠ A J 9 x x x   ♡ A K   ◇ Q J 10   ♣ x x

This hand had an original valuation of 17 points, and now that Spades have been supported, you add 1 point for the fifth Spade and 2 points for the sixth Spade, bringing it up to an adjusted value of 20 points. Therefore, even if partner has only 7 points, you will have sufficient and should contract for 4 Spades.

Your rebid need not be in the same suit. You may test out partner's raise by showing another suit or by bidding 2 No Trump, depending on the type of your hand.

♠ x   ♡ A Q 10 9   ◇ A J 10 x   ♣ A 10 9 x

You open with 1 Heart and your partner raises to 2. Your hand contains 15 high-card points and is valued at 17 for purposes of suit play. You cannot promise a game, but you should make a mild try to get there. You may bid 3 Clubs or Diamonds, hoping that partner will now be able to contract for game in Hearts on your display of additional strength. If he merely returns to 3 Hearts, you had better pass. That would mean that he had only a courtesy raise, of about 7 points, which would not be enough for game.

♠ A K Q 10   ♡ A Q 10   ◇ J 10 x x   ♣ Q x

This time your hand contains 18 points in high cards. (Observe that the 10s bring the hand above the limit for a 1 No Trump opening.) You open with 1 Spade and your partner raises to 2. Partner's hand may contain 8 high-card points. The suggested call is, therefore, 2 No Trump, asking partner to proceed to game in the denomination he considers best.

Rebids by opener after a 1 No Trump response

When partner responds to your opening bid by calling 1 No Trump, you must remember that he has a maximum of 10 high-card points and may have as little as 6. If it is not altogether likely that the partnership has 26 points, abandon hope of a No Trump game. To put it another way, if your hand was within the minimum range, game should not be contemplated after this response. If you have a balanced hand, do not rebid a five-card suit in this situation.

There are, generally speaking, three types of hands that belong to the No Trump family. They are distributed 4-3-3-3, 4-4-3-2, or 5-3-3-2. If your hand contains a singleton or two doubletons, you may look for an excuse to play in a suit, but even then it is not obligatory to do so. However, if your hand is unbalanced and not suited for No Trump, you may either rebid your suit or name some other suit. If your hand is within the qualification of what we have referred to as a good hand—in other words, above the minimum range—there may be a chance for game, depending upon the quality of partner's No Trump take-out. If you have 17 or 18 points, for example, you will be able to visualize the total of 26 if partner has a maximum No Trump response (in the vicinity of 9 points).[1] If you have 20 points yourself, then surely you proceed to 3 No Trump, for you know that partner has at least 6 points.

For example:

♠ A K J x x   ♡ x x   ◇ K J x   ♣ J x x

You open with 1 Spade, partner responds with 1 No Trump. Pass, despite the fact that you have a rebiddable Spade suit and a worthless doubleton in Hearts. You have a balanced hand which is suitable for play at 1 No Trump. You have only 13 high-card points, and even if partner has a near maximum, you will be far short of the number necessary for game.

♠ A K x x   ♡ 10 x x   ◇ A Q x x   ♣ x x

On the same sequence of bids you should pass. Do not bid 2 Diamonds. There is no hope for game and you have a balanced hand. *The best place to play an indifferent hand is 1 No Trump.*

♠ A K x x   ♡ A Q J x   ◇ x x x   ♣ x x

However, on this holding we advise a rebid of 2 Hearts to make allowance for those situations in which partner had a Heart suit which he was unable to show at the level of 2. If you pass 1 No Trump and his hand was something like:

♠ x x   ♡ K 10 x x x   ◇ x x   ♣ A 10 9 x

a laydown game contract would be missed.

♠ A K x x x x   ♡ A J x   ◇ x x x   ♣ x

Bid 2 Spades. Although your hand is minimum in high cards, it is unsuitable for play at No Trump and your six-card major suit should be rebid.

[1] Hands that count 17 or 18 should normally be opened with 1 No Trump, if the pattern is satisfactory, in preference to 1 of a suit.

♠ A K 10 x x ♡ A Q x ◇ A x x ♣ K x

Raise to 3 No Trump. You have 20 points in high cards and partner has at least 6. Note that this hand was too big to open with 1 No Trump and had to be opened with 1 of a suit.

Rebid by opener after take-out to 1 of a suit

When you open with 1 of a suit and partner responds with 1 of another suit, it is, of course, your duty to speak once more. It is at this point that you should clarify the nature of your opening bid, both as to type and as to strength. If your opening bid was of approximately minimum strength, this is the time to make the announcement. The message is conveyed to partner either by a rebid of 1 No Trump or by a rebid of 2 of your suit, whichever best describes your hand. Such a rebid sends the following message: "Partner, be on your guard. My opening may be an absolute minimum and in any case I have not much more than an opening bid. My hand ranges from 13 to 16 points."

♠ x x ♡ A K J x ◇ K J x ♣ K x x x

You open with 1 Heart and partner responds with 1 Spade. Your hand contains 15 high-card points, which places it in the minimum range. Your proper rebid is 1 No Trump.

♠ x x ♡ A K 10 x x ◇ A x x x ♣ x x

You open with 1 Heart and partner responds with 1 Spade. Again your hand is within the minimum range. It is worth 13 points, 11 in high cards and 1 for each doubleton, but it is of the suit type and is best described by a rebid of 2 Hearts.

These rebids are frequently referred to as "sign-offs," but the sign-off bid by the opener should not send a cold chill down his partner's back. Responder should not become obsessed by the notion that opener has a bad hand. He must not lose sight of the fact that partner did open the bidding, and the so-called sign-off merely announces that his hand ranges from 13 to 16 points.

♠ x x ♡ A K J 10 x x ◇ K x x ♣ x x

You open with 1 Heart and partner responds 1 Spade. Your rebid is 2 Hearts. Partner now bids 2 No Trump, denoting a desire to go game. The suggested action by you at this time is a 3 Heart bid. This is a warning bid which says, "Partner, be very cautious. I still have my opening bid, but it was based on minimum high-card strength. I have bid my suit three times to show extra length but no additional high-card strength."

♠ A Q 10 x   ♡ x x   ◇ x x x   ♣ A Q x x

You open with 1 Club and partner responds with 1 Diamond. Your proper rebid is 1 Spade. *The naming of a second suit at the level of 1 requires no additional strength.*

♠ x x   ♡ A Q 10 9 x   ◇ K Q J 10   ♣ x x

You open with 1 Heart and partner responds 1 Spade. You have a minimum hand which is not suitable for No Trump, because of the two worthless doubletons, and apparently you should rebid 2 Hearts. However, since a 2 Diamond rebid is just as cheap and permits partner to return to 2 Hearts, it is the recommended action. This will be particularly helpful when partner is very short in Hearts and has some length in Diamonds. Partner must realize that this is the cheapest possible level at which you could have shown this suit.

When you make it impossible for partner to return to 2 of your first suit, you advertise a very good hand. For example:

♠ x x   ♡ A Q 10 x   ◇ A K J x x   ♣ A x

You open with 1 Diamond and partner responds with 1 Spade. Your rebid should be 2 Hearts. To be sure, this makes it impossible for partner to return to 2 Diamonds, but if he is obliged to return to 3 Diamonds, you are in no danger, for you have a very good hand. Partner should realize that you have great strength when you choose this sequence of bids. In order to justify this sequence of bids, commonly known as a "reverse," your hand should be worth at least 19 points, including high cards and distribution. That is to say, in any bid of this character, which catapults the partnership into a nine-trick contract, the opener should have what we refer to as a very good hand, and a very good hand is described as one whose value is at least 19 points.

♠ A Q 10 x   ♡ x x   ◇ A Q 10 x x   ♣ x x

You open with 1 Diamond. If partner responds 1 Heart, you naturally rebid 1 Spade, but if, in response to your Diamond opening, partner bids 2 Clubs, you dare not bid 2 Spades, because this makes it impossible for partner to return to 2 Diamonds and your hand is not strong enough to relish a 3 Diamond contract. You must content yourself, therefore, with a rebid of 2 Diamonds, with the intention of showing Spades only if partner takes further aggressive action.

Raising partner's one-over-one response to 2

When your partner responds with 1 of a major suit for which you have some support, you must decide whether or not to offer partner an immediate raise. This raise by you does not require any great excess values, for it is important to announce the ability to play at partner's major suit early in the hand. Wherever your hand contains four of partner's trumps, or where it contains a singleton and normal trump support for partner, you may raise once even with a minimum hand. This is to make sure that the deal is played at the proper contract if partner has a weak hand and does not carry on. Where you have normal trump support for your partner and even slight additional values, you may give a single raise at once. Such a raise normally describes hands which are worth 14, 15, or 16 points in support of partner.

Even though you are the opener, when partner names a suit which you are about to raise, you start from scratch and value your hand as though you were the dummy for your partner's bid. Let us examine a few cases:

♠ A x x   ♡ x x   ◊ A K J x x   ♣ x x x

You open with 1 Diamond and partner responds with 1 Spade. A raise to 2 Spades is not recommended, because you have a minimum hand. Merely rebid to 2 Diamonds. However, if you hold:

♠ A x x   ♡ x   ◊ A K J x x   ♣ x x x x

a raise to 2 Spades is indicated. Observe that you have a singleton, which makes the Spade raise desirable. Furthermore, your hand is now worth 14 points in support of Spades and is therefore regarded as slightly above minimum.

♠ A x x x   ♡ x x   ◊ A K J x   ♣ x x x

In this case you have no additional honor strength, but the possession of four Spades makes it best to give an immediate raise, even though your hand is worth only 13 points in support of Spades.

Raising partner's response from 1 to 3

When the opening bidder raises his partner's take-out from 1 to 3, he describes a hand with substantial values in excess of the opening. Such hands should be worth, in support of partner's suit, 17, 18, or 19 points. To illustrate:

♠ A J 10 x   ♡ A K J x   ◇ x   ♣ Q J x x

You open with 1 Club and partner responds with 1 Spade. You have more than adequate trump support, and 19 points in support of Spades. You are therefore justified in jumping to 3 Spades.

This is not a forcing bid. Partner is permitted to pass if his 1 Spade response was of a shaded nature. If, for example, partner holds

♠ Q x x x x   ♡ x x x   ◇ Q J x   ♣ x x

he need not go on.

Raising partner's response from 1 to 4

A raise from 1 to 4 by the opening bidder is stronger than the raise from 1 to 3. There is a logical reason for this. If opener jumps to 3 and responder has a very weak hand, he may not go on. If, however, the opener is strong enough to insist upon a game contract, he should assume the entire responsibility himself. This requires a little more than is needed to jump from 1 to 3.

In this case opener shows a hand that is worth 20 or 21 points in support of partner's suit:

♠ A J x x   ♡ x x   ◇ A K J x   ♣ A Q x

You open with 1 Diamond and partner responds with 1 Spade. Your hand is worth 20 points in support of Spades. You should therefore assume responsibility for a game contract by going to 4 Spades. Partner might have nothing but five Spades to the King and would still have a play for game, yet he certainly would not bid it if you jumped to only 3 Spades.

The jump rebid to 2 No Trump

This rebid by the opener describes a hand that is well-suited to No Trump play and one that contains 19 or 20 high-card points.

This is a very important requirement to bear in mind. There is a tendency on the part of a great many players to jump to 2 No Trump whenever they hold slightly more than an opening bid. "Slightly more" is not sufficient. For example:

♠ J x   ♡ K J x   ◇ A K J x x   ♣ A Q x

You open with 1 Diamond and partner responds with 1 Spade. You have a hand that is well suited to No Trump play and one that contains 19 high-card points. Your proper rebid is 2 No Trump. If partner's Spade response included 6 high-card points, he should go on to 3 No Trump. If, however, part of partner's points were made up of distribution and he has less than 6 high-card points, he may pass the 2 No Trump bid, which, of course, is not forcing.

♠ x x   ♡ A x x   ◇ A K x x   ♣ A x x x

The opening bid has been 1 Diamond and the response 1 Spade. Some players commit the error of bidding 2 No Trump merely because they have more than a minimum opening. This is highly improper. This hand contains 15 high-card points, which places it, for rebid purposes, within the minimum range, and the proper rebid is 1 No Trump. Unless partner has 11 high-card points, there will be no game. And if partner has 11 high-card points, he will bid again even after the 1 No Trump rebid.

The jump rebid to 3 No Trump

It has been seen that when the opener's hand is suited for No Trump and contains 19 or 20 points in high cards, he should jump to 2 No Trump. When his hand contains slightly more than this—21 or 22 points—he should take the full responsibility upon himself and contract for 3 No Trump after a one-over-one response. For example:

♠ A x   ♡ A Q 10   ◇ A K J x   ♣ K 10 x x

You open with 1 Diamond and partner responds with 1 Spade. Your hand contains 21 high-card points, and you should jump to 3 No Trump, for which you should have a good play even if partner has less than 6 high-card points. Remember that if you jump to 2 No Trump and partner has a more or less balanced hand with only 5 high-card points, he will not go on to 3.

The jump rebid in opener's suit

When the opening bidder has a good six-card (or longer) suit and a hand that will produce about seven tricks in the play, he may make a jump rebid to 3 of that suit, provided the hand contains at least some high-card strength in excess of the opening. Expressed in terms of point count, the opening bidder's hand should be worth 19 to 21 points in rebid valuation. Perhaps an explanatory note regarding "rebid valuation" is in order at this point. You will recall that after partner has supported your suit, you add 1 point for the fifth trump and 2 for the sixth and each subsequent trump. These additional points were added because it was presumed that after the raise the trump suit became self-sustaining. Where the opening bidder himself has a self-sustaining suit, he may, for practical purposes, treat it as though partner had supported it, simply because it requires no support. In those cases, therefore, where opener has a long and powerful suit in addition to his original valuation, including high cards and distribution, he may add 1 point for the fifth trump, 2 points for the sixth, and so on, to determine the rebid value of the hand.

Let us see how this works with an example:

♠ x x   ♡ A K 10 9 x x   ♢ K x   ♣ A Q x

You open with 1 Heart and partner responds 1 Spade. The proper rebid is 3 Hearts. Your hand had an original valuation of 18 points, 16 in high cards and 1 for each doubleton. However, for rebid purposes, it is reasonable to consider the Heart suit self-sustaining, for you need no support in Hearts from partner. Therefore, in addition to your original valuation, you add 1 point for the fifth Heart and 2 for the sixth Heart, giving the hand a rebid valuation of 21 points. Expressed in other terms, this hand is worth about seven playing tricks and justifies the jump rebid.

Note that the jump rebid by opener in his own suit is not forcing where the response has been made at the level of one. If partner has made his Spade response on a hand of minimum values, which may not be helpful at the Heart contract, he is at perfect liberty to pass. A jump rebid in your own suit should not be made if your only excuse for doing so is the length of your suit. Remember that the jump rebid promises something additional in the way of high-card strength. If your hand contains a rebid valuation of 19, you will be within the required limits. Another way to state the requirement for a jump rebid in your own suit is: 16 to 19 original points with a solid five-card suit or a good six-card suit.

The jump rebid to game

Suppose you hold:

♠ x   ♡ A K Q J 10 x   ♢ A x x   ♣ K Q x

You open with 1 Heart and partner responds 1 Spade. No matter how weak a response partner has made, you should be unwilling to play this hand for less than game, and your proper rebid is 4 Hearts— not 3 Hearts, which partner might pass.

There are some players who raise an objection to such a rebid on the grounds that "it sounds too much like a shut-out." Let me hasten to point out that this department takes a dim view of the expression "shut-out." It is almost on the *verboten* list. When any player opens with 1 of a suit, he announces certain high-card values. When he subsequently jumps, he announces additional high-card values, or, what is more to the point, a great amount of playing strength. If the opening bidder jumps from 1 to 4, that is a stronger bid than a jump from 1 to 3. This is in sharp contrast with the technique of the responder. Where the responder jumps from 1 to 3, that shows high cards and distribution. But where the responder jumps from 1 to 4, it shows distribution but not high cards.

IN A NUTSHELL

A jump rebid to 4 of his suit (game) by the opening bidder denotes a very strong hand (about 8½ or 9 winners—22 rebid points). It is stronger than a jump rebid to 3, which is not forcing and shows 7 to 8 winners (19 to 21 rebid points).

There is no such thing as a "shut-out" rebid.

The jump shift by opening bidder

When the opening bidder wishes to insist upon a game he may do so in one of two ways: by jumping to game on the next round, as we have seen above; or by making a jump *in a new suit*. This, incidentally, is the only way the opening bidder can force the responder to speak again. A responder may pass if he hears a new suit mentioned. A responder may pass if he hears a jump in the same suit, or a jump in No Trump. But he has no option if partner jumps in a new suit. For example:

♠ K x x x   ♡ A K J x x   ◇ A K J   ♣ x

You open 1 Heart and partner responds 1 Spade. This hand has great possibilities. A jump bid of 3 Spades would be grossly inadequate. Partner might have nothing more than five Spades to the Queen Jack, in which case he would pass and a game in Spades might be missed.

A jump to 4 Spades might be acceptable, but even that does not do complete justice to your holding. This hand is worth 23 points in support of Spades, and partner will not need very much to produce a slam.

The recommended rebid is 3 Diamonds, a jump shift. *This forces partner to speak again, regardless of the nature of his hand.* It is your intention to contract for game in Spades on the next round. If partner has a good hand, the obligation to carry on (to a slam) will then be his. The jump shift by the opening bidder is made on hands that are worth, at the very least, 21 points.

Another case:

♠ J x   ♡ A K Q 10 x   ◇ x   ♣ A K Q x x

You open with 1 Heart and partner responds with 1 Spade. Surely you are unwilling to play this hand for less than a game, but you are not quite certain as to the exact contract. In order to be sure that partner does not pass and that game will eventually be reached, you must jump in a new suit, and your proper rebid is 3 Clubs.

Rebid by opener after take-out to 2 of a suit

If you choose your opening 1 bid properly, you will already have planned the rebid you will make if partner takes you out into 2 of his suit.

The principal things to remember are:

A rebid in the same suit you bid before, or a suit rebid which permits partner to return to your first suit at the level of 2, does not promise additional strength.

A bid of 2 No Trump, a raise of partner's suit to 3, a bid of 3 in a new suit, or any bid which makes it impossible for partner to return to 2 of your first suit shows a strong hand.

♠ J 10 x   ♡ A K x x   ◇ A 10 x x   ♣ x x

You bid 1 Heart. If partner responds 1 Spade, your rebid is 1 No Trump. But if partner should respond 2 Clubs, you must not bid 2 No Trump. You lack the high-card strength for such a call. You must bid 2 Diamonds, which permits partner—if his hand so indicates— to return to 2 Hearts.

♠ x x   ♡ A K x x x   ◇ Q x x   ♣ K J x

You bid 1 Heart, partner responds 2 Clubs. Rebid 2 Hearts. Your trump support is good enough to raise Clubs, but your hand as a whole is not strong enough. Your hand is worth only 13 points in support of Clubs and is therefore not good enough to raise to 3 of a minor suit. Such a bid requires 16 points.

A rebid of 2 No Trump by the opener when partner has taken out to 2 of a suit describes a good hand, one that ranges in high-card values from 15 to 18 points. The 2 No Trump rebid should not be used as a rescue of partner's response.

♠ A Q x   ♡ A Q J x x   ◇ K J x   ♣ x x

You bid 1 Heart. Over partner's response of 2 Clubs bid 2 No Trump, even though this prevents your telling immediately about your Heart suit. Remember, it is more important to describe the strength of your hand as a whole than to describe a particular suit. A rebid of 2 Hearts would announce that your hand was in the minimum range, 13 to 16 points. This hand is worth 17 points in high cards alone and must therefore be described in some other fashion.

A raise of the responder's take-out from 2 to 3 has been described as indicating a strong hand worth at least 16 points. There is, however, an exception. If you open with 1 Spade and partner responds with 2 Hearts, you may raise to 3 with only slight values above your opening bid, provided you are satisfied with Hearts. In other words, the raise may be based on 14 or 15 points.

Let us examine a few bidding sequences:

1.	OPENER	RESPONDER	2.	OPENER	RESPONDER
	1 Heart	2 Clubs		1 Spade	2 Clubs
	2 No Trump			3 Clubs	

3.	OPENER	RESPONDER	4.	OPENER	RESPONDER
	1 Spade	2 Diamonds		1 Heart	2 Clubs
	3 Clubs			2 Spades	

5. OPENER   RESPONDER
   1 Spade   2 Hearts
   3 Hearts

In the first four of the above sequences, opener has shown a strong hand. Note that in every case, if responder wishes to return to his partner's first suit, he must proceed to the level of 3. Opener, therefore, must have a hand which is based on at least 16 points.

Let us look at the cases individually:

1. Opener has promised at least 15 points in high cards and a well-distributed hand. He may even have a rebiddable Heart suit, but it is more important to describe the strength of the hand than the texture of the suit.

2. Opener must have at least 16 points in support of Clubs.

3. Opener's hand must be worth at least 17 points at one of his own suits, for he has reached the level of 3 without a fit having yet been established, which is a drastic step and must be supported by a strong hand.

4. This hand must be worth about 19 points at one of opener's suits. This type of bid is known as a "reverse" and shows great strength, for if partner wishes to prefer Hearts, he must go to the level of 3.

5. This is the exceptional case in which a player may go to the level of 3 without great additional strength. It applies when partner has taken out to 2 Hearts. Inasmuch as he has bid a major suit and opener has support for that suit, it is deemed expedient to give an early raise when opener has at least 14 points in support of Hearts. Remember that responder has presumably promised at least 10 points, so that the partnership will be assured of a minimum of 24 points, which is near game.

Choice between rebidding your own suit and raising partner's suit

The opener is frequently faced with the question: "Shall I rebid my suit or support my partner?" He may resolve the doubt by answering the following question: "What impression do I wish to make upon my partner: do I wish to appear aggressive or do I prefer to seem mild-mannered?"

If the opener wishes to display additional values, he should raise his partner. If, however, his hand is of the near minimum type, he should prefer to rebid his own suit as a mild warning. To illustrate:

1. ♠ A K J x x   ♡ A x x   ◇ x x x   ♣ x x
2. ♠ A K Q x x   ♡ K x x   ◇ K x x   ♣ x x

You open with 1 Spade and partner responds 2 Hearts. *With No. 1* your proper rebid is 2 Spades. You have an absolute minimum hand, and though you have normal trump support, your hand is not worth 14 points in support of Hearts. The safer procedure is to rebid your Spades to definitely identify your hand as being in the minimum range. But *with No. 2,* even though your Spades are somewhat stronger, they should not be rebid. You have adequate trump support for Hearts and distinctly more than a minimum hand, so that the major suit raise should be given at once.

Another form of this problem is presented when the opener has the choice of rebidding another suit or raising his partner. This is frequently a delicate question. Let us examine a few cases:

♠ K J x x   ♡ K J x   ◇ x x   ♣ A Q J x

You open with 1 Club and partner responds with 1 Heart. You have a choice of bidding 1 Spade or supporting your partner with 2 Hearts. Which is preferable? The hand is of moderate strength, and it would be doubtful strategy to bid both your suits and also support Hearts. Your partner would expect more strength. It is better, therefore, to raise to 2 Hearts, after which you may feel that you have done your full duty on the hand, which is worth only 15 points in support of Hearts. However, if you had slightly more strength, as with:

♠ A Q x x   ♡ K Q x   ◇ x x   ♣ A Q x x

a mere raise to 2 Hearts would not do justice to the hand. It is worth 18 points in support of Hearts, but inasmuch as you lack four trumps, the jump to 3 is not acceptable, and you are 1 point short for a jump to 2 No Trump. It is better tactics, therefore, to rebid 1 Spade, with the hope that partner will bid again (which he probably will do), after which you will also support Hearts. By naming two suits and supporting partner's suit, you will have given an adequate description of your hand.

When your partner's suit is a minor suit, it is not nearly so important to support it. For example, you hold:

♠ A J x x   ♡ x   ◇ J x x x   ♣ A K x x

You open with 1 Club; partner responds with 1 Diamond. You

may raise the Diamonds, if you choose, or you may show your four-card major. The latter bid is preferable. If over 1 Spade partner bids 1 No Trump, you intend to bid 2 Diamonds. If over 1 Spade partner bids 2 Diamonds, you intend to raise to 3 Diamonds, and partner will realize that you are short in Hearts.

Raising minor-suit take-outs

When the responder takes out into 2 Clubs or 2 Diamonds, the opener may find himself in possession of such good support for his partner that he is tempted to raise to 4 of that suit. In many cases this impulse should be suppressed in favor of a single raise, to allow partner the opportunity to bid 3 No Trump should he desire to do so. Eleven-trick game contracts should be avoided if there is a reasonable chance to bring in nine tricks at No Trump.

Suppose you open with 1 Heart and partner responds with 2 Diamonds.

♠ Q x   ♡ A Q J x x   ◇ A Q J x   ♣ K x

A jump to 4 Diamonds is not recommended. A raise to 3 affords partner the opportunity to try for 3 No Trump.

It is not nearly so desirable to raise a minor suit as to show other important features of the hand. For positional reasons you may elect to bid No Trump, concealing entirely your support for partner's minor, as in this case:

♠ K x   ♡ A K x x   ◇ K 9 x x   ♣ K x x

Assume that you have opened with 1 Heart (though most players would prefer 1 No Trump) and partner responds 2 Diamonds. Your rebid should be 2 No Trump rather than 3 Diamonds.

Rebid of 2 No Trump without the usual strength

It has been pointed out that when the opener's rebid is 2 No Trump, even though not a jump, a strong hand is indicated. However, an exception is to be noted in the case where your left-hand opponent has overcalled first and your partner has made a free bid at the level of 2, depriving you of some bidding space. In such a case, a rebid of 2 No Trump need not be quite so strong as usual, since partner by his free bid has deliberately placed you in this awkward position. For example, as South you hold:

♠ Q x   ♡ A K x x   ◇ A 10 x x   ♣ x x x

The bidding has proceeded:

SOUTH	WEST	NORTH	EAST
1 Heart	2 Diamonds	2 Spades	Pass
?			

You are forced to rebid and cannot support Spades or rebid Hearts. You are therefore obliged to rebid 2 No Trump. Partner must take into consideration the fact that his free bid at so high a level may have forced you to do so. When you opened the bidding you could not have foreseen that he was going to bid 2 Spades. You were prepared to rebid if his response were the expected 1 Spade or 2 Clubs, in which case you could have rebid 1 No Trump or 2 Diamonds respectively.

Third-round rebid with a two-suiter

It was observed in the chapter on opening bids that when two five-card suits are held, the normal procedure is to open with the higher-ranking and show the lower-ranking suit on the next round if it is convenient to do so. When both suits have thus been shown and it becomes the opener's third time to bid, assuming that he must insist upon one of his own suits, the proper procedure is to rebid the lower-ranking suit in order to permit the return to his first suit at the same level. For example, as South you hold:

♠ A J x x x   ♡ K Q 9 x x   ◇ K x   ♣ x

The bidding has proceeded:

SOUTH	WEST	NORTH	EAST
1 Spade	Pass	2 Diamonds	Pass
2 Hearts	Pass	2 No Trump	Pass
?			

At this point you wish to elicit from partner a choice between Spades and Hearts, since you are not enthusiastic about No Trump. The rebid of 3 Spades would be improper, because it makes it impossible for partner to return to 3 Hearts. It would therefore, by implication, deny that the Hearts are five cards long. The correct bid is 3 Hearts. This permits partner to return to 3 Spades, to pass 3 Hearts if he chooses, or to insist upon 3 No Trump if he must.

Rebids after forcing responses

When you have opened the bidding and your partner makes a jump response of any type—a double raise, a 2 No Trump response, or the more powerful jump shift—you can relax as far as game is concerned, but this does not make your choice of a rebid any less important.

Your guiding principle in rebidding over a forcing response should be this: Your rebid should show where, from your hand, you prefer that the hand should be played. For example:

♠ A J x x   ♡ A K 10 x   ◇ J x x x   ♣ x

You open with 1 Spade. Partner raises to 3 Spades. Rebid 4 Spades despite the four-card suit. You do not want to play this hand at No Trump with the singleton in Clubs. To bid 4 Hearts would be a slam try, and you do not have the necessary strength. But if partner responded 2 No Trump, your rebid would be 3 Hearts, again because you do not like a No Trump contract if a good suit contract can be found.

♠ J x   ♡ x x   ◇ A K x x x   ♣ A J x x

You open with 1 Diamond, partner responds 2 No Trump. Bid 3 No Trump. You do not want to play the hand in either Diamonds or Clubs, because your hand is too weak to relish the eleven-trick contract necessary for game in a minor.

When partner has made a take-out that is forcing to game, you need not concern yourself with bidding the full strength of your hand at this particular point if there is some descriptive bid which you choose to make. Remember that at this point you may wish to temporize, either by rebidding your own suit, to indicate its strength, or by naming some other suit. The mere rebid of your own suit might normally sound discouraging, but since you will be afforded another opportunity, you may correct that impression on a subsequent round.

Rebid when partner has refused to keep the bidding open

Courage is an essential ingredient in the composition of the successful player, but it is not to be confused with stubbornness.

You may recall the story of the headstrong cow who insisted upon her right of way against an oncoming freight train. After pausing awhile, the engineer at length plowed through and blasted the animal into eternity. An observer commented on the outstanding courage of the animal. "Great courage," came the reply, "but darn poor judgment."

When you open with 1 of a suit and partner fails to keep it alive, assume he has nothing, and do not carry on the fight unless you can virtually fulfill contract in your own hand.

You are South (vulnerable) and hold:

♠ A K 10 x x x   ♡ K x   ◇ x x   ♣ J x x

The bidding has proceeded:

SOUTH	WEST	NORTH	EAST
1 Spade	Pass	Pass	2 Hearts
?			

What should you do? It is foolhardy to contest the auction when you know your partner has nothing. You are not even close to fulfilling a 2 Spade contract unassisted. When I saw this hand played, the actual South stubbornly rebid 2 Spades, was doubled and set 800 points. The complete hand:

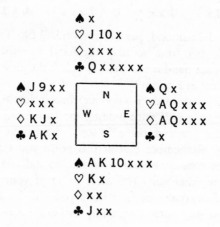

Similarly, as South you hold:

♠ A Q x x   ♡ A Q x x   ◇ x x   ♣ A Q x

The bidding has proceeded:

SOUTH	WEST	NORTH	EAST
1 Spade	Pass	Pass	2 Diamonds
?			

True, you have 18 high-card points, but since partner has announced a worthless hand, you will have to lead everything out of your own hand and may wind up taking no more than four tricks. You cannot reasonably expect to go places and should give up the fight. Any further action by you will result in a loss of 800 to 1,100 points, depending upon developments. The complete hand:

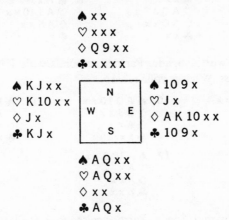

```
                      ♠ x x
                      ♡ x x x
                      ◊ Q 9 x x
                      ♣ x x x x

     ♠ K J x x                         ♠ 10 9 x
     ♡ K 10 x x        N               ♡ J x
     ◊ J x          W     E            ◊ A K 10 x x
     ♣ K J x           S               ♣ 10 9 x

                      ♠ A Q x x
                      ♡ A Q x x
                      ◊ x x
                      ♣ A Q x
```

When, however, you hold a hand like this:

    ♠ A K x x x   ♡ A K J x x   ◊ x   ♣ x x

and the bidding has proceeded:

SOUTH	WEST	NORTH	EAST
1 Spade	Pass	Pass	2 Diamonds
?			

Here you should bid 2 Hearts, because even though partner has no high-card strength, he may have some length in Hearts, in which case even a game in Hearts might not be beyond hope, and a contract of eight tricks should not be risky.

REBID QUIZ

You open with 1 Diamond. Partner responds with 1 Heart. The opponents pass. What is your rebid on each of the following hands?

1. ♠ x x
   ♡ Q x x
   ◊ A K J x
   ♣ K 10 x x

2. ♠ Q J x x
   ♡ x
   ◊ A K x x x x
   ♣ A x

3. ♠ x x
   ♡ K x x x
   ◊ A K Q x x
   ♣ A x

You open the bidding with 1 Heart. Partner responds with 1 Spade. The opponents pass. What is your rebid?

4. ♠ x x x x
♡ A K Q J x
◇ K x
♣ x x

5. ♠ Q x x
♡ A K x x x
◇ K x x x
♣ x

6. ♠ K x x
♡ A 10 x x x
◇ K x
♣ K x x

7. ♠ x x
♡ A Q J 9 x
◇ A Q x x
♣ x x

8. ♠ K x x
♡ A J 10 x x
◇ A K x x
♣ x

You open with 1 Spade. Partner responds with 1 No Trump. The opponents pass. What is your rebid?

9. ♠ Q J 10 x x
♡ x x
◇ Q x
♣ A K J x

10. ♠ A Q 10 x x
♡ Q J x x
◇ A x
♣ x x

11. ♠ K Q J 10 x x
♡ A
◇ A J 10 x x
♣ x

12. ♠ A 10 9 x x
♡ A x
◇ A x x
♣ K x x

You open with 1 Spade. Partner raises to 2 Spades. The opponents pass. What is your rebid?

13. ♠ A 10 9 x x x
♡ A
◇ K Q x x x
♣ x

14. ♠ A Q 10 9
♡ A K 10 x
◇ Q x x x
♣ x

You open with 1 Heart. Partner bids 2 Clubs. The opponents pass. What is your rebid?

15. ♠ A K 10 9 x
♡ x x
◇ Q x
♣ K x x x

16. ♠ A J 10 9 x
♡ x
◇ A x x
♣ A K x x

17. ♠ K J 10 9 x
♡ K 10 x
◇ A Q x
♣ Q 10

18. ♠ K Q 8 x x
♡ x x
◇ A K x x
♣ x x

In the following examples, you are South. The bidding has proceeded as indicated.

19. ♠ K 10
♡ Q x x
◇ A J 10 x x
♣ K J x

SOUTH	WEST	NORTH	EAST
1 Diamond	2 Clubs	2 Hearts	Pass
?			

20.	♠ x x	SOUTH	WEST	NORTH	EAST
	♡ x x	1 Diamond	1 Spade	1 No Trump	Pass
	◇ A K Q x x	?			
	♣ A K x x				

21.	♠ K J x	SOUTH	WEST	NORTH	EAST
	♡ Q x	1 Diamond	Pass	1 Heart	1 Spade
	◇ A 10 9 x	?			
	♣ A J 10 x				

22.	♠ x x x	SOUTH	WEST	NORTH	EAST
	♡ A K Q J x	1 Heart	Pass	1 Spade	2 Clubs
	◇ K 10 x	?			
	♣ x x				

23.	♠ K Q J x	SOUTH	WEST	NORTH	EAST
	♡ A x	1 Diamond	Pass	2 Clubs	Pass
	◇ K Q x x x	?			
	♣ x x				

24.	♠ A x	SOUTH	WEST	NORTH	EAST
	♡ K x x	1 Club	Pass	1 No Trump	Pass
	◇ x x	?			
	♣ A K Q x x x				

ANSWERS TO REBID QUIZ

1. Two Hearts.
A rebid of 2 Clubs is not recommended. This is a more or less minimum holding, which is worth 14 points in support of Hearts. In those cases an immediate raise is our choice. In fact, in all doubtful cases, the raise of partner's major suit is to be preferred.

2. One Spade.
The impression that a six-card suit must be rebid willy-nilly, before any four-card suit is shown is a hold-over from the Gay Nineties. Partner might have a hand which is quite well suited to play at Spades, and yet the Spade suit might be lost if partner is discouraged from continuing by your Diamond rebid. For example, he might hold:

> ♠ K 10 x x   ◇ x x
> ♡ A x x x x   ♣ x x

In this case, if your rebid is 2 Diamonds, partner might give up the

ghost, but if your rebid is 1 Spade, a game contract in that suit will almost surely follow.

3. Three Hearts.
Your hand is worth 19 points in support of partner's Heart bid and the jump raise might induce him to contract for game with just a shade more than the minimum requirement for keeping the bidding alive.

4. Two Spades.
You have a hand of more or less minimum proportion in support of the Spade contract (15 points). It would be unwise to permit the solidity of your Heart suit to goad you into making a jump raise. Surely partner will require at least an average hand or better if game is to be contemplated.

5. Two Spades.
As we have many times pointed out, the raise of partner's major suit is

D

to be preferred to most other calls. It is therefore not recommended that you bid 2 Diamonds, a call which could lead to complications.

6. One No Trump.
While it is true that you have good three-card support for partner, it is better tactics to show the balanced nature of your hand by calling 1 No Trump. You have the adverse suits guarded and your hand is quite minimum.

7. Two Diamonds.
The 2 Diamond bid is to be preferred to 2 Hearts, inasmuch as it offers an additional parking place should the hand develop to be some kind of misfit.

8. Two Diamonds.
This hand is a shade too good for a single raise (18 points), however, it lacks the normal trump support for a double raise. The compromise bid, therefore, is 2 Diamonds, which is calculated to obtain another bid from partner at which time you may return to Spades.

9. Two Clubs.
This bid is made in an effort to search for the best possible part score contract. If partner chooses to carry on by bidding 2 Hearts, or 2 Diamonds, it is your intention to let matters drop.

10. Two Hearts.
If partner prefers Spades, you will surely be in a playable contract, and if partner should raise Hearts, you will surely be in good strategic position.

11. Three Diamonds.
You have virtually nine winners in your own hand, and you should insist upon a game contract. This jump in a new suit is completely forcing.

12. Two Clubs.
This bid is made with a twofold purpose. It guarantees a five-card Spade holding in your hand since there is no holding with four Clubs and four Spades that you would elect to bid the Spade suit first. The added merit of the bid is that it permits partner to show a long Diamond or Heart suit should his hand be of an unbalanced nature. The knowledge that your hand contains five Spades will tip the scales in the direction of a Spade preference in any close decision.

13. Four Spades.
Your hand counts 20 points when partner raises your Spades. (The fifth and sixth cards in your suit obtain promotional values.) Since game is in view, there is nothing to be gained by mentioning your Diamond suit other than to point the way for the defense against your eventual Spade contract.

14. Three Hearts.
Your hand is worth 17 points, and partner's raise may have been based on 9. We suggest 3 Hearts, because partner may have offered his original raise on some hand containing only three Spades and four or perhaps five Hearts.

15. Two Spades.
Although you have excellent support for partner's suit, it would be indiscreet for you to raise him to the 3 level with such a minimum hand.

16. Three Clubs.
The raise to the 3 level shows substantially more than a minimum opening bid and gives partner the opportunity to search for the best ultimate contract.

17. Two No Trump.
With the adverse suits well guarded and a balanced hand containing 15 high-card points it is your intention to play 3 No Trump unless partner flashes the warning signal by repeated sign-off bids.

18. Two Diamonds.
It is our policy to offer partner a choice of suits, when it is economical to do so. This call promises no additional values.

19. Two No Trump.
While three-card support is not to be frowned upon, we prefer to designate No Trump when our hand is subject to attack on the opening lead.

20. Three No Trump.
Partner should have the adverse suits stopped, and his free bid of 1 No Trump shows 10 high-card points, bringing the partnership's assets up to 26, sufficient for game.

21. One No Trump.
You have 15 high-card points plus additional intermediate values. Since partner is expected to have 6 points for his response, your 1 No Trump call should be relatively safe. To pass

would be improper for it might place partner in an untenable position.

22. Pass.
Despite the splendid quality of your suit, you have a minimum opening bid and should not make a free bid at this point.

23. Two Diamonds.
This hand does not measure up to values required for a 2 Spade bid at this juncture, which would constitute a reverse. While your 2 Diamond call is a slight underbid it is reasonable to expect partner to carry the ball since he has carried on to the 2 level.

24. Three No Trump.
Partner's 1 No Trump response to your 1 Club opening shows values between 9 and 11 high-card points. With 16 high card points and a running six-card suit, there is no reason to place a burden upon him. Game should be reasonably certain.

4.

Rebids by responder

EARLIER it was pointed out that when the opener makes his rebid he is taking perhaps the most significant step in the auction. The opening bid of 1 in a suit covers a wide range of hands. It is the second bid that narrows down the range and places the hand in a specific category. This applies with equal force to the responder. His first response may have been temporizing and therefore covers hands valued from 6 to 18 points, and it is at his second call that he usually attempts to clarify the nature of his response. Any responder will do well to familiarize himself with the following table as his responding problems arise. This table will indicate in a general way the type of campaign which you should plan as responder, depending upon the amount of strength which you hold.

6 to 10 points

Your hand is of the minimum class and you should make a mild response. If you have 6 or 7 points, do not bid again unless your partner forces you to. If you have 8 or 9 points, you should bid once more if partner makes a strong bid urging you to proceed.

11 to 13 points

You have a good hand. It is worth two bids. In order to be sure that you have the opportunity to make a second bid, you should make some response which partner is not permitted to pass. In other words, a temporizing bid. You must not give a single raise or bid 1 No Trump, either of which partner may pass.

13 to 16 points

You have a very good hand which is a hand equal to an opening bid facing an opening bid. You must therefore see to it that you reach game if a suitable contract is available. You are assured that the partnership has 26 points. Therefore you should go to game yourself or continue to make forcing responses (new suits) until you reach a satisfactory game contract.

16 to 19 points

You have a strong hand. You must show that you have more than just an opening bid. You may do this (provided your hand is of the right type) by jumping to 3 No Trump or by bidding a suit and then making a big jump the next round.

19 points and up

This hand will produce a slam unless partner has a minimum. You must therefore give the immediate slam signal by jumping in a new suit. Note that even if partner has only 13 points, your 19 will bring the total to 32, which is 1 point away from a slam.

Let us examine a few examples:

♠ x x   ♡ A K x x x   ◊ J x x   ♣ K J x

You are responder. Your partner opens with 1 Spade. You note that your hand is equal to an opening Heart bid (13 points). You therefore estimate that there is a probable game in the hand, and you start investigating to determine the best contract and temporarily bid 2 Hearts. Partner makes the mild rebid of 2 Spades. Since you estimate a game on this hand, you do not give up. You search for that game by bidding 2 No Trump, even though you do not have complete protection in Diamonds.

♠ J x x   ♡ A K x x x   ◊ x x   ♣ K J x

Your partner bids 1 Spade. As in the previous case, you estimate there is game because you have the equivalent of an opening bid. Your hand is worth 13 points in support of Spades. However, you cannot properly jump to 3 Spades because you lack the necessary trump support for a jump bid, so you temporize by calling 2 Hearts. Partner now rebids 2 Spades, designating a hand of more or less minimum proportions, but you do know now that he has a good Spade suit for which three to the Jack is normal support. There is no further information which you require. You have found a suitable contract, Spades, and you know that you have the necessary values for game. You therefore bid 4 Spades.

♠ J x x   ♡ A K x x x   ◊ x x   ♣ Q x x

Your partner opens with 1 Spade. You respond 2 Hearts and partner rebids 2 Spades. You are now convinced that the best final contract will be Spades. Now for the question of how far you may go. You are not in position to predict that there is a game, because your hand is not the equal of an opening bid. It is worth 11 points in support, and therefore you must make another attempt. If partner has about 2 points to spare, you will have the necessary 26. You therefore raise to 3 Spades. If opener has a minimum, he should pass. If he has 15, game should be there; and even if he decides to go on with only 14, you will be in game with 25 points, which is by no means a lack of discretion.

♠ Q x x   ♡ A Q x x   ◊ K x x   ♣ Q 10 x

Partner opens with 1 Club. You respond 1 Heart. Partner's rebid is 1 No Trump, which may indicate an absolute minimum. Your hand is the equivalent of an opening bid (13 points), and since you are facing an opening bid, it is your duty to contract for game. You have found a convenient contract, No Trump. Therefore bid 3 No Trump. It would be improper for you to raise to only 2 No Trump, because partner, if he has only 13 points, will not be able to carry on.

♠ J x x   ♡ A K x x   ◊ K x x x   ♣ x x

Your partner opens with 1 Club. You respond with 1 Heart. Partner's rebid is 1 No Trump. While you are satisfied with No Trump you cannot promise game, because your hand is short of an opening bid in value (11 points). It is possible that the opening bidder has something to spare, in which case there should be game. Your proper procedure is to bid 2 No Trump; if partner has nothing to spare, he should pass. If he has a point or two in excess of his opening bid, he should go on to 3 No Trump.

♠ x x x   ♡ A x x x x   ◊ x x   ♣ A x x

Partner opens with 1 Diamond. You respond with 1 Heart. Partner's rebid is 2 Diamonds. What should you do? You should be persuaded that there is no hope for game. Therefore you pass. When the opener makes a minimum rebid, responder should not act again with less than 11 points, but he may occasionally do so with 10. This hand is worth only 8 points at No Trump and 9 points at Hearts. It does not, therefore, qualify for further action.

♠ Q J x   ♡ A x x x x   ◊ x x   ♣ A x x

Partner opens with 1 Diamond. You respond 1 Heart. Partner's rebid

is 2 Diamonds. This hand is worth 11 points at No Trump. You must
therefore make a second bid. There is still a chance that the partnership possesses 26 points. You therefore make one more move toward
game by bidding 2 No Trump. If partner does not contract for game,
you then retire gracefully.

When your hand is well suited to No Trump, which partner has
bid, you must not waste time by giving him the needless information
that you have a rebiddable suit. For example, you hold:

♠ x x   ♡ A x x   ◇ A K J x x   ♣ J x x

The bidding has proceeded:

NORTH	EAST	SOUTH	WEST
1 Club	Pass	1 Diamond	Pass
1 No Trump	Pass	?	

It is proper for you to go straight to 3 No Trump, undeterred by
your worthless doubleton in spades. You may assume that partner
has that suit protected. Your hand has the value of 13 points in high
cards alone and is well suited to No Trump play. Remember, a rebid
of 2 Diamonds would deny that your hand is suited for No Trump,
and partner could be expected to pass.

Responder clarifies his raise

When the responding hand has given his partner a single
raise in a major suit, he has given an approximate idea of his values
but not altogether an exact one. The raise may have been of a scanty
nature (7 or 8 points), made merely for the purpose of keeping the
bidding alive. On the other hand, it may have been a sound raise
(9 or 10 points). The opening bidder may determine which of these
two raises was given by inquiring in the form of another bid.

Let us assume that the bidding has proceeded:

OPENER	RESPONDER
1 Spade	2 Spades
3 Spades	?

If the responder has a good raise (9 or 10), he should bid again.
If he has a poor raise (7 or 8), he should pass.[1] For example, you

---

[1] With a capable declarer as partner you may casually go on to game with 8 points
if they are of the gilt-edged variety. It may then be that you are playing for game
with only 25 points, which should not be looked upon as a shot in the dark.

are the responder with each of the following hands. The bidding has proceeded as above:

1. ♠ Q x x x   ♡ x x   ◇ A Q x x   ♣ x x x
2. ♠ K x x   ♡ J x x   ◇ A Q x   ♣ x x x x
3. ♠ Q x x x   ♡ x x   ◇ K x x x   ♣ x x x

With NO. 1, you should bid 4 Spades. You have a sound raise containing 10 points. With NO. 2, you should contract for game. Your hand is worth 10 points, but inasmuch as it is evenly balanced you may try 3 No Trump. If partner does not find that suitable he may go on to 4 Spades. With NO. 3, you should pass. It contains only 7 points.

When the opening bidder tests out his partner's raise by a rebid of 2 No Trump, the same general principle applies.

OPENER	RESPONDER
1 Spade	2 Spades
2 No Trump	?

Again you are the responder. If your hand is evenly balanced and most of your points consist of high-card values, you should raise to 3 No Trump. If you have four trumps and your raise is worth 9 or more points, you should take your partner to 4 Spades. If you have not these requirements you should, as a rule, merely return to 3 of partner's suit. This bid does not amount to another raise. It is a preference and, to a certain extent, a sign-off. Its message is, "Partner, I had a raise of merely 7 or 8 points and I prefer Spades to No Trump."

With NO. 1 of the preceding examples, responder should leap from 2 No Trump to 4 Spades, announcing a good raise with 4 Trumps. With NO. 2, he should raise to 3 No Trump because he has 10 points in high cards alone. With NO. 3, he should merely return to 3 Spades, announcing that he prefers Spades to No Trump but had a light raise (7 or 8 points).

When the responder has given a single raise in a minor suit and the opener rebids to 3 of the same suit, the responder should try for game at No Trump even with an unstopped suit if he has about 8 or 9 points in high cards. For example, you hold:

♠ K x   ♡ x x x   ◇ A x x x   ♣ Q x x x

Partner opens with 1 Diamond, which you raise to 2. Partner rebids 3 Diamonds. You should try for 3 No Trump.

When a single raise has been given in a major suit and opener names another suit, responder is forced to speak at least once more. For example:

OPENER	RESPONDER
1 Heart	2 Hearts
3 Clubs	?

The 3 Club bid is a one-round force. It says, in effect, "Partner, I am trying to find out whether you had a good raise or a poor one. Please tell me now. Naturally you must not pass 3 Clubs, because we have agreed on Hearts thus far. If you can bid a game, please do so. If not, just quietly return to 3 Hearts." Responder should then go directly to 4 Hearts if he has a sound raise. For example, as responder you have:

♠ x x   ♡ K 10 x x   ◊ A x x x   ♣ x x x

In the bidding sequence above, after your partner's 3 Club bid, you should bid 4 Hearts, for you have a very fine raise worth 9 points. But if you substitute the Queen of Diamonds for the Ace, it would be a light raise and you would then merely return to 3 Hearts.

The rebid of 2 No Trump by the opener after a single raise is not forcing. In rare cases, with only three trumps and a weak but balanced hand, the responder should pass it.

Rebid by responder when opener gives a single raise

OPENER	RESPONDER
1 Heart	1 Spade
2 Spades	?

If the responder has a weak hand, he will naturally pass. If he has some slight unexpected strength, he may think in terms of game. He should rely upon the opener to have somewhat more than a minimum opening bid when he raises the response; that is, somewhere between 14 and 16. If responder's hand is worth 10 or more points, he may therefore feel that there is a possible game.

Suppose under the preceding bidding sequence you are the responder and hold:

1. ♠ A K J x x   ♡ x x x   ◊ J x x   ♣ x x
2. ♠ A K J x x   ♡ x x x   ◊ Q J x   ♣ x x
3. ♠ K J 9 x   ♡ x x   ◊ x x x   ♣ A Q 10 x

D*

With NO. 1, you may bid 3 Spades. The hand is worth 11 points, 10 points originally, plus 1 for the fifth Spade after partner supports the suit. Since opener might have 15, you must not abandon hope for game.

With NO. 2, you have enough to go to 4 Spades. Your hand is worth 13 points, and even if partner has an absolute minimum of 13, you will have the necessary count for game.

With NO. 3, your hand is worth 11 points. You must not therefore abandon hope for game, since partner may have 15. You should bid again by calling 3 Clubs. This may induce partner to contract for game in No Trump if he so chooses, and it may allow him to judge whether or not there is a game in Spades. If he merely returns to 3 Spades you should give up the ghost. However, he may be able to bid 4 Spades when you indicate that you have 11 points.

A somewhat similar case:

OPENER	RESPONDER
1 Spade	2 Hearts
3 Hearts	?

If your hand is worth 12 points, you should contract for game, for partner will surely have at least 14. Suppose you hold:

♠ x x x   ♡ A J x x x   ◊ K Q x   ♣ x x

With this hand you should bid 4 Hearts. Your hand is worth 12 points, 11 originally and 1 for the fifth Heart.

When a raise is to 3 in a minor suit the same considerations apply, except that the responder must fix his gaze on a No Trump game rather than an eleven-trick game in the minor suit, if his hand is at all suitable for No Trump play. For example:

OPENER	RESPONDER
1 Spade	2 Clubs
3 Clubs	?

Responder should chance a bid of 3 No Trump on:

♠ 10 x   ♡ A x x   ◊ x x x   ♣ A Q 10 x x

Rebid by responder after he has responded 1 No Trump

OPENER	RESPONDER
1 Spade	1 No Trump
2 No Trump	?

In this sequence of bids, opener has shown a very good hand. Opener's rebid of 2 No Trump states to partner, "Partner, if your No Trump response was on the lower side (6 or 7), we will not have enough. But if it was on the upper side (8 or 9), I should like you to contract for 3 No Trump."

Occasionally, with a capable declarer as partner, you may choose to go on with 7, but we wish to hear no complaints if you do so and go down a trick. For example, in the above bidding sequence you as responder hold:

♠ x x   ♡ 10 x x   ◇ K Q x x   ♣ K x x x

You should accept partner's invitation and bid 3 No Trump. You have 8, and your 1 No Trump response was therefore on the upper side.

Rebid by responder when opener names another suit

Responder takes his choice

A frequently misunderstood obligation of the responder is the one that involves showing a preference between partner's two suits. The responder should not assume the role of captain of the team. His duties are more akin to those of a servant, and he should indicate which of the two suits is preferable, according to his holdings.

A preference is sometimes indicated by passing, sometimes by returning to the first suit. In making a choice, length is far more important than high cards in the trump suit. As a rule, it is the duty of the responder to select the trump suit in which the partnership has the greater number.

For example, your partner has bid Spades and Hearts, and you have: ♠ x x x and ♡ A K. It is your solemn duty to take your partner back to Spades. You should never be heard to say, "But, partner, I have the two top Hearts." Those two top Hearts need not be trumps. They will be winners even with Spades as trumps. Spades will make the better trump suit, because if partner has a losing Heart he can use one of the little Spades to dispose of it.

When the same length is held in each of partner's suits, the practice is to prefer the suit he bid first. This has the advantage of giving partner one more chance, if that is your desire, and has the further advantage of returning to the suit in which the partnership will, more often than not, have the more trumps. For example:

♠ J x x   ♡ K x x   ◇ A x x x   ♣ x x x

Partner opens with 1 Spade. You respond 1 No Trump. Partner rebids 2 Hearts. You have no actual preference. The fact that you have a King in Hearts and only a Jack in Spades does not render Hearts any better for trumps. The two suits are exactly equal as far as you are concerned, but it would be a good practice to return to 2 Spades, because you have a very good 1 No Trump response and would like to give your partner another chance. In fact, should the opener make one more move, you will contract for game.

♠ J x   ♡ 10 x x   ◇ x x x x   ♣ A J x x

Your partner opened with 1 Heart. You respond with 1 No Trump. Partner's rebid is 2 Spades. This is a strong bid and shows that partner has five Hearts and four Spades. You naturally prefer Hearts, and it is your duty to return to that suit even though it increases the contract.

The responder must never refuse to show a preference for the partnership's best trump suit just because he is frightened. Where a preference actually exists he must indicate it. Occasionally there will be no actual preference and the responder may use his own judgment. It is my practice not to show an immediate preference for partner's first suit with a worthless doubleton. In those cases it is my policy either to pass or make some other bid. For example:

♠ A J x x x   ♡ x x   ◇ x x   ♣ 10 x x x

Partner opens with 1 Heart and you respond with 1 Spade. Partner bids 2 Diamonds. Since opener has been unable to make a jump bid you may conclude that there is no possible hope for game. I do not recommend a return to 2 Hearts, although it is partner's first suit, for I am not interested in giving partner any further chance. As far as I'm concerned, I have no preference between Hearts and Diamonds. Being too weak to make another bid in Spades, I pass. However, holding:

♠ A J x x x   ♡ x x x   ◇ x x x   ♣ x x

I would return to partner's first suit because, holding three trumps, I am at least mildly prepared to play it there.

Some additional cases:

A. ♠ x x x   ♡ K 10 9 x   ◇ A J x   ♣ x x x

Partner opens with 1 Club. You respond with 1 Heart. Partner bids
1 Spade. Note that this bid is not forcing upon you because you are
not the opening bidder. If your first response was based on barely 6
points and you like your partner's second suit as much as you do the
first, you may pass. Where, however, your partner's second suit is
shown at the level of 1, you should make every effort to bid again if
your hand is worth more than 6 points. In this case you have 8 points
and should therefore respond to his 1 Spade bid in the cheapest possible way, which is 1 No Trump. Note that if the Ace of Diamonds
were changed to the Queen, you would still have responded with 1
Heart, but you should pass 1 Spade.

B. ♠ x   ♡ x x x x   ◇ A J x x x   ♣ K Q x

Partner opens with 1 Spade. You respond 2 Diamonds. Partner rebids
2 Spades. Proper strategy is to pass. You have done your full duty by
this hand in responding at the 2 level and should take no further
action opposite a partner who has advertised a minimum-type opening.

C. ♠ K x x x   ♡ A x x   ◇ K x x   ♣ 10 x x

Partner opens with 1 Diamond. You respond with 1 Spade. Partner
bids 2 Clubs. You could, if you wish, return to 2 Diamonds. This
would be a mere preference, and since you have previously bid only
at the level of 1, it would still promise no more than 6 points. Your
hand has the value of 10 points, and they are gilt-edged points, for
the King of Diamonds is a more impressive King than any other.
You should exercise your judgment by making a second constructive
bid of 2 No Trump.

Rebids that force responder

It is essential for the responder completely to understand the
forcing principle. He must know the cases in which he is obliged to
bid further, whether he likes it or not, and the cases in which he may
pass if he chooses.

The responder is allowed a wider latitude than the opening bidder.
In most cases he has made no commitment. His partner is the one
with the strong hand, and responder may have been bidding just to
give the opener another chance. Consequently, he is at liberty to drop
the bidding at almost any time.

The fact that a responder hears his partner name a new suit does not force him to speak again. That obligation rests only on the shoulders of the opening bidder.

When a responder hears a jump in the same suit, that does not compel him to bid again, although such a jump is forcing on the opening bidder.

When a responder hears his partner jump in No Trump, he need not bid again if he does not choose to. Such a jump would be an unconditional obligation to rebid if he had been the opener.

But when a responder hears his partner jump in a new suit, then he has no right to opinions. He is absolutely bound to speak and to keep going until game is reached. A jump shift is a force to game whether it is made by opener or responder.

Let us examine a few cases. Suppose your partner has opened with 1 Diamond and you have responded with 1 Heart, holding:

♠ x x x x   ♡ K Q 10 x   ♢ x x   ♣ x x x

If your partner's rebid has been:

(A) 2 Clubs, you should pass. You prefer Clubs to Diamonds and have no interest in making any further bid. As responder you are not forced to speak again just because your partner named a new suit.

(B) 2 No Trump, you should pass. You did your full duty by this hand when you responded with 1 Heart. A jump in No Trump does not force the responder to bid again. Partner has 19 or 20, which is not quite enough. If he had 21 points he would have gone to 3 No Trump himself.

(C) 3 Diamonds. A jump rebid in the same suit does not force the responder. You should therefore pass.

(D) 3 Clubs. Now you have no choice. The jump in a new suit has forced you to bid again and to keep on going until game is reached. You cannot rebid your own suit. You are unable to support Diamonds. Your hand is not suitable for a Club raise. So there is only one call left for you—namely, 3 No Trump.

Partnership language

It is just as important to know what a bid means as to know how much strength it shows. As the bidding develops, the responder assumes the duty of directing the partnership into the proper contract as well as calculating the strength of the combined holdings. Some rebids are more engaging than others. For example, the constant repetition, at minimum stages, of the same suit indicates great length of suit but not very much strength. However, not every repetition of responder's suit is discouraging. Whenever responder is at perfect liberty to pass (or it has been suggested to him that he pass by partner's minimum rebids), and he keeps bidding even though it happens to be in the same suit, he is showing a willingness to go on. For example:

OPENER	RESPONDER
1 Heart	2 Clubs
2 Hearts	3 Clubs

You are asked to interpret the meaning of the 3 Club bid. It is a constructive bid. When opener rebids 2 Hearts he describes a hand in the minimum range and is willing to quit. When responder chose to go on to 3 Clubs it could hardly be construed as a refusal bid but plainly as a desire to go on. But if the bidding had proceeded:

OPENER	RESPONDER
1 Heart	2 Clubs
2 No Trump	3 Clubs

Responder's 3 Club bid in this case would not be encouraging to opener since his rebid of 2 No Trump has shown a strong hand and a desire to move toward game. If responder had a good hand he would raise partner to 3 No Trump. In this sequence the 3 Club bid announces, "Partner, I fear you will not find my hand useful at No Trump. There is a grave danger that you will not be able to run my Clubs." If responder in this sequence, for example, held:

♠ x x x   ♡ x x   ◇ x x   ♣ A K Q x x x

it would be highly improper to rebid 3 Clubs. This is a good hand for No Trump, and responder should raise to 3 No Trump.

A similar case:

OPENER	RESPONDER
1 Diamond	1 Heart
2 Clubs	2 Hearts
2 No Trump	3 Hearts

What is the meaning of the 3 Heart bid? It is very clear that responder has a weak hand with great length in Hearts, and even the Hearts cannot be very strong, because, if they were, by this time the responder could have been in a position to bid 4 Hearts after opener has shown such strength.

When your partner opens, and later rebids 2 No Trump, if you have a good hand you must not merely repeat your suit. You should either raise the No Trump or jump in your suit.

You are responder, holding:

♠ x x   ♡ A K Q x x x   ◇ x x x   ♣ x x

The bidding has proceeded:

OPENER	RESPONDER
1 Spade	2 Hearts
2 No Trump	?

You should bid either 3 No Trump or 4 Hearts. Definitely not 3 Hearts.

Some more cases:

OPENER	RESPONDER
1 Diamond	1 Spade
2 Clubs	2 Diamonds

The question arises: Is the 2 Diamond bid to be construed as encouraging? The answer is No. The responder has shown a mere preference for Diamonds over Clubs. He has never increased the contract, and the opener should be very cautious about carrying on.

In this case the 2 Diamond bid is not really constructive and does not denote additional values. Responder may still have only his 6 points, but it was his duty to return to Diamonds because he preferred that to Clubs. But if the bidding had proceeded:

OPENER	RESPONDER
1 Spade	2 Clubs
2 Diamonds	2 Spades

the 2 Spade bid in this sequence should be interpreted differently. On the surface it would appear to be a mere preference and therefore a sign-off. Actually it is not quite so. It is true that the responder has not given a Spade raise, but he has previously indicated that he has a fairly good hand by increasing the contract to 2 Clubs, indicating at least 10 or 11 points. Therefore the 2 Spade bid should not be treated as discouraging. After all, if responder's hand were not fairly good, he would have responded with an immediate raise to 2 Spades instead of taking the trouble to bid 2 Clubs. Responder may hold:

♠ Q J x   ♡ x x x   ◇ x x   ♣ A K x x x

It is apparent that this is the only reasonable bidding sequence for responder to adopt. He surely could not jump to 3 Spades after the 2 Diamond bid, for that would be forcing to game, and his hand is worth 11 points in support of Spades. Opener therefore should not give up if he has 14 or 15 points.

OPENER	RESPONDER
1 Spade	2 Spades
2 No Trump	3 Spades

What is the meaning of the 3 Spade bid? It is this: "Partner, I did not have a very strong raise. I know you are asking me to go game, but I am unable to do so. This hand must play at Spades as far as I am concerned, but I have only 7 or 8 points in support."

OPENER	RESPONDER
1 Heart	2 Diamonds
2 No Trump	3 Hearts

What is the meaning of the 3 Heart bid? Does it show a dislike of No Trump and a mere preference for Hearts, or is it a strong bid? It is a strong bid. The responder is merely saying, "I am not sure whether we should play this hand at 4 Hearts or at 3 No Trump. I wish to give you a choice, partner. You must know I have a good hand, because I first took the trouble to bid 2 Diamonds, increasing the contract, and then I again increased the contract to 3 Hearts. If my hand were not that good, I would have responded with a mere 2 Heart raise in the first place."

On this sequence of bids the 3 Heart call is forcing. The opener must select a game contract at either No Trump or Hearts. A typical hand justifying such bidding by responder is:

♠ x x   ♡ K x x   ◇ A K J x x   ♣ x x x

OPENER	RESPONDER
1 Heart	1 No Trump
3 Hearts	?

The responder holds:

1. ♠ x x x x   ♡ x x   ◇ K J x   ♣ Q x x x
2. ♠ K x x   ♡ x x   ◇ K x x x   ♣ Q x x x

With NO. 1, responder should pass; he has only 6 points, the absolute minimum, which he has already shown. With NO. 2, he should go on to 3 No Trump. He has a good No Trump response consisting of 8 points.

A semi-forcing bid need not be responded to, but if the responder does reply, it becomes a force to game:

OPENER	RESPONDER
1 Heart	1 Spade
3 Hearts	3 Spades

Responder was not forced to rebid 3 Spades. He could have passed. But since he accepted the semi-force, it now becomes a force to game, and neither partner may pass until game is reached.

Responder's new-suit rebids are forcing

When the responder names a new suit the opener must bid again, not only on the first round but on subsequent rounds. For example:

♠ A K J x x   ♡ A Q J x   ♢ x   ♣ x x x

Your partner opens with 1 Diamond. You respond with 1 Spade. Partner bids 2 Diamonds. You are quite set on going to game, but it is not essential for you to jump the bid in Hearts at this point. You may force another bid from partner by merely naming a new suit. Remember, the opening bidder must bid again every time he hears a new suit. On the next round you will be in a better position to judge where this hand should play.

This device may be employed by the responder as a temporizing measure when he wishes time to make up his mind about a hand. For example, you hold:

♠ x x   ♡ x x   ♢ A K J x x x   ♣ A J x

Your partner opens with 1 Spade. You respond with 2 Diamonds. Partner rebids 2 Spades. You know that this hand belongs in game, because you have distinctly more than an opening bid, but you are disinclined to assign this hand to an eleven-trick contract. If partner can stop Hearts, you would rather try for 3 No Trump.

You are perfectly safe, therefore, in bidding merely 3 Clubs, a one-round force. This is not intended as Ace-showing. As far as partner is concerned, you really have a Club suit. If he does not bid 3 No Trump, you will then decide whether to play for 4 Spades or 5 Diamonds.

Here is another interesting use of the new-suit force by responder to find the best contract. Responder holds:

♠ K Q J 9 x   ♡ K x x   ◇ x x   ♣ A x x

The bidding has proceeded:

OPENER	RESPONDER
1 Heart	1 Spade
2 Diamonds	?

The best game contract may be in Spades, Hearts, or No Trump, depending upon the texture of opener's hand. If opener has three Spades, that suit should be best. If he has five Hearts, that should be the final trump. In the absence of either, 3 No Trump appears to be the most suitable vehicle. How is responder to find out? Merely by bidding 3 Clubs. If opener prefers Spades he will bid 3 Spades and responder's worries are over. If opener rebids Hearts, that's the spot. If opener bids 3 No Trump, responder stops exploring.

When a player takes his partner out of a game contract, to which partner has voluntarily leaped, into a non-game contract, the inference is plain that he is looking for a slam. Otherwise the rescue would be senseless. For example, as responder, you hold:

♠ x x   ♡ x x   ◇ K J 10 x x x   ♣ x x x

The bidding has proceeded:

OPENER	RESPONDER
1 Club	1 Diamond
3 No Trump	?

What should you do? Pass, definitely. Do not make the mistake of bidding 4 Diamonds simply because you do not like No Trump. A player who has jumped to 3 No Trump does not have to be rescued.

Again, as responder, you hold:

♠ x x x   ♡ A Q x   ◇ x   ♣ K Q J x x x

The bidding has proceeded:

OPENER	RESPONDER
1 Spade	2 Clubs
3 No Trump	?

Here you have good reason to suspect that there is slam in the hand and wish to elicit further information from your partner. You may, if you choose, temporize by bidding 4 Clubs, which must be construed not as a rescue bid but as a slam try.

Cases in which a new-suit rebid by responder is not forcing

An exception is to be noted to the rule that the naming of a new suit by responder forces opener to speak once more. When the opener's rebid has been 1 No Trump, responder may show a new suit without forcing opener to bid again. For example, you are responder and hold:

♠ K J x x x   ♡ Q x x x x   ◇ x   ♣ x x

The bidding proceeds:

OPENER	RESPONDER
1 Club	1 Spade
1 No Trump	2 Hearts

The opener may pass; the 2 Heart rebid over 1 No Trump is not forcing. Suppose the bidding had proceeded:

OPENER	RESPONDER
1 Club	1 Spade
2 Clubs	?

If you held the above hand and the bidding had proceeded in this manner, it would be recommended that you give your hand up. In this situation a bid of 2 Hearts would be poor strategy because it would force opener to make another bid, a situation which you do not desire.

If the responder rebids in a higher-ranking suit, even over 1 No Trump, it is forcing:

OPENER	RESPONDER
1 Club	1 Diamond
1 No Trump	2 Spades

The 2 Spade bid makes it impossible for opener to return to 2 Diamonds; hence it is a strong bid, made in the expectation of getting to game, and opener must bid again.

A new suit by responder does not force the opener if either of the players has previously passed.

A new suit by responder does not force the opener when it is made directly over an adverse double. Suppose South holds:

♠ J x x   ♡ A Q J x x   ◇ A x x   ♣ x x

The bidding: SOUTH   WEST   NORTH   EAST
              1 Heart   Double   1 Spade   Pass
              ?

South may pass. Since North has not redoubled, he cannot visualize game, and Spades should be as safe a spot as any.

A new suit by responder does not force the opener when it is evident from the preceding bidding that responder is not trying to go places but is seeking a safe place to land. For example:

OPENER	RESPONDER
1 Heart	1 Spade
2 Hearts	2 Spades
2 No Trump	3 Diamonds

If responder had wished to force opener, he would have bid 3 Diamonds over 2 Hearts.

Observe the following sequence:

SOUTH	WEST	NORTH	EAST
1 Diamond	1 No Trump	2 Spades	Pass
?			

Is the 2 Spade bid, a new suit by responder, forcing on the opening bidder? This is an exceptional case in which it is not. The theory is this: North has a distributional hand rather than one containing high cards, because if he had high-card strength, he would have made a penalty double of West's overcall.

Meanings of bidding situations

The significance of the final bid in each sequence is indicated in the following chart:

1. | OPENER | RESPONDER |
   |---|---|
   | 1 Spade | 3 Spades ? |

   Game force
   (13–16)

2. | OPENER | RESPONDER |
   |---|---|
   | 1 Spade | 2 No Trump ? |

   Game force
   (13–15)

3. | OPENER | RESPONDER |
   |---|---|
   | 1 Spade | 2 Clubs ? |

   One-round force

4. | OPENER | RESPONDER |
   |---|---|
   | Pass | 1 Spade |
   | 3 Spades ? | |

   Not forcing
   Strongly invitational

5.
OPENER	RESPONDER
Pass	1 Spade
2 Hearts ?	

Not forcing

6.
OPENER	RESPONDER
1 Club	1 Diamond
1 Heart ?	

Not forcing

7.
OPENER	RESPONDER
1 Heart	1 Spade
3 Spades ?	

Semi-forcing
Strongly invitational

8.
OPENER	RESPONDER
1 Heart	1 No Trump ?

Weak bid (6–10)

9.
OPENER	RESPONDER
1 Heart	1 Spade
2 No Trump ?	

Semi-forcing
Strongly invitational

10.
OPENER	RESPONDER
1 Spade	2 Spades
3 Diamonds ?	

One-round force

11.
OPENER	RESPONDER
1 Heart	1 Spade
3 Hearts	3 Spades ?

Game force

12.
OPENER	RESPONDER
1 Heart	1 Spade
2 Clubs ?	

Not forcing

13.
OPENER	RESPONDER
1 Spade	2 Diamonds
2 Spades	3 Clubs ?

One-round force

14.
OPENER	RESPONDER
1 Heart	1 Spade
1 No Trump	2 Clubs ?

Not forcing

15.
OPENER	RESPONDER
1 No Trump	2 Clubs
2 Diamonds	2 Hearts ?

Not forcing

16.
OPENER	RESPONDER
1 No Trump	2 Spades ?

Weak bid

17.
OPENER	RESPONDER
1 Heart	2 Diamonds
3 Clubs ?	

One-round force

18.
OPENER	RESPONDER
1 Spade	2 Spades
2 No Trump	3 Spades

Sign-off

19.
OPENER	RESPONDER
1 Diamond	1 Spade
2 Clubs	2 Diamonds ?

Sign-off

20.
OPENER	RESPONDER
1 Spade	2 Hearts
2 Spades ?	

Not encouraging (13–15)

21.

OPENER	RESPONDER
1 Heart	1 Spade
1 No Trump ?	

Not encouraging (13–15)

22.

OPENER	RESPONDER
1 Spade	2 Clubs
2 No Trump ?	

Strength-showing (15–18)

23.

OPENER	RESPONDER
1 Spade	2 Diamonds
2 Spades	3 Diamonds ?

Mildly encouraging

24.

OPENER	RESPONDER
1 Spade	2 Diamonds
2 No Trump	3 Spades ?

Game force.

25.

OPENER	RESPONDER
1 Heart	1 No Trump
2 Spades ?	

Semi-forcing
Showing great strength

26.

OPENER	RESPONDER
1 Spade	2 Clubs
3 Spades ?	

Forcing

27.

OPENER	ADVERSARY	RESPONDER
1 Club	1 Heart	1 No Trump ?

Strength-showing bid (10–12)

28.

OPENER	ADVERSARY	RESPONDER
1 Diamond	Double	1 Spade ?

Not forcing

29.

OPENER	ADVERSARY	RESPONDER
1 Diamond	1 No Trump	2 Spades ?

Not forcing

30.

OPENER	RESPONDER
1 Club	1 Spade
1 No Trump	3 Spades ?

Forcing to game

31.

OPENER	RESPONDER
1 Club	1 Diamond
1 Heart	3 Clubs ?

Forcing to game

32.

OPENER	RESPONDER
Pass	1 Heart
2 Spades ?	

Forcing for one round

REBIDS BY RESPONDER QUIZ

1. ♠ x x
♡ K J 10 x
◇ x x
♣ A 10 x x x

OPENER	RESPONDER
1 Diamond	1 Heart
1 No Trump	?

2. ♠ K Q 10 x x
♡ Q x
◇ A J 10 x
♣ 10 x

OPENER	RESPONDER
1 Diamond	1 Spade
1 No Trump	?

3. ♠ A 10 x x x
♡ x
◇ J x x
♣ K Q x x

OPENER	RESPONDER
1 Heart	1 Spade
2 Clubs	?

4. ♠ K Q 10 9 x x
♡ A J x
◇ Q x
♣ x x

OPENER	RESPONDER
1 Diamond	1 Spade
1 No Trump	?

5. ♠ x x x
♡ x x
◇ A K Q 10 x
♣ Q 10 x

OPENER	RESPONDER
1 Heart	2 Diamonds
2 Spades	?

6. ♠ Q x x
♡ x x
◇ x x x x x
♣ A 10 x

OPENER	RESPONDER
1 Spade	2 Spades
3 Spades	?

7. ♠ K x x
♡ x
◇ A Q x x
♣ A K x x x

OPENER	RESPONDER
1 Spade	2 Clubs
2 Hearts	?

8. ♠ Q x x
♡ x x
◇ A K Q x x
♣ J x x

OPENER	RESPONDER
1 Spade	2 Diamonds
2 Hearts	?

9. ♠ x x
♡ K x x
◇ A x x
♣ K Q 10 x x

OPENER	RESPONDER
1 Heart	2 Clubs
2 No Trump	?

10. ♠ Q x
♡ K J x x x
◇ x x
♣ A Q x x

OPENER	RESPONDER
1 Diamond	1 Heart
1 Spade	?

11. ♠ Q x x
♡ A 10 x x x
◇ J 10 x
♣ x x

OPENER	RESPONDER
1 Diamond	1 Heart
1 Spade	?

12. ♠ Q x x x
♡ A K Q x x
◇ x
♣ x x x

OPENER	RESPONDER
1 Diamond	1 Heart
1 Spade	?

13. ♠ Q x
♡ J 10 9 x x
◊ K x x x
♣ x x

OPENER	RESPONDER
1 Spade	1 No Trump
2 Clubs	?

14. ♠ A J x
♡ A K Q x x
◊ x x
♣ x x x

OPENER	RESPONDER
1 Club	1 Heart
2 No Trump	?

15. ♠ A Q J x x
♡ x
◊ Q J 10 x
♣ x x x

OPENER	RESPONDER
1 Heart	1 Spade
2 Clubs	2 Diamonds
2 Spades	?

16. ♠ A 10 9 x x
♡ Q x
◊ K J x
♣ 10 x x

OPENER	RESPONDER
1 Heart	1 Spade
2 Clubs	?

17. ♠ A Q 10 x
♡ K Q 9 x
◊ x x
♣ x x x

OPENER	RESPONDER
1 Diamond	1 Spade
2 Clubs	2 Hearts
2 Spades	?

18. ♠ J 10 x
♡ x x
◊ A J 10 x
♣ Q 10 x x

OPENER	RESPONDER
1 Heart	1 No Trump
2 No Trump	?

ANSWERS TO REBIDS BY RESPONDER QUIZ

1. Two Clubs.
After a 1 No Trump rebid by the opener, the showing of a new suit by responder is not forcing. However, if responder in this sequence should bid 2 Spades (a reverse), that would constitute a force.

2. Three Diamonds.
You have the equivalent of an opening bid and must insist on game. If partner supports your Spades, you will carry on to game in that suit. If partner bids 3 No Trump, you will pass. On the other hand, if he bids 4 Diamonds, it is your intention to call 4 Spades, thus giving him an option of playing game at that designation or in 5 Diamonds.

3. Three Clubs.
Though your hand counts to 13 points in support of Clubs, it would be indiscreet to give partner a jump raise, for in so doing, you will have by-passed the desirable 3 No Trump game. If partner bids 3 Spades, you will, of course, carry on to 4.

4. Three Spades.
With an opening bid of your own, you must see that the partnership arrives at a game contract. Your jump rebid announces a strong suit, and gives partner the option of bidding 4 Spades or 3 No Trump.

5. Two No Trump.
While partner has shown an excellent hand by virtue of his "reverse," your hand is still nothing more than you promised when you bid freely at the level of 2. Do not make the mistake of jumping to 3 No Trump, for this call shows the equivalent of an opening bid. If slam is possible, partner will make. another move.

6. Pass.
Your single raise promised values between 7 and 10 points. Partner has

asked you to clarify the size of your raise. Since it is minimum, you should have nothing more to say.

7. Three Diamonds.

Your hand counts 19 points in support of partner's suit and is too good for a jump preference. By reversing as responder and then belatedly raising partner, you suggest the possibility of slam even though opener may have minimum values.

8. Three Spades.

Though we are normally reluctant to make the jump with only three trumps, however in this case, there appears to be no sound alternative. Since our hand is the equal of an opening bid in support of Spades, you indicate this fact by making a jump preference in partner's original suit.

9. Three Hearts.

This gives partner the option of playing game at Hearts or in No Trump. Do not fear that he will pass, for you have shown a good hand. With mediocre values, you would have suppressed your Club suit and raised Hearts immediately.

10. Two Clubs.

With 12 high card points plus a long suit, you are quite willing to risk a game opposite partner's opening bid. However, the question of which game to play can only be answered by partner's rebid. If he bids 2 Hearts, you will, of course, carry on to game in that suit. If, on the other hand, he raises your Clubs, you will proceed to 3 No Trump.

11. Two Diamonds.

Game is still possible if partner happens to fit Hearts. Should he give you a belated jump raise in Hearts, you intend to carry on to game in that suit. If partner passes, you probably are in your best contract.

12. Three Spades.

You have the standard requirements for a jump raise, four trumps to an honor and a hand that ranges between 13 and 16 points in support.

13. Two Spades.

While you have a meager preference, it would be unwise to mention your Heart suit with such poor holding. You are more or less certain that you have seven trumps between you. To bid Hearts runs the risk of partner's passing you with an unsuitable holding.

14. Six No Trump.

Partner has promised 19 or 20 high card points. Your 14 high-card points together with an excellent Heart suit make the slam odds-on since you have a minimum of 33 high-card points between you.

15. Three Spades.

Partner has shown a good hand with three-card support, for with an indifferent opening, he might well have raised your Spades immediately. Your bid invites him to go to game if his values are well placed.

16. Two No Trump.

While your hand is technically 1 point short of the standard requirement for this call, the long suit together with your good intermediate cards will give the partnership a fine play for game if partner chooses to continue.

17. Two No Trump.

Partner has the option of passing if his hand is the meagerest of openings. Do not make the mistake of bidding 3 Spades, for partner has only three-card support. With four-card support, he would have raised immediately.

18. Three No Trump.

Your original bid shows values between 6 and 10 high-card points. Partner is interested in game if the value of your hand is 9 or 10 points. Since you have 8 together with three ten-spots, you can evaluate your hand as maximum and accept the invitation.

5.   Slam bidding

I HAVE grave doubt as to the propriety of treating slam bidding as a distinct topic rather than as part of bidding tactics in general, but since that seems to be the accepted practice, I shall fall in line.

True enough, there are certain bids which by their very nature carry direct slam inferences. A jump in a new suit, for example, or a cue bid in a suit adversely bid. But the development of the bidding which reaches a slam should not differ widely from the style employed in getting to game. If we have a method for determining that a hand will take ten tricks, with Hearts as trumps, why is that method not equally suitable for determining that we have eleven tricks with Diamonds as trumps or twelve tricks at a Spade contract? The big thing in slam bidding is to determine whether or not the partnership resources amount to twelve tricks, a simple proposition indeed, but surprisingly difficult to sell.

What about Aces? you ask. You may find that your side can win twelve tricks but unfortunately the enemy can cash two tricks first. Naturally this is a condition to be avoided. After it is determined that the partnership has the necessary winning tricks, then comes the check-up. Various conventions have from time to time been devised for the purpose of making this checkup, but bear in mind that the purpose of these conventions is not to find out if you have a slam. Regular bidding methods are employed for that purpose. The conventions are calculated to find out if the opponents can win two tricks in a hurry. In other words, conventions like the Blackwood are not for the purpose of getting to a slam. They are for the purpose of staying out of one that cannot be made.

In other words, first find out that you have a slam. Then employ the slam convention for the purpose of checking up on Aces.

Slam valuation

In slam bidding the big thing is the diagnosis; that is, determination that the partnership has twelve or thirteen trick-winners. We have observed that when the partnership possesses the sum total of two opening bids (26 points), game will usually result. In other words, if both partners are satisfied with Spades as trump and each one has the equivalent of an opening bid, the hand should produce ten tricks. If the partnership has a surplus of a couple of tricks, it has the material for a slam. In other words, 33 or 34 points represents the trick-taking power of twelve tricks.

The following cases will illustrate how we determine that the partnership has the necessary trick-taking powers. You hold:

♠ K J x x x   ♡ A x   ◇ x x   ♣ K Q x x

Your partner opens with 1 Diamond. You respond 1 Spade. Your partner raises to 3 Spades. What is your diagnosis? You should diagnose a slam. Your hand is worth 16 rebid points (15 originally and 1 for the fifth Spade now that the suit has been supported). Partner has advertised a strong hand, probably 17 points or more. You therefore have the necessary 33 points. As a precautionary measure you may barge into a Blackwood bid, to protect against partner's holding some such hand as:

♠ A Q x x   ♡ K Q x   ◇ K Q x x x   ♣ x

Another example:

♠ 10 x x   ♡ A 9 x   ◇ A K J x   ♣ Q J x

Your partner opens with 1 Club, you respond with 1 Diamond. Partner's rebid is 2 No Trump. This is the classic case for simple addition. At No Trump we count only the high cards, so that your hand is worth 15 points. Partner, having made a jump to 2 No Trump, has promised 19 or 20 high-card points. You therefore know that you have at least 34, and you contract for 6 No Trump. What about Aces? you may ask. Should we check? In No Trump bidding it is impossible for the opponents to have two Aces if the partnership possesses 33 points, for there are only 7 points left in the pack.

The partner's hand was:

♠ A J x   ♡ K Q x   ◇ Q x x   ♣ A K x x

This leads us to the following conclusion: If you hold a responding hand which is as good as an opening bid and your partner opens the bidding and jumps, keep your eyes open for a slam. In other words, *an opening bid faced by an opening bid and followed by a jump equals a slam.* All of this, of course, assumes that there is a suitable contract and that the hand is not a misfit. I assume for the purpose of this rule that your partner's jump is in a declaration which you find to your taste.

We have seen that estimating slams on direct No Trump bidding is nothing more complicated than a simple addition of assets. With 37 or 38 points you should be willing to chance a grand slam (the opponents could not have an Ace). With 33 or 34, a small slam (the opponents could not have two Aces). This assumes a balanced hand. With a good five-card suit, you may get by with a point less; and with a six-card suit, with 2 or 3 points less. But in those cases it is wise to satisfy yourself as to the number of Aces held by the partnership.

If partner opens with a bid of 2 Spades, you may assume that he can take nine tricks in his own hand (and that he has at least 25 points with a five-card suit). By adding his assets to the total number of tricks you are confident your hand will produce, you will usually arrive with a fair degree of accuracy at the full trick-taking capacity of the combined holding.

Slam diagnosis by opener when responder jumps

You open, and partner jumps (1 Spade—3 Spades). If you have no excess values, you merely contract for game. Partner's response is based on a hand that is equivalent to an opening bid.

You have an opening bid. This spells game, and where you have excess values it follows that your hand may produce tricks in excess of game.

If your hand ranges in value from 13 to 16, it is regarded as of the minimum class. With those hands, slam will not be available and you simply contract for game.

If your hand is worth 17 points or more (don't forget to revalue your hand after partner supports it by adding 1 point for your fifth trump and 2 points for your sixth trump), then you may have a slam. If partner has a 3 Spade bid which is worth 16, you will have the necessary 33 points. With hands of this value, try once (by showing some Ace); if partner does not react favorably, quit at game.

If your hand is worth 20 points, you know that you have the necessary 33 and should not settle for less than a slam, provided you have checked for Aces. Hands that are worth 18 or 19 are usually safe enough to be taken to the level of 5, so that if you are concerned only with Aces, a Blackwood bid is permissible on hands of this strength. Remember, however, that to try Blackwood with holdings worth only 16 or 17 is a dangerous practice, for if the hand breaks badly, you may not be able to take eleven tricks if partner presents an unsuitable dummy.

Let us assume a few cases in each of which you open with 1 Spade and partner jumps to 3 Spades. You hold:

♠ A K J x x   ♡ x x   ◇ A x x   ♣ K x x

This hand is worth 17 rebid points. It had an original value of 16, but 1 point must be added for the fifth Spade now that partner has supported the suit. Inasmuch as partner's 3 Spade raise will be as much as from 13 to 16, it will be seen that if he has a maximum you will have the necessary 33 points. You should therefore try for a slam, but you must do so in a mild manner. A Blackwood call is not appropriate. First, because it will not provide you with enough information: even if partner has two Aces, you may be a long way from a slam, for you may not have the necessary tricks. Furthermore, a contract of 5 may not be safe if partner has a minimum raise of 13 points. You may make one try by bidding 4 Diamonds, showing the Ace. If partner wishes to proceed toward a slam, he may do so. If he returns to 4 Spades, you will retire gracefully.

You hold:

♠ A K J x x   ♡ x   ◇ A x x x   ♣ K x x

This holding is worth 18 rebid points. Now you may have a slam if partner has 15. You may therefore be slightly more aggressive than was recommended in the preceding example. A contract of 5 odd should now be safe, and you may make two tries for a slam.

♠ A K J x x   ♡ x   ◇ A J x x   ♣ K Q x

This hand is worth 21 rebid points, which, with partner's assured 13, brings the partnership up to 34 points, ample for a slam. You have merely to check for Aces now, and if partner has one, you may undertake to bid a slam.

In the following example you have opened with 1 Diamond, partner responds with 2 No Trump. You hold:

♠ A K x   ♡ K x x   ◇ A K J x   ♣ Q J x

You have 21 points, partner has 13, 14, or 15. You know, therefore, that you have at least 34 points, assuring you of a sound play for slam, and that you have a maximum of 36 points, so that you will not be inclined to contract for a grand slam. No checking for Aces is necessary, because the opponents cannot have two of them, and fu~~~thermore, even if your partner has two Aces and a King, you will not contract for a grand slam simply because you cannot count thirteen tricks.

Bids carrying slam implications

A jump shift in a new suit

A jump shift by the responder is the accepted method of announcing his early interest in a slam. Since the mere naming of a new suit by the responder forces the opener to speak again, it is unnecessary to jump in a new suit when game is responder's only objective. The jump shift is therefore reserved especially for those hands in which responder has slam aspirations. If responder sees that the partnership is surely within a point of a slam, he should make a jump shift. He can find himself in that position only if he has at least 19 points. He assumes for purposes of calculation that opener has 13 points. His 19 would bring it up to 32, the point at which he finds himself knocking on the slam door.

A jump from 1 of a suit to 3 No Trump

This bid is far from a signal for partner to subside. It is an exact descriptive bid which announces, "Partner, I have a high-card count of 16, 17, or 18. You can therefore calculate almost exactly on high-card assets. At the same time, I must warn you that my distribution is 4-3-3-3. With any other distribution a slam might better be available in one of our four-card suits."

Cue bids

Another bid carrying a definite slam inference is the cue bid; that is, a bid in the opponent's suit. This shows ability to win the first trick in that suit (either a void or the Ace).

A cue bid is made with the idea of reaching slam. Occasionally it may be used for the purpose of getting to 3 No Trump, when it is apparent from the bidding, which has not been vigorous, that the partnership cannot aspire to a slam. Normally, however, the cue bid is not used merely for the purpose of getting to game. Direct methods are more effective for such purposes. There are many slams, however, which cannot be reached unless partner is shown control of the adverse suit.

Before a cue bid is in order there must be an agreement on the trump suit, either expressed or implied. Let us take an illustration.

♠ none   ♡ K 10 x x x   ◇ A K x x   ♣ Q J x x

Your partner opens with 1 Heart and the opponent overcalls with 1 Spade. There is no question as to game in Hearts, and if your partner happens to have strength in Clubs, you will make either 6 or 7. At this point a cue bid of 2 Spades is in order. It says, "Partner, I can take care of your Spade losers. I have plenty of trump support. I absolutely guarantee a game and I am looking for a slam. Tell me more about your hand." If your partner rebids the Hearts, you should now call 4 Diamonds. If your partner follows this with a 5 Club bid, you may safely contract for 6 Hearts. You are not in a position to bid 7, because you may lose to the King of Clubs. If your partner's hand is as follows:

♠ x x x   ♡ A Q x x x x   ◇ x   ♣ A K x

he can contract for a grand slam.

A cue bid has an additional advantage. If partner's strength happens to be in the suit which you have cued, he will realize its lack of value. In the last case, assuming that your partner held:

♠ A K x   ♡ A Q x x x x   ◇ x   ♣ x x x

he would realize that his two tricks in Spades had little intrinsic value and a slam should be avoided.

It is important to bear in mind that a cue bid is not justified merely because of the void in the adverse suit. Such a bid must be supported by sufficient values to suggest a slam.

Choice between a cue bid and a suit bid

When you can either show your own suit or make an immediate cue bid, the former should be preferred. While it is very difficult to describe a good suit late in the bidding, it is never too late to show that you have control of the adverse suit.

For example, your partner opens with 1 Spade. The opponents bid 2 Clubs. You hold:

♠ K Q x x   ♡ A J x x x   ◇ x   ♣ A Q x

This hand certainly has a slam air about it and is strong enough to justify an immediate cue bid in Clubs, but that would not be the best strategy. The recommended bid is merely 2 Hearts. The hand is strong enough for a jump shift to 3 Hearts (19 points in support of Spades), but a simple one-round force is recommended in order to conserve bidding space, since there are so many features about your hand that you wish to describe. When on the next round you make a cue bid in Clubs, your partner will realize that you are headed for a slam. He will know also that you have a Heart suit. You will tell him later that you have very fine Spade support.

By way of exception it should be noted that occasionally a belated cue bid may be employed without intention of getting to slam. Where the bidding by partners has been relatively mild and one of the players cues an adverse suit it may be an effort to reach 3 No Trump.

The singleton in slam bidding

Aces and Kings alone do not make a slam. Quite as many slams are dependent upon the possession of a singleton.

Let us take an example. You are South and hold:

♠ A K Q x x   ♡ x x x   ◇ K x x   ♣ J x

The bidding has proceeded:

SOUTH	WEST	NORTH	EAST
1 Spade	Pass	2 Diamonds	Pass
2 Spades	Pass	3 Clubs	Pass
3 Diamonds	Pass	4 Spades	Pass
?			

What should South do?

The unimaginative player would pass, of course, because he would feel that he had already shown the full strength of his hand. The player with vision would stop to picture his partner's holding and would realize that there was only one Heart loser because partner must have a singleton or a void and the King of Diamonds would solidify that suit.

North holds:

♠ J 9 x   ♡ x   ◇ A Q J x x   ♣ A Q 10 x

The recognition of the singleton in Hearts is the interesting feature of the hand. It may be stated as a general principle of bidding that when a player names three suits and incorporates a jump in his sequence of bids he shows a singleton or void in the fourth suit.

If North held a doubleton Heart he might bid three suits, but then he would not be justified in jumping to 4 Spades. Over the 3 Diamond bid it would be sufficient to bid only 3 Spades.

Had South held precisely the same strength in high cards:

♠ A K Q x x   ♡ K x x   ◇ J x x   ♣ x x

he would have passed the 4 Spade bid. He would have then realized that his King of Hearts opposite his partner's singleton or void was of no great consequence and his Diamond holding was not such as to assure the partnership against losing a trick in that suit.

In the next case you are South and hold:

♠ J x   ♡ Q x x   ◇ K x   ♣ A K J x x x

The bidding has proceeded:

SOUTH	NORTH
1 Club	1 Diamond
2 Clubs	3 Spades
3 No Trump	5 Clubs
?	

What do you do?

Despite the fact that you have a minimum bid, you should contract for 6 Clubs. It will be seen that you have the right King. Had it been the King of Hearts, you would have had no reason to be optimistic. Your partner is marked with, at most, a singleton Heart. He has presumably shown five Diamonds, four Spades, and at least three Clubs. This is his hand:

♠ A Q x x   ♡ x   ◇ A Q J x x   ♣ Q 10 x

In this hand the important consideration was not the number of Kings which partner held, but specifically which ones.

Finding the singleton

A sudden leap beyond game, when nothing has previously been said about a suit the opponents have bid, should be taken as a request to partner to bid a slam if he has no more than one loser in the adverse suit. An illustration from a tournament:

NORTH:	♠ K Q x x x	♡ 10 x	◇ x	♣ K Q 10 x x
SOUTH:	♠ A J 10 9 x	♡ A K J x x	◇ x x	♣ A

The bidding is:

SOUTH	WEST	NORTH	EAST
1 Spade	2 Diamonds	3 Clubs	Pass
3 Hearts	Pass	4 Spades	Pass
5 Clubs	Pass	6 Spades	

The bidding follows routine lines up to South's 5 Club bid. This must be construed not as any desire to play Clubs, since Spades have been so vigorously supported. The bid therefore denotes possession of the Ace of Clubs and implies a desire for partner to bid a slam if he can take care of the adverse Diamonds. Had North's hand contained one Heart and two Diamonds he would have been obliged to return to 5 Spades; no slam could be made. The key to the slam was the singleton Diamond.

It is equally important to know when there is no singleton in the crucial spot:

OPENER: ♠ A K J 10 x x   ♡ Q x   ◊ A Q x x   ♣ x
RESPONDER: ♠ Q x   ♡ J x   ◊ K 10 x x x x   ♣ A Q 10

The bidding:

OPENER	RESPONDER
1 Spade	2 Diamonds
3 Spades	4 Clubs
4 Diamonds	4 Spades
5 Spades	Pass

When the opener jumped to 3 Spades, his partner had good reason to be slam-minded—his own hand was about equal to an opening bid, opposite an opening bid and a jump. The Spade suit is now accepted as trump by inference, and the responder's bid of 4 Clubs must be construed as an Ace-showing bid. This, incidentally, is the proper procedure even if you are playing the Blackwood convention. There should be no hurry about the 4 No Trump asking bid. Opener's showing of the Diamond support at this point is natural, and responder can do no better than show his Spade support in response. It is the opener's bid of 5 Spades that is the subject of our attention. What is its meaning?

Logically, it means this: "Partner, we have talked about everything else, and the only thing that worries me is the Heart situation. How are you fixed in that department? If you have only one Heart loser, I think we can make a slam." Responder must stop despite the strong bidding of his partner. With a singleton in Hearts he would, of course, have proceeded to a slam. Similarly, with a singleton Heart, opener would have bid 6 himself.

The right singleton—the right Ace

NORTH:	♠ x x	♡ Q	◇ A Q x x	♣ A K J 10 x x
SOUTH:	♠ A x x	♡ x x x	◇ K J 10 x x	♣ Q x

The bidding:

NORTH	EAST	SOUTH	WEST
1 Club	Pass	1 Diamond	1 Spade
3 Diamonds	Pass	3 Spades	Pass
6 Diamonds	Pass	Pass	Pass

South's cue bid, though aggressive, is justifiable. His hand closely approximates the value of an opening bid, and a slam is by no means a fanciful notion. Furthermore, if North manifests no interest in slam, information as to the Ace of Spades may permit him to bid 3 No Trump.

When North learns of the Ace of Spades he can bid a slam in Diamonds, relying on the establishment of the Club suit for discards. Note that South had the right Ace. Had it been the Ace of Hearts, the partnership would have been subject to the immediate loss of two Spade tricks. Note also that North had the right singleton. A short Spade holding would not have served the purpose.

Slam try below game

It would appear to be good business reasoning that it is better, when convenient, to try for a slam below the game level. You will have explored slam possibilities and have found yourself in position to quit, if necessary, without jeopardizing the game.

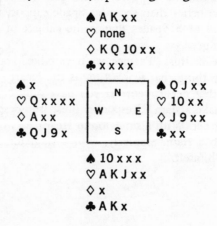

♠ A K x x
♡ none
◇ K Q 10 x x
♣ x x x x

♠ x
♡ Q x x x x
◇ A x x
♣ Q J 9 x

♠ Q J x x
♡ 10 x x
◇ J 9 x x
♣ x x

♠ 10 x x x
♡ A K J x x
◇ x
♣ A K x

The bidding is given as it actually took place:

NORTH	EAST	SOUTH	WEST
1 Diamond	Pass	1 Heart	Pass
1 Spade	Pass	3 Spades	Pass
4 Spades	Pass	5 Clubs	Pass
5 Spades	Pass	Pass	Pass

Down 1!

To be set 1 at a contract of 5 in a major suit which you have reached on your own power is equally devastating to the exchequer and the morale. There is nothing ignominious in being down 1 at a contract of 6. At least the victim may take a certain pride in the display of virility that led to the loss. He meets a soldier's death with important issues at stake. But he who climbs to 5 Hearts or Spades with no one in pursuit, and there encamps, is in a most unenviable position; he finds no hope of glory, no pride in having dared. South should have planned his bidding tactics so that he could try for a slam below the game level. South's second bid of 3 Spades is indefensible. Such a bid announces a willingness to contract for game but does not suggest a slam. Once the Spade bid is heard, South should visualize a slam and should at this point make a definite slam signal; that is, a *jump in a new suit*. His call should be 3 Clubs. North, a little nervous about his partner's Heart response, and having already described the values of his hand, may be reluctant to raise the Clubs and may step lightly by bidding 3 Diamonds. South now bids 4 Spades. By this time North will know very well that South has a powerful hand and is interested in big things, but North is still able to check out at a safe level.

Blasting

In many circles there is a lasting stigma attached to bidding a slam and being set one. This induces a tendency toward over-cautiousness which deprives these players not only of the increased revenue that is the reward of the daring, but, what is probably more important, the thrill of bringing in a big one. The bridge player, unlike the fisherman, derives no pleasure in telling about the one that got away.

The science of slam bidding is very fascinating. There are many ways in which ingenuity can be exercised in the effort to learn this, that, and the other thing about your partner's hand. There are other features than can be ascertained in a purely mechanical manner, such as by the showing of Aces (either wholesale or retail).

Occasionally a hand comes up in which no amount of science can help you to determine definitely that a slam can be made. Success may depend upon your partner's holding a doubleton of some suit or an odd Jack. In those cases blasting, or taking the bull by the horns, may be the best bet.

Occasionally unscientific treatment of the hand is apt to produce the best results. This is particularly true when everything depends on the luck of the opening lead. If the opposition is not given too many suggestions during the auction, there is at least an even chance that the opening lead will be favorable, as witness the following hand:

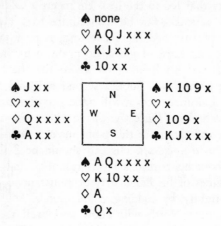

♠ none
♥ A Q J x x x
♦ K J x x
♣ 10 x x

♠ J x x
♥ x x
♦ Q x x x x
♣ A x x

♠ K 10 9 x
♥ x
♦ 10 9 x
♣ K J x x x

♠ A Q x x x x
♥ K 10 x x
♦ A
♣ Q x

The bidding:

NORTH	EAST	SOUTH	WEST
1 Heart	Pass	1 Spade	Pass
2 Hearts	Pass	6 Hearts	

South knew that it might depend on the opening lead, which would be either Diamonds or Clubs. Of course partner might have the Ace of Clubs, in which case South would certainly wish to be in a small slam, although not necessarily in a grand slam. North might have the King of Clubs, which would make the chance of fulfillment very bright. Finally, East might not lead a Club. In the actual case, East elected to lead the 10 of Diamonds and the contract was brought home without any difficulty. A Club lead, of course, would have defeated the contract, but there are many players who would not have led a Club with East's hand.

Positional slams

A slam can frequently be made when played from one side of the table but not when played from the other. Let us examine a case or two:

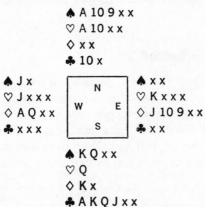

```
                    ♠ A 10 9 x x
                    ♡ A 10 x x
                    ◇ x x
                    ♣ 10 x

    ♠ J x                              ♠ x x
    ♡ J x x x        ┌─────────┐       ♡ K x x x
    ◇ A Q x x        │    N    │       ◇ J 10 9 x x
    ♣ x x x          │ W     E │       ♣ x x
                     │    S    │
                     └─────────┘
                    ♠ K Q x x
                    ♡ Q
                    ◇ K x
                    ♣ A K Q J x x
```

South opened with 1 Club, and when North responded with 1 Spade, he properly leaped to 4. Note that a jump bid to 3 Spades by South would not have been forcing, and if North happened to have responded with a shaded bid of 1 Spade, containing perhaps 5 points, he would surely not carry on. South was willing to bid the 4 Spades however weak a response North had made. North, on the other hand, having two Aces and knowing that partner could hardly rely upon him for more than 6 points, tried for a slam by bidding 5 Hearts, designating the Ace. South now elected to bid 6 Clubs. North, it seems to me, should have passed. North actually went on to 6 Spades, which was defeated with a Diamond opening and the unfortunate location of the Ace. South's technique had been faultless. When there was merely game in contemplation he was satisfied to be in 4 Spades, but when it became apparent that a slam was available he realized the importance of becoming declarer himself, in order to protect the King of Diamonds from attack on the opening lead.

South reasoned that if North happened to have five Spades, a discard of a Diamond could be made on North's long Spade. North should have realized that his partner had a specific reason for bidding 6 Clubs rather than 6 Spades, and North's own weakness in Diamonds should have suggested to him that his partner might be trying to protect the King of the suit. True enough, South could have saved the day by bidding 6 No Trump, but such action was hardly indicated.

In the bidding of powerhouses, when a player holds King x of a suit he should make any reasonable effort to become declarer himself; and by way of corollary, when he holds two worthless cards of any unmentioned suit he should try to permit partner to play the hand just in case his partner should happen to have the King or a tenace position.

The case method

A bid which frequently leads up to a slam is the double raise. If you name any other suit after a double raise, it is a definite slam try and partner is requested to give you any valuable information he may possess. If his double raise has been a minimum, he merely returns to 4 of the original suit. If he has additional values, he may take action in various ways. Let us examine a few cases.

♠ A K x x x   ♡ x   ♢ K x x x   ♣ A x x

You open with 1 Spade, partner raises to 3. Your hand has the value of 17 rebid points. If partner's bid is maximum (16 points), you will have the necessary 33. This means that while there is a chance for slam it is not a very bright one, and you should make a mild try. This you do by bidding 4 Clubs, which designates the Ace. Remember that Spades have been agreed upon and the naming of a new suit is forcing. If partner merely returns to 4 Spades, you relax in the knowledge that you have done your duty. If he shows the Ace of Hearts, you can do no more than return to 4 Spades, but you will be in position to answer a further invitation should it be extended by partner.

♠ A K x x x   ♡ A J x   ♢ x x   ♣ A x x

You open with 1 Spade, partner raises to 3. Your hand has a rebid value of 18 points. This gives you a reasonable chance for slam if partner has more than a minimum. If, for example, he has 15 points, the slam should be assured, for your points are all gilt-edged. The proper procedure is to bid 4 Clubs, showing the Ace. This affords partner the chance to bid 4 Diamonds, which in turn will allow you to bid 4 Hearts. In this manner you have succeeded in showing both your Aces below the game level. Notice in this case it was easier to show the Ace of Clubs first. Had you shown the Ace of Hearts over the 3 Spade bid, partner would have had to bid 5 Diamonds if he chose to show the Ace of Diamonds. If he did show it, you would have had considerable qualms about showing the Ace of Clubs at the level of 6. In situations such as this where there is an unnamed suit, holding two Aces, it is usually more convenient to show the lower Ace first.

♠ K Q J x   ♡ K x x x   ◇ A x   ♣ x x x

Your partner opens with 1 Diamond. You respond with 1 Spade. Now opener jumps to 3 Spades. What is your diagnosis? This hand possesses slam possibilities. Your hand is worth 14 points. If partner's jump was based on 19, you will have the necessary ingredients. Since he might have that much, you should make a try by bidding 4 Diamonds. This indicates merely possession of the Ace, not a desire to play Diamonds (since Spades have been agreed upon). The rest you should leave more or less to your partner.

♠ x x   ♡ A K J x x   ◇ K Q x   ♣ x x x

Your partner opens with 1 Spade. You bid 2 Hearts. Partner raises to 4 Hearts. Here again you should recognize slam possibilities. Your hand is worth 15 rebid points, 14 originally and 1 for the fifth Heart now that that suit has been supported. Partner may have as many as 18 or 19 points for his jump. Inasmuch as you have no Ace to show, you indicate your desire for slam in the only way open to you, by bidding 5 Hearts.

♠ A K J x x   ♡ J x   ◇ x x x   ♣ K Q x

Your partner opens with 1 Heart. You respond with 1 Spade. Partner jumps to 2 No Trump. Inasmuch as the final contract will definitely be in No Trump, you value only your high cards and observe that you have 14. Partner's jump rebid to 2 No Trump shows 19 or 20. Therefore you are assured of the necessary 33 or 34 points and should assume the responsibility. The proper call is 6 No Trump. Don't make an attempt to play this hand at Spades. Your Spades will win tricks at No Trump.

♠ x   ♡ K Q x x x   ◇ K x x x   ♣ K x x

Partner opens with 1 Club. You respond with 1 Heart, which partner raises to 3. You should recognize slam possibilities. Your hand is worth 14 rebid points at Hearts, and partner, for his jump to 3, may have 19 points. You have no Aces to show, but bidding 4 Clubs will serve the same purpose. In view of partner's opening in that suit and subsequent jump, partner probably has the Ace of Clubs and will

E*

recognize that you are showing the King. If your partner's next bid is 4 Diamonds, you should gamble it out for a slam. This action is based on the possession of a singleton Spade. Remember partner may be unable to bid the slam because of the possession of two small Spades. This hand is suitable for Blackwood because your prime concern is with the Aces. His complete hand was:

♠ x x   ♡ A J x x   ◇ A x   ♣ A Q J x x

OPENER:	♠ K Q x	♡ A Q J x x x	◇ A x	♣ x x
RESPONDER:	♠ A 10 9 x x x	♡ K x	◇ x x x	♣ A x

The bidding:

OPENER	RESPONDER
1 Heart	1 Spade
3 Hearts	3 Spades
4 Spades	5 Clubs
5 Diamonds	5 Hearts
7 No Trump	

The 3 Heart rebid by opener is not an absolute force, but partner is expected to bid if his hand is not hopeless. Responder's rebid of 3 Spades is just marking time. Opener raises to 4 Spades, showing that his previous jump was influenced by Spade support. Responder now shows the Ace of Clubs, whereupon opener shows the Ace of Diamonds. At this point responder, by his bid of 5 Hearts, is attempting to indicate the King of that suit, Spades having already been agreed upon. The opener is now able to count thirteen tricks, relying on six Hearts, five Spades (as far as he knows), and the two Aces.

OPENER:	♠ A Q J x x	♡ K x	◇ K Q	♣ K 10 x x
RESPONDER:	♠ K 10 x x x	♡ Q J 10	◇ x	♣ A Q J x

The bidding:

OPENER	RESPONDER
1 Spade	3 Spades
5 Spades	?

In actual play responder accepted the invitation and contracted for a slam in Spades because he had a very good 3 Spade bid. Naturally two Aces were lost and the slam defeated. The question arose as to the place of the guilt. In this hand the Blackwood Convention, to be sure, would have kept the partnership from error, but still the pitfall should have been avoided. Responder contended that opener should have been satisfied merely to contract for game and should not have invited the slam. The opener argued that he had a full trick over and above his bid and was justified in issuing one invitation. With this I concur. Responder should have realized that the opponents had both the red Aces, else South would have bid 4 Diamonds or 4 Hearts as a slam try. South's 5 Spade bid was very clear. It said, "Partner, I have a fine hand but I have no Aces to show you, other than in trumps." The moral: If partner has a reasonable opportunity to show an Ace and fails to do so, you are to assume that he does not have it.

The Blackwood Convention

This is perhaps the most widely used of all the slam conventions and, I venture to say, the most subject to abuse. On the surface it appears to be a very simple device. In actual practice, however, the exercise of very fine judgment is required to attain the ultimate in results by its use. Unfortunately there has been broadcast the notion that the Blackwood Convention is easy to learn and to apply. Nothing can be farther from the truth. In fact, Blackwood is a very difficult convention, though a highly useful one, and students should not be lulled into a sense of complacency by being told of the ease with which it can be applied. It requires a great deal of study, a great deal of practice, and the exercise of very delicate judgment. The difficulty arises in making the decision whether or not to use Blackwood or the other methods. I know one dear little lady, when asked why she did not proceed toward slam, replied, "I couldn't; she didn't ask me for Aces."

This convention should not be employed as a substitute for thinking. The conduct of certain bridge players gives one the impression that they have a desire to insert a nickel in the Blackwood juke box and expect a slam to come bursting forth.

The original sin is in the assumption that the Blackwood Convention may be employed in all slams. This is most emphatically not so. Permit me to quote from the writings of Easley Blackwood, the man who originally introduced this device:

"We do not pretend that the Blackwood Convention will solve all your slam problems, because there are certain types of hands that cannot be covered by Blackwood.

"In some deals both the Blackwood Convention and cue bidding are impossible, because an exchange of information between the partnership is either unnecessary or unobtainable. When that happens a player must use his own initiative and jump directly into a slam.

"The Blackwood Convention is so easy and simple that it can be learned in less than five minutes, and for that reason it is subject to abuse, and players are warned against trying it too often.

"During the preliminary rounds a player must make certain that Blackwood will produce better results than either cue bidding or a direct try for slam."

When the preliminary rounds of bidding have indicated that a slam is probable, and a suit has been agreed upon, either player may institute the convention by calling 4 No Trump. No special holding is required, but the player making the 4 No Trump bid must be quite convinced that the hand will play safely for eleven tricks; in other words, that the partnership assets are approximately 33 points.

The responses are as follows:

> With no Aces bid 5 Clubs.
> With one Ace bid 5 Diamonds.
> With two Aces bid 5 Hearts.
> With three Aces bid 5 Spades.
> With four Aces bid 5 Clubs.

Observe that the answer with four Aces is the same as the one employed to show no Aces. This is for economy of space. An ambiguity could not possibly develop, because the previous bidding will make it clear that the responder (where he has four Aces and bids 5 Clubs) could not possibly be Aceless. The Blackwood bidder may then ask for Kings, which he could conveniently not do if partner responded 5 No Trump.

After Aces have been shown, the 4 No Trump bidder may ask for Kings by bidding 5 No Trump. However, there is the very distinct proviso that the 5 No Trump bid must never be made unless it has been previously determined that the partnership is in possession of all four Aces.

In other words, the opener late in the bidding calls 4 No Trump. Responder bids 5 Diamonds, showing one Ace. The opener now bids 5 No Trump, asking for Kings. Responder knows that the opener has three Aces. Otherwise he could not tell that the partnership has all four Aces and would not be privileged to call for Kings.

The responder to the 5 No Trump bid shows the number of his

Kings exactly as he shows the number of his Aces in response to 4 No Trump.

Not every 4 No Trump bid is part of the convention. A suit must have been mentioned on the way up. If an opening No Trump bid is raised to 4 No Trump, that is simply an assist and is not part of the convention.

The player who makes the conventional 4 No Trump bid must be careful to plan so that any response by partner will not embarrass him. Such might be the case when the agreed suit, for example, is Clubs. The 4 No Trump bidder must in that case have at least two Aces, because otherwise the partnership will be in a slam after a 5 Diamond response and the opposition will hold two Aces.

It is essential to determine whether or not information as to how many Aces partner has will solve your problem. After all, many a hand with all the Aces has no chance to produce a slam. A singleton in partner's hand may be the decisive factor.

Another important consideration is which of the two players should start the convention. As a general rule, the stronger of the two hands should be given the opportunity to do so, because he can better judge what the hands will produce. For example:

NORTH: ♠ A x x   ♡ K x x   ◇ A x x x   ♣ A J x
SOUTH: ♠ K Q J x x   ♡ A Q x   ◇ K Q J   ♣ K x

After Spades have been agreed upon, which of these two players should start the 4 No Trump bid? If North does it, he will find out that the partnership has all the Aces and Kings, but he will be worried about a losing Diamond and possibly a losing Heart. If, however, South is the one who starts the convention, he will be able to bid 7 No Trump immediately he learns that partner has three Aces and one King.

Note that hands containing voids do not lend themselves to Blackwood treatment, for partner's Ace may be in your void suit, where it would be useless. Hands containing worthless doubletons or trebletons very frequently do not react favorably to Blackwood treatment. This is another way of saying that when your only concern is how many Aces has my partner, Blackwood is ideal. But when you must know specifically which Aces your partner has, Blackwood should not be employed, but the Ace-showing method resorted to, hoping that partner will voluntarily show you specifically which Aces he holds.

Let us turn back to a hand previously discussed on page 120.

NORTH: ♠ K Q x x x   ♡ 10 x   ◊ x   ♣ K Q 10 x x
SOUTH: ♠ A J 10 9 x   ♡ A K J x x   ◊ x x   ♣ A

You are South. During the bidding partner has bid Clubs and jumped in Spades, while the opponents have bid Diamonds. Would it be proper for you to employ the Blackwood Convention? The answer is a distinct "No." In order for your side to produce a slam, your partner need not have an Ace, but second-round control in Diamonds, which he would have whether he held a singleton or a King and Queen. This slam does not necessarily depend upon an Ace. In the actual holding you will observe that North has the singleton Diamond and the slam is spread. But North, consistent with his previous bidding, might have had two Diamonds and one Heart. Remember that the Blackwood Convention cannot ferret out a singleton.

Observe the hand previously discussed on page 122.

NORTH: ♠ x x   ♡ Q   ◊ A Q x x   ♣ A K J 10 x x
SOUTH: ♠ A x x   ♡ x x x   ◊ K J 10 x x   ♣ Q x

Presume that you are North and that you have bid Clubs and jumped your partner's Diamond response, whereas the adversaries have bid Spades. Is North in a position to employ Blackwood? Here again the answer is "No," for if partner has the Ace of Hearts you will not choose to undertake a slam, because of the two Spade losers. But if partner has the Ace of Spades, you will be glad to commit your team to a slam on the theory that the losing Spade can be discarded on the Club suit. In other words, here your problem is not "Does partner have an Ace?" but "Which Ace is it?"

Let us observe the case of the void:

NORTH: ♠ J 9 x x   ♡ A x x   ◊ K x   ♣ x x x x
SOUTH: ♠ A K Q x x   ♡ K Q J x   ◊ A Q J x   ♣ none

You are South and open with 2 Spades. Partner raises to 3 Spades. Would it be proper for you to employ Blackwood? The answer again is a distinct "No," for if partner admits that he has an Ace you will be unable to tell whether it is a Club or a Heart. You should therefore *tell*, rather than *ask*. Since Spades have been agreed upon, you bid 4 Diamonds, showing the Ace. Partner will now bid 4 Hearts, showing the Ace of that suit. You now show the Club control, after which he will show the King of Diamonds and you can safely contract for 7 Spades.

NORTH: ♠ A 10 x x   ♡ K J 9 x x x   ◇ x x   ♣ x
SOUTH: ♠ K Q J x   ♡ A Q x   ◇ A J x x   ♣ x x

South opens with 1 Spade, opponent overcalls with 2 Clubs, North bids 2 Hearts. South gives a jump raise to 4 Hearts, and North bids 4 Spades. South, of course, recognizes slam possibilities. Is a Blackwood call appropriate? No, for if South learns that his partner has only one Ace he will be unable to bid a slam, because of the two losing Clubs. North, too, cannot profitably call 4 No Trump, because when he learns that South has two Aces he cannot bid a slam with assurance, for partner might have the Ace of Hearts and the Ace of Clubs. Instead of "asking" for Aces, South instead chooses to "tell" by bidding 5 Diamonds. This permits North to bid 6 Spades (not Hearts).

NORTH: ♠ A K J 10 x x   ♡ x x   ◇ A x   ♣ Q x x
SOUTH: ♠ Q x x   ♡ K x   ◇ x x   ♣ A K J 10 x x

South opened with 1 Club, North bid 1 Spade. South raised to 2 Spades. North, in an effort to ferret out a slam, chose to bid 4 No Trump. Was this a sound call? When South acknowledged one Ace, North faced an impossible problem. He chose to risk that South could stop the Heart suit and bid 6 Spades. He was defeated when a Heart lead netted the defense two tricks. The worthless doubleton in Hearts should have warned North away from Blackwood. Had he chosen instead to temporize by "showing" the Ace of Diamonds and subsequently followed it up with a bid of 5, South, having second-round control of Hearts, could then try 6 Clubs, a contract which could not be defeated.

To Blackwood players:
beware of the worthless doubleton

NORTH: ♠ x x   ♡ A J x x x x   ◇ K Q J   ♣ x x
SOUTH: ♠ A K J x x   ♡ K Q 9 x   ◇ x   ♣ K Q x

South opens 1 Spade, North responds 2 Hearts. South, willing to gamble on the ability to establish the Spade suit without loss, knows that his only concern is with the number of Aces North holds, and it matters not which ones. His proper call is 4 No Trump. This will imply satisfaction with Hearts as the "agreed" suit. If North shows three Aces, South should risk a grand slam; if two Aces, he will be content with a small slam. When North actually comes up with just one Ace, South is forced to sign off at 5 Hearts.

When it may be desirable for partner to start the 4 No Trump bid, the bidding may be steered in that direction by making temporary bids of various types to afford him the opportunity, when the 4 level is reached, to ask for Aces.

Assuming that the bidding has proceeded in a very aggressive manner and that a slam becomes probable, is it desirable for you or your partner to initiate the 4 No Trump bid with these hands?

♠ A x x x   ♡ x x x   ◇ A 10 x   ♣ A K x

With this hand you should permit partner to bid the 4 No Trump, because you can give specific information about your hand which will help partner decide. If you bid the 4 No Trump and find out that your partner has one Ace and three Kings, you will still be worried about small-card losers; in other words, the trick-taking potentialities of the hand.

♠ A Q J x x   ♡ A Q x x   ◇ x   ♣ A x x

With this hand you may initiate the Blackwood Convention, because specific information about Aces and Kings will permit you to judge the possibilities of the hand. This is assuming, of course, you have previously determined that the partnership assets amount to 33 points.

♠ Q J x x   ♡ A 9 x x x   ◇ x x x   ♣ A

With this hand it is much better for your partner to start the convention, because information about Aces and Kings will not solve your problem.

It is an integral part of the Blackwood Convention that the 4 No Trump bidder is the captain of the team. When he hears the response, he, and he alone, decides on the final contract, and the responder must abide by his decision.

There is one exception: When the bidding has shown that the partnership has all four Aces, the responder may exercise his own judgment as to the final contract. Occasionally the responder, instead of telling how many Aces he has, may bid a slam directly when his hand contains a void. This might be done in a case where, let us say, Diamonds are the agreed suit and partner has asked for Aces. The Blackwood response would be 5 Diamonds, showing one Ace, but the responder has a void in an unmentioned suit and he fears that the

Blackwood bidder will be discouraged and pass the 5 Diamond bid. He may exercise his discretion by bidding a slam directly over the 4 No Trump bid. For example:

♠ A K x x x   ♡ Q x x   ◇ Q J 10 x x   ♣ none

Your partner has opened with 1 Heart, has vigorously supported your Diamonds, and then bids 4 No Trump (Blackwood). Your conventional response would be 5 Diamonds, showing one Ace. This may discourage partner from bidding a slam, so you may take control of the situation and bid 6 Diamonds instead of telling about your Ace.

There is an important amendment to the Blackwood Convention employed by many players. When cue bids have been made on preliminary rounds to show Aces or voids, and subsequently the Blackwood 4 No Trump is called, any Ace that has previously been cue-bid or any Ace in a suit that partner has cued must not be shown. For example, you hold:

♠ K Q J   ♡ 10 9 x x x   ◇ A x x x   ♣ x

Your partner has opened with 1 Heart, which you have jumped to 3. Your partner now bids 4 Clubs, an obvious cue bid. You bid 4 Diamonds, showing the Ace. Partner now bursts forth into Blackwood. Your normal response would be 5 Diamonds, showing one Ace, but since you have previously made a cue bid indicating this Ace, it does not count and you are obliged to respond with 5 Clubs, showing no Ace other than Diamonds. If instead of the King of Spades you held the Ace, your proper response would be 5 Diamonds, showing one Ace other than the one which you cued.

Blackwood response after interference bid

Occasionally, after a 4 No Trump bid, an adversary will insert an overcall in order to interfere with the normal response. If you do not choose to double for a penalty, the Aces are indicated as follows:

The responder starts to count Aces from the suit in which the overcall has been made. For example: After the Blackwood 4 No Trump bid an opponent bids 5 Diamonds. You have two Aces which you wish to show, so you start counting at 5 Diamonds; a pass would show no Aces, 5 Hearts would show one Ace, 5 Spades would show two Aces, 5 No Trump would show three Aces, and 6 Clubs would show all four.

There is one other exception which permits the responder to set up the final contract. When the 4 No Trump bidder mentions an unbid suit at the level of 5 after partner's response, the responder is forced to call 5 No Trump, which becomes the contract. This is done in cases where it is learned that the adversaries have two Aces but that No Trump will be the best contract.

The Gerber 4 Club Convention

Sometimes a grand slam can be made with a great many points less than the normal 37, when responder holds a very long suit.

In cases of that kind, of course, it will be desirable to check on Aces—since the opposition may have as many as 10 points. At such times the Gerber Convention (4 Clubs) will be useful.

Your partner opens 1 No Trump and you hold:

♠ x ♡ x x ◊ A K J x x x x ♣ A x

You know that you will play for at least 6 Diamonds, but if partner has the key cards you can make a grand slam. It is possible that partner has a maximum No Trump but lacks one of the Aces. For example, he might hold:

♠ K Q J ♡ A Q J ◊ x x x ♣ K Q x

In order to determine this, you burst into 4 Clubs (the Gerber Convention). This is a request for Aces. If partner shows two Aces and two Kings, you may contract for 7 No Trump. Even if he shows two Aces and only one King, you may, if you choose, take the reasonable risk that he has a Queen with one of his Kings and bid 7 anyhow.

A response of 4 Clubs over an opening bid of 1, 2, or 3 No Trump is artificial and is treated in the Blackwood manner as a request for Aces. The responses are:

4 Diamonds	No Aces
4 Hearts	One Ace
4 Spades	Two Aces
4 No Trump	Three Aces
4 Diamonds	Four Aces

Where the 4 Club bidder desires information as to partner's Kings, he employs 5 Clubs as his asking bid. The response is made in the same fashion as above.

SLAM BIDDING QUIZ

The bidding is indicated in each of the following cases. You are South. What is your bid?

1. ♠ K x x
    ♡ A x x x
    ◇ Q 10 x
    ♣ A x x

NORTH	EAST	SOUTH	WEST
1 Diamond	Pass	1 Heart	Pass
2 No Trump	Pass	?	

2. ♠ A K
    ♡ K Q J 10 9 8
    ◇ x x
    ♣ A K Q

SOUTH	WEST	SOUTH	EAST
2 Hearts	Pass	3 Hearts	Pass
?			

3. ♠ K Q 10 9 x
    ♡ K Q 10 x
    ◇ x
    ♣ A K x

SOUTH	WEST	NORTH	EAST
1 Spade	Pass	3 Spades	Pass
?			

4. ♠ A J 10
    ♡ K Q 9 x x x
    ◇ A x
    ♣ x x

SOUTH	WEST	NORTH	EAST
1 Heart	Pass	3 Hearts	Pass
?			

5. ♠ K 10 x
    ♡ x x
    ◇ K Q J 10 x
    ♣ A x x

NORTH	EAST	SOUTH	WEST
1 Spade	Pass	2 Diamonds	Pass
3 Spades	Pass	?	

6. ♠ A Q 10 x x
    ♡ none
    ◇ x x
    ♣ A K Q x x x

SOUTH	WEST	NORTH	EAST
1 Club	Pass	1 Spade	Pass
?			

7. ♠ K Q J x x
    ♡ x x x
    ◇ K x
    ♣ A x x

SOUTH	WEST	NORTH	EAST
1 Spade	Pass	2 Diamonds	Pass
2 Spades	Pass	3 Clubs	Pass
3 Diamonds	Pass	4 Spades	Pass
?			

8. ♠ K Q 10
    ♡ A K 10 x x
    ◇ Q x
    ♣ x x x

SOUTH	WEST	NORTH	EAST
1 Heart	Pass	2 Clubs	Pass
2 Hearts	Pass	3 Diamonds	Pass
3 No Trump	Pass	4 Hearts	Pass
?			

9. ♠ A 10 9 x x
    ♡ A Q 10 x
    ◇ A K
    ♣ x x

SOUTH	WEST	NORTH	EAST
1 Spade	2 Clubs	2 Diamonds	Pass
2 Hearts	Pass	4 Hearts	Pass
?			

10. ♠ K 10 9 x x
    ♡ A K Q x x
    ◇ A x x
    ♣ none

SOUTH	WEST	NORTH	EAST
1 Spade	Pass	3 Spades	Pass
?			

11. ♠ Q x	NORTH	EAST	SOUTH	WEST
♡ x x	1 Spade	Pass	1 No Trump	Pass
◇ K x x x	3 Clubs	Pass	4 Clubs	Pass
♣ Q J x x x	4 Hearts	Pass	?	

12. ♠ K Q x x x x	NORTH	EAST	SOUTH	WEST
♡ K Q x x	2 No Trump	Pass	?	
◇ x				
♣ x x				

13. ♠ K Q 10 x	SOUTH	WEST	NORTH	EAST
♡ A Q x	1 Diamond	Pass	1 Heart	Pass
◇ K Q 10 x	1 Spade	Pass	3 Spades	Pass
♣ x x	?			

14. ♠ K Q 10 x	NORTH	EAST	SOUTH	WEST
♡ x x	1 Club	Pass	1 Diamond	Pass
◇ A K 10 x x	1 Spade	Pass	3 Spades	Pass
♣ x x	5 Spades	Pass	?	

15. ♠ A 10 x x	NORTH	EAST	SOUTH
♡ A x x	1 Heart	2 Clubs	?
◇ K Q J 10 x x			
♣ none			

16. ♠ K x x	NORTH	EAST	SOUTH	WEST
♡ Q 10 9 8	2 Diamonds	Pass	2 No Trump	Pass
◇ 10 x	3 Hearts	Pass	?	
♣ x x x x				

17. ♠ Q 10 9 x x	NORTH	EAST	SOUTH	WEST
♡ K x x	1 Diamond	Pass	1 Spade	Pass
◇ K x x	2 Hearts	Pass	3 Diamonds	Pass
♣ x x	4 Spades	Pass	?	

18. ♠ K x	NORTH	EAST	SOUTH	WEST
♡ K Q 10 9 x	1 Spade	Pass	2 Hearts	Pass
◇ A x x	4 No Trump	5 Diamonds	?	
♣ x x x				

ANSWERS TO SLAM BIDDING QUIZ

1. Four No Trump
(or conceivably 5 NT).
You have 13 points, and partner's jump rebid promises 19 or 20 points. Partner will bid the slam if he has maximum values for his rebid.

2. Four Clubs.
It is your intention to bid 4 Spades over partner's expected 4 Heart rebid. In this manner you express a desire to reach slam if partner has second round control of the Diamond suit. If part-

ner rebids 4 Diamonds, you will bid the slam directly.

3. Four No Trump.
Your primary interest is the number of Aces that partner owns. If he shows two Aces, you will bid the small slam. If he shows three Aces, it is your intention to bid the grand slam.

4. Three Spades.
Your hand is worth 19 rebid points which together with partner's an-

nounced holding (13-16 points), places the hand in the slam range. Should partner respond with 4 Clubs, you will bid the slam. If, on the other hand, he rebids 4 Hearts, you will bid 5 Diamonds, urging partner to contract for the slam if he can take care of the Club suit.

5. Four Clubs.

You have the ingredients for a slam since an opening bid facing an opening bid plus a jump indicates slam possibilities. If partner bids 4 Hearts, you will take the bit in your mouth and bid 6 Spades. If, instead, he merely rebids 4 Spades, your raise to 5 will convey the message that you are concerned about his Heart holding.

6. Six Spades.

This is one of those hands that do not lend themselves to scientific approach. It can make anywhere from 4 to 7 and a direct bid of 6 Spades will place the onus upon the enemy to find the correct defense if perchance we are off the first two Diamond tricks. We recognize that this technique will sometimes result in missing a laydown grand slam, but regard this as a calculated risk.

7. Four No Trump.

Partner has marked himself with a singleton Heart for he has bid two suits and jumped in the third. The only hazard to the slam is the lack of Aces. If partner turns up with two, we will bid the Spade slam.

8. Pass.

Partner's bidding has indicated that he has a singleton Spade (he has shown five Clubs, four Diamonds and surely three Hearts), which turns the bulk of our hand into jelly so far as slam is concerned. While it is true that slam is still a possibility if partner were to hold something like

♠ x   ◇ A x x x
♡ Q J x   ♣ A K Q x x

this combination, it is definitely too much to hope for.

9. Five Diamonds.

Partner has indicated a robust free bid and slam may be in sight so long as he can stop Clubs. Your Ace and King of Diamonds are priceless.

10. Five No Trump.

When the trump suit has been more or less agreed upon, a jump to 5 No Trump commands partner to bid a grand slam in that suit if he holds two of the top three honors and a small slam if he has less. In this hand, South's only concern is his partner's trump holding since the two little Diamonds should be easily disposed of by partner's high cards.

11. Four No Trump.

When this sequence is properly analyzed, it becomes apparent that we are not intending to make a Blackwood call. It must be therefore that we are intending to show a value in Diamonds in a natural way, and this value must presumably be the King of Diamonds, for if it were the Ace, we would show it directly.

12. Four Clubs.

The Gerber Convention is quite useful when partner has opened the bidding in No Trump and you are desirous of inquiring for Aces. Should partner's response show all the Aces, you will bid 5 Clubs requesting information about his Kings.

13. Four Hearts.

Slam is quite possible if partner has a maximum jump raise. A 5 Club cue bid by him will be rewarded with a jump to 6 Spades by you.

14. Pass.

Partner's bid requests a command performance from you, which is that you contract for a slam if you can stop the run of the unbid suit. Since your hand is helpless in that respect, you must resign.

15. Three Diamonds.

It would be bad timing on your part to cue bid 3 Clubs immediately for it would consume priceless bidding space. For example partner might be indiscreet enough to call 3 No Trump, making it virtually impossible for you to show the excellent Diamond suit and convince partner that it can stand alone. It is your intention, of course, to cue-bid your void at a later stage in the auction.

16. Five Hearts.
Your original response denoted a hand that could conceivably be a Yarborough. If you were to rebid merely 4 Hearts, partner would imagine that you have only fulfilled your obligation to carry on to game. Since your hand is worth 7 points in support, you should jump to 5 Hearts to stir the embers of what appeared to partner to be a dying fire. His hand was

♠ none   ◇ A K Q J x x
♡ A K J x   ♣ A Q x

17. Four No Trump.
Partner has shown a hand with splendid Spade support and a singleton in the Club suit. (He has opened with 1 Diamond, reversed in Hearts and jumped in Spades, hence he can have at most one Club in his hand.) You are primarily concerned with the number of Aces in his hand.

18. Five Hearts.
When the opponents intervene over a Blackwood request, you pass to show no Aces, and bid the next suit to show one Ace. A double on your part would be interpreted for penalties.

6.   Overcalls

THE PROPER USE of the overcall may spell the difference between a winning and a losing player. Losses incurred by indiscriminate overcalling may at times be so staggering that a somewhat lengthy dissertation on this topic is in order.

An overcall is a competitive bid made when an opponent has opened the bidding. It must not be confused with a response made when partner opens the bidding and an opposing call is inserted, for example:

NORTH	EAST	SOUTH
1 Spade	2 Clubs	2 Diamonds

South's 2 Diamond bid is not regarded as an overcall. It is simply a free response and is discussed in the chapter on Responses. But in this sequence:

EAST	SOUTH
1 Spade	2 Diamonds

the 2 Diamond bid is an overcall.

Naturally, with a partner who has opened the bidding you are in a position to take a certain amount of liberty, but when an opponent opens the bidding and you may be all alone in the world, the exercise of greater care is indicated. The idea developed some years ago that if the bidding is opened adversely and you hold 1½ honor tricks and a biddable suit, you should make your presence felt by overcalling. That was in the days before the public had familiarized itself with the penalty double.

Every overcall should serve some specific purpose. There are several considerations that might induce you to enter the bidding. One of the most important is to suggest a lead to your partner. For example, you hold:

♠ K Q J 9 x   ♡ A x x   ◊ x x x   ♣ x x

Your right-hand opponent opens with 1 Club. The potentialities of the hand are as yet unknown, but it is not looking too far ahead to visualize a possible adverse 3 No Trump contract, or possibly a game contract in Hearts. As far as you are concerned, the lead most ardently desired is a Spade, a suit which your partner could hardly be expected to select for his opening shot should it become his duty to lead. An overcall of 1 Spade is therefore in order, even though you have no real expectation of playing the hand or a desire to go places. This suggests a danger in overcalling with Jack- or 10-high suits.

On some hands you may be able to outbid the opponent for a part score. You may hold a fairly good hand on which, for some reason or other, you do not choose to make a take-out double. For example:

♠ x   ♡ A K 10 9 x   ♢ A J 9 x x   ♣ J x

Your opponent bids 1 Spade. It is usually not good policy to double with two-suiters, because the bidding might become too involved before you have a chance to show both suits. Your best bet is to overcall with 2 Hearts. The next time it will probably be convenient to show the Diamonds, and partner can exercise his choice without increasing the contract. With hands that are stronger or more flexible, strength-showing bids other than overcalls are made. They will be discussed some pages hence.

You have heard much about nuisance or bother bids. Many times the person most bothered by your bid is your patient partner. Remember this: Unless you are playing against someone who has been attacked by Dracula, you must not expect him to fold up and collapse into his shelter just because you overcall his 1 Club bid with 1 Diamond.

Overcalls can have a certain nuisance value. This is when they deprive the opponents of some bidding space. Suppose, for example, the bidding is opened with 1 Diamond and you overcall with 2 Clubs. You have deprived the opponent of the opportunity to respond at the level of 1 in either Hearts or Spades. This may prove embarrassing to him. If, however, the opening bid is 1 Spade and you overcall with 2 Clubs, you have deprived the responder of nothing, because he would have had to bid at that level anyhow. In such cases a 2 Club overcall gives the enemy all the best of the bargain. They can either double you (even on suspicion, because a fulfilled 2 Club contract will not yield a game) or they can go on.

There is the further disadvantage of providing the declarer with clues that will be of assistance to him in the play of the hand. An overcall, far from being a nuisance to the opponents, will many times be of actual assistance in the bidding. Let us suppose that you are South and hold the following hand:

♠ Q x x   ♡ Q x x   ♢ x x   ♣ A Q x x x

The bidding has proceeded:

NORTH	EAST	SOUTH
1 Spade	2 Diamonds	?

What should you do? For one thing, you should inwardly acknowl-
edge your indebtedness to East for helping to clarify the situation.
You can now be content to bid 2 Spades. In the absence of the overcall
you would have been in some quandary about your response. The
giving of a mere single raise would have been inadequate, and yet a
bid of 2 Clubs, followed by a subsequent Spade raise, would have
been somewhat on the aggressive side. The overcall by East clarified
your response because it made it clear that you had a hand on which
you were willing to make a free raise.

If you have come to the conclusion that you have a sound purpose
in overcalling, you should then inquire into the risk. You must expect
to be doubled every time you overcall and you must be prepared to
find a very anemic dummy. Figure out what the damages are going
to be. If they come to more than 500 points, you cannot afford the
luxury of overcalling. This little guide takes care of such questions
as vulnerability and the level of your bid.

In overcalling, the number of high cards held is of minor importance. When you go down 700, do not ever be heard to sing the song
of a sucker, "But, partner, I had 14 points." The important consideration is the type of trump suit you have, not the number of points in
your hand. I should like to repeat that in order to overcall you should
have a good trump suit or plenty of credit with the local bank. A
good rule of thumb *is not to overcall at the level of 2 unless you can
promise that you will not lose more than two trump tricks.*

Suits like these are treacherous:

A Q 9 4 2

K J 7 3 2

Such suits may produce very few tricks against an unfortunate trump
break, whereas the following combinations, no richer in point count,
give you the comfort of a well-heated home.

K Q J 9 7

Q J 10 9 8

With trump suits like these there can be no feeling of impending
disaster.

When playing with a partner of the type who constantly wishes to "get into the act," extreme caution should be exercised in making overcalls on hands which contain a singleton in some side suit. To illustrate, you hold:

♠ A x x x   ♡ x   ◇ A Q J x x   ♣ J 10 x

If the opening bid by your right-hand opponent is a Spade and you overcall with 2 Diamonds, there is always the risk that your eager-beaver partner will feel it his duty to show his five-card Heart suit. This will place you in an awkward position, for a rebid of 3 Diamonds would be attended with great danger and the pass of 2 Hearts would place you in anything but a comfortable position.

Note that if the opponent had opened the bidding with 1 Heart, action by you is not attended with nearly the same risk, for even if partner chooses to act on his own initiative, you will have some support for any suit that he chooses to bid.

Reopening the bidding

When an opponent opens the bidding and his partner fails to keep it alive, you may take great liberties in competing for the part score. You have the distinct comfort of knowing that one of your opponents is "broke" and the other was not able to open with a demand bid. It follows, therefore, that your partner probably has a smattering of strength. In this position you may compete on a prayer. For example, you are South with this hand:

♠ Q 10 x x x   ♡ K Q x   ◇ Q x x   ♣ x x

The bidding has proceeded:

WEST	NORTH	EAST	SOUTH
1 Club	Pass	Pass	?

You should contest the auction by bidding 1 Spade. Partner must not expect too much of you in this situation.

Use of the 1 No Trump bid to reopen

When an adverse opening bid of 1 in a suit has not been kept alive and you are in fourth position, it has been pointed out that you can take great liberty in competing for the part score. You may do so in some cases by calling 1 No Trump. Partner must not con-

strue this as a normal 1 No Trump call, but merely as a refusal to
sell out cheaply. For example, you are South and hold:

♠ A Q   ♡ Q x x   ◇ K 9 x x   ♣ J x x x

The bidding:

WEST	NORTH	EAST	SOUTH
1 Spade	Pass	Pass	?

You may bid 1 No Trump. If partner has values, he may speak. If
he hasn't much, you may as well play it at 1 No Trump. Partner must
realize that you cannot have a really good hand, else you would have
doubled first and then bid No Trump later. He must not raise the
No Trump unless he passed with a very good hand.

The jump overcall

Over a considerable period of time the jump overcall has been
used as a strength-showing bid when an adversary has initiated the
auction. It described a hand with a strong trump suit, and one that
would produce game with only a smattering of strength from partner.

On such occasions as it could profitably be employed, the merits of
this call were undeniable, so that the bid survived for a great number
of years. However, it eventually became manifest that the frequency
with which this weapon could be employed was not great enough to
warrant giving up an otherwise useful weapon.

Interference with the enemy, when it appears that they may have
the preponderance of strength, is a far more useful purpose to which
to put the jump overcall. The bid furthermore has the merit of
pointing out to partner that defensive values are lacking, and that an
eventual sacrifice bid should be given serious consideration.

It may be in order to outline briefly the specifications for the pre-
emptive jump overcall. (See page 160 for treatment of hands that
formerly called for a strong jump overcall.)

(A) The bid should be based on a fairly good suit, at least six cards
long.

(B) The hand should contain no more than 9 points in high cards,
regardless of vulnerability.

(C) The strength of the hand should be concentrated in the bid
suit.

(D) The pre-emptive bidder should have the reasonable expectation of winning within three tricks of his contract when not vulner-

able and within two tricks when vulnerable, that is to say the limit of loss ought normally not to exceed 500 points.

Let us examine a few cases in which you are South. The previous bidding has been set forth in each instance.

♠ K Q J 9 8 x x   ♡ x   ◇ x   ♣ J 10 9 x

WEST	NORTH	EAST	SOUTH
1 Heart	Pass	1 No Trump	?

3 Spades. This is an ideal holding for the pre-emptive overcall. Your maneuver may deprive the opponents of space for further exploratory bidding. If they do go on, they may stumble into the wrong contract. If they double you for "a small profit," partner could produce a card or two in Clubs which might enable you to fulfill the contract.

♠ A J 10 x x x   ♡ K x   ◇ x x x   ♣ x x

Neither side vulnerable.

EAST	SOUTH
1 Heart	?

1 Spade. Jump overcalls should be avoided on hands that contain any significant defensive strength. This hand has the equivalent of two quick tricks and will be better described by a simple overcall.

♠ x x   ♡ x   ◇ A J x   ♣ K Q 10 9 8 x x

Both sides are vulnerable.

EAST	SOUTH
1 Heart	?

2 Clubs. You have sufficient playing strength for a jump to 3 Clubs, but here also there is too much defensive strength. The pre-emptive overcall should be based on a hand containing not more than nine high-card points, most of which should be concentrated in the bid suit.

♠ K Q J x x x   ♡ J 10 9 x x   ◇ x x   ♣ none

East-West are vulnerable.

EAST	SOUTH
1 Diamond	?

1 Spade. The jump overcall should be avoided, if possible, on a two-suited hand. Partner may fit Hearts but not Spades. A pre-emptive bid would greatly reduce the chances of finding a possible Heart fit.

♠ x   ♥ x x   ♦ A x x x x   ♣ K J 9 x x

WEST	NORTH	EAST	SOUTH
1 Heart	3 Clubs	Pass	?

5 Clubs. Since partner has announced a hand containing little defensive strength, the opponents are assuredly spread for at least a game in one or both of the majors. A premature sacrifice bid by you will put them to the guess concerning their proper action. You may be able to "steal" the hand for a relatively modest fee.

♠ J x x x x   ♥ none   ♦ A 10 x x x   ♣ x x x

WEST	NORTH	EAST	SOUTH
1 Heart	3 Diamonds	4 Hearts	?

Pass. It is not at all improbable that the enemy has a slam in this hand. Whatever strength you have is in a suit of which partner has at least six or seven cards, so that defensively your hand may be regarded as nonexistent. We would not be inclined to make any bid that might goad the enemy into aggressive action.

♠ Q J 10 x   ♥ K J 9 x   ♦ A x   ♣ K Q 9

East and West are vulnerable.

WEST	NORTH	EAST	SOUTH
1 Club	2 Diamonds	2 Spades	?

Pass. It would be unwise to act prematurely. You have been warned that partner's hand is of doubtful value, so that your offensive potentialities are distinctly limited. It should be borne in mind that East's response is forcing and proper strategy is to lie in wait for further developments. Your silence combined with partner's announced weakness may induce the enemy to overreach themselves.

Double jump overcalls

The single jump overcall is a bid of exactly one more than necessary and shows five or six tricks according to the conditions of vulnerability. A double jump overcall, e.g. as 3 Spades over 1 Diamond, does not show any greater high-card strength. It is also a pre-emptive bid made on the same type of hand, but containing one additional winner. For example, the opening bid on your right is 1 Heart. You are not vulnerable, and hold:

♠ Q J 10 x x x x   ♥ x   ♦ Q J 9 x   ♣ x

You may overcall with a jump to 3 Spades. This bid may have the effect of keeping the opponents out of a 4 Heart contract. However, if you are vulnerable the double jump overcall might prove too costly and a bid of just 2 spades is recommended.

The 1 No Trump overcall

This bid denotes a strong hand. While an opening 1 No Trump bid should never contain more than 18 points, a 1 No Trump overcall may be based on hands ranging between 16 and 19 points inclusive, with the proviso that the adversaries' suit must be safely stopped. It is a bid to use when you are prepared to play at 1 No Trump, if partner is weak, and are willing to go on to game if partner raises. The hand will, as a rule, meet with the technical requirements for a take-out double, but the double has the disadvantage of compelling you to bid No Trump on the next round, when a higher level will have been reached. Suppose you hold:

♠ K Q x   ♡ A K x   ◇ A Q J x   ♣ 10 x x

Your opponent opens the bidding with 1 Spade. If you double and partner responds with 2 Clubs or 2 Diamonds, you will feel obliged to try 2 No Trump, which may not be safe if partner is weak. The best strategy is to overcall the Spade bid with 1 No Trump. If partner is weak, you are prepared to play it there. If he raises, you are willing to try for game.

The unusual No Trump overcall

Among the more recent developments in contract bridge, perhaps one of most colorful is the "Unusual No Trump Convention," which provides that where a player makes a bid of any number of No Trumps which could not possibly mean what it says, then the No Trump bid is to be construed as a take-out double, and partner is expected to respond in his better minor suit. The common sense of the situation is this: if a player makes a take-out double of one major suit, it is reasonable to suppose that he would like to hear his partner respond in the other major. But where the prospective doubler is not prepared for the other major, he obtains the effect of doubling for a minor-suit response by using an unnatural overcall in No Trump.

It is important to emphasize that overcalls in No Trump have not lost their natural significance. For example, the bidding has proceeded:

EAST	SOUTH
1 Spade	1 No Trump

South's bid of 1 No Trump is a good old-fashioned overcall, describing a balanced hand with 16 to 19 points and sound protection in Spades. Similarly:

EAST	SOUTH
1 Spade	2 No Trump

South's bid is not unusual. It describes a balanced hand with about 22 to 24 high-card points and adequate stoppers in Spades.

Let us examine a few other illustrations:

WEST	NORTH	EAST	SOUTH
1 Heart	Pass	Pass	1 No Trump

This is a natural bid and designates a hand of moderate strength on which South does not wish to "sell out" to the opponents. It does not require the same amount of strength as a standard No Trump bid.

WEST	NORTH	EAST	SOUTH
3 Hearts	Pass	Pass	3 No Trump

This overcall is used in its natural sense and indicates a desire to play at that contract. It is by no means a request to partner to show any suit, and he should resist the impulse to show even a six-card suit, unless he has a most extraordinary hand from the standpoint of distribution.

WEST	NORTH	EAST	SOUTH
1 Heart	Pass	2 Hearts	2 No Trump

This is an unusual overcall in No Trump and requests a minor suit take-out. With a good hand and strength in Hearts, South might have chosen either to double or to make a jump bid of 3 No Trump.

WEST	NORTH	EAST	SOUTH
1 Spade	Pass	3 Hearts	3 No Trump

This cannot be a natural bid inasmuch as West has opened the bidding and East has announced slam aspirations. Therefore, South must have a minor two-suiter, and is laying the groundwork for a possible sacrifice.

It is not always easy to determine whether a No Trump overcall is unusual or not. This can best be decided on a logical basis.

Normally, any overcall in No Trump at the level of 2 or higher, made after the opener and his partner have both bid, is unusual and asks for the better minor. To delve into the matter further and to clarify this definition, it is best to deal in terms of specific examples. Let us examine some specimen cases.

In the following examples you are South, and the bidding has proceeded as indicated:

♠ Q 10 x   ♡ x   ◇ A Q J x x   ♣ K Q J x

WEST	NORTH	EAST	SOUTH
1 Spade	Pass	2 Spades	?

Bid 2 No Trump. This is nearly the classic example of an unusual No Trump overcall. You have two excellent minor suits and no interest in the other major. The fine texture of your suits is necessary to justify forcing partner to enter the auction at the 3 level.

♠ x x   ♡ none   ◇ A J 10 9 x x   ♣ A Q 10 x x

EAST	SOUTH
1 Heart	?

Bid 2 Diamonds. Do not make the mistake of making an unusual call of 2 No Trump. This bid, when employed immediately over an opening bid, has a natural meaning and shows a relatively balanced hand of about 22 points. In the present instance, you should plan on showing both suits yourself if the opportunity presents itself.

♠ A   ♡ x   ◇ A 10 x x x x   ♣ J x x x

EAST	SOUTH
3 Hearts	?

You should pass. A No Trump overcall in this position is a natural bid, indicating a desire to play the hand in No Trump. Note that if partner reopens the auction with a double or a bid of 3 Spades, you must not bid No Trump, for that would also be a natural bid.

♠ J 9 x x x   ♡ x x   ◇ A K Q x   ♣ Q x

WEST	NORTH	EAST	SOUTH
1 Heart	Pass	2 Hearts	Pass
Pass	2 No Trump	Pass	?

Bid 4 Diamonds. Partner is employing the unusual No Trump overcall requesting your better minor suit. You have a fine hand with

a very good fit for partner, and some interest in game should be manifested. A mere 3 Diamond bid would sound forced and might easily be passed out.

♠ 10 9 x x x   ♡ x x x x   ◇ Q   ♣ A x x

WEST	NORTH	EAST	SOUTH
1 Heart	Pass	2 Hearts	Pass
4 Hearts	4 No Trump	Double	?

Bid 5 Clubs. Partner is asking for your best minor and you have a distinct preference for Clubs. A pass would be courting disaster, for partner would be forced to pick the suit himself, and if he chose Diamonds you would have to enter the 6 level to bid Clubs.

♠ x x x   ♡ 10 9 x x x   ◇ Q x x   ♣ x x

WEST	NORTH	EAST	SOUTH
4 Spades	4 No Trump	Pass	?

Bid 5 Hearts, not 5 Diamonds. The 4 No Trump overcall of a pre-emptive bid of 4 Spades is not treated as an unusual No Trump overcall but rather as a "super" take-out double, and asks for your best suit which is, of course, Hearts. Partner's hand should look something like this:

♠ x   ♡ A K Q x   ◇ K J 10 x   ♣ A K J x

♠ x x   ♡ K 10 9 x x   ◇ none   ♣ Q J 9 x x x

EAST	SOUTH	WEST	NORTH
Pass	Pass	1 Spade	Pass
2 Diamonds	Pass	2 Spades	Pass
Pass	?		

Bid 2 No Trump. While the unusual No Trump overcall is conventionally employed to ask partner to bid his better minor suit, there are occasional instances where the common sense of the situation makes it apparent that while the No Trump bidder is asking his partner to take the bid out, his choice should be made from the two unbid suits rather than the two minors. This is just such an example. South does not wish to abandon the fight, yet he is too weak to make a take-out double. So he makes an unusual bid in No Trump. East's 2 Diamond call should make it apparent that South is not interested in that suit, so the inference is clear that it is either in Clubs or Hearts that he wishes his partner to make a choice.

F

Action by partner of overcaller

Partner of an overcaller is many times in a strategic position to judge the entire possibilities of the hand. He knows approximately how much partner has; knows that he has a good trump suit and that he can come within two or three tricks of making his bid. The partner is therefore in a position to add his own assets to those shown by the overcaller, and thus to form a conclusion as to game possibilities.

There is seldom any point in raising an overcall unless there is a chance for game. If the partner believes there is a chance for game, he may raise, assuming, of course, that he is satisfied with the trump named in the overcall.

Normal trump support for an overcall is less than that required to support an opening bid, because, while an opening bid may be based on a four-card suit, an overcall usually is not. The overcaller's partner may presume that the overcaller has a good five-card suit, so three small trumps are sufficient support, or even Queen x, particularly if the overcaller's side is vulnerable. For example, you are South and hold:

♠ x x x   ♡ Q 10   ◇ K J 9 x x   ♣ K Q x

With both sides vulnerable, the bidding has proceeded as follows:

SOUTH	WEST	NORTH	EAST
Pass	1 Spade	2 Hearts	Pass
?			

What should you do? Your partner's vulnerable overcall has shown the ability to take at least six tricks and is based upon a good Heart suit. Your hand should develop at least three tricks for partner, which means that you have some reasonable prospects of going game. What do you bid? Surely not 3 Diamonds. In the first place, partner might pass. He is not the opener. Secondly, if he is placed in a position where he is obliged to rebid Hearts, you will not know whether he had any additional values or whether he just couldn't stand 3 Diamonds, and you will be called upon to bid 4 Hearts blindly, if at all. Your proper procedure is to raise to 3 Hearts. If partner wishes to leave it, he may do so. If partner wishes to go on, you have given him an inducement to do so.

Similarly, you are South and hold:

♠ x x x   ♡ 10 x x   ◇ K Q x   ♣ A K x x

With North and South vulnerable, the bidding has proceeded:

WEST	NORTH	EAST	SOUTH
1 Spade	2 Hearts	Pass	?

What should you do? You have normal trump support for a vulnerable overcall at the level of 2, and your hand has a reasonable chance to develop four playing tricks. Since partner has promised to take six, the total reaches ten, and you should bid 4 Hearts. A bid of 3 Clubs would be little short of an atrocity. Partner might pass. He did not open the bidding and is not obligated to make any further bids.

Another illustration. You are South and hold:

♠ A K x   ♡ x x x x   ◇ x x x x   ♣ K x

North and South are vulnerable. The bidding has proceeded:

WEST	NORTH	EAST	SOUTH
1 Heart	1 Spade	Pass	?

What should you do? Your partner has guaranteed to take five tricks. You can take three. The hand should be safe for eight tricks. You therefore raise to 2 Spades.

Again, as South you hold:

♠ K 9 x x   ♡ x   ◇ A 10 x x   ♣ Q 10 x x

North and South are vulnerable. The bidding has proceeded:

WEST	NORTH	EAST	SOUTH
1 Diamond	1 Spade	Pass	?

What should you do? Partner has promised to take five tricks. You can produce at least four. You should therefore jump to 3 Spades. This is not forcing, since partner was not the opener. He may drop it if he has a questionable overcall, but he should be given a strong inducement to go on to game if he chooses.

If you are satisfied with your partner's overcall but have a suit of your own, you should think twice before showing it. Remember that he has not invited you to bid, that he has not shown a hand of general strength; all his values may be massed in his own suit, and he may not have the slightest interest in yours. It is usually not good policy to show your own suit unless you have such a hand that you would have overcalled independently of your partner. To illustrate, as South you hold:

♠ A K 10 9 5   ♡ x x   ◇ K 10 x   ♣ x x x

The bidding has proceeded:

WEST	NORTH	EAST	SOUTH
1 Club	1 Heart	Pass	?

Prospects for game appear dim unless partner has a fit in Spades with you. Nevertheless, you should bid 1 Spade for a dual purpose. If partner has three-card support and a reasonably sound overcall, he may decide to raise you, in which case game possibilities are lurking on the horizon. On the other hand, should the opposition outbid you on this hand (a prospect which though remote is still possible), your Spade bid has prepared the basis for the defense of the hand.

When partner overcalls and your hand is rather strong though lacking in normal support for his suit, you can test game possibilities by offering a No Trump contract, assuming that you have the adverse suit protected. As South you hold:

♠ K 10 x   ♡ A J 10 x   ◊ J x   ♣ A J 9 x

The bidding has proceeded:

WEST	NORTH	EAST	SOUTH
1 Club	1 Diamond	Pass	?

Since you have an opening bid in your own right, you are quite willing to risk a game contract at No Trump providing partner is willing to carry on. You should therefore bid 2 No Trump.

When you approve of partner's overcall, and your values may be subject to attack on the opening lead, you can offer partner a choice. As South you hold:

♠ K J x   ♡ Q x   ◊ A J x x   ♣ 10 9 x x

The bidding has proceeded:

WEST	NORTH	EAST	SOUTH
1 Spade	2 Hearts	Pass	?

What should you do?

Your values in Spades suggest that you try 2 No Trump. If partner defects to Hearts, you will retire also. If, on the other hand, partner carries on to 3 No Trump, there should be a reasonable play for that contract.

Where you have a choice between showing your own suit and supporting your partner's overcall, if your partner has bid a major suit, by all means support him. If your partner has bid a minor suit, you may try the major if your hand is sufficiently strong. To illustrate, as South you hold:

♠ Q x x   ♡ x x   ◇ A Q J x x   ♣ x x x

The bidding has proceeded:

WEST	NORTH	EAST	SOUTH
1 Heart	1 Spade	2 Hearts	?

Here your problem is whether to compete by bidding 3 Diamonds or by raising to 2 Spades. The bid of 2 Spades is recommended. But if you held:

♠ A Q J x x   ♡ x x   ◇ Q x x   ♣ x x x

and the bidding proceeded

WEST	NORTH	EAST	SOUTH
1 Heart	2 Diamonds	2 Hearts	?

you should try 2 Spades, inasmuch as you are prepared to raise to 3 Diamonds in any event.

Do not rescue an overcall when it is not doubled

As South you hold:

♠ x x   ♡ x   ◇ 10 x x   ♣ K 10 9 x x x

The bidding has proceeded:

WEST	NORTH	EAST	SOUTH
1 Spade	2 Hearts	Pass	?

What should you do? This is no hand with which to seek involvements. Offer up a prayer of thanksgiving that you have not been doubled and don't do anything that might put such ideas in the enemy's mind. Pass quickly. If you permit matters to rest, you will probably learn that West, the opener, who rather likes his hand, will rescue your partner and save you the trouble. But if partner is doubled at 2 Hearts, you might give serious consideration to bidding 3 Clubs.

MORAL: *Do not rescue a partner who has not been doubled.*

Rescuing

What if partner's overcall has been doubled for penalties? Should you rescue? That involves the use of good, sound judgment. "Never rescue" would be just as bad advice as "Always rescue."

Suppose you are South and hold:

♠ x   ♡ x x x   ◇ A K 10 9 x   ♣ J x x x

The bidding has proceeded:

WEST	NORTH	EAST	SOUTH
1 Heart	1 Spade	Double	?

Should you rescue to 2 Diamonds? By all means *No*. In the first place, you have no means of knowing that 2 Diamonds will be a better contract than 1 Spade. Secondly, a rescue would increase the commitment to eight tricks. And finally, your hand as dummy will produce two tricks for your partner, which is as many as he had the right to expect. Again, as South you hold:

♠ x x   ♡ x x x   ◇ Q J 10 9 x x   ♣ x x

The bidding has proceeded:

WEST	NORTH	EAST	SOUTH
1 Spade	2 Clubs	Double	?

Should you rescue to 2 Diamonds? As a dummy your hand is completely useless. If you rescue to 2 Diamonds, you are sure of winning four tricks in your own hand plus whatever high cards partner might contribute. Since you will be developing four tricks which would not otherwise exist, a rescue to 2 Diamonds is recommended.

Showing adverse stoppers when partner has overcalled

Bidding No Trump for the sole purpose of showing stoppers in the suit adversely bid is not good policy. Remember, when partner has merely overcalled, you should take no action unless you think there is some chance for game. Do not keep the overcaller's bid open as though he were the opener. For example, as South you hold:

♠ x x x x   ♡ x x   ◇ A Q x   ♣ Q x x x

The bidding has proceeded:

WEST	NORTH	EAST	SOUTH
1 Diamond	1 Heart	Pass	?

What should you do? Nothing. Do not bid 1 No Trump to show that you have Diamonds stopped. That would indicate a desire to go on, a desire which you do not have. At least, you shouldn't.

IT IS STRANGE that the take-out double, one of the most valuable tools in the bridge player's kit, should be so much neglected and yet so frequently abused.

Before delving into the refinements of the take-out double, it may be well to pause for a second for purposes of identification. How is the student to distinguish between a take-out and a penalty double? Here's how!

The double of 2 No Trump is always for penalties.

The double of 1 No Trump is intended primarily for penalties, but partner is permitted the wide exercise of judgment and may refuse to leave the double in if his hand contains a long suit and has little defensive values.

What about the double of an opening 3 bid? In the methods herein recommended, *the double of a 3 bid is treated in the same manner as the double of a 1 bid.* It is intended primarily for take-out, but naturally, at this high level, the partner may exercise a certain amount of discretion and may pass if he thinks it more profitable to play for penalties.

A double, in order to be for a take-out, must be made at the player's first opportunity to double that suit. For example:

SOUTH	WEST	NORTH	EAST
1 Spade	Pass	1 No Trump	Pass
2 Spades	Double		

This is a double for penalties. The logic of the situation is this: If West had been desirous to hear from partner, he would not have passed 1 Spade but would have doubled then and there, requesting partner to bid.

After partner has made any bid, all doubles are for penalties. For example:

SOUTH	WEST	NORTH	EAST
1 Club	1 Diamond	Double	

This is a penalty double, since North's partner has already bid.

Requirements for the take-out double

The take-out doubler announces that his hand is at least as good as an opening bid, or, to put it in another way, a take-out double over an opening bid of 1 in a suit should be based on no less than 13 points, including high cards and distribution. If the double is made after a 1 No Trump opening, doubler should have at least 16 points in high cards.

There are other factors to be weighed when contemplating a take-out double. Some hands which contain a great many more than 13 points are not suitable for a take-out double, as will presently be seen.

The take-out doubler should never lose sight of the fact that he is forcing partner to bid, a partner who may be completely devoid of values. If you are contemplating a take-out double, it is rather good practice for you to try to guess in what suit your partner will make his response (let's face it, more likely than not it will be your worst suit). If that response is apt to prove embarrassing to you, something is wrong with your take-out double. You ought not to force your partner into a position which you might find distasteful yourself. For example:

♠ A Q x x   ♡ x   ◇ A J x x   ♣ A x x x

Both sides are vulnerable. Your right-hand opponent opens with 1 Spade. What should you do? The casual player, without pausing to visualize partner's probable response and impressed by his high-card holding, would make a take-out double, a step which we do not recommend. Let's be realistic about it. It is almost a moral certainty that partner will reply with 2 Hearts. What then? The natural inclination will then be to bid 2 No Trump. Attempting to win eight tricks at No Trump with a partner who may have nothing is a highly hazardous undertaking. At the moment there is no safe avenue of escape for you. What is wrong? You should have thought of all this before you doubled. You might then have foreseen this awkward situation and, instead of doubling, might have decided to employ "snake-in-the-grass" tactics, just waiting around for something to turn up.

In other words, it is the doubler's position, in addition to promising certain high-card strength, to offer safety to his partner. He announces, in effect: "You will find my hand to be a satisfactory dummy for you" or "I have a very convenient suit in which I myself can play the hand."

F*

Take the following example:

♠ K 10 x x   ♡ K 10 x x   ◇ A Q x x   ♣ x

Your opponent opens with 1 Club. Though your hand contains only 12 high-card points, it is a highly acceptable double. Regardless of which suit your partner names in response, your dummy will be more than adequate for him because, valued as a supporting hand, it is worth about 15 points.

Possession of a good five-card suit is no bar to the use of the double. For example:

♠ A K J 10 x   ♡ K x x x   ◇ x x   ♣ A x

Your opponent opens the bidding with 1 of a minor suit. To make a mere overcall in Spades would not describe the strength of your hand and would risk partner's passing with a smattering of values sufficient to produce game. This hand has the value of 17 points, and some affirmative action must be taken. The best procedure is to double first and to bid Spades thereafter. This will inform partner that you have better than an opening bid. The double has the added advantage of providing two possible final contracts. Partner might be short in Spades and have some length in Hearts, in which case a game might be available in the latter suit.

The take-out double is a technical bid announcing, "I have a good hand, partner; it is at least as good as an opening bid. I will tell you more about it later. Meanwhile, just answer my questionnaire."

Now that the jump overcall has been relegated to the category of "pre-emptive-type" bids, hands which formerly called for such treatment are now included under the heading of the take-out double. For example, as South you hold:

♠ K x   ♡ A K J 10 x x   ◇ A J 10 x   ♣ x

East opens the bidding with 1 Diamond. You must resist the temptation to bid 2 Hearts, since that call now shows 9 high-card points or less. The proper strategy is to double first, and then bid an appropriate number of Hearts on the following round.

A double to reopen the bidding

There is one instance in which a take-out double may be made with less than 13 points. That is to prevent the bidding from dying out when the adversaries have quit at a low level. For example, as South you hold:

♠ A J x x   ♡ K x x x   ◇ K x x   ♣ x x

The bidding has proceeded:

WEST	NORTH	EAST	SOUTH
1 Club	Pass	Pass	?

What should you do? It is not at all uncommon in situations of this type to hear a player give forth some such utterance as this: "They didn't bid a game, so there is no use fighting against 1 Club. That won't get them very far." We do not admire such lack of enterprise. As we view it, it is more becoming for a player in this situation to express himself in some such fashion as this: "Why should we permit them to play a hand so cheaply when it is likely that we can obtain a part score?" South, in this sequence, may deduce that partner has a certain amount of strength. East is woefully weak, since he was unable even to keep open a Club bid. He quite probably has a good deal less than 6 points. North's hand may have been just short of the requirements for a take-out double or an overcall. You should give your partner a chance to compete by making a take-out double. North must make allowances in situations of this kind and should not presume that you have a normal type of double. You should be very careful not to proceed further after doubling, because in that case partner will assume that your double was of the standard variety.

Responses by partner of doubler

When partner makes a take-out double, it is your absolute duty to respond irrespective of the weakness of the hand. *The only excuse for passing is the ability to defeat the opponents in the bid which your partner has doubled.* Do not be afraid to bid with a "bust" hand. Your partner has assumed full responsibility. If you suffer a loss, blame it on him.

If your response can be made at the level of 1, a four-card major should be shown in preference to a five-card minor, provided the four-card major is headed by a high honor. For example:

♠ x x x   ♡ Q x x x   ◇ x   ♣ K x x x x

Your partner has doubled 1 Diamond. You should respond with 1 Heart rather than 2 Clubs.

Consideration of safety may dictate a departure from this rule. Suppose that as South you hold:

♠ J x x x   ♡ x x   ◇ J x x x x   ♣ x x

The bidding has proceeded:

WEST	NORTH	EAST	SOUTH
1 Club	Double	Pass	?

With a hand this weak it is better policy to respond with 1 Diamond rather than 1 Spade.

Some players make an exception to the above rule when they have a fairly good hand and hope to get a chance to show both suits in response. For example:

♠ K 10 x x   ♡ x x   ◇ x x   ♣ A x x x x

Partner doubled an opening bid of 1 Heart. The above rule calls for a response of 1 Spade. Some players, however, prefer to respond with 2 Clubs, hoping to get another chance, at which time they will bid 2 Spades. This will give partner an accurate description of the hand; he will know responder held five Clubs, four Spades, and a good hand, containing about 9 points.

There is one objection to this type of strategy. When you respond in a minor suit, partner may become discouraged and not carry on the bidding; whereas if you respond with a major suit, you are much more likely to get another chance.

When the responder holds two suits and a good hand, the practice is to show the higher-ranking suit first, with the intention of showing the other suit on the next round. For example:

♠ x x x   ♡ x x   ◇ A 10 x x   ♣ K Q x x

Partner has doubled a bid of 1 Heart. You should respond with 2 Diamonds. This hand is worth 10 points and therefore is strong enough to warrant two bids from you. Clubs should be shown on the next round if the opportunity presents itself.

♠ K 10 x x   ♡ A J x x   ◇ x x x   ♣ x x

Partner has doubled a bid of 1 Diamond. Respond with 1 Spade, fully intending to bid Hearts on the next round unless Spades are vigorously supported. Your hand is worth 9 points, 8 in high cards and 1 for distribution, and is therefore worth two bids.

Occasionally you will find that the only four-card suit in your hand has been bid by the opponents. This presents an embarrassing problem. Do not respond with No Trump unless you can very safely stop the adverse suit. Rather than bid No Trump you may be obliged to respond in a three-card suit. In that case you should select the cheapest possible bid you can make. For example:

♠ 10 x x   ♡ J x x   ◇ Q x x x   ♣ x x x

Your partner has doubled a bid of 1 Diamond. Do not respond with 1 No Trump. Your Diamond stopper is too sketchy. Respond with your cheapest three-card suit. In this case, 1 Heart.

The response of 1 No Trump denotes a fairly good hand and should be based on not less than 8 or 9 points in high cards and a stopper in the opposing suit. There was an old school of players who treated the 1 No Trump response to a double as a specialized bid announcing certain high-card strength but making no promises as to a stopper in the adverse suit. This practice has been abandoned by all experienced players. The No Trump response normally shows a stopper in the adverse suit, and the doubler need not have an additional stopper to support the No Trump if his hand is otherwise suitable.

If your hand contains four cards in a major and also a safe stopper in the opponent's suit, a choice of response is presented. As a rule, it is better policy to name a major than to respond in No Trump. For example:

♠ J 10 x x   ♡ K J x   ◇ Q J x   ♣ x x x

Partner has doubled a bid of 1 Heart. Respond with 1 Spade rather than 1 No Trump. If partner displays any enthusiasm, you may bid No Trump later.

But when you have the adversaries' suit well stopped and your hand contains about 8 or 9 points, you may respond in No Trump in preference to showing a four-card minor suit. For example:

♠ K 10 9 x   ♡ x x   ◇ Q x x   ♣ K 10 x x

Partner has doubled 1 Spade. This is a fairly good hand under the circumstances. You have a little better than 8 points, and the adversaries' suit is safely stopped. You could respond with 2 Clubs, but that will probably lead nowhere, and a better response is 1 No Trump. It will be noted that the No Trump response to partner's double denotes a fairly good hand. In some quarters the unsound practice exists of using the No Trump response to partner's double to indicate a bad hand. This should be avoided.

Responding with strong hands

Among the shortcomings of the average bridge player, few are more outstanding than his inability to judge the value of his hand when partner has made a take-out double. Most players are inclined to underestimate the value of their hands in this position.

The following table should be of assistance, in a general sort of way, in judging the value of the responding hand:

If you have 6 points, you have a fair hand.

If you have 9 points, you have a good hand.

If you have 11 points, you have a probable game.

When you have more than 11 points, game becomes a moral certainty, provided you reach the proper contract. When you hold a hand in which you have a probable game (11 points), it is generally good strategy to so advise your partner at once. This is done by bidding one more than is necessary, in response. You may bid one more than necessary even though your suit is not very robust.

For example:

♠ Q J x x   ♡ A J x   ◇ x x x   ♣ K J x

Partner has doubled a bid of 1 Diamond. You have 12 points, which means that you no doubt have a game. The proper response is 2 Spades, one more than necessary. This does not promise a good Spade suit.

When your best suit is a minor and you hold 11 points or more, the same principle should be followed. That is, your strength should be shown by bidding one more than necessary. But if this would require a jump to 3, you ought to have a fairly good minor suit. Holding minor-suit strength, as well as protection in the suit adversely bid, a jump should be made in No Trump, thus:

♠ Q J 10   ♡ J x x   ◇ K J x   ♣ K J x x

Partner has doubled 1 Diamond. You have 12 points and a jump is indicated. The recommended response is 2 No Trump, rather than a jump in the minor suit. But:

♠ x x   ♡ Q J 10   ◇ A 10 x   ♣ K Q J x x

Partner has doubled a bid of 1 Spade. The proper response is 3 Clubs.

The business pass of partner's take-out double

It has been pointed out above that doubler's partner is under an absolute duty to respond, however weak his hand may be. The double should be passed only when responder is quite sure he can defeat the contract.

This does not refer to doubles of 1 No Trump which are essentially for penalties and should usually be left in. Reference is being made to take-out doubles of suit contracts.

The double of 1 in a suit should never be left in with less than three sure trump tricks. Bear in mind that if you pass the double of 1 in a suit, partner will select a trump for his opening lead. Are you prepared for it? If you are not, then definitely your business pass is improper.

Inexperienced players will sometimes pass a take-out double on the ground that "Partner, I didn't have a thing to bid." This is anathema. Basic in the principles of bridge is this: That one never passes a take-out double out of a sense of fright. The pass of partner's take-out double is an aggressive step and indicates a desire to conquer. The person who passes, therefore, should be well equipped.

Procedure by doubler's partner after an intervening bid

When your partner has doubled the opening bid and opener's partner, who speaks before you, takes action, you are no longer under the duty to respond. You have been relieved of that obligation by the enemy. A bid by you at this point is therefore voluntarily made and denotes some measure of strength. It is not, however, regarded as a free bid in the general meaning of that term. The requirements are not nearly so stringent as they would be if partner had opened the bidding and second hand had overcalled. By doubling, partner is trying to get a message from you, and the opponents are trying to obstruct your communications. You will sometimes find it necessary to stretch a point to get the message through to your partner.

Bear in mind that if your hand is worth about 7 or 8 points, you should regard it as fair to middling and ought to feel justified in making a free bid. For example, you hold:

♠ A Q x x x   ♡ x x   ◇ x x x   ♣ x x x

Your partner has doubled a bid of 1 Heart. Opener's partner bids 2 Hearts. You may make a free bid of 2 Spades.

♠ x x x   ♡ K x x   ◇ A Q x x   ♣ x x x

Partner has doubled a bid of 1 Spade. Opener's partner bids 2 Clubs. You should make a free bid of 2 Diamonds. Your hand is worth 9 points.

♠ x x   ♡ x x x   ◇ Q J 10   ♣ A 10 9 x x

Partner has doubled a bid of 1 Heart. Opener's partner bids 1 Spade. You should make a free bid of 2 Clubs. Had the opener's partner bid 2 Hearts, it would have required a bid of 3 to show your suit, which in this case would have been somewhat doubtful wisdom but still a close question. Your hand is worth 8 points.

Where your free bid may be made at the level of 1, the requirements may be shaded if you have a long major suit.

Procedure by doubler's partner when an opponent redoubles

If your partner makes a take-out double and the opener's partner redoubles, you are relieved of the obligation to bid, because the auction reverts to your partner and permits him to take himself out. A pass by you indicates, in most cases, that you have nothing to say at the present time and you would prefer to have your partner take himself out of the redouble. It implies that you are more or less willing to have him select any of the suits, that you have no special choice. However, a bid at this point does not promise strength and should not be regarded as a free bid. Partner has asked you for your best suit. If you can afford to show it, the chances are you should. If you have a five-card suit, it is generally good practice to show it regardless of its texture. Even a four-card suit may be shown if it does not consume any bidding space. For example:

♠ x x x   ♡ K J x x   ◇ x x x   ♣ x x x

Partner has doubled a bid of 1 Diamond. The next hand redoubles. It is proper for you to bid 1 Heart. This does not consume any bidding space. If partner wishes to bid 1 Spade or 2 Clubs, he can do so at the same level as if you had passed. Had the opening bid been 1 Club, doubled by your partner and redoubled, it is doubtful that you should bid the Heart with a hand this weak, inasmuch as partner's suit might be Diamonds. A Heart bid would force him to the level of 2 to name his suit, whereas had you passed he could have rescued himself from the redouble by a bid of 1 Diamond.

Action by doubler after partner responds

A great many players are able to visualize partner's possible strength. Few, however, learn to visualize partner's probable weakness. Generally speaking, a doubler who has already advertised his strength should underbid on subsequent rounds, and the responder, who has made no promises, should adopt an aggressive attitude. In actual play, however, for some strange reason, the opposite seems to be true. The doubler keeps rebidding his values, while his partner, who never did care for his hand, rarely seems to work up any enthusiasm.

The advice I hand out for general consumption reads something like the following: "If you are the take-out doubler, I suggest that you bid about half as much as it has been your habit to. If you are the partner of the take-out doubler, it is my recommendation that you bid twice as much as you have been in the habit of doing."

Let us take an illustration. As South you hold:

♠ A K 10   ♡ x x   ♢ K 10 x   ♣ A K J 10 x

The bidding has proceeded:

WEST	NORTH	EAST	SOUTH
1 Heart	Pass	Pass	Double
Pass	2 Clubs	Pass	?

What do you do?

Most players could not resist the impulse to make a jump raise in Clubs. They do not stop to realize that with an opening bid on your left and opposite a partner who may be extremely weak, an eleven-trick contract would not have a very good prospect of success. However, if partner can manage to stop the Heart suit, a game contract at No Trump might be worth risking. The proper procedure, therefore, is to bid only 3 Clubs. A jump to 4 Clubs would be improper on another ground, the simple one that you have no assurance that your partner will not lose four tricks. Let us examine the complete hand:

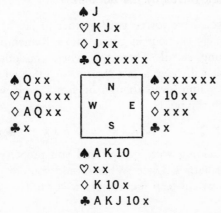

```
              ♠ J
              ♡ K J x
              ♢ J x x
              ♣ Q x x x x x
♠ Q x x                      ♠ x x x x x x
♡ A Q x x x        N         ♡ 10 x x
♢ A Q x x      W       E     ♢ x x x
♣ x                S         ♣ x
              ♠ A K 10
              ♡ x x
              ♢ K 10 x
              ♣ A K J 10 x
```

It will be observed that a contract of 3 No Trump can be fulfilled, the bid which North should hazard after partner raises to 3 Clubs. The singleton Spade should not act as a bar to such action, inasmuch as partner's strong bidding clearly indicates that he has some strength in that suit.

Sometimes the doubler can tell from partner's response that chances for game are very remote and that the bidding should therefore not be continued. For example, as South you hold:

♠ A Q x x   ♡ x x   ◇ A 10 x   ♣ K J x x

The bidding has proceeded:

EAST	SOUTH	WEST	NORTH
1 Heart	Double	Pass	2 Diamonds
Pass	?		

What should you do?

Your double was on moderate values; partner was unable to jump the bid, so you are to assume that he has less than 11 points. Inasmuch as partner failed to respond with 1 Spade, it is not to be expected that he will have four of that suit. It would therefore be risky, if not altogether pointless, for you to try 2 Spades. If you did so, partner would be justified in looking for a five-card Spade suit in your hand and might base his subsequent action on that assumption. Furthermore, partner was unable to bid 1 No Trump, so that you know he either has insufficient high-card values or lacks a Heart stopper. Since game in Diamonds is out of the question, there is nothing for you to do but pass.

Major-suit raises by the doubler

When you have forced your partner to bid by doubling, you should be extremely cautious in giving raises. Remember that partner may have nothing at all. Therefore, when you offer a raise you represent that he will have a fair chance to fulfill whatever contract you impose upon him, even though he has a very weak hand. For example, as South you hold:

♠ A K Q x x   ♡ K x x   ◇ A J x   ♣ x x

East opens the bidding with 1 Club and you properly double. Your partner responds with 1 Spade. What should you do?

Many players would leap impulsively to 4 Spades. A little analysis will show such action to be unsound. Partner was forced to speak and may be trickless. In that case even a contract of 3 Spades will not be safe. This hand in support of partner's Spade bid is worth 18 points. Let us examine the complete hand:

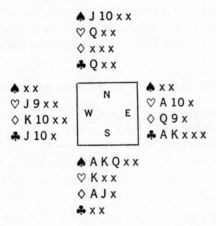

It will be noted that declarer, against proper defense, will be obliged to lose two tricks in each of the side suits and could barely fulfill a contract of 1 odd.

No sounder advice can be given the doubler than this: *When partner's response has been forced, never jump to any contract which you cannot reasonably expect to fulfill in your own hand.*

When a doubler follows up his original double with a free raise (after his right-hand opponent has bid again), he confirms a fine double and a hand that possesses game-going possibilities. For example, as South you hold:

♠ x   ♡ A 9 x x x   ◇ A Q x   ♣ K Q x x

The bidding has proceeded:

EAST	SOUTH	WEST	NORTH
1 Spade	Double	Pass	2 Diamonds
2 Spades	?		

What should you do? Nothing. No action would be safe. A raise to 3 Diamonds, when partner may have nothing, may prove disastrous, as may likewise a bid of 3 Hearts. You have done justice to your holding by making an immediate double. You can afford to pass the bid around to partner, who, if he has anything at all, will not forget that you made a double and surely will not permit the opponents to run off with the contract at this bargain price.

When contemplating a raise after having forced partner to bid, it is well to examine the following table:

> Don't raise to the 2 level unless you have at least 16 points.
> Don't raise to the 3 level unless you have at least 19 points.
> Don't raise to the 4 level unless you have at least 22 points.

Action by doubler's partner when doubler raises

With an indifferent hand the doubler's partner will have no problem when the doubler raises his response, but if he holds a good hand, it will be his duty to take further action.

It should be borne in mind that if responder to the doubler has about 9 points, he must consider that he has a good hand. For example:

♠ J x x x   ♡ A x x   ◇ x x x   ♣ K J x

Your partner has doubled an opening bid of 1 Diamond. You have responded with 1 Spade, which partner raises to 2. Holding 9 points, you have a good hand. A player holding a good hand should make one more bid if the doubler gives him a raise. Your proper procedure is to bid 3 Spades. Remember that partner has offered to fulfill an eight-trick contract, though he knows you may have little or nothing, and you should surely be safe for nine tricks.

Remember that since partner raised to the 2 level, he has promised at least 16 points. You therefore have almost enough to see a game. If he has an extra point somewhere, you should have a good gamble for the game contract.

♠ J x x x   ♡ K Q x   ◇ x x   ♣ Q J x x

The bidding has proceeded as in the previous example. Your hand is worth 10 points valued at Spades, and partner, by raising, has shown that his hand is worth 16. The necessary 26 are in sight, and you should be willing to contract for 4 Spades. Remember that a probable game becomes a biddable game when your partner raises. Do not be concerned about the complexion of your trump suit. Remember, as far as partner can tell, you have nothing more than four small Spades, and it is not good practice for him to raise your suit unless he, too, has four trumps.

Action by opener's partner

The redouble

When your partner's opening bid has been doubled by your right-hand opponent, your proper procedure is not always clearly indicated. What you do at this point may determine the success or failure of the hand.

A superstition that seems to have gained popularity is the one to the effect that "a bid over a double shows weakness." This is an unsound doctrine, but it is easy to see how the confusion has arisen. It has for many years been a definitely accepted convention that when partner opens the bidding and the next hand doubles, a redouble by the third player denotes a good hand. It may or may not denote support for partner, but the paramount consideration is the desire to get across this information, "Partner, do not be intimidated by the double. I think we have the best hands. I'll tell you more about mine later."

If, therefore, the partner of the opening bidder fails to redouble, the implication is quite plain that he does not have a very strong hand. However, if the opener's partner chooses to bid rather than redouble, it does not imply that he has a weak hand. It may be that he has certain values which he finds it expedient to show at this time. It may be that he cannot afford to wait, for fear that the bidding will mount too high before his next chance to call.

In a condensed form the principle may be stated as follows: When your partner opens the bidding and the next hand doubles:

WITH A GOOD HAND, YOU REDOUBLE

The question arises as to what constitutes a good hand in this sense. A hand is considered to be good enough for a redouble if it is above average in strength. An average hand is worth 10 points. If the hand is worth less than 10 points and you have anything to say, say it at once. If it is worth more than 10 points, then you should redouble first to advise partner that you have the balance of power.

WITH A BAD HAND, YOU PASS

To bid for the sole purpose of announcing you are broke does not seem to make good sense. Yet there is one situation in which the partner of the opening bidder may speak with a bad hand, and that is when he has trump support for partner and is able to give a raise.

This merely serves as an obstructive measure and intends to interfere with the opposition without incurring any risk.

WITH AN IN-BETWEEN HAND, YOU USUALLY BID AT ONCE

(Sometimes, with a hand that is not quite good enough to redouble, you may decide to await developments and enter the auction later, but in such cases you ought to be very sure that you can afford to bid later.)

Let us take a few practical examples:

♠ x ♡ K Q 10 x ◇ A Q x x ♣ A 10 x x

Your partner's opening bid of 1 Spade has been doubled by your right-hand opponent. Although you do not like Spades, you have a very good hand. The proper procedure is to redouble to announce your strong holding. If you contend, "What if this hand should be played at 1 Spade redoubled?" the answer is that with all your high cards your partner will surely be able to take seven tricks and the redouble of 1 Spade will produce a game. If, however, as is more probable, the opponents elect to bid, they will fall into your trap and you will be in position to make a devastating penalty double of any suit which they choose to play.

Here it is essential to point out a very important convention which applies to this case: A player who redoubles becomes the temporary captain of the team. The opening bidder is requested to pass the next bid around to the redoubler, who promises to double or bid.

♠ 10 x x ♡ A K J x x ◇ K x x ♣ x x

Again your partner's opening bid of 1 Spade has been doubled. You have a good hand and your proper procedure is clearly defined. You should redouble. There will be plenty of time to show the Hearts later, if expediency so dictates.

♠ J x x x ♡ x ◇ x x x ♣ Q x x x x

Again your partner's opening bid of 1 Spade has been doubled. With this hand you should bid 2 Spades, not for the purpose of showing weakness but with the intention of taking this opportunity to show some Spade support. This may make it possible for partner eventually to sacrifice at 4 Spades, if he believes such procedure will be profitable. The bid has the further advantage of making it somewhat more difficult for the doubler's partner to respond. He must now bid 3 of some suit and may fear to do so. If in a similar bidding situation you hold:

♠ Q J x x x   ♡ x   ◇ x x x   ♣ J x x x

you might be justified in bidding 3 Spades. You will note that while this is a jump it cannot be interpreted as showing strength, because over a double the accepted way to indicate strength is by a redouble. Since you fail to redouble, your partner must realize that you do not have a good hand. The 3 Spade bid is made merely as a barricade. In most cases it will make it more embarrassing for the partner of the doubler to enter the auction, under circumstances in which you do not welcome competition from the enemy. It is hardly necessary to point out that the jump in this situation is not forcing.

♠ x x   ♡ x x x   ◇ x x x   ♣ A K J x x

Your partner's opening bid of 1 Spade has been doubled by your right-hand opponent. Your hand is neither good nor bad. It might be called an in-between hand. If you do not bid now, you will find no convenient opportunity to show your values at a later stage. The proper procedure, therefore, is to bid 2 Clubs. Note that your hand valued at Clubs is worth only 9 points, 8 in high cards and 1 for distribution. It is therefore considered of mediocre strength, and immediate action must be taken if ever you intend to let your voice be heard.

♠ A K x x x   ♡ x x   ◇ x x x   ♣ A Q x

As South you open the bidding with 1 Spade. West doubles. Your partner bids 3 Spades and East passes. What should you do?

You should pass. Your hand is worth only 14 points, and you know to a certainty that your partner cannot have more than 10 points, else he would have redoubled. Partner's jump to 3 Spades was intended as a barricade against East. The complete hand:

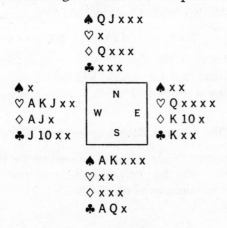

♠ Q J x x x
♡ x
◇ Q x x x
♣ x x x

♠ x
♡ A K J x x
◇ A J x
♣ J 10 x x

♠ x x
♡ Q x x x x
◇ K 10 x
♣ K x x

♠ A K x x x
♡ x x
◇ x x x
♣ A Q x

It will be seen that even a 3 Spade contract is down one. But the opponents can make 4 Hearts if they are permitted to get together in the bidding.

As previously stated, with a poor hand the opener's partner should pass the take-out double. For example:

♠ x x   ♡ x x x   ◇ Q x x   ♣ K x x x x

Your partner opened with 1 Spade. The next hand doubles. It is poor strategy for you to bid 2 Clubs. Nothing is to be gained by taking action. Your hand is worth only 6 points at Clubs, and a pass is clearly indicated.

Occasionally, when partner's opening bid is doubled, you will have just a smattering of strength and your course of action will not be clear. For example:

♠ x x   ♡ A x x   ◇ K x x x   ♣ J x x x

Your partner's opening bid of 1 Spade has been doubled by the next hand. What should you do? Your high-card holding, in conjunction with your partner's bid (you have 8 points in high cards), is such that you are quite persuaded that you can prevent the opponents from going game. In other words, this hand may develop into a dogfight for a part score. If you advise partner that you have a little something, he may be able to carry on the fight for a round or two. This bit of information you may convey by an immediate bid of 1 No Trump. If you do not act immediately, it may not be very practical for you to bid on a later round, and the opponents may steal a part score from you.

There is one case in which opener's partner would do well to take out with a very weak hand containing a long suit. That is when the opener's 1 No Trump bid has been doubled. For example:

♠ x   ♡ x x   ◇ J x x x   ♣ Q 10 x x x x

Partner opened with 1 No Trump. Next hand doubles. There is a very distinct danger that the double will be left in and may prove costly. In this case a rescue to 2 Clubs is recommended.

Use of the take-out double by opening bidder

The take-out double may also be used by the opening bidder to force a partner who has previously declined the opportunity to make a bid. For example, as South you hold:

♠ K J x x   ♡ A K 9 x   ◇ x   ♣ K Q x x

The bidding has proceeded:

SOUTH	WEST	NORTH	EAST
1 Club	1 Diamond	Pass	Pass
?			

What should you do?

Naturally you are going to carry on the fight, and it would be pointless for you to guess whether to rebid in Spades or in Hearts. There is no necessity for you to do so. Inasmuch as partner has not yet spoken, a double by you is for a take-out. There is a tendency in some quarters to confuse this with a business double because the *doubler* has previously bid. That is not the test. The test is whether the partner of the doubler has previously bid. If he has, the double is for penalties; if he has not, it is to be construed as a take-out double. In this case, since North has not bid, South's double insists that he do so. Here the double will provide for every contingency. If partner has either Hearts or Spades, he will name the suit. If he has neither, he may return to 2 Clubs, or if he has great length in Diamonds, he may elect to pass and play the hand at 1 Diamond doubled. Such practice almost entirely eliminates guesswork.

A few specialized situations

Exposing the psychic bid

As South you hold:

♠ x x x   ♡ K 10 9 x x   ◇ A x x x   ♣ x

The bidding has proceeded:

WEST	NORTH	EAST	SOUTH
1 Club	Double	1 Heart	?

What should you do?

Had East not bid, your response would have been 1 Heart—a response, incidentally, which you would have made with good cheer, inasmuch as your hand is worth 9 points when valued at Hearts. If partner has a sound double, East will be unable to fulfill the contract of 1 Heart. You should therefore double for penalties. It is not unlikely that East is playing "horse" and is attempting to rob you of your bid. Remember that a double by you at this point is for penalties, inasmuch as your partner has already bid. Remember, too, that a take-out double is classified as a bid for this purpose. In this situation North will realize that you have a sound Heart response yourself and will act accordingly.

To put it in another way: *Whenever your partner has shown strength by either an opening bid or a double, and your right-hand opponent makes the bid which you had the desire to make, double for business.*

Cue bidding as a response

As South you hold:

♠ A   ♡ 10 9 x x   ◇ Q 10 9 x   ♣ K J x x

What should you do if the bidding has proceeded:

WEST	NORTH	EAST	SOUTH
1 Spade	Double	2 Spades	?

Valued as a dummy, your hand is worth 13 points, 10 in high cards and 3 for distribution. Consequently there is no doubt in your mind that you should reach game in one of your three suits. At a quick glance it would seem that a bid of 3 Hearts is in order, but this call meets with several objections. The weakness of the Heart suit renders the bid at this level somewhat awkward. There is always the danger that partner will expect a somewhat better trump suit. Furthermore, there is the objection that partner may not carry on. True enough, a free bid at this level, while it portrays a really good hand, does not necessarily promise a game. It seems that the best procedure is to force partner to select the suit himself. This may be done by a cue bid in the adverse suit. The recommended call is 3 Spades, asking partner to select the suit in which the game contract will be played.

Occasionally a cue bid may be made even with one or two losers in the adverse suit when the hand is strong enough to warrant insistence on game. For example, as South you hold:

♠ Q J x x   ♡ K 10 x x   ◇ A x x   ♣ x x

EAST	SOUTH	WEST	NORTH
1 Club	Pass	2 Clubs	Double
Pass	?		

We recommend a bid of 3 Clubs, since you are prepared to carry on to game in either major suit.

The immediate cue bid

This is the strongest of all defensive bids. It is absolutely forcing to game and announces practically the equivalent of an opening 2 bid. It promises the ability to win the first trick in the suit adversely bid, either with the Ace or by ruffing.

For example, an opponent opens with 1 Diamond. You hold:

♠ A K Q x   ♡ A J 10 x x   ◇ none   ♣ K Q J x

You are unwilling to play for less than game (and conceivably a slam) in one of your three suits. You prefer not to make a take-out double: first, because of the slight risk that partner might have sufficient strength in Diamonds to make a penalty pass, and you have no special desire to play against 1 Diamond doubled; secondly, because if you double and partner responds with a weak hand, he may lose his nerve somewhere along the line and drop the bidding short of game. The proper procedure, therefore, is an immediate cue bid of 2 Diamonds. This forces partner to keep bidding until game is reached, and you may then proceed to display your wares in leisurely fashion without the necessity for resorting to jump bids on the way up.

Partner is expected to respond to the cue bid exactly as he would to a take-out double.

8.

The penalty double

AN OUTSTANDING SOURCE of unrealized wealth is the penalty double, made when an opponent overcalls at the level of 1 or 2. The average player never contemplates penalizing the opponents until they reach the upper levels, and appears to be completely oblivious of the fact that by far the most profitable penalties are gathered at the very low levels. The reason for this seems clear. When your opponents eventually reach a contract of 4, 5, or 6, it is usually as the result of some exploration. While they may have misjudged their strength, they have, more often than not, succeeded in finding a reasonable place to play the hand. But when your partner has opened with 1 Spade and next hand bids 2 Clubs, he has many times just tested his luck with what has come to be known as a "nuisance bid." The question of who more frequently finds him to be a nuisance has not been definitely cleared up. Penalties at this point can be devastating.

First of all, it is important to differentiate between a penalty double and one intended for a take-out. This problem we discussed in the chapter on take-out doubles. Here is a restatement:

Doubles of all No Trump contracts are intended for penalties. All doubles, even at the level of 1, are intended for penalties if made after partner has bid. There is no such thing as a take-out double after partner has made a bid.

The question arises: How is the inexperienced player to tell when to double an adverse bid for penalties? Generally speaking, this is done on a simple arithmetic basis. You count those tricks which you may reasonably expect to win, add them to those partner is expected to deliver, and if the total is sufficient to defeat the contract, let the ax descend. In the higher brackets this calculation is not very difficult, but it is not quite so easy to judge in doubling contracts of 1 and 2.

Perhaps the following suggestion may serve as an effective guide. At least it possesses the merit of simplicity:

When your partner opens the bidding (or in any other way shows strength, as by a take-out double) and your right-hand opponent overcalls in the suit which you wanted to bid, you should double for business. For example, you hold:

♠ K J 9 x   ♡ J 10   ◇ A J 10 x   ♣ x x x

Partner opens with 1 Heart. Opponent overcalls with 1 Spade. You should double, and your adversary isn't going to enjoy it. You are doubling not merely to show that you have the Spades. Had second hand passed, you would cheerfully have responded with 1 Spade. That is the test. It is not whether you might have responded with 1 Spade. It is whether you *wanted* to. For example, in the same situation, you hold:

♠ K J x x   ♡ x x x   ◇ K x x   ♣ x x x

In this case you would have responded to partner's opening bid of 1 Heart with 1 Spade, only because you felt it was your duty; for with 7 points, it was incumbent upon you to keep the bidding open. If second hand overcalls with 1 Spade, a double on this hand is not recommended.

Another simple guide: Partner opens with 1 of a suit and the next hand overcalls with 2 of some other suit. On hands which tempt you to call 2 No Trump, pause for five seconds and maybe you will change your mind. Double instead and watch your savings grow. For example, your partner opens with 1 Spade, the next hand overcalls with 2 Diamonds, and you hold:

♠ J x   ♡ A x x   ◇ Q 10 x x   ♣ K x x x

While you are seized with the temptation to bid 2 No Trump, my suggestion is that you resist it. That your hand will produce at least four tricks in defense is a reasonable assumption. These, coupled with your partner's expected three tricks, will account for a two-trick penalty. Assuming the opponents are not vulnerable, this will yield 300 points.

What, you will contend, about the situation in which you will be abandoning game, for which 300 points would not be adequate compensation? The answer is really very simple. If your partner has a minimum hand, you will have no game. Suppose the second hand had not overcalled. Would you have been willing to suggest that you have a good chance for game? I think not, for you have only 10 points facing the opening bid. But if your partner has more than a minimum and a game is probable, it follows that the penalty will be correspondingly greater. In other words, the more your partner has, the more the opponents are going to suffer.

There is this consideration of paramount importance: When the contract which you double will yield a game if fulfilled, you must exercise greater caution and allow yourself a trick leeway for margin of error or for the arrows of outrageous fortune. In other words, don't double a contract of 2 or 3 Spades or 3 or 4 Diamonds unless you expect to defeat it two tricks. But when your partner opens the bidding, and next hand overcalls with 2 Clubs or 2 Diamonds, great latitude is allowed in the exercise of the double "on suspicion." The risk is not great. The doubled contract, though fulfilled, does not yield the enemy a game. An illustration from real life:

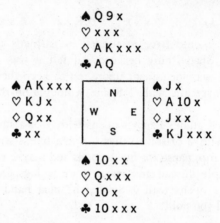

```
                ♠ Q 9 x
                ♡ x x x
                ◇ A K x x x
                ♣ A Q
  ♠ A K x x x    ┌───────┐    ♠ J x
  ♡ K J x        │   N   │    ♡ A 10 x
  ◇ Q x x        │ W   E │    ◇ J x x
  ♣ x x          │   S   │    ♣ K J x x x
                └───────┘
                ♠ 10 x x
                ♡ Q x x x
                ◇ 10 x
                ♣ 10 x x x
```

West opened the bidding with 1 Spade. North was vulnerable and overcalled with 2 Diamonds. East was presented with a problem. He had what he regarded as a little too much to pass, but after the 2 Diamond overcall the thought of a 3 Club bid could not be entertained for even a moment, and there was no other available bid for him. Reasoning that his hand would probably develop at least three tricks in defense, and counting on his partner for the usual minimum of three, he elected to double, relaxing in the knowledge that even if the opponents fulfilled the contract they could not score game. The result was an 800-point penalty, and what is more remarkable about it is that East and West could not have scored game.

Tricks for a penalty double

In counting your expected tricks for the purpose of making a penalty double, too much reliance must not be placed on the Point Count Table. Common-sense methods of deduction should be resorted to.

Sometimes you may allow a greater value than that suggested by the table. Ace Queen is regarded as 1½ quick tricks, but if that suit has been strongly bid on your right, you may be justified in counting on two winners. Similarly, a guarded King is regarded as ½ quick trick, but if your right-hand opponent may reasonably be expected to hold the Ace, you may rely upon the King as a winner. However, when the suit has been bid on your left, the Ace Queen should not be valued at much more than a trick and a King should be discounted almost entirely.

It is rarely sound to count more than two tricks in any one suit, and if you have great length in the suit, it is dangerous to rely on more than one defensive trick from that source. Occasionally none should be counted, as might be the case if you held A K Q x x x and partner had vigorously supported the suit.

Be quick to double when short in partner's suit. Be more cautious when holding as many as four of your partner's suit.

An item of value that may escape the attention of some players is the possession of four cards of the adverse suit. For defensive purposes this may be regarded as one trick, even though no honor card is held. The nuisance value of four small trumps should not be underestimated. It means that if declarer is to exhaust trumps, he must make four pulls, which he will rarely find it convenient to do. If declarer is forced to ruff once, he will probably be brought down to your size in trumps.

On this basis observe the following hand. As South you hold:

♠ A K J 9 ♡ x x x x ◇ x x ♣ A K J

The bidding has proceeded:

SOUTH	WEST	NORTH	EAST
1 Spade	2 Diamonds	Double	2 Hearts
?			

What should you do? The recommendation is to double. The defensive tricks may be estimated as follows: Since partner doubled 2 Diamonds, it is unlikely that he has any length in Spades, which makes it probable that two tricks will be cashed in that suit. At least two tricks may be counted in Clubs, and one trick should be counted for the possession of four Hearts. This brings the tally up to five tricks, or book. Anything partner produces will be velvet. You may contend, What if partner has nothing but Diamonds and produces no tricks against a Heart contract? The answer is, in that case your partner has made a very unsound business double.

In doubling the opponents one must always be conscious of the question, "Is there apt to be a rescue, and if so, can I do any damage to that rescue bid?"

When counting on partner's expected tricks to defeat the contract, one must have regard for the type of action that partner has previously taken. If he has opened the bidding with 1 of a suit, it is reasonable to expect him to produce about three tricks in the play of the hand. If he has opened with 1 No Trump, he may be depended on for four tricks. If he has made a take-out double, he may be relied upon to take at least three tricks. When partner has merely overcalled, it may be somewhat incautious to count on him for more than one defensive trick. Similarly, when partner has raised your suit, his raise may be based to a certain extent on distribution and he should not be counted on for more than one trick. And when partner has opened with a pre-emptive bid, you must base no business double on his action. Do not count on him for much of anything. In that case, any business double must be based entirely on your own hand.

Taking partner out of a business double

One of the most popular cartoons by H. T. Webster holds up to ridicule the player who takes his partner out of a business double. This has come to be regarded in many circles as contract's outstanding crime. I fear that this is somewhat in the nature of subversive crime. Since ignorance of the law is no excuse, it is of course a crime, and sometimes of major proportions, to take partner out of a business double from ignorance that it was intended for penalties. But the refusal to stand for partner's penalty doubles in the interest of the partnership is a matter involving the exercise of good judgment, without which no player can succeed at the card table.

Even though you make a business double, your partner may still be entitled to his opinion, though little toleration is to be held out for his whims. If a player's hand is completely unsuitable for defensive purposes, he is at perfect liberty to decline to stand for the double. However, the burden of proof is on the person who overrides his partner's judgment. Let us observe an illustration or two. As South you hold:

♠ x x   ♡ K Q J 10 x x   ◇ A x x x   ♣ x

The bidding has proceeded:

SOUTH	WEST	NORTH	EAST
1 Heart	2 Clubs	Double	Pass

What should you do? Of course partner has made a business double, but your hand is bound to be a disappointment to him in defense against 2 Clubs. Actually your hand may develop only one trick. You should therefore issue a warning by bidding 2 Hearts, at which contract you should be in no serious danger. However, on the same sequence of bidding, if you hold:

♠ x   ♡ K Q J x x   ◇ A K x x   ♣ J x x

you would naturally pass the double and start clipping coupons. Your hand is very well suited for defensive play. You should not be concerned about the possible loss of a game, because your penalty double will be adequate to repay you.

If your hand is unsuited to defense at a contract which partner has doubled, but is a very fine hand from the offensive standpoint, you should, in refusing to stand for the double, jump the bid to make this point clear to partner. For example, as South you hold:

♠ x   ♡ A Q J 10 x x   ◇ A K J x x   ♣ x

The bidding has proceeded:

SOUTH	WEST	NORTH	EAST
1 Heart	2 Clubs	Double	Pass

What should you do? In this hand you have good defensive values despite your shortage in Clubs, and you do not fear the fulfillment of the adversaries' contract, but there is a question in your mind whether it will be adequate compensation, inasmuch as your prospects for scoring a game are very bright. It is not recommended that you stand for the double, but in taking out the double you should make a jump—you should bid 3 Diamonds—to indicate to your partner that you are bidding aggressively and not merely because your hand is not suitable for defensive play.

It will be seen, therefore, that the mere circumstance that the enemy can be defeated is not always sufficient justification for doubling. You must always inquire, Will it be worth while? If you can score more points by going on with the bidding, naturally the double should be eschewed; but in doubtful cases lean toward the double on the theory that you will never go broke by taking sure profits.

Close doubles

Occasionally we must desist from doubling the adversaries in a close situation where it is feared that our double will locate

G

certain strength for the declarer and permit him to play the hand in a somewhat unnatural manner. It is a good principle not to double a close contract if your double is apt to cost you a trick. When your trump holding is something like Q 10 x x, for example, a double may warn the declarer of the adverse trump distribution and may permit him to play that suit unnaturally on the basis of your warning.

On the same line of reasoning, close doubles of slams should never be made. There is not enough profit in them compared to the risk of affording declarer an occasional clue to the successful fulfillment of the contract.

Sometimes a doubtful double must be made in the competitive situation when it is definitely wise for your side to discontinue bidding. In such cases, if you pass the bid to your partner, there is a mild suggestion that you are willing to have him go on.

Doubles of slam contracts

It has been pointed out that few points are gained above the line by doubling slam contracts. As a result of this experience, a convention has been developed in modern times relating to the double of a slam contract by a player who does not have the opening lead. The purpose of the convention is to guide the opening leader in the selection of his attack.

When partner doubles a slam, you must not make your normal opening lead. If you and your partner have bid any suit or suits, these suits should not be led, and obviously a trump lead is out of the question where a suit slam has been reached. The convention makes the following provisions:

1. If dummy has bid any suit or suits (other than trump), the double demands the lead of the first suit bid by dummy.

2. If dummy has bid no side suit, but declarer has bid another suit, the double demands the lead of the first side suit bid by declarer.

3. If neither dummy nor declarer has bid any side suit, but the defensive side has, the double demands the lead of one of the unbid suits.

In other words, the opening leader must not lead his own or his partner's suit. It follows, therefore, that you must not double a slam contract if you are anxious to have your partner make his normal lead. Of course, if the opponents have stepped so far out of line that the opening lead will not matter very much, you might as well strike and collect a bonus. But where it is a question of just another 50 or 100 points, you must forego the luxury.

For example, as South you hold:

1. ♠ A x x   ♡ K Q J 10 x x   ◇ x x x x   ♣ none
2. ♠ Q J 10   ♡ A Q J x x x   ◇ x x   ♣ x x

The bidding has proceeded:

WEST	NORTH	EAST	SOUTH
1 Spade	Pass	3 Clubs	3 Hearts
3 Spades	Pass	4 Spades	Pass
6 Spades	Pass	Pass	?

What should you do?

With NO. 1 you should double. This demands the lead of dummy's first suit, Clubs, which you ruff and defeat the contract.

With NO. 2 you must not double. If you do, partner has instructions not to lead a Heart, which is the lead you want to get.

Doubles of 3 No Trump contracts

The double of a 3 No Trump contract by a player not on lead carries with it certain implications.

1. If the doubler has bid a suit, his partner must unconditionally lead that suit, even though he may have but a singleton in it and a very fine suit of his own.

2. If the opening leader has bid a suit, partner's double requests him to lead that suit.

3. When neither the leader nor the doubler has bid, the double is a suggestion to partner to lead the dummy's first bid suit, unless he has a very fine opening lead of his own.

COMPETITIVE BIDDING QUIZ

Your right-hand opponent has opened with 1 Diamond. What action do you take with the following hands?

1. ♠ A K 10   ♡ Q x x x x   ◇ x x   ♣ A Q x

2. ♠ Q J 10 9 x x   ♡ A x   ◇ x   ♣ x x x x

3. ♠ x x   ♡ A K Q 10   ◇ K x x   ♣ J 10 x x

4. ♠ A K J 10 x   ♡ K x   ◇ x x x   ♣ Q x x

5. ♠ A x   ♡ A 10 x   ◇ A Q 9 x   ♣ K 10 x x

6. ♠ x   ♡ A J 10 x   ◇ A K 10 9   ♣ Q 10 9 x

You are South in the following problems and the bidding has proceeded:

WEST	NORTH	EAST	SOUTH
1 Club	Double	Pass	?

7. ♠ K x x
♡ K x x
◇ x x
♣ Q J 7 6 x

8. ♠ A K 10 x
♡ K Q x x
◇ x x
♣ x x x

.9. ♠ x x x
♡ A x x
◇ x
♣ Q J 10 9 x x

10. ♠ 10 9 x
♡ J x x
◇ A Q 10 x
♣ A 10 x

In the following problems, you are South. The bidding has proceeded:

NORTH	EAST	SOUTH
1 Heart	Double	?

11. ♠ Q J 10 x
♡ x
◇ A Q 10 x
♣ Q x x x

12. ♠ Q x x
♡ x x
◇ K Q x x
♣ J 10 x x

13. ♠ x
♡ 10 9 x x
◇ A Q x x
♣ x x x x

14. ♠ J 9 x x x
♡ 10 x
◇ K x x
♣ 10 9 x

In the following problems, you are South. The bidding has proceeded as indicated.

15. ♠ J 9 8 x x
♡ K 9 8 x x
◇ Q x x
♣ none

WEST	NORTH	EAST	SOUTH
1 Heart	2 Clubs	Double	?

16. ♠ K 10 9 x x
♡ A K x x
◇ x x
♣ A Q

SOUTH	WEST	NORTH	EAST
1 Spade	2 Diamonds	Pass	Pass
?			

17. ♠ A x
♡ x
◇ J 10 9 x x
♣ Q J 9 8 x

EAST	SOUTH	WEST	NORTH
1 Heart	Pass	2 Hearts	Pass
Pass	?		

18. ♠ Q J x
♡ x x x x
◇ A K J x
♣ x x

WEST	NORTH	EAST	SOUTH
1 Heart	1 Spade	Pass	?

19. ♠ Q x
♡ x x
◇ K J x x x
♣ A Q 10 x

WEST	NORTH	EAST	SOUTH
1 Spade	Pass	1 No Trump	Pass
2 Hearts	Pass	Pass	?

20. ♠ A 10 9 x
    ♡ K Q 10 x
    ◇ x x
    ♣ K J x

EAST	SOUTH	WEST	NORTH
1 Diamond	Double	Pass	1 Heart
2 Diamonds	?		

21. ♠ A x x
    ♡ K x
    ◇ Q 10 9 x
    ♣ 10 9 x x

NORTH	EAST	SOUTH
1 Heart	2 Diamonds	?

22. ♠ A Q J 10 x x
    ♡ A K Q x
    ◇ x
    ♣ A x

SOUTH	WEST	NORTH	EAST
2 Spades	Pass	2 No Trump	3 Clubs
?			

23. ♠ A K 10 x
    ♡ 10 9 x x
    ◇ Q x x
    ♣ K x

SOUTH	WEST	NORTH	EAST
1 Spade	2 Diamonds	Double	Pass
?			

24. ♠ A 10 x x x
    ♡ K Q J x x
    ◇ x
    ♣ Q x

SOUTH	WEST	NORTH	EAST
1 Spade	2 Diamonds	Double	Pass
?			

25. ♠ A 10 x
    ♡ Q J x x
    ◇ 10 9 x
    ♣ K x

WEST	NORTH	EAST	SOUTH
1 Heart	2 Clubs	Pass	?

26. ♠ A J 10 9 x
    ♡ K x
    ◇ K x x
    ♣ x x x

WEST	NORTH	EAST	SOUTH
1 Club	1 Heart	Pass	?

27. ♠ x x x
    ♡ A Q 10 x x
    ◇ x x
    ♣ Q x x

WEST	NORTH	EAST	SOUTH
1 Spade	Pass	2 Spades	Pass
Pass	2 No Trump	Pass	?

28. ♠ K J x
    ♡ A K J
    ◇ K Q 10 x
    ♣ A J 9

WEST	NORTH	EAST	SOUTH
Pass	Pass	1 Spade	?

29. ♠ x x
    ♡ A Q 10 x
    ◇ A J 10 x
    ♣ Q 10 x

WEST	NORTH	EAST	SOUTH
1 Heart	2 Spades	Pass	?

30. ♠ x
    ♡ A 10 9 x x x
    ◇ x x
    ♣ K Q 10 x

EAST	SOUTH	WEST	NORTH
1 Diamond	1 Heart	Pass	3 Hearts
Pass	?		

31. ♠ x x x
    ♡ K Q x
    ◇ K 10 9 x
    ♣ A x x

NORTH	EAST	SOUTH
1 Heart	3 Spades	?

32.

♠ x	NORTH	EAST	SOUTH
♡ Q x x	1 Diamond	Double	?
◊ K 10 x x x			
♣ A x x x			

33.

♠ A Q 10 9 x	WEST	NORTH	EAST	SOUTH
♡ x x	1 Heart	Pass	Pass	?
◊ A 10 x				
♣ x x x				

34.

♠ x x	WEST	NORTH	EAST	SOUTH
♡ x	1 Heart	Pass	1 Spade	?
◊ A 10 x				
♣ Q J 10 9 x x x				

35.

♠ x	EAST	SOUTH
♡ A K J 10 x x	1 Spade	?
◊ A K J x		
♣ x x		

ANSWERS TO COMPETITIVE BIDDING QUIZ

1. Double.
Your hand contains 15 high-card points in addition to 1 point for distribution, and we veto a bid of 1 Heart, first because the suit is not sufficiently robust for an overcall and secondly the hand has too much strength for a non-vulnerable overcall.

2. Two Spades.
You have the textbook requirements for a pre-emptive jump overcall — a good six-card suit and less than 9 high card points.

3. One Heart.
This is one of the rare instances where an overcall with a four-card suit is suggested. Had the enemy begun with 1 Spade, a take-out double would have been preferred.

4. One Spade.
You have a healthy five-card suit and the equivalent of an opening bid. However, it would be indiscreet to double and then call Spades after partner's 1 Heart response, for such action would indicate a stronger hand.

5. One No Trump.
The overcall of an opening bid with 1 No Trump requires the equal of a normal 1 No Trump opening and the adverse suit must be well stopped.

6. Pass.
Your hand is too strong for an overcall, and lacks the values in Spades for a take-out double. On hands where a considerable portion of your strength lies in the adverse suit it is best to reserve action until the later stages of the auction. You might, perhaps, be able to extract a sizable penalty from the opposition.

7. One No Trump.
To pass would be presumptuous, for it is highly unlikely that you will defeat the contract more than one trick. If you cannot answer the question of "Would I be happy to play this 1 contract myself opposite a singleton or void in partner's hand?" with a resounding "Yes," you should not pass for penalties.

8. Two Clubs.
This may seem somewhat irregular and indeed it is with the worst possible

The penalty double

holding in the Club suit. However, this procedure is indicated in order to paint the best possible picture of your powerful holding. You have the strength required to insist upon a game after partner's take-out double. If partner's next call is in either major suit, you intend to proceed to game. If your partner bids No Trump it should be not on the basis of a cue bid, but rather on his own values.

9. Pass.
If partner makes the expected trump opening, your side should obtain a handsome profit. You have five winners with Clubs as trump. Remember, when partner leaves in a take-out double of 1 of a suit, he is pleading for a trump opening.

10. One No Trump.
The response of 1 No Trump to the double of an adverse suit shows roughly 8-10 high-card points where responder has room to call a suit at the one-level. Since opener needs 16 points in his hand for game to be in sight, there is no purpose in calling 2 No Trump, which might induce partner to stretch a point and bid 3 with a minimum hand.

11. Redouble.
While you lack one high card point for this call, you are prepared to double the opposition in any contract they choose to assume. Incidentally, the redouble in this sequence does not necessarily indicate acceptance in partner's suit. It is rather calculated to announce "please do not be intimidated by the adverse double, I am convinced that we have the balance of power."

12. One No Trump.
With moderate values (8 or 9 points) and a balanced hand, it is best to announce your values immediately. Thus fortified, partner may be in a position to compete. Whereas if you pass, you run the risk of being shut out of the auction.

13. Three Hearts.
Your hand is worth 9 points in support and it does no harm to muddy up the waters for the enemy. They might be embarrassed for a bid at this level in the auction.

14. Pass.
There is no reason to bid your shabby Spade suit. Let nature take its course.

15. Pass.
Don't be a nursemaid. Partner should have a good suit for his 2-level overcall. There is no reason to believe that Spades offer a safer haven. Frequently you will find that the opening bidder will not be in a position to pass and that will relieve you of any responsibility in the hand.

16. Double.
It is true that you do not have a desirable holding should partner bid Clubs, but if he does, he will probably have length in that suit, and A-Q doubleton may prove to be adequate support. Partner may, on the other hand, convert the take-out to penalties, a prospect which would not be distasteful.

17. Two No Trump.
This is the unusual No Trump overcall and requests partner to bid his better minor suit.

18. Three Spades.
You have 11 points and excellent support for partner's suit. Game should prove to be laydown if he is inclined to bid it.

19. Double.
While the unusual No Trump overcall is available, it permits the opposition to retire from the auction unscathed. A double, on the other hand, shows interest in the unbid suits and gives partner the opportunity to pass for penalties. This action would meet with your approval.

20. Pass.
Your double has evinced an interest in the unbid suits. Since it was based

upon minimum values, any further action must originate from partner.

21. Double.

You have a trick expectancy of four winners which, together with the three partner is expected to supply, will produce a minimum of a two-trick penalty.

22. Pass.

Your original bid has made it incumbent upon the partnership to reach game or double the opponents. Partner may be disposed to handle this adverse call and should be given the opportunity to do so.

23. Pass.

Almost any hand containing three trumps is good enough to allow a penalty double to stand for it usually means that your side will have a trump majority since partner is expected to hold four trumps for his double.

24. Two Hearts.

While we usually are inclined to let penalty doubles stand, our reason for initiating proceedings was the possession of ten cards in the major suits. Partner could hold something like ♠ x ♡ A 10 x x x ◇ Q 10 x x ♣ K 10 x, whereupon 4 Hearts would be a laydown, with no reasonable guarantee that the adverse contract would be defeated.

25. Two No Trump.

Our fit in Clubs should make a No Trump game a substantial favorite if partner deems it wise to continue.

26. One Spade.

If partner can raise Spades, game is on the horizon. We prefer this call to the direct raise of partner's suit with K x when our own major suit is reasonably sound.

27. Three Clubs.

Despite our fine Heart holding, it is imperative that we obey partner's command and take our choice of the minor suits. If partner wished us to bid Hearts he would have made a take-out double in preference to the unusual No Trump overcall.

28. Two No Trump.

This call is natural and is not to be construed as the unusual No Trump overcall which, incidentally, is a request for the minors only when the natural meaning of the bid is pointless when based upon the complete scope of the auction.

29. Pass.

Partner's pre-emptive call will normally produce six winners. While we have the makings of three with our cards, game is out of sight. Besides, the opposition might feel disturbed about being preempted and venture forth once again. This would not meet with our displeasure.

30. Four Hearts.

If partner's cards fit well, a game will be in sight. On the other hand, if we are defeated, we can find solace in the fact that our opposition might have a game or a part score in one of their suits.

31. Double.

Admittedly we might be euchred out of a game—or a slam, for that matter, but the pre-emptive action has snipped our lines of communication too short for us to enjoy any luxuries. The penalty double will yield a profit, perhaps even a handsome one.

32. Three Diamonds.

While you have a reasonable share of the high cards, your length in Diamonds minimizes the defensive possibilities of your hand. Your jump raise shows a hand of average strength with excellent Diamond support and might prove embarrassing to the opponents in terms of their seeking a possible fit in one of the major suits.

33. One Spade.

Our own Heart holding indicates that partner may have been trapping.

While the Spade overcall denies the ability to reopen the bidding with a double (10 high-card points), we cannot afford to double and then show our suit with such scant values.

34. Three Clubs.
With seven winners assured in our own hand, the pre-emptive jump overcall may embarrass the opposition as well as light the way for a defense against an eventual 3 No Trump contract.

35. Double.
It is not our policy to double when we have a two-suited hand, but since the strong jump overcall is no longer available to us, we must, of necessity, double with the intention of jumping in the Heart suit at our next opportunity to speak.

9.   Advanced bidding situations

Misfits

RIFTS in friendships of long years' standing, as well as sizable financial disasters, are frequently brought about on hands in which each partner is short of the other's suit. One denies the other for round after round, until one of the opponents finds it high time to enter the auction with a resounding double.

Success at the bridge table involves not only making the most of your good cards but holding your losses to a minimum on hands that were not destined to show a profit. A willingness to take a short loss on hopeless hands is one of the distinguishing features of the experienced player.

In cases of misfits, which one of the partners should quit? You have all listened at one time or another to bidding like this:

OPENER	RESPONDER
1 Spade	2 Hearts
2 Spades	3 Hearts
3 Spades	4 Hearts

and so on ad infinitum.

Now who should quit in this case? I have sought for some time to hit upon a practical solution. At one time I recommended that it be done on a priority basis. The younger of the two partners, it was suggested, should be the first to resign. This practice was not endorsed by the Bureau of Vital Statistics, which was burdened by too heavy a demand for birth certificates. So that possible solution had to be abandoned.

In any such case the exercise of good judgment is called for. A few general principles, however, may be laid down.

1. The player who can buy the hand at the cheapest price should, as a rule, be given the courtesy of the road. It is not always wise in these cases to look for the best possible contract. In case of a storm, an inferior contract, undoubled, is better than a superior one that is doubled and down. When it is probable that a loss must be taken, a

player with Spades should have priority over a player with Hearts, for the one holding Hearts must bid to a new level to buy the hand.

2. The player with high cards should be willing to become dummy, permitting the player with the long suit to be declarer. Let us see how this applies to a case from real life.

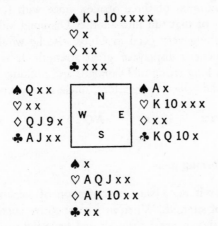

```
                    ♠ K J 10 x x x x
                    ♡ x
                    ◇ x x
                    ♣ x x x

      ♠ Q x x        ┌─────────┐        ♠ A x
      ♡ x x          │    N    │        ♡ K 10 x x x
      ◇ Q J 9 x      │  W   E  │        ◇ x x
      ♣ A J x x      │    S    │        ♣ K Q 10 x
                     └─────────┘
                    ♠ x
                    ♡ A Q J x x
                    ◇ A K 10 x x
                    ♣ x x
```

The bidding:

SOUTH	WEST	NORTH	EAST
1 Heart	Pass	1 Spade	Pass
2 Diamonds	Pass	2 Spades	Pass

What should South do? When I saw this hand played, South went on. In fact, he went on indefinitely, as is the tendency of most players who hold two five-card suits. That holding seems to instill in them some pride of possession.

South should have realized that game was hopeless when North failed to support one of his red suits and also was unable to bid No Trump. Despite his shortage in Spades, South should have passed the 2 Spade bid, realizing that game was hopeless. South's hand makes a good dummy because of its high-card content. North must have length in Spades to repeat them in the face of an announced two-suiter. North's hand will probably be a useless dummy, so South should be inclined to permit North to be declarer.

A splendid opportunity for the thoughtful handling of a misfit was presented to the holder of the following hand:

♠ K Q 10 x   ♡ A Q x x x   ◇ none   ♣ A J x x

He opened with 1 Heart and partner responded with 2 Diamonds. His rebid was 2 Spades and partner bid 3 Diamonds. What should he do? He knows that his partner has a maximum of two Hearts, since with three it would have been his duty to return to the opener's first suit, the opener having shown a five–four. The responder is known to have a maximum of three Spades, since with four he would not have gone out of that suit into another Diamond bid. Responder cannot have anything very good in Clubs, else he would have tried No Trump on opener's display of great strength. It is evident that responder has a long string of Diamonds and nothing else and that it is a hopeless hand. Opener, therefore, made a very fine pass. His mate held:

♠ x x   ♡ x x   ◇ A Q 10 x x x x   ♣ Q x

The forcing pass

A pass is not always a confession of weakness. It may be a definite sign of strength. When in a competitive auction you and your partner have shown great strength and have bid up to 4 Hearts, and your right-hand opponent now makes an obvious sacrifice bid of 4 Spades, a pass by you does not indicate fear, because it is quite apparent that you could double a 4 Spade bid if you chose. If you double, you are in effect saying to your partner that you do not care to go on to 5 Hearts. If, however, you feel that the penalty may not be adequate compensation, and you believe that you may have a fair chance to make 5 Hearts, you pass and permit partner to make the decision.

In such a sequence of bids, of course, partner is obliged to act. If he does not choose to bid 5 Hearts, he must, without reference to the merits of his own hand, automatically double, which you would have done yourself had you been quite sure there was no chance for 5 Hearts. A pass by you at this point is known as a forcing pass. It forces partner either to double the opponents or to go on with the bidding.

It is not always easy to identify a forcing pass. Not every pass in a competitive auction is forcing. A pass becomes a force when it is quite evident from the common sense of the situation that your side has the better holding and that the opponents are trying to wrest it from you. Let us take an illustration or two.

You are South and vulnerable. The opponents are not. You hold:

♠ A x x x   ♡ x x   ◇ K Q x x   ♣ x x x

The bidding has proceeded:

NORTH	EAST	SOUTH	WEST
1 Spade	2 Hearts	2 Spades	3 Hearts
4 Spades	5 Hearts	?	

What should you do?

You are quite convinced that the opponents cannot make 5 Hearts. Should you double? Since you have a very fine raise, should you try 5 Spades? You are not sure. In that case, why not let partner decide? You should pass. This is not a confession of weakness; you made a free raise early in the auction, and thus showed strength. On the contrary, it is an announcement of strength. Your pass says, "Partner, I think we have a fair chance to fulfill a contract of 5 Spades. What do you think?" If partner does not think so, he will double the 5 Heart bid.

Another case. The opponents are vulnerable. You are not. As South you hold:

♠ x x   ♡ A K Q x   ◊ 10 x x x   ♣ A Q 10

The bidding has proceeded:

SOUTH	WEST	NORTH	EAST
1 Heart	Pass	3 Hearts	3 Spades

What do you do?

Had East passed, you would have bid 4 Hearts in routine manner. It is true that East's 3 Spade bid does not prevent you from bidding 4 Hearts if you choose to. Should you so choose? The answer is No. Your partner has made a bid that is forcing to game. Each of you is committed to a final game contract (unless the opponents pay an adequate price for taking it from you). Your proper procedure is to pass it around to your partner. He will do one of three things, whichever is most suitable to his hand. He may go on to 4 Hearts, which he announced the partnership could make. He may decide to play for 3 No Trump, to which you will have no objection. Or—and this is the important consideration—he may be able to double a 3 Spade bid, and if he wishes to do so, you would find it quite delectable.

In the actual case, the 3 Spade bid was doubled by North and defeated 1,100 points.

In the next case it is you who have made a game-forcing bid. You are South and hold:

♠ x   ♡ A K Q 10 x x   ◊ A K x   ♣ A Q x

The bidding has proceeded:

SOUTH	WEST	NORTH	EAST
2 Hearts	Pass	2 No Trump	3 Spades

What should you do?

In my opinion there is only one proper call at this point, and that is a pass. Your opening 2 bid was forcing to game and remains so. You should not crowd the bidding by calling 4 Hearts, for three reasons. First, partner may wish to show one of the minor suits at the level of 4, and a 4 Heart bid will make it impossible for him to do so. Secondly, partner may wish to double the 3 Spade bid if he considers that profitable. Finally, he may have a Spade stopper and desire to play the hand at 3 No Trump. He will be in a better position to judge than you. You have announced the approximate strength of your hand by your original 2 Heart bid and no further announcements from you are necessary.

Another interesting example:

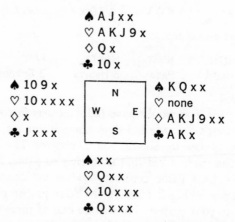

♠ A J x x
♡ A K J 9 x
◇ Q x
♣ 10 x

♠ 10 9 x
♡ 10 x x x x
◇ x
♣ J x x x

♠ K Q x x
♡ none
◇ A K J 9 x x
♣ A K x

♠ x x
♡ Q x x
◇ 10 x x x
♣ Q x x x

With North and South vulnerable, the bidding has proceeded:

NORTH	EAST	SOUTH	WEST
1 Heart	2 Hearts	Pass	3 Clubs
3 Hearts	?		

What should East do at this point? Only one call may be regarded as correct, and that is a pass. A bid of 4 Diamonds or a raise of the Clubs would be little short of an atrocity. There is no need for East to act when his previous cue bid committed the partnership to game, and West in his next turn is duty bound to take some action, either by doubling the enemy or by going on with the bidding as best he can.

In the actual case, West doubled and East passed. As the cards lay, it may be seen, East and West could not have made a game. We pass lightly over North's bid of 3 Hearts. Those things will happen, and no one will ever completely stamp out such practices.

Part-score bidding

A number of the bidding principles which we have discussed in the preceding pages must be modified to a certain extent when the bidding side has the benefit of a part score. Similarly, defensive bidding tactics must be adjusted somewhat when it is the opposition that has possession of the part score. Note the use of the expression "modified" and "adjusted," and those in a mild sense. I do not recommend a complete upheaval of normal bidding methods in part-score situations, as is the unsound practice in certain quarters.

The new-suit (by responder)-forcing principle does not apply where the responder's bid is sufficient to complete the game. For example, with 60 on score, opener bids 1 Spade and responder bids 2 Clubs. Opener need not bid again. If responder has mild slam aspirations, he must jump to 3 Clubs. The jump shift in these conditions is forcing for only one round.

An opening demand bid is still a demand, despite the part score, and responder must reply once. He need not bid again unless opener jumps in a new suit, in which case the obligation to speak once more arises.

When an advanced score of 60 is held, responder should be willing to stretch a point to keep the bidding alive, since a contract of 1 No Trump will complete the game.

The possession of a part score by either side will frequently influence decisions as to opening bids. Part scores of 20 and 30 should, for practical reasons, be disregarded, and the bidding should proceed, except for the final call, as though such a score did not exist. But when an advanced score is held, such a consideration as preparing for a rebid disappears entirely. For example, you hold:

♠ A K x x   ♡ A J x   ◊ J x x   ♣ x x x

With a clear score a pass is recommended on this hand. It is worth only 13 points and is almost sure to present a difficult rebidding problem on the next round. However, with a part score of 60, this hand should be opened with 1 Spade, since any response of 2 by partner may be dropped.

Similarly, holding:

♠ A K 10 x   ♥ x x x   ♦ x x x   ♣ A Q x

With a clear score it is recommended that this hand be opened with 1 Club, but with a part score such action is impractical. The proper procedure is to open with 1 Spade.

When the opponents have a part score and it is to be presumed that they will try to "sneak out," doubtful hands must be opened against them. Holding:

♠ A Q x x   ♥ x x   ♦ x x x   ♣ K Q 10 x

you should open against a part score with 1 Club, because otherwise you may expect the opponents to open and it will be difficult for you to compete at a later stage.

Since slams are available even to players with part scores, our tactics must be adjusted to this condition. An opening demand bid is permissible with slightly less playing strength than is normally required. For example, either of the following hands should be opened with a demand bid when you have a part score of 40 or 60:

♠ A x x   ♥ A K Q J x x   ♦ A x x   ♣ x
♠ A x   ♥ K Q J 10 x x   ♦ A x x x   ♣ x

When you have an advanced score of 70 or 80 and partner opens with 1 of a suit, you should not pass simply because the bid completes game. You should give partner a mild chance if you have a good hand. For example, with a 70 part score, partner opens with 1 Spade and you hold:

♠ A 10 x   ♥ K x   ♦ A Q x x   ♣ x x x x

If partner has a very fine hand, you may have a chance for big things. your proper procedure is to bid 2 Spades. This is overbidding the game and suggests that you might be interested in going places if partner chooses to act aggressively. If he does not, 2 Spades will surely be safe. You must not make the mistake of responding with 2 Diamonds, which partner, in view of the part-score situation, may pass.

Observe that the range of the 2 Spade bid with the advanced part score is much larger than normal, for although we might, with a clear

score, offer a single raise on a mediocre holding, we would not in this
situation shade the raise. For example, you hold:

♠ A Q x   ♡ x x   ◊ J 10 x x   ♣ x x x x

With a clear score you would "eke out" a single raise with this hand
if partner opened 1 Spade. However, with a 70 part score, the recommended procedure is to pass.

Similarly, under the same conditions you hold:

♠ A x x x   ♡ Q x x   ◊ A K Q x x   ♣ x

With a clear score you would have responded with 2 Diamonds,
intending to jump in Spades on the next round, but in this case you
dare not bid 2 Diamonds, and it is suggested that you do one of two
things—either overbid the game with 3 Spades or, preferably, make
a jump shift to 3 Diamonds. This forces partner for one more round.
You will show Spade support subsequently.

Protection bidding

A further modification of standard practices takes place in
certain so-called "protective" situations. When the bidding is about
to die out at a low level and the opponents have clearly indicated
that they do not have the balance of strength between them, great
liberties may sometimes be exercised to reopen the bidding. The
requirements for both the take-out double and the overcall are considerably reduced in a reopening situation. Let us examine a few typical cases. You are South. West opens the bidding with 1 Heart and
the next two hands pass. What action do you take on each of the
following hands:

1. ♠ Q x x x   ♡ x x   ◊ A J x x   ♣ K x x
2. ♠ K J x x   ♡ x x   ◊ A x x x x   ♣ x x
3. ♠ x x   ♡ K x   ◊ A Q J 9 x x x   ♣ K x
4. ♠ Q x x x   ♡ K Q x x   ◊ Q J 9 x   ♣ x

1. **Double.** The requirements for a take-out double may be reduced
to 11 points for purposes of reopening the bidding.
2. **Bid 1 Spade.** Competition should be offered and the safest course
of action is to bid 1 Spade rather than 2 Diamonds. It is cheaper, and
affords competition in a higher-ranking suit.
3. **Bid 3 Diamonds.** A 2 Diamond call would merely sound com-

petitive. This is an excellent hand for offensive purposes and a display of strength is indicated. Note that when used in a protective position, the jump overcall is not considered pre-emptive.

4. Pass. Partner does not figure to have much strength, since he clearly has nothing in Hearts and yet was unable to overcall the opening bid. To reopen the bidding would run the risk of permitting the opponents to find a better contract.

You are South and the bidding has proceeded:

EAST	SOUTH	WEST	NORTH
1 Heart	Pass	1 No Trump	Pass
Pass	?		

1.	♠ x	♡ A J x x	◇ K Q 10 x	♣ Q J x x
2.	♠ K 10 x	♡ K x	◇ J 10 x x	♣ A J 10 x

With HAND 1 we would advise a pass, for while you have the necessary values to double, your partner is too likely to bid Spades.

With HAND 2 a double is recommended. You had nearly enough for a double originally, and the slight distributional feature is in your favor.

Again you are South and the bidding has proceeded:

EAST	SOUTH	WEST	NORTH
1 Heart	Pass	2 Hearts	Pass
Pass	?		

1.	♠ A J 10 x x	♡ x x x	◇ K 10 x	♣ J x
2.	♠ A 9 x x	♡ A x x x	◇ A x x	♣ Q 10

With HAND 1 we would bid 2 Spades. Partner is marked with a few high cards and is probably short in Hearts. Competition is therefore reasonably safe.

With HAND 2 we would double. Partner can have no more than 1 Heart. Game is a distinct possibility if he has any length in Spades. If partner should bid Clubs, he is very apt to have at least five, but in any event, the risk is reasonably well calculated.

Four opposite four

The advantages of a four-four fit in trumps are not lost on the experienced player, but the average declarer prefers the feeling of security that a five-card suit gives him. The following is an illustration to point up the principle of the "four-four."

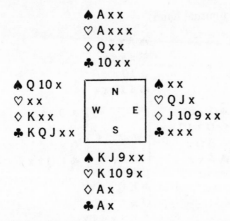

♠ A x x
♡ A x x x
◊ Q x x
♣ 10 x x

♠ Q 10 x   ♠ x x
♡ x x   ♡ Q J x
◊ K x x   ◊ J 10 9 x x
♣ K Q J x x   ♣ x x x

♠ K J 9 x x
♡ K 10 9 x
◊ A x
♣ A x

The bidding actually proceeded:

EAST	SOUTH	WEST	NORTH
Pass	1 Spade	Pass	2 Spades
Pass	3 Spades	Pass	4 Spades
Pass	Pass	Pass	

In the play of the 4 Spade contract, declarer lost a trick in each suit and was defeated a trick. The players consoled each other with the observation that it all depended on the Spade finesse. However, a little resourcefulness on the part of South would have landed the game despite the unfavorable Spade distribution.

Instead of rebidding 3 Spades, South could have seized an additional chance by trying 3 Hearts, a one-round force. Partner is offered the opportunity of choosing between two possible suit contracts. There is always the chance that partner has raised with only 3 Spades on a hand containing 4 Hearts.

At Hearts the game could not be lost, because the fourth and fifth Spades would provide discards for the two losing Diamonds out of dummy after trumps were extracted.

It is apparent, therefore, that provided each of the partners has four trumps, the five-card suit is much more desirable as a side suit than as trump, because the long suit will provide discards for losers in the other hand.

This principle does not apply, however, to a choice between eight trumps divided five–three and eight trumps divided six–two. *The six–two division is better,* because declarer, with six trumps, can stand repeated forces in any adverse long suit. This he could not do with only five trumps in his hand.

Observe this unusual hand:

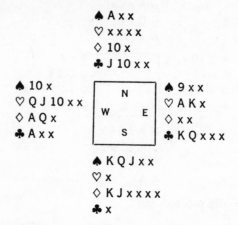

♠ A x x
♡ x x x x
◇ 10 x
♣ J 10 x x

♠ 10 x
♡ Q J 10 x x
◇ A Q x
♣ A x x

♠ 9 x x
♡ A K x
◇ x x
♣ K Q x x x

♠ K Q J x x
♡ x
◇ K J x x x x
♣ x

East opened with 1 Club and South overcalled with 1 Diamond. South thereafter bid Spades twice, showing that he had six–five distribution (see on page 9). When East and West got to 4 Hearts, South chose to sacrifice, bidding 4 Spades and thus giving North a choice between Spades and Diamonds.

Though he had three Spades as against two Diamonds, *and though Diamonds required a contract one trick higher,* North should have preferred Diamonds, the six–two suit, as a safety measure. At Spades, South would be forced on the second trick by a Heart opening and continuation. He could play safe for down four, but would probably go over to the trump Ace and try a finesse for the Diamond Queen, after which he would be forced in Hearts again. Now he could not both draw trumps and establish his Diamonds, and he would probably win only five tricks, going down 900. At Diamonds, however, South would have plenty of trumps for Heart ruffs and would lose only his two singletons and two trump tricks, going down 300 points even at a higher contract. (Even the double-dummy defense of a Spade opening and continuation by West, without touching Hearts, could beat South only 500 points.)

In this case, therefore, the five–three Spade suit produced only five tricks as against nine tricks for the six–two Diamond suit, a difference of four tricks; and it will be noted that neither suit broke badly.

CONVENTIONS

In an effort to approach completeness it is our purpose to present some of the bidding "gadgets" which have made their appearance in recent years. Among the more popular with a limited group of tournament players are the "weak 2 bid" and the "weak No Trump," the Drury Convention, the Landy Convention, the Texas Convention, the Michaels Cue Bid, the 2 Club-2 Diamond Convention, and the "Grand Slam Force."

The weak No Trump

The "weak No Trump" is really not at all new. In the early days of contract bridge it was standard procedure in various circles to open the bidding with 1 No Trump on modest holdings of balanced distribution. The practice flourished for a time, faded out and in isolated spots has recently been revived.

The "weak No Trump" has certain advantages. It covers hands ranging in high-card strength from 12 to 14, and has a tendency to crowd the opposition out of a certain amount of bidding space without unduly exciting partner. It achieves its best results when the outstanding strength is evenly divided and the opponents can be goaded into entering the auction. It is subject to the risk, however, of incurring severe losses when the No Trumper's partner has a bad hand, and should be used very sparingly when vulnerable.

In discussing defense to the "weak No Trump," let us examine a few specimen cases: You are South on each of the following hands and East has opened with 1 No Trump. What action do you take?

1. ♠ x   ♡ A J 10 x x x   ◊ K Q J x   ♣ x x
2. ♠ K Q x x x   ♡ A Q x x x   ◊ x x   ♣ 10
3. ♠ K x x   ♡ A x x   ◊ A J x x   ♣ J 10 9
4. ♠ A J 9 x x   ♡ A 10 x x   ◊ J   ♣ A x x

1. Bid 2 Hearts. In order to overcall, you should have the requirements for a normal overcall at the 2 level.

2. Pass. Your suits do not have a good enough texture to make any offensive action a reasonable risk. Even a 2-level contract could prove very costly. If, however, your partnership is employing the Landy Convention, an artificial 2 Club overcall is recommended, for it asks partner to bid one of the major suits. The hand is reasonably safe so long as you do not have to guess which one of your suits to bid.

3. Pass. In order to make an immediate take-out double you should have at least 14 high-card points. Remember that the take-out doubler's hand should normally be at least as strong as the hand of the player whose bid he is doubling. Where the hand is completely balanced an additional point should be required for safety's sake.

4. Double. While it is true that you wouldn't like to contend with a Diamond response from partner, your side has a fair prospect to score either a game or a substantial set, so some risk must be assumed. If partner does bid Diamonds, you may fall back on the Spade suit.

The weak 2 bid

A certain group of players employ an opening 2 bid in Spades, Hearts, and Diamonds as a pre-emptive measure. The 2 bid describes a hand which contains a fairly good suit, but which has less than the standard high-card requirement for an opening bid of one in a suit. In playing strength the "weak 2 bid" rates to take from five to seven tricks varying with conditions of vulnerability.

An opening bid of 2 Clubs is an artificial call employed to cover all hands that would normally qualify for a demand bid. The negative response is 2 Diamonds—not 2 No Trump—and the opener shows his suit when he rebids. The bidding now proceeds as it would after a normal demand opening.

Whatever success the "weak 2 bid" has achieved stems largely from the effect it produces on players who feel they are being "shut out" of the auction and are consequently goaded into taking action at unnecessarily high levels on meager values. In order to properly defend against the "weak 2 bid," soundness of approach should be stressed. The reader should be cautioned in the exercise of restraint.

An adverse pre-empt has a tendency to stir up resentment and induce action on insufficient values. Don't be obstinate merely because you are conscious that the enemy is trying to barricade you.

A take-out double should be based on a hand that revalues to at least 16 points as a dummy. It should contain either good support for all unbid suits or a good suit that the doubler can bid conveniently over his partner's response. Let us look at a few instances where the player on your right has opened with a weak bid of 2 Hearts.

1. ♠ A Q x	♡ K 10 x	◇ A x x	♣ J 10 x x
2. ♠ A J 10 x	♡ 10 x	◇ K Q 9 x x	♣ A J
3. ♠ K Q 10 9 x	♡ x x	◇ x x	♣ A Q J x

1. Pass. The distribution on this hand is too balanced to make any offensive action a reasonable risk. This would barely qualify for a take-out double over an opening bid at the 1 level.

2. Double. This holding qualifies for offensive action of some sort and the take-out double gives the most flexible approach. You are

well prepared for a Spade response and if partner should bid Clubs instead, you can decide subsequently whether or not to show the Diamonds.

3. 2 Spades. This holding figures to produce at least six tricks, which, along with the good sound structure of the Spade suit, qualifies it as a reasonable overcall.

Drury Convention

It has been our practice through the years to employ a light opening bid in third position after two passes. Properly managed, this works very well, but there are certain disadvantages to the practice. They stem principally from the circumstance that a player who has passed originally is subjected to the urge to explode in an effort to compensate for his prior pass. The Drury Convention was designed to curb such unwarranted enthusiasm and it works in the following manner.

Let us assume that, having previously passed, you have the desire to offer a double raise when your partner opens in third position with, let us say 1 Spade. Under the Drury Convention you refrain from giving a jump raise and resort instead to an artificial response of 2 Clubs. This is the conventional manner of asking the opener about the quality of his third-hand bid (in this case 1 Spade). If the third-hand bid was shaded the opener is expected to rebid 2 Diamonds, which allows the responder to sign off at 2 Spades. If the third-hand bid happens to have been sound then the opener must rebid anything other than 2 Diamonds. For example, you are third hand after two passes and open the bidding with 1 Spade holding:

♠ A K J x x   ♡ A J x   ◊ x x   ♣ x x x

Partner employing the Drury Convention responds 2 Clubs. This is an inquiry as to the quality of your Spade bid. Inasmuch as you have a sound opening bid of 1 Spade, you rebid 2 Spades and partner proceeds in accordance with his values.

Let us assume that you had made a shaded opening bid of 1 Spade on:

♠ K J x x x   ♡ K J x   ◊ K x x   ♣ x x

surely reasonable in third position; partner responds 2 Clubs. Having a shaded opening your rebid should be 2 Diamonds and partner takes it up from here.

Partner opens in third position with 1 Heart. Next hand passes. What is your action with the following hands?

1. ♠ A K J x   ♡ x x x   ◇ Q 10 x x   ♣ Q x
2. ♠ x x   ♡ K x x x   ◇ A J x   ♣ K x x x
3. ♠ Q J x x   ♡ x x   ◇ x x   ♣ A K Q x x x

1. 1 Spade. While you have the point count to justify a double raise after passing, you lack the normal trump support. If partner rebids 1 No Trump or 2 Hearts, you intend to raise him.

2. 2 Clubs. If partner rebids 2 Diamonds, denoting a subminimum opening, there is no reason to venture higher than the 2 level. If partner rebids 2 Hearts, announcing a sound opening, you will, of course, raise to 3.

3. 2 Clubs. While this response will be interpreted as the Drury Convention, your subsequent rebid of 3 Clubs will announce a Club suit with the values required for a 2-level response.

Bearing in mind that the initiation of this conventional call announces a fit in partner's major suit, certain by-products are effected.

You have passed originally, and partner opens 1 Spade. Next hand passes.

♠ Q x x   ♡ A K x x x   ◇ x x   ♣ Q 10 x

You respond 2 Clubs. Partner calls 2 Diamonds, indicating a subminimum hand. Since you have shown your Spade support by responding with 2 Clubs, you should bid 2 Hearts allowing for the possibility that partner may have opened a hand with four Spades and three Hearts.

Partner opens third hand with 1 Heart and next hand passes. You hold:

♠ x   ♡ K Q 10 x   ◇ A 10 9 x x   ♣ Q x x

What is your bid?

3 Hearts. This call promises a minimum of four trumps and the equivalent of an opening bid. Had your trump holding been less formidable, you would have employed the Drury Convention. Observe that the jump to 3 Hearts has afforded you a certain advantage; it may have barricaded the opposition from entering the auction with a competitive bid of 2 Spades.

Landy Convention

The Landy Convention is a device developed by my friend Alvin Landy, the managing director of the American Contract Bridge League. It was originally designed as a defensive measure to be employed against players who were using the weak No Trump opening and was subsequently enlarged in scope.

The convention calls for the use of an artificial 2 Club overcall against adverse 1 No Trump opening bids to elicit a bid from partner. The reason for the convention is to avoid complications which may develop from the casual use of the take-out double. Observe that the double of a 1 No Trump opening has always been something of a two-way bid. The player making the double somehow wishes his partner will have a hand which justifies leaving in the double for penalties, so that when a player has a holding not suited to this type of action, he should be wary of employing the double. When he wishes to insist upon a take-out, he therefore employs the artificial bid of 2 Clubs, a bid which suggests a length in the major suits with not enough high card strength to warrant a double for penalties. To illustrate, against a vulnerable 1 No Trump opening made by your right-hand opponent, you would overcall 2 Clubs with the following hands:

1. ♠ A 10 9 x x   ♡ Q J 9 x x   ◇ x x   ♣ x
2. ♠ K Q 10 x   ♡ J 10 9 x x   ◇ A x x   ♣ x
3. ♠ A J 9 x   ♡ K Q 10 x x   ◇ K 9 x   ♣ x

Naturally, the vulnerability has everything to do with your daring, and whereas you might taunt the opposition with the vulnerability in your favor, you keep something in reserve when you are susceptible to a vulnerable penalty. Vulnerable, against a strong No Trump opening, what is your call with the following?

1. ♠ A Q 10 x x   ♡ A Q 10 9 x   ◇ x   ♣ x x
2. ♠ K Q 10 x   ♡ A K Q x   ◇ J 10 9 x   ♣ x
3. ♠ K 9 x x   ♡ A J 9 x x   ◇ K x   ♣ x x
4. ♠ Q 9 x x   ♡ A K J 10 x x   ◇ A x   ♣ x

1. 2 Clubs. Should partner respond with 2 Diamonds, it is your intention to bid 2 Hearts. Partner, holding 3 Spades and 2 Hearts, will know enough to prefer your Spades. Even though you are vul-

nerable, the take-out figures to be a safe call since partner will normally have a fit in one of your suits. To overcall in either Spades or Hearts is placing all your eggs in one basket.

2. Double. You are quite willing to defend with a hand this strong, and have no reason to insist that partner pick his better major.

3. Pass. This is not a propitious time for you to get into the act. If your left-hand opponent has a reasonably good hand, you will be in danger of sustaining a serious injury should you choose to compete. If the enemy permits the bidding to die, your partner will be in a position to protect the fort.

4. 2 Hearts. The purpose of the Landy Convention is to offer partner a choice of suits. You are quite willing to play your contract opposite a singleton in preference to forcing partner to bid an inferior three-card suit.

In the pass-out position, Landy is often used to reopen the auction with mediocre unbalanced hands, thereby preserving the sanctity of the penalty double, which actually is lowered in requirement to 11 or 12 points to pick up partner who may have had to pass with 12 to 14 points and a balanced hand. The 2 Club call in this "dead" position is still an urgent request for one of the major suits.

With neither side vulnerable, your left-hand opponent opens 1 No Trump, which is passed around to you. What action do you take with the following hands?

1. ♠ 6 2	♡ K 9 8 5	◇ A J 8 4	♣ J 9 3
2. ♠ J 10 9 6 2	♡ A J 7 4	◇ A 7 4	♣ 5
3. ♠ 4	♡ K Q 10 9 4 2	◇ A 6 2	♣ J 10 9
4. ♠ K 9 3	♡ A K 6 2	◇ Q J 4 2	♣ 10 7

1. Pass. You do not have the requirements for a reopening double, and to institute the Landy Convention would prove to be embarrassing if partner elects to respond in Spades.

2. 2 Clubs. You are quite content to contract for a part score in any other suit. Since your hand is worth approximately 12 or 13 points, it is quite possible that your assets combined with partner's will be enough to achieve a plus result.

3. 2 Hearts. You do not have the values for a penalty double, and are only interested in the Heart suit. While there is a slight degree of risk involved, the knowledge transmitted to partner by virtue of your bid might lead to the defeat of an adverse contract should the opposition choose to compete further.

4. Double. If partner leaves it in, you can start clipping coupons.

If, instead, he takes out in a suit, his call will not meet with your displeasure.

Texas Convention

The object of this convention is to transfer the play of the hand to the opening bidder when his original opening was either 1 or 2 No Trump so that any tenaces contained in his hand would not be subject to an attack on the opening lead.

If partner opens with 1 or 2 No Trump and it is your intention to contract for game immediately in one of the majors, you jump to the 4 level in the suit which ranks immediately below your true suit. Thus, if you wish to play 4 Hearts, you bid 4 Diamonds, if you wish to play 4 Spades, you bid 4 Hearts. Partner must oblige and bid the next ranking suit regardless of his holding and becomes declarer.

Partner opens 1 No Trump. You hold:

1. ♠ Q J 10 9 x x   ♡ A x x   ◇ Q 10 x   ♣ x
2. ♠ x x   ♡ A Q J 10 x x   ◇ K x   ♣ x x x

1. 4 Hearts. Partner must call 4 Spades.
2. 4 Diamonds. Partner is forced to bid 4 Hearts.

If it is your intention to employ this convention, make absolutely sure that you remember the transfer principle. The main drawback to its use is that one member of the partnership usually forgets and makes a natural call over the No Trump opening or the opener is caught napping and forgets to make the transfer to the true suit.

Michaels Cue Bid

There are certain hands of mediocre proportions on which there appears to be a desire on the part of the holder to take some action. The hand may not measure up to the specifications for a take-out double, yet the urge to act is definite. To answer the need suggested by these hands, my friend and associate, Mike Michaels, has devised a procedure known as the Michaels Cue Bid. Here are its provisions.

A direct cue bid of a minor suit opening shows a hand that is primarily distributional with the majority of its strength (usually from 8–14 points) concentrated in the major suits. It is employed only when a take-out double or an overcall will not furnish an accurate description of your holding. Thus, with the following hands, you would cue-bid 2 Clubs over an initial 1 Club opening made by your right-hand opponent.

1. ♠ K 9 x x x   ♡ Q J x x x   ◇ x x   ♣ x
2. ♠ A K 10 x   ♡ A 10 x x x   ◇ x x   ♣ x x
3. ♠ x x x x x x   ♡ A J x x   ◇ x   ♣ x

If the opening bid is in a major suit, a subsequent cue bid denotes a two-suited hand with at least a five–five distribution. One of the suits is the opposing major, and the other, one of the minors. If responder does not have three card support for the implied major suit, he calls 2 No Trump, which conventionally asks the cue bidder to name his minor suit.

Partner has cue bid 2 Spades over the initial 1 Spade opening, and next hand passes. What action do you take with the following hands?

1. ♠ x x x x x   ♡ Q x   ◇ A x x   ♣ 10 x x
2. ♠ x x x x   ♡ A x x x   ◇ K x   ♣ Q x x
3. ♠ x x x   ♡ x x   ◇ A K J 10 x x   ♣ x x

1. 2 No Trump. Since you do not have three card support for partner's Hearts, your Two No Trump command call will uncover a convenient trump suit when partner obliges you by naming his five-card minor.

2. 4 Hearts. Partner has forced you to take a preference at the level of three and has shown a five-card Heart suit and a five-card minor. Your supporting cards in his suits should make a game bid odds-on to make regardless of the relative weakness of his hand.

3. 3 Diamonds. There is no point in inquiring for partners minor suit when your own suit can stand on its own merits. Partner will realize your suit is quite good, for otherwise you would have made the conventional 2 No Trump response asking him to name his minor.

The conditions of vulnerability are of paramount importance when employing the Michaels Cue Bid. The length and strength of suits tend to be stronger when vulnerable and are relaxed as the vulnerability conditions vary.

2 Club-2 Diamond Convention

A method of inquiring for the possibility of a major suit fit when partner opens the bidding with 1 No Trump is the 2 Club-

2 Diamond convention. Both of the possible responses of 2 Diamonds or 2 Clubs request the opening no trumper to show a four card major if he has one. The 2 Diamond response establishes a game forcing situation while the response of 2 Clubs is considered forcing for one round only.

This procedure was devised by David Carter of St. Louis and developed by my friend John Gerber, of Houston, Texas, captain of the American International Team.

Since the 2 Diamond response is unconditionally forcing to game, the minimum requirements for this bid are 10 points which will assure the partnership's assets amounting to at least 26 points. There is no special requirement for the 2 Club call, which ranges from about 2 up to 9 points.

Partner has opened the bidding with 1 No Trump. What is your response with the following hands?

1. ♠ x x x x	♡ A K J x	◇ K x	♣ x x x
2. ♠ A Q J x x x	♡ A x	◇ x x	♣ Q x x
3. ♠ J x x x	♡ A x x x x	◇ x x	♣ x x
4. ♠ x x x x	♡ Q x x x	◇ K x x	♣ x x

1. 2 Diamonds. If partner rebids in either major, it is your intention to raise him. Note that it is not necessary for you to jump to game, since your original response of 2 Diamonds demands that the partnership arrive at some game contract. If partner chooses to bid 3 No Trump when you raise his major suit, the balanced nature of your hand should render that contract agreeable.

2. 3 Spades. There is no point in using the 2 Diamond call when you have a self-sufficient suit and you know where you are headed. Use the direct approach. If partner displays an interest in slam by cue-bidding an Ace, you will be quite willing to continue the probe for a slam.

3. 2 Clubs. If partner rebids in a major suit, you will content yourself with that part score contract. If, instead, his rebid is 2 Diamonds, you will then mention your Hearts. Partner will raise you only if he has a maximum No Trump and a good fit, for you have forewarned him of the limited nature of your hand when you responded with 2 Clubs rather than 2 Diamonds.

4. Pass. There is no point in searching for a possible major suit fit when you have a balanced hand and game is quite out of the question. The best place to play an indifferent hand is 1 No Trump.

Grand slam force

When trumps have been agreed upon, either by inference or directly by a raise or a jump raise, a leap to 5 No Trump, by-passing a 4 No Trump Ace-asking bid is a direct request that partner bid a grand slam in the agreed trump suit if he holds two of the three top honors (Ace, King or Queen). For example, holding:

♠ A J 10 x x   ♡ A K Q x x   ♢ none   ♣ A x x

You open with 1 Spade, and partner jumps to 3 Spades. Your one and only concern is the texture of his trump holding, for surely his outside values will take care of your two little Clubs. You therefore bid 5 No Trump, the grand slam force. Partner will dutifully bid 7 Spades if he holds the King and Queen of that suit, or settle for a small slam if he has but one or none.

Variations

The Romans use an interesting variation of this convention. When the grand slam force is introduced, responder jumps to 7 if he has two of the top three honors, bids 6 in the agreed suit with one of the top three honors, and bids 6 Clubs if he has none. This variation clarifies what may be a rather difficult situation if you have opened the bidding with one Heart, and partner jump-raises to 3. Your hand is:

♠ A K Q x   ♡ K Q J 10 x x   ♢ A x x   ♣ none

If you call 5 No Trump and partner bids 6 Hearts, you will not be certain whether he has the Ace of trumps or not. Playing the Roman variation, you know you are off the Ace of trumps when partner bids 6 Clubs, and you do not have to suffer the humiliation of being in a grand slam off the trump Ace. Naturally, if Clubs are the agreed suit, this information is not available.

Another interesting version of the grand slam force arises when partner has shown some sign of strength, but you are concerned about Aces. Modifying the first example to

♠ A J 10 x x   ♡ A K Q x x   ♢ x   ♣ A x

After partner jump-raises your Spades, you call 4 No Trump (Blackwood). Suppose partner responds with 5 Diamonds. Since you are in possession of all the Aces, you are ready to introduce the grand slam force. You do so by bidding 6 in the unbid minor, which in this instance is 6 Clubs. Partner then leaps to the grand slam if he holds both the King and Queen of trumps, or contracts for the small slam if he does not.

ADVANCED BIDDING SITUATIONS

You are South in each of the following cases. The previous bidding is indicated. What is your bid?

1. ♠ K 10 x

	NORTH	EAST	SOUTH	WEST
♡ K 9 8 x	1 Heart	1 Spade	2 Hearts	Pass
◇ K J x	3 Hearts	Pass	?	
♣ x x x				

2. ♠ J x

	NORTH	SOUTH
♡ K Q 9 8 x	1 Spade	1 No Trump
◇ x x x x	2 Clubs	?
♣ x x		

3. You have an 80 part score. Partner opens with 1 Heart.

   ♠ A K 10
   ♡ Q J 10 x
   ◇ A x
   ♣ x x x

4. Both sides have 30 part score.

	NORTH	EAST	SOUTH
♠ A K 10 x	Pass	Pass	?
♡ Q J 10 9 8 x			
◇ A x			
♣ x			

5. ♠ K Q 10 x

	NORTH	EAST	SOUTH	WEST
♡ K 10 x x	1 Spade	Pass	2 Spades	Pass
◇ x x x	3 Hearts	Pass	?	
♣ x x				

6. ♠ Q J x

	EAST	SOUTH	WEST	NORTH
♡ A x	1 Heart	Pass	4 Hearts	4 Spades
◇ Q x x x	5 Clubs	?		
♣ x x x x				

7. ♠ x

	SOUTH	WEST	NORTH	EAST
♡ K Q 10 x x	1 Heart	2 Spades	3 Hearts	4 Spades
◇ A 9 x	5 Hearts	(Pre-emptive)	Pass	5 Spades
♣ A K x x	?	Pass		

8. ♠ K J 10 x

	NORTH	EAST	SOUTH
♡ Q 10 9 x	1 No Trump	2 Clubs	?
◇ x x		(take-out)	
♣ Q 10 x			

9.		WEST	NORTH	EAST	SOUTH
♠ x		1 Spade	Pass	3 Spades	?
♡ x					
◇ K Q J 10 x					
♣ A K 10 9 x x					

10.		NORTH	EAST	SOUTH	WEST
♠ Q		1 Spade	Pass	1 No Trump	Pass
♡ A x x x		2 Spades	Pass	Pass	3 Clubs
◇ J x x		3 Diamonds	Pass	?	
♣ x x x x x					

11.		EAST	SOUTH	WEST	NORTH
♠ x x		Pass	Pass	1 Spade	Pass
♡ K 10 9 x x		2 Clubs	?		
◇ A Q 10 9 x					
♣ x					

12.		NORTH	EAST	SOUTH
♠ A K x x		3 Hearts	Pass	?
♡ none				
◇ A K x x				
♣ A x x x x				

13.		WEST	NORTH	EAST	SOUTH
♠ K x x x x		1 No Trump	Double	2 Diamonds	?
♡ Q J x x					
◇ x					
♣ A x x					

14.		NORTH	EAST	SOUTH
♠ A x x		1 No Trump	2 Clubs	?
♡ x x				
◇ Q x				
♣ K J 10 9 x x				

15.		WEST	NORTH	EAST	SOUTH
♠ J 10 9 x x x		1 Heart	Pass	Pass	1 Spade
♡ x		2 Hearts	Double	Pass	?
◇ x x x					
♣ A Q J					

16.		EAST	SOUTH	WEST	NORTH
♠ x x		Pass	Pass	1 Heart	2 Clubs
♡ x x		3 Clubs	?		
◇ A Q J x x					
♣ Q 9 x x					

17.		WEST	NORTH	EAST	SOUTH
♠ Q x x		1 Heart	Double	4 Hearts	?
♡ A J 10 x					
◇ x x					
♣ x x x x					

18.		NORTH	EAST	SOUTH	WEST
♠ J x x		1 Heart	2 Spades	3 Clubs	Pass
♡ x x		3 Diamonds	Pass	?	
◇ A Q x					
♣ A K x x x					

ANSWERS TO ADVANCED BIDDING SITUATIONS

1. Three No Trump.
You have made a perfectly sound free raise, and obviously Hearts is your first choice since you failed to bid No Trump at your first opportunity. But if partner is willing to accept a No Trump contract, a nine trick effort might be more acceptable.

Advanced bidding situations

215

2. Two Hearts.
I prefer to bid 2 Hearts because this is about as good a Heart suit as I would ever be apt to suppress in a normal auction. If partner is not in a position to accept Hearts, the door is open for him to bid Spades. It is to be pointed out that partner is known to have a five-card Spade suit, for if he had held four Spades and four Clubs, his opening bid would have been 1 Club.

3. Three Hearts.
This would be a maximum jump raise without the part score, so that even though a 2 Heart bid is over game, a jump is recommended. Do not temporize with 1 Spade. Since this call closes out the part score, it is not forcing upon partner.

4. Three Hearts.
This is a tactical bid, of course. Since partner has passed, the chances for slam are remote, but there is a bright prospect of goading the opponents into the auction where you may be able to inflict a sizable penalty.

5. Four Hearts.
Although you greatly prefer Spades, the four-four trump contract should not be disregarded since partner's possible five-card Spade suit may give you a valuable discard with Hearts as trump. Partner's hand was:

♠ A J 9 x x   ◇ A J 9
♡ A 9 8 x   ♣ x

6. Five Hearts.
Partner may have had a terrific hand and have been regrettably subdued because of the rapid transit of the auction. Since you have an excellent raise, it does no harm to mention the Heart control on the way. Partner held:

♠ A K 10 9 x x   ◇ A K x x x
♡ x x   ♣ none

7. Pass.
You will be quite willing to contract for slam if partner chooses to bid it. The pass promises a second-round

H

Spade control and forces partner to double or bid on.

8. Double.
It is your intention to wield the ax against any major suit contract. Partner may be able to double Diamonds if the enemy calls that suit.

9. Four No Trump.
Partner is virtually busted, according to the auction and the size of your hand. Nevertheless, a game bid in either of the minors should not prove costly, and a contract at the 5 level by the opposition might be defeated.

10. Three Spades.
Partner has shown six Spades and four Diamonds, so that your singleton Queen is sufficient reason for returning him to the major suit. Repeated Club leads might play havoc with a Diamond contract.

11. Double.
In view of your original pass, your partner is not apt to place you with too many high cards for this call. Your hand does have some defensive strength, and the take-out double permits you to locate a fit in one of the red suits at the level of 2. A 2 No Trump overcall would ask partner to bid either Hearts or Diamonds, but this bid forces the auction to the level of 3, which may prove to be too costly. The artificial bids should be employed only when a natural bid is not adequate to cope with the situation at hand. In this particular case, the common sense of the take-out double is clear. Since the opposition has bid Spades and Clubs, it says, "Naturally, partner, I wish you to select between Hearts and Diamonds." The conversation then proceeds in a conventional manner without the use of artificial bids.

12. Four Hearts.
While it seems like a heroic gesture to raise partner with a void in his suit, it appears to be the only reasonable action. 3 No Trump is out of the

question, and our arsenal of high cards is too strong to hope that the opponents will compete.

13. Three Diamonds.

Partner has indicated a holding which is equivalent to an opening bid of 1 No Trump, which together with your 10 points should produce a game. Your cue bid is an effort to locate a possible major suit fit.

14. Three No Trump.

It is senseless to double for it gives the enemy time to discover a fit for a possible save. Since it was your intention to bid a game without interference bidding, waste no time in doing so now.

15. Pass.

Partner is clearly marked with a good hand plus Heart strength since he chose to make a trap pass on the first round of bidding. This means he is doubling primarily on his own values. You have a trick and a half defen-sively and your hand should not prove to be a disappointment.

16. Three Diamonds.

Your length in Clubs suggests that the opposition may be headed for big things on this hand, and it would be advisable to bid 3 Diamonds as a lead directing bid. If it becomes necessary, you hold in reserve a return to Clubs in the search for safety.

17. Double.

Partner has shown an excellent hand, and it would place too much of a burden upon him to pass. You have an expectancy of two tricks defensively. Partner should be able to furnish the balance.

18. Three Spades.

It is your intention to play the hand in No Trump if partner can furnish some sort of a guard in the adverse suit. Since you failed to cue the suit immediately, partner should have no trouble deciphering the urgency of your message.

10.   Opening leads

THE TERM "LEAD" refers to the first card played at each trick, whether by defense or declarer. In this chapter, however, we shall be concerned only with the defensive lead to trick one. In other words, the opening lead.

There are a number of bromides current advocating such ideas as "Never lead away from a King," or "Never lead away from an Ace," "Always lead the highest of your partner's suit," et cetera. Some of these have a sound basis. Others have none. However, this general truth should be borne in mind by the reader: that the selection of the opening lead is not an exact science. There is great room for the exercise of the imagination, and on a given hand a number of experts might disagree in the choice of an opening lead.

Only general advice can be given, though indeed there are certain principles which are fundamental and from which deviation should not be made.

In selecting opening leads, it is advisable to get into the habit of classifying various hands. A lead may be proper against a No Trump contract which, with the same hand, would be improper against a suit contract. You must ask yourself, "Am I leading against a part score, a game, or a slam contract? Has my partner bid? Has my partner suggested a lead to me? Will the opponents probably make this hand or will they go down?"

It is improper, as so many players are in the habit of doing, to submit a hand to an expert and ask what is the correct opening lead. That question cannot be answered unless you also provide Mr. Expert with the complete bidding. Incidentally, a knowledge of the personal habits of the players will frequently influence the choice of the lead. Where your right-hand opponent is notorious for opening the bidding with suits that he does not have, many times serious consideration should be given to the lead of that suit, even though it might not otherwise be the first choice.

The choice of the lead should frequently depend upon the manner in which the opponents have reached their contract. If the bidding has progressed smoothly and the chances of defeating the contract appear to be remote, desperate measures are in order. If the opponents appear to have staggered in the bidding and you feel that the prospects of defeating the contract are good, then conservatism is the best policy, and you ought to play safe.

Leads at No Trump

We shall take up those hands where no specific information has been obtained from the bidding. For example: 1 No Trump, 2 No Trump, 3 No Trump.

Against No Trump contracts it is essential to develop tricks out of small cards.

Against a suit contract, if you hold A Q 7 4 3, you would hardly expect to take more than the Ace and the Queen. But at No Trump there is a very good chance that you will take tricks with the small cards. Therefore your longest suit should usually be selected as the opening lead.

It is not always a privilege to have the opening lead. Sometimes it is a hardship. If you hold an honor which is not in sequence with another honor, it is usually a disadvantage to lead, because in the majority of cases it will enable the declarer to make an additional trick. For example:

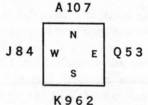

Notice that if you are either East or West, and lead this suit, North and South will take all the tricks. If, however, either North or South leads the suit, East and West cannot be prevented from taking a trick, which illustrates the point that unless you hold a sequence it is disadvantageous to start a suit.

One of the outstanding weaknesses of the ordinary player is a tendency to lead new suits each time he obtains the lead. It has been estimated that every time the defense leads a new suit they average to lose a half trick, so that it is generally a good policy to stick to the suit you open unless you have a good reason for shifting. For it is better, with Hamlet, to "bear those ills we have than fly to others that we know not of."

The most desirable lead is from the top of a complete sequence.

♠ 9 6 4   ♡ 7 3   ◇ J 10 9 8   ♣ K J 5 2

In this hand the Jack of Diamonds is a much more desirable lead than the 2 of Clubs, because it is certain not to lose a trick regardless of the adverse holding; whereas the Club lead might permit declarer to win a trick with the Queen, which he might not otherwise have been able to do. Where you have a choice between two suits of exactly the same texture, the bidding having given you no information, it is the general practice to lead the major suit rather than the minor, the theory being that the opponents will sometimes conceal a long minor suit but they are less likely to conceal a long major suit.

If, however, the choice lies between a major and minor and the texture of the minor suit holding is better, it should be given preference. For example:

♠ Q 6 3 2   ♡ 9 6 3   ◇ 8 2   ♣ Q 10 8 3

I would recommend a Club lead rather than a Spade, because the Club holding is more nearly a sequence. Notice that if your partner holds only the Jack of Clubs, you have not lost a trick. In fact, you are well on your way to develop two tricks in the suit. If, however, you lead a Spade and again find your partner with the Jack, you are still not certain to build up a trick unless your partner also has the 10.

♠ Q 9 6 5   ♡ 10 9 8 5   ◇ 7 3   ♣ 8 5 3

If I were forced to choose my opening lead between the Spade and the Heart, I would select the Heart, because it is less likely to cost a trick. Sometimes you have a choice between two suits. One is longer, the other is more solid. It is sometimes difficult to select the proper lead. Usually, however, quality should take precedence over quantity. For example:

♠ Q J 10 9   ♡ 8 3   ◇ Q 7 4 3 2   ♣ 6 3

The Queen of Spades is the proper lead. The Spade lead cannot lose a trick, whereas the Diamond lead may permit declarer to win with the Jack, which he might not otherwise have been able to do.

The statement "leads from a tenace should be avoided" is frequently heard. This is an unsound generalization. Leads from four-card suits containing a tenace are not attractive, but when your suit contains five or more cards the objection does not exist.

The lead from A Q 6 2 is very undesirable, but the lead from

A Q 6 4 2 is extremely desirable, for this reason: in the first case you are almost sure to give up a trick to declarer, and yet you will gain only one additional trick if you succeed in making good your small card. Whereas in the second case you are giving up the same trick with the very good expectancy of gaining two tricks with the small cards. After you have given up a trick, if your partner can gain the lead and come through, the contract of 3 No Trump will almost certainly be defeated, because you will probably win four tricks in your suit in addition to your partner's entry trick. Notice how well this principle operates on the following hand:

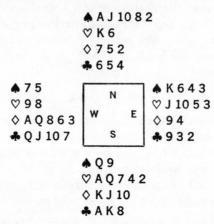

♠ A J 10 8 2
♡ K 6
◇ 7 5 2
♣ 6 5 4

♠ 7 5   ♠ K 6 4 3
♡ 9 8   ♡ J 10 5 3
◇ A Q 8 6 3   ◇ 9 4
♣ Q J 10 7   ♣ 9 3 2

♠ Q 9
♡ A Q 7 4 2
◇ K J 10
♣ A K 8

If West should open the Queen of Clubs, declarer will win and take the Spade finesse, which loses to East. Now a Diamond shift comes too late, and the defense can take only two Diamonds and the King of Spades. But if the 6 of Diamonds is opened, declarer is forced to win with the 10. Now when he takes the Spade finesse and East gets in, a Diamond return defeats the contract.

Similarly, holding K J 4 3, the suit does not provide a desirable lead, but the holding of K J 4 3 2 is considerably more attractive. The following combinations are all regarded as undesirable holdings from which to lead. Lest the reader forget, he should be reminded as he goes along that these leads are against No Trump contracts.

J 8 6 4   K 7 4 3   Q 9 4 2   K Q 7 3   K J 6 3   A Q 8 2

Where you have several high cards for entries your longest suit invariably should be selected. For example:

♠ A 8 4 3   ♡ 7 5   ◇ Q 7 6 4 2   ♣ A 5

The proper lead is the 4 of Diamonds, because even though you lose a trick at the opening, you hope to build up several tricks in that suit while you still have two Aces as entry cards.

♠ Q 8   ♡ K J 5 3   ◇ 10 4   ♣ J 8 5 3 2

You have a choice between a weak five-card minor and a strong four-card major. The choice should be in favor of the Club, because there is a chance to develop more tricks with this suit if the suit breaks well for your side. Furthermore, a four-card suit headed by a tenace is not an attractive lead even though it be a major suit. When you have a choice between two suits of the same length, it is not always easy to select the proper lead. For example:

♠ 7 4   ♡ 8   ◇ A 9 6 4 3   ♣ Q 7 5 3 2

Many players prefer to lead a Club from this holding rather than a Diamond, on the theory that the Ace of Diamonds may prove to be an entry after the Clubs are established.

Leading from bad hands

It is a sound policy not to waste efforts on a hopeless hand. That does not mean that you should not pay attention to the defense because you have no values. It simply means that if you have no trick-taking possibilities don't bother to lead your long suit. For example:

♠ 10 9 4   ♡ 10 8 5 4 2   ◇ 7 3   ♣ 5 3 2

Your hand, to all intents and purposes, is dead. It is poor policy to lead the fourth best Heart. Your side's only trick-taking possibilities are in your partner's hand. The only thing you can do, therefore, is to give him a fairly decent start in the race to take tricks. Your best bet is the 10 of Spades, hoping (somewhat against hope) that you may strike your partner's best suit. This is frequently called the short-suit lead. Some players would lead a Diamond because that is the shortest suit. This is definitely unsound. You select the suit not because it is short but almost in spite of the fact that it is. In choosing beween a two- and a three-card suit you should generally select the three-card suit, particularly when, as in this case, you hold the 10 and the 9, which may be helpful cards to promote partner's holding.

Objection to the lead of the fourth best Heart is that such a lead suggests to your partner that you are trying to build up that suit and obviously invites him to continue it. You do not wish to induce your partner to exert any effort in building up the Heart suit. If, by chance, the Hearts do become established, you will have no means of getting in to cash them. It surely does not pay to deposit money with a bank whose doors are closed.

The short-suit lead

We have just observed the use of the short-suit lead on hopeless hands. That type of lead is also made on hands where you fear to lead anything else because you have great hopes of taking tricks. For example:

♠ K 10 8   ♡ J 4 3 2   ◇ A Q 10 4   ♣ 10 9

This presents no desirable opening lead. I regard the Diamond as the most undesirable. If you adopt waiting tactics, the declarer will probably never be able to win a trick in that suit. If you lead the Diamond, he will almost surely take at least one trick. The next in order of undesirability is the Spade. In the first place, your partner will probably misread the lead of the 8; second, you may very easily sacrifice a trick by that lead. The Heart lead, therefore, appears to be the logical one. However, experience has shown that a lead from the Jack and three small cards is, in the long run, not very profitable. From holdings such as those in Spades, Hearts, and Diamonds, the best results are obtained by waiting. By the process of elimination, therefore, we arrive at the Club lead, and the 10 of Clubs should be selected. This is not a case, as in the previous example, where you hope to do anything for partner, but it is the one lead which will probably not lose a trick, and your prospects of defeating the contract are so good that you do not choose to give the declarer even the slightest advantage. If the Heart holding included the 10 of Hearts as well as the Jack, I would recommend the lead of that suit, because if partner has even so much as the 9 of Hearts, not to mention the Queen, the lead will not cost a trick. Obviously, if an additional Diamond were held, making five in all, a Diamond would be the best lead in the hand.

The card to lead

When you have determined the proper suit to lead, the selection of the proper card becomes important. Where you have a complete sequence (a complete sequence is considered three cards next to each other, such as the K Q J, Q J 10, J 10 9), you always lead the top card. A two-card sequence is not treated as such for our purposes. In other words, K Q 3 2, Q J 3 2, J 10 3 2 are not considered complete sequences, and the proper card is the fourth from the top.

There are certain combinations which, though not a complete sequence, are treated as such for the purpose of the opening lead. For example: K Q 10 2, Q J 9 2, J 10 8 2. You will notice that these are within a card of being a complete sequence. The proper leads are the King, the Queen, and the Jack, respectively. The rule is that where the third card is only one removed from the perfect sequence it may be promoted, so that the K Q 10 equals K Q J; Q J 9 equals Q J 10; and J 10 8 equals J 10 9. See Table of Leads for proper card to lead, page 247.

When your partner has made a bid against No Trump declaration

Naturally you do not always lead the suit your partner has bid, though in the long run it is best to do so.

Assuming that you are about to lead your partner's suit, it is important to select the proper card. There is a false impression that you are obliged to lead the highest card of the suit your partner has bid. This is a very unsound and illogical bromide. As a matter of fact, experienced players very rarely lead the highest of partner's suit. In fact, the only time it is correct to do so is when you have only two cards of that suit, or three unimportant cards, or where you have a holding containing two honors in sequence. In all other cases the low card is the correct lead.[1]

Assuming that you are about to lead your partner's suit from any of the following combinations, the underlined card is the proper lead at No Trump:

A 2	K 2	Q 2	9 2	9 8 2
6 5 4	A 6 2	K 6 2	Q 6 2	10 6 2
K 6 3 2	Q 6 3 2	J 6 3 2	9 6 3 2	J 6 2
9 6 4 3 2	Q J 6 2	K Q 6 2	J 10 6 2	5 4 3 2

In other words, where you have four or more of your partner's suit, you lead the fourth from the top. Where you have three of

---

[1] When leading partner's suit, many players prefer to lead low from three small. This is purely a partnership matter.

H*

your partner's suit headed by an honor, you lead the lowest. This lead has two purposes. First, to show the number of cards you hold in the suit, so that your partner can read the number of cards that are out against him; second, the more important, when you have a high card it is better not to waste it on the opening lead, but to keep it behind the declarer in order to kill one of his important cards. In other words, an Ace will capture declarer's King, a King will capture his Queen, a Queen will capture his Jack, and the Jack will take his 10. Note also that when you have a sequence of high honors in your partner's suit, you lead the top of the sequence, regardless of the number of cards held.

Observe the following very usual holding:

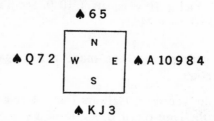

East has bid Spades and South No Trump, expecting to take two Spade tricks. If West leads the Queen, South will win two tricks. The lead of the 2 of Spades enables the defense to capture South's Jack.

Whether to lead partner's suit or your own

When you are in doubt whether to lead your partner's suit or your own, resolve all doubts in favor of your partner's suit for two reasons:

1. The best results are usually obtained by having a suit led up to rather than having a suit led away from.

2. The psychology is all in favor of leading partner's suit. If it should develop that your failure to lead his suit permitted the opponents to fulfill their contract, you are bound to have a disgruntled partner on your hands. Whereas if the lead of your partner's suit turns out to be less successful than your own, you will rarely hear your partner complain.

In this department of the game many close questions will arise, and a number of factors must be taken into consideration. Did your partner open the bidding with that suit, or did he overcall? Strangely enough, there is a greater inducement to lead partner's suit when he overcalled, for the reason that the opening bid shows a generally strong hand though the suit itself may be very weak. Whereas the overcall, while it may not denote a generally strong hand, almost always should be based upon a strong suit. Furthermore, more often than not, the purpose of the overcall is to induce partner to lead that suit. Therefore your partner's suggestion should not lightly be disregarded. In order to do so, you should have a very good excuse.

You should be guided, too, by the number of tricks for which your partner contracted when he mentioned his suit. If he named it at a high level, you can be certain that he has a very fine suit. If he bid the suit more than once, you can depend upon its being very strong, and you may reason that the opponents have contracted for game with only one stopper in his suit.

We come to the consideration of what constitutes a good excuse for not leading partner's suit. Holding a singleton is usually a good excuse, provided you have some hope of establishing tricks in your own hand. Even a singleton of partner's suit should be led if your hand is entirely hopeless. For example:

$$\spadesuit 10 \qquad \heartsuit 8\,6\,4\,3 \qquad \diamondsuit 9\,6\,4\,2 \qquad \clubsuit 7\,4\,3\,2$$

Your partner has bid Spades. Do not lead one of your three worthless suits. Lead the 10 of Spades. For example:

$$\spadesuit 8 \qquad \heartsuit Q\,J\,10\,7\,3 \qquad \diamondsuit 9\,5\,3\,2 \qquad \clubsuit 7\,6\,2$$

Partner has bid Spades. Lead the Queen of Hearts, a perfectly safe lead which has some remote hope if partner has strength in Hearts.

Holding two small cards of your partner's suit, you have a slight excuse for not leading the suit. However, any five-card suit does not constitute that slight excuse; for example:

$$\spadesuit 6\,2 \qquad \heartsuit 9\,7\,3 \qquad \diamondsuit J\,8\,6\,4\,2 \qquad \clubsuit 7\,5\,2$$

Partner has bid Spades. The Diamond lead is not to be considered. Lead the 6 of Spades.

Another consideration is, did the opponents bid No Trump immediately over your partner's bid, or did they contract for No Trump later and rather reluctantly?

Suppose you held the following hand:

$$\spadesuit Q\,6\,2 \qquad \heartsuit Q\,J\,7\,4\,3 \qquad \diamondsuit 9\,3\,2 \qquad \clubsuit 8\,6$$

Partner has bid Spades. Your supporting cards in Spades makes the lead of that suit obligatory. Do not experiment with the Hearts.

However, suppose you held this hand:

♠ Q 6 2   ♡ K Q J 7 3   ◇ 9 4 2   ♣ 7 5

Partner has bid Spades. The Heart suit, being probably within one trick of establishment, offers a good excuse for not leading partner's suit. You will very likely be permitted to hold the trick, and you may then decide whether to continue the Heart suit or now shift to partner's suit.

Leading the opponent's suit

Where your best suit contains a complete sequence it should be led though the opponents have bid it. For example:

♠ Q J 10 9 4   ♡ Q 10 7 3   ◇ 8 4   ♣ 4 3

You should lead the Queen of Spades even though that suit has been bid by your right-hand opponent. If, however, your holding is:

♠ K J 8 3 2   ♡ Q J 9 3   ◇ 6 4   ♣ 7 5

you have an entirely different situation. The lead of a Spade will probably be into declarer's Ace Queen, thus presenting him with a trick. In this case the Queen of Hearts is the proper lead.

Here knowledge of declarer's habits is important. Some players have a flair for bidding suits which they do not really have, hoping to deter their opponents from leading that suit in a subsequent No Trump contract. Against such players it frequently pays to take a chance and lead that suit if it appears to be your best. Particularly is this true if your holding is Clubs or sometimes Diamonds. Modern bidders very frequently open the bidding with a Club when they do not really have that suit. Therefore, when a Club lead is normal from your hand, as a general rule, you should not refrain from leading it simply because the suit has been bid by your right-hand opponent. For example:

♠ K 9 2   ♡ 8 6   ◇ A 4 3   ♣ K J 9 4 3

If the bidding is opened on my right with a Club and declarer subsequently plays No Trump, I would open the 4 of Clubs. If partner has the Queen of the suit, it will be established at once. If he has the 10, there is a good chance to build up the suit while I still have two likely entries.

Leads against No Trump when partner has doubled the final contract[2]

A double of a No Trump contract made by a player who does not have the opening lead carries certain inferences.

A. If the doubler has bid a suit, the leader must absolutely lead that suit even if he has but a singleton and has a good suit of his own. For example:

♠ 7   ♡ K Q J 8 5   ◇ 7 3 2   ♣ 8 6 4 3

Your partner has bid Spades and subsequently doubled 3 No Trump. You must lead the 7 of Spades, not the King of Hearts. Partner has stated, "If you lead Spades, I will defeat contract."

B. If the opening leader has bid a suit, partner's double requests him to lead that suit. For example:

♠ K J 8 6 3   ♡ K Q J 3   ◇ A 5   ♣ 6 5

You have bid Spades. Partner, who has not bid, doubles the final contract of 3 No Trump. Without the double your best lead would be the King of Hearts, but partner's double is based on the belief that you will lead Spades. Don't disappoint him.

Here is an illustration from "real life":

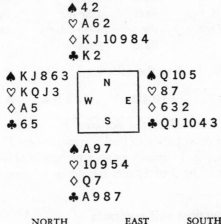

```
                    ♠ 4 2
                    ♡ A 6 2
                    ◇ K J 10 9 8 4
                    ♣ K 2

   ♠ K J 8 6 3     ┌─────────┐      ♠ Q 10 5
   ♡ K Q J 3       │    N    │      ♡ 8 7
   ◇ A 5           │ W     E │      ◇ 6 3 2
   ♣ 6 5           │    S    │      ♣ Q J 10 4 3
                    └─────────┘
                    ♠ A 9 7
                    ♡ 10 9 5 4
                    ◇ Q 7
                    ♣ A 9 8 7
```

WEST	NORTH	EAST	SOUTH
1 Spade	2 Diamonds	Pass	2 No Trump
Pass	3 No Trump	Double	Pass
Pass	Pass		

[2] Exclusive of slam contracts. See page 243, Leads against doubled slams.

I am not arguing in favor of East's double. It is extremely risky and lays his side open to the sting of a devastating redouble, but East was willing to run the risk because he felt that if partner did not lead a Spade all hope was gone. Notice that a Heart lead would have permitted the fulfillment of the contract.

C. If both partners have bid, it is not easy to determine which suit to lead when partner doubles. Use your own judgment.

D. When neither the leader nor the doubler has bid, the doubler is suggesting to partner to lead the dummy's first-bid suit unless the leader has a very good opening of his own. But bear in mind that this is only a suggestion—*not a command.* There is current among many players the belief that when the 3 No Trump is doubled in these circumstances the opening leader must lead dummy's suit. There is no *must* about it. You should use your own judgment, and if the dummy's suit has been rebid, it is extremely doubtful that you should lead it. Your partner's double simply states he expects to defeat the contract. He hopes you have a good lead to make. But, if not, probably the safe one would be to lead the dummy's suit. The thing to bear in mind in these circumstances is that it is essential not to waste time trying to establish some indifferent suit of your own.

Presume the bidding to have progressed as follows:

SOUTH	WEST	NORTH	EAST
1 Heart	Pass	1 Spade	Pass
2 No Trump	Pass	3 No Trump	Double
Pass	Pass	Pass	

You are West, holding the following hand:

♠ 9 2   ♡ J 10 4 3   ◊ 10 7 5 4   ♣ K 8 4

Hearts have been bid by the declarer. You do not select that suit. It would not be good policy to lead the fourth best Diamond, hoping to establish that suit. Inasmuch as your partner doubled and you have no indicated lead, the 9 of Spades should be selected.

Leads against suit contracts

Many of the principles applicable to leads against No Trump will not apply if the opposition is playing a suit contract. Against No Trump contracts considerable attention must be devoted to building up tricks from small cards. The length, therefore, of the suit selected is frequently the most important consideration. Against suit contracts, however, your attention is principally concentrated on the first two or three rounds of the suit. The holding of A K Q J against No Trump must produce four tricks, while at a suit contract you are usually safe in assuming that you will take but two. You might take three, but almost certainly you will be unable to take four. It will be observed that against suit contracts the defense must exercise greater haste in building up tricks, because sooner or later good tricks get ruffed.

Holding K Q 6 4 2 against No Trump, the correct lead is the 4. Against a suit contract you lead the King, to be sure that you build up at least one trick. Holding A K 6 4 2 against No Trump, the correct lead is the 4, hoping you will take tricks with the remaining cards. Against a suit contract that lead would be absurd. You do not hope to take more than two tricks.

You have heard a great deal about never leading away from a King against a suit contract. Forget it. The same principle applies here as in No Trump. It is unattractive to lead away from any honor, King, Queen, or Jack, when that honor is not part of a sequence. However, in one respect there is a difference. At No Trump we quite properly lead away from an Ace. At a suit contract, to lead away from an Ace is unorthodox and should be avoided. If that suit must be led, lead the Ace, not the small one. The reason is, at No Trump you cannot lose your Ace. At a suit contract, if you lead away from it, it may be trumped the next time.

Leading partner's suit

In leading partner's suit against trump declarations there is a popular belief that you always lead the highest. This is not true. If you have two cards of a suit, you lead the higher. If you have three worthless cards, you lead the highest. If you have a sequence in your partner's suit, you lead the top of the sequence, but if you hold four small cards of your partner's suit, you lead the lowest in order that your partner will have a count on how many cards are against him. If, however, the Ace is held, regardless of how many cards are with it, the Ace should be led.

Holding three cards headed by an honor, the choice is optional. Some players lead the honor, some lead low, others vary their tactics, depending upon the bidding. As a general rule, I find it more profitable to lead low from the honor of partner's suit because I believe that leading high cards is less productive than waiting with high cards.

The importance of retaining a high card in the suit bid by partner instead of tossing it thoughtlessly out on the table is illustrated in the following hand:

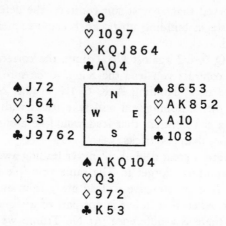

```
                    ♠ 9
                    ♡ 10 9 7
                    ◊ K Q J 8 6 4
                    ♣ A Q 4
  ♠ J 7 2                              ♠ 8 6 5 3
  ♡ J 6 4           N                  ♡ A K 8 5 2
  ◊ 5 3          W     E               ◊ A 10
  ♣ J 9 7 6 2       S                  ♣ 10 8
                    ♠ A K Q 10 4
                    ♡ Q 3
                    ◊ 9 7 2
                    ♣ K 5 3
```

South became declarer at a contract of 4 Spades on bidding which does not have my endorsement. East had opened the bidding with 1 Heart, so West led the Jack. East was obliged to win with the King and Ace and continued the suit. Since the 10 was high in dummy, declarer took a discard. Trumps were drawn, and the Ace of Diamonds conceded. How different had West led a low Heart! Now declarer would have to ruff the third round of Hearts and would be unable to draw trumps, so that West would be enabled to make his Jack of trumps on an overruff of the fourth Heart.

When you have great length in partner's suit it is sometimes advisable not to lead it, because of the likelihood that you will not realize any tricks in that suit. Whereas you might utilize the time in developing some other suit. For example:

♠ 6 2   ♡ K 9 5 4 3   ◊ Q J 10 4   ♣ 7 5

The opponents are playing a Spade contract, your partner having bid Hearts. The proper lead is the Queen of Diamonds. One of the opponents surely has a singleton Heart. If your partner has the Ace, he can win with it later. If the opponents have the Ace, no Heart trick is available to your side. Inasmuch as this may be your only chance to lead, you should use the opening to attempt to build up

Diamond tricks. You might be lucky enough to capture the King of that suit in dummy.

Be very cautious about leading an important card in a suit you have forced partner to bid by doubling.

♠ A Q 2   ♡ 7 3   ◊ Q J 9 5   ♣ A Q 8 4

You have doubled the opening bid of 1 Heart and partner has responded with a Spade. Do not lead Spades against the final contract. It is very likely that the opening bidder, who sits under you, holds the King. Wait for that suit to come through. Remember your partner was forced to bid and may have a 10-high suit. Lead the Queen of Diamonds.

The singleton lead

The question is frequently asked, "Is the singleton a good lead?" In some cases it is the perfect lead. In others it is the worst. The mere lead of a singleton just because it is a singleton is not good. You should have some reason for doing so. It is objectionable because, more often than not, you are helping to develop a long suit in the declarer's hand and at the same time giving him a clear picture of the whole suit.

There are times when the singleton lead is ideal. The conditions are as follows:

A sure trump trick

The reason is this. The singleton lead, being a shot in the dark, may not have worked out well; in which case the declarer can usually draw the trumps and discard his losers on the suit which you have led into. If, however, you have a sure trump trick, you can regain the lead early in the play and proceed to lead into your partner's hand to obtain the ruff, or at least to cash whatever tricks you can. In other words, when you hold a sure trump trick the declarer cannot "run away with the hand."

Surplus trumps

When holding A 8 4, K 9 7, A 6 of trumps, the small trumps accompanying an Ace are otherwise useless, as well as the 7 with the K 9 7, because only one small card is necessary to guard the King. When holding the K 5 or Q 9 3, the small trumps are necessary to guard your honor. Therefore, with this holding, the singleton lead is undesirable. Similarly, holding Q J 4 of trumps, you do not desire to ruff because you have a natural trump trick.

Partner has bid

The lead of a singleton is not apt to be productive unless you are able to reach partner's hand to obtain the ruff. If partner has not bid, you cannot rely on being able to put him into the lead. But where he has entered the auction, the chances that you can do so are good. You hold:

♠ A 5 3   ♡ K 9 7 5   ◊ 4   ♣ 9 7 4 3 2

Your partner has bid Hearts and the opponents have reached the contract of 4 Spades. This is an ideal hand on which to lead a singleton. All three conditions exist. You have a quick trump trick. You have two otherwise useless trumps. You have a reasonable certainty you can put your partner into the lead because he has bid. Therefore you should lead the singleton Diamond rather than Hearts which your partner bid, intending, when you win with the Ace of Spades, to lead the Heart to your partner so that he will return a Diamond.

When the lead of a singleton is unattractive

Whenever you have at least four trumps it is generally undesirable to lead a singleton. You should not be anxious to ruff. Rather lead your longest suit, hoping to force declarer to ruff. When he does so, your four trumps will be a serious menace.

Suppose you hold:

♠ A 10 7 5   ♡ 9   ◊ Q J 10 8 5   ♣ A K 3

The contract is Spades. Do not lead the single Heart. Your trumps are so strong that you wish to weaken the declarer's trumps, and the best procedure is to lead Diamonds. The declarer will eventually have to trump, and when he does so your trumps will become stronger than his. The same reasoning applies to the lead of a doubleton with the idea of obtaining ruffs. For example:

♠ K Q 8 5   ♡ 8 5   ◊ Q J 9 3 2   ♣ A K

Against a Spade contract you might be tempted to lead out the Ace and King of Clubs, hoping to get a third-round ruff. The temptation should be resisted. Try to force declarer by leading the Queen of Diamonds, your longest suit.

You have been warned that leads away from tenaces are unattractive against a suit contract. That rule is subject to the exception that when you have four trumps you should lead your long suit. For example, if you hold:

♠ K J 8 5   ♡ A Q J 5 4   ◇ 7 3   ♣ 9 4

Against a contract of 4 Spades, I would make a lead which most players would shrink violently from: namely, the Ace of Hearts, under other circumstances the worst lead possible, but my trumps are so strong that I desire to force the declarer to use one of his early in the game.

The blind lead of a singleton is, generally speaking, unattractive. However, remember that the lead of a singleton of the suit that partner has bid does not come under the same objection. It is usually an attractive lead.

A singleton lead becomes somewhat more attractive in a hand that would seem otherwise hopeless. If the opponents have arrived smoothly at a 4 Spade contract, your partner not having bid, and you hold very little in the way of high cards, your cause is more or less hopeless. You must therefore make a desperate effort of some sort, and the singleton in this case answers the description. For example:

♠ 9 6 4   ♡ 7 4 3   ◇ 8   ♣ K 9 6 4 3 2

The opponents have reached a 4 Spade contract, which appears hopeless from your standpoint. Only a miracle will defeat it, and the nearest contribution that you have to a miracle is the singleton Diamond. It should be led, with a prayer. A singleton lead against a small slam contract is sometimes effective. It succeeds whenever partner has the Ace of the suit led or the Ace of trumps.

The lead of a singleton Ace can be recommended only in cases where you are convinced that your partner can obtain the lead early. If you have no reason to be sure, the lead of a singleton Ace is very undesirable.

The lead of a singleton King comes under the head of my "Never lead." Too many singleton Kings make on finesses for that card to be given up without a fight. The same reasoning applies, though not quite so strongly, to the singleton Queen. When I think that the lead of a singleton is attractive I will lead it, even though it be a Jack, though I would not if it were a Queen.

The preceding paragraph refers to the singleton honors in unbid suits. It has no application if your partner has bid that suit, in which case the lead is entirely proper.

It does not apply to the situation where a trump lead is mandatory. Where it is indicated that a trump must be opened, that should be done even though your trump happens to be a singleton. This will be further discussed in a succeeding paragraph on the trump lead.

Taking a look at the dummy

Laying down an Ace rates as one of the most unattractive leads. Aces were meant to capture Kings and Queens; when led, they pick up deuces and treys. Many players lead an Ace just to look at the dummy. Remember, they must show you the dummy even if you lead a deuce. This look is an exaggerated advantage. The lead of an Ace will frequently give declarer two tricks in a suit in which he would otherwise have taken only one.

The lead of a King from an Ace King has for a long time ranked at the top of the list. Note, however, that if the Ace King is at the head of a short suit, it is not nearly so attractive as many players believe. Many times it will aid declarer in the establishment of one of his cards, such as a Queen. It is much more important to retain the Ace and King of such a suit as entries to build up tricks in your own hand. For example:

♠ 9 7   ♡ A K 4   ◇ Q 4 3 2   ♣ Q J 10 3

Against a Spade contract the lead of the King of Hearts is not desirable. You must build up a trick in Clubs in a hurry and retain the Ace and King of Hearts as entries to cash the Club trick eventually.

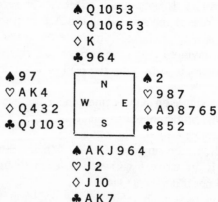

```
                   ♠ Q 10 5 3
                   ♡ Q 10 6 5 3
                   ◇ K
                   ♣ 9 6 4
    ♠ 9 7                        ♠ 2
    ♡ A K 4          N           ♡ 9 8 7
    ◇ Q 4 3 2    W     E         ◇ A 9 8 7 6 5
    ♣ Q J 10 3       S           ♣ 8 5 2
                   ♠ A K J 9 6 4
                   ♡ J 2
                   ◇ J 10
                   ♣ A K 7
```

Another lead that is classified high in the table by other writers is the lead of the Queen, holding Q J 9 5. This is a somewhat dangerous lead, especially if partner has not bid, because many times the dummy comes down with A 10 2, or K 10 2, and the declarer has the other honor. This permits your Jack to be finessed later. One of the most attractive leads is the Queen from the Q J 10 9. If two leads are necessary to establish your trick, you have gotten the start, and you cannot lose a trick by the lead in any event.

The trump lead

There is another maxim, "When in doubt lead trumps." This is not sound advice. Trumps should very frequently be led, but not when you are in doubt. You should do so because you are sure that it is the proper lead. The trump lead is proper when you think that the dummy has a short suit. If, therefore, you start removing dummy's trumps you will be destroying the principal value of that hand.

How can you tell that the dummy will have a short suit? Only by the bidding. If the declarer has bid two suits, Spades and Hearts, and the dummy has taken him back to Spades, it is probable that the dummy will be short in Hearts. Declarer will plan to trump small Hearts in dummy. That being the case, a trump lead will spoil his plans. It becomes, therefore, more or less an axiom that against two-suiters a trump opening is indicated.

Another case in which a short suit in dummy can be visualized is where the bidding has proceeded as follows:

DECLARER	DUMMY
1 Spade	2 Spades
4 Spades	

If you hold some strength in high cards, you may deduce on simple reasoning that the dummy will have a short suit.

Declarer obviously has a good hand because he jumped to 4 Spades as soon as he received a raise. You have a good hand yourself, and there is not much left in high cards for the dummy to have. You have further corroboration by the fact that dummy made a somewhat weak bid. The raise must have been based on a short suit rather than on high cards.

There is a situation of somewhat frequent occurrence which indicates that the dummy will have a very short suit and therefore the ability to ruff. It is the case where there has been competitive bidding and during the auction the declarer has doubled for penalties a bid made by you or your partner, but the dummy has refused to stand for the double and has gone on in declarer's suit.

In this situation a trump lead is almost mandatory. The reason is plain. The dummy will probably have a singleton or void of the suit which his partner has doubled. (If it were otherwise, he would not have taken his partner out of the business double.) The declarer will obviously have a number of cards in the suit you and your partner have bid, which he could dispose of by trumping in the dummy. Repeated trump leads, therefore, are calculated to leave declarer with a number of your suit that he will be unable to ruff out. For example:

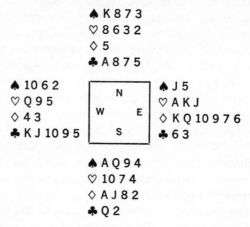

North and South—60 Part Score.

SOUTH	WEST	NORTH	EAST
1 Spade	Pass	2 Spades	3 Diamonds
Double	Pass	3 Spades	Pass
Pass	Pass		

Trump leads are usually very effective when your partner has opened with 1 No Trump and the opponents subsequently play the hand. The reason is evident. Your partner has a majority of the high cards. If the opponents are to make the hand, they must take advantage of favorable distribution, which means a short suit in the dummy, and the use of those trumps for ruffing purposes. Therefore, in order to kill this asset of the dummy and to protect your partner's high cards, lead a trump and keep doing so unless the appearance of the dummy makes you change your mind.

Another case of somewhat frequent occurrence in which a short suit may be diagnosed in the dummy is when the opening bid has been on your right, you have doubled for a take-out, and the dummy has given a raise. For example:

SOUTH	WEST	NORTH	EAST
1 Spade	Double	2 Spades	Pass
4 Spades			

It is evident from North's bid that he has no particular strength in high cards but that his raise must have been based on trumps and a short suit. In this situation a trump lead will probably be effective.

Timing

There is one case in which trump openings should be avoided and that is when you suspect from the bidding that the dummy will have a good suit which you are unable to stop. A trump lead is dangerous because with the trumps extracted declarer will obtain discards upon dummy's good suit. In such cases attacking leads are in order. In other words, you must try to establish your tricks in a hurry.

A trump opening is advisable, even though you have only one, in cases where you have made a take-out double of a suit bid and your partner has left it in. In fact, this advice is close to being an always rule and trumps should be led blindly.

As a corollary to this principle, if I may be permitted a diversion, it is virtually a rule that when your partner doubles a suit bid of 1 for a take-out, you should not leave it in unless you are anxious to have your partner open a trump. The reason is this: When you leave in a double of 1 you are predicting that you will make more tricks than the declarer. In other words, you have converted your side into the declarer's with that trump. Now, if you were playing the hand, what would you do? You would pull trumps to protect your high cards, so that the opponents would not make any of their small trumps. Similarly, in this one, you should attempt to keep the declarer from making any of his small trumps by starting to pull them early.

Doubleton leads

The question is frequently asked, "Is the doubleton a bad lead?" As in the case of the singleton, it depends on the circumstances.

A doubleton lead in the blind, and only because it is a doubleton, is even worse than a pointless singleton lead. But under certain circumstances the doubleton lead may not only be very satisfactory but can actually be the one and only lead in a hand.

The doubleton lead is made for one of two purposes:

A. With the hope of obtaining a third-round ruff.

B. For the purpose of avoiding other embarrassing leads. In other words, as an exit.

All the requirements regarding the singleton lead should apply in the case of the doubleton: namely, a quick trump trick, some otherwise useless trumps, and the ability to enter partner's hand.

The doubleton lead is more frequently employed as a protective lead; that is, to protect your holdings in other suits that you do not desire to lead.

For example:

♠ K Q 5   ♡ 9 4   ◇ A Q 8 2   ♣ Q 9 7 3

Against a Spade contract we immediately rule out Spades and Diamonds as opening leads, which leaves the choice between Hearts and Clubs. The Club lead from an unsupported honor is not attractive. I therefore recommend the lead of the Heart. Here the lead is made, not because you desire a ruff, because you actually do not want it, but as a graceful exit in order to wait for the other suits to be led to you. The doubleton lead in this respect bears a close resemblance to the trump opening made when all other leads are unattractive. In the same hand, if Hearts were trump, I would still open that suit, as I consider the lead of the other three suits unattractive.

Under this heading comes also the lead of a worthless three-card suit. The top of a worthless three-card suit is frequently led for the same purpose.

For example:

♠ K Q 6   ♡ 9 8 4   ◇ A Q 3 2   ♣ Q 9 5

In this case, if Spades were trumps, no other lead having been indicated, I would recommend the lead of the 9 of Hearts.

The lead of a doubleton containing the J x, or Q x, is too frequently resorted to. I consider it one of the worst of all leads. Queens and Jacks are much too important to give up without a fight. Too many tricks are won with Queens and Jacks for them to be tossed idly upon the table. I even dislike to lead the 10 from the doubleton, because that card frequently becomes a winner. However, my objection to it is not nearly so strong as in the case of the Jack or Queen.

A popular opening lead is the Ace from A x, hoping to find your partner with the King and to obtain an immediate ruff. Unless the situation is desperate, I dislike this lead. It might be called a "prayer lead." I repeat: Aces were meant to capture Kings and Queens and not to be led out indiscriminately. You will find many times that even though you have obtained an immediate ruff, you will achieve better results by giving up the ruff and retaining the killing power of the Ace.

Another doubleton lead sometimes resorted to is the King from the K x. Only if the situation is very desperate should such a lead be attempted, for the reasons indicated above. However, when the defeat of the contract seems hopeless, the lead of the King from K x may sometimes save a desperate situation.

Another case in which the King might profitably be led from the K x is where your partner has shown distributed strength, such as by making an informatory double or by bidding No Trump, so that you are persuaded that he must have one honor in that suit.

If you lead the Ace and follow it with the King, it is an abnormal opening, because the conventional lead is the King and you therefore give partner the specific information that you have only two of the suit and desire to ruff the third round.

Against suit contracts where you have a choice between leading a worthless doubleton or a worthless tripleton, by all means select the doubleton, because in addition to all other features that they have in common, the doubleton does have the outside chance of bringing home the third-round ruff.

Note here the difference between suit and No Trump contracts. In No Trump you should select the three-card suit rather than the two-card.

When the doubleton is opened for the purpose of obtaining a third-round ruff, the co-operation of partner is frequently required. Naturally it will be difficult sometimes for the partner of the opening leader to determine whether the lead is a singleton or a doubleton. It will involve a certain amount of guessing. Clues can often be obtained from the bidding.

Where the partner of doubleton leader has the Ace and no other quick-entry card, he should be careful not to win the first trick but should wait for the second trick. Observe how this works in the following hand.

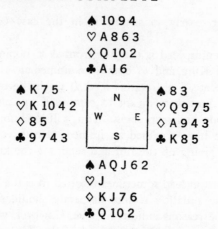

♠ 10 9 4
♡ A 8 6 3
◇ Q 10 2
♣ A J 6

♠ K 7 5   ♠ 8 3
♡ K 10 4 2   ♡ Q 9 7 5
◇ 8 5   ◇ A 9 4 3
♣ 9 7 4 3   ♣ K 8 5

♠ A Q J 6 2
♡ J
◇ K J 7 6
♣ Q 10 2

South is declarer at a contract of 4 Spades, and West leads the 8 of Diamonds. If East wins this trick with the Ace and returns the suit, the dummy will win and take the Spade finesse, which loses to the King. Now West will shift to a Club. Declarer will climb up with the Ace and pull trumps, fulfilling the contract. Note the difference if East refuses to take the first Diamond trick. (East should, however, signal with the 9, suggesting to his partner to continue the suit.) Declarer wins and takes the Spade finesse. Now when West is in he has another Diamond to lead and so obtains the ruff. Note that if East had held the Ace of Clubs instead of the King, it would not have been necessary for him to hold up. He could have taken the first trick with the Ace and returned the suit, hoping to get in with the Ace of Clubs to give partner a ruff.

Whether to lead partner's suit or your own

Against a trump contract it is much easier to decide whether to lead your own or partner's suit.

When you have a great many of your partner's suit it will not be a very good weapon on the defense, because declarer will no doubt be short, and unless you are playing the forcing game (when you have four or more trumps) it is better to look about for a sequence lead in some other suit.

♠ 4 3   ♡ K 7 3 2   ◇ Q 6 4   ♣ Q J 10 9

You are on lead against a contract of 4 Spades, your partner having bid Hearts. It is doubtful whether you will take more than one Heart trick, and that only if partner has the Ace, because one of the opponents almost surely has a singleton. Since you probably will not be on lead again, the best opening is the Queen of Clubs. This will be particularly effective if the King is in dummy and partner holds the Ace.

Holding A K J, with or without others in a side suit, a good idea is to lead the King of that suit first and then shift to partner's suit so that if the Queen is in the closed hand, your partner can lead through and capture it.

Some writers recommend the lead of the King from the A K x, just to have a look at the dummy. I am decidedly against this. It is usually not that important to have a look at the dummy.

Leading from a three-card suit

Sometimes you will be obliged to lead from a three-card suit. If my choice is between K 6 2 and Q 6 2, I always lead from the King rather than the Queen. Because if I lead into an A Q, my King may still live to take a trick, but if the lead from the Queen has lost to a lower honor, I have no hope for the future. In other words, a King is strong enough to survive a bad lead, a Queen probably not. Even if declarer learns where the King is located, he may be able to do nothing about it. But if he finds out where the Queen is, he can very frequently pick it up by finessing in either direction. If you are obliged to lead from a three-card suit which contains an honor, it is important to select the proper card to lead. Holding Q 9 2, if that suit is to be led, the proper card is the 2. It may be argued that partner will be deceived into thinking you have four cards of the suit. That is true, but unfortunately cannot be avoided. Some players have formed the practice of leading the middle card from a holding such as this. That practice has been found to be unprofitable for various reasons. In the first place, the middle card may be too important; as, for example, the 9 in this case, which may develop into a winning card and therefore cannot be spared. In the second place, the lead of the 9 may place partner under the impression that you are leading the "top of nothing" and he will not read you for an honor in that suit. All in all, it is better to deceive your partner as to the exact number of your cards in the suit, in order not to confuse him as to the type of holding you have. How important a card the 9 may be is illustrated by the following diagram:

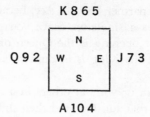

K 8 6 5

Q 9 2   J 7 3

A 10 4

Notice that the lead of the 9 permits declarer to win all the tricks in the suit. The lead of the deuce will not produce the same result.

Leads against slams

Against slam bids a very popular lead is an Ace. This practice, however, does not have the approval of the experts. It takes two tricks to defeat a slam, and cashing an Ace will not attain your end unless, of course, partner appears to have the King. Leading an Ace makes the declarer's work so much easier. It is my policy not to lead an Ace unless I have somewhere a probability of a second trick or infer the probability of a second trick in my partner's hand. For example:

♠ Q 6 5   ♡ A 9 7 4   ◊ 5 3 2   ♣ 8 6 2

The opponents have reached a contract of 6 Spades. I feel that I have a fair chance to make my Queen. Therefore I would cash the Ace of Hearts.

♠ 7   ♡ A 9 6 4   ◊ 8 6 4 2   ♣ 7 6 4 2

If Spades were not vigorously supported by dummy, I would reason there is a fair chance that my partner has a trump trick and I would cash my Ace in that case. But where no immediate trick is in sight it is important to try to build one up before the Ace is released. For example:

♠ 8 5 4   ♡ A 9 5   ◊ 10 9 8 4   ♣ 5 3 2

The only prospect of a trick against a 6 Spade contract is if partner can take one in Clubs or Diamonds. Therefore I would lead the 10 of Diamonds, hoping that my partner might have something like the King behind dummy's Ace, so that I can build up a trick for him before my Ace is released. The lead of the Ace might establish some Heart tricks in dummy upon which declarer can discard a losing Diamond or Club.

♠ 8 6 5   ♡ A 7 4 2   ◊ 9 7 3   ♣ Q 3 2

If the dummy has bid Hearts, the proper opening on this hand is a Club, with the hope that the partner holds at least the King of that suit. It is urgent to build up a trick before your Ace is driven out, so that declarer cannot obtain discards on dummy's Heart suit.

Trump leads against slams are not recommended, although occasionally they turn out well. For example, if declarer has bid two suits and you have the other one well under control, a trump lead may cut down dummy's ruffing power.

The singleton lead against a slam contract from a completely worthless hand is very attractive. Partner probably holds a trick. If it happens to be the Ace of that suit, the hand is immediately defeated. Also, if partner happens to hold a quick trump trick, he will return the suit in time to defeat the slam.

Aggressive leads as a rule are not desirable against No Trump slams. In other words, unless you have a complete sequence do not take a chance to build up tricks. It is better to wait. For example:

♠ 9 8 6   ♡ J 6 4 2   ◇ Q 6 5 3   ♣ J 4

Against 6 No Trump, I would lead the 9 of Spades even though the suit had been bid.

Leads against doubled slams (in a suit)

Where partner has doubled the slam contract and you have the opening lead, the accepted modern convention is that you are not entitled to your own opinion. The double calls for a certain specific lead. The convention is based upon the theory that when the opponents have reached a slam contract they will rarely go down more than a trick, and a double should not be made merely for the purpose of scoring an additional 50 or 100 points but should be made strictly for the purpose of directing your partner's opening lead. The doubler of a slam contract says: "Partner, please do not make the normal opening lead." The leads required by partner's double are as follows:

A. If dummy has bid any suit other than trumps, the doubler demands the lead of that suit. If the dummy has bid more than one suit, it demands the lead of the first suit bid by dummy.

B. If dummy has bid no side suit, but the declarer has, the doubler demands the lead of the first side suit bid by declarer.

C. If declarer and his partner have bid no side suit, the doubler demands the lead of an unbid suit. (In other words, you absolutely must not lead trumps.)

D. If the doubler or his partner has bid a suit, the doubler announces, "Partner, please do not lead that suit." For example: you are North and hold:

♠ 6 5 2   ♡ A 9 7   ◊ 7 4 3   ♣ 10 9 4 2

The bidding has proceeded:

WEST	NORTH	EAST	SOUTH
1 Spade	Pass	3 Clubs	3 Hearts
3 Spades	Pass	4 Spades	Pass
6 Spades	Pass	Pass	Double

A Club is demanded of you.

Underleading Aces

From auction days we have the rule, "Never lead away from an Ace." This refers, of course, to the opening lead. As a general principle it is almost as true today. But even to this rule there are certain exceptions which the experienced player may sometimes recognize. The underleading of an Ace may produce very good results on certain type hands. The conditions are these: You suspect that the King of the suit will be in the dummy. And your suspicions can be obtained, of course, only from the bidding. You may suspect that the King may be in the dummy when the dummy has constructively bid No Trump or when the dummy has made a take-out double showing distributed strength. Now if the declarer has the Jack, possibly he will expect that you are leading from the Queen instead of the Ace and may very likely misguess the situation.

However, the underleading of an Ace is usually done from the Ace and two cards and sometimes from the Ace and three cards, but never when holding more, because the danger of the declarer having a singleton becomes too great, so that the Ace may subsequently be trumped. Suppose you hold:

♠ Q 9 4   ♡ Q 10 5   ◊ K 10 8 4   ♣ A 6 2

The dummy has opened with a No Trump, and the declarer subsequently plays a Spade contract. The dummy will almost surely have the King of Clubs. If the Jack of Clubs is either in the closed hand or in the dummy, the declarer will undoubtedly misguess it. Furthermore, the lead of either Spades or Hearts or Diamonds is unattractive. Therefore the low Club would appear to be the best lead.

What about leading from Kings?

Some years ago an authority broadcast to a very gullible public that one must never lead away from a King. I know how he is going to spend eternity. It is going to be in the hot nether regions, the declarer is always going to be at his right, and our victim will eternally hold four Kings. It will serve him right! I don't contend that you should go out of your way to lead from a King, but when the bidding indicates that the particular suit should be attacked, don't refuse to lead it only because it contains a King.

Deceptive leads

Opportunities to practice deception successfully on the opening lead are not very frequent in occurrence.

Deceptive tactics at this point are likely to become boomerangs, inasmuch as partner is more apt to be deceived than declarer.

Declarer knows his own twenty-six cards. Your partner is looking at only thirteen and requires your assistance to suggest the other thirteen.

In certain cases, however, it may become apparent to you that partner's hand is probably hopeless and that information concerning the exact structure of your own will not be of great interest to him. It is at such times that the opportunity for a deceptive lead may present itself.

One of the oldest chestnuts, which still occasionally proves effective, is the lead of the Jack from the Q J doubleton, particularly in trumps. This is to induce declarer to believe that your partner has the Queen, and sometimes results in your making that card on a finesse. It is somewhat more risky to make this play in a side suit, because there is a chance your partner may have strength in that suit and misread your holding, whereas in trumps it is extremely unlikely that your partner can have any holding where the unorthodox lead will upset him.

A more subtle type of false carding is the lead of the fifth best instead of the fourth best against a No Trump contract. For example: Holding A K 6 4 2, some players will frequently lead the 2 for the purpose of inducing declarer to believe that the lead was from a four-card suit. This may cause declarer to plan the play of the hand in some manner other than that which he might have done had he suspected the possibility of a five-card suit against him. This type of false lead, however, may occasionally prove unfortunate, because partner might reason that you have only four of the suit and may abandon it when he obtains the lead. Probably the best case for that type of false lead is when your partner is not a particularly alert player, whereas the declarer is a keen card reader. In that case your partner will probably not be conscious of whether you have led from a four- or five-card suit, whereas the declarer might be impressed.

Another popular type of deceptive opening lead which is successful many times is the lead of a high card through the suit that the dummy has bid when the opening leader holds the King and is trying to discourage declarer from taking the finesse. For example: The dummy having bid Spades and you hold the K 8 6 2. The lead of the 8 may intimidate declarer into believing that your lead is a singleton. He may, therefore, decline the finesse and try another line of play which is somewhat inferior.

Opening lead table

HOLDING IN SUIT	AGAINST NO TRUMP	AGAINST TRUMP BIDS
A K Q J	A	K
A K Q x x x	A	K
A K Q x x	K	K
A K Q x	K	K
A K x	K	K
A K J 10	A	K
A K J x	K	K
A K J x x	x	K
A K J x x x x	A	K
A K x x x x	x	K
A K 10 9 x	10	K
A K 10 9 x x	10	K
A K x x x	x	K
A Q J x x	Q	A
K Q J x x	K	K
K Q 10 x x	K	K
K Q 7 4 2	4	K
Q J 10 x x	Q	Q
Q J 9 x x	Q	Q
Q J 7 4 2	4	4
J 10 9 x x	J	J
J 10 8 x x	J	J
J 10 7 4 2	4	4
10 9 8	10	10
10 9 7 4	4	10
A Q 10 9 x	10[3]	A

Opening lead table (continued)

HOLDING IN SUIT	AGAINST NO TRUMP	AGAINST TRUMP BIDS
A Q 8 7 4 2	7	A
A J 10 8 2	J	A
A 10 9 7 2	10	A
K J 10 7 2	J	J
K 10 9 7 2	10	10
Q 10 9 7 2	10	10
A 7 4	4	A
K J 4	4[4]	4
K 7 4	4	4
Q 10 4	4	4
J 7 4	4	4
10 7 4	4	4
K 9 8 7	7[5]	7

OPENING LEAD QUIZ

You are West and hold each of the following hands. The bidding has proceeded:

SOUTH	NORTH
1 No Trump	2 No Trump
3 No Trump	

What is your opening lead?

1. ♠ K Q J
    ♡ 10 7 5 4 2
    ◇ A 7
    ♣ 6 5 4

2. ♠ 6 4
    ♡ K Q 10 9
    ◇ Q 8 6 4 2
    ♣ J 7

3. ♠ 7 3
    ♡ A Q 8 4 2
    ◇ K 10 9 8 5
    ♣ 7

4. ♠ A 10
    ♡ Q 8 6 4
    ◇ K 9 5 2
    ♣ K 4 2

5. ♠ J 10 7 5 2
    ♡ 9
    ◇ K 10 6 4 3
    ♣ K 2

6. ♠ J 10 7
    ♡ 7 5 4 3
    ◇ A J 8 2
    ♣ K J

7. ♠ 10 9
    ♡ K 6 4
    ◇ A Q J 5
    ♣ J 10 6 4

8. ♠ Q 4 3
    ♡ Q 5 2
    ◇ K Q 9 8 4
    ♣ 7 3

9. ♠ Q 9 6 5 4
    ♡ 10 7 2
    ◇ 10 6
    ♣ 7 5 2

10. ♠ A Q J 9 5
    ♡ J 10 9 7
    ◇ Q 5 2
    ♣ 8

[3] The Queen is led when you suspect the King is in dummy.
[4] Unattractive lead, but made necessary by the bidding.
[5] Do not treat the 9 8 7 as the top of an interior sequence, because partner may improperly read it as the top of nothing.

I

You are West holding each of the following hands. The bidding has proceeded:

SOUTH	NORTH
1 Spade	2 Spades
4 Spades	

What is your opening lead?

11. ♠ 7 5
♡ Q J 9 7
♢ K J 6
♣ A J 10 5

12. ♠ Q 9 8 6
♡ A J 9 8 6
♢ J 10
♣ 8 5

13. ♠ 6
♡ 8 7 3
♢ A 8 6 5
♣ K J 9 6 2

14. ♠ A 7 5
♡ Q 4 3
♢ Q 10 6 3
♣ Q 8 7

You are West. The bidding is indicated under each problem. What is your opening lead?

15. ♠ J 10 9 8 7 3
♡ K J 4
♢ J 5
♣ 8 3

16. ♠ A 4
♡ J 6
♢ K 7 3 2
♣ K J 9 7 2

15.
The bidding:

SOUTH	WEST	NORTH	EAST
1 Heart	Pass	2 Clubs	2 Diamonds
2 No Trump	Pass	3 No Trump	Pass
Pass	Pass		

16.
The bidding:

SOUTH	WEST	NORTH	EAST
1 Club	Pass	1 Heart	Pass
1 No Trump	Pass	3 No Trump	Pass
Pass	Pass		

17. ♠ Q J 10 9 8 6
♡ 4 3
♢ 2
♣ 10 9 8 3

18. ♠ 10 9 7
♡ K 9 8 7 3
♢ A J 6 2
♣ 6

17.
The bidding:

SOUTH	WEST	NORTH	EAST
1 Heart	Pass	2 Clubs	2 Diamonds
2 No Trump	Pass	3 No Trump	Double
Pass	Pass	Pass	

18.
The bidding:

NORTH	EAST	SOUTH	WEST
1 Club	Pass	2 No Trump	Pass
4 No Trump	Pass	6 No Trump	Pass
Pass	Pass		

19. ♠ 10 7 2
♡ J 9 8 7 2
♢ 9 3
♣ 10 6 2

20. ♠ 8 6
♡ A Q 10 9 6
♢ 9 7
♣ K J 6 3

19.

The bidding:

SOUTH	WEST	NORTH	EAST
1 Club	Pass	1 Spade	Pass
2 Diamonds	Pass	2 Spades	Pass
3 No Trump	Pass	6 No Trump	Double
Pass	Pass	Pass	

20.

The bidding:

SOUTH	WEST	NORTH	EAST
1 Diamond	1 Heart	1 No Trump	Pass
3 Spades	Pass	3 No Trump	Pass
6 Diamonds	Pass	Pass	Pass

21. ♠ A 2
♡ K Q J 6
♢ 9 7 4
♣ 8 6 5 2

22. ♠ K Q J 10
♡ 8
♢ A K 8 6
♣ K 10 3 2

21.

The bidding:

SOUTH	WEST	NORTH	EAST
1 Spade	Pass	2 Clubs	Pass
4 Clubs	Pass	4 Hearts	Pass
5 Diamonds	Pass	5 Spades	Pass
6 Spades	Pass	Pass	Pass

22.

The bidding:

SOUTH	WEST	NORTH	EAST
1 Heart	Double	Pass	Pass
Pass			

23. ♠ K 6
♡ 9 7 2
♢ J 8 2
♣ A K 7 3 2

24. ♠ K J 5
♡ 6 5
♢ A J 10 8 3
♣ 8 6 3

23.

The bidding:

SOUTH	WEST	NORTH	EAST
1 Spade	Pass	1 No Trump	Pass
2 Hearts	Pass	4 Hearts	Pass
Pass	Pass		

24.

The bidding:

NORTH	EAST	SOUTH	WEST
1 Club	Pass	1 Heart	Pass
3 Clubs	Pass	3 Hearts	Pass
4 Hearts	Pass	Pass	Pass

25. ♠ 7 4 3
♡ K Q 3 2
♢ 6
♣ Q J 7 5 4

26. ♠ K 9 8 7
♡ 10
♢ 7 4 3
♣ K Q J 9 2

25.

The bidding:

NORTH	EAST	SOUTH	WEST
1 Diamond	Pass	1 Spade	Pass
3 Spades	Pass	3 No Trump	Pass
4 Diamonds	Pass	4 Spades	Pass
Pass	Pass		

26.

The bidding:

NORTH	EAST	SOUTH	WEST
1 Diamond	1 Heart	1 Spade	Pass
2 Spades	Pass	Pass	Pass

27. ♠ K 9 5
♡ J 6 3
◇ 3
♣ J 10 9 5 4 3

28. ♠ 4 3
♡ Q
◇ Q 4 3 2
♣ K J 10 8 6 2

27.
The bidding:

SOUTH	WEST	NORTH	EAST
1 Diamond	Pass	1 No Trump	2 Hearts
2 Spades	Pass	4 Spades	Pass
Pass	Pass		

28.
The bidding:

SOUTH	WEST	NORTH	EAST
1 Diamond	Pass	1 Heart	Pass
1 Spade	Pass	1 No Trump	Pass
3 Diamonds	Pass	3 Spades	Pass
4 Spades	Pass	Pass	Pass

29. ♠ A Q 3 2
♡ 7 2
◇ A Q J 10
♣ J 10 8

30. ♠ 6 3
♡ A 10 9 3
◇ A K Q
♣ Q J 10 7

29.
The bidding:

SOUTH	WEST	NORTH	EAST
1 Heart	Double	Pass	1 Spade
3 Hearts	Pass	4 Hearts	Pass
Pass	Pass		

30.
The bidding:

SOUTH	WEST	NORTH	EAST
1 Spade	Double	3 Spades	Pass
Pass	Pass		

31. ♠ J 10 9 8 6 3
♡ 7
◇ Q 10
♣ 7 5 3 2

32. ♠ K 7 4 3 2
♡ A 6 3
◇ 7 2
♣ J 10 9

31.
The bidding:

SOUTH	WEST	NORTH	EAST
1 Heart	Pass	3 Clubs	3 Diamonds
3 Hearts	Pass	4 Hearts	Pass
6 Hearts	Pass	Pass	Double
Pass	Pass	Pass	

32.
The bidding:

SOUTH	WEST	NORTH	EAST
1 Diamond	Pass	2 Hearts	Pass
3 Diamonds	Pass	3 Spades	Pass
4 Clubs	Pass	5 Diamonds	Pass
6 Diamonds	Pass	Pass	Pass

33. ♠ K J 7
♡ 6 3
◇ A 8 6
♣ K 10 6 4 3

34. ♠ 10 9 5 2
♡ A Q J 6 3
◇ A
♣ Q J 3

33.
The bidding:

SOUTH	WEST	NORTH	EAST
4 Hearts	Pass	Pass	Pass

34.
The bidding:

SOUTH	WEST	NORTH	EAST
1 Diamond	1 Heart	2 Diamonds	2 Hearts
3 Diamonds	3 Hearts	4 Diamonds	Pass
Pass	Pass		

35. ♠ J 7 6 3
♡ 10 7
◇ Q 8 5 4
♣ A 6 2

36. ♠ K 10 8 6 3 2
♡ K 7 3
◇ K 10 5 2
♣ none

35.
The bidding:

NORTH	EAST	SOUTH	WEST
1 No Trump	Pass	3 Spades	Pass
4 Spades	Pass	Pass	Pass

36.
The bidding:

SOUTH	WEST	NORTH	EAST
1 Heart	1 Spade	3 Hearts	3 Spades
4 Hearts	4 Spades	5 Hearts	Pass
Pass	Pass		

37. ♠ A 6 3
♡ K J 2
◇ 9 7 4 3
♣ 8 6 4

38. ♠ A 7
♡ J 6 4
◇ 5 2
♣ Q 10 8 6 4 3

37.
The bidding:

WEST	NORTH	EAST	SOUTH
Pass	Pass	1 Spade	Pass
1 No Trump	2 Diamonds	2 Hearts	3 Clubs
3 Spades	Pass	Pass	4 Clubs
Pass	Pass	Pass	

38.
The bidding:

SOUTH	WEST	NORTH	EAST
1 Spade	Pass	2 Diamonds	Pass
2 Hearts	Pass	3 Spades	Pass
4 Hearts	Pass	4 Spades	Pass
6 Spades	Pass	Pass	Pass

ANSWERS TO OPENING LEAD QUIZ

1. The 4 of Hearts.
With at least two entries, an effort should be made to establish a five-card suit.

2. The King of Hearts.
With a near-solid suit, preference should be given to the four-card holding. If the Diamond suit included the Jack, we would lean toward leading from that suit.

3. The 4 of Hearts.
The Heart suit makes a better lead because even if partner has no high

cards in the suit, you may be able to set it up with one lead. Even if declarer has K J 10 of Hearts, you will merely have to find an entry in partner's hand to get a Heart lead through to run the balance of the suit.

4. The 2 of Diamonds.
This is a better choice than the 4 of Hearts, because it is less apt to cost a trick. Even though declarer learns that you have the King of Diamonds, he may not be able to do anything about it, but if you help

him locate the position of the Queen of Hearts, he may be able to finesse it either way.

5. The 5 of Spades.
With no great disparity between the two five-card suits, we lean toward the Spade opening, for if either opponent had a Spade suit, he would probably have made an effort to explore for a possible major-suit fit in the bidding.

6. The Jack of Spades
with the 3 of Hearts a rather doubtful second choice. It is not especially desirable to attempt to set up a Heart trick, because the chances of doing so are remote. A Diamond lead is unattractive because it is likely to cost a trick.

7. The 10 of Spades
but 4 of Clubs is a second choice. The Heart and Diamond leads are not favored.

8. The King of Diamonds.
If the 9 of Diamonds were a smaller spot, the lead of the fourth best would be recommended, but with the present holding, if declarer has the A J x and partner can be found with as little as the 10 of Diamonds, it may be possible to hold declarer to one trick in the suit.

9. The 2 of Hearts
(although the 7 of Clubs is an alternate choice). There appears to be no future in the Spade suit, for even if you should succeed in getting it established, there is not the remotest prospect of your getting in to cash it. Your best chance, therefore, is to try to find partner's suit and send him off to a fairly good start. It is preferable to lead from a three-card holding rather than a doubleton, and since the Heart suit contains an honor, the deuce is the correct choice.

10. The Jack of Hearts.
On the bidding it is clear that the opponents do not have any values to spare and a Spade lead is too likely to present declarer with his ninth trick. The Heart opening is perfectly safe, and if partner can get in, he may be in position to lead Spades profitably in an effort to trap declarer's King.

11. The 7 of Spades.
This is the type of bidding on which trump leads are effective, because dummy will have distribution rather than high cards. The Queen of Hearts, while it is a second choice, is far off the pace, in our view.

12. The Ace of Hearts.
With four trumps it is desirable to try and shorten declarer's trump holding. Your best prospect is in your long suit, Hearts. The Ace of that suit is, therefore, the proper opening.

13. The 6 of Clubs.
As a general principle it is desirable to lead from your strength in suit contracts, even though you lack a sequence. The purpose is to set up a fast trick before declarer has acquired complete control of the hand. In the present case there appears to be a fair chance that partner has four trumps, and if he also has some values in Clubs, you may be able to shorten declarer's trump holding.

14. The 5 of Spades.
The trump lead is the safest choice and is also constructive, as dummy is likely to contain a ruffing value. The 5 of Spades is chosen in preference to the Ace because partner is unlikely to have more than two trumps, and if he is the first one to get in, he will still retain a trump to return in an effort to clear away the dummy's Spades.

15. The Jack of Diamonds.
You should resist the temptation to lead Spades even though you have a good sequence and two probable Heart entries. Possession of the

Jack of Diamonds makes it probable that partner's suit can be established with one lead and surely he must have an entry. Remember he over-called at the level of 2.

16. The 7 of Clubs.
Even though this suit has been bid, it is preferred to the Diamond. If you hit partner with the Queen, the suit may be readily establishable and even if he has just the 10, you have two probable entries with which to set up the suit.

17. The 2 of Diamonds.
While the Queen of Spades is an inviting lead, nevertheless, with a sound partner, it is mandatory to lead the Diamond. It is conventional that when partner bids a suit and then doubles the opponent's No Trump contract, he demands uncon-ditionally that you lead his suit. On the actual hand, the lead of the Queen of Spades permitted declarer to fulfill the contract.

18. The 10 of Spades.
On this particular bidding partner is unlikely to have any strength and you should not make a lead that is likely to sacrifice a trick. Under no circumstances should a lead be made from one of the red suits. Aggressive action is not advisable against No Trump slams. It is better to protect your holdings.

19. The 2 of Spades.
Partner obviously has some good Spade holding behind the dummy and feels that unless you attack that suit, declarer may have time to de-velop twelve tricks. Your hand would tend to confirm his judgment and the Spade should, therefore, be led.

20. The 3 of Clubs.
Unless partner has the Queen of Clubs your cause is lost. You must set up a Club trick before dummy's King of Hearts is established.

21. A Club.
While the lead of the King of Hearts is very tempting, it is probable that one of the opponents has a singleton Heart. A better chance to defeat the contract is to give partner a Club ruff. North's first take-out was to 2 Clubs, which indicates he probably has at least four. South's jump to 4 Clubs marks him with four of that suit, which means that partner can-not have more than one. Therefore, when West obtains the lead with the Ace of trumps, partner can be given the ruff.

22. The 8 of Hearts.
When your partner leaves in your take-out double of 1 in a suit, he announces that his trumps are good enough to defeat the contract. There-fore you should start pulling trumps immediately.

23. A trump.
This does not mean you should first lead the King of Clubs to look at the dummy. The lead of the King of Clubs may permit declarer to make the hand. You do not need a look at the dummy to know it will be short in Spades and have four Hearts. Your partner probably has some good Spades which you should protect by leading trump as often as possible. Keep the Ace and King of Clubs to get in with to lead more trump.

24. The 5 of Spades.
This lead is suggested because the dummy has shown a very good Club suit which will provide discards un-less your tricks are taken in a hurry. It is pointless to make a waiting lead where dummy has a good long suit. You must trust that your partner has either the Ace or Queen of Spades. If not, in all probability there is no hope to defeat the con-tract.

25. The King of Hearts.
Although dummy has been marked with a highly unbalanced hand, a

trump lead is inadvisable, since the Diamond suit will probably soon be available for discards. The singleton lead is ruled out on the same ground. Your best hope is that partner has the Ace of Hearts and that you will be able to cash tricks in that suit immediately.

26. The King of Clubs.

Your trump holding is so strong that you do not desire to obtain Heart ruffs. You are more interested in forcing the declarer, and the Club suit offers a very bright prospect of establishing that force. If subsequent developments show that ruffs are required, you will have the opportunity to lead Hearts later.

27. The 3 of Diamonds.

Here the singleton should be preferred to the lead of your partner's suit. You have the ideal condition for such a lead: a trump stopper, one superfluous trump, and the ability to give your partner the lead to obtain the ruff.

28. The Jack of Clubs.

A singleton honor is not generally an attractive lead and should be avoided in this instance. Declarer has shown only four Spades, since he failed to rebid the suit, and North probably has just three, since he failed to raise the suit immediately. This means your partner is likely to have four and your best hope is to force declarer's trump holding with repeated Club leads.

29. The Jack of Clubs.

It is not advisable to lead a suit which you have forced partner to bid. It may cost a trick. The Club lead is safer and offers some prospect of developing a trick for your side.

30. A Spade.

North has shown possession of a highly distributional holding, and repeated trump leads represent the only effective means of cutting down the dummy's trick-taking ability.

31. A Club.

The lead of partner's suit is ruled out by the double. Nor should you select the unbid suit. The double of the slam calls for an abnormal lead, and in this particular case it appears that the abnormal lead is the dummy's first suit. You may wager a tidy sum that partner can ruff the opening lead.

32. A low Spade.

North obviously has a very good Heart suit and you must try to develop a trick in Spades before your Ace of Hearts is driven out. Unless partner shows up with the Queen of Spades, your cause is probably hopeless.

33. The 7 of Spades

is the recommended lead. First, because it is more nearly a sequence than the Clubs; second, because preemptive bids in one major frequently indicate the fear that the opponents have the other major.

34. The Queen of Clubs.

It is imperative to build up tricks in a hurry. The Hearts will take care of themselves. As between Spades and Clubs, the Clubs are the better choice, because you have something in the suit to help develop tricks, whereas the Spade lead requires that your partner have considerable Spade strength himself.

35. The deuce of Clubs.

This is one of the rare cases where the underlead of an Ace is recommended. You have no attractive lead. The dummy has bid 1 No Trump and more than likely has the King of Clubs. Your lead may therefore induce declarer to play low from dummy, permitting your partner to make one of the lesser honors.

36. The deuce of Spades.

In order to defeat the contract, it may be necessary to obtain a Club ruff. In order to make partner aware of your void in that suit, a somewhat unnatural lead is suggested. The deuce of Spades could hardly be fourth best (you would not have overcalled and rebid in a four-card suit), so the inference should be plain that you are attempting to get partner in to make some special lead. The fact that you selected the deuce would suggest to him the lower ranking of the two plain suits, Clubs.

37. The 2 of Hearts.
Do not lead the Ace of Spades. If partner's Spade suit is headed by the Queen Jack, this lead might cost a

trick. Whereas the Heart lead will prove safe if partner has either the Ace or Queen.

38. The 5 of Diamonds.
The normal inclination to lead the unbid suit should be stifled here, because South's bidding makes it clear that he is not worried about Clubs. Your best chance is that partner has something like the King of Diamonds behind the dummy and that you can set up a trick in that suit while you still retain the Ace of trumps.

FOR THE PURPOSE of this discussion the partner of the opening leader will be referred to as the third hand. The play of the third hand to the first trick is the turning point of the hand many times. Partner's opening lead has been more or less in the blind, and it may be the duty of the third hand to guide the opener as to the subsequent play. This will be discussed at greater length in the chapter on signals and discards. For the present we are concerned with the handling of various card combinations by third hand.

There is an old bromide to the effect that third hand must play high. This is only partially true, and in this chapter we will consider various deviations from this principle. The object of third hand's playing high is to force out a still higher card from the declarer's hand, so that the opening leader's cards will be promoted in rank.

Rule of 11

The first thing to observe is that the Rule of 11 is not a rule at all. It is a sugar-coated method of rapid calculation when your partner has opened the fourth best of a suit. This merely enables you to calculate rapidly how many cards (higher than the one led) are held by second, third, and fourth hands combined. This is how it is done. Take the size of the card led, subtract it from 11. The balance represents the number of cards (higher than the one led) that are held by second, third, and fourth hands. For example:

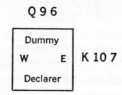

Q 9 6

Dummy	
W E	K 10 7
Declarer	

West leads the 5.

Assuming that you are East and you recognize partner's lead of the 5 as his fourth best, your problem is to determine how many cards South (the declarer) holds that are better than the 5. The process is as follows: 11 minus 5 equals 6. That means that the second, third, and fourth hands together hold six cards better than the 5. North and East each have three. South therefore has none, and your 7 will win the trick. West has obviously led from A J 8 5.

This device is also available to the declarer. To illustrate:

A Q 2

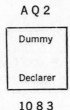

10 8 3

West leads the 7. You are South and declarer. Assuming that West's lead is his fourth best, your problem is to determine how many higher cards East holds. Take the card led and subtract it from 11; 11 minus 7 equals 4. North, East, and South together, therefore, have four cards higher than the 7. Since North and South each have two, East can have none, so you play low from dummy, knowing that the 8 will win the trick. West's lead has been from K J 9 7.

How does this Rule of 11 come about? It is really very simple. There are thirteen cards in a suit, whose numbers range from 2 to 14, the Jack being 11, the Queen 12, the King 13, and the Ace 14. This represents their rank. Since the opening leader automatically has three cards higher than the one led (remember we are presuming he has led his fourth highest), those three do not enter into the calculation, which reduces the top number from 14 to 11.

Another way to state the rule is as follows: When a particular card is led, such as the 7, you ask yourself how many cards higher than the 7 are in the deck. The answer, obviously, is seven. This includes all the cards from the 8 to the Ace. Since three of them are known to be in the opening leader's hand, that leaves four of them out around the table; 11 minus 7 equals 4.

Another way to state the case is to subtract the card led from 14 and you will have the number of cards in the deck that are higher than the one led. Now subtract the three which the opening leader is always known to possess and you have the total in the hands of the other three players.

This rule will sometimes help third hand to determine whether to play his highest card.

Here is an important principle. If the dummy has no vital card that you are interested in capturing, you, as third hand, should always play high, but if there is an important card in the dummy that you would like to trap, it frequently pays for third hand to wait for that card to be played before playing his highest. In other words, third hand acts as a guard over dummy. For example:

K 6 3

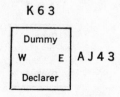

A J 4 3

West leads the 5. Dummy plays low. What should you (East) play? If you play third hand high and win with the Ace, dummy's King becomes established. Proper play is the Jack, in the hope that partner has led from the Queen. If it proves that declarer holds the Queen, you will not have lost anything by your play, because had you played the Ace, declarer would have won with both the King and the Queen. As it is, your Ace stands guard to capture the King.

This play is sometimes erroneously referred to as a finesse against partner. You are not finessing against partner at all. You are finessing against the dummy, which is quite proper. In other words, the dummy contains a high card which you are anxious to capture and you keep the Ace to stand guard over the King.

In cases where third hand is to play high there is a slight variation where his two highest cards are in sequence. In that case the second best card is just as high as the best card, and when following suit it is proper to follow with the bottom of the sequence. This is the reverse of the rule that applies to the leader who must lead the top of a sequence. For example:

6 5 4

K 10 7 3
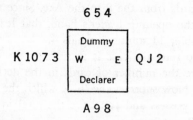
Q J 2

A 9 8

West leads the 3. As East you properly play the Jack, not the Queen. This will prove informative to partner, for when the Jack forces the Ace, partner will realize you have the Queen. But if, thinking it makes no difference, you play the Queen, your partner will have no way of knowing you have the Jack and may fear to continue his suit.

If partner leads a low card of a suit in which you hold the J 10 9 8, you must follow suit with the 8. It is the equal of the Jack, but when the 8 forces out the other high card your partner will then be in a position to know that you have the 9 10 J.

Lead from top of a sequence; follow suit from bottom of a sequence.

Q 6 2

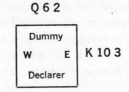

You are East. Your partner West leads the 5, and North, the dummy, plays low. What card do you play? The answer is the 10, not the King. If you play the King, the Queen must eventually be established. If you play the 10, it may possibly drive out the Ace. If the 10 loses to the Jack, you have lost nothing, because the play of the King would permit the declarer subsequently to take a trick with either the Jack or the Queen or possibly both.

If the contract is No Trump, it is barely possible that your partner is leading from the Ace and Jack, in which case your 10 will actually win the trick. If your partner is leading from the J 9 7 5 and you play the King, declarer will win two tricks. If, however, you play the 10, declarer's Ace will be forced out and he will be able to take no further tricks in the suit because you will wait for partner to lead through the Queen.

The same principle applies in the following diagram:

Q 6 2

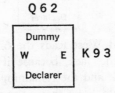

If West leads the 5 and dummy plays low, East should play the 9, retaining the King to capture the Queen.

A case calling for exceptional treatment by third hand is the following:

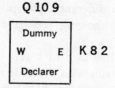

Against a 4 Heart contract your partner West leads the 4 of Spades. Dummy plays the 9. What card should you play?

Declarer definitely holds the Ace, since it is very remote that partner would have underled the Ace against a 4 Heart contract. If you play the King, the declarer will win and subsequently finesse the 10 against your partner, making three tricks in the suit. If you duck the 9, declarer will win the trick and will still have the Ace. This will give him two tricks instead of three. The complete holding is as follows:

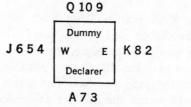

Unblocking by third hand

When your partner has opened a long suit and you have high cards in that suit, you must be careful not to retain them too long lest they interfere with your partner running that suit. For example:

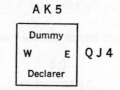

It is No Trump and West leads the 6. Declarer plays the King. East's proper play is the Jack, because if he plays low he will be certain to win one trick and the remaining cards of partner's will be blocked out. East should hope that partner is leading from the 10, and when the Ace is subsequently played he should follow with the Queen in order to get out of partner's way. The same principle also applies when third hand holds an honor and one other card of partner's suit.

4 3 2

It is No Trump. Partner leads the Jack. East should play the Queen in order to get out of partner's way.

4 3 2

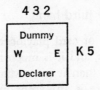

West leads the Queen. East should play the King for the same reason. However, where East can see that by unblocking he will definitely lose a trick, he must refuse to unblock.

9 7 4 3

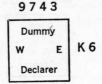

West leads the Queen. East cannot afford to unblock by playing the King, because if he does so, the 9 will subsequently become a winner. He must, therefore, reluctantly play low.

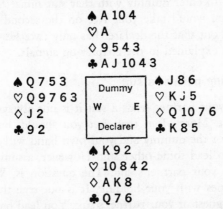

♠ A 10 4
♡ A
◇ 9 5 4 3
♣ A J 10 4 3

♠ Q 7 5 3   ♠ J 8 6
♡ Q 9 7 6 3   ♡ K J 5
◇ J 2   ◇ Q 10 7 6
♣ 9 2   ♣ K 8 5

♠ K 9 2
♡ 10 8 4 2
◇ A K 8
♣ Q 7 6

South is the declarer at a contract of 3 No Trump. West leads the 6 of Hearts, dummy plays the Ace. East should play the Jack of Hearts and not the 5. The play serves a dual purpose:

1. It signals to partner that a continuation of the suit is desired.

2. And, more important, it starts unblocking for partner, who no doubt has a five-card suit. Note the difference if East retains the Jack of Hearts. When he is in with the King of Clubs he will cash the King of Hearts and follow with the Jack, which West cannot afford to overtake, but if the 5 were retained at this point, a lead through declarer's 10 8 of Hearts would clear up the entire suit.

Holding up by third hand

It is an axiom of card playing that Aces were meant to capture Kings and Queens, and it is much better to put your Ace on the opponent's honor card than it is to wait and subsequently play it on a deuce. However, there is an exception. Where declarer has a long suit in dummy without any entries, it is frequently wise not to take your Ace until such time as declarer has no more of the suit. For example:

♣ K Q J 10 2

Dummy	
W E	♣ A 7 4
Declarer	

You are East. Dummy has no other high cards. When South leads a Club you must refuse to take your Ace and wait until the third round in case South has three of the suit. If you take the Ace earlier, he will be able to enter dummy with that suit himself.

Sometimes you would take your Ace on the second round because you have found out that the declarer has only two. How you can find this out will be explained in the chapter on signals.

Returning partner's suit

When your partner leads a suit it is not always necessary for you to return it. More often than not you should, but many times the appearance of the dummy and your own hand will show you that it is advisable to lead some other suit. However, assume that you are about to return your partner's suit. The question is, Which card to select? That varies with your holding. It is not true that you always lead back the highest of your partner's suit. You lead back the highest if you originally held three cards or less, but where you originally held four or more cards of the suit it is conventional to return the fourth highest. This enables your partner to know the exact distribution of the suit around the table. It is true that sometimes your partner will be in doubt when you return a low card. He may think it is the highest and that you therefore have no more, but nine times out of ten something in the bidding or the appearance of the dummy will tell him that you cannot be short-suited, therefore you are returning your fourth best. The following hand illustrates the principle:

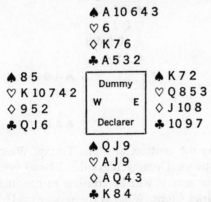

```
                    ♠ A 10 6 4 3
                    ♡ 6
                    ◊ K 7 6
                    ♣ A 5 3 2
   ♠ 8 5          ┌──────────┐      ♠ K 7 2
   ♡ K 10 7 4 2   │  Dummy   │      ♡ Q 8 5 3
   ◊ 9 5 2        │ W      E │      ◊ J 10 8
   ♣ Q J 6        │ Declarer │      ♣ 10 9 7
                  └──────────┘
                    ♠ Q J 9
                    ♡ A J 9
                    ◊ A Q 4 3
                    ♣ K 8 4
```

Against the contract of 3 No Trump, West leads the 4 of Hearts, East plays the Queen, and South wins with the Ace. The Spade finesse is then taken and East wins. He naturally returns Hearts. If he should lead the 8, South would play the 9 and West would win with the 10. Inasmuch as there would be absolutely no way for him to know that the Jack would fall the next time, he might fear to lead the King lest the Jack might become established in the South hand. East therefore should return the 3 instead of the 8. This will tell West that he originally had four cards of the suit, and when he knows this it will be evident that South has only one more, which must fall.

There is an exception to this principle. Where third hand holds a sequence of high cards in the suit partner has led, and there is danger that the suit may become blocked, the top of the sequence should be returned.

```
                        6
                   ┌─────────┐
                   │    N    │
   K J 7 5 4       │ W     E │   A 10 9 3
                   │    S    │
                   └─────────┘
                       Q 8 2
```

West opens the 5. East wins with the Ace. If he should return the 3, South will play the 8 and West will win with the Jack. The King drops the Queen, but East has left only the 10 9 and must block the run of the suit.

Third hand defensive play

When the third hand decides to lead a new suit it is important to select the proper card, especially where honors are involved. Assume that you are East:

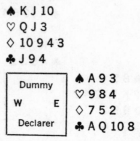

♠ K J 10
♡ Q J 3
◇ 10 9 4 3
♣ J 9 4

	♠ A 9 3
Dummy	♡ 9 8 4
W E	◇ 7 5 2
Declarer	♣ A Q 10 8

South is playing the contract at 3 No Trump. West, your partner, opens the 2 of Spades. Dummy plays the 10 and you win with the Ace. It is apparent that it will be fruitless to continue with Spades, so you decide to lead Clubs. What is the proper card? The answer is, the Queen, because you believe that South has the King. This will force him to win the trick, and when your partner regains the lead and comes back with a Club you will win all the tricks in that suit. The complete hand is as follows:

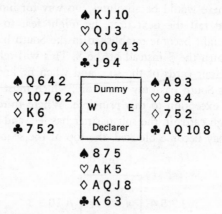

♠ K J 10
♡ Q J 3
◇ 10 9 4 3
♣ J 9 4

♠ Q 6 4 2		♠ A 9 3
♡ 10 7 6 2	Dummy	♡ 9 8 4
◇ K 6	W E	◇ 7 5 2
♣ 7 5 2	Declarer	♣ A Q 10 8

♠ 8 7 5
♡ A K 5
◇ A Q J 8
♣ K 6 3

Notice that if East had led his fourth best, South would have played low and North would win with the 9, and the King of Clubs would subsequently produce another trick. The way for East to remember the proper card to lead from this combination is as follows: When you sit over the dummy (that is, the dummy plays before you) and you surround one of dummy's honor cards (in this case your Queen and 10 of Clubs surround dummy's Jack), and you have another higher card, you should lead as though the surrounded card is in your own hand. In other words, you lead as though you held A Q J 10, from which the proper lead would be the Queen. Another illustration of this principle is the following:

You are East. South is the declarer at a contract of 3 No Trump. Your partner, West, leads the Jack of Spades. Dummy plays low. You win with the King and decide the Heart suit must be attacked. The proper card to lead is the Jack. Notice that your Jack and 9 of Hearts surround the dummy's 10 and you have a higher heart—the King. Therefore you should lead as though you held K J 10 9. The complete hand is as follows:

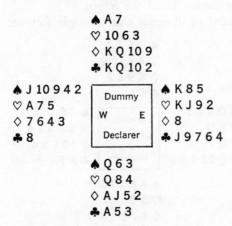

Notice that had you led the 2 of Hearts, South would have played low, West would have been forced to win with the Ace, and now the Queen would stop the suit.

There is a popular belief that when on subsequent defense you find it expedient to lead a suit in which you hold two cards, the higher of the two must be led. This is not always true. When your two cards are immaterial, the higher of the two is led.

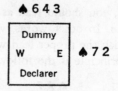

♠ 6 4 3

If East finds it desirable to lead Spades, the 7 is the proper card. But if, in the diagram which follows below, East desires to lead Spades, he should not lead the 10. It is too important a card. Note that if the 10 is led, West will win with the Ace but will be unable to return the suit.

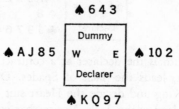

♠ 6 4 3

♠ A J 8 5   ♠ 10 2

♠ K Q 9 7

As a general proposition, the lead of a small card by a defender suggests mildly that he can "stand" the return of the suit because he has a supporting card. The lead of a high intermediate card suggests that he probably cannot stand the return.

A complete hand to illustrate this principle follows:

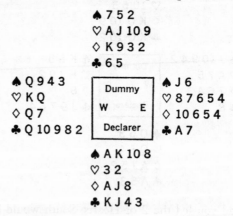

♠ 7 5 2
♡ A J 10 9
◇ K 9 3 2
♣ 6 5

♠ Q 9 4 3   ♠ J 6
♡ K Q   ♡ 8 7 6 5 4
◇ Q 7   ◇ 10 6 5 4
♣ Q 10 9 8 2   ♣ A 7

♠ A K 10 8
♡ 3 2
◇ A J 8
♣ K J 4 3

South is the declarer at a contract of 3 No Trump. West leads the 10 of Clubs, which is won with the Ace. The 7 is returned, and declarer permits this to hold the trick. At this point, naturally, East must shift, and logically the only shift is to Spades. East does not make the mistake of leading the Jack. Instead he leads the 6, in order to retain the Jack as a forcing card should West find it expedient to lead that suit later on. Declarer wins this trick and starts on the Hearts. When West is in, he is able to return a Spade. Declarer wins this trick and cashes the Hearts. It is true that South can still make the hand by guessing the adverse holding, but there is a good chance that he will not do so. Note that if East returns the Jack of Spades instead of the 6, now, when West is in with the Heart he will be unable to return Spades without giving declarer his ninth trick.

Leading up to strength

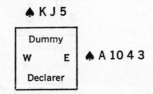

♠ K J 5

Dummy
W   E   ♠ A 10 4 3
Declarer

It goes against the grain of many players to lead into dummy's strength. It is habitual with them to lead through strength. The above diagram represents a holding which frequently comes up in play. East has the lead and arrives at the conclusion that the defense must cash several Spade tricks to defeat the contract. Naturally this can be done only if partner holds the Queen. The proper attack, therefore, is the 3 of Spades. If declarer has the Queen, the chances are that nothing is lost. If partner has the Queen, East will now have a tenace position over dummy and can wait for partner to come through and clear up the suit.

The complete hand follows:

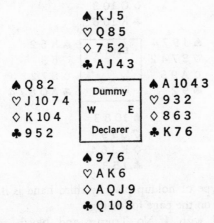

```
                    ♠ K J 5
                    ♡ Q 8 5
                    ◇ 7 5 2
                    ♣ A J 4 3
  ♠ Q 8 2      Dummy      ♠ A 10 4 3
  ♡ J 10 7 4              ♡ 9 3 2
  ◇ K 10 4    W    E      ◇ 8 6 3
  ♣ 9 5 2      Declarer   ♣ K 7 6
                    ♠ 9 7 6
                    ♡ A K 6
                    ◇ A Q J 9
                    ♣ Q 10 8
```

South is declarer at a contract of 3 No Trump. West leads the 4 of Hearts. East plays the 9, and declarer wins with the Ace. This is a very ineffective false card because it cannot possibly fool anyone. The Club finesse is taken, and East, knowing the declarer still holds the King of Hearts, must attack some other suit. Therefore he leads the 3 of Spades, and West's Queen forces the dummy's King. When West subsequently regains the lead on the Diamond finesse, a Spade comes through and three more tricks are cashed by the defense.

You are East defending against South's contract of 3 No Trump. West leads the 4 of Spades, dummy plays the 6, you win with the King, and declarer plays the 3. What is your proper return?

The Spade suit offers no future. If the contract is to be defeated, Clubs are the only hope. The proper return is the 7 of Clubs. This will permit declarer to win a trick cheaply, but if partner gains the lead and can return a Club, the balance of the suit will be cashed. The complete holding is as follows:

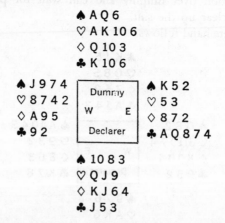

An unusual type of holdup play by third hand is illustrated in the holding depicted on the page following.

South opened with 1 No Trump, and North raised to 3 No

Trump. West led the 3 of Spades, and dummy played the 4. East's play to the first trick settles the fate of the hand. Since there is nothing in dummy to capture, it may appear that third hand should

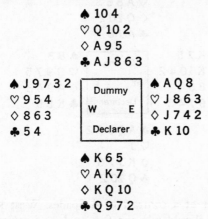

♠ 10 4
♥ Q 10 2
♦ A 9 5
♣ A J 8 6 3

♠ J 9 7 3 2
♥ 9 5 4
♦ 8 6 3
♣ 5 4

Dummy

W   E

Declarer

♠ A Q 8
♥ J 8 6 3
♦ J 7 4 2
♣ K 10

♠ K 6 5
♥ A K 7
♦ K Q 10
♣ Q 9 7 2

play high, but a moment's reflection will show that an exceptional play is called for at this point. It is quite obvious from the bidding that West can have no high cards. The lead of the 3 shows that West has either four Spades or five, if he also has the deuce, but he cannot have more than five, which means that declarer must have at least three Spades, one of which is the King. If the Ace is put up, declarer will naturally refuse to take the King until the third round and West's Spades will be shut out. East therefore should play the Queen of Spades. This will surely force declarer to win with the King. It is true that declarer could circumvent this defense by refusing to take the Queen, but declarer is not blessed with X-ray eyes and such a play would be virtually impossible. Now when the Club finesse is taken into East he follows with the Ace and another Spade to defeat the contract.

Co-operating with the leader of a doubleton

Third hand is frequently called upon to co-operate with his partner in cases where a doubleton lead has been made against a suit contract. The difficulty lies, of course, in diagnosing that the lead is a doubleton. It is frequently difficult to determine whether partner's lead is from one or two. Many times the bidding will furnish a clue. However, let us assume that you have determined that partner's lead is a doubleton. It is frequently good policy when you have the Ace of that suit to duck the first round, so that partner will retain a card of that suit to return to you should he obtain the lead before trumps are exhausted.

An example:

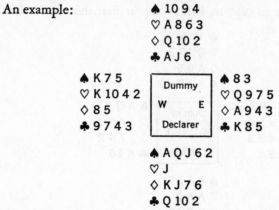

```
                  ♠ 10 9 4
                  ♡ A 8 6 3
                  ◊ Q 10 2
                  ♣ A J 6
♠ K 7 5        ┌─────────┐        ♠ 8 3
♡ K 10 4 2     │ Dummy   │        ♡ Q 9 7 5
◊ 8 5          │ W     E │        ◊ A 9 4 3
♣ 9 7 4 3      │ Declarer│        ♣ K 8 5
               └─────────┘
                  ♠ A Q J 6 2
                  ♡ J
                  ◊ K J 7 6
                  ♣ Q 10 2
```

South is declarer at a contract of 4 Spades. West leads the 8 of Diamonds. If East should win the first trick and return a Diamond, the trick will be won in dummy and a Spade finesse taken. West will win with the King and will shift to a Club in an effort to reach partner's hand for a Diamond ruff. Declarer will refuse to take the finesse and will pull the remaining trumps, giving up in all a Club, a Diamond, and a Spade. Note how different the play develops if East refuses the first trick. (East should, however, signal with the 9 of Diamonds, so that partner will not be discouraged from continuing the suit.) When declarer takes the trump finesse, West still has a Diamond to lead while he has a trump, and a ruff is obtained.

If the partner of the doubleton leader has a quick entry card, the holdup is unnecessary. In the above hand, if East had held the Ace of Clubs instead of the King, he could afford to win the first Diamond trick and return the suit, West being able to enter his hand later with the Ace of Clubs for the ruff.

Third hand frequently has the opportunity to make a neat though very simple ducking play with the following combination of cards:

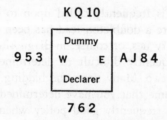

```
              K Q 10
           ┌─────────┐
           │ Dummy   │
  9 5 3    │ W     E │   A J 8 4
           │ Declarer│
           └─────────┘
              7 6 2
```

West leads the 9, dummy plays the Queen. East should refuse to win the trick but signal with the 8. Now when West obtains the lead, East can cash the balance of the tricks.

If East has the lead he should avoid, if possible, leading a Spade. In the vast majority of cases it will cost him a trick to touch this suit. The cards may be distributed as follows:

Example A   Example B

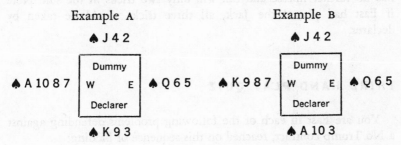

In EXAMPLE A, if East leads a low Spade, declarer will play low and the Ace will follow, giving the declarer one trick. If he is left to play the suit himself, he can win no tricks.

In EXAMPLE B, if declarer led the suit himself, he can win only the Ace, inasmuch as the Jack, if led, will be covered by the Queen. If East leads the suit, declarer will play low, forcing the King, and then a finesse is available against East's Queen, yielding the declarer two tricks.

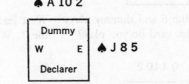

The contract is 4 Hearts. West leads the 3 of Spades and dummy plays the 2. What card should East play? Inasmuch as West cannot hold the King and Queen, since, against a suit contract, he would have led the King, declarer is marked with a high honor. The play of the Jack, therefore, cannot be sound. If declarer has the King, West's Queen will be subject to finesse and three tricks taken by declarer. If declarer has the Queen, West's King will be subject to finesse. The complete holding is as follows:

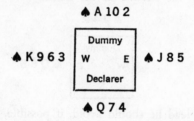

♠ A 10 2

♠ K 9 6 3   **Dummy** W   E   ♠ J 8 5
             Declarer

♠ Q 7 4

The play of the 8 by East will go to South's Queen, but now he has no further finesse and can win only two tricks in the suit. Note if East had played the Jack, all three tricks would be taken by declarer.

THIRD HAND PLAY QUIZ

You are East in each of the following problems defending against a No Trump contract, reached on this sequence of bidding:

SOUTH   NORTH
1 No Trump   3 No Trump

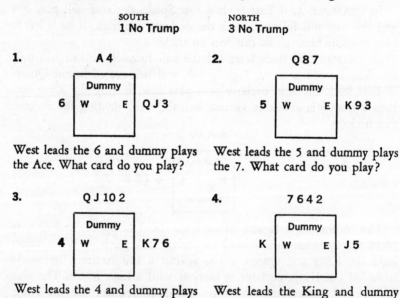

1.   A 4

6   **Dummy** W   E   Q J 3

West leads the 6 and dummy plays the Ace. What card do you play?

2.   Q 8 7

5   **Dummy** W   E   K 9 3

West leads the 5 and dummy plays the 7. What card do you play?

3.   Q J 10 2

4   **Dummy** W   E   K 7 6

West leads the 4 and dummy plays the 10. What card do you play?

4.   7 6 4 2

K   **Dummy** W   E   J 5

West leads the King and dummy plays the 2. What card do you play?

5.   A 7

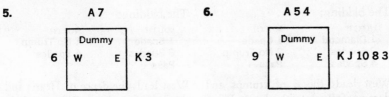

West leads the 6 and dummy plays
the Ace. What card do you play?

6.   A 5 4

West leads the 9 and dummy plays
the 4. What card do you play?

In the following problems South, the declarer, is playing a Spade
contract. You are sitting East in each instance.

7.   ♡ A 10 9

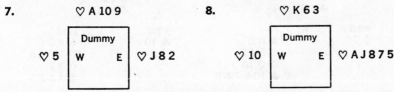

West leads the 5 and dummy plays
the 9. What card do you play?

8.   ♡ K 6 3

West leads the 10 of Hearts and
dummy plays the 3. What card do
you play?

9.   ♡ K 10 6

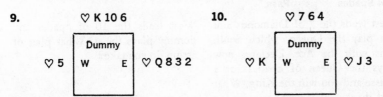

West leads the 5 of Hearts and
dummy plays the 6. What card do
you play?

10.   ♡ 7 6 4

West leads the King of Hearts and
dummy plays the 4. What card do
you play?

You are East in each of the following problems.

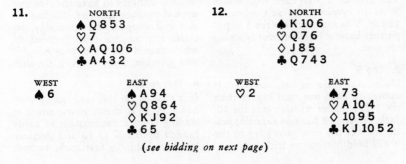

11.   NORTH
                  ♠ Q 8 5 3
                  ♡ 7
                  ◇ A Q 10 6
                  ♣ A 4 3 2

WEST   EAST
♠ 6   ♠ A 9 4
                  ♡ Q 8 6 4
                  ◇ K J 9 2
                  ♣ 6 5

12.   NORTH
                  ♠ K 10 6
                  ♡ Q 7 6
                  ◇ J 8 5
                  ♣ Q 7 4 3

WEST   EAST
♡ 2   ♠ 7 3
                  ♡ A 10 4
                  ◇ 10 9 5
                  ♣ K J 10 5 2

(*see bidding on next page*)

The bidding:

NORTH	SOUTH
1 Diamond	1 Spade
2 Spades	2 No Trump
4 Spades	Pass

West leads the 6 of trumps and dummy follows with the 3. What card do you play?

The bidding:

SOUTH	NORTH
1 Spade	1 No Trump
3 Spades	4 Spades
Pass	

West leads the deuce of Hearts and dummy plays the 6. What card do you play?

13.

NORTH
♠ A 5
♡ A K J 6
♦ 9 6 4 3 2
♣ J 2

WEST
♦ 7

EAST
♠ K 6
♡ 8 4 3
♦ Q 10 5
♣ 10 8 7 6 5

The bidding:

NORTH	SOUTH
1 Heart	1 Spade
2 Diamonds	3 Spades
4 Spades	Pass

West leads the 7 of Diamonds and you play the Queen, which South wins with the Ace. Declarer now plays the Queen of Spades for a finesse and you win the King. What card do you play next?

14.

NORTH
♠ Q J 4
♡ Q 4 3
♦ J 8 7 5
♣ K Q 5

WEST
♠ 10

EAST
♠ A 3 2
♡ 9 7 6 5
♦ 9 3
♣ A J 7 6

The bidding:

NORTH	SOUTH
Pass	1 No Trump
3 No Trump	Pass

West leads the 10 of Spades and dummy plays the 4. What plan of action do you take?

ANSWERS TO THIRD HAND PLAY QUIZ

1. The Jack.
The play of a high card will induce West to continue the suit when he gets in. You should retain the 3 to put partner back in later without blocking the suit.

2. The 9.
Under the rule of 11, declarer is known to have one card higher than the 5. No matter whether it is the 10, Jack, or Ace, he has one sure stopper. But if it is the Ace, your play of the 9 will hold him to one trick only.

3. The 6.
West is unlikely to have the Ace and even if he does, declarer still has the suit well stopped. More probably, declarer has the Ace once guarded, in which case if you waste your King, it will give him three tricks in the suit.

4. The Jack.
It is vital to get this card out of your hand. If, as is likely, your partner is leading from a combination of cards headed by the K Q 10 and declarer lets him hold the first trick, he will

be unlikely to continue the suit for fear that declarer holds the A J, unless you release the latter card.

5. The 3.

You cannot afford the luxury of unblocking. It is true that declarer is not likely to have either the Queen or Jack, for in that case, he would have permitted the lead to come around to his hand. However, he may have 10 9 x x, in which case discarding the King would cost your side a trick.

6. The 8 or even the 10.

Declarer has the Queen and at least one other (partner has obviously led the top of nothing), which gives declarer two stoppers in the suit. The purpose of ducking is to maintain communication with partner in case he obtains the lead first.

7. The deuce or the 8

but not the Jack. If you play the Jack and declarer has the Queen, it will automatically give him three tricks in the suit.

8. The 8 is the proper play.

The 10 will force the Queen and you will still retain a position over dummy's King with your A J. The play of the Ace would be profitable only if partner had led a singleton. Yet, even if that happens to be the case, the chances are that your play of the 8 will not prove costly.

9. The 8.

There is no assurance that this play will succeed, but if partner has led from a combination of cards including the 9 and Jack, your 8 will force the Ace. To play the Queen would surely be surrendering three tricks in the suit to declarer, for dummy's holding would now permit a finesse against West's Jack.

10. The 3.

You cannot afford to play the Jack, for if partner is leading from the K Q, that might cost a trick. Against a No Trump contract, he would lead the King only if he had the 10 as well as

the Queen to back it up. But against a suit contract, you have no such assurance.

11. The 9.

The purpose of the defense can best be served by extracting as many of dummy's trumps as possible. If you win the first trump trick, you may not regain the lead soon enough to lead a third round of trumps. Since partner may be able to get in before you do, it is well to see that he retains another trump in his hand, which purpose you may accomplish by ducking the first lead.

12. The 10.

West is leading from a three- or four-card holding headed by an honor. If he has the King and Jack, your 10 will hold the trick. If declarer has one of these honors, your 10 will force it. The play of the Ace would cost a trick if partner held the missing high honors.

13. The 6 of Clubs.

The Diamond suit holds no great future, because from partner's lead it is clear that you can expect to win, at most, one more trick in that suit. The only hope of setting the contract is to find partner with a good Club holding. The Club shift at this point is vital, for the dummy's Heart suit may be immediately available for discards. The complete holding was:

```
              NORTH
              ♠ A 5
              ♡ A K J 6
              ◇ 9 6 4 3 2
              ♣ J 2
WEST                        EAST
♠ 8 3 2                     ♠ K 6
♡ 10 9 7                    ♡ 8 4 3
◇ K J 7                     ◇ Q 10 5
♣ A Q 4 3                   ♣ 10 8 7 6 5
              SOUTH
              ♠ Q J 10 9 7 4
              ♡ Q 4 2
              ◇ A 8
              ♣ K 9
```

14. Win the Ace of Spades and shift to the 6 of Clubs.

The Spade suit obviously has no future, and your only hope of developing sufficient tricks to set the contract lies in the Club suit. Since dummy has a sure stopper in the suit, a trick must be conceded to declarer. You should, therefore, return a low Club immediately, hoping that partner holds the 10. If he also has a card of entry in the red suits, he will subsequently be able to return a Club for you to run the suit.

The complete holding was:

NORTH
♠ Q J 4
♡ Q 4 3
◊ J 8 7 5
♣ K Q 5

WEST
♠ 10 9 8 5
♡ A 10 8 2
◊ 6 4
♣ 10 3 2

EAST
♠ A 3 2
♡ 9 7 6 5
◊ 9 3
♣ A J 7 6

SOUTH
♠ K 7 6
♡ K J
◊ A K Q 10 2
♣ 9 8 4

12.   Second hand play

AN ADAGE from the days of Whist recommends the play of "second hand low." This is sound advice in the vast majority of cases. It is subject, of course, to the exception that when the opponents lead an honor you may desire to cover, with the hope of building up a trick for yourself or partner. It is also subject to the exception that you may play a high card second hand—as, for example, where you have both the King and Queen—in order to be sure to build up a trick in a hurry. The rule, therefore, is that if you are second hand you should play low unless you have a very definite reason for not doing so.

A simple illustration is the following:

Q 6 4 2

AJ3   ┌─────────┐
       │ Dummy │
       │ W   E │
       │   S   │
       └─────────┘

South, the declarer, leads a small one. You are West. What do you play? The answer is, low. If you play low, the dummy will be forced to play the Queen. Either your partner will win with the King or, if the Queen holds the trick, you now retain the Ace Jack over the declarer's King and will be able to take two tricks.

The complete holding is as follows:

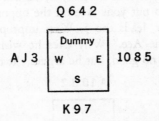

Q 6 4 2

AJ3   ┌─────────┐ 10 8 5
       │ Dummy │
       │ W   E │
       │   S   │
       └─────────┘

K 9 7

It is quite obvious that if you had played the Ace, the declarer would have lost only one trick in the suit.

The same reasoning would apply if North held:

```
              K 6 4 2
              +-------+
              |   N   |
      A J 3   | W   E |
              |   S   |
              +-------+
```

Here again West would play low, except in the rare case where he suspects that South has a singleton and is trying to steal a trick with the King.

```
              K J 9 4
              +-------+
              |   N   |
    A 10 3 2  | W   E |
              |   S   |
              +-------+
```

South leads a small one. West would play low, not the Ace. If partner has the Queen, he should be given a chance to make it. If the declarer has the Queen, it is useless to come up with the Ace, because the declarer will lose only one trick in the suit. The complete holding might be as follows:

```
              K J 9 4
              +-------+
              |   N   |
    A 10 3 2  | W   E |  8 7
              |   S   |
              +-------+
               Q 6 5
```

It is a good general policy to make your Aces catch big ones. *The place for the Ace is on a King.* If you cannot catch a King, try to catch a Queen. If you cannot do that, try to win a Jack, because it is usually losing play to put your Ace on the opponent's deuces.

South, the declarer, leads the 5. West improperly plays the Jack, in order "to force the Ace." Why does he wish to force the Ace? Surely it will do him no good, but he argues, "It might do my partner

```
              A 10 3 2
              +-------+
              |   N   |
       J 4    | W   E |
              |   S   |
              +-------+
```

some good." This is a fallacious argument. It can do your partner
some good only if he has the King or Queen, in which case he won't
need your help. Either the Ace must come up or your partner will
win the trick.

However, the play of the Jack might do your partner a lot of
harm, because the complete holding might be as follows:

A 10 3 2

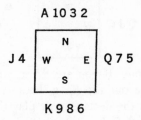

J 4   Q 7 5

K 9 8 6

South leads the 6. If West plays the Jack, declarer wins with the
Ace and returns the 10, finessing against East's Queen. If West holds
on to his Jack, the defense must win a trick regardless of how declarer
plays.

A Q 10 4 2

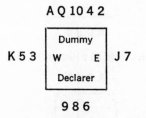

K 5 3

South, the declarer, leads a small one. I have seen West play the
King (in order to force out the Ace) because "my King is gone in
any event." Why does West wish to force out the Ace? It surely will
not do him any good. But he argues, "I wanted to build up my partner's Jack." The answer is, your partner's Jack needs no building up.
Nature will take care of that. Suppose, for example, the complete
holding were as follows:

A Q 10 4 2

	Dummy	
K 5 3	W E	J 7
	Declarer	

9 8 6

Now if the declarer plays the Queen next time, your side wins no
trick. If you had played low, regardless of which card was played
κ

from dummy, either your partner would win with the Jack or you subsequently would win with the King.

To repeat: *Do not put your honor cards on deuces.*

Another frequent error is as follows:

A K 10

Q J 6 | N W E S

South leads a low one. If you are West, you should not play the Jack in order to force out the King, because it does you no good. Do not be afraid that the declarer will play the 10, because, first of all, he may not; second, if he does, there is nothing you could ever do about it.

Change the situation slightly:

A 10 2

Q J 6 | N W E S

When South leads low, the play of the Jack is proper in order to force out the Ace, because now you will be sure of a trick in that suit. Whereas if the declarer inserts the 10 and wins, you may lose your trick. The complete holding may be:

A 10 2

Q J 6 | N W E | 7 5 3

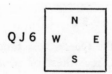

K 9 8 4

If, however, the holding were as follows:

A 7 5 3

Q J 6 | N W E S

and South led the deuce, it would be improper to play the Jack in order to force out the Ace, because it is highly improbable that the declarer intends to play the 7, and if he does, your partner would no doubt have some card that could beat it. One of the dangers of playing the Jack in that case is that your partner might have the singleton King. To recapitulate: Do not split your honors unless by so doing you are sure of building up a trick.

There are cases in which second hand should play high. They will be treated presently.

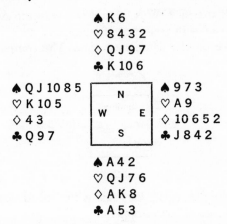

♠ K 6
♡ 8 4 3 2
♢ Q J 9 7
♣ K 10 6

♠ Q J 10 8 5   ♠ 9 7 3
♡ K 10 5   ♡ A 9
♢ 4 3   ♢ 10 6 5 2
♣ Q 9 7   ♣ J 8 4 2

♠ A 4 2
♡ Q J 7 6
♢ A K 8
♣ A 5 3

South is the declarer at a contract of 3 No Trump. West leads the Queen of Spades, which dummy wins with the King. The 2 of Hearts is led from dummy. East should not play second hand low. He should come right up with the Ace of Hearts, in order to clear partner's Spade suit and so partner can retain any entry cards that he may hold. Note the difference if East plays second hand low. Declarer will put up the Jack, and West will win with the King. The Spade will be continued, and declarer will refuse the trick. Now when the Spades are established West will have no entry card.

The general principle of defense is as follows: When your partner has opened a long suit at No Trump, which he is obviously trying to establish, you should rush in full speed, using every possible effort to win a trick early in the play in order to clear your partner's suit while he still holds entry cards.

In the above example, if East had held the K 9 of Hearts instead of the A 9, he should still play the King of Hearts, in the hope that it will hold the trick. There is really no danger in this play, since if the declarer has the A Q, the King was doomed from the beginning.

Second hand should sometimes play high when an honor card can be captured.

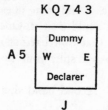

KQ743

Dummy
A 5 | W   E
Declarer

J

Declarer leads the Jack. West should win with the Ace. It is better to capture an honor with your Ace. If you duck, you will find yourself placing your Ace on the deuce next time. The complete holding is as follows:

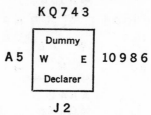

KQ743

Dummy
A 5 | W   E | 10 9 8 6
Declarer

J 2

If you duck the first trick, your side is limited to one trick. If you take it, your partner still has a stopper.

Combinations

A somewhat advanced situation in which second hand should play high occurs in the following hand:

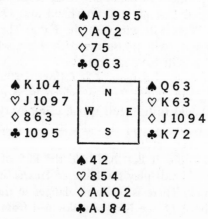

♠ A J 9 8 5
♡ A Q 2
◇ 7 5
♣ Q 6 3

♠ K 10 4
♡ J 10 9 7
◇ 8 6 3
♣ 10 9 5

N
W   E
S

♠ Q 6 3
♡ K 6 3
◇ J 10 9 4
♣ K 7 2

♠ 4 2
♡ 8 5 4
◇ A K Q 2
♣ A J 8 4

South is playing 3 No Trump. West leads the Jack of Hearts, dummy plays the Queen, and East wins and returns the suit. Declarer ducks the second round and is forced to win the third round with the Ace. He returns to his hand with a Diamond and leads the 2 of Spades. If West plays the 4, the 8 will no doubt be played from dummy and East will win with the Queen. Declarer will subsequently finesse the Jack of Spades and bring in the entire suit. West's proper play is the King of Spades. This prevents the declarer from running the suit. The play appears to be drastic but in fact is not so, inasmuch as declarer almost certainly does not have the Queen of Spades. If he does, there is really no chance to defeat the contract. There is the further chance that declarer will think you are false-carding from the K Q 4 and may permit you to hold the trick, subsequently finessing the Jack of Spades. This will result in the complete collapse of the hand.

Covering honors

We are all familiar with the old adage "Cover an honor with an honor," which means that whenever an honor card is led by the declarer or dummy and you are in second position holding a higher honor, you should cover the one played by the opponent. This would appear to contradict the other bromide, "Second hand low." As in most other departments of play, there is no such thing as *always* or *never*. If you always cover an honor with an honor you will lose a great many tricks. It is important to understand why the opponent's honor should be covered. Put briefly, it is this: If you do not cover the honor, it is apt to win a trick. If you do cover, you will force the opponents to play two of their high cards on the same trick. There is the further and more important consideration that by forcing them to play two honors on that trick you may build up a later trick for either your partner or yourself. Each case must be decided by the particular situation, but it is wise to decide quickly, so as to avoid giving away information by hesitation. When it appears that an honor will soon be led, make up your mind in advance and be ready when the declarer plays that card. The simplest case is as follows:

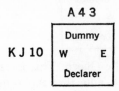

You are West. South, the declarer, leads the Queen. Obviously you must cover with the King, forcing the Ace and converting both your Jack and 10 into winners.

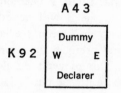

South leads the Queen. Here you cover with the King, forcing the declarer to play the Ace and Queen on the same trick. You may not profit by this procedure if the declarer has the Jack and 10 as well, but, on the other hand, you will not lose. You will build up a trick if it happens that your partner has the Jack or the 10. This time, therefore, you are covering not to promote your own cards but to promote some card that your partner might have. It will do you no good to retain the King, for you know perfectly well that the Queen will win the trick if you do not cover. The complete holding might be as follows:

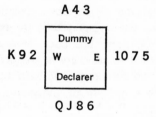

In which case you actually have gained nothing by covering the Queen, but, on the other hand, you have lost nothing. If you cover the Jack when it is played, declarer will have to give up a trick in the suit.

These examples have been relatively simple. There is one, however, which is more difficult to judge. Take the following holding:

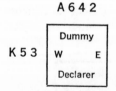

South, the declarer, leads the Queen. This is apparently the same situation as the one above, but note that this time you do not have the 9. The proper procedure in this case will depend upon the type of player who is declarer. If he is a sound player, you may depend upon it when he leads the Queen that he also has the Jack. Therefore it will do no good to cover the Queen, and you should wait for the Jack to be led. An inferior player, however, might lead the Queen when he does not have the Jack, in which case the better procedure is to cover.

The objection to covering the Queen against a good player will appear from the following diagram:

A 6 4 2

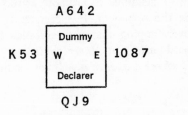

K 5 3

10 8 7

Q J 9

Notice that if you cover the Queen, dummy will win with the Ace and subsequently finesse the 9, losing no tricks in the suit. However, if you refuse to cover the Queen, but wait and cover the Jack, your partner's 10 will subsequently prove to be a winner.

Notice that in the combinations just under consideration the dummy has been to your left and the closed hand has led first. Let us take the other situation where the dummy is at your right, as follows:

Q 6 2

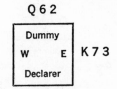

K 7 3

The Queen is led. The proper procedure is to cover with the King. You know that your King is lost in any event, and you hope that partner has, if not the Jack, at least the 10. The complete holding may be as follows:

Q 6 2

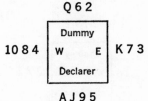

10 8 4

K 7 3

A J 9 5

Notice that failure to cover the Queen will result in declarer's making all the tricks.

Q J 4

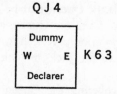

K 6 3

When dummy leads the Queen, you should not cover, because the the only card you can hope to promote at this time is the Jack, and that is held by the opponent. If subsequently the Jack is led, then you should cover, hoping that partner holds the 10. Which brings us to this general principle: *Never cover a sequence of honors until the lowest card of the sequence is led.* For example:

Q J 10 2

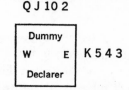

K 5 4 3

When dummy leads the Queen, do not cover. When the Jack is continued, also refuse to cover, because there is no card that you can positively develop for partner. By covering, you can lose a trick if the complete holding were as follows:

Q J 10 7

9 8 2 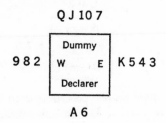 K 5 4 3

A 6

To repeat: *Never cover the first time if it is just as convenient to cover the second time or the third.*

J 10 2

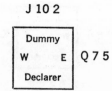

Q 7 5

The Jack is led from dummy. Do not cover. Here the rule not to cover a sequence of honors applies. If subsequently the 10 is led, that should be covered, with the hope that partner has the 9. Notice how badly the cover will result if the complete holding were as follows:

J 10 2

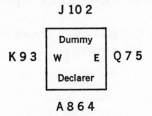

K 9 3

Q 7 5

A 8 6 4

If you cover the Jack with the Queen, your side will take only one trick. If you wait, your partner will win the first trick with the King and when you subsequently cover the 10 your partner will win another trick with the 9.

It is a good general doctrine not to cover an honor unless you have in your mind the possibility that your partner holds a certain card which can be promoted.

Therefore do not cover an honor without making a wish. For example:

A J 3

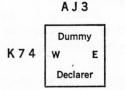

K 7 4

South, the declarer, leads the 10. If you play low, it is probable that the declarer intends to duck in dummy and your partner will probably win with the Queen. That will be your side's last trick, because subsequently, no doubt, your King will be finessed. The proper play is to cover, and as you do so make a wish that your partner holds the Queen 9 and another card. Let us see how this will work:

A J 3

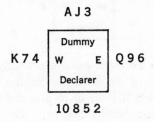

K 7 4

Q 9 6

10 8 5 2

K*

Notice if you fail to cover the 10, your side will win only one trick, but if the 10 is covered, declarer must win with the Ace and your partner's Queen and 9 will both be winners.

The above considerations do not apply as broadly when the suit in question is trump. Partner is then less apt to have any strength in the suit.

Where you can see that your honor cannot be captured, it will be apparent that a cover is not in order.

For example:

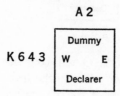

A 2

K 6 4 3

Dummy
W   E
Declarer

Assuming the contract to be No Trump, you know that your King cannot be captured. Therefore, when South leads the Queen, you must not cover. This will, of course, give the declarer the occasional opportunity to fool you by leading the Queen when he does not really have the Jack, but the chances of the occurrence are so remote that for all practical purposes it should be disregarded.

A good general plan to remember is that you should cover when the dummy leads an honor that is not part of a sequence and you are second hand containing an honor which you know cannot win a trick in any event.

To the rule that you never cover a sequence of honors there is an exception—that is when you have just two of the suit. The reason is that the next time you may be forced to place your honor on a small card.

For example:

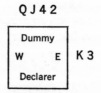

Q J 4 2

Dummy
W   E   K 3
Declarer

When the Queen is led from dummy normally we do not cover a sequence of honors, but if we duck, the declarer may lead the deuce the next time, which would force us to play the King. Therefore the cover is proper. The complete holding may be:

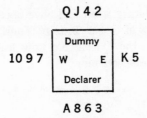

Q J 4 2

10 9 7 | Dummy |
           | W   E | K 5
           | Declarer |

A 8 6 3

In the combinations just considered for covering we had in mind principally the side suits. When the question of trumps is involved there may be other considerations, and many times where the cover might ordinarily be proper it would be otherwise if the suit led were trumps, because the bidding may have indicated to you that your partner could not possibly have a card which would be promoted by your cover. For example: Suppose the declarer had bid Spades several times, showing a long suit.

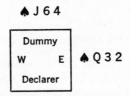

♠ J 6 4

| Dummy |
| W   E | ♠ Q 3 2
| Declarer |

You are East. When the Jack is led and you contemplate covering you must make a wish, and that wish would be that your partner holds the 10 and two others, but this is impossible, because that would give the declarer only a four-card suit and he would not have bid the suit several times. Therefore declarer must have at least five or six, which would give your partner either one or two. Your cover cannot gain. If your partner has the King, he will make it in any event. If he has the 10, it will fall too soon to be a winner. There is the bare possibility that your partner has the lone King. The complete holding will then have been as follows:

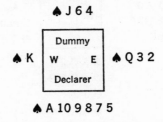

♠ J 6 4

♠ K | Dummy |
        | W   E | ♠ Q 3 2
        | Declarer |

♠ A 10 9 8 7 5

In the next hand, you are West and have opened the 10 of Spades against South's contract of 3 No Trump. Your partner plays the 8, and declarer wins with the Queen. He now leads the Jack of Diamonds. What card should you play?

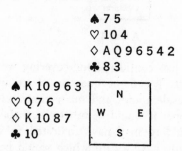

♠ 7 5
♡ 10 4
◇ A Q 9 6 5 4 2
♣ 8 3

♠ K 10 9 6 3
♡ Q 7 6
◇ K 10 8 7
♣ 10

The bidding has proceeded as shown below:

SOUTH	NORTH
1 Club	1 Diamond
1 Heart	2 Diamonds
2 No Trump	3 No Trump

The answer is, if you are playing against anyone but a most inferior player, a low Diamond. The reason is that if declarer has any knowledge of card combinations he will permit your King of Diamonds to hold if you cover, and your partner will definitely show out on this lead. Declarer, having bid No Trump enthusiastically, surely has two Diamonds. Now when East shows out, the declarer will be able to finesse the 9 on the next round and pick up the entire suit. The complete holding is as follows:

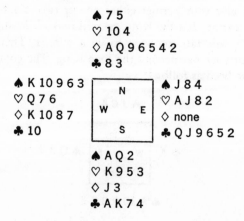

♠ 7 5
♡ 10 4
◇ A Q 9 6 5 4 2
♣ 8 3

♠ K 10 9 6 3
♡ Q 7 6
◇ K 10 8 7
♣ 10

♠ J 8 4
♡ A J 8 2
◇ none
♣ Q J 9 6 5 2

♠ A Q 2
♡ K 9 5 3
◇ J 3
♣ A K 7 4

You are West defending against South's contract of 4 Spades. The Jack of Diamonds is opened, won in dummy, and the trump Ace driven out. What is your proper lead?

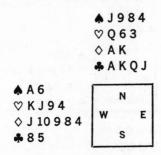

♠ J 9 8 4
♡ Q 6 3
◇ A K
♣ A K Q J

♠ A 6
♡ K J 9 4
◇ J 10 9 8 4
♣ 8 5

It is apparent that your side has no more tricks in Spades, Diamonds, or Clubs. Obviously, therefore, you must shift to a Heart, but which Heart? The proper card is the Jack. If declarer has the Ace, it makes no difference, but if your partner has the Ace and not the 10, a low Heart lead will permit declarer to win one trick in that suit.

The complete holding is as follows:

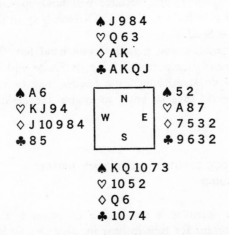

♠ J 9 8 4
♡ Q 6 3
◇ A K
♣ A K Q J

♠ A 6
♡ K J 9 4
◇ J 10 9 8 4
♣ 8 5

♠ 5 2
♡ A 8 7
◇ 7 5 3 2
♣ 9 6 3 2

♠ K Q 10 7 3
♡ 10 5 2
◇ Q 6
♣ 10 7 4

To the general principle that second hand should play low there is one outstanding exception. When the opponents are playing a No Trump contract and your partner opens his longest suit, it is essential for you to assist him in its establishment. It is your duty to win tricks as quickly as possible, in order to establish his suit before his entry cards are taken away from him.

For example:

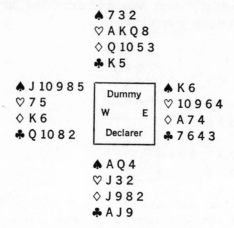

♠ 7 3 2
♡ A K Q 8
◇ Q 10 5 3
♣ K 5

♠ J 10 9 8 5   ♠ K 6
♡ 7 5   ♡ 10 9 6 4
◇ K 6   ◇ A 7 4
♣ Q 10 8 2   ♣ 7 6 4 3

Dummy
W   E
Declarer

♠ A Q 4
♡ J 3 2
◇ J 9 8 2
♣ A J 9

You are East. South is playing 3 No Trump. West leads the Jack of Spades, and your King falls to declarer's Ace. The dummy is entered with the Queen of Hearts and a small Diamond led. You must win this trick in a hurry, in order to clear the Spade suit for your partner. Upon a Spade return, declarer will hold up and West will clear the suit. He now has the King of Diamonds as an entry to cash the setting tricks in Spades.

Note the difference if you played second hand low. The Jack of Diamonds will force your partner's King. A Spade will be returned, and declarer will duck. Although the Spades may be cleared, your partner will have no card of entry to enable the cashing of these tricks.

Maintaining communication with partner at No Trump

Where a defender is attempting to establish a suit at No Trump, it is important for him to bear in mind that unless he has a card of entry the long suit will be worthless even when it becomes established. Partner may be able to obtain the lead but will have none of the suit to return to the opening leader. In such cases it is vital for the opening leader to play the hand in such a manner that partner will retain a card of that suit with which to communicate after the suit is established.

For example:

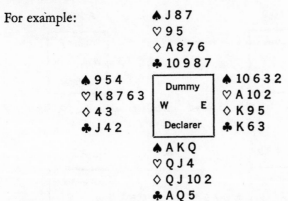

```
                  ♠ J 8 7
                  ♡ 9 5
                  ◇ A 8 7 6
                  ♣ 10 9 8 7
   ♠ 9 5 4      ┌─────────┐      ♠ 10 6 3 2
   ♡ K 8 7 6 3  │ Dummy   │      ♡ A 10 2
   ◇ 4 3        │ W     E │      ◇ K 9 5
   ♣ J 4 2      │ Declarer│      ♣ K 6 3
                └─────────┘
                  ♠ A K Q
                  ♡ Q J 4
                  ◇ Q J 10 2
                  ♣ A Q 5
```

South is the declarer at a contract of 3 No Trump. West leads the
6 of Hearts. East wins with the Ace and returns the 10. Declarer
plays the Jack. West can win this trick and clear the suit, but he
would never be able to cash the two long Hearts, because he has no
entry card, and, besides, partner will have no Heart left to return to
him. The proper procedure is for West to permit declarer's Jack to
hold the trick. One trick must be lost in any event. Now when East
obtains the lead with the King of Diamonds he will have a Heart
left to return to West and the setting tricks are cashed.

SECOND HAND PLAY QUIZ

What is the proper play in the defense of the following hands?

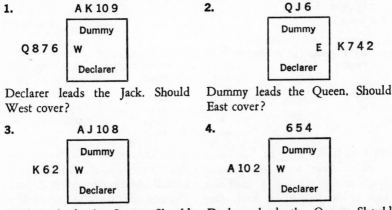

1.
```
            A K 10 9
          ┌─────────┐
 Q 8 7 6  │ Dummy   │
          │ W       │
          │ Declarer│
          └─────────┘
```
Declarer leads the Jack. Should
West cover?

2.
```
            Q J 6
          ┌─────────┐
          │ Dummy   │
          │       E │ K 7 4 2
          │ Declarer│
          └─────────┘
```
Dummy leads the Queen. Should
East cover?

3.
```
            A J 10 8
          ┌─────────┐
 K 6 2    │ Dummy   │
          │ W       │
          │ Declarer│
          └─────────┘
```
Declarer leads the Queen. Should
West cover?

4.
```
            6 5 4
          ┌─────────┐
 A 10 2   │ Dummy   │
          │ W       │
          │ Declarer│
          └─────────┘
```
Declarer leads the Queen. Should
West cover?

5.

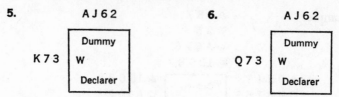

A J 6 2

Dummy
W
Declarer

K 7 3

Declarer leads the 10. Should West cover?

6.

A J 6 2

Dummy
W
Declarer

Q 7 3

Declarer leads the 10. Should West cover?

7.

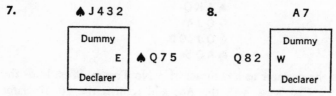

♠ J 4 3 2

Dummy
E   ♠ Q 7 5
Declarer

Declarer is playing a 4 Spade contract. Dummy leads the Jack. Should East cover?

8.

A 7

Dummy
W
Declarer

Q 8 2

Declarer leads the Jack. Should West cover?

In the following hands you are West, and the play has proceeded as indicated in each problem.

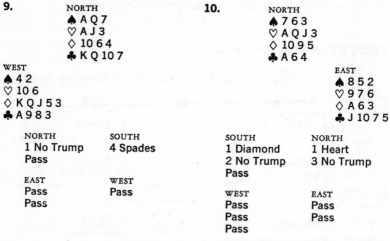

9.

```
              NORTH
              ♠ A Q 7
              ♡ A J 3
              ◇ 10 6 4
              ♣ K Q 10 7
WEST
♠ 4 2
♡ 10 6
◇ K Q J 5 3
♣ A 9 8 3
```

NORTH	SOUTH
1 No Trump	4 Spades
Pass	

EAST	WEST
Pass	Pass
Pass	

West leads the King of Diamonds which declarer wins. He plays a Spade to the Ace and a small one back to the Jack in his hand. Declarer now plays a small Club. What should West do?

10.

```
              NORTH
              ♠ 7 6 3
              ♡ A Q J 3
              ◇ 10 9 5
              ♣ A 6 4
                                    EAST
                                    ♠ 8 5 2
                                    ♡ 9 7 6
                                    ◇ A 6 3
                                    ♣ J 10 7 5
```

SOUTH	NORTH
1 Diamond	1 Heart
2 No Trump	3 No Trump
Pass	

WEST	EAST
Pass	Pass
Pass	Pass
Pass	

West leads the King of Spades. Declarer wins with the Ace and plays a small Heart to the Jack in dummy. Dummy now leads the 10 of Diamonds. What should East play?

11.

NORTH
♠ A 6
♡ A J 9 8 3
◇ 7 6 4
♣ K 8 4

WEST
♠ J 10 9 3 2
♡ K Q 4
◇ 8 5 3
♣ 6 5

SOUTH	WEST	NORTH	EAST
1 Diamond	Pass	1 Heart	Pass
1 No Trump	Pass	3 No Trump	Pass
Pass	Pass		

West leads the Jack of Spades. Dummy plays
low and East wins with the King and a
Spade is returned, driving out the Ace.
Dummy leads a small Diamond and declarer
puts in the 10 holding the trick. Now South
leads the deuce of Hearts. What should
West play?

ANSWERS TO SECOND HAND PLAY QUIZ

1. It would be silly for West to cover.
That would simply give declarer the
rest of the tricks.

**2. East should not cover the Queen,
but wait for the Jack.**
Never cover a sequence of honors until the last of the sequence is played.

3. West should cover.
Partner might have the 9 and three
others of the suit, which will act as
a stopper if the Queen and Ace are
used on the same trick.

4. West should duck.
If partner has the King, the defense
will take three tricks. If declarer has
it, it will still be subject to capture.
If West wins the Queen with the Ace,
South will be able to win a trick in
the suit if his original holding was
Q J x.

5. West should cover.
Partner might have the Queen, 9, and
a small one, which would develop

two tricks if West covers, because if
the 10 is permitted to ride, partner
will win with the Queen, and the
King will subsequently be captured
anyhow.

6. This is a difficult problem.
It might be that declarer has the King
and 10 and has led the 10 to coax you
to cover. If, however, you think your
partner has the King of that suit, you
should definitely cover in the hope
that he also has the 9 and another,
which would develop two tricks.

7. East should not cover.
Declarer has either four or five
Spades, which means that your partner has either one or two and your
cover cannot help him. In fact, he
might dislike a cover if his one happened to be the King.

8. West should not cover.
If East has the King, he will win the
trick, and since the Ace must be played

the next time, West will still retain his Queen. If South led from K J 10 9, a duck will still leave him to guess which defender has the Queen. If declarer has something like K J 6 5 2, the cover of the Queen would be proper, but from that combination he would hardly have led the Jack.

9. West should play a small Club.

Although declarer probably has a singleton and this will temporarily cost a trick, it is the only hope for setting the contract. The defenders must be able to cash two Diamonds and two Hearts, and if West takes the Ace of Clubs, South will have a ready parking place for his small Hearts.

The complete hand.

NORTH
♠ A Q 7
♡ A J 3
◇ 10 6 4
♣ K Q 10 7

WEST
♠ 4 2
♡ 10 6
◇ K Q J 5 3
♣ A 9 8 3

EAST
♠ 8 3
♡ K Q 9 8 5
◇ 8 2
♣ J 6 5 4

SOUTH
♠ K J 10 9 6 5
♡ 7 4 2
◇ A 9 7
♣ 2

10. The Ace.

West's lead marks him with at least K Q 10 of Spades so that that suit is ready to run. If East ducks, declarer may be able to sneak off with his ninth trick.

The complete hand.

NORTH
♠ 7 6 3
♡ A Q J 3
◇ 10 9 5
♣ A 6 4

WEST
♠ K Q J 9 4
♡ 8 5 2
◇ 7 2
♣ 9 8 3

EAST
♠ 8 5 2
♡ 9 7 6
◇ A 6 3
♣ J 10 7 5

SOUTH
♠ A 10
♡ K 10 4
◇ K Q J 8 4
♣ K Q 2

11. The 4.

Under no circumstances should West split his honors. That might give away the show. If South has the 10 of Hearts, West's play will not cost anything, but if East has the 10 he will probably make it if West plays low. South is almost certain to finesse West for that card. When East gets in, another Spade lead will drive out the Queen, and West will still retain a Heart entry to run his now established suit.

The complete hand.

NORTH
♠ A 6
♡ A J 9 8 3
◇ 7 6 4
♣ K 8 4

WEST
♠ J 10 9 3 2
♡ K Q 4
◇ 8 5 3
♣ 6 5

EAST
♠ K 8 5
♡ 10 7 6
◇ K 9 2
♣ Q J 10 2

SOUTH
♠ Q 7 4
♡ 5 2
◇ A Q J 10
♣ A 9 7 3

13.   Signals

THERE IS a tendency on the part of a great many casual players to pay no attention to the cards being played, except when they are winning tricks. By such practice they lose many opportunities to score points. Bridge is a partnership game, and during the defense of a hand the partnership angle is extremely important. You should try to make every play and every card have a special meaning. Sometimes, even with a completely useless hand, you may be of great assistance to your partner by giving him information he may need to conduct the defense. Signals have something in common with traffic lights. They may be red, which say stop. They may be green, which say go ahead, or they may be yellow, which say hesitate. In the last instance the signaler is not quite sure.

It is to be borne in mind that even when a card cannot possibly win a trick it might tell an important story to partner. There should be no meaningless play in contract. A card played by you when not attempting to win a trick should state to partner at least your desire as to whether or not the suit should be led again by your side. You may be very anxious for its continuance, in which case an unnecessarily high card is played. You may be very anxious that it be discontinued, in which case the lowest possible card is played, or you may not be sure, in which case you might play a card that is not quite your lowest.

Your desire to have the suit continued may be for one of several reasons. You may wish to trump a subsequent round of the suit. You may wish to win a trick in that suit. You may wish your partner to force the declarer by the continuance of that suit, or you may occasionally wish to force the dummy to trump that particular suit. You may even desire the continuance of that suit because you fear your partner might make a damaging shift.

However, regardless of your reason, when you have expressed it, it is not for your partner to reason why, but for him to "do or die." Otherwise bridge is not his game and he should take up 500 or gin rummy.

One of the most effective means by which the defense conveys information is the "come-on" signal. The signal is made when not attempting to win a trick. The "come-on" signal is made on the defense by playing an *unnecessarily* high card. For example, if the King and then the Ace of a suit are led by the defender and his partner follows suit first with the 7 and then with the 5, that would complete the signal and would be the "come-on" message, because the 7 was an *unnecessarily* high card, since the normal procedure would be to play the low one first and then the higher one. The departure from the normal procedure is intended as a signal. The "come-on" signal suggests to partner the continuance of that suit. Discards in the ordinary manner, such as first the 5 and then the 7, suggest that a continuance of that suit is not desired.

It is to be noted that the high-low signal is used whenever you wish partner to "come on," and you may wish him to "come on" for several reasons, as indicated above. When a defender fails to signal, there is the suggestion that he wishes some other suit led. It is not a command, but the opening leader should think twice before continuing a suit in the face of such discards by partner.

A signal may be given by a defender, not only on the lead by his partner, but also when the declarer is playing a suit. Here again the play of an unnecessarily high card suggests the desire that partner lead that suit if he gets in.

The play of the deuce or of any card which the leader can read as being the lowest assumes that partner does not wish that suit led. This may be told although partner has bid a suit.

Suppose your partner has bid Spades and you led the Ace. He follows suit with the deuce. It is quite obvious to you that he must have been able to spare some higher card when he bid the suit. Therefore it must be a violent message to you to lead some other suit even though he bid Spades.

If a defender is extremely anxious to have the suit continued, he should play the highest card he can afford for the purpose.

There is a tendency on the part of some players to say arbitrarily that a 6 or better is a come-on signal. This is unwise. You cannot help the cards that have been dealt to you. The 7 might be a discouraging card and a 4 might be an encouraging card, depending on the cards that have been dealt to you.

If partner leads the Ace and you urgently desire the suit continued, assuming that you hold the K 8 6 2, you should signal with the 8 rather than the 6, because your signal will then be more emphatic. If you signal with the 6, it might be understood by partner but there might be a doubt in his mind, whereas a signal with the 8 is more apt to impress him.

When you want a suit led and are playing with a mediocre or inattentive partner, it is better to shout rather than to whisper. That is, make your signals as violent as you reasonably can. He may not notice the mild or subtle signals. He may pay attention if you drop a 10.

Signaling at No Trump

Signaling at No Trump is slightly different from signaling at a suit declaration. The distinction must be borne in mind during this discussion. A simple illustration of an encouraging signal at No Trump is the following:

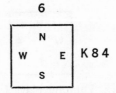

Declarer is playing No Trump. West leads the Queen. What card should East play? The answer is definitely the 8. Your partner is leading from either the Q J 10 or the Q J 9, and you must encourage him to continue the suit. If you play the 4, your partner will not know where the remaining cards are and may fail to continue the suit. The complete holding may be as follows:

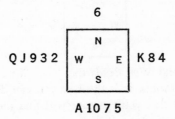

Another illustration:

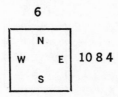

West leads the Queen. East should play the 8. Partner's lead is from the Q J 9, and as your partnership contains all the cards except the Ace and King your partner should be encouraged to continue the suit. Another example:

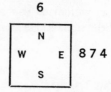

West leads the Queen. East should play the 4. He does not wish to give West any undue encouragement to continue the suit. If West's suit is solid, such as the Q J 10 9, he will not need encouragement and will go ahead anyhow.

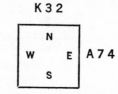

West leads the Jack. Dummy plays low. East should play the 7. If he plays the Ace, it permits declarer to win both the King and the Queen. The Jack forces declarer's Queen, and the Ace subsequently captures the King. However, partner must be encouraged to continue, and the 7 will provide that encouragement.

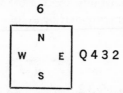

It is No Trump and West leads the Jack. What card should East play? The 4 by all means. It is the best you can do in the way of a signal, and you trust that your partner will find the 3 and 2 missing and suspect you of holding one of them.

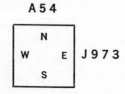

West leads the King and dummy plays low. What card should East play? The answer is the 9, violently calling for a continuance of the suit.

A 4 2

	N	
W		E
	S	

9 8 5 3

West plays the King. Dummy plays low. What card should you play as East? If partner has led from K Q J, you wish to encourage a continuation. If he has led from K Q 10 7, it would be dangerous for him to continue with a small card, for declarer would have J 6. Inasmuch as you are undecided, you should take no definite position. Do not signal violently for a continuation by playing the 8, nor should you shout discouragement by playing the 3. Rather, you ought to say, "Partner, I am not sure." This message you may convey by a temporizing discard of the 5. It is up to partner to decode your message. He can probably tell that the 5 is not your lowest, and should realize that you are in some doubt. He may then be resourceful enough to realize that the holding which would place you in doubt would be four small, because if you had the Jack you would surely say, "Come on." If you had three small ones, you would certainly shout, "Whoa." He should therefore lead the Queen, which will drop the Ace and Jack together. The complete holding is as follows:

A 4 2

K Q 10 7
	N	
W		E
	S	
9 8 5 3

J 6

5 3

	N	
W		E
	S	

9 6 4 2

You are East defending against a No Trump contract. West leads the King. You are not sure whether you wish your partner to continue the suit or not. If your partner has a complete sequence, he will continue it even though your discard is discouraging. If he has a holding such as A K J 7, you certainly do not wish him to continue the suit. Therefore, with this holding, you should play the 4. When partner notices that the 2 is missing he may realize that your discard says, "I'm not quite sure."

Signals must not be given indiscriminately merely to show high cards. They must be given to suggest leads. In other words, if I should signal with the 7 of Spades, I would not merely be telling my partner that I have the Ace of Spades, let us say. I would be saying, "Partner, please lead Spades for some reason which I know best. I may not even have the winning Spade, but desire that suit to be led."

A signal may be given even on a suit that is being led by the opponents. For example, if the dummy leads a low card, you are second hand and hold A 7 3 but do not wish to put up the Ace, you should play the 7. This will serve as a signal to partner that you have something important in the suit.

Playing against a 4 Spade contract, you are East.

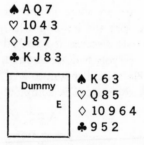

♠ A Q 7
♡ 10 4 3
◇ J 8 7
♣ K J 8 3

Dummy E

♠ K 6 3
♡ Q 8 5
◇ 10 9 6 4
♣ 9 5 2

Partner leads the King of Hearts. You should signal with the 8, because you wish your partner to continue with three rounds of that suit. But, playing against a Club contract, suppose the holding were as follows:

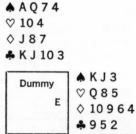

♠ A Q 7 4
♡ 10 4
◇ J 8 7
♣ K J 10 3

Dummy E

♠ K J 3
♡ Q 8 5
◇ 10 9 6 4
♣ 9 5 2

Your partner leads the King of Hearts. You must not signal with the 8, because when your partner follows with the Ace you will have

to play the 5 and your partner will think that you desire a third
round of the suit, which is exactly what you do not wish, because the
declarer may possibly be out of the suit and ruff in the dummy and
discard a loser from the closed hand. Your proper play is, therefore,
the 5 of Hearts. You do not signal to show the Queen. You signal
because you wish a suit continued for three rounds.

Discards

Signals may be given when not following suit—that is, when
discarding. Various artificial methods of signaling have from time to
time been devised, such as an even-number card indicating one thing
and an odd-number card another. None of these has passed the test of
experience, and common-sense methods of signaling have survived.

The discard of a low card from weakness is sound. If you have
some suit in which you are not interested and you have a low card,
then there is no objection to discarding it.

When in discarding you play first a high card and then a low card,
that is drawing your partner's attention to that suit and is calling for
its lead. To illustrate: If you first discard the 3 and then the 5, that
indicates you have nothing in that suit; but if you first discard the 5
and then the 3, that would draw your partner's attention to that suit
and request its lead.

It is apparent that a signal by discarding will shorten your strong
suit. If you do not desire to do this—as, for example, at No Trump,
where you wish to retain a number of cards in your best suit—you
may signal by inference. Let us suppose, for example, Spades are
being run, to which you cannot follow. You wish Hearts led by your
partner. You may indicate this by discarding a low Club (stating, "I
do not wish Clubs") and then a low Diamond (stating, "I do not
wish Diamonds"), and by this time your partner should be able to
figure out that you prefer to have Hearts led.

Spades are being led by the opponents at No Trump. You have,
for example:

♠ none   ♡ A K 10 8 6   ◇ 9 6 4 3   ♣ 8 7 5 2

You would like to signal for a Heart lead but you do not wish to
waste one of your Hearts by playing the 8. You may signal for a
Heart lead inferentially by first discarding the 2 of Clubs and then
the 3 of Diamonds. If you do not wish either Clubs or Diamonds, it
is probable that you desire a Heart.

However, if there is an emergency and you want to be quite sure that your partner leads Hearts, you should not signal by inference but should discard the 8 of that suit. This is especially true if you happen to be playing with a partner who is not particularly alert. In fact, if the emergency is great enough, you should discard the 10. He might not notice the 8.

An illustration of a case in which partner desires a continuance of the suit because he wants the dummy to ruff is provided by the following hand:

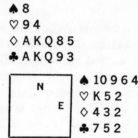

    ♠ 8
    ♡ 9 4
    ◊ A K Q 8 5
    ♣ A K Q 9 3

                    ♠ 10 9 6 4
                    ♡ K 5 2
                    ◊ 4 3 2
                    ♣ 7 5 2

South is declarer at a contract of 6 Hearts, and West leads the King of Spades. What should East play? East knows that the King of Hearts may be captured on a finesse, but if the Spade is continued and one of dummy's trumps must be used early, declarer will not be able to come through the King of Trumps twice. He should therefore signal for a continuance of the Spades and should play the 10, a violent signal to his partner. This 10 of Spades does not mean *maybe*. It means *positively!* Note the difference if West fails to continue with a Spade.

The complete hand is as follows:

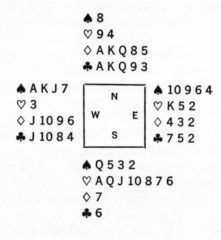

                    ♠ 8
                    ♡ 9 4
                    ◊ A K Q 8 5
                    ♣ A K Q 9 3

    ♠ A K J 7   ♠ 10 9 6 4
    ♡ 3   ♡ K 5 2
    ◊ J 10 9 6   ◊ 4 3 2
    ♣ J 10 8 4   ♣ 7 5 2

                    ♠ Q 5 3 2
                    ♡ A Q J 10 8 7 6
                    ◊ 7
                    ♣ 6

It has been shown that a signal can be made with an unnecessarily high card. The word *unnecessarily* is important, because sometimes we have actually no high card. If we have A 4 2 and wish the suit continued, we are obliged to play the 4. It is not actually a high card, but in point of fact it is an *unnecessarily* high card because we have the 2. At the time it is played partner may not recognize it, but when the 2 subsequently appears the signal will become apparent.

When, therefore, you are the defender and you win the first trick and your partner follows with a card like the 4, look around the table for the 3 and the 2. If neither one of them appears, there is the chance that your partner holds one of them and the 4 may be the beginning of a signal. Or it may be that the declarer is deliberately concealing the 3 and the 2 to give you the impression that your partner is signaling. In that case you will sometimes have to guess, but more often than not, if the 3 and 2 are missing, the chances are that your partner has begun an echo.

You are West playing against a Spade contract. You have, for example:

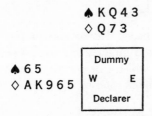

♠ K Q 4 3
◊ Q 7 3

♠ 6 5
◊ A K 9 6 5

Dummy
W   E
Declarer

You lead the King of Diamonds, and partner follows with the 4. Declarer plays the 8. What would your next play be? Is there any danger that the Ace of Diamonds will be trumped? The answer is no. It all depends on who has the 2. If your partner has it, the 4 is the beginning of a signal. If the declarer has it, then your Ace will not be trumped.

Signaling with honors

There is a slogan that reads "Never signal with a honor." Like so many others, this is only a partial truth. A better way to state the principle is, "Never signal with a card that might later on take a trick." When, however, your honor card cannot possibly win a trick and must fall in any event, there is no objection to signaling with it. For example:

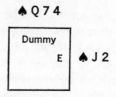

♠ Q 7 4

Hearts are trumps, and West leads the King of Spades. What should East play? He is anxious to ruff the third round, and his Jack cannot possibly win a trick. Therefore he should signal with it. Partner will continue with the Ace, and East will ruff the third round. If East should play the 2 on the first trick, West might lead some other suit and the Spade ruff would be lost.

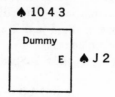

♠ 10 4 3

West leads the King of Spades, Hearts are trumps. East must not play the Jack, because that card might win a trick. Partner's lead may be from the King Queen, in which case the Jack could not be spared. The complete holding might be as follows:

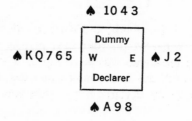

♠ A 9 8

The Queen is never used as a signal. If, therefore, the defender follows suit with the Queen, it must be a singleton or that player must also have the Jack.

It is a definitely accepted convention that against a suit contract, if a player leads the King of a suit and partner follows with the Queen, the opening leader must absolutely underlead at trick two and in no case lead his Ace.

An illustration of this principle is provided in the hand which follows:

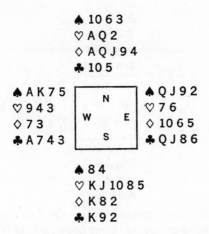

♠ 10 6 3
♡ A Q 2
◇ A Q J 9 4
♣ 10 5

♠ A K 7 5   ♠ Q J 9 2
♡ 9 4 3   ♡ 7 6
◇ 7 3   ◇ 10 6 5
♣ A 7 4 3   ♣ Q J 8 6

♠ 8 4
♡ K J 10 8 5
◇ K 8 2
♣ K 9 2

South is the declarer at a contract of 4 Hearts. West leads the King of Spades. East must realize that in order to defeat the contract West will have to have the Ace of Clubs (West has bid a Spade). Therefore East plays the Queen of Spades on the opening lead. West is obligated to lead a low one, which East wins with the Jack, and the Queen of Clubs comes through, defeating the contract.

As for the rule that one must not signal with honors, an exception must be noted in the case where you are deliberately unblocking for for your partner at No Trump. It is very vital not to let your high cards block partner's suit.

Trump echo

When a defending player follows high-low in trumps, it is a signal to his partner which states as follows: "Partner, I have three trumps and I can ruff something." The trump echo can also be applied when trumps have not been led but when one of the defenders is actually ruffing. When holding only two trumps, the defender should ruff with his lowest trump. When holding three or more trumps, the first trick should be ruffed with a card that is not the lowest, and the second one should be ruffed with the lowest. This will signal your partner that you have another trump. It may be important for your partner to know this, because he will not know whether to give you a third ruff or not. The following hand illustrates this principle:

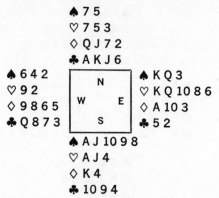

You are West. Your partner opens the bidding with 1 Heart. South plays the hand at Spades. Your opening lead is the 9 of Hearts, which draws your partner's Queen, the trick going to declarer's Ace. Entry to dummy is gained through a Club lead to enable declarer to lead trumps toward his own hand. Your partner "splits his equals" by playing his Queen of Spades, the trick being won by declarer's Ace. The declarer next proceeds to clear his trump suit by letting your partner win with the King of Spades.

Your three-trump echo (first playing your 4, then your 2) shows East that you still hold a trump. Your play of his suit (9, then 2, when he leads out his Heart King) clearly discloses that you hold no more Hearts. Consequently your partner will lead a third round of Hearts for you to trump, giving your side a third trick; your partner's Ace of Damonds will win a fourth trick.

Unless you use the three-trump echo, your partner may lose game by laying down his Diamond Ace and leading a second round of that suit, hoping that you hold the King. In any event, your use of the echo makes your partner's proper play perfectly clear. Another example:

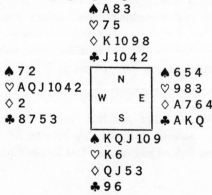

You are West. South is playing 4 Spades doubled. You open the singleton Diamond. East wins and returns the 4 of Diamonds, which you ruff with the 2 of Spades. A Club lead is won by East's Queen and another Diamond is ruffed with the 7 of Spades. When East is back in with the King of Clubs he knows there is no use trying to give you another ruff, because your play of the trumps shows you have no more. Therefore he leads a Heart, and you take two more tricks. If you held three trumps, you would have ruffed first with the 7 and then with the 2.

Echoing with an honor

When partner opens a fourth best at No Trump and dummy plays a high card which you cannot beat, if you have some mild support in the suit you may convey the information on the first trick by the play of your second best card. If your holding includes two adjacent honors, it is customary to signal with your highest card. This serves the dual purpose of giving advice and also unblocking for future plays of the suit.

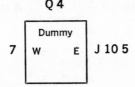

You are East. Partner opens the 7 and dummy plays the Queen. You should follow with the Jack, and partner will know that you have the 10. Furthermore, your play will prevent the possible blocking of the suit. Similarly, if you held J 9 5, your proper play would be the 9. But if you held 6 3 2, you should play the 2, which would indicate to partner that you are not interested in the suit.

Special high-low signal at No Trump

There is a specialized use of the high-low signal at No Trump which occurs under the following condition: The declarer is playing No Trump, and the dummy has the long suit with no side entries. One of the defenders holds the Ace of the dummy's long suit and he wishes to hold off until such time as the declarer has no more of the suit. How long should he hold up?

The defender wishes naturally to take his Ace at exactly the time when declarer has no more of that suit. It would be disastrous to take it too soon, leaving declarer with a card of that suit, and it might be fatal to hold up too long, for declarer might in this manner sneak away with his contract-fulfilling trick. The number of cards held by declarer may be determined by the following signals.

If the player who does not have the Ace follows suit in regular order, it shows that he has three. If the player follows suit in the reverse order—that is, high-low—it shows that he has two. Occasionally that player may have four, but that is rare. In such case he must not play his lowest. In other words, an ambiguity arises, and partner will not be sure whether it is four or two, but the bidding will usually make that clear. It will not very often be four in any event. An example follows:

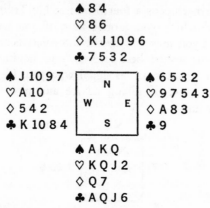

```
                   ♠ 8 4
                   ♡ 8 6
                   ◇ K J 10 9 6
                   ♣ 7 5 3 2
  ♠ J 10 9 7                        ♠ 6 5 3 2
  ♡ A 10          N                 ♡ 9 7 5 4 3
  ◇ 5 4 2      W     E              ◇ A 8 3
  ♣ K 10 8 4       S                ♣ 9
                   ♠ A K Q
                   ♡ K Q J 2
                   ◇ Q 7
                   ♣ A Q J 6
```

South is the declarer at 3 No Trump. He wins the opening Spade lead and leads the Queen of Diamonds. When West plays the 2, East knows that he should hold up his Ace just once but not any more, because if declarer had three Diamonds, West would have only two and would therefore have started the high-low. If West has a singleton Diamond, so that he is helpless to signal, it makes no difference, because the declarer will have four and the holdup will do no good anyhow. Notice that if East would wait until the third round to take his Ace, the declarer would have enough tricks. Taking the Ace on the second round prevents declarer from fulfilling the contract.

When declarer is running a suit at No Trump, discarding finally becomes quite embarrassing, and it is extremely undesirable for both partners to hold the same suit. Early in the play, therefore, each player should indicate which suit he really has and the other partner should let go of that suit even though he has something important in it. If East discards a high Club, he is announcing that he has something in Clubs, and West therefore should not worry about that suit.

If West discards a high Diamond, he is announcing strength in that suit, and East should not bother to protect Diamonds. This avoids the common error of both partners' keeping the same suit and both discarding what they should have kept.

Make it a point not to discard until void of a suit if it appears that the declarer may have some guessing to do as to the location of the missing honors in that suit. For example:

♣ A J 6 2

♣ 5 4 | W | N

You are West. It is undesirable to let go a Club if there is some other discard to make. Declarer may require a finesse against the Queen, and your discard will "tip off" your partner's hand. Your partner might hold the Q 7 3 and declarer K 10 9 8. If you hold on doggedly to your two Clubs, he may suspect that you have the Queen. Another example:

```
              ♠ J 5 2
              ♡ K J 10
              ◇ K Q 9 4
              ♣ 7 5 3
♠ A 10 8 7 4      N       ♠ Q 9 3
♡ Q 5 3       W     E     ♡ 8 7 4 2
◇ 8 6 2           S       ◇ J 5
♣ K 2                     ♣ Q 10 9 4
              ♠ K 6
              ♡ A 9 6
              ◇ A 10 7 3
              ♣ A J 8 6
```

South is the declarer at a contract of 3 No Trump, having opened the bidding with 1 No Trump. West leads the 7 of Spades, and East's 9 forces declarer's King. The Diamonds are now run, and East must make two discards. He naturally must keep both Spades, and should refuse to discard a Heart but rather elect to throw two Clubs. This, on the surface, appears to be a very daring discard. Actually it is not so. The declarer surely has the Ace of Hearts and the Ace of Clubs. If he also has the King of Clubs he has nine top-card tricks. East's best chance, therefore, is that the declarer will misguess the

L

location of the Queen of Hearts. If East elects to discard Hearts, the guess will be a cinch.

Be very careful to avoid, if possible, discarding from a suit in which you have the same length as the dummy or a suit in which you have the same length that you suspect the declarer of holding in the closed hand. Take the following:

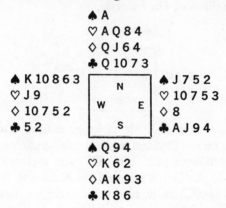

```
                 ♠ A
                 ♡ A Q 8 4
                 ◊ Q J 6 4
                 ♣ Q 10 7 3
♠ K 10 8 6 3                        ♠ J 7 5 2
♡ J 9              N                ♡ 10 7 5 3
◊ 10 7 5 2    W       E             ◊ 8
♣ 5 2             S                 ♣ A J 9 4
                 ♠ Q 9 4
                 ♡ K 6 2
                 ◊ A K 9 3
                 ♣ K 8 6
```

South is the declarer at a contract of 3 No Trump. West leads the 6 of Spades, and East plays the 7. As the declarer runs the Diamonds, East can afford to discard one Spade, or even two Spades, provided he lets go the Jack for unblocking purposes. His other discard must be from his good Club holding, but not from the Hearts. If the declarer has both the King and Jack of Hearts, nothing can stop 3 No Trump, but if partner has the Jack of Hearts, it is necessary for East to retain four Hearts in order to stop that suit.

A hand which illustrates the danger in discarding until void of a suit is the following:

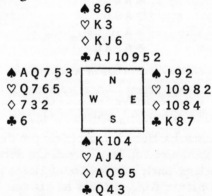

```
                 ♠ 8 6
                 ♡ K 3
                 ◊ K J 6
                 ♣ A J 10 9 5 2
♠ A Q 7 5 3                        ♠ J 9 2
♡ Q 7 6 5          N               ♡ 10 9 8 2
◊ 7 3 2       W       E            ◊ 10 8 4
♣ 6               S                ♣ K 8 7
                 ♠ K 10 4
                 ♡ A J 4
                 ◊ A Q 9 5
                 ♣ Q 4 3
```

South is playing 3 No Trump, and West leads the 5 of Spades. East's Jack forces the King. The declarer has a total of eight top-card tricks, with any number of extra tricks if the Club finesse succeeds. If, however, the Club finesse fails, the contract is immediately defeated. Declarer bided his time by cashing the King of Hearts and running off the four Diamonds. On the fourth Diamond, West thoughtlessly let go the 6 of Clubs because "it was no good to him." Declarer now led the Queen of Clubs, originally intending to finesse, but when West showed out, that play was naturally abandoned. Now a Spade threw West into the lead. He was able to cash four Spades but in the end had to lead up to declarer's Ace Jack of Hearts.

West could easily have spared a Heart discard in order to keep the 6 of Clubs, and there is a fair chance that he would have defeated the contract. It is true that declarer could still have made it by first cashing the Ace of Clubs, but it is doubtful whether he would have made that play without seeing the hands exposed.

Discarding partner's suit

After having led the highest of partner's suit, it is conventional to discard from the top down. For example: if you hold the 9 6 2 in a suit your partner has bid and you lead the 9 of that suit, the 6 should be played the next time and finally the 2. At this point partner will know that you have no more of the suit. This method of discarding is usually more important at a suit contract than it is at No Trump, but even at No Trump it may be very informative.

Discarding to Ace led at No Trump

Another convention which dates back to auction days is the one calling for your play of the highest card when partner leads the Ace at No Trump. You are unconditionally required to drop your highest card, though it be the King or Queen, unless the appearance of the dummy makes it evident that your play will cost a trick.

Suit-preference signal

The purpose of the suit-preference signal in playing against suit declarations is to eliminate the guess as to which of two suits partner should return if he obtains the lead. The statement "which of two suits" may not be very clear, but in actual play there is usually no doubt which two suits are involved. When partner obtains the lead his problem as to the correct return will almost never involve a choice of three suits. For the purpose of this discussion the trump suit is immediately eliminated, and the suit that is being led when the preference signal is being made does not count, which leaves for the player's consideration a choice between the other two suits. Which to lead will frequently be a guess, and the following convention is devised in an effort to remove the doubt.

The play of an unnecessarily high card *which obviously is not a come-on signal* asks partner to return the higher-ranking of the two plain suits.

Emphasis is placed on the phrase "which obviously is not a come-on signal" because numerous abuses have been committed by players who have recently learned to employ this convention. A signal still remains a signal. If you lead an Ace of Diamonds and partner follows with a very high card, it means that he wants you to continue Diamonds, not that he wishes you to shift to Spades. An illustration of the abuse follows:

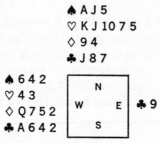

♠ A J 5
♡ K J 10 7 5
◇ 9 4
♣ J 8 7

♠ 6 4 2
♡ 4 3
◇ Q 7 5 2
♣ A 6 4 2

♣ 9

South is playing a Spade contract. West leads the Ace of Clubs, and partner plays the 9. I have heard many players say, "When you played a high Club, I thought you wanted a Heart shift through strength." This is absurd. The normal come-on signal applies here. Partner wants you to lead some more Clubs. How else can he tell you? The suit-preference convention would apply only if from the appearance of the dummy your common sense tells you that he cannot want a Club led.

Sometimes an ambiguity will arise, but not often. Bidding, combined with common sense, will usually furnish the solution to the problem.

A situation in which partner's signal cannot possibly be intended in the normal sense is the following:

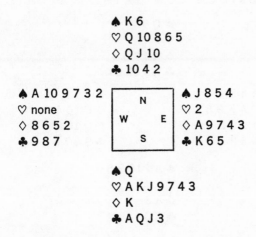

♠ K 6
♡ Q 10 8 6 5
◇ Q J 10
♣ 10 4 2

♠ A 10 9 7 3 2
♡ none
◇ 8 6 5 2
♣ 9 8 7

♠ J 8 5 4
♡ 2
◇ A 9 7 4 3
♣ K 6 5

♠ Q
♡ A K J 9 7 4 3
◇ K
♣ A Q J 3

South is the declarer at a contract of 6 Hearts. Spades have been bid and supported. West leads the Ace of Spades. Unless the Diamond Ace is cashed at this point, declarer will win the hand. West does not know whether to shift to the Diamonds or Clubs, but it is quite apparent to everyone at the table that a shift is in order, because nothing could possibly be gained by the Spade continuance. East's discard of the Jack of Spades indicates that a diamond shift should be made—the higher-ranking suit. If Clubs were desired, the 4 would be played. Notice this principle applies only when it is quite evident that another Spade lead is not desired. The Jack of Spades is not a normal come-on signal, but a suit-preference signal.

Normal signal

There are cases in which it might be that a Spade continuance would be logical. Then the signal would be interpreted in its normal sense. In the hand that follows South is playing 6 Spades. West leads the King of Hearts. It will be seen that another Heart lead will defeat the contract by forcing dummy to trump, and now East's King of Trumps cannot be picked up. East's discard of the 10 of Hearts should be regarded as a normal come-on signal and not as a suit-preference signal, because the appearance of the dummy does not make it clear that a shift is indicated. It is perfectly logical that East may wish dummy to trump a Heart. If dummy had a great many trumps it would be different. Then there could be no logical reason to wish dummy forced.

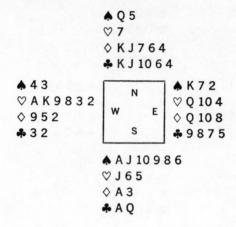

```
              ♠ Q 5
              ♡ 7
              ◇ K J 7 6 4
              ♣ K J 10 6 4
♠ 4 3                        ♠ K 7 2
♡ A K 9 8 3 2                ♡ Q 10 4
◇ 9 5 2                      ◇ Q 10 8
♣ 3 2                        ♣ 9 8 7 5
              ♠ A J 10 9 8 6
              ♡ J 6 5
              ◇ A 3
              ♣ A Q
```

Entry at No Trump

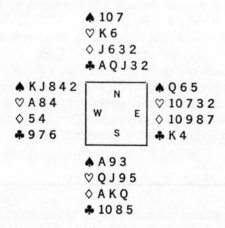

```
              ♠ 10 7
              ♡ K 6
              ◇ J 6 3 2
              ♣ A Q J 3 2
♠ K J 8 4 2                  ♠ Q 6 5
♡ A 8 4                      ♡ 10 7 3 2
◇ 5 4                        ◇ 10 9 8 7
♣ 9 7 6                      ♣ K 4
              ♠ A 9 3
              ♡ Q J 9 5
              ◇ A K Q
              ♣ 10 8 5
```

South is playing 3 No Trump. West leads the 4 of Spades. East wins with the Queen and returns the 6. South plays the 9, and West wins with the Jack. West has the option of knocking out the Ace with either the deuce or the King. It does not really matter. Since it does not matter, the choice of the card that West selects will be a signal to his partner advising what suit to return should East obtain the lead. His proper play is to drive out the Ace of Spades with the King. This is a signal to lead back the higher-ranking suit—Hearts rather than Diamonds. Notice that when declarer wins the Spade trick he will take the Club finesse. East will win with the King, and if he should return a Diamond, the contract would be fulfilled. West's suit-preference signal of the King of Spades makes it clear to East that he should return a Heart. The suit-preference signal applies here because West had a choice of cards to lead back. If it were necessary to lead back the King in order to surely force the Ace, then, of course, the suit-preference convention would not apply. Another example:

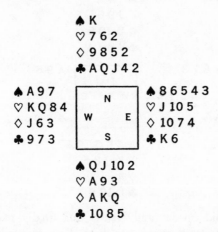

♠ K
♡ 7 6 2
◊ 9 8 5 2
♣ A Q J 4 2

♠ A 9 7   ♠ 8 6 5 4 3
♡ K Q 8 4   ♡ J 10 5
◊ J 6 3   ◊ 10 7 4
♣ 9 7 3   ♣ K 6

♠ Q J 10 2
♡ A 9 3
◊ A K Q
♣ 10 8 5

South is the declarer at a contract of 3 No Trump. West leads the 4 of Hearts. East follows with the 10 and is permitted to hold the trick. The Jack is continued, and declarer again ducks. A third round is led, and declarer wins with the Ace. West has remaining the King and Queen, and which one he drops is immaterial. Therefore he selects the one which will suggest to partner the suit in which he holds his entry. He follows with the King of Hearts. Partner knows that he has the Queen, and therefore he has made an unnatural discard. The suit-preference convention applies, and the higher-ranking suit is suggested to partner. Notice that when a Club finesse loses, the contract will be made unless East returns a Spade.

Ruffs

The most frequent application of the suit-preference convention is in obtaining ruffs. The situation is one in which you know your partner is about to trump your lead, and inasmuch as he will desire subsequent ruffs, he must know how to regain entry into your hand for the purpose of obtaining the desired ruffs. The size of the card which you lead for your partner to trump flashes the signal as to which suit he must return to you. If the card led is an unnecessarily high one, it suggests to partner a return of the higher-ranking of the two remaining side suits. If the card led to be ruffed is the lowest one, it suggests the return of the lower-ranking suit. As an example:

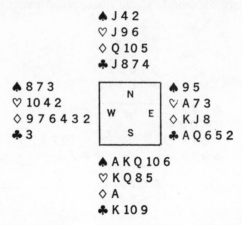

           ♠ J 4 2
           ♡ J 9 6
           ◊ Q 10 5
           ♣ J 8 7 4

♠ 8 7 3   ♠ 9 5
♡ 10 4 2   ♡ A 7 3
◊ 9 7 6 4 3 2   ◊ K J 8
♣ 3   ♣ A Q 6 5 2

           ♠ A K Q 10 6
           ♡ K Q 8 5
           ◊ A
           ♣ K 10 9

South has bid Spades and Hearts and finally plays the hand at 4 Spades. West leads the 3 of Clubs. East wins with the Ace and reads it as a singleton lead. East may return any Club he wishes, but when West ruffs the Club he will be in doubt as to the method of re-entering his partner's hand. Since Hearts have been bid, West will no doubt elect to lead a Diamond, and the contract will be easily fulfilled. East, therefore, must suggest to his partner to return a Heart, and this he does by returning the unnecessarily high Queen of Clubs. When West ruffs he knows he must lead a Heart, the higher-ranking of the two side suits. If East held the Ace of Diamonds, he would return the 2 of Clubs for his partner to ruff.

The use of the suit-preference convention may also be employed in an opening lead. In leading a suit that does not contain a complete sequence, it is customary to open with the fourth highest. If that fourth highest happens to be a deuce, the opening leader is marked with a four-card suit.

Let us suppose that your partner has opened the deuce of a suit in which you know from the bidding that he has more than four. It is apparent, therefore, that he is making an unnatural lead, and this unnatural lead must be interpreted as part of the suit-preference convention, intending to communicate to you the suggestion that he wishes the lowest-ranking suit returned. An illustration of this principle appears in the following hand:

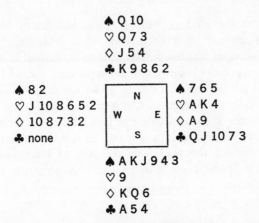

```
              ♠ Q 10
              ♡ Q 7 3
              ◇ J 5 4
              ♣ K 9 8 6 2
♠ 8 2                        ♠ 7 6 5
♡ J 10 8 6 5 2    N          ♡ A K 4
◇ 10 8 7 3 2   W     E       ◇ A 9
♣ none            S          ♣ Q J 10 7 3
              ♠ A K J 9 4 3
              ♡ 9
              ◇ K Q 6
              ♣ A 5 4
```

East has opened the bidding with 1 Club. South doubled, and West bid 1 Heart. South later became the declarer at 4 Spades.

West opened the 2 of Hearts, which East won with the King. He realized that his partner would not bid a four-card suit as a sign of weakness over the double. Therefore the lead of the 2 must have some other significance; namely, that a Club return was desired. East also realized that it was perfectly possible that his partner had six Hearts, in which case his Ace of Hearts would not be a re-entry. Therefore he showed his partner that the proper return was a Diamond by playing the 3 of Clubs instead of the Queen. This was ruffed by West, and even though his partner was marked with the Ace of Hearts, West followed the suit-preference convention and returned a Diamond, thus putting East in to give West another ruff. (It might be good policy for East to win the first lead with the Ace of Hearts, in order to give partner the impression that the King is held by South.)

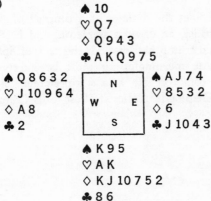

```
              ♠ 10
              ♡ Q 7
              ◇ Q 9 4 3
              ♣ A K Q 9 7 5
♠ Q 8 6 3 2                  ♠ A J 7 4
♡ J 10 9 6 4    N            ♡ 8 5 3 2
◇ A 8        W     E         ◇ 6
♣ 2             S            ♣ J 10 4 3
              ♠ K 9 5
              ♡ A K
              ◇ K J 10 7 5 2
              ♣ 8 6
```

L*

North opens the bidding with 1 Club, and South becomes the declarer at a contract of 5 Diamonds. West leads the 2 of Clubs, which is an obvious singleton. The Queen is played from dummy, and at this point East should make an unnatural discard in order to suggest to his partner how he can be given the lead in order to provide a ruff. Under the Queen of Clubs he should play the Jack. The bidding will make it evident that the Jack cannot be a singleton, so that it must be interpreted by partner as a suit-preference signal. When West obtains the lead with the Ace of Diamonds, he will know to lead a Spade, because of partner's unnecessarily high Club, rather than a Heart.

Directing a safe lead

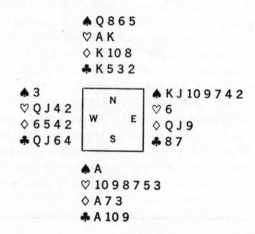

```
              ♠ Q 8 6 5
              ♡ A K
              ◊ K 10 8
              ♣ K 5 3 2
 ♠ 3                          ♠ K J 10 9 7 4 2
 ♡ Q J 4 2        N           ♡ 6
 ◊ 6 5 4 2    W       E       ◊ Q J 9
 ♣ Q J 6 4        S           ♣ 8 7
              ♠ A
              ♡ 10 9 8 7 5 3
              ◊ A 7 3
              ♣ A 10 9
```

South becomes the declarer at a contract of 4 Hearts. West leads the 3 of Spades, an obvious singleton, and East's 7 forces the Ace. On the second trump East discards the Jack of Spades. Since this would be otherwise meaningless, it must be interpreted not as a normal signal to come on, but as a suit-preference signal, meaning it is safe to lead Diamonds. Notice if West leads Clubs the hand can be made.

SIGNALS QUIZ

1.
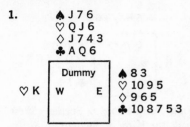

♠ J 7 6
♡ Q J 6
◊ J 7 4 3
♣ A Q 6

♡ K | Dummy   W   E |

♠ 8 3
♡ 10 9 5
◊ 9 6 5
♣ 10 8 7 5 3

South is playing 4 Spades. West leads the King of Hearts. What card should East play?

2.
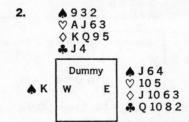

♠ 9 3 2
♡ A J 6 3
◊ K Q 9 5
♣ J 4

♠ K | Dummy   W   E |

♠ J 6 4
♡ 10 5
◊ J 10 6 3
♣ Q 10 8 2

South is playing 4 Hearts. West leads the King of Spades. What card should East play?

3.
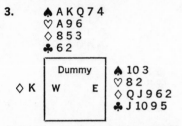

♠ A K Q 7 4
♡ A 9 6
◊ 8 5 3
♣ 6 2

◊ K | Dummy   W   E |

♠ 10 3
♡ 8 2
◊ Q J 9 6 2
♣ J 10 9 5

South is playing 4 Hearts. West leads the King of Diamonds. What should East play?

4.
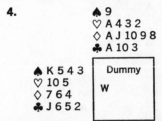

♠ 9
♡ A 4 3 2
◊ A J 10 9 8
♣ A 10 3

♠ K 5 4 3
♡ 10 5
◊ 7 6 4
♣ J 6 5 2

| Dummy   W |

South is playing 4 Spades, East having bid Hearts. West leads the 10 of Hearts, dummy plays the Ace, East the 7, and South the 6. When West wins the King of Spades, what should he lead?

5.
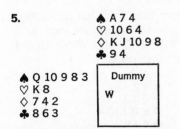

♠ A 7 4
♡ 10 6 4
◊ K J 10 9 8
♣ 9 4

♠ Q 10 9 8 3
♡ K 8
◊ 7 4 2
♣ 8 6 3

| Dummy   W |

South is playing 3 No Trump. West leads the 10 of Spades. East wins with the King and continues the suit. Declarer takes the third round in dummy, and then plays to the Queen of Diamonds in his own hand. What card should West play?

6.
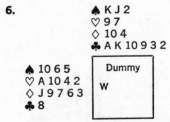

♠ K J 2
♡ 9 7
◊ 10 4
♣ A K 10 9 3 2

♠ 10 6 5
♡ A 10 4 2
◊ J 9 7 6 3
♣ 8

| Dummy   W |

South is playing 3 No Trump. West leads the 6 of Diamonds. East's King goes to South's Ace. South plays Ace, King, and another Club. East wins the third round with the Queen as South follows with the Jack. What cards should West discard?

7.
♠ Q 10 4
♡ 10 7 4
◇ A 9 6 5
♣ J 8 3

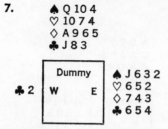

♣ 2 | Dummy W E | ♠ J 6 3 2
♡ 6 5 2
◇ 7 4 3
♣ 6 5 4

South is playing 3 No Trump. West leads the 2 of Clubs. Dummy's Jack wins and the 4 of Spades is led. What should East play?

8.
♠ A K
♡ A 10 9 3 2
◇ 9
♣ A K Q 8 5

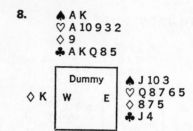

◇ K | Dummy W E | ♠ J 10 3
♡ Q 8 7 6 5
◇ 8 7 5
♣ J 4

South is playing 6 Spades. West leads the King of Diamonds. What should East play?

9.
♠ Q J
♡ 7 6 4 3
◇ K 10 6 5
♣ K 10 9

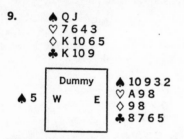

♠ 5 | Dummy W E | ♠ 10 9 3 2
♡ A 9 8
◇ 9 8
♣ 8 7 6 5

South is playing 3 No Trump after having opened the bidding with 1 No Trump. West leads the 5 of Spades and dummy plays the Jack. What card should East play?

10.
♠ A 8
♡ J 7 6
◇ 9 6 5
♣ A Q J 10 3

♠ J 9 6 4
♡ 8 5 2
◇ Q 7 4 3
♣ 8 2 | Dummy W

South is playing 3 No Trump after North opens with 1 Club and East overcalls with 1 Heart. West leads the 8 of Hearts, East plays the 10, which holds the trick. The King then drives out declarer's Ace. As declarer runs five Club tricks, East discards the 2 of Spades, then the 2 and 8 of Diamonds. What should West's discards be?

11.
♠ K Q J
♡ Q 8 3
◇ K 7 5 2
♣ A 7 3

♠ 7 5
♡ J 5 2
◇ 9 8 6 3
♣ J 10 9 4 | Dummy W

South is playing a contract of 6 No Trump, having opened the bidding with 1 No Trump. West leads the

12.
♠ 4 2
♡ Q J 3
◇ K Q J 10 4
♣ A J 6

♠ Q | Dummy W E | ♠ K 9 5
♡ 9 8 7 5
◇ 9 5
♣ 8 7 5 3

South is playing 3 No Trump after North opened with 1 Diamond and South responded 2 No Trump. West

Jack of Clubs. Dummy plays the 3, East the 8, and South the King. Declarer now runs five Spade tricks, East follows for three rounds and then discards a Heart. What should West discard?

13.   ♠ Q 8 6
      ♡ Q 9 2
      ◇ K Q J 9 8 5
      ♣ 6

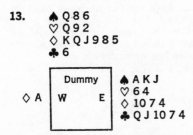

◇ A   Dummy   ♠ A K J
         W   E   ♡ 6 4
                    ◇ 10 7 4
                    ♣ Q J 10 7 4

South is playing 4 Hearts, after East opened the bidding with 1 Club. South overcalled in Hearts and North bid Diamonds. West leads the Ace of Diamonds. What card should East play?

leads the Queen of Spades. Declarer holds off the Ace until the third round, discarding the 3 of Hearts from dummy. He next runs five Diamond tricks. He and West follow for three rounds and then they each let go a small Heart. What should East discard?

14.

♠ 7 5
♡ 9 7 4 3 2
◇ A 8 6
♣ Q 5 3

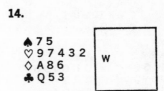

W

The contract is 6 Spades. Both opponents have bid Hearts. You suspect partner is void. What card do you lead?

ANSWERS TO SIGNALS QUIZ

1. The 9 of Hearts.
Nothing must be done that might induce West to shift to some other suit. A switch to either Diamonds or Clubs might prove fatal to the defense. When partner now cashes the second Heart, you will follow with the 10 so that he will realize that you are not in position to ruff the third round.

2. The 6 of Spades.
West should be encouraged to continue. If he has led from King and Queen, it may be essential to establish at least one additional trick in that suit.

3. East should play the Queen of Diamonds
which demands that his partner underlead the Ace. This may permit East

to win the trick early enough to come through with a Club. With the solid Spades in dummy available for discards, the defense must try to take Club tricks in a hurry.

The complete hand:

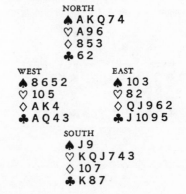

                    NORTH
                    ♠ A K Q 7 4
                    ♡ A 9 6
                    ◇ 8 5 3
                    ♣ 6 2

WEST   EAST
♠ 8 6 5 2   ♠ 10 3
♡ 10 5   ♡ 8 2
◇ A K 4   ◇ Q J 9 6 2
♣ A Q 4 3   ♣ J 10 9 5

                    SOUTH
                    ♠ J 9
                    ♡ K Q J 7 4 3
                    ◇ 10 7
                    ♣ K 8 7

4. West should lead the 2 of Clubs.
East's 7 was his lowest Heart and asked partner not to lead the suit. Since nothing could be gained by attacking dummy's strong suit, obviously the Club lead must be desired by partner. (Any Diamond tricks East may have cannot be lost.)

The complete hand:

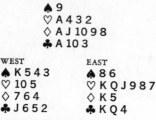

```
            NORTH
            ♠ 9
            ♡ A 4 3 2
            ◇ A J 10 9 8
            ♣ A 10 3

WEST                    EAST
♠ K 5 4 3               ♠ 8 6
♡ 10 5                  ♡ K Q J 9 8 7
◇ 7 6 4                 ◇ K 5
♣ J 6 5 2               ♣ K Q 4

            SOUTH
            ♠ A Q J 10 7 2
            ♡ 6
            ◇ Q 3 2
            ♣ 9 8 7
```

5. West should play the 2.
The lowest card is proper, holding three of the suit. East, if he holds three Diamonds to the Ace, will therefore know that the declarer has only two and can afford to take the second trick rather than wait for the third. Note that if declarer is permitted to take two Diamond tricks, he makes his contract.

The complete hand:

```
            NORTH
            ♠ A 7 4
            ♡ 10 6 4
            ◇ K J 10 9 8
            ♣ 9 4

WEST                    EAST
♠ Q 10 9 8 3            ♠ K 2
♡ K 8                   ♡ Q J 5 3 2
◇ 7 4 2                 ◇ A 5 3
♣ 8 6 3                 ♣ 10 7 5

            SOUTH
            ♠ J 6 5
            ♡ A 9 7
            ◇ Q 6
            ♣ A K Q J 2
```

6. West should discard the 3 and 7 of Diamonds
to advise partner that it is useless to continue that suit, since the declarer is marked with nine sure tricks made up of five Club tricks, the Ace and Queen of Diamonds, and the Ace and King of Spades. (If the declarer did not have the Ace of Spades, he would not have cleared his own hand of Clubs.) The only hope now is the Heart suit, and partner should be given an inducement to lead this suit if he has strength in it.

The complete hand:

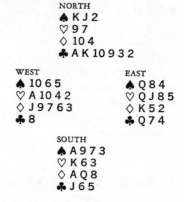

```
            NORTH
            ♠ K J 2
            ♡ 9 7
            ◇ 10 4
            ♣ A K 10 9 3 2

WEST                    EAST
♠ 10 6 5               ♠ Q 8 4
♡ A 10 4 2             ♡ Q J 8 5
◇ J 9 7 6 3            ◇ K 5 2
♣ 8                    ♣ Q 7 4

            SOUTH
            ♠ A 9 7 3
            ♡ K 6 3
            ◇ A Q 8
            ♣ J 6 5
```

7. East should follow with the 6 of Spades,
which is a mild signal that he holds something in the suit. Partner will be able to realize as the play develops that it must be the Jack.

8. East should play the 8 of Diamonds.
This is a signal to partner to continue the suit if he holds the Ace, in order to force a trump out of dummy. This will assure East a trump trick.

9. The 10.
If West has led from a holding headed by the King, he must be offered every inducement, when he regains the lead, to lay down the King to bump the Ace and Queen together.

The complete hand:

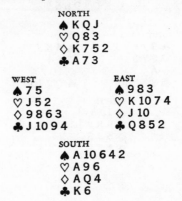

NORTH
♠ Q J
♡ 7 6 4 3
◊ K 10 6 5
♣ K 10 9

WEST
♠ K 7 6 5
♡ Q J 10
◊ 4 3 2
♣ A 3 2

EAST
♠ 10 9 3 2
♡ A 9 8
◊ 9 8
♣ 8 7 6 5

SOUTH
♠ A 8 4
♡ K 5 2
◊ A Q J 7
♣ Q J 4

10. West should not let go his Heart.
He must discard no more than two
Diamonds, or preferably one Diamond and two Spades. There is no
need to protect Spades, because if the
declarer has the King and Queen of
Spades, his contract is assured. Similarly, there is no need to keep two
small Diamonds to guard the Queen,
for if the declarer has the Ace and
King of Diamonds, nine tricks can be
counted.

The complete hand:

NORTH
♠ A 8
♡ J 7 6
◊ 9 6 5
♣ A Q J 10 3

WEST
♠ J 9 6 4
♡ 8 5 2
◊ Q 7 4 3
♣ 8 2

EAST
♠ K Q 2
♡ K Q 10 4 3
◊ K 8 2
♣ 9 4

SOUTH
♠ 10 7 5 3
♡ A 9
◊ A J 10
♣ K 7 6 5

**11. The 2 of Hearts and then the 4
and 9 of Clubs.**
Diamonds must be saved at all costs,
as it is too dangerous to discard from
a suit in which you have the same
length as the dummy. If West dis-

cards even one Diamond, the contract
will be fulfilled.

The complete holding:

NORTH
♠ K Q J
♡ Q 8 3
◊ K 7 5 2
♣ A 7 3

WEST
♠ 7 5
♡ J 5 2
◊ 9 8 6 3
♣ J 10 9 4

EAST
♠ 9 8 3
♡ K 10 7 4
◊ J 10
♣ Q 8 5 2

SOUTH
♠ A 10 6 4 2
♡ A 9 6
◊ A Q 4
♣ K 6

12. The 5, 7, and 8 of Hearts.
He must hold the Clubs for dear life.
Any Heart finesses must be made into
West's hand, but since the Clubs may
be finessable either way, East must
protect his partner's holding in that
suit. The discard of even one Club
may give the hand to declarer.

The complete holding:

NORTH
♠ 4 2
♡ Q J 3
◊ K Q J 10 4
♣ A J 6

WEST
♠ Q J 10 8 7
♡ A 6
◊ 8 7 2
♣ Q 9 2

EAST
♠ K 9 5
♡ 9 8 7 5
◊ 9 5
♣ 8 7 5 3

SOUTH
♠ A 6 3
♡ K 10 4 2
◊ A 6 3
♣ K 10 5

13. The 10.
Partner's lead is obviously a singleton.
Since the 10 cannot mean "come on,"
it must mean "shift to the higher-
ranking suit—Spades, not Clubs."

The complete hand:

NORTH
♠ Q 8 6
♡ Q 9 2
◇ K Q J 9 8 5
♣ 6

WEST
♠ 9 7 5 4 2
♡ 8 7 3
◇ A
♣ 8 5 3 2

EAST
♠ A K J
♡ 6 4
◇ 10 7 4
♣ Q J 10 7 4

SOUTH
♠ 10 3
♡ A K J 10 5
◇ 6 3 2
♣ A K 9

14. The 9.
Partner will be able to read this as an unnecessarily high Heart and will therefore return the higher-ranking suit—Diamonds, rather than Clubs.

14.

The uppercut

COLORFUL EXPRESSIONS from all walks of life ultimately find their way into the picturesque lingo of the cardplayer. One of the most descriptive of these expressions is the term "uppercut," which is borrowed from the prize-fight ring and used to describe the trumping of one of your partner's cards, even though it may be high, in order to force out a high trump from declarer. This is done with the hope of building up a trump trick for partner.

For example:

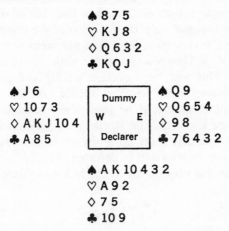

```
              ♠ 8 7 5
              ♡ K J 8
              ♢ Q 6 3 2
              ♣ K Q J
♠ J 6                          ♠ Q 9
♡ 10 7 3      Dummy            ♡ Q 6 5 4
♢ A K J 10 4  W        E       ♢ 9 8
♣ A 8 5       Declarer         ♣ 7 6 4 3 2
              ♠ A K 10 4 3 2
              ♡ A 9 2
              ♢ 7 5
              ♣ 10 9
```

South is the declarer at a contract of 4 Spades, West having over-called with 2 Diamonds. West cashes the King and Ace of Diamonds, East completing the signal. West then plays the Ace of Clubs and follows with the Jack of Diamonds, declarer playing low from dummy. East should realize that declarer is going to ruff, both from the 2 Diamond bid and from the fact that West cashed his Ace of Clubs first. Therefore he should trump his partner's good trick with the Queen of Spades, since it is of no value to him and may force a high trump from declarer. In this way West's Jack becomes promoted to a winner and the contract is set.

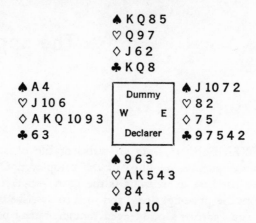

South opened the bidding with 1 Heart and became declarer at a game contract in that suit. West leads the King and Queen of Diamonds, upon which East plays high-low. What should he play next?

It is quite evident that declarer has the Ace of Clubs for the opening bid, so that the only hope to defeat the contract is for the defense to gain a trump trick. This does not seem very likely, unless East holds the 8 of Hearts and can be made to trump a Diamond with that card. This will force declarer's King and promote West's holding to a winner. West, therefore, should cash the Ace of Spades and lead a small Diamond. If he leads the Ace of Diamonds, East will probably not know that he should ruff. When a low Diamond is led, East will naturally wake up to the necessity of ruffing with his high Heart and the contract will be defeated.

A variation of this play occurs in the following hand:

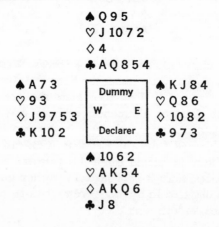

The bidding:

SOUTH	WEST	NORTH	EAST
1 Heart	Pass	2 Clubs	Pass
2 Diamonds	Pass	3 Hearts	Pass
4 Hearts	Pass	Pass	Pass

South is the declarer at a contract of 4 Hearts. West leads the Ace of Spades, and the defense cashes three tricks in that suit. East continues with the thirteenth Spade because he knows that a discard can do the declarer no good. (Declarer has bid Hearts and Diamonds and therefore can have no more than two Clubs after he follows to three rounds of Spades.) Declarer discards a Club, and West ruffs with the 9 of Hearts, forcing dummy's 10. It matters not how declarer plays; East's 8 of Hearts must now become a winner.

An extreme case of the repeated use of the uppercut to defeat the contract is the following:

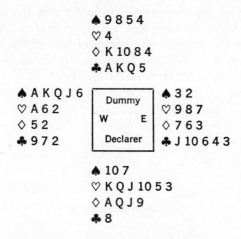

```
                ♠ 9 8 5 4
                ♡ 4
                ◇ K 10 8 4
                ♣ A K Q 5
♠ A K Q J 6   ┌──────────┐   ♠ 3 2
♡ A 6 2       │  Dummy   │   ♡ 9 8 7
◇ 5 2         │ W      E │   ◇ 7 6 3
♣ 9 7 2       │ Declarer │   ♣ J 10 6 4 3
              └──────────┘
                ♠ 10 7
                ♡ K Q J 10 5 3
                ◇ A Q J 9
                ♣ 8
```

South was declarer at a contract of 4 Hearts on strong bidding which included showing the Diamond suit, and apparently must lose only two Spades and the Ace of Hearts. However, inspired defense was able to defeat the contract. After two Spades were cashed, West led the 6 of Spades, East ruffed with the 7 of Hearts, and South overruffed with the 10. The King of Hearts was led, taken with the Ace, and another Spade, although high, was trumped by East with the 9 of Hearts. This forced declarer's Jack, and the 6 of trumps was developed into the setting trick.

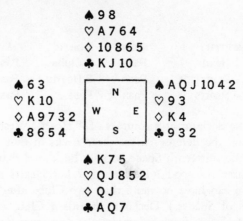

                    ♠ 9 8
                    ♡ A 7 6 4
                    ◇ 10 8 6 5
                    ♣ K J 10

    ♠ 6 3   ♠ A Q J 10 4 2
    ♡ K 10   ♡ 9 3
    ◇ A 9 7 3 2   ◇ K 4
    ♣ 8 6 5 4   ♣ 9 3 2

                    ♠ K 7 5
                    ♡ Q J 8 5 2
                    ◇ Q J
                    ♣ A Q 7

    Declarer is playing a contract of 4 Hearts, doubled by West, East having overcalled with Spades. The 6 of Spades was led; East won with the Ace and, hoping that partner had the Ace of Diamonds, led his King at trick two. The Diamond was continued and won by West's Ace. Now on the surface it appears that the defenders can take no more tricks, because West's King of Hearts can be finessed and the suit picked up. However, the third lead of Diamonds can be trumped by East with the 9 of Hearts, forcing out the Jack, and now West is assured of a trump trick by merely covering anything that declarer leads.

15. Elementary card combinations

Declarer

IT IS an elementary principle of card playing that the best results can be obtained by forcing an opponent to play ahead of you. This is especially true when you are attempting to capture one or more of his high cards. A simple illustration is the following.

```
                 9 4 2
               ┌─────────┐
               │    N    │
     8 7 5 3   │ W     E │   K J 6
               │    S    │
               └─────────┘
                 A Q 10
```

Your object is to win tricks with the Queen and the 10. This you will succeed in doing only if the King and Jack are held by East, and also if you compel East to play before you are obliged to do so. Therefore the proper procedure is to enter the North hand and lead a small card, covering whatever East plays. By repeating this procedure you will win tricks with both the 10 and the Queen. Note if you play first from the South hand you would win only the Ace and lose the other two.

```
                 8 5 3
               ┌─────────┐
               │    N    │
    10 9 7 6   │ W     E │   A J 4
               │    S    │
               └─────────┘
                 K Q 2
```

Similarly, here you are trying to win tricks with both the King and the Queen. This can be done only if East holds the Ace, and provided he is compelled to play before you. The proper procedure is to lead a small card from the North hand. If East plays the Ace, your troubles are over. If he plays small, you win with the Queen and enter the North hand again to repeat the process. Note that if you had led the King out of your hand you could have taken only one trick, with the Queen.

8 6 5 3

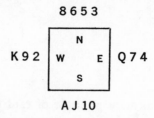

K 9 2

Q 7 4

A J 10

Your object is to win two tricks in the suit. If you lead from the South hand, this is impossible, but if you lead from the North hand and play the 10, West will win a trick with the King. You subsequently enter the North hand and lead the suit again. If East plays small, you win with the Jack. Here again you have obtained the maximum by compelling the opponent to play before you use your high card.

A 6 4

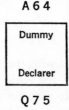

Q 7 5

Your object is to win two tricks in the suit. Assuming that the outstanding cards are normally divided against you, the Ace will naturally win one of them, but to win a trick with the Queen you must force the opponent who holds the King to play ahead of you. Your only hope is that East has that card, so that after cashing the Ace you lead a small one. If East plays low, you play the Queen, hoping it will win. If it develops that West holds the King, you will not succeed, but then it was impossible to make two tricks in any event.

The inexperienced player sometimes leads the Queen from the South hand, expecting to win a trick with it. This is impossible, because if West plays properly he will place his King on your Queen, and now you can win only one trick in the suit.

It is important to bear in mind that it is almost impossible to win a trick with a card that you lead. You must try to compel the opponent who has the missing card to make his play before you make yours.

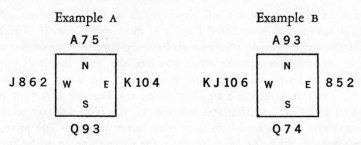

Example A   Example B

and two tricks are needed *in a hurry,* it now becomes proper to lead the Queen, because if West has the King and covers, your Jack will immediately become good. If he fails to cover, the Queen will win a trick. The difference in this case is that you retain the equivalent of the card that you lead.

Notice that in **EXAMPLE B** you are helpless to take more than one trick no matter how you play, but in **EXAMPLE A**, if you lead a small card from the North hand toward your Queen, you will win two tricks in the suit. Note how different it would be if South improperly played the Queen first.

If we add a Jack to the South holding, producing the following combination:

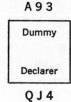

and two tricks are needed *in a hurry,* it now becomes proper to lead the Queen, because if West has the King and covers, your Jack will immediately become good. If he fails to cover, the Queen will win a trick. The difference in this case is that you retain the equivalent of the card that you lead.

It is important to bear in mind that a finesse is not so much an effort to get an opponent's high cards out of the way as it is an attempt to win tricks with your own high cards. It is rarely possible to win a trick with a card that you lead unless you have the card next below it. Whenever you take a finesse you must make a wish and say, "I wish the outstanding card to be in such and such a position. If it is, I will win the trick with such and such a card."

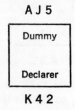

Your problem is to win all three tricks with this combination. What is the proper procedure? First, you must make a wish. Which one of the opponents do you wish to have the Queen? If East has it, luck is not with you, because when you lead the Jack, East will play the Queen and you will be forced to win with the King. Now you can win only two tricks. You have made the mistake of trying to win a trick with a card that you led; second, you have not compelled the opponent with the high card to play before you did. The proper procedure is to wish for West to have the Queen and to make him play ahead of you. A small card, therefore, should be led from the South hand, and if West plays low, insert the Jack, hoping it will win a trick. In other words, the card played third hand to a trick has a fair chance to win. The card played first hand to a trick has practically none. By the addition of one more card, the 10, we have the following position:

A J 10

K 4 2

With this holding you can win all three tricks, provided you can guess which one of the opponents holds the Queen. This is a mere guess, and if you believe that West has it you should lead a small card from the South hand, making West play before North. The 10 will then win the trick. If, however, you think that East has the Queen, you should first play the Ace and then lead the Jack. If the Queen covers, the 10 will be good. If East plays low, the Jack is permitted to ride and will win the trick. In this case the lead of the honor card to the first trick will succeed because you have the next card.

K J 10

```
      N
   W     E
      S
```

4 3 2

Your problem is to win two tricks with this holding. Obviously one must be lost to the Ace, so that it does not much matter which opponent has it. The important question is, "Who has the Queen?" If East has it, you will be obliged to lose two tricks, but if West holds it, you may win two tricks by compelling West to play before you. The proper procedure, therefore, is to lead a low card from the South hand and, if West plays low, to follow with the 10. This will succeed in forcing out the Ace. The South hand is subsequently re-entered and another small card led, with the assumption that the Jack will win the trick. Here again you are leading toward your high cards, compelling the opponent who may have the missing honor to play before you use your high cards.

Q 10 9

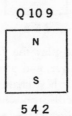

5 4 2

Your object is to win one trick in the suit. If West holds both the Ace and the King, you will be successful if you lead from the South hand. If West plays the King, North will play the 9 and subsequently re-enter the South hand in order to lead again toward the Queen. However, inasmuch as it is improbable that West has both the Ace and the King, the better procedure is to wish that he holds the Jack. A small card is led from the South hand, and when West plays low North follows with the 9, hoping that this will drive out the King or the Ace. The South hand is entered and another small card is led, and since West is known to hold the Jack one trick must be built up.

A K 9 4

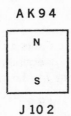

J 10 2

Your object is to win all four tricks. This can be done if West holds the Queen. The Jack, therefore, is led from the South hand. If West covers, all your cards are high. If West plays low, the small card is played from the North hand and the process repeated. If East has the Queen, this play will not succeed. It is true that if East has the

Queen and one other, the finesse will have been a losing play, but you have no way of telling this, and in the long run the finesse is the better play with this combination, as will be seen in the chapter on probabilities.

If, however, the 10 is not held, so that your holding is the following:

A K 4 2

J 6 3

it would now be improper to play the Jack, because if West has the Queen he will presumably cover, and now one of the opponents must win a trick with the 10. Your best chance is that the Queen has only one small card with it and will drop when you play the Ace and the King. In any event, it is impossible to win all four tricks no matter how you play the cards, because if the Queen drops, it will mean that one of the opponents has the 10 9 x x and must win the fourth round of the suit. This is apparent from the following example:

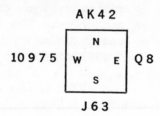

A K 4 2

10 9 7 5   Q 8

J 6 3

Finesses

In taking finesses, there comes a time when there are very few entries in the dummy and it is desirable to retain the lead in the hand from which you are leading for the finesse.

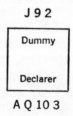

J 9 2

Dummy

Declarer

A Q 10 3

The lead is in the dummy and there are no other entries. What is the proper card to lead? The 9. This is the same in value as the Queen, but if the finesse succeeds, the lead is still retained in the North hand, where it is desired. At the next trick the Jack should be led, so that if the finesse wins, the third lead can come from the dummy hand. Notice that if the Jack were led and it held, South playing small, the next lead would have to be won by declarer and you would be unable to come through again. This would be disastrous if the actual holdings were as follows:

J 9 2

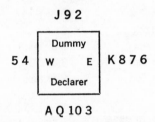

5 4   K 8 7 6

A Q 10 3

Notice, too, that if you led the Jack you could not afford to unblock with the 10, because East, as above, might have the K 8 7 6 and, by covering the 9, subsequently would succeed in taking a trick with the 8.

Finesses to capture an honor

Where declarer holds A K J and others, and the dummy several others, the object is to capture the opponent's Queen. This may be done by leading out the Ace and the King, with the hope that the Queen will drop, or by finessing the Jack, hoping that the Queen is located under the King. Which is the better play? That depends on the number of cards that are out against you. If there are only four cards out, for the purpose of finessing you assume that they are equally divided. (In point of actual fact the chances are they will not be so divided. (See chapter on Percentages.) However, for the purpose of finessing only, we work on the theory that the suit will break.) Therefore, with four out, the better play in the long run is to try to drop the Queen. If there are five cards out against you, you assume that they will be divided three–two and that the Queen is probably in the hand that holds three cards. Therefore the lead of the Ace and the King will probably not drop the Queen, and the finesse becomes the better play.

The same principle applies in attempting to capture the King.

There is a common conception that holding ten trumps, without the King, the proper play is to lead the Ace. This is not sound. Since there are three cards out against you, they will probably be divided two–one, and the King is more apt to be in the hand that holds two. Therefore the Ace will probably not drop the King and the finesse would be the better play.

HOLDING	TOTAL CARDS OF SUIT IN DECLARER'S TWO HANDS	PLAY
Ace Queen	11	Ace
Ace Queen	10 or less	Queen
Ace King Jack	9 or more	King
Ace King Jack	8 or less	Jack
Ace Queen Ten	9 or 10	Queen
Ace Queen Ten	8 or less	Ten

The double finesse

A Q 10 9 2

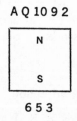

6 5 3

What is the proper play to realize the maximum number of tricks with this holding? The correct procedure is for South to play a low card, intending to finesse the 9 in the North hand. If this succeeds in driving out the King, your troubles are over. If the 9 loses to the Jack, the South hand is re-entered and the finesse is repeated, hoping that West now holds the King. The complete holding may be as follows:

A Q 10 9 2

K 8 7 W N E J 4
          S

6 5 3

At first appearances it might seem that the finesse of the 9 was a losing play, as it allowed East to win with the Jack, but it is apparent that no matter how you play this holding you must lose one trick. If you had played the Queen first, it would have held the trick, but then the Ace would succeed in dropping the Jack and the opponent's King would still be good. In other words, the opponents have five cards of the suit, so that one of them must have at least three. The play of the Queen and the Ace to the first two tricks cannot possibly clear the suit, so that unless West has both the King and the Jack, the opponents must take one trick. However, if West had held both, you would have won all the tricks by playing the 9 first. A certain number of players dislike giving up tricks during the play of the hand. When there is no emergency, do not have any objection to giving the opponents a trick early in the play if it is not possible to prevent them from winning it in any event.

Make it a point always to give away cheerfully that which the opponents are going to take from you anyway.

If you had held nine of the suit instead of eight, the reasoning would be somewhat different. Now the opponents would have only four cards, and it is possible that each might have two, in which case, if the Queen wins the trick, the Ace will drop both the King and the Jack and you need not lose any tricks.

Perhaps an easy way to remember when to take the single finesse with the Ace, Queen, and 10 and when to take the double finesse is as follows:

Divide the outstanding cards as equally as possible. If one of the opponents must have at least three cards, you finesse them three deep; that is, the 10. If one of the opponents may have only two cards, finesse two deep; that is, the Queen.

Elementary card combinations when the opponent has led a suit

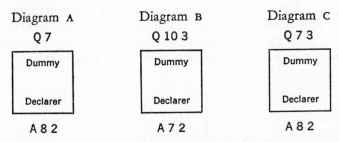

Diagram A	Diagram B	Diagram C
Q 7	Q 10 3	Q 7 3
Dummy	Dummy	Dummy
Declarer	Declarer	Declarer
A 8 2	A 7 2	A 8 2

You are South, the declarer at No Trump. West leads the 5 of Hearts. What card do you play from dummy?

In DIAGRAM A obviously the Queen must be played. Your only hope is that West is leading from the King and that the Queen will hold. If it does not win this trick, it can never win a later one, as it will now be alone. If you make the mistake of playing the 7 from the North hand, East will not play the King even if he has it, so that either a 9, 10, or Jack will force your Ace, and the Queen will then be lost to the King.

In DIAGRAM B the 10 is the proper play, in the hope that it will force the King from East. You will win with your Ace, and the Queen will be high. If the 10 is covered by the Jack, you will win with the Ace and, hoping that West has the King, you will subsequently lead toward the Queen, expecting to win a trick with it.

In DIAGRAM C the proper play from dummy is small. There is no hurry about playing the Queen, because if West has the King, the Queen will still be protected and can be developed into a winning trick later on. The reason for playing low is that there is a bare possibility that East will play the King, relieving you of any further anxiety.

Q 10

Dummy
Declarer

A 8 2

You are South, the declarer. West leads the 5 of Hearts. Here the proper play from dummy is very difficult to determine and is really a guess. If you think West is leading from the King, you should play the Queen, hoping it will win the trick. If you think West is leading from the Jack and that East has the King, the play of the 10 will force East's King and give you two tricks. But to repeat—this is a mere guess. When you are playing No Trump it is a better guess that West is leading from the King. If you are playing a suit contract it is better to guess that West is leading from the Jack, because so many players have an aversion to leading away from a King at suit contracts.

K 7 2

Dummy
Declarer

Q 6 4

West leads the 5 of Hearts. In this case obviously the correct play from dummy is a low card. The play of the King could not gain, but if East should happen to play the Ace, both your King and Queen will be good. If West led from the Ace, you will win with the Queen, and the King will subsequently be good for another trick.

K 7

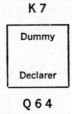

Q 6 4

In this case the proper play is the King, hoping it will hold the trick. The play of the 7 will hardly be successful, because even if East has the Ace he should not put it on the 7 but should wait to capture the King. East, therefore, will play some intermediate card on dummy's 7 that will force the Queen and will leave the King alone in dummy.

If the lead happens to be from the Ace, the King will hold the trick, and now West will be unable to lead that suit again, if he gets in, without permitting you to win a trick with the Queen.

Ducking

♠ A K 7 6 3

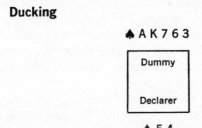

♠ 5 4

Assume that you are playing a No Trump contract and that the North hand has no other high cards. You are anxious to take four tricks in Spades. How is this to be done? Since your opponents have six Spades, your only hope is that each of them will have three. If you play the Ace, King, and another, the two remaining Spades will be good, but you will have no means of getting over to the dummy to use them. The proper procedure, therefore, is to give the opponents their trick at the beginning, rather than at the end. If you play a small Spade from your hand and a small one from the dummy, one of the opponents will be obliged to win. You now hope that each will have two cards left in the suit, so that when you play the Ace and the King it will clear all the Spades and the two small ones will be good.

This play of conceding the first trick is known as "ducking." Notice that had there been an Ace on the side in the North hand, it would not be necessary to duck. You could, if you choose, play the Ace and the King and another Spade, hoping that the opponents each had three, and then you could subsequently enter the North hand with the Ace to cash the two good Spades.

♠ A 9 7 6 3

♠ 5 4 2

Sometimes it is necessary to duck twice in order to establish a suit. In the above example, no matter how the cards are distributed, the opponents must win at least two Spade tricks. Assuming that the North hand has no entry, it will be futile to play the Ace of Spades first and then two more, because if the remaining two become established, there is no way to cash them. In order that the opponents be given their two tricks early in the play, a small Spade is led by South and a small one played from dummy. This is won by the opponents. When declarer regains the lead he leads another low Spade and again plays small from dummy. This trick, too, goes to the opponents. Now there is only one more Spade out, and it must fall upon the Ace, giving the declarer three tricks in the suit.

If it should develop that the opponents' five cards are four in one hand and one in the other, your play will not succeed, but then nothing could have been done about it and you are the victim of a "bad break."

♠ A Q 2

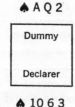

♠ 10 6 3

West leads the 4 of Spades. What is the proper play from dummy? The correct play is the deuce. This is the one way to make all three tricks in case West has both the King and the Jack. If West is leading from the King and East has the Jack, nothing is lost, because the finesse of the Queen can be taken next time. If West is leading from the Jack and East has the King, the gain is obvious.

♡ K J

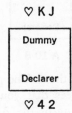

♡ 4 2

The contract is Spades. West leads the 5 of Hearts. What card do you play from dummy? That depends on who you think has the Ace. If you believe that East has it, the Jack is the correct play, hoping that it will force out the Ace. Since it is a suit contract, the chances are that West would not lead away from the Ace, so that the best play is the Jack. In a majority of cases the opening leader will not underlead an Ace against a suit contract. If, however, the contract is No Trump, then West might very well lead from the Ace, and since most persons select their best suit for the opening lead, possibly the chances favor the play of the King instead of the Jack.

In DIAGRAM A West leads the 6. With this particular holding you might just as well play the King, because if it does not win the trick now, it never will.

In DIAGRAM B West leads the 5. The contract is No Trump. Play the Queen. If it does not win the trick on the opening lead, it has no hope. It will do no good for dummy to play low, because no matter what East has to play, you can take no tricks.

Diagram A	Diagram B	Diagram C
K 2	Q 4	J 2
Dummy	Dummy	Dummy
Declarer	Declarer	Declarer
7 4 3	1 0 9 6	A 9 4

In DIAGRAM C Contract: No Trump. West leads the 5. The proper play from dummy is the Jack. Your only hope is that the lead was from the King Queen. Otherwise it will be impossible to take two tricks.

M

Diagram D	Diagram E	Diagram F
J 2	J 2	J 2

Dummy	Dummy	Dummy
Declarer	Declarer	Declarer

| Q 5 3 | A 10 3 | A K 3 |

In DIAGRAM D West leads the 4. The proper play from dummy is the small one. This guarantees that you will win a trick, because East must play either the King or the Ace, and the Jack will drive out the other honor. Many players thoughtlessly play the Jack from the dummy, which cannot possibly gain and which now lays the Queen open to capture.

In DIAGRAM E West leads the 4. Do not make the mistake of playing the Jack from dummy. If you do, it will probably be covered by the King or the Queen, forcing you to win with the Ace. Now if East obtains the lead he will come through your 10 and you will be held to one trick in the suit. The play of the deuce from dummy guarantees that you will win two tricks, because East will be forced to play either the King or the Queen, in which case the Jack will drive out the other honor and the 10 will be good.

In DIAGRAM F West leads the 5. Dummy must play the Jack. If it does not win a trick now, it never can.

10 7 3

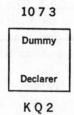

Dummy
Declarer

K Q 2

West leads the 8. The proper play from dummy is the 10. If East has the Ace, the play is immaterial, but if West has both the Ace and the Jack, the 10 will win the trick and will guarantee two tricks for the declarer. If West is leading his fourth best, the 10 will definitely win the trick. (See Rule of 11, pages 256-57.)

16.   Advanced card combinations

NOW WE COME to the question of more difficult combinations of the cards.

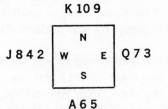

K 10 9

J 8 4 2   W E   Q 7 3

A 6 5

With the above holding, if you are South and must lead the suit yourself, you can win only with the Ace and the King; but if one of the opponents can be induced to lead that suit, you can win three tricks by developing a finessing situation. For example: If West should lead the 2, dummy's 9 is played, and East will have to cover with the Queen. This is won by South's Ace. Now the 5 of Spades is returned, and when West plays low North's 10 wins the trick.

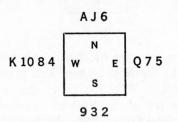

A J 6

K 10 8 4   W E   Q 7 5

9 3 2

If you are South and are obliged to lead this suit, you can win only one trick if the opponents play properly. If you led the 9, West would cover with the 10 and the Jack would lose to the Queen. The only trick available is the Ace. If, however, West should lead the 4, your best play is not to play the Jack, because it is improbable that West has both the King and the Queen, but you can hope that West has the 10 and one of the other picture cards. In that case, if you play small from the dummy, East will be obliged to win with the Queen. The South hand is subsequently re-entered, and now the finesse can be taken against West's King.

AJ9

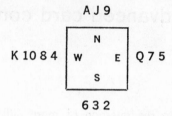

K 10 8 4   Q 7 5

632

You are South and wish to win two tricks with this holding. What is the proper play? You should lead a small one from the South hand and when West plays low insert the 9, hoping that this will force an honor.

This is a better play than trying to win the trick with the Jack. The Jack play will be proper in only one case, that is where West has both the King and the Queen, whereas the play of the 9 will succeed in two cases, where West has the Queen and 10 or the King 10. The 9 forces a high honor from the East hand, and then the Jack can be successfully finessed on the next round.

K 10 9 8

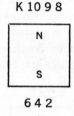

642

You are anxious to win two tricks with this holding. The proper play is a small card by South, and when West plays low insert the 8. This play will succeed if West has either the Jack or the Queen, regardless of how the rest of the cards are distributed, because the 8 will force, let us say, the Queen. Now the South hand is re-entered and another small card led, inserting the 9 from dummy. Since West has the Jack, this will force the Ace, and the North hand now has the tenace of King 10 over West's Jack.

NORTH: K 6 4 2   SOUTH: Q 7 5 3

Is it possible for you to win three tricks with this combination? The answer is yes, provided the player who has the Ace has only one guard with it and that his partner has three cards of the suit. If you believe that West holds the Ace you should lead a small one from the South hand and, when West plays low, go up with the

King. Now a small one is returned from North and ducked completely, hoping that the Ace will fall. If it does not, there is nothing you can do about it. If you believe that East has the Ace of the suit, the first lead should come from the North hand. When East plays low, the trick is won with the Queen and the return is ducked. In the first case the holding will have been as in DIAGRAM A, in the second case as in DIAGRAM B.

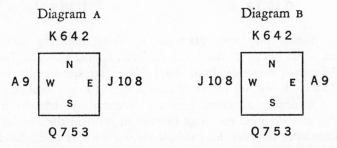

With DIAGRAM A, following, your object is to win three tricks in the suit. This may be done in two ways, depending on who you believe has the King. If you think East has it, you should play the Ace and then lead a small one toward the Queen. If you think West has it, then your only hope is that it will fall on the second round. In that case you should play the Ace and a small one and duck the second round. The holding will then have been as in DIAGRAM B, following.

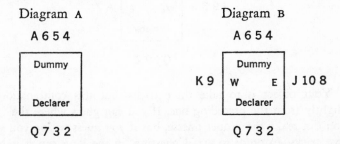

With DIAGRAM A below you are trying to win three tricks. If you think that East has the King, you should play as in the previous example. If you think that West has the King, then it may be that East has the Jack, in which case you should lead low from the North hand and finesse the 10 after the play of the Ace, hoping that this will drive out the King.

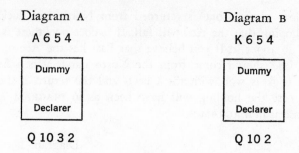

Diagram A

A 6 5 4

Dummy

Declarer

Q 10 3 2

Diagram B

K 6 5 4

Dummy

Declarer

Q 10 2

The normal play with DIAGRAM B, above, assuming plenty of entries, is the finesse of the 10 by declarer, hoping that East has the Jack. Suppose, however, from the bidding you are morally certain that East holds the Ace but are not quite sure as to the location of the Jack. A somewhat abnormal play will frequently be effective if you are able to determine the exact number of cards in the suit held by the adversaries. Suppose, for example, during the play of the hand you are able to determine that West holds four cards of this suit. That would leave East with only two cards, one of which you are morally certain is the Ace. The proper play is to lead the 4 from dummy and win with the Queen. At the next trick the 2 is led and ducked in dummy, hoping the Ace will fall. The complete holding will be as follows:

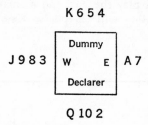

K 6 5 4

J 9 8 3   Dummy
         W   E   A 7
         Declarer

Q 10 2

Your object is to take three tricks, but this combination differs slightly from the preceding one. If you can guess where the cards are you can make the proper finesse, but if you guess wrong you will lose two tricks. In order to avoid guessing, in the long run it is better to play upon the theory that two high cards adversely held will usually be found in different hands. You should therefore lead first from the South hand, intending to lose the finesse to East if West does not cover, and subsequently enter the South hand and finesse again. It does not matter who has the King or the Jack. Just so long as they are in different hands, you will succeed. (See chapter on Percentages.)

A 6 5 4

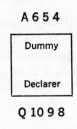

Q 10 9 8

Diagram A

A 6 5 4

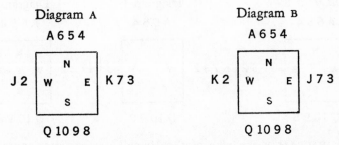

Q 10 9 8

Diagram B

A 6 5 4

Q 10 9 8

In either of these cases, if the Ace is played first and then a small one, when East plays low declarer must guess whether to play the 10 or the Queen, and the wrong guess will be fatal. Where two finesses are taken, only one trick will be lost in both these cases.

In DIAGRAM C, when an honor is led through, the automatic cover will hold the defenders to one trick, whereas in DIAGRAM D the recommended play will lose two tricks. On the other hand, the play of the Ace first will succeed in DIAGRAM D but will lose in DIAGRAM C. These cases cancel each other in frequency. The advantage to be gained is that the declarer is saved the hazard of misguessing which card to play on the second round when the Ace is led first.

Diagram C

A 6 5 4

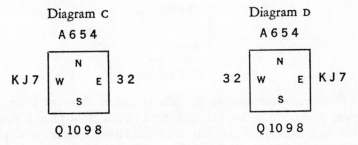

Q 10 9 8

Diagram D

A 6 5 4

Q 10 9 8

The question arises which card to lead first—the Queen or the 10. This is a mere guess and will matter only where there is a singleton Jack or singleton King outstanding. If East has a singleton Jack, the lead of the Queen will win all four tricks. Without any information, these two chances are equal. If the bidding tells you that East is probably short, you must hope that it is the singleton Jack. If East has the lone King, West's Jack will be protected and win a trick in any event. If it is West who is short, you should lead a lower honor from the South hand. This is illustrated by the following diagrams:

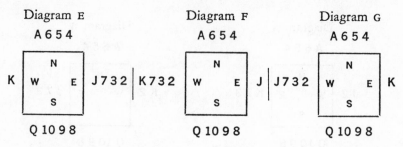

| Diagram E | Diagram F | Diagram G |
| A 6 5 4 | A 6 5 4 | A 6 5 4 |

In DIAGRAM E the play of the 10 will succeed in winning four tricks.

In DIAGRAM F, if the Queen is led, the King and the Jack will drop together and all four tricks will be taken in that manner.

In DIAGRAM G there is no way to take all the tricks.

Generally speaking, the play of the 10 is slightly superior to the lead of the Queen because it takes care of the remote contingency that West is void, in which case the Ace will be played from dummy and three tricks won in that manner.

Another frequently occurring combination follows:

A J 3 2

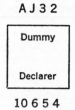

10 6 5 4

If three tricks are required by declarer and no clues are available, the best play is for declarer to lead the 4 and, if West plays low, put up the Jack from the dummy. If this should lose, declarer's next play would be the Ace, hoping that West had a doubleton honor which would now fall or that East had King Queen alone. The Jack play will, of course, also succeed where West has K Q x.

If you have reason to believe that East has only two cards of the

suit and West has three, it is better to lead the 2 from dummy, for
if one of East's two cards happens to be the King, he will almost
surely come up and you will now have a finesse of the Jack on the
next round.

Here is another illustration:

A 4 2

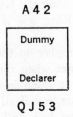

Q J 5 3

Your object is to win three tricks in the suit. The popular lead of
the Queen in this case is not correct, because if West has the King
he will cover and you must lose a trick to the 10 in any event. You
will now win three tricks only if the opponents' cards are divided
three–three. Your best chance is for East to have the King. Then the
distribution will not matter, because you will lose only one trick by
leading the Ace, then a small one toward the Queen. If it wins, the
North hand is re-entered and the process repeated.

Suppose the adverse holdings were as follows:

A 4 2

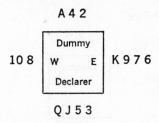

Q J 5 3

It will be noticed that in this case the lead of the Queen will limit
the declarer to only two tricks. The proper play will yield three.

J 9 2

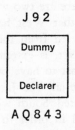

A Q 8 4 3

M*

The correct play is to lead first the small card from the North hand, intending to finesse the Queen. If this succeeds, you must now guess how the remaining cards are distributed. If you think that the King is now alone, you should play the Ace. If you think that the King is still guarded in the East hand, you have a hope that West's 10 will now fall, so that you enter the North hand and lead the Jack. This will be covered by the King, and if the 10 drops, all the tricks are yours.

In the long run the better play on the second lead of the suit is the Jack, because while it loses when the King is alone in the East hand, it gains when the 10 is alone in the West hand. These two combinations cancel each other, but if all the remaining cards are in the East hand, the play of the Jack will gain a trick, while playing the Ace will permit East to win both the King and the 10. The complete holding will be as follows:

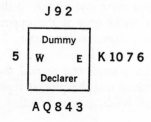

J 9 2

5 — K 10 7 6

A Q 8 4 3

Here is another example:

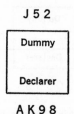

J 5 2

A K 9 8

Your object is to win all four tricks in the suit. It should be noted that this is very unlikely. There are two ways in which to accomplish this result. One is to hope that West has the singleton Queen, in which case the high card is led from the South hand and the rest becomes routine. This, however, is extremely unlikely, so that your best chance is to hope for East to have both the Queen and the 10, and the distribution is immaterial. The Jack, therefore, is led through and will presumably be covered. South will win with the King, and the North hand is re-entered in order to lead a small card for the

purpose of finessing the 9. This will succeed if the original holdings
are as follows:

J 5 2

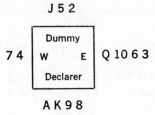

7 4   Q 10 6 3

A K 9 8

Your object is to win all the tricks.

J 5 2

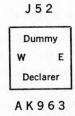

A K 9 6 3

If you believe that East has the Queen and 10, you may play as
in the previous example, but this is not the best play. Since there are
five cards out, your most reasonable hope is that the Queen will fall
on the second round from either hand, which gives you two chances.
The best play, therefore, is to lead out the Ace and the King.

Declarer has the lead and has now only one more entry: What is
the proper card to lead in the combination below?

A J 10 8

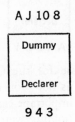

9 4 3

The 3, not the 9. Declarer plans to take two finesses, the first of
which must lose. If the 9 is led at the first trick, the second finesse
will have to be won in dummy, and declarer has no further entries
to repeat the finesse. When the 3 is led and the 10 loses to the Queen,
on the second finesse the 9 is led and, if it is not covered, will hold
the trick, since dummy can underplay the 8. A hand illustrating this
principle is as follows:

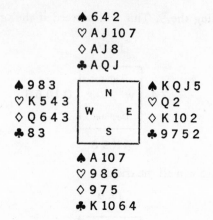

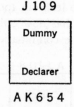

Declarer is playing 3 No Trump. West leads the 9 of Spades, and the Ace wins the third round of the suit. If the 9 of Hearts is led and ducked in dummy, East will win with the Queen. Declarer can subsequently regain the lead with the King of Clubs to take the Heart finesse, but now the 10 will win and South's hand cannot be re-entered to repeat the Heart finesse. Declarer could have saved the day if after leading the 9 he had played the 10 from dummy at the first trick. This would leave the 7 for the subsequent underplay of the 8.

Assuming plenty of entries, what is the correct way to play this suit?

J 10 9

Dummy

Declarer

A K 6 5 4

While normally the finesse for the Queen is postponed for the second round, in this case it is not proper to do so, because the play of the Ace first sacrifices an important card from dummy, and a trick will be lost if the complete holding were as follows:

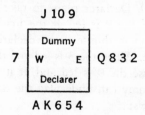

With this holding, therefore, a first-round finesse should be taken. In other words, the chances of East holding four to the Queen are greater than West holding the singleton Queen.

Your object is to win two tricks.

6 5 3

A Q 9

The casual play is to lead from the North hand and finesse the Queen, hoping that East has the King. This is not correct. If East has the King, he will have it a trick or two later just as well, and you can avail yourself of an additional chance by first finessing the 9. This might possibly drive out the King, but if it fails to do so, the North hand can be re-entered and the finesse of the Queen tried at the next lead of that suit. The principle illustrated here is that a finesse is never taken early in the play when it is just as convenient to take it somewhat later. The complete holding may be as follows:

6 5 3

K 8 4 2 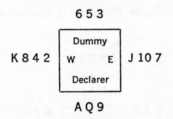 J 10 7

A Q 9

Assuming that you need all four tricks with this combination, what is the proper procedure?

J 6 4 2

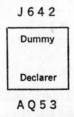

A Q 5 3

The lead obviously must come from the North hand, but you must not make the mistake of leading the Jack, because no matter where the rest of the cards are located you will have to lose at least one trick, since if East has the King he will cover and the 10 or 9 must become good. If West has the King, naturally your finesse will lose. The proper play is to lead a low card from North, and when East follows the Queen should be played. When this wins there is no further finesse. Either the King will drop or it won't. If it drops when you play the Ace, the rest are yours. If it does not, then there was no possible way to attain your end. The holdings might have been as follows:

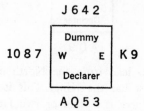

Notice that the lead of the Jack would have compelled declarer to lose one trick when East covered. The presence of the 9 in either the North or South hand would have modified this advice somewhat. Now you would have a choice of plays on the second round, because West might be left with the lone 10, in which case the lead of the Jack will pick up another trick.

An interesting hand that illustrates a number of finesse positions is the following:

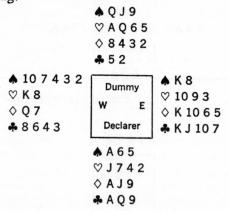

Declarer is playing 3 No Trump, and West leads the 3 of Spades. Dummy plays the Queen, East the King, and declarer the Ace. The 2 of Hearts is led and the Queen finessed in dummy. The Ace of Hearts drops West's King. The Diamond suit is now attacked. Dummy leads the 2, and declarer finesses the 9, which drives out West's Queen. West continues with a Spade, and dummy's 9 is finessed. The Diamond finesse is now taken and the Ace led, in the hope that the suit will break three–three, but West fails to follow. Now dummy's high cards are run and East must reduce his hand to three cards. Since one of them must be the King of Diamonds, he is obliged to come down to the King and Jack of Clubs. When declarer takes the Club finesse the balance of the tricks are his.

Leading toward high cards

It has previously been shown that in order to obtain full advantage of your high cards you must lead toward them and compel your opponent to play first.

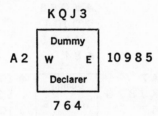

K Q J 3

A 2 | Dummy |
      | W   E | 10 9 8 5
      | Declarer |

7 6 4

Your object is to win three tricks in the suit. Do not make the mistake of leading the King from the North hand. If you do so, you will win three tricks only if the opponents' cards are divided three–three. The proper procedure is to lead a low card from the South hand, playing an honor from the North. If this wins, the South hand is re-entered and the process repeated. This forces West to play ahead of you, and if he is obliged to follow with the Ace, North's small card will be used instead of an honor.

Another illustration of repeated leads toward high cards is the following:

♠ K Q 8 6
♡ Q 10 4
♢ A K Q 5
♣ 8 4

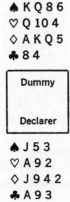

Dummy

Declarer

♠ J 5 3
♡ A 9 2
♢ J 9 4 2
♣ A 9 3

You are South, the declarer at a contract of 3 No Trump. West, having opened the bidding with 1 Heart, leads the 2 of Clubs. East plays the 10 and you win with the Ace. You must lead a low Spade toward the Queen, which holds the trick. What is your next play?

You must not lead the Spade back to your Jack, because if the Spades do not break even, you will not have nine tricks. The proper play is to return to the South hand with the Jack of Diamonds and lead a small Spade toward the King. This may compel West to play his Ace, and three Spade tricks are assured. If West does not play the Ace, you will win with the King, and then you must hope that the Spades will break three–three.

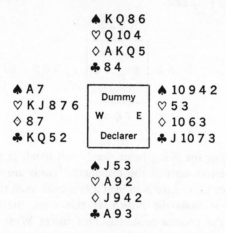

```
                    ♠ K Q 8 6
                    ♡ Q 10 4
                    ◇ A K Q 5
                    ♣ 8 4
    ♠ A 7          ┌─────────┐      ♠ 10 9 4 2
    ♡ K J 8 7 6    │ Dummy   │      ♡ 5 3
    ◇ 8 7          │ W     E │      ◇ 10 6 3
    ♣ K Q 5 2      │ Declarer│      ♣ J 10 7 3
                   └─────────┘
                    ♠ J 5 3
                    ♡ A 9 2
                    ◇ J 9 4 2
                    ♣ A 9 3
```

Your object is to win three tricks. What is the proper play?

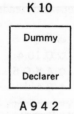

K 10

```
┌─────────┐
│ Dummy   │
│         │
│ Declarer│
└─────────┘
```

A 9 4 2

South must lead a small one and play the 10 from the North hand. No other play is correct. This will succeed if West has both the missing honors or the Queen twice guarded or the Jack twice guarded. Against almost any other holding it is impossible to make three tricks. The only time the play of the 10 will not work is if East has a singleton honor, which is too remote to be considered.

♠ A

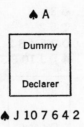

♠ J 10 7 6 4 2

This is your trump holding. You have plenty of entries in both hands, and your object is to lose only two trump tricks. Naturally the Ace of Spades is cashed first and the South hand re-entered. What card should South play? The answer is a low one and not the Jack. In order to succeed, declarer hopes that the six adversely held trumps will be divided three–three. In that case the card that he plays to the second trick is immaterial, because on the third trick the trumps will fall together; but if the adverse trumps are four–two, the play of a low card will succeed if the doubleton contains an honor, whereas the play of the Jack will lose under those conditions. The complete hand is as follows:

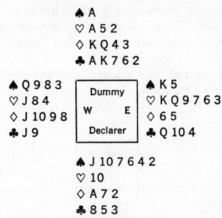

♠ A
♡ A 5 2
◇ K Q 4 3
♣ A K 7 6 2

♠ Q 9 8 3
♡ J 8 4
◇ J 10 9 8
♣ J 9

♠ K 5
♡ K Q 9 7 6 3
◇ 6 5
♣ Q 10 4

♠ J 10 7 6 4 2
♡ 10
◇ A 7 2
♣ 8 5 3

Another case to illustrate the principle of economy in the play of honor cards is the following:

South is the declarer at a contract of 4 Spades. West leads the King of Hearts. Declarer wins. What should his first play be? The answer is a low Spade, not the King. This seems to be somewhat unorthodox and may require an explanation. Declarer must lose one Heart trick and pins his hope on the chance that he will lose only two Spade tricks, which will be the case if the adverse trumps are

♠ 3
♡ 5 2
◊ 7 5 4 3 2
♣ Q J 10 8 3

```
+-------------------+
|      Dummy        |
|                   |
|                   |
|     Declarer      |
+-------------------+
```

♠ K Q 8 7 6 5 2
♡ A 3
◊ A K
♣ A K

divided three – two. Then declarer's play will be immaterial, since the hand can't be lost, but if the trumps are four – one, the play of the King will lose the hand, since the opponents cannot be kept from cashing three Spade tricks. There is, however, one chance for the declarer even if the trumps are four – one, and that is that the Ace of trumps may be alone. Since nothing can be lost by trying, a low trump is the correct play. There is a possible argument that the play of a low trump risks a subsequent ruff in either Clubs or Diamonds, but this argument is not reasonable. No one is trying for a ruff, and furthermore, if the ruff takes place, it will probably cost the defense a natural trump trick anyhow.

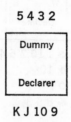

5 4 3 2

K J 10 9

Assuming that dummy has no entries, what is the proper card for declarer to play? The answer is the King. It is almost certain that declarer will have to lose two tricks, but there is one remote chance that he can hold his losses to one trick, and that is if the Queen is alone. The argument that the Ace might just as well be alone carries no weight, because even if the 9 succeeds in forcing out the Ace, there is no way to capture the Queen without any entry in dummy.

J 10 8 6 4 2

```
┌─────────────┐
│   Dummy     │
│             │
│             │
│  Declarer   │
└─────────────┘
```

K 9 7 5

Declarer has the lead and there are no entries in dummy. Declarer is trying to hold his losses to one trick. What is the best play? This is an absolute guess. In order to lose only one trick, declarer must find either the Ace or Queen alone and must make the proper guess. If the Ace is alone, obviously declarer should play a low card. If the Queen is alone, of course the King should be led. In the next case there is no guess.

J 10 8 6 4

```
┌─────────────┐
│   Dummy     │
│             │
│             │
│  Declarer   │
└─────────────┘
```

K 9 7 5

There are no entries in dummy and declarer can afford to lose only one trick. The proper play is the King, because unless the Queen is alone, there is no way to win four tricks. If the Ace is alone, it is true that a small card will drive it out, but the Queen would still be good and could not be captured.

J 6

```
┌─────────────┐
│   Dummy     │
│             │
│             │
│  Declarer   │
└─────────────┘
```

A 9 7 4 3 2

With plenty of entries in both hands, the declarer's object is to lose only one trump trick with this holding. What is the correct play? Declarer's chances are not very good. He will succeed only where West holds specifically the King 10 doubleton or the Queen 10 doubleton. On no other holding is it possible for declarer to win against proper defense. Therefore he should lead the 2 toward dummy. If West wins, dummy is entered and the Jack led through, hoping that West's 10 will drop on the trick. The complete holding is as follows:

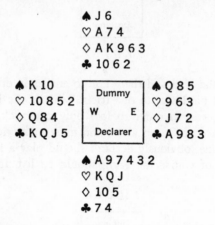

```
                    ♠ J 6
                    ♡ A 7 4
                    ◇ A K 9 6 3
                    ♣ 10 6 2
   ♠ K 10        ┌──────────┐      ♠ Q 8 5
   ♡ 10 8 5 2    │  Dummy   │      ♡ 9 6 3
   ◇ Q 8 4       │ W      E │      ◇ J 7 2
   ♣ K Q J 5     │ Declarer │      ♣ A 9 8 3
                 └──────────┘
                    ♠ A 9 7 4 3 2
                    ♡ K Q J
                    ◇ 10 5
                    ♣ 7 4
```

Declarer is playing a somewhat unsound contract of 6 Hearts, and West cashes the Ace of Spades and continues the suit. Declarer's object is to lose no trump tricks. What is the proper play?

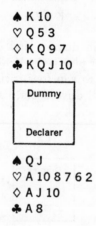

```
                    ♠ K 10
                    ♡ Q 5 3
                    ◇ K Q 9 7
                    ♣ K Q J 10
                 ┌──────────┐
                 │  Dummy   │
                 │          │
                 │ Declarer │
                 └──────────┘
                    ♠ Q J
                    ♡ A 10 8 7 6 2
                    ◇ A J 10
                    ♣ A 8
```

I do not like declarer's chances very much. He has one faint ray of hope, and that is that West holds the singleton Jack of Hearts. On no other holding is it possible for declarer to fulfill his contract against proper defense. The Queen of Hearts, therefore, should be led. If East covers, the Jack will drop, and dummy is entered for the finesse of the 8 of trumps. The play of the Queen of Hearts also has the merit that occasionally East, holding the King and one Heart, will make the error of refusing to cover the Queen, in which case all the tricks will be won. The complete holding is as follows:

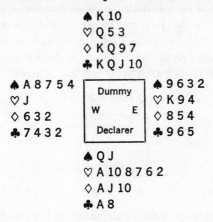

```
                    ♠ K 10
                    ♡ Q 5 3
                    ◇ K Q 9 7
                    ♣ K Q J 10
♠ A 8 7 5 4    ┌──────────┐    ♠ 9 6 3 2
♡ J            │  Dummy   │    ♡ K 9 4
◇ 6 3 2        │ W      E │    ◇ 8 5 4
♣ 7 4 3 2      │ Declarer │    ♣ 9 6 5
               └──────────┘
                    ♠ Q J
                    ♡ A 10 8 7 6 2
                    ◇ A J 10
                    ♣ A 8
```

Ducking

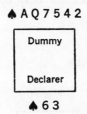

```
              ♠ A Q 7 5 4 2
         ┌──────────────┐
         │   Dummy      │
         │              │
         │   Declarer   │
         └──────────────┘
              ♠ 6 3
```

The North hand has no entries other than Spades, and your object is to win five tricks. It can be seen that regardless of how the adverse cards are distributed one trick must be lost in any event. Therefore a trick should be conceded to the opponents at once. Now our only hope is for West to have the King. The finesse is taken the next time, and if the King is in the West hand, dummy's Spades will all be good. It is true that if the finesse loses you will succeed in taking no Spade tricks instead of one, but it was your only hope and it was worth spending an extra trick to try it.

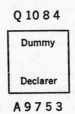

```
              Q 10 8 4
         ┌──────────────┐
         │   Dummy      │
         │              │
         │   Declarer   │
         └──────────────┘
              A 9 7 5 3
```

Assuming that you need all the tricks, is there any hope? There is, but not a very likely one. If East has the singleton King, the play of the Ace will win all the tricks. If West has the singleton King, a trick must be lost to the Jack in any event. There is one other hope. If West has the singleton Jack, all the tricks can be won by leading the Queen from the North hand. Which to do is a guess.

Suppose, however, your combined holding contains ten cards:

Q 10 8 4 2

```
┌──────────┐
│ Dummy    │
│          │
│ Declarer │
└──────────┘
```

A 9 7 5 3

Now the correct play is definitely the Ace, because it will succeed if either of the opponents has a singleton King, whereas if the Queen is led through, it will succeed in only one case, and that is where West has the singleton Jack.

The backward finesse

K 8 7

```
┌──────────┐
│ Dummy    │
│          │
│ Declarer │
└──────────┘
```

A J 9

It has been demonstrated that in order to take three tricks in the suit you should wish for East to hold the Queen. The play, therefore, is first to the King and to return by finessing the Jack. Suppose, however, that you are quite certain that West holds the Queen of the suit and therefore the finesse will fail. How are you certain? Well, West might have opened the bidding with 1 No Trump, which marks him almost certainly with that card. Is it hopeless for you to make three tricks? No, you have one chance, and that is that East has the 10. Therefore you execute what is known as the backward finesse, leading the Jack first. Notice that you must not lead the Ace first. When the Jack is covered by the Queen, you win with the King and return a low card, finessing the 9, with the hope that East holds the 10. If West holds both, there is nothing you can do about it.

The complete holding:

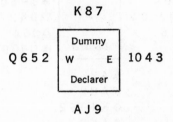

K 8 7

Q 6 5 2   W   E   10 4 3

A J 9

The backward finesse may sometimes be employed to keep the dangerous hand out of the lead.

For example:

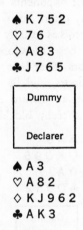

♠ K 7 5 2
♡ 7 6
◇ A 8 3
♣ J 7 6 5

♠ A 3
♡ A 8 2
◇ K J 9 6 2
♣ A K 3

You are South, the declarer at 3 No Trump. The King of Hearts is led, and you win the third round of the suit. The normal Diamond finesse may permit West to obtain the lead, and he is the one you fear. Your proper play, therefore, is to lead the Jack of Diamonds, intending to let it ride to the East hand, which has no more Hearts. This would normally be an improper play except that you must do anything to keep West out of the lead. If West covers, you win with the Ace and then come back to the King, hoping that the 10 will fall or that East has the 10.

The complete holding is as follows:

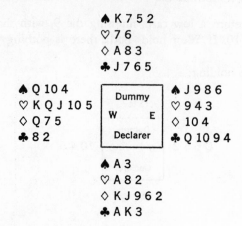

♠ K 7 5 2
♡ 7 6
◇ A 8 3
♣ J 7 6 5

♠ Q 10 4   ♠ J 9 8 6
♡ K Q J 10 5   ♡ 9 4 3
◇ Q 7 5   ◇ 10 4
♣ 8 2   ♣ Q 10 9 4

♠ A 3
♡ A 8 2
◇ K J 9 6 2
♣ A K 3

Blocking the opponents' suit

Preventing the run of opponents' suit by blocking it is a play which does not come up very often, but when it does it operates in a very neat fashion. The diagnosis is usually made on the opening lead. The leader has led a fourth best, therefore you conclude that he did not have a sequence of honors. That being the case, his partner must have one of the missing honors, and by refusing to duck you may compel the third hand either to discard his high card, which gives you a trick, or to retain it, thereby blocking the suit. For example:

♠ A 8
♡ K Q 9 5
◇ A J 7
♣ Q 9 5 2

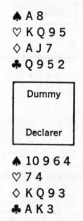

♠ 10 9 6 4
♡ 7 4
◇ K Q 9 3
♣ A K 3

You are playing a contract of 3 No Trump. West leads the 3 of Spades. You will notice that you have eight immediate tricks and the ninth is available in Hearts, but the only danger is that the

Advanced card combinations

367

opponents might run four Spades and the Ace of Hearts. This can be done only if West has a five-card suit. If he has only a four-card suit, there is no danger. If West has five, East can have only two, but the important point is that East must have either the King, Queen, or the Jack, because if West had all three, the proper lead would not have been the low card but the King, so that by playing the Ace to the first trick you will compel East to unblock, which gives you an additional Spade stopper. If East retains his honor card, the suit will be blocked. The complete hand is as follows:

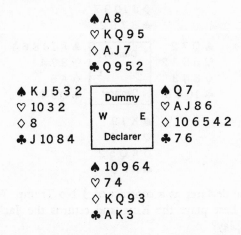

Declarer is playing a contract of 3 No Trump. East having bid 1 Spade, West leads the 2 of Spades. East plays the Ace and returns the 6. What should declarer play?

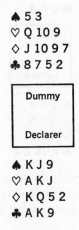

He must first determine the meaning of the deuce of Spades lead. It is quite evident that West has led from either four small cards or three headed by an honor, since if he had a singleton deuce he would probably lead some other suit. If East has only four Spades, there is nothing to fear, but if he has five, West will have three to the Queen and declarer can block the suit by going up with the King and driving out the Ace of Diamonds. The complete holding is as follows:

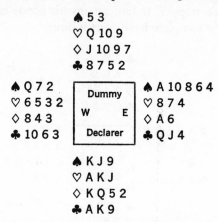

```
              ♠ 5 3
              ♡ Q 10 9
              ◇ J 10 9 7
              ♣ 8 7 5 2
♠ Q 7 2                       ♠ A 10 8 6 4
♡ 6 5 3 2     Dummy           ♡ 8 7 4
◇ 8 4 3      W       E        ◇ A 6
♣ 10 6 3      Declarer        ♣ Q J 4
              ♠ K J 9
              ♡ A K J
              ◇ K Q 5 2
              ♣ A K 9
```

South is the declarer at a contract of 3 No Trump. West leads the 5 of Spades. East plays the King and returns the Jack. What card should South play?

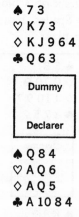

```
          ♠ 7 3
          ♡ K 7 3
          ◇ K J 9 6 4
          ♣ Q 6 3

          Dummy

          Declarer

          ♠ Q 8 4
          ♡ A Q 6
          ◇ A Q 5
          ♣ A 10 8 4
```

South's only hope is to block the opponents' suit. Under the Rule of 11, East is known to have one more card higher than the 5. (Eleven minus 5 equals 6.) Dummy has one, declarer has two, which leaves East with three cards better than the one led, two of which have already been shown. If East's remaining Spade happens to be the 10, the suit will be blocked and declarer can run enough tricks for contract. The proper play, therefore, is to cover the Jack. The complete hand is as follows:

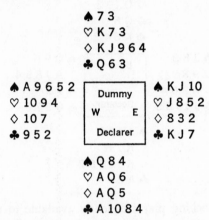

♠ 7 3
♡ K 7 3
◊ K J 9 6 4
♣ Q 6 3

♠ A 9 6 5 2   ♠ K J 10
♡ 10 9 4   ♡ J 8 5 2
◊ 10 7   ◊ 8 3 2
♣ 9 5 2   ♣ K J 7

♠ Q 8 4
♡ A Q 6
◊ A Q 5
♣ A 10 8 4

South is playing a contract of 3 No Trump. West leads the 9 of Hearts. What card should declarer play from dummy?

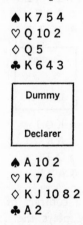

♠ K 7 5 4
♡ Q 10 2
◊ Q 5
♣ K 6 4 3

♠ A 10 2
♡ K 7 6
◊ K J 10 8 2
♣ A 2

This is an obviously short-suit lead, and East is marked with the Ace and the Jack. If declarer plays low from dummy, East will duck and the King will be forced. If West gains the lead with the Ace of Diamonds, he will be able to continue through the Queen of Hearts. Declarer has a certain way to prevent any such attack, and that is by the simple expedient of playing the Queen from dummy. This will force East to win with the Ace and he will be unable to continue the suit with the 10 in dummy. This gives declarer plenty of time to drive out the Ace of Diamonds. The complete holding is as follows:

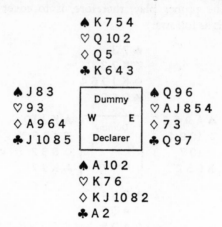

```
                    ♠ K 7 5 4
                    ♡ Q 10 2
                    ◊ Q 5
                    ♣ K 6 4 3
   ♠ J 8 3      ┌──────────┐    ♠ Q 9 6
   ♡ 9 3        │  Dummy   │    ♡ A J 8 5 4
   ◊ A 9 6 4    │  W    E  │    ◊ 7 3
   ♣ J 10 8 5   │ Declarer │    ♣ Q 9 7
                └──────────┘
                    ♠ A 10 2
                    ♡ K 7 6
                    ◊ K J 10 8 2
                    ♣ A 2
```

A type of unblocking play frequently available to the declarer is the following:

```
                    ♠ 10 7 5
                    ♡ 9 7 4 2
                    ◊ A 9 5
                    ♣ 10 7 6

                ┌──────────┐
                │  Dummy   │
                │          │
                │ Declarer │
                └──────────┘

                    ♠ K Q J
                    ♡ A K Q J 10
                    ◊ Q 3
                    ♣ A 9 5
```

South is the declarer at a contract of 4 Hearts. West leads the Jack of Diamonds. Dummy plays the 5, and East wins with the King. What card should South play? The answer is the Queen. This play would not be necessary if dummy had a quick entry, but since dummy cannot be entered and since West is morally certain to hold the 10 of Diamonds, the unblocking play will permit the subsequent finesse of the 9 and discard of the losing Club on the Ace of Diamonds.

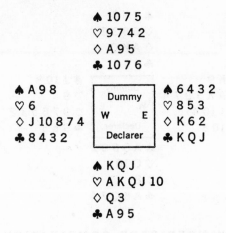

♠ 10 7 5
♡ 9 7 4 2
◇ A 9 5
♣ 10 7 6

♠ A 9 8   ♠ 6 4 3 2
♡ 6   ♡ 8 5 3
◇ J 10 8 7 4   ◇ K 6 2
♣ 8 4 3 2   ♣ K Q J

♠ K Q J
♡ A K Q J 10
◇ Q 3
♣ A 9 5

Occasionally the normal method of play should be departed from because of information gleaned from the auction.

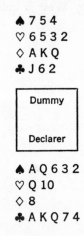

♠ 7 5 4
♡ 6 5 3 2
◇ A K Q
♣ J 6 2

♠ A Q 6 3 2
♡ Q 10
◇ 8
♣ A K Q 7 4

South is declarer at a contract of 4 Spades, West having opened the bidding with 1 Heart, and East, his partner, having failed to keep the bidding open. West leads the King and Ace, then the Jack of Hearts, which declarer ruffs. What is the proper way to play the trumps? It is a moral certainty that West holds the King of Spades as part of his opening bid. Therefore the finesse is bound to fail. Declarer has one chance, and that is that West holds exactly two Spades. If he holds more or less, there is no hope for declarer. Therefore the proper play is the Ace, followed by a small trump, with the hope that the King will fall. The complete hand is as follows:

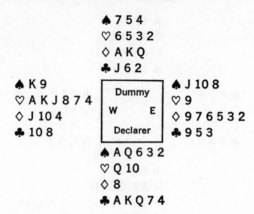

```
              ♠ 7 5 4
              ♡ 6 5 3 2
              ◇ A K Q
              ♣ J 6 2
♠ K 9                        ♠ J 10 8
♡ A K J 8 7 4    Dummy       ♡ 9
◇ J 10 4       W       E     ◇ 9 7 6 5 3 2
♣ 10 8          Declarer     ♣ 9 5 3
              ♠ A Q 6 3 2
              ♡ Q 10
              ◇ 8
              ♣ A K Q 7 4
```

QUIZ ON ADVANCED CARD COMBINATIONS

In each of the following cases you are South, the declarer, at No Trump. The opening lead by West is indicated. What is the proper play from dummy?

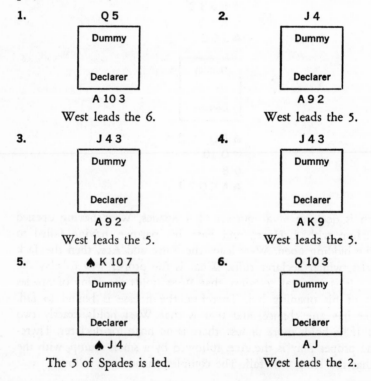

1.

Q 5

Dummy

Declarer

A 10 3

West leads the 6.

2.

J 4

Dummy

Declarer

A 9 2

West leads the 5.

3.

J 4 3

Dummy

Declarer

A 9 2

West leads the 5.

4.

J 4 3

Dummy

Declarer

A K 9

West leads the 5.

5.

♠ K 10 7

Dummy

Declarer

♠ J 4

The 5 of Spades is led.

6.

Q 10 3

Dummy

Declarer

A J

West leads the 2.

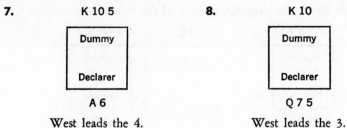

7. K 10 5

Dummy

Declarer

A 6

West leads the 4.

8. K 10

Dummy

Declarer

Q 7 5

West leads the 3.

In the following problems you are South, the declarer, at No Trump. It is your lead unless otherwise stated. The dummy has no other entries. How do you play these combinations in order to make the number of tricks indicated under each problem?

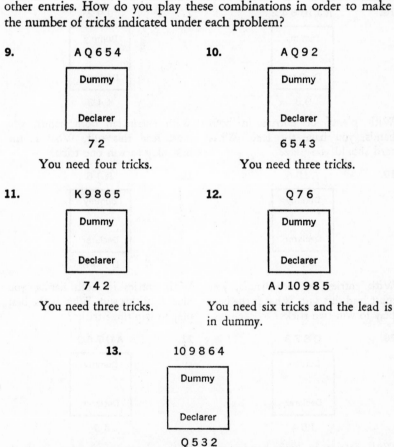

9. A Q 6 5 4

Dummy

Declarer

7 2

You need four tricks.

10. A Q 9 2

Dummy

Declarer

6 5 4 3

You need three tricks.

11. K 9 8 6 5

Dummy

Declarer

7 4 2

You need three tricks.

12. Q 7 6

Dummy

Declarer

A J 10 9 8 5

You need six tricks and the lead is in dummy.

13. 10 9 8 6 4

Dummy

Declarer

Q 5 3 2

You need three tricks and the lead is in your hand.

You are South, the declarer, in each of the following examples.

14. K Q 8 7 5

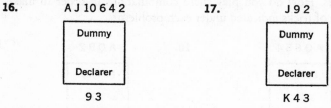

J 9 3 2

With plenty of entries in both hands, what is the proper way to play this combination?

15. K Q 9 6 3

A 7 5 2

With entries in both hands, what is the proper way to play this combination?

16. A J 10 6 4 2

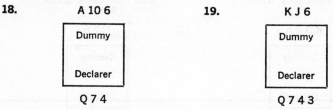

9 3

With plenty of entries in both hands, you have the lead. What card should you play?

17. J 9 2

K 4 3

With entries in both hands, you must lead this suit. What is the best play to win one trick?

18. A 10 6

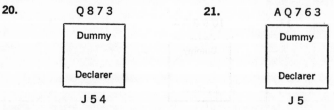

Q 7 4

With entries in both hands, you must lead this suit. What is the best play to win two tricks?

19. K J 6

Q 7 4 3

With entries in both hands, you must lead this suit. What is the best play to win three tricks?

20. Q 8 7 3

J 5 4

With entries in both hands, you must lead this suit. What is the best way to win one trick?

21. A Q 7 6 3

J 5

With plenty of entries in both hands, what is the best play to win four tricks?

22.

K 9 7 5 4

Dummy
Declarer

A J 10

Dummy has no entries. What is the best way to play this suit to win five tricks?

23.

A K J 10 4 3

Dummy
Declarer

7 5

With entries in both hands, what is the best way to play this suit to win all six tricks?

In each of the following hands you are South, the declarer.

24.

♠ A 8 3
♡ K 3 2
◇ K Q J 4
♣ A Q 3

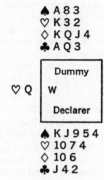

♡ Q | W

Dummy
Declarer

♠ K J 9 5 4
♡ 10 7 4
◇ 10 6
♣ J 4 2

You are playing a contract of 4 Spades after West opened the bidding with 1 No Trump. West leads the Ace, followed by the Queen of Hearts. Plan your play.

25.

♠ J 9 3
♡ A K 7
◇ Q 10 3
♣ Q J 10 4

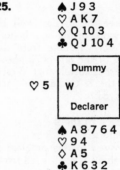

♡ 5 | W

Dummy
Declarer

♠ A 8 7 6 4
♡ 9 4
◇ A 5
♣ K 6 3 2

You are playing a contract of 4 Spades with no adverse bidding. West leads the 5 of Hearts. Plan your play.

26.

♠ K 7 4 3
♡ K Q
◇ J 4 2
♣ A Q J 10

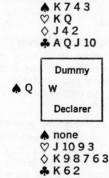

♠ Q | W

Dummy
Declarer

♠ none
♡ J 10 9 3
◇ K 9 8 7 6 3
♣ K 6 2

You are playing a 5 Diamond contract reached on the following sequence:

NORTH	SOUTH
1 Club	1 Diamond
2 Diamonds	4 Diamonds
5 Diamonds	Pass
Pass	

EAST	WEST
Double	Pass
Pass	Pass
Double	Pass

West leads the Queen of Spades. Dummy plays the 3, East the 8, and you ruff. Plan your play.

ANSWERS TO QUIZ ON ADVANCED CARD COMBINATIONS

1. The 5.
No matter what East plays, you must win two tricks. If you go up with the Queen and East covers with the King, a subsequent lead through your 10 may hold you to just one trick.

2. The Jack.
The only hope is that the lead is from the K Q. Otherwise the Jack can never take a trick.

3. The 3.
Since you have the 9, East will be forced to play one of the high honors whenever West is leading from the Q 10 or the K 10 and others. Without the 9, your best chance is that West's lead is from the K Q, and the Jack should be played.

4. The presence of the 9 in your hand
makes the answer to this problem a guess. If you think West has led from the Queen, you should put up the Jack. If you believe he has led from the 10, you should play low.

5. The 7
hoping to win two tricks if West has led from the Queen. If East wins with the Ace, you should play the Jack in order to be able to finesse the 10 the next time.

6. The Queen.
With this holding you are always assured of two tricks, but if East has the King, and he can be induced to cover the Queen, a third trick will be set up.

7. The 10.
Your best chance of winning a third trick in the suit is that West is leading from a combination of cards headed by the Q J. If you play the 5 from dummy, East will surely play some intermediate card to force out your Ace and thus hold you to two tricks.

8. The 10 is the best play.
If West is leading from the A J or the Jack, you will have two stoppers. If West has the Ace and East the Jack, the play of the King would temporarily prevent West from safely attacking the suit, but that possibility is counterbalanced by the instance where he holds both high honors.

9. There is only a remote chance
to win four tricks with this holding, but since there is a mathematical possibility, you should give it the old college try. You should, therefore, give up a trick and then finesse the second time. If the finesse fails, it will mean that you have lost your Ace, but in view of the possible gain it is worth the risk.

10. You should lead the 3
and if West plays low, insert the 9 from dummy. If this does not draw out the King, the finesse of the Queen should be taken on the next round. If the 9 goes to East's 10, you have lost nothing.

11. Your only chance
is to find a doubleton Ace in either hand. Therefore, you must concede the first two tricks in the suit by playing low from both hands. If the Ace falls on the second lead, dummy's King will pick up the remaining outstanding card.

12. Lead the 6 from dummy
and, if East plays small, play the 5 from your hand. Or you may lead the Queen, provided you underplay with the 8 from your own hand in the absence of a cover.

13. Lead the Queen from your hand.
This is to cover the possibility of either defender holding a singleton Jack in the suit. If the suit breaks 2–2, it doesn't matter what you do, and if either opponent holds a singleton high honor, there is no way to avoid three losers.

14. The King should be played first so that if either opponent has the A 10 and two others, the 10 can be captured by a finesse either way.

15. Lay down the Ace from your hand.

If East shows out you can finesse West out of his J 10 by leading twice toward the dummy. You should not lay down a high honor from the dummy initially, because if East is the one with J 10 x x, he cannot be prevented from winning a trick in the suit.

16. You should play the 3 and not the 9

intending to finesse the 10. When it loses, your hand will be re-entered and the 9 led in order to finesse the Jack. The 9 should not be played to the first trick, because West might have a singleton honor, in which case East will have the Q 8 and two others or the K 8 and two others, and the 8 will be promoted to a second winner.

17. You should lead the 3

and if West plays low, follow with the 9 from dummy. If this forces the Queen, there is no further problem. If it loses to the 10, dummy should be entered and the 2 led toward the King with the hope that East has the Ace. This play will lose only if West has the A Q and a small one and ducks the first lead. Many times West, holding the A Q and another, will fear to play low and will come up with the Queen.

18. Lead low from dummy toward the Queen.

If this loses to the King, when you regain the lead play low toward dummy, intending to finesse the 10 if West plays low.

19. Lead low toward the dummy.

If the Jack holds, you should return to your hand to lead low toward the King. This protects against the holding of A x in the West hand.

20. It is better not to start operations on this suit.

But, if you must play it yourself, your best chance is to find one defender with a doubleton honor. You should lead a low card through that player. If you think it is East, play low to the Jack. This will presumably drive out a high honor. Now, when you regain the lead, play a low Heart to dummy and duck it hoping the other high honor will fall from the East hand.

21. Lead low from dummy toward the Jack.

If either hand has the K x x, you will make four tricks regardless of how you play the suit, but if East has the K x, the play toward the Jack is necessary. It has the added advantage that if East has four to the King, he may make an error and go up with his King.

22. Lead the 10

intending to finesse if West plays low. If you play the Ace first, then continue with the Jack and West covers with the Queen, you would be forced to let him hold the trick in order to avoid blocking the suit. If the 10 holds, you will then be in position to cash the Ace and overtake the Jack.

23. Lead the 5 from your hand

and finesse the 10 in dummy. This play will lose a trick if East has a singleton Queen, but it will succeed when West has Q x x x. If East does have a singleton, it is much more likely to be one of the small spots rather than the Queen.

24. Win the King of Hearts

and since West is marked with all the missing high cards for his 1 No Trump opening, he must have the Queen of Spades and an unusual play in the trump suit is indicated. Lead a low Spade to the King and play the Jack of Spades now, hoping that East has the 10 x of trumps. When the finesse succeeds, you draw the last trump and drive out the Ace of Diamonds, claiming the remaining tricks.

The complete holding:

NORTH
♠ A 8 3
♡ K 3 2
◇ K Q J 4
♣ A Q 3

WEST
♠ Q 7 6
♡ A Q J 9
◇ A 8 2
♣ K 10 7

EAST
♠ 10 2
♡ 8 6 5
◇ 9 7 5 3
♣ 9 8 6 5

SOUTH
♠ K J 9 5 4
♡ 10 7 4
◇ 10 6
♣ J 4 2

25. Since you have a marked loser in Diamonds and Clubs, you must hold your loss in trumps to one trick. The best chance is to find West with either the K 10 or Q 10 doubleton. You should, therefore, play to the Ace of Diamonds, and lead a low Spade to dummy. West wins the King and leads another Heart. You win in dummy and lead the Jack of Spades through. When this smothers West's 10, the contract is home.

The complete holding:

NORTH
♠ J 9 3
♡ A K 7
◇ Q 10 3
♣ Q J 10 4

WEST
♠ K 10
♡ J 8 6 5 2
◇ K 8 7
♣ 9 8 5

EAST
♠ Q 5 2
♡ Q 10 3
◇ J 9 6 4 2
♣ A 7

SOUTH
♠ A 8 7 6 4
♡ 9 4
◇ A 5
♣ K 6 3 2

26. It seems probable
that East has both major-suit Aces and the A Q of Diamonds. Your one hope is to find West with a singleton 10 of trumps. You should lead a Club to the dummy and return the Jack of Diamonds. (This play will save a trick for you even if East has all the missing trumps.) East plays the 5, you play the 6, and West drops the 10. Another Diamond lead brings forth the Ace from East, and when you regain the lead his last trump is drawn and a trick conceded to the Ace of Hearts.

The complete holding:

NORTH
♠ K 7 4 3
♡ K Q
◇ J 4 2
♣ A Q J 10

WEST
♠ Q J 9 5 2
♡ 7 5 2
◇ 10
♣ 9 8 7 3

EAST
♠ A 10 8 6
♡ A 8 6 4
◇ A Q 5
♣ 5 4

SOUTH
♠ none
♡ J 10 9 3
◇ K 9 8 7 6 3
♣ K 6 2

17.   Safety plays

THE SAFETY PLAY is very much what the name indicates, a means of protection against a bad break. It is a method of play which is calculated to hold your losses in a particular suit within certain limits, in the event of unforeseen distribution.

One line of play, for example, may have the prospect of winning five tricks, but if you attempted to win these five tricks and the cards broke badly, you might find yourself taking only three tricks.

Let us presume that to fulfill your contract you need four tricks. In that case it would be extremely unwise for you to attempt to win the maximum if there were a safer way to guarantee that you will win four tricks. This is the theory of the safety play.

In other words, safety plays many times deliberately sacrifice one trick in order to run the least possible risk of losing two tricks.

Failure by declarer to exercise caution in what are considered normal situations has resulted in staggering losses at the bridge table. "Partner, I was helpless against such a bad break in trumps" is frequently another way of saying, "Partner, I took too much for granted. I should have exercised more caution."

While it is true that optimism in the play of a hand is a great asset, nevertheless there are certain situations in which pessimism is a sounder attitude. When a contract can be fulfilled only on one distribution of the cards, even though it is highly unlikely, by all means be an optimist and play for that break, but when a contract can be fulfilled against any distribution of the adverse cards, however unexpected, pessimism pays big dividends.

When a contract appears to be "in the bag," pause a moment and ask yourself what bad breaks of the cards might prove embarrassing. If there is such a division, guard yourself against it. Do not presume that suits will break unless it is absolutely necessary to do so. When there is danger, however slight, it does not pay to try for the maximum. (A possible exception may be noted by duplicate players. These are referred to in the chapter on Percentages.)

Certain combinations in the safety field have become standardized. Others you may be called upon to figure out for yourself as the situation develops. Mastering safety plays requires steady practice to fix in mind all the outstanding cards in the suit. An hour of private practice with one suit will help more than weeks of actual play. One or two combinations will at first appear to go against your natural instincts, but upon study you will observe their soundness.

Let us take first one of the simplest cases of all:

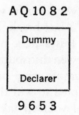

A Q 10 8 2

Dummy

Declarer

9 6 5 3

If you need five tricks, you play for West to hold King and another Spade and lead from South to finesse the Queen. But if you need only four tricks and play in the same manner, you may come a cropper. If the Queen loses to the King, what do you do next time? If you play the Ace, it may turn out that East is now void and you will lose to West's Jack, which would be the case if the original holdings were as follows:

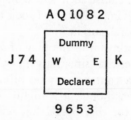

A Q 10 8 2

J 7 4   Dummy   K

W   E

Declarer

9 6 5 3

If, however, you decide to finesse again the next time, it is barely possible that you will lose to the Jack, in which case the original holdings can be as follows:

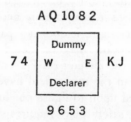

A Q 10 8 2

7 4   Dummy   K J

W   E

Declarer

9 6 5 3

In other words, if you misguess you will be lost. To guard against such a misguess the absolute insurance play is the Ace first. Notice in the first case you would drop the singleton King, and your play would win all the tricks. In the second case you would drop the Jack, and your troubles would be over. Assume, however, that on the play of the Ace two small cards fell. Now the South hand would be re-entered and a small one led toward the Queen. If West follows, it must be with either the Jack or the King, and your troubles are over. If West shows out, you will lose two tricks, but then nothing could ever have been done about it. You would have had to lose two tricks in any event. If it is possible for the contract to be fulfilled, the play of the Ace guarantees that you will do so and protects you against a possible misguess which would result from finessing. Bear in mind that this method applies where you can afford to lose one trick but cannot afford to lose two.

A variation of this play is seen in the following situation:

A Q 6 4 3

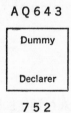

7 5 2

With this combination, no matter how favorable the distribution of the opponents' cards, one trick will have to be lost in any event.

Assume that the King is in the West hand. East will then have the J 10 9, and the Jack must eventually win one trick.

Now this holding may prove very treacherous. Assume, for example, that East has the singleton King. The first-round finesse will lose, and the opponents will take three tricks against you. If East has the King and one other Spade, and the finesse is taken, the opponents will win two tricks against you.

Assume that you have plenty of time and plenty of entries. The play of the Ace first will in the long run be profitable. If West holds the King, he will hold it a trick or two later, and the Queen will still be a winner, because the South hand will be re-entered and a small card led toward the Queen. Occasionally when you play the Ace the Jack will fall from the East hand, which may lead you to suspect that the King will fall on the next lead.

Suppose, for example, the adverse holdings were:

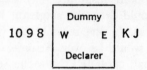

When you play the Ace and follow up with a small card you will lose only one trick in the suit. Whereas if you take the finesse immediately you will be obliged to lose two tricks.

It must be understood that these discussions assume that there is no anxiety to prevent the opponents from obtaining the lead in a hurry. If, for example, you need two tricks at once without letting the opponents in, you would naturally have to take the finesse.

There are certain safety plays that cost nothing. They are merely precaution plays. One of them we learned when the elements were being taught to us. For example:

A 9 4 3

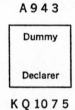

K Q 10 7 5

Having nine cards, the only way you could lose a trick in the suit is for one opponent to have all four, including the Jack. If, however, you find out which one has the four, you can finesse against the Jack either way. Therefore the safety play is to lead first the King from the South hand. If West shows out, the 10 can subsequently be finessed against East. If East shows out, then the 9 can be finessed in the North hand. This is the first safety play which beginners are taught.

A slight variation of the above is the following:

K 9 6 5

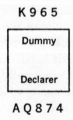

A Q 8 7 4

With this combination of cards can you lose a trick? The answer is yes, if one of the opponents has all four outstanding cards. The next question is, can you do anything about it? The answer is, it all depends on which one of them has all four. If West has them, nothing can be done about it with any line of play. Look at *Diagram A*. But if East has them (*Diagram B*), you need not lose a trick. You first play the King and then find that West is void. Then play the 5 from the North hand, and East will be obliged to play the 10. This is won by South's Queen. The North hand is re-entered, and now the 9 is led in order to pick up East's Jack.

Diagram A

K 9 6 5

J 10 3 2 | Dummy W E Declarer | none

A Q 8 7 4

Diagram B

K 9 6 5

none | Dummy W E Declarer | J 10 3 2

A Q 8 7 4

The important thing, however, is to find out early whether East has all four. The instinctive play, to lead the high card from the hand that has the two honors, is not correct in this case, because if you find out that West has them all, it does you no good. There is no use finding out something when you can't do anything about it.

When a hand seems to be a cinch, that is the time to stop and say, what misfortune can befall me? And if that misfortune occurs, can I do anything about it? If there is nothing to be done about the holdings, give it no further thought, as in the case where West holds all four. Do not bother to find out, because you cannot do anything about it. Therefore the proper play is the King from the North hand, to find out if East has all four, because something can be done about that.

A Q 9 5

Dummy

Declarer

J 8 7 6 3 2

If you are attempting to win all the tricks in this suit, which card do you lead from the South hand?

First of all, the proper play with ten cards is to finesse. (For dis-

N*

cussion of this principle see Chapter 24 "Percentages.") The question is, should the Jack be led or a small one? If the adverse three cards are divided two–one, it will make no difference which card you lead. If East has all three, it will be immaterial, but if West has all three, you will be able to find it out by leading the Jack. West presumably will cover, and North will win with the Ace. When East shows out, the rest is easy. Notice if you had played a small one first, West would have followed with the 4, dummy would have played the Queen, and East would show out, and now West would hold the K 10 over your Jack and cannot be prevented from taking a trick. Needless to say, if on the lead of the Jack, West shows out, the 5 will be played from dummy and East permitted to take his one and only trick. The complete holding:

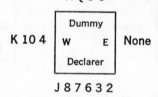

A Q 9 5

K 10 4   Dummy / W E / Declarer   None

J 8 7 6 3 2

The above is the type of safety play which cannot possibly lose a trick but might gain a trick. It might be described as a precaution play.

In this holding you are willing to lose one trick but not two. What is the correct play?

J 7 5 2

Dummy

Declarer

A Q 8 4 3

Since the opponents have four cards, you intend to take the finesse. The normal play would be to lead the 2 from the North hand and finesse the Queen. If West should show out, East could not be prevented from winning two tricks. The original holding would have been:

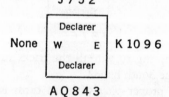

J 7 5 2

None   Declarer / W E / Declarer   K 10 9 6

A Q 8 4 3

If West originally had all four of the suit, nothing could ever have been done about it. He would naturally be entitled to two tricks in the suit.

Notice in the first case, however, that had North led the Jack, East could have been limited to one trick in the suit. He would be obliged to cover with the King, South would win with the Ace, and West would show out. Now the 3 is led toward the 7, and East wins the trick with the 9, but the North hand is entered with some other suit, and the finesse is taken against East's guarded 10.

It is true that the play of the Jack might cost an extra trick. That is where East holds a singleton King. The lead of the small one would permit you to take all five tricks, whereas the lead of the Jack permits West to win a trick with the 10. However, in the case where you are willing to lose one trick because you want to be quite sure not to lose two, the Jack is the proper play.

K 10 7 4

A 9 6 5 3

Assume that you are playing a slam contract in Hearts and this is your trump suit. You have no other losers in the side suits. You will, therefore, succeed in your contract if you lose only one Heart trick. If you play properly, you will be successful no matter how the cards are distributed. What is the correct play? If you should first play the King from the North hand, you will meet with defeat if East shows out. If you lead the Ace from the South hand, it will be disastrous if West shows out. When a hand seems as easy as this you must stop and say, what disaster can possibly overtake me? The answer is, of course, all four trumps in one hand. You must, therefore, play in such a manner as to find out which one is void. The proper play is a low card from either hand. Let us assume that the lead is in the North hand. The 4 should be played first. If East shows out, the Ace will win, and a small one led toward the King 10 will hold West to only one trick. If East should play the 2 on the 4, then South would play the 9. This will take care of the situation if West shows out. If West wins the trick, your troubles are over, because the rest of the trumps must fall.

Remember the only thing you feared was all four in one hand. It must also be remembered that you were not trying to make all the tricks. You wanted to be quite certain not to lose two. If, indeed, it turned out that each of the opponents had two Hearts, you will have spent a trick needlessly, but that is a small premium to pay for an insurance policy.

K 9 5

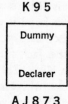

A J 8 7 3

With this holding, if you can afford to lose one trick but cannot afford to lose two, what is the proper play? If you lead the King from the North hand, you will lose two tricks if it turns out that West had originally Q 10 6 2. The proper play is first the Ace, then the 3, and when West plays low follow with the 9 from the North hand. If East wins the trick with the 10, your troubles are over, because the Queen must fall next time. If West plays the 10, of course that is the end of the problem. If on the second lead West shows out, North wins with the King and now leads the 9 toward the Jack. East will then have held the Q 10 6 2 and will win only with the Queen. The complete hands follow:

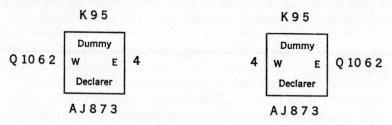

Assuming that you can afford to lose one trump trick but not two, what is the correct play?

K J 3 2

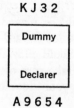

A 9 6 5 4

The answer is the King first. If you play the Ace first and West shows out, East cannot be prevented from taking two tricks with the Queen and the 10. On the play of the King, if West shows out, the 2 will now be led. This forces East to put up his 10 and he can take only one trick. If it is East who shows out instead of West, nothing is lost by the play of the King, because then the 2 is led toward the Ace and the 5 is led toward the Jack, holding West to only one trick, the Queen.

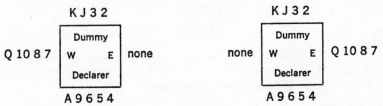

The following diagram contains an interesting combination of cards, but the proper play depends upon just how many tricks you are after. If you need three tricks, there are two different ways of handling it, which have already been discussed on page 350.

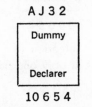

If, however, you are satisfied with only two tricks in the suit but wish to be quite sure not to lose three, another line of play is necessary. The 100 per cent play to guarantee the taking of two tricks is the Ace first, followed by a small one toward the 10. This will guarantee two tricks against any possible distribution of the remaining cards.

If the King, Queen, and a number of others are under the Ace, a low one to the 10 will draw out the Queen. The South hand is then re-entered and a low one is led toward the Jack.

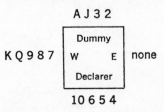

If the five cards are behind the Ace, the Queen will have to come up on the second trick, and the Jack and 10 between them will produce one more trick for the declarer.

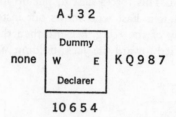

This play avoids misguessing where a single honor is held by the adversary. If, for example, the 10 is led, declarer will lose three tricks if West happens to have the singleton honor.

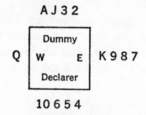

If the 4 is led, with the intention of playing the Jack from the North hand, declarer will win only one trick if East has a singleton honor.

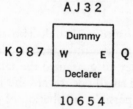

Of course if the adverse cards are divided three–two, any line of play will succeed in winning two tricks.

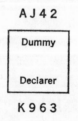

The problem is to insure the taking of three tricks. The common way of playing this holding is to lead the King first and then toward the Jack. This play will lose two tricks whenever East has four or more headed by the Queen 10. The proper play will guarantee the taking of three tricks regardless of the adverse distribution. The correct method is to play the Ace first and then the 2. If East follows, the 9 is played by declarer. If it loses to the 10, the Queen must fall next time. If, on the 2, East shows out, declarer wins with the King and leads toward the Jack. If on the very first play of the Ace, West shows out, the 2 is led to the King 9 and East will be forced to play an honor.

If you need all four tricks, the finesse is the proper play. Very little is to be gained by playing the King first, since if you drop a singleton Queen from the East hand, it is impossible to take four tricks in any event. Whereas if the 3 is led and West holds a singleton Queen, the 10 in the East hand can now be captured.

10 4 3

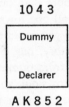

A K 8 5 2

In playing this hand South leads the King and West drops the Jack. What is the next proper play? Assume that you can afford to lose one trick but not two. It is true if the Queen is now alone in the West hand you can win all the tricks by playing the Ace, but if West should show out, it would mean that East's Queen 9 would both be winners. What is the sure play? The answer is, a small one toward the 10. If West has the Queen alone, the rest of the suit must now fall. If West shows out, the 10 will force East to play the Queen, and while he still has the 9 protected, you can enter the North hand with some other suit and finesse the 8 against him. The holding will have been:

10 4 3

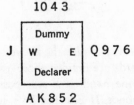

A K 8 5 2

Would you play any differently if on the lead of the King it was East who played the Jack? The answer is no. The same play is indicated. If East's Jack is accompanied by the Queen, he is welcome to one trick, because the rest will now be good; but if East's Jack was a singleton, then West would now hold the Q 9 7, and a low card toward the 10 will either force him to play the Queen or permit the 10 to win.

A combination of very frequent occurrence is the following:

A 10 6 5 2

```
+-----------+
|  Dummy    |
|           |
|           |
|  Declarer |
+-----------+
```

K 7 4

Your object is to lose no more than one trick in the suit. The King should be led first, then a small one toward the Ace 10. If West does not follow, there was nothing you could ever have done about it. The loss of two tricks was obligatory, but if West follows with a small card, you should play the 10 from dummy. If it loses, the rest of the tricks are now good. If East shows out, your precaution will have been rewarded. In other words, do not take for granted that a suit will break three–two and play the Ace the next time on the theory that it makes no difference. It is true that if they break three–two it will not matter, but just in case West has the Queen Jack and two others, it costs you nothing to play the 10. This is another way of stating that when the opponents must take a trick in any event, it frequently pays to be cheerful about it and give it to them early.

Q 8 4 3

```
+-----------+
|  Dummy    |
|           |
|           |
|  Declarer |
+-----------+
```

A K 9 5

What is the proper way to play the above combination if you need all four tricks? If the cards are divided three–two, the play is immaterial. If they are four in one hand, it is still possible to make the hand if the singleton is an honor. If East has four, including the Jack 10, it is true that we could make all the tricks if we knew it, but unfortunately there is no way to find out. The best play, therefore, is the King from the South hand. If West should drop the 10, the correct continuation would be the 5 toward the Queen, and if West shows out, the 9 can be finessed against East's Jack. If both opponents follow, of course there is no further problem. If, however, on the play of the King, East drops the 10, the proper continuation is the Ace, and if East shows out, the 8 can be finessed in the North hand.

9 7 6

A K 10 3 2

Assuming that you are willing to give up one trick in the suit, what is the proper way to play this combination? If the cards are divided three–two, there will be no problem. You must, therefore, guard merely against four important cards in the East hand. The proper play is the Ace first. If an honor drops, there is no further problem. If only small ones appear, you must not lead out the King. You should either enter the North hand to lead through for a finesse of the 10 or lead a small one toward the 9. If West shows out, the 9 forces the Jack, and the North hand is entered later on for a finesse against East's Queen.

♠ A 5 3

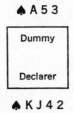

♠ K J 4 2

With this holding the declarer wishes to take three tricks but cannot afford to lose two. The proper play is the King first. Then the 2 is led to the Ace and the 5 returned toward the Jack. If the Queen was located with East, where the finesse would have succeeded, the Jack will still be good for the third trick. If the Spades were three–three, regardless of the location of the Queen, a third trick will become established. If West had four, including the Queen, there was never any way to take more than two tricks. When three tricks are needed, the finesse of the Jack is not the proper play, because West might have a doubleton Queen.

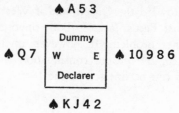

♠ A 5 3

♠ Q 7   Dummy   ♠ 10 9 8 6
W   E
Declarer

♠ K J 4 2

QUIZ ON SAFETY PLAYS

You have plenty of entries in both hands. How would you manage each of the following combinations of cards to limit yourself to one loser?

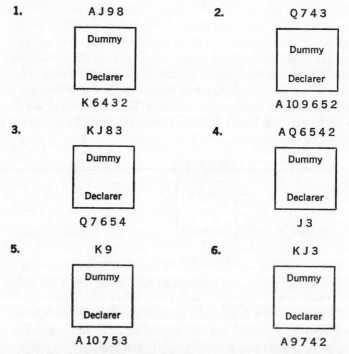

1. A J 9 8

Dummy

Declarer

K 6 4 3 2

2. Q 7 4 3

Dummy

Declarer

A 10 9 6 5 2

3. K J 8 3

Dummy

Declarer

Q 7 6 5 4

4. A Q 6 5 4 2

Dummy

Declarer

J 3

5. K 9

Dummy

Declarer

A 10 7 5 3

6. K J 3

Dummy

Declarer

A 9 7 4 2

In each of the following hands you are South, the declarer. Plan the safest line of play to assure your contract.

7.
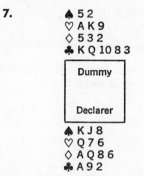

♠ 5 2
♡ A K 9
◇ 5 3 2
♣ K Q 10 8 3

Dummy

Declarer

♠ K J 8
♡ Q 7 6
◇ A Q 8 6
♣ A 9 2

The contract is 3 No Trump. West leads the 6 of Spades and East plays the Queen.

8.
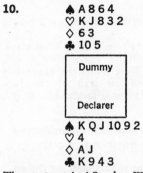

♠ J 6 3 2
♡ A 4 2
◇ A Q 3
♣ 8 7 6

Dummy

Declarer

♠ A K 9 8 4
♡ K 8 7
◇ K 6 2
♣ K 3

The contract is 3 No Trump. West leads the Jack of Diamonds.

9.
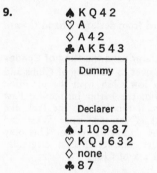

♠ K Q 4 2
♡ A
◇ A 4 2
♣ A K 5 4 3

Dummy

Declarer

♠ J 10 9 8 7
♡ K Q J 6 3 2
◇ none
♣ 8 7

The contract is 6 Spades. West leads the Queen of Clubs.

10.

♠ A 8 6 4
♡ K J 8 3 2
◇ 6 3
♣ 10 5

Dummy

Declarer

♠ K Q J 10 9 2
♡ 4
◇ A J
♣ K 9 4 3

The contract is 4 Spades. West over-called in Diamonds. He leads the Queen of Clubs. East wins with the Ace and returns the deuce.

11.
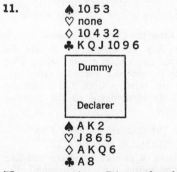

♠ 10 5 3
♡ none
◇ 10 4 3 2
♣ K Q J 10 9 6

Dummy

Declarer

♠ A K 2
♡ J 8 6 5
◇ A K Q 6
♣ A 8

The contract is 5 Diamonds after West overcalled in Hearts. He leads the King of Hearts.

12.
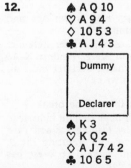

♠ A Q 10
♡ A 9 4
◇ 10 5 3
♣ A J 4 3

Dummy

Declarer

♠ K 3
♡ K Q 2
◇ A J 7 4 2
♣ 10 6 5

The contract is 3 No Trump. West leads the 5 of Spades.

13.
    ♠ 2
    ♡ A 10 9 3
    ◇ Q 10 5 4
    ♣ 9 8 6 2

```
┌──────────┐
│ Dummy    │
│          │
│          │
│ Declarer │
└──────────┘
```

The contract is 4 Hearts. West leads the King of Clubs.

♠ K J 5 4
♡ K Q J 8 7
◇ A 3 2
♣ A

ANSWERS TO QUIZ ON SAFETY PLAYS

1. Declarer should lead low from his hand

and cover whatever card West plays. If East follows, the suit must now break. If West shows out, the Ace is played and the lead of the Jack through East will restrict him to one trick.

2. Lead a small card from dummy and cover whatever East plays.

3. Declarer should lead the Queen. This will assure only one loser if West has A 10 9 2 as he can subsequently be finessed out of his intermediate cards. If East has A 10 9 2, then two tricks must always be lost.

4. The correct play is the Ace and then a small card.

This will succeed if either defender has a singleton King. Against K 10 9 x in either hand, declarer must always lose two tricks.

5. Barring a three-three break declarer's best hope to hold himself to one loser is by leading a small card toward dummy and inserting the 9. This play will succeed if West has either Q x or J x.

6. The correct play is the King followed by a subsequent lead of a

low card from declarer's hand toward the J 3.

7. Declarer wins the King of Spades crosses over to the King of Clubs and leads a low Club with the intention of playing the 9 from his hand if East follows. If this loses to the Jack, the contract is assured, since West can make no damaging return. This play saves the contract if East originally had J x x x of Clubs.

8. The Diamond opening is won in dummy

and a low Spade is led. South will cover whatever East plays. If West wins this trick, the suit will break establishing declarer's ninth trick, and the Clubs will be safe from attack.

9. After the Club lead is won the Ace of Diamonds should be played and a Club discard taken. This is to prevent one defender from giving the other a Club ruff when the lead is surrendered to the Ace of trumps.

10. The Club return should be ducked to dummy's 10.

This is to protect against a possible second-round ruff. A Diamond discard can subsequently be taken on the King of Clubs after trumps are drawn.

11. Declarer should ruff the Heart lead

play a trump to the Ace and then a low trump from his hand. This is to protect against a four-one trump break in which case the run of dummy's Club suit could be interrupted in the absence of the safety play.

12. Declarer has eight tricks off the top

and can assure his contract by playing Ace and a small card in either minor suit. The Ace should be played first in case either defender has a singleton honor.

13. Declarer wins the Ace of Clubs

and, in order to assure his contract, leads a Spade from his hand. If he should enter dummy with a trump to lead toward the King of Spades, a second round of trumps by one of the defenders might prevent him from trumping all of his Spade losers.

18.

Entries

WE HAVE previously observed that in order to take full advantage of our high cards the lead must come toward them. In order to accomplish this result we must be able to enter the other hand in order to make the lead. Cards which enable a player to reach at will into the hand from which he wishes to lead are called entries. The most obvious entry is an Ace, or King of the suit in which the other hand holds the Ace. There are less obvious ones which we shall discuss presently.

There are certain combinations of cards which require repeated leads from the dummy, in which case more entries will be needed. For example:

4 3 2

A Q J

In this case it will be necessary to lead twice from the dummy in order to finesse successfully against the King. Two entries must be found for the purpose. Though we are sometimes carelessly inclined to look at this combination as just one finesse, it actually involves two finesses.

At the start of a hand it is wise for the declarer to determine how many such leads he requires. This will lead him naturally to the number of entries he requires. That number of entries may be obvious. If not, there may be certain later entries which we might call "hidden." A "hidden entry" is one which does not appear on the surface.

K Q 10

A J 9 4

The simplest development of a hidden entry is the establishment of a low card in a suit when the opposition can no longer follow.

In this case it is apparent that the dummy has three entries, all three of dummy's cards being capable of winning tricks. These are obvious entries. Some entries are certain and some are problematical.

Diagram A	Diagram B	Diagram C
A K J	K 3	A Q
Dummy	Dummy	Dummy
Declarer	Declarer	Declarer
4 3 2	4 2	3 2

In DIAGRAM A the dummy has two certain entries in the Ace and King and one problematical entry in the Jack. This will prove to be an entry only if the finesse succeeds.

In DIAGRAM B the King is a problematical entry. If the Ace is on the left, the King will be an entry, but if it is on the right, it will not be.

In DIAGRAM C dummy has one certain entry in the Ace and one possible entry in the Queen, which will prove to be such if the finesse succeeds.

Declarer wishes to finesse Clubs. How many times must he lead the suit?

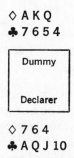

♢ A K Q
♣ 7 6 5 4

Dummy

Declarer

♢ 7 6 4
♣ A Q J 10

It is impossible to tell. Maybe once, if the King shows up at the first trick. Perhaps twice and possibly three times, which would be the case if East held the King and at least three other Clubs. However, the declarer is prepared for such a contingency, because he can enter the dummy just three times in order to make the required three Club leads.

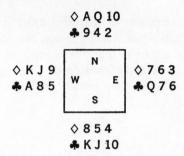

$\diamond$ A Q 10
$\clubsuit$ 9 4 2

$\diamond$ K J 9 $\diamond$ 7 6 3
$\clubsuit$ A 8 5 $\clubsuit$ Q 7 6

$\diamond$ 8 5 4
$\clubsuit$ K J 10

Assuming that the lead is in the South hand, Diamonds should be led first. North has one sure entry and two problematical ones. If the King and Jack of Diamonds are both with West, dummy will have three entries. The 10, therefore, is played from dummy. This holds the trick, and now the dummy leads a Club, finessing the 10 from the closed hand. This is won by West's Ace. Assuming that West returns a Diamond, you win with the Queen in dummy, and now, having determined the location of the Queen of Clubs, you lead a Club and play the Jack.

Diagram D	Diagram E	Diagram F	Diagram G
$\spadesuit$ K Q 6	$\spadesuit$ A J 10	$\spadesuit$ A K Q 3	$\spadesuit$ A 6 4 2
$\diamond$ 5 4 3	$\diamond$ 5 4 3		
Dummy	Dummy	Dummy	Dummy
Declarer	Declarer	Declarer	Declarer
$\spadesuit$ 5 4 3	$\spadesuit$ 5 4 3	$\spadesuit$ J 10 9 2	$\spadesuit$ K Q 7 3
$\diamond$ K Q 6	$\diamond$ A J 10		

In DIAGRAM D assuming that the lead is in the declarer's hand, how many entries has the dummy? The answer is, one certain one and one problematical one. If West has the Ace of Spades, dummy can be entered with both the King and Queen. If East has it, the dummy will possess only one entry. A low Spade is played toward dummy. If it should win, a low Diamond is led toward the closed hand for the same process.

In DIAGRAM E how many entries has the dummy? One certain one and one problematical one. The Ace, of course, is certain, and if West has at least one of the honors, a second trick can be won in the dummy. A low Spade, therefore, is led and the 10 played from dummy. This loses to the Queen, and a Diamond is returned. The 10 is played by declarer and loses to the Queen. Now a Spade comes back, and the Jack is finessed in the dummy. If it wins the trick, this process is repeated in Diamonds.

In DIAGRAM F the declarer wishes to make four leads from the dummy. The three obvious entries are the Ace, King, and Queen. However, if both opponents follow to the first two leads, there will be no more of the suit left at the fourth lead, and if declarer has been careful to retain the deuce, he can enter the dummy at that time with the 3. This is known as a hidden entry because it does not appear on the surface. If declarer should carelessly use the deuce of Spades early in the play, he will lose his hidden entry.

If, as the declarer overtakes the Spades, he learns at the second trick that one of the opponents has four of the suit, he will not be able to continue the overtaking process and will, therefore, find that the 3 in dummy will not become an entry.

The most frequent occurrence of a hidden entry is where each of the hands has four cards of the suit. The result is that in the vast majority of cases at the end of the third lead of the suit neither of the opponents will have any, so that the fourth one is a winner in either hand.

In DIAGRAM G the declarer will no doubt very likely win all four Spade tricks. Let us assume that he desires to enter the dummy twice. He can obviously do so once with the Ace, but if the suit breaks reasonably, he can subsequently make an entry out of the 6. This can be done by playing first the King, then the Queen, and to the third trick the 7 instead of the 3. Notice if the 3 is not retained, the 7 will be too large a card with which to enter dummy, inasmuch as it is higher than the 6.

In the next illustration it will be obligatory to give up one trick to the opponents, regardless of the distribution:

♠ A 5 3 2

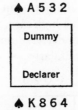

♠ K 8 6 4

Assuming that two entries are desired in the dummy, declarer can retain the 4 of Spades so that the 5 will be a late entry. The King naturally wins a trick. The 6 is led to the Ace, which provides one entry. Subsequently the 8 of Spades is given up to the opposition. This clears the suit, and the 4 may be used to enter the dummy with the 5.

Many times the declarer can win the opening lead very cheaply, but should refuse to do so in order to retain a low card to enter dummy subsequently. Let us take a few simple illustrations:

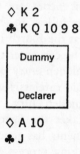

$\diamond$ K 2
$\clubsuit$ K Q 10 9 8

$\diamond$ A 10
$\clubsuit$ J

West leads the 6 of Diamonds. East plays the 9. South should win with the Ace. The purpose is to retain the King of Diamonds as an entry to dummy to cash the Clubs after they become established. The Jack of Clubs is overtaken and the suit continued until the Ace falls.

A case that is not quite so obvious is as follows:

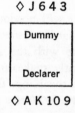

$\diamond$ J 6 4 3

$\diamond$ A K 10 9

West leads the 5 of Diamonds. Dummy plays the 3 and East the 2. South can win the trick with the 9, but if it is important to enter dummy for some other purpose, declarer should win the trick with the King, because it is apparent that West has led from four Diamonds (Q 8 7 5) and that the Jack can be converted into an entry after the first trick is won with a high card.

Notice that this play costs declarer nothing, because he will still make three tricks in the suit. Similarly:

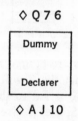

$\diamond$ Q 7 6

$\diamond$ A J 10

West leads the 4 of Diamonds, dummy plays low, and East plays the 8. If a subsequent entry is required into the dummy, declarer should win the first trick with the Ace, retaining the Queen for such time as dummy must be entered. In the above illustrations we have been assuming that the contract was No Trump.

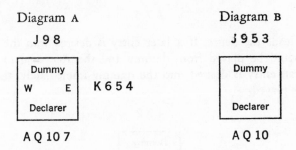

Diagram A

J 9 8

Dummy
W   E   K 6 5 4
Declarer

A Q 10 7

Diagram B

J 9 5 3

Dummy

Declarer

A Q 10

Assume that dummy has no further entries:

In DIAGRAM A the 8 should be played from the dummy and (if East does not cover) the 7 from the closed hand. This permits the trick to be held in the dummy, where the lead is desired. The next play would be the Jack, not the 9, because if the 9 is led, the trick would be won in the closed hand, whereas it is desirable to retain the lead in the dummy.

In DIAGRAM B the Jack should be led from the dummy, so that if it is not covered, the lead will be retained there for the next finesse.

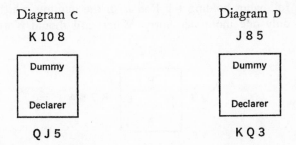

Diagram C

K 10 8

Dummy

Declarer

Q J 5

Diagram D

J 8 5

Dummy

Declarer

K Q 3

In DIAGRAM C, West leads the deuce, East wins with the Ace. If South needs entries in the dummy, the Jack should be played from the closed hand. This will subsequently make both the King and 10 winners.

In DIAGRAM D, West leads the 10, East plays the Ace. If an entry is required in the dummy, declarer would play the Queen, permitting the Jack to become the commanding card.

Q J 6

A 7 5

West leads the deuce. If a later entry is desired into the dummy, the 6 should be played from dummy and the Ace used to win the trick. If an entry is desired into the dummy immediately, the Queen should be played.

4 3 2

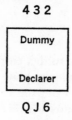

Q J 6

In order to build up a trick with this holding, the declarer must lead twice from the dummy. If he should lead from his own hand, it would be impossible for him to win a trick. Two entries, therefore, are required for this purpose, unless when the first lead comes from dummy East comes up with the Ace or King.

In the following holding the lead is in the dummy, which at this time has only one more side entry. What card should North play?

9 6 2

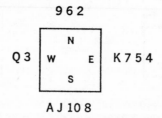
Q 3   K 7 5 4

A J 10 8

He should not make the mistake of leading the 9. Since the 9 will serve a useful purpose later on, it should be retained. The proper play is a small one, inasmuch as declarer intends to lose this trick. He should play the 10 in his own hand, and when it loses to the Queen, dummy should be subsequently entered and the 9 led. If East covers, there is no further problem. If East ducks, South underplays

with the 8 and repeats the finesse. To put it briefly, since a trick must
be lost, it is idle to waste the 9 on that trick.

By the proper handling of certain card combinations an additional
entry may be created when none appears to exist:

♠ 6 4
♣ Q 10 9

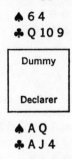

♠ A Q
♣ A J 4

In this case dummy has the lead with no other entry cards. Declarer
wishes to take a finesse in both Spades and Clubs. The proper procedure
is to lead the Queen. If it is covered, the 10 is an entry to permit the
Spade finesse. If East plays low, the Jack should be dropped under the
Queen. Now the 10 is continued, and if East still refuses to cover, the
lead remains in dummy and the Spade finesse can be tried.

Occasionally entries can be created by ruffing good tricks in order
to cross to the other hand.

♠ J 4 3
♡ 7
◇ A K Q 8 4
♣ 10 9 4 3

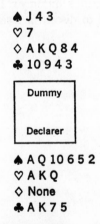

♠ A Q 10 6 5 2
♡ A K Q
◇ None
♣ A K 7 5

Declarer is playing a Spade contract. West leads the Queen of
Clubs, which declarer wins with the King. He desires to enter the
dummy, first to discard his two Clubs on the good Diamonds and,
second, to take the Spade finesse. The simplest way to do it is to
trump the Queen of Hearts even though it is good.

In order to preserve entries in a hand which is short of them, the proper management of certain finesse combinations will be helpful.

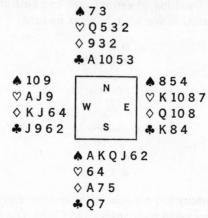

♠ 7 3
♡ Q 5 3 2
◇ 9 3 2
♣ A 10 5 3

♠ 10 9
♡ A J 9
◇ K J 6 4
♣ J 9 6 2

♠ 8 5 4
♡ K 10 8 7
◇ Q 10 8
♣ K 8 4

♠ A K Q J 6 2
♡ 6 4
◇ A 7 5
♣ Q 7

South is declarer at a contract of 3 Spades. West leads the deuce of Clubs, dummy plays low, and East wins with the King. Since there is no entry in the dummy to take a discard on the Ace of Clubs, it is apparent that the declarer will lose two Hearts, two Diamonds, and a Club, and be defeated one trick. His proper procedure is to hope that West led from the Jack of Clubs, and he should play the Queen under the King. This permits dummy's 10 of Clubs to be finessed, and the Ace can be used to discard a losing Diamond.

19. The holdup

THE HOLDUP PLAY consists of refusing to take a trick early in the hand where it is desirable to take the trick later. It is most frequently employed in No Trump contracts, but it is occasionally used with profit at a suit declaration.

The purpose in holding up (that is, not taking a trick at once) is to run one of the opponents out of that suit. In other words, you plan to take the trick at such time that the partner of the opening leader will have no more of that suit to return to the leader. A suit may have been led against you at No Trump which you feel will eventually become established. If, however, the person with the established suit is unable to regain the lead later on in the play, he will not be a menace. You plan, therefore, to exhaust his partner of that suit and then hope that only the partner of the opening leader can obtain future leads.

Whether or not to hold up is the question which the declarer is frequently called upon to answer early in the play. Perhaps the best way to learn when to hold up is to learn the converse, that is—when not to hold up.

1. When it is apparent that the partner of the opening leader cannot be exhausted of that suit. In other words, when something in the hand tells you that the partner of the opening leader has more of that suit than you do.

2. When the hand is so managed that the leader's partner can never obtain the lead.

Another case where it would be pointless to hold up is where the important finesse of the hand, if it loses, must go to the leader himself, so that the number of cards held by the leader's partner is immaterial. For example:

South is the declarer at a contract of 3 No Trump. West leads the 7 of Spades, and East plays the Queen. It is pointless to hold up, because we are indifferent as to the number of Spades that East has, inasmuch as East cannot possibly obtain the lead. All finesses must be taken against him and into West. If they lose, we are down anyhow. If they win, we might be able to take all the tricks. The East hand is dead. It does not pay to disarm a corpse.

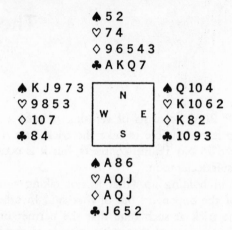

♠ 5 2
♡ 7 4
◇ 9 6 5 4 3
♣ A K Q 7

♠ K J 9 7 3   ♠ Q 10 4
♡ 9 8 5 3   ♡ K 10 6 2
◇ 10 7   ◇ K 8 2
♣ 8 4   ♣ 10 9 3

♠ A 8 6
♡ A Q J
◇ A Q J
♣ J 6 5 2

3. Frequently declarer must refuse to hold up, because there might be a greater menace in the hand in the form of a shift to some other suit by the leader's partner. For example:

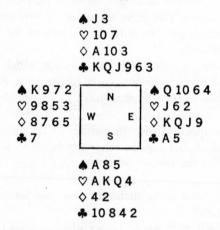

♠ J 3
♡ 10 7
◇ A 10 3
♣ K Q J 9 6 3

♠ K 9 7 2   ♠ Q 10 6 4
♡ 9 8 5 3   ♡ J 6 2
◇ 8 7 6 5   ◇ K Q J 9
♣ 7   ♣ A 5

♠ A 8 5
♡ A K Q 4
◇ 4 2
♣ 10 8 4 2

South is the declarer at a contract of 3 No Trump. West leads the 2 of Spades, the Jack is played from the dummy, and East plays the Queen. Unless West is false-carding, he has only four Spades and there is no danger in the hand. If East is permitted to win the trick, he may shift to Diamonds, which would defeat the contract. The first trick, therefore, should be taken, since there is a greater danger in another suit.

4. When declarer can see that he is able to insure the contract by taking the trick, he should postpone the attempt for extra tricks until the contract is "in the bag."

5. When by not holding up you can develop an additional trick by lower cards in the suit which would lose if you hold up. For example:

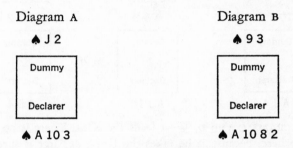

In DIAGRAM A, West leads the 5 of Spades. Dummy plays the 2, and East plays the Queen. It would be absurd for South to hold up, because he would then be able to take only one trick in the suit, whereas if he takes the Queen with the Ace he is assured of an additional trick, because the Jack will drive out the King and thus establish the 10.

In DIAGRAM B, West leads the 5 of Spades. Dummy plays the 3, East plays the Queen. Here again the holdup would be unsound, because by taking the first trick declarer is assured of another trick, inasmuch as the 8 and 9 will drive out the Jack and King, establishing the 10 as a winner.

The play known as the Bath Coup is simply a holdup when declarer has the Ace, Jack, and another and the King has been led by his left-hand opponent. In this particular case the purpose of the holdup is not so much to exhaust the partner of the opening leader as to force the opening leader to make a return that will be favorable to declarer.

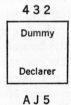

In this case, if West leads the King, assuming that there is no other suit that South is worried about, he should permit West to hold the trick, for if that suit is continued, declarer will win with both the Jack and the Ace.

o

If, however, the 10 is in either hand, it would be pointless to use the Bath Coup.

Diagram C	Diagram D		Diagram E
10 3 2	4 3 2		J 3 2
Dummy	Dummy	or	Dummy
Declarer	Declarer		Declarer
A J 4	A J 10		A 5 4

In DIAGRAMS C AND D, West leads the King. There is no sense to a holdup here, because if he takes the King, declarer is sure of two tricks.

In DIAGRAM E, the King should be taken, and a subsequent lead toward the Jack will produce another trick.

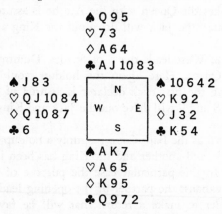

```
                    ♠ Q 9 5
                    ♡ 7 3
                    ◇ A 6 4
                    ♣ A J 10 8 3
   ♠ J 8 3                        ♠ 10 6 4 2
   ♡ Q J 10 8 4      N            ♡ K 9 2
   ◇ Q 10 8 7      W   E          ◇ J 3 2
   ♣ 6              S             ♣ K 5 4
                    ♠ A K 7
                    ♡ A 6 5
                    ◇ K 9 5
                    ♣ Q 9 7 2
```

You are South, the declarer; the contract is 3 No Trump. West leads the Queen of Hearts. East signals encouragingly with the 9. This is the suit which you fear may defeat your contract. If you should take the first trick and subsequently lose the lead, the opponents will cash four Heart tricks and the King of Clubs. You refuse, therefore, to take the Heart trick until the third round, hoping by this time that East will have no more Hearts. Now if the Club finesse loses to East, he will be unable to return his partner's suit. You are able, therefore, to take the rest of the tricks yourself. Notice if you had taken the first or second Heart, East would have had one left to return to his partner when he won with the King of Clubs.

Changing the holdings slightly, we have:

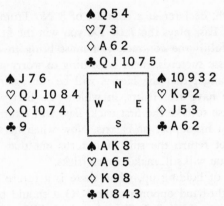

```
            ♠ Q 5 4
            ♡ 7 3
            ◇ A 6 2
            ♣ Q J 10 7 5
♠ J 7 6              ♠ 10 9 3 2
♡ Q J 10 8 4        ♡ K 9 2
◇ Q 10 7 4          ◇ J 5 3
♣ 9                 ♣ A 6 2
            ♠ A K 8
            ♡ A 6 5
            ◇ K 9 8
            ♣ K 8 4 3
```

Here again the Queen of Hearts is opened, and the question is whether to win with the Ace immediately. You know that you will have to surrender the lead to the Ace of Clubs. If West happens to have that card, there is nothing you can do about it. He is bound to win four Heart tricks and the Ace of Clubs, but you have the hope that East may have the Ace. In that case you must not win the Heart trick until such time as East has no more of the suit to return. The same principle applies here as in the preceding example, except that there is no certainty about it, because West might have the Ace of Clubs, in which case you have not gained or lost anything. But if East has it, you have insured the safety of the hand.

In the preceding example you were certain to fulfill the contract no matter who held the missing Club King.

The holdup play may be employed not only when you hold the Ace. It can be used in cases where your stopper is the King, Queen, and another. For example:

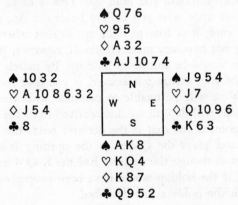

```
            ♠ Q 7 6
            ♡ 9 5
            ◇ A 3 2
            ♣ A J 10 7 4
♠ 10 3 2            ♠ J 9 5 4
♡ A 10 8 6 3 2     ♡ J 7
◇ J 5 4            ◇ Q 10 9 6
♣ 8                ♣ K 6 3
            ♠ A K 8
            ♡ K Q 4
            ◇ K 8 7
            ♣ Q 9 5 2
```

You are South, declarer at a contract of 3 No Trump. West leads the 6 of Hearts, East plays the Jack. Do you win the first trick?

In order to fulfill the contract, you must bring in the Club suit. If the Club finesse succeeds, there is nothing to worry about, but if it loses, there is danger that the Hearts will be run against you. However, West may have six Hearts, in which case East will have only two. If you refuse to take the first trick, East will return the suit, but that will exhaust his supply of Hearts. Now when he wins the Club finesse he cannot return the suit. If it turns out that West has the King of Clubs, you will still make eleven tricks.

For purposes of holding up, when there is a future lead that you fear by your right-hand opponent, the K Q 4 should be regarded in the same manner as the A 3 2. Changing the holdings slightly:

♠ Q 9 5
♡ 8 7
◇ A 7 6
♣ Q J 10 4 3

Dummy

Declarer

♠ A K 7
♡ K Q 5
◇ K 9 8
♣ K 8 7 2

Here again the 6 of Hearts is led, and East plays the Jack. Should you win the trick or should you hold up? This is more or less of a guess and depends upon who you believe holds the Ace of Clubs. If East holds that card, it is wise to hold up, so that when he obtains the lead he may not have any more Hearts. If, however, West has the Ace of Clubs, it would be suicide to hold up. By merely giving him the Ace of Clubs your contract is assured, if you take the first Heart trick, because West will be unable to continue with Hearts. Which procedure to adopt will depend on clues derived from the bidding.

It has been poinetd out that if the declarer holds the K J 4, and East in third hand plays the Queen to the opening lead, the same principle applies as though the declarer had the K Q 4 or the A 3 2. In other words, if the holdup would have been proper with the Ace, it is proper with the holding just described.

The fact that your stoppers (King Queen), instead of being both

in your hand, are divided between your hand and the dummy does not
alter the principle of play.

Q 5

K 8 6

With this holding, if the holdup is indicated, then you should play
low from both hands in order to be sure not to win the first trick.
For example:

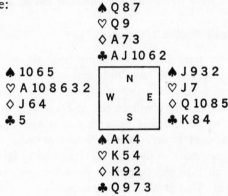

       ♠ Q 8 7
       ♡ Q 9
       ◇ A 7 3
       ♣ A J 10 6 2

♠ 10 6 5   ♠ J 9 3 2
♡ A 10 8 6 3 2   ♡ J 7
◇ J 6 4   ◇ Q 10 8 5
♣ 5   ♣ K 8 4

       ♠ A K 4
       ♡ K 5 4
       ◇ K 9 2
       ♣ Q 9 7 3

West leads the 6 of Hearts. Since the Club finesse must be taken
into East, we desire to exhaust him of Hearts. The proper play, therefore, is to refuse the first trick. If the Queen is played from dummy,
you cannot help winning the trick. (East should take the precaution
to unblock with the Jack.) Therefore you should play low from both
hands.

A somewhat unusual type of holdup is demonstrated here:

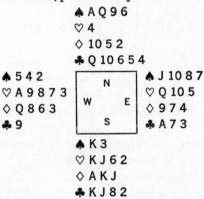

       ♠ A Q 9 6
       ♡ 4
       ◇ 10 5 2
       ♣ Q 10 6 5 4

♠ 5 4 2   ♠ J 10 8 7
♡ A 9 8 7 3   ♡ Q 10 5
◇ Q 8 6 3   ◇ 9 7 4
♣ 9   ♣ A 7 3

       ♠ K 3
       ♡ K J 6 2
       ◇ A K J
       ♣ K J 8 2

South was the declarer at 3 No Trump, with no adverse bidding. West opened with the 7 of Hearts. East played the Queen. South ducked, and when the 10 of Hearts was continued he ducked again. (If South had played the Jack, West would have ducked, permitting partner to retain the Heart for a "come-through.") A third Heart was led, and this one West took and cleared the suit. When East won with the Ace of Clubs, he was unable to return a Heart. The question might occur to you, what if West held the Ace of Clubs? Then declarer's strategy would have been wrong. But South reasoned that if West had the Ace of Clubs in addition to the Heart suit headed by the Ace, he would have overcalled the opening bid of 1 Club.

Holdup with double stopper

Thus far we have been considering holdups on the opening lead at No Trump when you have only one stopper in the suit led. Occasionally you will have two stoppers, such as the Ace and King, and still the proper procedure will be not to take the first trick. How can you recognize when you hold up with two stoppers in the adversaries' suit? The answer is very simple. When in order to build up your nine tricks you must relinquish the lead twice, it is generally good strategy not to take the first trick, even though you have two stoppers in the suit. This is also with the proviso that there is not some other suit that you fear will be attacked in the meantime.

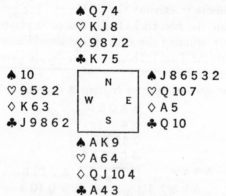

```
                    ♠ Q 7 4
                    ♡ K J 8
                    ◇ 9 8 7 2
                    ♣ K 7 5
      ♠ 10                         ♠ J 8 6 5 3 2
      ♡ 9 5 3 2         N          ♡ Q 10 7
      ◇ K 6 3        W     E       ◇ A 5
      ♣ J 9 8 6 2       S          ♣ Q 10
                    ♠ A K 9
                    ♡ A 6 4
                    ◇ Q J 10 4
                    ♣ A 4 3
```

You are South, at a contract of 3 No Trump. West leads the 6 of Clubs, East plays the Queen. You should allow the Queen to hold. The suit will be continued. Then the Ace of Diamonds is driven out and East has no Clubs to return. If West wins the first Diamond trick, his Clubs will become harmless, because he will have no entry to use them. Observe that if you hold up on the second lead of Clubs instead

of the first, you cannot make the hand. You lead a Diamond, which
East wins with the Ace and returns the 10 of Clubs. West overtakes
with the Jack and continues the suit. Now when he obtains the lead
with the King of Diamonds his Clubs are established. Notice here
you have a double stopper in the suit led and two important cards to
drive out. In such cases a holdup on the first round with two stoppers
is indicated.

Another example of holding up with a double stopper which at
first blush would appear to contradict some advice previously given is
the following:

                ♠ A K 7
                ♡ A J 4
                ◇ 10 5 3
                ♣ Q J 10 2

                N

                S

                ♠ Q 9 3
                ♡ K 6 2
                ◇ A J 4
                ♣ 9 8 7 3

South is playing 3 No Trump, after East overcalled in Diamonds.
West leads the 9 of Diamonds, and East plays the Queen. What
should South do?

Since East is marked with both the King and Queen he will have
two Diamond tricks even if he refuses this trick. Notice that two
important cards must be driven out, the Ace and King of Clubs. If
East has them both, the hand cannot be made, but if West has one
of them, it is important to hold up even with a double stopper.

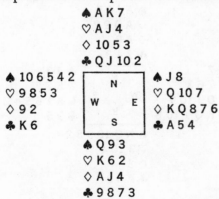

                ♠ A K 7
                ♡ A J 4
                ◇ 10 5 3
                ♣ Q J 10 2

♠ 10 6 5 4 2   N   ♠ J 8
♡ 9 8 5 3   W   E   ♡ Q 10 7
◇ 9 2   S   ◇ K Q 8 7 6
♣ K 6   ♣ A 5 4

                ♠ Q 9 3
                ♡ K 6 2
                ◇ A J 4
                ♣ 9 8 7 3

Note if declarer takes the first trick and leads a Club, West will win with the King and return a Diamond. East will clear the suit while he still retains the Ace of Clubs. If declarer refuses the first Diamond trick, the suit will be continued and won with the Jack. Now when West wins with the King of Clubs he has no Diamond to return. It is interesting to note that East could have defeated the contract if he had played the 8 of Diamonds instead of the Queen to the first trick.

Holdup at suit play

Thus far we have been discussing the holdup as it applies to No Trump play. It is applicable as well with a suit as trumps.

South has been pushed to a contract of 5 Spades by his nonvulnerable opponents, West having overcalled with 2 Clubs and East having bid Diamonds. The King of Clubs is led. What should declarer do?

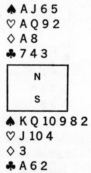

♠ A J 6 5
♡ A Q 9 2
◇ A 8
♣ 7 4 3

♠ K Q 10 9 8 2
♡ J 10 4
◇ 3
♣ A 6 2

He should refuse to take it, for if East happens to have the King of Hearts he will then have no Clubs to return to partner, assuming that West has five Clubs. (If West has six Clubs, the play will not succeed unless the Heart finesse wins.) The complete hand:

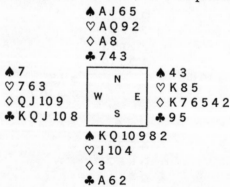

♠ A J 6 5
♡ A Q 9 2
◇ A 8
♣ 7 4 3

♠ 7
♡ 7 6 3
◇ Q J 10 9
♣ K Q J 10 8

♠ 4 3
♡ K 8 5
◇ K 7 6 5 4 2
♣ 9 5

♠ K Q 10 9 8 2
♡ J 10 4
◇ 3
♣ A 6 2

South is the declarer at a contract of 4 Hearts. West leads the 6 of Spades, and East plays the King. What should declarer do?

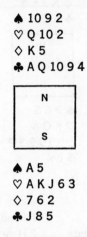

♠ 10 9 2
♡ Q 10 2
◇ K 5
♣ A Q 10 9 4

N

S

♠ A 5
♡ A K J 6 3
◇ 7 6 2
♣ J 8 5

The trick should be refused. The danger in the hand lies in West subsequently obtaining the lead and coming through the King of Diamonds. The only card that West could possibly use as an entry is the Queen of Spades, and if the first trick is refused, the Queen of Spades is killed as an entry.

The complete holding is as follows:

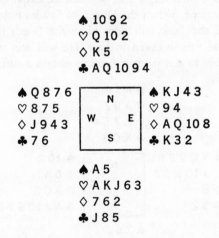

♠ 10 9 2
♡ Q 10 2
◇ K 5
♣ A Q 10 9 4

♠ Q 8 7 6   N   ♠ K J 4 3
♡ 8 7 5   ♡ 9 4
◇ J 9 4 3   W   E   ◇ A Q 10 8
♣ 7 6   S   ♣ K 3 2

♠ A 5
♡ A K J 6 3
◇ 7 6 2
♣ J 8 5

The holdup at suit play is sometimes employed to avoid an adverse ruff.

An interesting illustration is the following:

o*

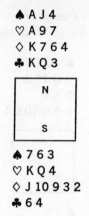

♠ A J 4
♡ A 9 7
◇ K 7 6 4
♣ K Q 3

♠ 7 6 3
♡ K Q 4
◇ J 10 9 3 2
♣ 6 4

The bidding has been as follows:

EAST	SOUTH	WEST	NORTH
1 Club	Pass	1 Spade	Double
Pass	2 Diamonds	2 Hearts	3 Diamonds
Pass	Pass	Pass	

West leads the 8 of Clubs, and the Queen goes to the Ace. The 10 of Spades is returned by East, and West plays the Queen. What should dummy play? The answer is, the dummy should duck. West probably has five Spades, and East, therefore, has a doubleton. East surely has the Ace of trumps, and he must be exhausted of Spades if a ruff is to be avoided. When the Queen of Spades holds, a Spade will be returned and the Jack will win. Now the South hand is entered and the Diamond finesse taken to East. He will win with the Queen but will be unable to put partner back to obtain a ruff. The complete hand is as follows:

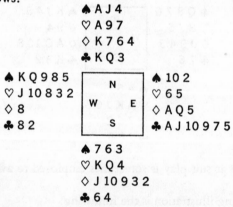

♠ A J 4
♡ A 9 7
◇ K 7 6 4
♣ K Q 3

♠ K Q 9 8 5
♡ J 10 8 3 2
◇ 8
♣ 8 2

♠ 10 2
♡ 6 5
◇ A Q 5
♣ A J 10 9 7 5

♠ 7 6 3
♡ K Q 4
◇ J 10 9 3 2
♣ 6 4

20.

The crossruff

AS A GENERAL PRINCIPLE it is not profitable for declarer to use up his own trumps for the purpose of ruffing losing cards. The theory of the ruff is to make a trick with a trump which would otherwise be useless. If declarer has five solid trumps in his own hand, they are naturally good tricks, and he need not ruff anything to convert any one of those five trumps into a winner. Where, however, the dummy has three trumps, let us say, and if one or more of the dummy's three trumps can be used *separately* before trumps are drawn, they will be tricks in addition to the five already counted in the declarer's hand.

However, there are cases in which the declarer may find it expedient to make all the trumps in declarer's hand and dummy's hand separately. That type of play is known as the Crossruff.

Declarer frequently is called upon to decide whether to establish a side suit and draw trumps or whether to try to make his trumps separately.

The crossruff is indicated whenever the declarer, by counting up his high cards and the number of ruffs, reaches the sum total of tricks required.

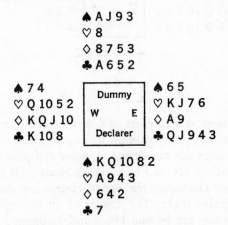

South is the declarer at a contract of 4 Spades. The defense cashes the first three Diamond tricks and shifts to the trumps. Since declarer has three losing Hearts he must use every one of dummy's trumps for the purpose of ruffing these losers. Even one more lead of trumps will ruin the hand, so declarer's play is to ruff Clubs and Hearts back and forth, since ten tricks can be counted.

The bookkeeping process is one Club trick, one Heart trick, five trumps in the South hand, and three ruffs in dummy—a total of ten tricks.

The danger in the crossruff is that sooner or later one of the opponents will be able to overruff either you or the dummy. In this hand that danger virtually disappears, since after the dummy ruffs one Heart and the declarer ruffs one Club the rest of the trumps are high.

There is this important principle to bear in mind in the playing of the crossruff. Where two suits are being ruffed back and forth and a third suit contains high cards such as the Ace and King, it is usually desirable to cash them early in the play. The reason is that as you continue your crossruff one of the opponents may run out of the suit that is being ruffed and discard one of his cards of the suit in which you have the Ace and King.

For example:

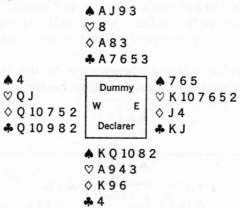

```
                    ♠ A J 9 3
                    ♡ 8
                    ♢ A 8 3
                    ♣ A 7 6 5 3
   ♠ 4            ┌──────────┐      ♠ 7 6 5
   ♡ Q J          │  Dummy   │      ♡ K 10 7 6 5 2
   ♢ Q 10 7 5 2   │ W     E  │      ♢ J 4
   ♣ Q 10 9 8 2   │ Declarer │      ♣ K J
                  └──────────┘
                    ♠ K Q 10 8 2
                    ♡ A 9 4 3
                    ♢ K 9 6
                    ♣ 4
```

South is declarer at a contract of 6 Spades, and West leads the 10 of Clubs. If declarer draws trumps, he cannot count to twelve tricks. However, if trumps are not drawn, declarer can plan to cash as follows: five Spades in his own hand, three Heart ruffs in dummy, the Ace and King of Diamonds, the Ace of Hearts, and the Ace of Clubs —a total of twelve tricks. The danger of an overruff is negligible, since declarer must get by one Heart ruff in dummy and one Club ruff in his own hand, at which point all his trumps are high.

Before starting the crossruff, however, it is vital for declarer to cash both the Ace and King of Diamonds. Note that if he fails to do so

before starting to crossruff Clubs and Hearts at once, on the third
Club lead East will discard one of his Diamonds and declarer will be
unable to cash both the Ace and King.

To repeat: Cash all high cards in side suits as promptly as is convenient before starting the crossruff.

In playing the crossruff, the drawing of even one round of trumps
will frequently be fatal where a lead must be subsequently relin-
quished, because at that time the defense may lead another trump.

For example:

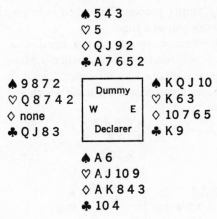

```
                    ♠ 5 4 3
                    ♡ 5
                    ◇ Q J 9 2
                    ♣ A 7 6 5 2
 ♠ 9 8 7 2        ┌──────────┐      ♠ K Q J 10
 ♡ Q 8 7 4 2      │  Dummy   │      ♡ K 6 3
 ◇ none           │ W      E │      ◇ 10 7 6 5
 ♣ Q J 8 3        │ Declarer │      ♣ K 9
                  └──────────┘
                    ♠ A 6
                    ♡ A J 10 9
                    ◇ A K 8 4 3
                    ♣ 10 4
```

South is declarer at a contract of 5 Diamonds. West leads the 2 of
Spades. In order to crossruff, declarer will be obliged to give up a
Club trick. If he makes the mistake of pulling even one trump, when
East is in with the King of Clubs, he will lead another trump, and
now eleven tricks cannot be counted. Immediately on winning the
Ace of Spades declarer should play the Ace and another Club. East
will lead a trump, but declarer can still cash five Diamonds in his
own hand, three Heart ruffs in dummy, the Ace of Spades, the Ace of
Hearts, and the Ace of Clubs, for a total of eleven tricks.

COUNTING OUT the opponents' hands, i.e., their original suit distributions, is one of the declarer's first problems. It is not so complicated a procedure as the average player is led to believe. Sometimes it is really a very simple process. The point is to go about it systematically, counting one suit at a time.

There are two elements in counting a hand. One consists of the facts that are proven absolutely, such as when a player fails to follow suit. Other counts are obtained by inference. These clues are gathered from the bidding and sometimes from leads which you have no reason to believe are false.

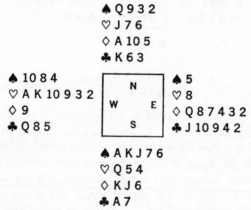

♠ Q 9 3 2
♡ J 7 6
◇ A 10 5
♣ K 6 3

♠ 10 8 4
♡ A K 10 9 3 2
◇ 9
♣ Q 8 5

♠ 5
♡ 8
◇ Q 8 7 4 3 2
♣ J 10 9 4 2

♠ A K J 7 6
♡ Q 5 4
◇ K J 6
♣ A 7

The bidding:

SOUTH	WEST	NORTH	EAST
1 Spade	2 Hearts	2 Spades	Pass
4 Spades	Pass	Pass	Pass

Declarer is playing a contract of 4 Spades. West leads the King and Ace of Hearts, upon the second of which East discards a Club. East ruffs the third round of Hearts and returns the Jack of Clubs. Declarer's problem now is to guess the location of the Queen of Diamonds. The Ace of Clubs wins the return, and three Spades are drawn. At this point the definite information for the declarer is that West held six Hearts and three Spades. This has been proven by the fall of the cards. Declarer leads a Club to the King and ruffs a Club in his own hand, for no other purpose than to find out how many Clubs West had. When West follows to the third round the count reads:

Three Spades, six Hearts, and at least three Clubs.

There is only one unknown card in his hand, which may be a Diamond or a Club. The 6 of Diamonds, therefore, is led to the Ace, and when West follows suit he does so with his last unknown card. The complete count is:

Three Spades, six Hearts, one Diamond, and three Clubs. East, therefore, must have the Queen of Diamonds.

Another example:

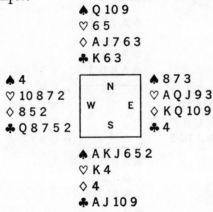

♠ Q 10 9
♡ 6 5
◊ A J 7 6 3
♣ K 6 3

♠ 4
♡ 10 8 7 2
◊ 8 5 2
♣ Q 8 7 5 2

N
W   E
S

♠ 8 7 3
♡ A Q J 9 3
◊ K Q 10 9
♣ 4

♠ A K J 6 5 2
♡ K 4
◊ 4
♣ A J 10 9

The bidding:

EAST	SOUTH	WEST	NORTH
1 Heart	Double	Pass	3 Diamonds
Pass	3 Spades	Pass	4 Spades
Pass	4 No Trump	Pass	5 Diamonds
Pass	6 Spades	Pass	Pass
Pass			

West leads the deuce of Hearts. East wins with the Ace and returns the King of Diamonds, which is won in dummy with the Ace. The success of the contract hinges upon declarer's ability to locate the Queen of Clubs, which may be finessed in either direction. A Diamond is led from dummy, and South ruffs with a trump. This play has no other purpose than to find out how many Diamonds each opponent has. A low trump is returned to dummy's 9 and another Diamond ruffed. The Jack of trumps is taken by dummy's Queen and a fourth

Diamond is ruffed out with the King of Spades. Now the Ace of Spades is cashed to draw the last trump, and at this point declarer has a perfect count on East's hand. Since West has shown just one trump, East is known to have had three. The play of the Diamonds showed that East had four. These two counts are definite. The count of the Heart suit comes by inference. West led the deuce of his partner's bid suit, which indicates that he held four. East had five Hearts (by inference), three Spades (by actual count), four Diamonds (by actual count), and, therefore, can have only one Club. The Ace of Clubs is played first, in case East's Club happened to be the Queen. When it proved to be the 4, the Jack of Clubs is led and finessed with perfect confidence.

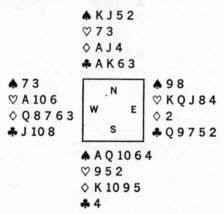

```
                    ♠ K J 5 2
                    ♡ 7 3
                    ◇ A J 4
                    ♣ A K 6 3
        ♠ 7 3                         ♠ 9 8
        ♡ A 10 6          N           ♡ K Q J 8 4
        ◇ Q 8 7 6 3    W     E        ◇ 2
        ♣ J 10 8          S           ♣ Q 9 7 5 2
                    ♠ A Q 10 6 4
                    ♡ 9 5 2
                    ◇ K 10 9 5
                    ♣ 4
```

The bidding:

NORTH	EAST	SOUTH	WEST
1 Club	1 Heart	1 Spade	Pass
3 Spades	Pass	4 Spades	Pass
Pass	Pass		

Declarer's contract of 4 Spades was not in danger. The problem centered around the Diamond play in an effort to make an overtrick. West opened the Ace of Hearts and continued the suit. East won and led a trump. Declarer drew the remaining trumps, playing the Ace and King of Clubs and ruffing one in the closed hand. The last Heart was ruffed in dummy and the remaining Club ruffed in the closed hand. On the last Club lead West showed out and East's hand was an open book. He is known to have held five Clubs (actual count), two Spades (actual count), and surely five Hearts for his vulnerable overcall, which was bad enough (inference), which would leave him with only one Diamond. The King of Diamonds, therefore, was led from the South hand and the Jack finessed from dummy with the complete assurance that it would work.

A more involved case is the following:

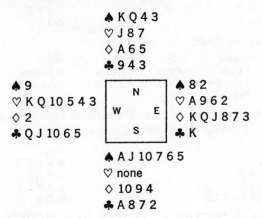

```
                    ♠ K Q 4 3
                    ♡ J 8 7
                    ◇ A 6 5
                    ♣ 9 4 3
    ♠ 9                          ♠ 8 2
    ♡ K Q 10 5 4 3      N        ♡ A 9 6 2
    ◇ 2            W       E      ◇ K Q J 8 7 3
    ♣ Q J 10 6 5       S         ♣ K
                    ♠ A J 10 7 6 5
                    ♡ none
                    ◇ 10 9 4
                    ♣ A 8 7 2
```

The bidding:

EAST	SOUTH	WEST	NORTH
1 Diamond	1 Spade	2 Hearts	2 Spades
3 Hearts	4 Spades	Pass	Pass
Pass			

West, no doubt, should have gone to 5 Hearts, but the bidding is given as it actually took place. The 2 of Diamonds was opened, an obvious singleton, and the Ace took the trick. A Heart was ruffed in the closed hand and dummy entered with a trump. Another Heart was ruffed and dummy re-entered with the second high trump, and the final Heart was ruffed by South. At this point declarer stopped to count out the hand. West was known to have one Diamond and one Spade. He therefore had started with eleven cards in Hearts and Clubs. These were, no doubt, six Hearts and five Clubs, since with a seven-card Heart suit he would surely have bid once more (inference), and if he held a six-card Club suit he would certainly have risked a 5 Club bid over 4 Spades (by inference). East, therefore, is marked with only one Club. Declarer hit upon a means of avoiding the loss of two Club tricks. He cashed the Ace of Clubs, so that East could not return that suit, and then led the 10 of Diamonds, presenting East with the lead. He was able to cash two Diamond tricks and was then obliged to lead a red card, which permitted South to ruff, while dummy discarded one of the losing Clubs.

QUIZ ON COUNTING

1.

NORTH	SOUTH
♠ K 10 7 5	♠ A Q J 9 6 4
♡ 8 3	♡ J 2
◇ A Q 9	◇ J 6 3
♣ A 7 4 2	♣ J 5

The bidding has gone:

NORTH	EAST	SOUTH	WEST
1 Club	Pass	1 Spade	3 Hearts
3 Spades	Pass	4 Spades	Pass
Pass	Pass		

West leads the King and Ace of Hearts as East plays up the line, then shifts to a trump. How do you proceed?

2.

NORTH	SOUTH
♠ 8 6 5	♠ K Q 7 3
♡ A 10 2	♡ K 9 3
◇ 4 2	◇ A K 5 3
♣ A 10 6 4 3	♣ Q 5

You are in 3 No Trump and West leads the Jack of Spades. You win the Queen and run the Queen of Clubs to East's King. East returns the 9 of Diamonds. You win the Ace on which West drops the Jack and finesse the 10 of Clubs in dummy, which holds. When you cash the Ace, East discards a Heart. West wins and leads the Queen of Diamonds. How do you continue?

3.

NORTH	SOUTH
♠ 8 7 6 5 4	♠ K Q 9
♡ Q J 9 3	♡ A 10 8 7 5
◇ Q 3	◇ 5 2
♣ A J	♣ K Q 5

After three passes, you open the bidding with 1 Heart. West passes and partner jumps to 3 Hearts, and you carry on to game. West leads the Diamond Jack and East wins your Queen with the King, and cashes the Ace then exits with a Club. What is your intended campaign?

4.

NORTH	SOUTH
♠ J 10 8 4	♠ K 9 6 5
♡ 6 2	♡ A 8 5
◇ K 10 9 4	◇ A J 7
♣ A 7 3	♣ K Q J 4

North-South vulnerable.

SOUTH	WEST	NORTH	EAST
1 No Trump	2 Hearts	2 No Trump	Pass
3 Spades	Pass	4 Spades	Pass
Pass	Pass		

West opens the King of Hearts. You win the Ace as East begins an echo by playing the 9. Dummy is entered with a Club and the Spade Jack is finessed, losing to West's Queen. The Queen of Hearts is cashed, and the 10 is continued. Dummy ruffs with the Spade 10 and East overruffs with the Ace. He then leads another Spade. You win the King as West follows with the last outstanding trump. How do you carry on?

5.

WEST	NORTH
♠ J 6 5	♠ 10 8 7 4 3
♡ Q 10 7 2	♡ 5
◇ K 6 5 2	◇ Q 4
♣ 4 3	♣ A J 9 8 5

You are West defending 3 No Trump after the following auction.

SOUTH	NORTH
1 Diamond	1 Spade
3 No Trump	Pass

You open the Deuce of Hearts and declarer wins partner's Jack with the King. South plays a Club to dummy's Jack and partner drops the Ten. The Queen of Diamonds is led, partner playing the Eight, and you win the King. How do you defend?

6.

WEST	NORTH
♠ K 9 3	♠ 10 7 6 4
♡ A 7 6 2	♡ Q J
◇ 6 4	◇ A Q J
♣ 9 8 6 3	♣ A J 10 2

The bidding:

NORTH	SOUTH
1 Club	1 Heart
1 Spade	2 No Trump
3 No Trump	

Not savoring any lead, you open the Club 9. Dummy's 10 holds as partner plays low. The Queen of Hearts is led, partner producing the 10, and you duck. Hearts are continued and partner's 9 falls. What is your defense?

You are South playing 3 No Trump after the following auction:

7.

NORTH	SOUTH
♠ A 10 5	♠ K 7 3
♡ 6 5 2	♡ A 9 4
◇ A 8 6 4	◇ K 9 7
♣ K 10 3	♣ A Q 8 4

The bidding:

SOUTH	NORTH
1 No Trump	3 No Trump

West opens the deuce of Hearts. East plays the King and you duck. The 10 is returned as you hold up once more, and East leads another Heart, clearing the suit. How do you continue?

ANSWERS TO QUIZ ON COUNTING

1. Your efforts should be aimed toward discovering the number of Diamonds West has, for should he prove to have two, a successful finesse followed by cashing the Diamond Ace will pull the King and bring home the contract. If, on the other hand, West turns up with three or four Diamonds, a double finesse against the King and the 10 in the West hand will be necessary.

After winning the trump lead in dummy, you lead a low Club to your Jack. West will win the King and return a Club. Dummy's Ace wins and you trump a Club high. Dummy is re-entered with a trump and the fourth Club is ruffed. When West fails, he is known to have had one Spade, three Clubs, and five or six Hearts (inference), therefore, he either has three or four Diamonds. Hence you must hope that he began with both the King and 10 of that suit, and lead the Diamond Jack. When West covers, you win the Ace and re-enter your hand with a trump to finesse West for the 10 of Diamonds. Here is the complete hand:

NORTH
♠ K 10 7 5
♡ 8 3
◊ A Q 9
♣ A 7 4 2

WEST
♠ 3
♡ A K Q 10 7 5
◊ K 10 4
♣ K 9 6

EAST
♠ 8 2
♡ 9 6 4
◊ 8 7 5 2
♣ Q 10 8 3

SOUTH
♠ A Q J 9 6 4
♡ J 2
◊ J 6 3
♣ J 5

2. Obviously West started with five Spades

for otherwise East would surely prefer to continue the attack on Spades (if he had one) rather than shift to Diamonds from what subsequently appears to be an anemic holding. West's play of the Jack marks him with either the J 10 doubleton or an original holding of Q J 10 x

After winning the fourth round of Clubs, West leads the Diamond Queen. Therefore, he is known to have the 10 left in his hand (inference from East's initial lead of the 9 of Diamonds). West has only one unknown card in his hand. By cashing the King of Hearts, he is stripped out of all exits and can be thrust on play with a Diamond. His forced Spade return gives you your ninth trick. The complete hand follows:

NORTH
♠ 8 6 5
♡ A 10 2
◊ 4 2
♣ A 10 6 4 3

WEST
♠ A J 10 9 2
♡ J
◊ Q J 10
♣ J 9 8 2

EAST
♠ 4
♡ Q 8 7 6 5 4
◊ 9 8 7 6
♣ K 7

SOUTH
♠ K Q 7 3
♡ K 9 3
◊ A K 5 3
♣ Q 5

3. Since you must lose the Ace of Spades

as well as the two Diamond tricks, you must assume that East has the Heart King. Accordingly, you win the Club return with Dummy's Jack and take the vital trump finesse.

Counting the hand

427

East ducks, and you continue trumps, picking up the King. It would seem that your contract now hinges upon finding East with the Ace of Spades to thereby limit your losses to one trick in that suit, but is this possible? Remember East has shown up with the Ace and King of Diamonds as well as the King of Hearts. If he had the Ace of Spades as well, he surely would have opened the bidding.

It would seem that the only logical chance for success would be to locate the Jack and 10 of Spades in the East hand, and dummy should be re-entered with the Club Ace with the intention of playing a low Spade and finessing your 9 should East fail to split his honors. If in fact he does, and West wins the Ace, you win the subsequent return and cross over to dummy to finesse once again for the missing intermediate honor. The complete hand is shown:

NORTH
♠ 8 7 6 5 4
♡ Q J 9 3
◇ Q 3
♣ A J

WEST
♠ A 2
♡ 4 2
◇ J 10 9 8 4
♣ 9 6 4 2

EAST
♠ J 10 3
♡ K 6
◇ A K 7 6
♣ 10 8 7 3

SOUTH
♠ K Q 9
♡ A 10 8 7 5
◇ 5 2
♣ K Q 5

4. West has turned up with six Hearts

(his partner and dummy failed on the third lead of that suit) and two Spades. Your problem on this deal is centered upon locating the Queen of Diamonds. You can do this by playing off your Club winners in an effort to discover how many Clubs he began with. For example, if he fails on the second lead, you will know that he had four Diamonds to begin with, and since this would leave East with only two, the odds

would be two to one in favor of finding West with the missing Queen. In actual play, West will follow to three rounds of Clubs, thereby marking himself short in Diamonds. The King of Diamonds is then cashed and East subsequently finessed for the missing Queen. The complete hand follows:

NORTH
♠ J 10 8 4
♡ 6 2
◇ K 10 9 4
♣ A 7 3

WEST
♠ Q 7
♡ K Q J 10 7 3
◇ 6 2
♣ 8 6 5

EAST
♠ A 3 2
♡ 9 4
◇ Q 8 5 3
♣ 10 9 2

SOUTH
♠ K 9 6 5
♡ A 8 5
◇ A J 7
♣ K Q J 4

5. Declarer can be counted for five Club winners,

two Heart tricks, and four Diamond tricks should he be left unmolested. Therefore, the only possibility of setting the contract rests with the Spade suit.

The play of a low Spade will hit the jackpot as partner's Ace drops declarer's King, and his subsequent lead to your Jack permits you to lead your third Spade to pierce dummy's guard.

The complete hand follows:

NORTH
♠ 10 8 7 4 3
♡ 5
◇ Q 4
♣ A J 9 8 5

WEST
♠ J 6 5
♡ Q 10 7 2
◇ K 6 5 2
♣ 4 3

EAST
♠ A Q 9 2
♡ J 9 8 6 4
◇ 8 7
♣ 10 2

SOUTH
♠ K
♡ A K 3
◇ A J 10 9 3
♣ K Q 7 6

6. If you are counting
declarer has nine winners if he is allowed to win this Heart trick. Surely he must have the King of Diamonds, giving him three Diamond tricks, four Club tricks, and one Heart trick ready to cross home plate.

You have inferentially placed declarer with the King of Diamonds and observed that he has the King, Queen of Clubs as well as the King of Hearts. Your only hope is that he has only a doubleton honor in Spades —not the Ace.

If this is fact, you must take care to smooth the base path for your partner by leading the Spade 9, for if you fail to do so, you will block the suit in the rundown.

Partner wins the Ace and returns the deuce, as declarer's Queen loses to your King. Your lead of the trey retires the side.

The complete hand follows:

NORTH
♠ 10 7 6 4
♡ Q J
◇ A Q J
♣ A J 10 2

WEST
♠ K 9 3
♡ A 7 6 2
◇ 6 4
♣ 9 8 6 3

EAST
♠ A J 8 2
♡ 10 9
◇ 10 8 5 3 2
♣ 7 5

SOUTH
♠ Q 5
♡ K 8 5 4 3
◇ K 9 7
♣ K Q 4

7. You have eight tricks available
in the form of two Spades, one Heart, two Diamonds and three Clubs. Your ninth trick may come

from a long Diamond or a long Club. Accordingly, you should duck a Diamond into the East hand. His best defense is to return a Diamond, and West's 10 is topped by dummy's Ace. A low Diamond discloses that West began with four of that suit as well as four Hearts. Therefore, his last five cards are most likely to be three Clubs and two Spades; or two Clubs and three Spades. To complete the count, you duck a Spade into the East hand. The Spade return is won in dummy, and when West follows to a third round, he can have at most two Clubs. You now cash the Club Ace. When West plays low you play Dummy's 10, for that card will be a roadblock should West's next card prove to be the 9 or Jack of Clubs. When West follows to the next trick with the Club 9, it is the last unknown card in his hand and the marked finesse against East's Jack wins you the contract. If you had failed to jettison the Club 10, you would be unable to reach your hand after your finesse succeeded.

The complete hand follows:

NORTH
♠ A 10 5
♡ 6 5 2
◇ A 8 6 4
♣ K 10 3

WEST
♠ J 6 2
♡ Q J 8 2
◇ Q 10 5 3
♣ 9 5

EAST
♠ Q 9 8 4
♡ K 10 7
◇ J 2
♣ J 7 6 2

SOUTH
♠ K 7 3
♡ A 9 4
◇ K 9 7
♣ A Q 8 4

22.   Dummy reversal

ONE of the cardinal principles of declarer's play is not to force the
strong trump hand to ruff. While ruffs in dummy are to be sought,
ruffs in the closed hand are usually to be avoided. Yet even so fundamental a doctrine as this has its exceptions. The most common exception is where the hand is played at a crossruff, when all of declarer's
and dummy's trumps are to be made separately. Another exception is
in the type of play known as Dummy Reversal. Let us illustrate the
meaning of dummy reversal with a hand:

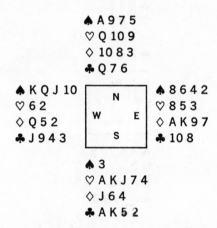

```
              ♠ A 9 7 5
              ♡ Q 10 9
              ◇ 10 8 3
              ♣ Q 7 6
♠ K Q J 10   ┌──────────┐   ♠ 8 6 4 2
♡ 6 2        │    N     │   ♡ 8 5 3
◇ Q 5 2      │ W     E  │   ◇ A K 9 7
♣ J 9 4 3    │    S     │   ♣ 10 8
             └──────────┘
              ♠ 3
              ♡ A K J 7 4
              ◇ J 6 4
              ♣ A K 5 2
```

South is declarer at a contract of 4 Hearts, and West leads the
King of Spades. If trumps are drawn, declarer will lose the three Diamonds and one Club unless the Clubs break three–three. Since they do
not, declarer will be down. There is a better way to play this hand,
and that is to make the dummy the master hand. When the Spade is
won, the 5 is returned and trumped with an honor. Dummy is entered
with the 9 of trumps and the 7 of Spades is ruffed with an honor.
Dummy is entered with the 10 of Hearts and the 9 of Spades ruffed
with South's remaining trump. Dummy is entered with the Queen of
Clubs and the last trump pulled, on which South discards a Diamond.
At the end declarer will lose two Diamonds and a Club, fulfilling the
contract for ten tricks. The execution of the play is relatively simple.

It is the diagnosis to play this hand as a dummy reversal that is important.

How does one diagnose that the situation is present for such a play? The answer is, first: dummy's trumps must be good enough to draw the adverse trumps.

In the above example there are five trumps out. The probability is that they will be divided three–two. Therefore the outstanding trumps can be drawn with the Q 10 9. That fulfills the first condition.

The second condition is that the declarer's hand should have the short suit, as in this case South has a singleton Spade.

You are declarer at a contract of 6 Spades. West leads the King of Hearts and continues with the Ace. How do you plan the play?

> ♠ Q J 2
> ♡ 7 6 5 4
> ◊ K 5 4
> ♣ K Q J

```
        N
   W         E
        S
```

> ♠ A K 10 9 3
> ♡ 2
> ◊ A 3 2
> ♣ A 10 9 3

Apparently there is no way to get rid of the losing Diamond, and the declarer appears to be doomed to a one-trick set until he notices that the hand meets with the requirements for dummy reversal, or making the dummy the master hand. Notice the two prevailing symptoms. Dummy's trumps are strong enough to pull the opponents' trumps, assuming that they do not break badly. The short suit is in the long trump hand. The proper procedure for the declarer upon trumping the second Heart is to play first the Ace of Spades, then a small Club to the Jack. A Heart is ruffed with the King of Spades. A Spade is led to dummy's Jack, and the last remaining Heart is trumped with the 10 of Spades. Dummy is entered with the King of Diamonds to pull the last trump, on which declarer discards his losing Diamond. The complete holding follows:

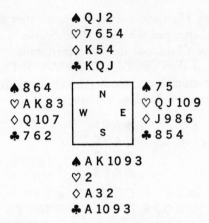

```
              ♠ Q J 2
              ♡ 7 6 5 4
              ◇ K 5 4
              ♣ K Q J
♠ 8 6 4                      ♠ 7 5
♡ A K 8 3    ┌─────────┐     ♡ Q J 10 9
◇ Q 10 7     │   N     │     ◇ J 9 8 6
♣ 7 6 2      │ W     E │     ♣ 8 5 4
             │   S     │
             └─────────┘
              ♠ A K 10 9 3
              ♡ 2
              ◇ A 3 2
              ♣ A 10 9 3
```

You are South, the declarer at a contract of 7 Spades. West leads the King of Hearts. What is your plan of play?

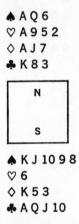

```
              ♠ A Q 6
              ♡ A 9 5 2
              ◇ A J 7
              ♣ K 8 3

             ┌─────────┐
             │   N     │
             │         │
             │   S     │
             └─────────┘

              ♠ K J 10 9 8
              ♡ 6
              ◇ K 5 3
              ♣ A Q J 10
```

Apparently everything depends upon the successful finesse of the Jack of Diamonds, which, to be sure, offers a fifty-fifty chance of success. There is, however, a play for the hand which offers a better chance than the mere even-money bet of the Diamond finesse. If the Spades are divided three–two, which is probable, the hand can be made without the Diamond finesse by resorting to dummy reversal, or making the dummy the master hand. Let us examine the symptoms. Dummy's trumps are good enough to draw the opponents' trumps, and the short suit is in declarer's hand. The Heart is returned at once and ruffed. The King of Spades is cashed and another Spade led to the Ace. If the trumps do not break at this point, declarer will be obliged to try the Diamond finesse, but when they do break, another Heart is led and trumped with the 10 of Spades. Dummy is entered with the King of Clubs and the last Heart ruffed with the Jack of Spades. Dummy is then entered with the Ace of Diamonds, in order to play the last trump, on which declarer discards his only losing Diamond. The complete holding follows:

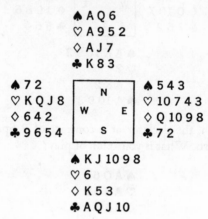

```
                  ♠ A Q 6
                  ♡ A 9 5 2
                  ◇ A J 7
                  ♣ K 8 3

   ♠ 7 2              N          ♠ 5 4 3
   ♡ K Q J 8                     ♡ 10 7 4 3
   ◇ 6 4 2         W    E        ◇ Q 10 9 8
   ♣ 9 6 5 4          S          ♣ 7 2

                  ♠ K J 10 9 8
                  ♡ 6
                  ◇ K 5 3
                  ♣ A Q J 10
```

23.   Deception

BY THIS TIME it is to be hoped that we have mastered the general principles of the play of various card combinations. In some cases the proper procedure is clearly defined. In others a guess must be presented to a player, and where he is put to a guess the principle of percentages or probabilities should be applied in determining which guess is more apt to be successful. Occasionally, however, we are confronted with a situation in which no amount of technical correctness can save us. In other words, regardless of the adverse distribution of the cards, if the opponents play properly we are doomed to failure. In such cases the only hope is that the defense will err.

That being the case, it is our duty to make it easy for the opposition to make mistakes. The attempt to prevail by psychology is open not only to the declarer, it is available also to the defense. If you see that the declarer will surely make his contract with normal play, you should try to induce him to form a false theory about your holding. This type of strategy may take the form of a false discard or winning with a higher card when a low card would have done the work just as well. However, when you are defending, attempts at deception may prove to be a boomerang because of the fact that your partner may be fooled as readily as your opponents. Where you are the declarer you are under no such handicap, inasmuch as you have no partner to deceive. Generally speaking, therefore, a defender should practice deception only when he knows that the false-carding cannot be harmful to partner but may induce the declarer to err. False-carding by the defenders is less apt to be dangerous when done in the trump suit, because it is unlikely that partner will have such a holding that your false information will set him off stride.

Certain types of deception will be effective against experienced players but will have little or no effect against the novice, because he is probably not noticing what cards you play. It calls to mind the remark of the late Joe Penner of stage, screen, and radio fame. "You can't fool me," he once said; "I'm too ignorant."

Don't waste subtleties on an unwitting opposition.

It is important to bear in mind that when you practice deception you are really telling a lie, and in doing so you are not apt to deceive the opponents if you stutter. Speed is an essential qualification of both a liar and a false-carder. Make up your mind in advance and act promptly.

Deception may be practiced on the opening lead; as, for example, the strategy of underleading an Ace or leading a very high card from the King, in order to convey the impression to the declarer that you are leading a short suit. These have been discussed in the chapter on leads.

One of the oldest chestnuts known to bridge, but one which can still occasionally be employed with effect, is the lead of the Jack from the Queen Jack doubleton. This should be done only in the trump suit. The following diagram will illustrate the point:

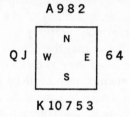

A 9 8 2

QJ　　64

K 10 7 5 3

The declarer holds nine trumps. If left to his own resources, he will probably play for the suit to break. If you lead the Jack, he may reach the mistaken belief that your partner has the Queen and finesse to his disaster. However, you must not get the reputation for doing this constantly, because your opponents will be less likely to fall for your deception. Occasionally, with this holding, you should "cross them up" by leading the Queen. In other words, it is well to keep the opposition guessing.

The advice has been given to use this type of strategy only in the trump suit. The reason it should not be employed in the side suit is the possibility that partner will have one of the high honors and waste the card because he believes that the declarer has the Queen. For example, the dummy may show up with a great many, including the King. Your partner may have the Ace and suspect that you are leading a singleton. He may, therefore, play his Ace, establishing dummy's King. First consider declarer's tactics.

At this point it may be appropriate to point out that there is current in certain circles the practice of leading the second best of two touching honors, such as the Queen from the King Queen, the Jack from Queen Jack, et cetera. Where partners have such an understanding, it is regarded as a private convention and should be announced to the opposition. Where, however, the partnership has no such agreement, there is no objection to the deception tactics suggested above.

In considering deception practices let us first concentrate our attention on the tactics of the declarer.

When declarer has a choice of cards with which to win a trick, the selection of the proper one, although on the surface it makes no difference, may have a vital effect on the subsequent play.

Suppose you are playing a No Trump contract. West leads the 5 of Spades. East follows with the Jack. You are South, the declarer, and hold A K Q. You are naturally anxious to have West continue when he subsequently regains the lead, but there is some other suit that you fear. If you win with the Queen, he will know that you have both the Ace and the King, else East would have played one of the higher ones. You must not give him this impression. Is it, therefore, proper for you to win with the Ace? The answer is definitely no, because you will be suspected of deception. The play of the Ace would be the truth only if East had the K Q J, which will no doubt appear improbable to West when you win the first trick without holding up. Your best play is the King. This will be an admission that you hold the Ace but will lead West to believe that his partner is following suit with the Jack, holding the Queen Jack.

When the Queen is led at No Trump and you, as declarer, hold the Ace and King, it will not be deceptive to win with the Ace. You should win with the King, which will leave the partner of the opening leader guessing. He will not know whether the opener has led from A Q J or Q J 10, but if you play the Ace he will know you have the King as soon as partner leads the Queen, because the Queen is not led from the King Queen.

In the following case you are South, playing a suit contract, and hold in a side suit:

8 7 4

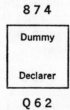

Q 6 2

West leads the King, and East follows with the 3. You know that this is East's smallest card and that he has discouraged partner from continuing the suit. Since you never can win a trick with the Queen unless West lays down his Ace, you must play in a manner which might induce him to do so. If you can make him suspect that the 3 is not his partner's lowest card, he may read it as the beginning of an echo and continue the suit. You would, therefore, follow with the 6. This might induce West to believe that his partner holds the deuce and is starting a signal. If he continues with the Ace, all is well. If not, you have lost nothing. The complete holding is as follows:

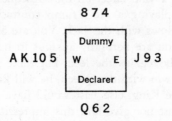

874

AK105 | Dummy / W E / Declarer | J93

Q62

Assume that the holding was somewhat different, as follows:

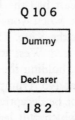

Q106

Dummy / Declarer

J82

Against a suit contract West leads the King, and East follows with the 4. This time you are not anxious to have the suit continued. Therefore it would be suicide to false-card with the 8, because West would realize that the deuce is missing and may think that partner has it, which would indicate the start of a down-and-out signal. Your best procedure is to make the normal play of the deuce. West may be in some doubt as to who has the 3 and, feeling that declarer may have it, will read the 4 as a discouraging card and shift to some other suit. The complete holding is as follows:

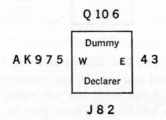

Q106

AK975 | Dummy / W E / Declarer | 43

J82

You are South, the declarer, and hold the following combination:

K 9 5

Dummy

Declarer

A J 10 8

You are desirous of picking up the Queen but have no clues whatsoever as to its location. You might as well guess one way as the other, but since you have no indication, on the principle of percentages you should play East for the Queen. The reason is that if East has four of the suit, including the Queen, you will still be able to pick up the suit without finessing on the first round. Whereas if it should turn out that West has four of the suit to the Queen, you would lose one trick in any event, unless you decided to take the first-round finesse, which is improbable.

Since it is desirable to postpone finesses wherever possible, it is just as well to guess East for the Queen. However, with all the cards right down to the 8, it costs nothing for South to lead the Jack, fully intending to go up with the King. The purpose of the play is to induce West to cover with the Queen if he holds it. This is apt to be very effective, inasmuch as so many players automatically cover an honor with an honor. It should be pointed out that if South has a card smaller than the 8 he could not afford to lead the Jack and overtake with the King, because an opponent's 8 spot might be developed into a winner even though the finesse succeeded.

The converse of this, a case in which it is not desired to have the opponents cover, is present in the following:

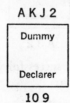

A K J 2

Dummy

Declarer

10 9

This combination is held near the end of the hand, when dummy has no more entries and four tricks are required in the suit. If the 10 is led and covered by the Queen, four tricks are not obtainable, because the 9 happens to be in the South hand and one of the opponents has at least four cards, so that the deuce cannot possibly stand up. If, however, West holds the Queen and does not cover, all four tricks are available. If the 10 is led, West will surely cover. The proper play, therefore, is the 9, which gives the declarer the best chance to capitalize on a defensive error. It is true that if West can see through your plot, the cover of the 9 by his Queen will defeat your purpose, but he is less apt to cover the 9 than he is the 10.

A somewhat ordinary card holding on which success depends upon an error by the opposition is the following:

J 10 5 4

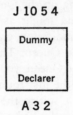

A 3 2

Assuming that you have plenty of entries and you are anxious to lose only one trick in the suit, what is your play? Technically, your only hope is that the King and the Queen are doubleton or that East has a doubleton honor, but this appears to be very unlikely, and the better chance is to hope that the honors are divided and that West can be induced to make the mistake of taking the trick early. The best play is a low card from the South hand toward dummy. If West goes up with an honor, dummy is subsequently re-entered and a finesse taken against East's remaining honor. The complete hand is as follows:

J 10 5 4

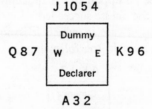

A 3 2

After a play of this kind is successful you may obtain good results with the following combination:

J 7 2

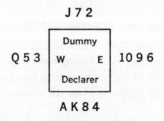

A K 8 4

South has the choice of playing out the Ace and the King, in the hope that the Queen will drop doubleton. This, however, is not very likely, and declarer decides to lead a low spot toward dummy. If West is the player who has been caught on the previous hand, he may duck, hoping that his partner has the King. If he does, you will win all four tricks. Note that your play of a low card is not apt to lose, but if West has the Queen, you will win three tricks in the suit, regardless of the distribution. If East has the Queen and one, your play will have lost, but it is worth the risk.

A somewhat kindred holding is the following:

10 2

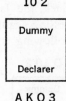

A K Q 3

You find it necessary to win all four tricks in this suit. Unless the Jack is singleton, there is no straightforward way of doing it. The singleton Jack is such a remote possibility that it may be ignored. What is the best procedure? Obviously to play a small one toward dummy. If West holds the Jack and several others, he may not come up. In fact, he probably will not, and the 10 may win the trick. This is the only way you can accomplish your purpose.

A play that works much more often than it should is:

9 7 4 3 2

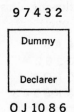

Q J 10 8 6

This is the trump suit and, as you see, two tricks must be lost unless a mix-up occurs. The proper technique is not to lead from dummy. You have practically no hope that the Ace and the King will fall together, for if East has the Ace and another one and West has the singleton King, East will surely play low. Your only hope is to lead the Queen from the South hand. If West holds the King and a small one, you will be surprised at how many times the King will come up only to be smothered by partner's Ace. I agree with you that

P

West should not play the King. It borders on the absurd to do so, because if declarer had the Ace and the Queen, it would be rather silly for him to lead the Queen instead of either playing out the Ace or taking the finesse. The fact remains that a great many players do not stop to analyze and are in dread fear of losing their King. It costs you nothing to try.

Another old chestnut that still keeps working is the following: You are playing a Spade contract and hold the singleton King of Diamonds. Your dummy has the J 10 6 2. All other suits are under control, but you are anxious to steal the King of Diamonds. This can be done only if second hand ducks the lead from dummy. In order to make it more sporting to duck, the Jack should be led, to create the impression that you are finessing against the Queen. This can also be effectively done with the following combination:

Q 10 2

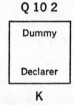

K

Assuming the rest of the hand is solid and no discards are needed, here the Queen or the 10 might be led from dummy. This gives you a much better chance that East will duck with the Ace.

As declarer you will sometimes find it necessary to steal a trick in order to win your contract. In such cases act quickly, before the opponents are organized. The following illustration, provided by Louis Watson, is a very instructive one:

♠ A 6
♡ J 6 2
◇ A Q 4
♣ K 8 5 4 3

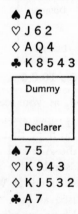

♠ 7 5
♡ K 9 4 3
◇ K J 5 3 2
♣ A 7

You are South, the declarer at a contract of 3 No Trump. West leads the 10 of Spades. You see eight tricks readily available, and it appears pointless to hold up with the Spade. It is hardly likely that West has seven of them, since they were not bid. It would be very pusillanimous to take your eight tricks and give up for down one. If East holds the Ace of Hearts, you have a fair chance to steal a trick before the defense knows that you are wide open in Spades. Your proper play is the immediate lead of the Jack of Hearts. This will make it appear to East that you are starting a finesse, and he may not come up with the Ace. If he does not, you boldly put up the King. If it holds, you are home. If not, you will be down several tricks. The question arises, does it pay to take this risk? That would depend upon how much you stand to lose if your strategy fails. If you are not vulnerable and not doubled, 50 points a trick is a cheap price to pay for the chance of fulfillment. If you are doubled, I would not like to give my out-and-out advice. That would depend somewhat on your bank balance.

Assume that you are the declarer at a contract of 4 Hearts on strong bidding, which East has doubled without hearing from his partner:

♠ A Q 2
♡ 10 8 6 4
◊ A 8 4 2
♣ Q 10

```
+----------+
| Dummy    |
|          |
| Declarer |
+----------+
```

♠ J 7
♡ K Q J 7 5 2
◊ 9 3
♣ A 6 5

West leads the 5 of Diamonds, which North wins. It is reasonable to suppose that East holds the King of Spades, and therefore the finesse will fail. The proper procedure when South obtains the lead is to play the 7 of Spades and go right up with the Ace, returning the deuce immediately. It is true that East will know that you are up to something, but he may not know what you are trying to get him to do. It may be that you have a singleton and are trying to trap him into playing the King. On the other hand, if you have the Jack, he must come up. He may guess wrong. If he does, you are home. The complete hand is as follows:

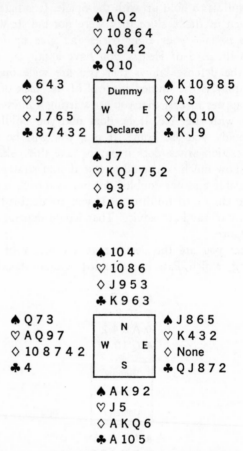

```
                    ♠ A Q 2
                    ♡ 10 8 6 4
                    ◇ A 8 4 2
                    ♣ Q 10
   ♠ 6 4 3      ┌──────────┐      ♠ K 10 9 8 5
   ♡ 9         │  Dummy   │      ♡ A 3
   ◇ J 7 6 5    │ W     E  │      ◇ K Q 10
   ♣ 8 7 4 3 2  │ Declarer │      ♣ K J 9
              └──────────┘
                    ♠ J 7
                    ♡ K Q J 7 5 2
                    ◇ 9 3
                    ♣ A 6 5
```

```
                    ♠ 10 4
                    ♡ 10 8 6
                    ◇ J 9 5 3
                    ♣ K 9 6 3
   ♠ Q 7 3      ┌──────────┐      ♠ J 8 6 5
   ♡ A Q 9 7    │    N     │      ♡ K 4 3 2
   ◇ 10 8 7 4 2 │ W     E  │      ◇ None
   ♣ 4         │    S     │      ♣ Q J 8 7 2
              └──────────┘
                    ♠ A K 9 2
                    ♡ J 5
                    ◇ A K Q 6
                    ♣ A 10 5
```

South was the declarer at a contract of 3 No Trump on bidding which is not sanctioned here. West opened the 4 of Diamonds, which dummy held with the Jack, East discarding the 8 of Clubs. It is apparent that only eight tricks are available without building up a Club trick, and if the lead is surrendered, the defense will surely shift to Hearts.

It is psychologically true that the defense will usually avoid a suit that the declarer is working on. Capitalizing on this principle, the declarer immediately led the 6 of Hearts, playing the Jack from his own hand. West won with the Queen and responded to his partner's signal by leading the 4 of Clubs. The Jack forced the Ace, and the 10 of Clubs was returned, losing to East's Queen. East calling to mind that declarer had first led Hearts, decided to shift to the Spades, and declarer was home.

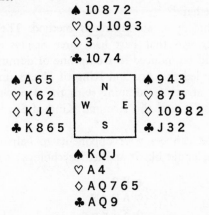

```
                    ♠ 10 8 7 2
                    ♡ Q J 10 9 3
                    ♢ 3
                    ♣ 10 7 4
    ♠ A 6 5         ┌──────────┐      ♠ 9 4 3
    ♡ K 6 2         │    N     │      ♡ 8 7 5
    ♢ K J 4         │ W     E  │      ♢ 10 9 8 2
    ♣ K 8 6 5       │    S     │      ♣ J 3 2
                    └──────────┘
                    ♠ K Q J
                    ♡ A 4
                    ♢ A Q 7 6 5
                    ♣ A Q 9
```

South was declarer at a contract of 3 No Trump. West led the 5 of Clubs, dummy played low, East followed with the Jack, and declarer, recognizing that he had no entry in the dummy, hit upon an ingenious method of getting there. He won the opening trick with the Ace of Clubs instead of the Queen. This naturally gave West the impression that East held originally the Jack Queen of Clubs, since the Jack had forced the Ace. Now declarer's hope was that West held the King of Hearts. Therefore he played the Ace and another Heart. When West took the third trick in Hearts he led the 6 of Clubs. The 10 was put up from dummy holding the trick, and declarer was able to cash the remaining Hearts.

The following hand is a classic of deception. It illustrates, too, the principle that the most hopeless hands can be brought home if you maintain a stiff upper lip:

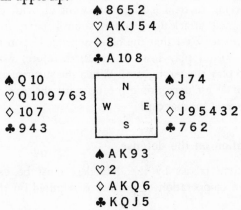

```
                    ♠ 8 6 5 2
                    ♡ A K J 5 4
                    ♢ 8
                    ♣ A 10 8
    ♠ Q 10          ┌──────────┐      ♠ J 7 4
    ♡ Q 10 9 7 6 3  │    N     │      ♡ 8
    ♢ 10 7          │ W     E  │      ♢ J 9 5 4 3 2
    ♣ 9 4 3         │    S     │      ♣ 7 6 2
                    └──────────┘
                    ♠ A K 9 3
                    ♡ 2
                    ♢ A K Q 6
                    ♣ K Q J 5
```

Through a series of aggressive bids South found himself in the impossible contract of 7 Spades. West led the 10 of Diamonds. How would you play the hand?

This declarer hit upon an ingenious method. The only hope to fulfill the contract was that East had three Spades and West two, and that East could be induced to trump one of dummy's good cards. Declarer therefore led the Ace and King of Hearts immediately, and East fell into the error of trumping with the 4 of Spades. Declarer overruffed with the 9, and the Ace and King of Spades dropped the adverse trumps.

Occasionally you can get your opponents to help you make your guess. Here is a splendid bit of applied psychology:

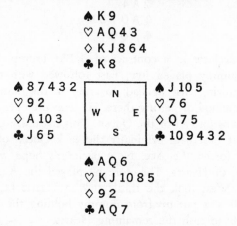

```
              ♠ K 9
              ♡ A Q 4 3
              ◇ K J 8 6 4
              ♣ K 8
♠ 8 7 4 3 2    ┌─────────┐    ♠ J 10 5
♡ 9 2          │    N    │    ♡ 7 6
◇ A 10 3       │ W     E │    ◇ Q 7 5
♣ J 6 5        │    S    │    ♣ 10 9 4 3 2
              └─────────┘
              ♠ A Q 6
              ♡ K J 10 8 5
              ◇ 9 2
              ♣ A Q 7
```

The contract was 6 Hearts. West led a Spade, which declarer won in his own hand with the Ace, and before touching any other card led the 2 of Diamonds. West was caught flat-footed, and, fearing that declarer was trying to steal a singleton, went up with the Ace. Had declarer postponed attacking Diamonds until later, it might have become apparent to West that the hand depended upon the Diamond guess, and he would play low. Declarer, therefore, would have an even chance to play the wrong card. When the surprise attack is made at trick two, if West does not come up with the Ace it is a better gamble to play East for that card.

Deception on the defense

Deceptive tactics by the defenders must be exercised with caution. Where co-operation of partner is required on the defense, it is important not to confuse him. Occasionally these tactics may be employed without confusing partner.

Declarer plays the King. What card should East play?

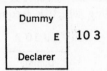

It is very likely that your partner holds the Queen and that the declarer intends to finesse the Jack—a play which you know will be successful. If you can induce the declarer to believe that the Queen might fall, you have some hope. Since the card is immaterial to you, you should follow suit with the 10 instead of the 3. It costs you nothing and may cause declarer to believe that you also have the Queen.

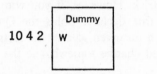

You are West. South plays the King, on which all hands play low. He follows with a small one. You are convinced that your partner has the Queen and fear that the declarer might decide to play for the drop instead of the finesse. Your best play to the second trick is the 10, since it is of no use to you and will tend to make the declarer believe that you have the Queen alone at this point or, if your partner has it, that it cannot fall. This type of false-card will almost always induce the declarer to take the finesse instead of playing for the drop.

A more advanced type of false-carding is the following:

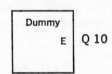

You are East. Declarer plays the Ace from dummy. If you play the 10, declarer may suspect that the Queen will fall next time and refuse the finesse. The play of the Queen instead may be very effective, if you suspect that the declarer has only two cards of the suit. He will then be certain that your partner has the 10 and will no doubt finesse the 9 on the next round. Of course there is no assurance that this type of play will succeed, because declarer might have three of the suit, but if he has only two, it is bound to work.

A type of false-carding which is frequently abused is:

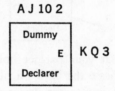

South, the declarer, plays a small one and finesses the 10. Many players false-card with the King (in order to induce declarer to believe that West has the Queen). This is usually unsound strategy, because generally you do not care what the declarer believes. He is going to have to take the finesse again in any event. If he does not, you are sure of the trick. However, if you win with the King, your partner will believe that declarer holds the Queen and may subsequently defend upon a mistaken idea of the facts.

The situation would change somewhat if the holding were:

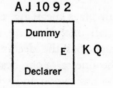

Declarer finesses the 10; you, as East, win. You fear the possibility that declarer will not finesse again but will play for the drop. Now you should try to induce South to believe that your partner has one of the honors. This you may do by winning with the King, but here again you must vary your tactics. Do not always follow the same procedure. Sometimes you should win with the King, sometimes with the Queen. It is very unprofitable to get yourself spotted as a notorious false-carder.

You are East:

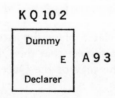

South leads the 4, West follows with the 5, and declarer plays the King. Assume that you do not fear a singleton in the declarer's hand. Your policy is to duck. If you win the trick, declarer will surely finesse against the Jack on the next round, and you know that it will succeed. If you play low, declarer may form the mistaken belief that West has the Ace and may be induced to come up with the Queen next time. But please do not go into a brown study as you make the play. Determine in advance what your action is to be. In ducking, the 9, rather than the 3, should be played.

The complete holding was:

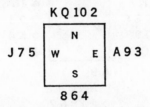

Another brilliant deceptive lead which is worthy of study was one made by my friend Albert H. Morehead. It has the merit of tending to deceive declarer without hurting partner:

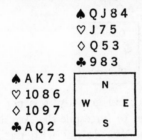

The bidding has been:

SOUTH	WEST	NORTH	EAST
1 Heart	Pass	1 Spade	Pass
2 Diamonds	Pass	2 Hearts	Pass
4 Hearts	Pass	Pass	Pass

West led the Ace of Spades, a deliberate false-carding, because he did not wish the declarer to know that he had both the Ace and the King with the Spade bid behind him. Partner played the deuce. The bidding indicated that South might have five Hearts and five Diamonds, and the only hope from Mr. Morehead's standpoint was that one of his partner's two Diamonds was the King. If declarer were left to his own resources, he would surely play a low Diamond from

P*

dummy and the entire suit would be picked up. In order to induce a false theory of the Diamond distribution, he led the 9. Declarer placed East with the King 10 and one other, and played the Queen. This was covered by the King and the Ace, and West could not be prevented from taking a trick with the 10. The complete hand follows:

♠ Q J 8 4
♡ J 7 5
◇ Q 5 3
♣ 9 8 3

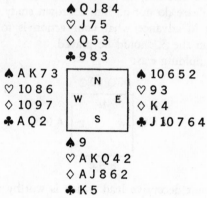

♠ A K 7 3   ♠ 10 6 5 2
♡ 10 8 6   ♡ 9 3
◇ 10 9 7   ◇ K 4
♣ A Q 2   ♣ J 10 7 6 4

♠ 9
♡ A K Q 4 2
◇ A J 8 6 2
♣ K 5

South leads the 3. What should you play as West?

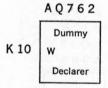

A Q 7 6 2

K 10 | Dummy
     | W
     | Declarer

It is apparently immaterial, but actually it is not so. The proper play is the King, not in order to force out the Ace, because nothing is to be gained by doing so. You do not wish the Ace forced out unless partner has the Jack and two others, and if partner has that holding, no matter what card you play your side cannot be prevented from ultimately winning a trick. The reason for your play is strategic. Since it makes no difference to you, you wish to give the declarer the impression that your King is alone. This may induce him to play your partner for the 10—particularly if the complete holding were:

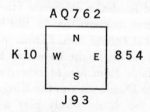

A Q 7 6 2

K 10 | N | 8 5 4
     | W   E |
     | S |

J 9 3

Deception 449

At No Trump, South leads the deuce of this suit. What should West play?

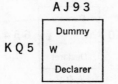

A J 9 3

The answer is the 5. It is pointless to climb up with the Queen to insure one trick, unless that should happen to be the setting trick or unless you should desire the lead in great haste. With this holding it is very likely that your partner holds the 10, and if so, declarer's probable play from dummy will be the 9, unless you "tip your hand" and tell him plainly that you have the King and the Queen. If the declarer has the 10, you will not have lost your trick, you will simply have postponed winning it.

Another holding in which an opportunity for the double-cross is presented is the following:

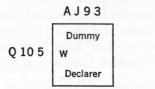

A J 9 3

Declarer leads the deuce. What should West play? West knows that if declarer has the King, the finesse of the Jack will surely be taken. If partner has the King and declarer plays properly, the defenders will take only one trick, because the correct play from the dummy will be the 9, forcing out the King, and the subsequent finesse against West's Queen will take up the entire suit. West therefore should try to induce declarer to believe that he holds both the King and the Queen. This can be done by playing the Queen second hand. It is very difficult now for declarer to believe that West does not have the King, and he almost surely will play the Jack next time. The complete holding is as follows:

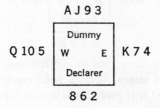

A J 9 3

South leads the deuce. What should West play?

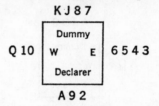

It might be profitable to play the Queen. Surely declarer intends to play the Jack from dummy and your holding will soon be apparent to him. Your play of the Queen may induce declarer to finesse the 9 on the return. Here's another:

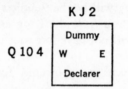

Declarer leads the 5. You are West and play the 4. Dummy's Jack holds the trick, and then the King is cashed. Notice you should drop the Queen. Declarer knows that you have it, and the 10 is the same value. If he can be induced into playing your partner for the 10, you may win a trick. The complete holding is as follows:

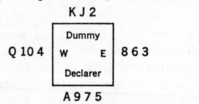

A defensive false-card which has nothing to lose and may occasionally gain a trick could be employed by West against a No Trump contract in the following situation:

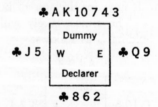

Dummy has a sure entry card in another suit. When declarer leads the 2 of Clubs, West might obtain a good result by playing the Jack. Declarer will win and will probably return to his hand to lead another

Club. When West follows with the 5, declarer may suspect him of
having originally held the Q J 5.

A slight variation of this play occurred on the following hand
taken from a tournament:

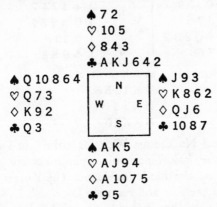

```
                    ♠ 7 2
                    ♡ 10 5
                    ◇ 8 4 3
                    ♣ A K J 6 4 2
   ♠ Q 10 8 6 4    ┌──────────┐    ♠ J 9 3
   ♡ Q 7 3         │    N     │    ♡ K 8 6 2
   ◇ K 9 2         │  W    E  │    ◇ Q J 6
   ♣ Q 3           │    S     │    ♣ 10 8 7
                   └──────────┘
                    ♠ A K 5
                    ♡ A J 9 4
                    ◇ A 10 7 5
                    ♣ 9 5
```

South was playing 3 No Trump. West led the 6 of Spades. South
won and played the 5 of Clubs, intending to finesse. West promptly
played the Queen, and declarer paused for a moment. If the Queen
were singleton, East would have 10 8 7 3 and would stop the suit.
Declarer therefore was obliged to make a safety play by permitting
the Queen to hold. In this way declarer was held to 3 No Trump.

Boldness combined with quick thinking may prove very effective in
cases like the following:

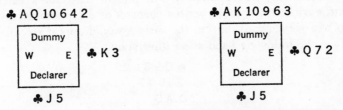

```
  ♣ A Q 10 6 4 2              ♣ A K 10 9 6 3
 ┌──────────────┐           ┌──────────────┐
 │    Dummy     │           │    Dummy     │
 │  W      E    │  ♣ K 3    │  W      E    │  ♣ Q 7 2
 │  Declarer    │           │  Declarer    │
 └──────────────┘           └──────────────┘
      ♣ J 5                      ♣ J 5
```

You are East. Declarer is playing No Trump, dummy has no entry
cards. Declarer, who is suspected of having only two Clubs, leads the
Jack and plays low from dummy. If you win, the declarer has the
balance of the suit. It is good tactics to duck. The finesse will almost
surely be repeated, and the dummy may be shut out. Of course, if you
have a "lunging" partner, your strategy will fail. A "lunging" partner
is one who lunges toward the trick every time declarer takes what
appears to be a losing finesse. The reflex action of his forearm may
prove very costly.

Here is a ruse that may work in less astute circles:

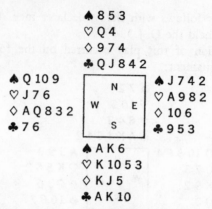

♠ 8 5 3
♡ Q 4
♢ 9 7 4
♣ Q J 8 4 2

♠ Q 10 9   ♠ J 7 4 2
♡ J 7 6   ♡ A 9 8 2
♢ A Q 8 3 2   ♢ 10 6
♣ 7 6   ♣ 9 5 3

♠ A K 6
♡ K 10 5 3
♢ K J 5
♣ A K 10

South is playing 3 No Trump. West leads the 3 of Diamonds, and South wins with the Jack. Since only eight tricks are available, declarer must build up the ninth in Hearts. The danger, however, is that East will hold the Ace and return a Diamond. If West has that card, the contract is safe, but if East has it, he may be induced to hold off once if he is given the impression that dummy has no other entries. The Ace and the King of Clubs should be played and the suit discontinued, to give the impression that declarer has no more. Then the King of Hearts is played. Naturally East should take this trick, but your play may give him the false impression that you are trying to build up the Queen as an entry and induce him to hold off one round.

Occasionally an opportunity will present itself for a defender to win a trick very cheaply, yet for purposes of deception he may decide to win with a card that on the surface would appear to cost a trick. Take the following hand as an illustration:

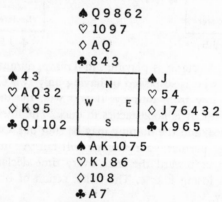

♠ Q 9 8 6 2
♡ 10 9 7
♢ A Q
♣ 8 4 3

♠ 4 3   ♠ J
♡ A Q 3 2   ♡ 5 4
♢ K 9 5   ♢ J 7 6 4 3 2
♣ Q J 10 2   ♣ K 9 6 5

♠ A K 10 7 5
♡ K J 8 6
♢ 10 8
♣ A 7

The bidding has proceeded:

SOUTH	WEST	NORTH	EAST
1 Spade	Pass	2 Spades	Pass
3 Hearts	Pass	4 Spades	Pass
Pass	Pass		

West leads the Queen of Clubs, East signals with the 9, and declarer wins with the Ace. Two rounds of trumps are drawn, winding up in dummy. The 10 of Hearts is led, declarer playing low. West sees that he can cash two Heart tricks, probably one Club, and no Diamonds, inasmuch as declarer will be forced to take the Diamond finesse. If, however, the declarer can be persuaded that East holds the Queen of Hearts, he will certainly not try the Diamond finesse but will plan to discard dummy's Queen of Diamonds on his own good Heart. So reasoned, West won the trick with the Ace instead of the Queen, cashed the Jack of Clubs, and shifted to a low Diamond. Declarer, convinced that the Heart Queen was with East, naturally refused the Diamond finesse and went up with the Ace. When the succeeding Heart finesse lost to West's Queen, the King of Diamonds was cashed for the setting trick.

A very pretty case of camouflage is the following:

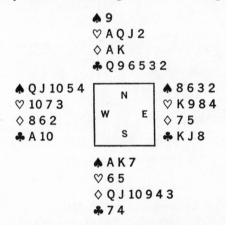

```
              ♠ 9
              ♡ A Q J 2
              ◇ A K
              ♣ Q 9 6 5 3 2
♠ Q J 10 5 4              ♠ 8 6 3 2
♡ 10 7 3        N        ♡ K 9 8 4
◇ 8 6 2      W   E       ◇ 7 5
♣ A 10          S        ♣ K J 8
              ♠ A K 7
              ♡ 6 5
              ◇ Q J 10 9 4 3
              ♣ 7 4
```

Declarer is playing 3 No Trump, and West leads the Queen of Spades. Declarer is in the unhappy predicament of having a great many tricks but not being able to use them, because the Diamond suit is blocked and West's lead has taken out declarer's only entry. Another Spade in dummy would be worth a great many points. However, South hit upon an almost "sure-fire" ruse. He quickly ducked the Queen of Spades, and West can hardly be blamed for continuing with the Jack. Now dummy's two high Diamonds were discarded on the Ace and King of Spades, which permitted the uninterrupted run of six Diamond tricks from the closed hand. It is true that if West had led no more Spades, declarer could not have made the hand, but it is a play that the defense could not have foreseen without X-ray eyes.

24.   Percentages

I HESITATE to use the title "Percentages," as it may frighten off some of my readers. Let me hasten to explain that no alarm need be felt; this is not to be a lesson in mathematics.

A great many players have the mistaken notion that to be a successful bridge player one must be very good in arithmetic. Nothing could be farther from the truth. Strange to say, in the select circle of bridge experts very few are mathematicians. If you are able to count thirteen and are willing to exercise ordinary common sense (not that mysterious unknown quantity frequently called card sense), you will not find this chapter difficult to wade through.

"Playing percentages" is another way of saying that where there are two ways to do a thing it is better to select that way which offers you the greater chance. If the first method offers you three chances of success and the second method offers you only one, obviously the former should be selected. But how are you to determine these chances?

I shall not burden you with the mathematics of the various situations. The mathematicians who have come before us have done all the hard work, and we must take their word for the details.

The simple way to remember their conclusions will be pointed out to you in the succeeding pages.

I should like to point out very early that the principle of percentages—or "the odds," to use a more common expression—is employed only when there are no other clues as to the distribution of the cards. The things that took place at the table during the bidding and the play are far more important than any abstract probabilities. If, for example, you are concerned with the distribution of five Spades that may be out against you, the probability is that they will be divided three in one hand and two in the other. But if the player to your left has bid a great many Hearts and a great many Diamonds, he will not have room in his hand for many Spades, and you must not be surprised if he has only one Spade, though the table of probabilities indicates that on the average he should have at least two. Remember that the man who wrote this table was not present during the bidding. When, however, you have no information from the bidding, and have nothing else to go by, the probabilities should guide you in your play.

At this point it is appropriate to say a word or two about the element of luck. It is freely conceded that luck cannot be eliminated. In a certain number of cases the correct play will lose while the improper one will succeed. This is to be expected. If you play properly, luck will be with you more often than against you. When you hear a player saying, "My finesses always fail," "My suits never break," there is a strong probability that the player is not availing himself of the proper odds. Lady Luck requires a little assistance from the persons on whom she is to shower her blessings.

It is fortunate for the game of bridge that, however scientific we may make it, the element of chance cannot be eliminated, and on a given number of hands the veriest tyro might outguess the super-expert.

While there are certain fixed principles for the management of various combinations, the play of the hand can never be reduced to an exact science. Which finesse to take or what suit to develop will many times be a sheer guess, one offering as good a prospect as the other. If, however, you find that you are guessing wrong in a majority of the cases, there is a strong suspicion that your technique has been faulty.

Bridge players at times exercise an extraordinarily peculiar sense of business. I have known men to refuse a wager on a football game at 6–5 odds when they felt the odds should be 6½–5, and yet that night they would sit down at the card table and accept a 40 per cent chance where they could have gotten 60 per cent for the same price of admission. Lady Luck usually gets the blame. Various methods are popularly employed to change the course of luck. These attempts include such well-calculated plans as sitting on a handkerchief or walking around a chair, and in some circles even more drastic acts, which cannot be discussed here.

A simple study of percentages will be more effective in changing luck than all these acts of magic.

The application of the principle is illustrated in the play of the following hand:

NORTH:	♠ 4 3	SOUTH:	♠ A 8 5
	♡ A Q 4		♡ 8 7 6 2
	◇ A K Q		◇ 10 5 4 3
	♣ A K Q 3 2		♣ 6 4

You are South, the declarer at a contract of 3 No Trump. West leads the Queen of Spades and receives an encouraging signal from

East. You duck the first round, and the Jack is continued. Now let us assume that you decide to win the second trick. You have a choice of plays. If the Clubs will break, you have ten running tricks. If they do not break, you have only eight, and the ninth might be available through a Heart finesse. But if you try one and it fails, it is too late to try the other. Which is the better chance?

If West had participated in the bidding, you would be inclined toward the belief that he held the missing King. But since there is no clue, you must fall back on the law of probability. If you try the Heart finesse, you have exactly a 50 per cent chance. In other words, West is just as apt to have the King as East, and half the time that play will succeed. Now the question is, what are the chances of the Clubs breaking 3 and 3? The answer is that the chances are distinctly against it. To put it in the form of a rule, *when there are an even number of cards out against you they will probably not break.* Therefore on the above hand the proper procedure is to take the Heart finesse.

In the next example, you are declarer at a contract of 3 No Trump. West leads the King of Spades. You have a total of eight top-card tricks, and the question arises how to develop the ninth. In Hearts you have a chance for a finesse. In Diamonds you have a chance that the suit will break 3–3, which will provide two additional tricks. In Clubs you have a chance that the suit will break 3–3, in which case the 5 of Clubs will be the ninth trick. It is obvious that the lead must not be surrendered, for in that case a sufficient number of Spades may be cashed to defeat the contract.

NORTH: ♠ 4 3   SOUTH: ♠ A 2
♡ 7 6 5 4 3   ♡ A Q 2
◇ K 5   ◇ A Q 4 3 2
♣ 5 4 3 2   ♣ A K Q

The first thing to do is to try the Clubs. If they break, your troubles are over. However, when you lead them you find that one opponent has four Clubs. Therefore you must decide to either lead out your Diamonds, in the hope that the suit will break, or enter dummy to take the Heart finesse. Which has the better chance of success? The opponents hold six Diamonds—an even number. It is probable, therefore, that they will not be divided 3–3. The percentages are against an even number of cards breaking. The Diamond suit, therefore, offers less than a 50–50 chance.

The Heart finesse is an exactly even gamble. That play, therefore, should be tried in preference to the Diamonds.

Changing the hand slightly, we have:

DUMMY: ♠ 5 4   SOUTH: ♠ A 3 2
       ♡ 6 5 4 3   ♡ A Q 2
       ◇ K 5 4   ◇ A Q 3 2
       ♣ 5 4 3 2   ♣ A K Q

Again you are South playing at 3 No Trump, and again West leads the King of Spades. You have eight top-card tricks. In this case you need not worry about percentages. You can discover the facts and do not need to resort to probabilities.

First you try the Clubs. They fail to break. You then try the Diamonds, making sure to win the third Diamond trick in dummy with the King. If the Diamonds have broken, your troubles are over. If they fail to break, you have only one hope left, and that is the Heart finesse.

As a corollary to the above principle it may be stated that *when there are an odd number of cards out against you they probably will break as evenly as possible.*

The principle of percentages, to repeat, means simply selecting that play which offers the greater chance of success.

Holding eight cards of a suit, missing only the Queen, the best chance to capture the Queen is by finessing rather than playing the Ace and King.

NORTH: A K J 6   SOUTH: 5 4 3 2

The reason is this. The five cards out will probably be divided 3–2. The missing card, the Queen, has a greater chance of being with the 3 than with the 2. This is a fundamental principle of percentage. *The person with the greater number of cards is the one more likely to have the card you are looking for.* Since, therefore, the Queen is probably in the hand that holds three, the play of the Ace and King will not succeed in dropping it.

As we have seen above, the proper play in an attempt to capture the Queen with five missing cards is the finesse, but here you have a choice of finessing either way:

NORTH: A J 10 2   SOUTH: K 9 7 4

You must make up your mind which one of the opponents probably has the Queen. Here I might pause for a moment to point out that there is a popular superstition to the effect that the Queen lies over the Jack, and some players always finesse in that manner. This policy has about as much merit as some such doctrine as "Always finesse toward City Hall." If any of your friends would like to wager, ask them to give you odds of 11 to 10 on their belief, and you have my assurance that in very short order your friends will run out of chips.

In handling this combination you should try to ascertain which of your opponents has more Spades (let us say). There are various ways to do this. If you can find out how many of the other suits your opponents have, you will, by simple subtraction, determine the number of Spades. If you find out that one player is very long in a certain suit, there is a good chance that he will be short in Spades. Consequently his partner should be played for the Queen. If the player on your left has bid Hearts and Diamonds, there is a great likelihood that he is short in Spades. In that case the Ace should be played first (the singleton Queen may drop) and the Jack led through for the finesse, because the player on your right is more likely to have the Queen.

When you use the words "more likely" you are practicing the principle of percentages.

You are South, the declarer at a contract of 4 Spades. West leads the King of Clubs, which of course you win in dummy with the Ace. Now you have a choice of finessing either the Diamonds or the Spades. Which is the correct play?

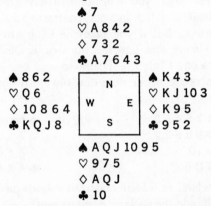

```
              ♠ 7
              ♡ A 8 4 2
              ◇ 7 3 2
              ♣ A 7 6 4 3
♠ 8 6 2          N          ♠ K 4 3
♡ Q 6                       ♡ K J 10 3
◇ 10 8 6 4    W     E       ◇ K 9 5
♣ K Q J 8        S          ♣ 9 5 2
              ♠ A Q J 10 9 5
              ♡ 9 7 5
              ◇ A Q J
              ♣ 10
```

Obviously the Diamond, because it must be finessed twice, and you have another entry to do so. The Spade finesse would be improper, because even if it wins, you may not have gained anything, since the King will probably not fall anyhow. If you take the Diamond finesse, you are simply wishing for the King to be on the right. If you take the Spade finesse, you are wishing for the King to be on the right and also for it to fall on the second round. Which is more likely? The answer is obvious. One prayer is easier to have answered than two.

NORTH:	♠ A 10 6	SOUTH:	♠ Q J 9
	♡ J 8 5		♡ A K 6 4 2
	◊ 9 6 4		◊ K 7 5 3
	♣ A K J 5		♣ 3

You are South, the declarer at a contract of 4 Hearts. West leads the 4 of Spades. You play low from the dummy and win in your own hand. You lead the Ace and King of Hearts, and everyone follows, but the Queen does not drop. What is your proper play at this point?

Your choices appear to be:

(a) To take the Club finesse in order to discard two of South's Diamonds.

(b) To hope for the Ace of Diamonds to be with East.

Which is the better choice? Mathematically, the chances are exactly the same. There is a 50 per cent chance that the Queen of Clubs is with West, and there is also a 50 per cent chance that the Ace of Diamonds is with East. On the surface, therefore, it would appear that the choice is a mere guess.

Actually, however, this is not quite so. If you play properly, you can give yourself both chances instead of only one. If you try the Diamond and that loses, you will immediately give up three Diamonds and a Heart and fail in your contract. You have, therefore, had only one chance. But if you take the Club finesse and it loses, you still have a chance that East has the Ace of Diamonds, in which case you will lose one Club, one Diamond, and one Heart. Since two 50 per cent chances are better than one, obviously the Club finesse is the correct play.

NORTH:	♠ 7 5 4 3 2	SOUTH:	♠ none
	♡ 9 8 5 3 2		♡ 7
	◊ 10		◊ A K Q J 9 8 7
	♣ Q 6		♣ A K 4 3 2

South is the declarer at 6 Diamonds. West leads the King of Spades, and South ruffs. Should the declarer draw trumps?

Everything will depend on the Clubs breaking. Here percentages are not necessary. The Queen of Clubs should be cashed, then the King, and a small Club ruffed with the 10, since there is no danger of an overruff. If it is argued that the second Club might be trumped by the opponents, the answer is that if one opponent held five Clubs, the hand could never have been made even if trumps had been drawn, because two Clubs and a Heart would have been lost.

A very neat illustration of the principle of percentages is provided by the following hand:

NORTH: ♠ A 9 7 5 SOUTH: ♠ 3
♡ Q 10 9 ♡ A K J 7 4
◇ 10 8 3 ◇ J 6 4
♣ Q 7 6 ♣ A K 5 2

You are South, the declarer at a contract of 4 Hearts, and West leads the King of Spades, which of course you win in dummy. You see that the loss of three Diamonds is inevitable. Should you pull the trumps? If you do so, everything will depend upon the Clubs breaking 3–3. Since an even number of Clubs will probably not break, the chances are you will not fulfill your contract. Is there a better way to play this hand?

Yes. Since there are five trumps outstanding, an odd number, they will probably be divided 3–2, so that dummy's trumps may be used to draw those held by the adversaries and declarer's trumps may be used for ruffing Spades. The play will proceed as follows:

The Ace of Spades is won, and the 5 of Spades is ruffed with the King of Hearts. The 4 of Hearts is led to dummy's 9, and the 7 of Spades is ruffed with the Ace of Hearts. The 7 of Hearts is led to dummy's 10, and the remaining Spade is ruffed with the Jack of Hearts. Dummy is entered with the Queen of Clubs and the last trump drawn with the Queen of Hearts, declarer discarding a Diamond. The Ace and King of Clubs will be the ninth and tenth tricks, and if the Clubs happen to break, an eleventh trick is available with the 5 of Clubs. (See chapter on Dummy Reversal.) The complete hand follows:

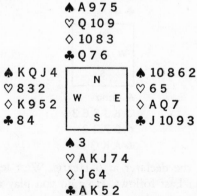

Let us consider the same hand with the Queen of Clubs transferred to declarer's hand.

Should trumps be drawn? Everything will depend on the Clubs breaking, since there are three losing Diamonds. This hand cannot be played in the same manner as the previous one, since dummy can-

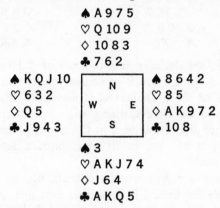

♠ A 9 7 5
♡ Q 10 9
◇ 10 8 3
♣ 7 6 2

♠ K Q J 10
♡ 6 3 2
◇ Q 5
♣ J 9 4 3

♠ 8 6 4 2
♡ 8 5
◇ A K 9 7 2
♣ 10 8

♠ 3
♡ A K J 7 4
◇ J 6 4
♣ A K Q 5

not be entered a sufficient number of times to ruff out the Spades and also to pull the trumps. The proper procedure is to play only two trumps and then A K Q of Clubs. If the Clubs have broken, the last trump is drawn. If the Clubs do not break, there is the chance that the player who was short in Clubs does not have the remaining trump, in which case the 5 of Clubs can be ruffed in dummy. If it is argued that the Queen of Clubs might be trumped, then the answer is that there was no possible way to make the hand.

♠ A J 8 6 3
♡ Q 10 4
◇ A K 8 4
♣ 4

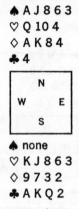

♠ none
♡ K J 8 6 3
◇ 9 7 3 2
♣ A K Q 2

You are South, the declarer at 6 Hearts. West leads the Ace and another trump, and East follows. How do you play the hand?

Do not pull the remaining trump. Do not attempt to establish the Spades. For that play to succeed, the Spades would have to be four-

four, which is very improbable. It is better to trust that the Diamonds will be three–two, which is probable. Therefore you cash the Ace and King of Diamonds, play A K Q of Clubs, discarding two Diamonds from dummy. Lead a Diamond and ruff. The South hand is entered by ruffing a Spade and the last trump pulled. The complete hand:

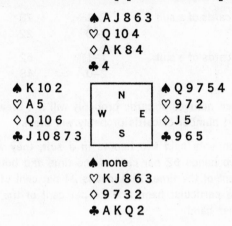

$$\spadesuit \text{ A J 8 6 3}$$
$$\heartsuit \text{ Q 10 4}$$
$$\diamondsuit \text{ A K 8 4}$$
$$\clubsuit \text{ 4}$$

$\spadesuit$ K 10 2   N $\spadesuit$ Q 9 7 5 4
$\heartsuit$ A 5   W   E $\heartsuit$ 9 7 2
$\diamondsuit$ Q 10 6   S $\diamondsuit$ J 5
$\clubsuit$ J 10 8 7 3 $\clubsuit$ 9 6 5

$$\spadesuit \text{ none}$$
$$\heartsuit \text{ K J 8 6 3}$$
$$\diamondsuit \text{ 9 7 3 2}$$
$$\clubsuit \text{ A K Q 2}$$

Table of probabilities

YOU AND PARTNER HOLD BETWEEN YOU		THE ADVERSE CARDS WILL BE DIVIDED % OF THE TIME
6 cards of a suit	4–3	62
	5–2	31
	6–1	7
	7–0	Less than ½
7 cards of a suit	4–2	48
	3–3	36
	5–1	15
	6–0	1
8 cards of a suit	3–2	68
	4–1	28
	5–0	4
9 cards of a suit	3–1	50
	2–2	40
	4–0	10

Table of probabilities (continued)

YOU AND PARTNER HOLD BETWEEN YOU	THE ADVERSE CARDS WILL BE DIVIDED	% OF THE TIME
10 cards of a suit	2–1	78
	3–0	22
11 cards of a suit	1–1	52
	2–0	48

Note: An even number of cards probably will not break.
An odd number of cards probably will break.

Note: If opponents hold two honors in a suit, they will be divided between the two hands 52 per cent of the time and both in the same hand 48 per cent of the time. That means 24 per cent of the time they are both in one particular hand and 24 per cent of the time they are both in the other hand.

Discussion of the percentage table

The following is a common holding which is very frequently misplayed:

A K Q 7 4

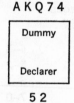

5 2

Assuming no entries in dummy, it is better to concede the first trick by playing small from both hands. Then when A K Q are played, declarer has an excellent chance of catching all the outstanding cards and thus making four tricks. Many players feel confident that such a holding will produce five tricks unless they are unlucky enough to get a bad break in the suit. Actually their reasoning is false. To take five tricks depends on a 3–3 split, which occurs just 36 times in 100. A 4–2 split, which will cause ruination if you play the A K Q, occurs about 48 times in 100, and is, therefore, to be expected.

There is a popular belief that with ten cards in a suit, missing the King, the Ace play is superior to the finesse. This is a misconception.

Unless you have some specific clue, the finesse is the proper play. The percentage table shows that the 2–1 split occurs 78 per cent of the time, but the King is much more apt to be in the larger group. The exact figures are:

The King will be singleton 26 per cent of the time—of these, 13 per cent in one hand and 13 per cent in the other. In other words, 13 times in 100, by refusing to finesse, you will pick up a singleton King behind you. When a singleton King is ahead of you, all plays succeed because the finesse becomes unnecessary.

The King will have one card with it 52 per cent of the time.

The King will have two cards with it 22 per cent of the time, which means the finesse will work 26 per cent plus 11 per cent of the time—a total of 37 per cent.

Fifty per cent of the time the play is immaterial. It will fail or work on either play. When eleven cards are held, the question is very close. There is a 2 per cent advantage in favor of the drop rather than the finesse. Two per cent is so slight that any clue at all is a better bet. Even a suspicious look in the eye of an opponent or a nervous twitch is worth more than 2 per cent.

When nine cards are held:

A particular card will be alone 12 per cent of the time (6 per cent on each side).

A particular card will have one card with it 40 per cent of the time (20 per cent on each side).

A particular card will have two cards with it 38 per cent of the time (19 per cent on each side).

If two pivotal cards are adversely held, such as the King and Queen, for example, either the King or Queen will be alone 24 per cent of the time (12 per cent on each side); there will be a doubleton King Queen 14 per cent of the time (7 per cent on each side), or they will be split between the two hands 52 per cent of the time.

When eight cards are held:

A particular card will be alone 6 per cent of the time (3 per cent on each side).

A particular card will have one card with it 28 per cent of the time (14 per cent on each side).

A particular card will have two cards with it 40 per cent of the time (20 per cent on each side).

A particular card will have three cards with it 22 per cent of the time (11 per cent on each side).

If two pivotal cards are adversely held, such as the King and Queen, for example, either the King or Queen will be alone 12 per cent of the time (6 per cent on each side); there will be a doubleton King Queen 6 per cent of the time (3 per cent on each side), or they will be split 52 per cent of the time. (This is constant.)

When seven cards are held:

When a particular card is out, the chances of its being singleton are extremely remote.

The particular card will be doubleton 18 per cent of the time (9 per cent on each side).

It will have two small cards with it 54 per cent of the time (27 per cent on each side).

If two pivotal cards are out, such as the King Queen, as always they will be split 52 per cent of the time; there will be a singleton King or Queen 8 per cent of the time (4 per cent on each side); there will be a doubleton King Queen 4 per cent of the time (2 per cent on each side), or they will both appear by the third lead 50 per cent of the time.

A simplified way to figure the odds

Naturally no one but a mathematician could be expected to memorize the table of probabilities. For practical purposes only an approximate idea of the odds is required. The following will serve as a useful guide.

In order to determine the probability of a certain distribution, take the two figures involved and subtract one from the other. For example: The opponents have five cards and you wish to determine the probability of their being divided 4–1. You subtract 1 from 4, leaving 3. You divide 100 by the result, which produces about 33. The probability of the distribution 4–1 will be slightly less than 33 per cent. (The mathematical tables will show the figures to be 28 per cent.)

Let's try it again. The opponents have seven cards of a suit. You wish to determine the chances of a 5–2 division. Five minus 2 equals 3. One hundred divided by 3 equals 33. The chances are slightly less than 33 per cent. (The mathematical tables will show that the exact figure is 31 per cent.)

What are the chances of a 6–2 split of eight outstanding cards?

Six minus 2 equals 4. One hundred divided by 4 equals 25. The actual chances are slightly less than 25 per cent.

This rule obviously will not work for distributions such as 3–2, 4–3, 5–4, et cetera, where the difference is 1, because 100 divided by 1 equals 100 per cent, which naturally could not be.

Let us apply this rule practically:

NORTH:	♠ A 8 6	SOUTH:	♠ 5 4 3 2
	♡ A K Q J		♡ 9
	◊ J 10 7		◊ A Q 9 8 6
	♣ A 6 4		♣ K Q 7

Declarer is playing a contract of 5 Diamonds. The opening lead is the King of Spades, taken by dummy's Ace. The danger of the hand lies in losing the Diamond finesse while holding two losing Spades. If declarer undertakes to discard Spades on Hearts before drawing trumps, he runs the risk of a Heart ruff. The percentage player, therefore, compares the chances of a Diamond finesse with the chances of escaping a Heart ruff on discarding Spades.

Declarer needs two Spade discards. An opponent would be able to ruff Hearts only if the outstanding Hearts are divided 8–0, 7–1, or 6–2. The chances of the 8–0 or 7–1 distribution are small enough to be of no consequence. This leaves the 6–2 split to be considered. What are the chances of its occurrence? Six minus 2 equals 4. One hundred divided by 4 equals 25. It will occur about 25 per cent of the time. In other words, the two Spade discards can be safely taken 75 per cent of the time. The Diamond finesse will work only 50 per cent of the time. Therefore the better play is to take the discards immediately. There is the further consideration that if East happens to be the one who is short in Hearts, he can be overruffed by declarer and the Diamond finesse may still be tried.

NORTH:	♠ A K Q 2	SOUTH:	♠ 7 4
	♡ 8 6 4		♡ K Q J 10 9 7
	◊ 9 7		◊ K 8
	♣ K Q 8 2		♣ J 10 3

The declarer is playing 4 Hearts with no adverse bidding. West leads the Jack of Spades. As declarer has three Aces to lose, he must lose no other trick.

There are two ways in which to play the hand. The first is to draw trumps and hope that East has the Ace of Diamonds or that, if West holds it, East will not lead a Diamond. The second is to lead high

Spades and take a Diamond discard at once, before giving up the lead. What line of play has a better chance of success?

The first line of play has about a 50 per cent chance of success because it is fifty-fifty on who has the Ace of Diamonds (plus the slight chance that East will not lead a Diamond). The second line of play depends for its success on the chances that three rounds of Spades will live. What Spade distribution does declarer fear? There are seven Spades out. Declarer fears that the Spades might be 5–2, so that the third round will be ruffed by the opposition.

What are the chances of a 5–2 split? Five minus 2 equals 3. One hundred divided by 3 is 33. About 33 per cent of the time the third round of Spades will be ruffed, which would apparently leave 67 per cent of the time for the play to succeed. From this must be deducted the slight possibility of a 6–1 split, which will also be detrimental to our cause. This still leaves over 60 per cent, which is better than a 50 per cent chance provided by the first line of play. Actually the second line of play has better than a 60 per cent chance of winning, because the doubleton Spade might be in the East hand, in which case declarer could overruff and still try to make the Diamond King.

Another situation in which the consideration of the odds is vital is one in which you find yourself in a very hazardous contract. Let us suppose the contract is 3 No Trump, redoubled and vulnerable. You can take eight tricks with certainty and give up for down 400, or you may try a finesse early in the play which, if it wins, will bring home the contract. If it fails, you will be down 2,800. What should you do? If there is no clue as to the location of the particular card, it is better percentage at rubber bridge to take the short loss. In other words, an attempt to make the contract would be risking the loss of 2,400 points, which is considerably more than the contract itself is worth if fulfilled.

NORTH:	♠ none	SOUTH:	♠ 9 5 4
	♡ A 9 7 4 2		♡ K 8 3
	◇ A 7 4 3		◇ K Q J 5
	♣ A Q J 8		♣ K 10 6

South is the declarer at the rather overambitious contract of 7 Diamonds. West leads the King of Spades, which is ruffed in dummy with the 3 of Diamonds. South's hand is entered with the King of Hearts, and the 5 of Spades led and ruffed with the 4 of Diamonds. Declarer returns to his own hand with the 10 of Clubs and leads the last Spade. At this point he has a decision to make. He may ruff with the 7 of Diamonds, cash the Ace of trumps, and return to his hand with the King of Clubs to draw the remaining trump, or he may trump the Spade with the Ace of Diamonds and return to his hand with a trump.

The first line of play will fail if someone has a singleton Club. The second line of play will fail if the Diamonds are 4–1. Which is the better play? It is a question of matching the probability of a 4–1 Diamond break against the probability of a 5–1 Club break. Since obviously the 5–1 Club break is less probable, declarer should ruff in dummy with the 7 of Diamonds, cash the Ace of trumps, and return with a Club. The complete hand follows:

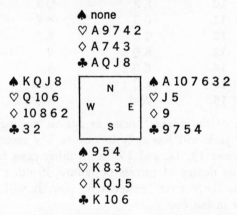

```
              ♠ none
              ♡ A 9 7 4 2
              ◇ A 7 4 3
              ♣ A Q J 8
   ♠ K Q J 8              ♠ A 10 7 6 3 2
   ♡ Q 10 6        N      ♡ J 5
   ◇ 10 8 6 2   W     E   ◇ 9
   ♣ 3 2            S      ♣ 9 7 5 4
              ♠ 9 5 4
              ♡ K 8 3
              ◇ K Q J 5
              ♣ K 10 6
```

The proper play of the following very common holding is the subject of considerable discussion:

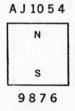

```
        A J 10 5 4
           N

           S
         9 8 7 6
```

Assuming that you have plenty of entries to the South hand, the best play is to take two finesses, on the principle that the two outstanding honors will probably be split. If you have finessed the first time, by all means finesse the second time. If, however, you find yourself short of entries, so that it is inconvenient to finesse twice, the next best play is to lead the Ace first and then the Jack. This will succeed whenever the suit is split 2–2 or a singleton honor falls.

To illustrate the basis for this conclusion let us examine the possible adverse distributions and combinations:

	WEST	EAST
1.	K	Q 3 2
2.	Q	K 3 2
3.	K Q	3 2
4.	K 3 2	Q
5.	Q 3 2	K
6.	3	K Q 2
7.	2	K Q 3
8.	3 2	K Q
9.	K 3	Q 2
10.	K 2	Q 3
11.	Q 3	K 2
12.	Q 2	K 3
13.	K Q 3	2
14.	K Q 2	3
15.	K Q 3 2	Void
16.	Void	K Q 3 2

The taking of the double finesse as against playing the Ace first and then the Jack will lose only in case 8. The recommended play will gain in cases 13, 14, and 15. In all other cases both plays will attain the same degree of success or failure. In other words, taking two finesses is the correct "percentage" play. It will gain in three cases and lose in but one.

Here the lead is from the South hand, and West plays low. The problem is whether to go up with the King or play the Jack:

K J 10 4 3

7 6 5 2

A clue will very frequently be found in the bidding, but if there is no clue, the percentage guess is to play the Jack, hoping it will drive out the Ace. If West originally had the Ace and one other, the recommended play will lose, but it will gain if West had the Queen and one other. These two probabilities cancel each other. There is the further case in which West had the Ace and Queen; here the Jack will prove to be the superior play. If West has bid, he probably holds the Ace, and it is better to come up with the King.

QUIZ ON PERCENTAGES

1.

NORTH
♠ A K J 4
♡ 10 5 2
◊ 10 6 3
♣ K J 8

WEST
♡ 6

EAST

SOUTH
♠ 9 8
♡ A K
◊ Q J 8 4 2
♣ A Q 10 5

You are South playing 3 No Trump. West leads the 6 of Hearts. East plays the 9. What is your next play?

2.

NORTH
♠ Q 7 2
♡ 2
◊ K J 10 9 8
♣ Q 6 5 4

WEST
♠ 9

EAST

SOUTH
♠ A K 6
♡ A Q 10 6 4
◊ none
♣ A K 10 7 2

You are South playing 6 Clubs. West leads the 9 of Spades. How do you play the hand?

3.

NORTH
♠ 8 6 3
♡ A Q 10 6
◊ A 8 4
♣ K 9 4

WEST
♠ 7

EAST

SOUTH
♠ A 2
♡ J 9 3
◊ K J 9 6 3
♣ A 6 2

You are South playing 3 No Trump. West leads the 7 of Spades, East plays the King, and South wins the second round of the suit. Plan the play.

Q

4.

NORTH
♠ 10 3
♡ K 4
◇ A 10 8 6 2
♣ J 9 4 3

WEST
♡ 6

EAST

SOUTH
♠ A K 7 5
♡ A 7 5
◇ K Q
♣ A 7 6 2

You are South playing 3 No Trump. West leads the 6 of Hearts, East plays the 10. Plan the play.

5.

NORTH
♠ 10 7 2
♡ Q 5
◇ K J 10 8
♣ A 9 4 3

WEST
♠ 6

EAST

SOUTH
♠ A 5 4
♡ A 10 9 4
◇ A Q 5
♣ K 5 2

You are South playing 3 No Trump. West leads the 6 of Spades and you hold up till the third round. East discards the 4 of Diamonds at the third trick. Plan the play.

6.

NORTH
♠ K 4
♡ 6 5 3
◇ A 8 6 4 2
♣ A J 7

WEST
♠ 5

SOUTH
♠ Q 10 6
♡ A J 10 9
◇ K 5
♣ K 8 6 5

You are South playing 3 No Trump. West leads the 5 of Spades. East wins with the Ace and returns the 8. Plan the play.

7.

NORTH
♠ 10 7
♡ A J 5
◇ A 6 3
♣ A K J 7 2

WEST
◇ J

SOUTH
♠ K J
♡ K Q 10 9 4 3
◇ K Q 4
♣ 8 6

You are South playing 6 Hearts. West leads the Jack of Diamonds. Plan the play.

8.

NORTH
♠ K Q 10 4
♡ A J 3 2
◇ A 5
♣ 10 9 6

WEST
◇ K

SOUTH
♠ A J 9 8 6 5
♡ K 4
◇ 6 2
♣ A K Q

You are South playing 7 Spades. West leads the King of Diamonds. Plan the play.

9.

NORTH
♠ A 7 6 3
♡ J 8 5
◇ 8 5 4 2
♣ 10 4

WEST   EAST
♠ Q

SOUTH
♠ K 5 2
♡ A Q 6 4 3 2
◇ K Q
♣ A Q

You are South playing 4 Hearts. West leads the Queen of Spades, which you take with the Ace. What is your next play?

10.

NORTH
♠ Q 8 5
♡ 8 6
◊ J 9 4 2
♣ A 9 7 5

WEST
♡ 3

EAST

SOUTH
♠ A K J
♡ K Q 9
◊ A Q 10 8
♣ Q J 10

Declarer plays 3 No Trump. West leads the 3 of Hearts. East plays Jack, South wins. What is your next play?

11.

NORTH
♠ A 9 6 3
♡ K 6
◊ A Q 10 5 2
♣ A 8

WEST
♣ K

EAST

SOUTH
♠ K Q J 10 8
♡ A J 9 8
◊ K 8 6
♣ 9

Declarer is playing 7 Spades. West, having bid and rebid Clubs, leads the King of that suit. The Ace wins and a low Spade is led from dummy, East discarding a Club. Plan the play.

12.

NORTH
♠ A 9 7 5
♡ Q 10 9
◊ 10 8 3
♣ 7 6 2

WEST
♠ K

EAST

SOUTH
♠ 3
♡ A K J 7 4
◊ J 6 4
♣ A K Q 5

Declarer is playing 4 Hearts. West leads the King of Spades. Plan the play.

ANSWERS TO QUIZ ON PERCENTAGES

1. You should lead the 8 of Spades and let it ride.

If West has the 10, the Queen will be forced out and your nine tricks are available. If the Eight loses to the Ten, you can subsequently try the finesse of the Jack of Spades. This line of play will succeed whenever the Queen and the 10 are in different hands, or if they are both in the West hand. If you finesse the Jack of Spades at once, you have only a 50 per cent chance of winning. If you first finesse the 8 of Spades, you have a combination of two 50 percent chances, which amounts really to about 75 per cent. Complete hand follows:

```
            NORTH
            ♠ A K J 4
            ♡ 10 5 2
            ◇ 10 6 3
            ♣ K J 8

WEST                  EAST
♠ 10 7 5              ♠ Q 6 3 2
♡ Q 8 7 6 3          ♡ J 9 4
◇ A 9 7              ◇ K 5
♣ 9 6                ♣ 7 4 3 2

            SOUTH
            ♠ 9 8
            ♡ A K
            ◇ Q J 8 4 2
            ♣ A Q 10 5
```

2. South should win the first trick and play the Ace of Trumps. Both opponents follow. Declarer should play to set up the Diamonds rather than the Hearts, because the Diamond play will succeed whenever the Ace and Queen of Diamonds are in different hands, or when they are both in the East hand. Trumps are drawn, winding up with the Queen in Dummy. The King of Diamonds is led and permitted to ride if not covered. If it is covered, there is no further problem. If it should lose to the Ace, dummy is entered with the

Queen of Spades and the Jack of Diamonds led through, trusting East to have the Queen. This is a much better line of play than hoping for the King of Hearts to fall on the third round. Complete hand follows:

```
            NORTH
            ♠ Q 7 2
            ♡ 2
            ◇ K J 10 9 8
            ♣ Q 6 5 4

WEST                  EAST
♠ 9 8 5              ♠ J 10 4 3
♡ K J 9 5 3          ♡ 8 7
◇ 5 4 3 2            ◇ A Q 7 6
♣ 9                  ♣ J 8 3

            SOUTH
            ♠ A K 6
            ♡ A Q 10 6 4
            ◇ none
            ♣ A K 10 7 2
```

3. South should first play the Ace and King of Diamonds.

There is a slight chance that the Queen will drop. If it does not, the Heart finesse should be tried. This gives declarer two chances to make the hand. The immediate Heart finesse would place all your eggs in one basket, as would the immediate Diamond finesse.

```
            NORTH
            ♠ 8 6 3
            ♡ A Q 10 6
            ◇ A 8 4
            ♣ K 9 4

WEST                  EAST
♠ Q 10 8 7 4         ♠ K J 5
♡ 8 5 2              ♡ K 7 4
◇ Q 7               ◇ 10 5 2
♣ Q 8 5              ♣ J 10 7 3

            SOUTH
            ♠ A 2
            ♡ J 9 3
            ◇ K J 9 6 3
            ♣ A 6 2
```

4. Declarer should win the trick in his own hand.

Play the King of Diamonds, then the Queen, and overtake with the Ace. This play will succeed

(a) If the 9 of Diamonds drops on the second round.

(b) If the Jack of Diamonds drops on the second round.

(c) If the Diamonds are three–three.

The improper play is the King and Queen of Diamonds, trusting that the suit will clear in three rounds with the Heart as an entry. Remember that six outstanding cards will probably break four–two. Complete hand follows:

```
            NORTH
            ♠ 10 3
            ♡ K 4
            ◇ A 10 8 6 2
            ♣ J 9 4 3

WEST                      EAST
♠ 8                      ♠ Q J 9 6 4 2
♡ Q 9 6 3 2              ♡ J 10 8
◇ J 7 5 3               ◇ 9 4
♣ K 10 8               ♣ Q 5

            SOUTH
            ♠ A K 7 5
            ♡ A 7 5
            ◇ K Q
            ♣ A 7 6 2
```

5. Declarer's best chance is to play West for the Jack of Hearts.

(If West has the King of Hearts, the contract is probably doomed.) This is better than hoping to build up the ninth trick in Clubs, because in order to do so the six outstanding Clubs would have to fall three–three, which is against percentages. Second, you would have to be sure to keep West out of the lead, which is by no means a good gamble. There is a 50 per cent chance that West has the Jack of Hearts and that the 10 will force out East's King. That is the best play.

```
            NORTH
            ♠ 10 7 2
            ♡ Q 5
            ◇ K J 10 8
            ♣ A 9 4 3

WEST                      EAST
♠ K J 9 6 3              ♠ Q 8
♡ J 8 7                  ♡ K 6 3 2
◇ 6 3 2                 ◇ 9 7 4
♣ J 8                  ♣ Q 10 7 6

            SOUTH
            ♠ A 5 4
            ♡ A 10 9 4
            ◇ A Q 5
            ♣ K 5 2
```

6. Declarer should work on the Heart suit.

The two outstanding honors will probably be in different hands. It is improper to work on the Diamond suit, which will probably not break, inasmuch as an even number of cards (six) are out against the declarer. Complete hand follows:

```
            NORTH
            ♠ K 4
            ♡ 6 5 3
            ◇ A 8 6 4 2
            ♣ A J 7

WEST                      EAST
♠ J 9 7 5 3             ♠ A 8 2
♡ K 7 2                 ♡ Q 8 4
◇ J 9                  ◇ Q 10 7 3
♣ 9 3 2               ♣ Q 10 4

            SOUTH
            ♠ Q 10 6
            ♡ A J 10 9
            ◇ K 5
            ♣ K 8 6 5
```

7. Declarer should win the Diamond in his own hand

and play to establish the Club suit, rather than to try to win a Spade trick. All the trumps, therefore, should not be drawn. The only risk incurred is that someone has a singleton Club. This would mean that the Clubs were divided five–five, an extremely remote holding. Complete hand follows:

NORTH
♠ 10 7
♡ A J 5
◇ A 6 3
♣ A K J 7 2

WEST
♠ A Q 5 2
♡ 8 7 2
◇ J 10 9 7
♣ 5 4

EAST
♠ 9 8 6 4 3
♡ 6
◇ 8 5 2
♣ Q 10 9 3

SOUTH
♠ K J
♡ K Q 10 9 4 3
◇ K Q 4
♣ 8 6

8. You have the choice of ruffing out the Hearts

with the hope that the Queen will drop for a Diamond discard, or finessing the Jack of Hearts. The finesse of the Jack is the proper play, because that has a 50 per cent chance. That the Queen of Hearts will drop on the third round is less than an even gamble, because there are seven cards out which are probably divided four–three with the further probability that the missing card, the Queen, is in the hand with the greater number. There is less than a 50–50 per cent chance that the Queen will fall on the third round.

NORTH
♠ K Q 10 4
♡ A J 3 2
◇ A 5
♣ 10 9 6

WEST
♠ 7 3
♡ Q 9 7 5
◇ K Q J 8
♣ 8 5 3

EAST
♠ 2
♡ 10 8 6
◇ 10 9 7 4 3
♣ J 7 4 2

SOUTH
♠ A J 9 8 6 5
♡ K 4
◇ 6 2
♣ A K Q

9. The Club finesse should be taken rather than the Heart.

If that wins (50 per cent chance), your contract is virtually assured. If you decide to take the Heart finesse and it works, you may still have to lost a Heart trick, unless the Hearts are divided two–two, which is improbable. Complete hand follows:

NORTH
♠ A 7 6 3
♡ J 8 5
◇ 8 5 4 2
♣ 10 4

WEST
♠ Q J 10 8
♡ 9
◇ A J 10 9
♣ J 7 6 3

EAST
♠ 9 4
♡ K 10 7
◇ 7 6 3
♣ K 9 8 5 2

SOUTH
♠ K 5 2
♡ A Q 6 4 3 2
◇ K Q
♣ A Q

10. Declarer should first enter Dummy

and finesse the Diamond. If this succeeds, his troubles are over. If it fails, he still has the chance for a Club finesse. If he tries the Club finesse first and that fails, he is down immediately. Two chances are obviously better than one. Complete hand follows:

NORTH
♠ Q 8 5
♡ 8 6
◇ J 9 4 2
♣ A 9 7 5

WEST
♠ 7 4 3
♡ A 10 7 3 2
◇ 6 5
♣ 8 3 2

EAST
♠ 10 9 6 2
♡ J 5 4
◇ K 7 3
♣ K 6 4

SOUTH
♠ A K J
♡ K Q 9
◇ A Q 10 8
♣ Q J 10

11. Declarer should play to ruff out two Hearts in the dummy.

This is a better chance than hoping for the Diamonds to be three—two. While that distribution of the Diamonds is normal, nevertheless it has been ascertained that West has four Spades and probably six Clubs, because he rebid them, which would leave him only three red cards. The best chance is that two of them are Hearts. In order for this play to lose, the adverse Hearts would have to be divided six—one, which is less likely than that the Diamonds will be four—one or even five—none.

NORTH
♠ A 9 6 3
♡ K 6
◇ A Q 10 5 2
♣ A 8

WEST
♠ 7 5 4 2
♡ Q 3 2
◇ none
♣ K Q J 10 7 5

EAST
♠ None
♡ 10 7 5 4
◇ J 9 7 4 3
♣ 6 4 3 2

SOUTH
♠ K Q J 10 8
♡ A J 9 8
◇ K 8 6
♣ 9

12. Declarer should not draw trumps

and trust everything to a Club break. If the Clubs do not break, there is no use pulling trumps. If Clubs do break, there is no need to pull trumps. Two trumps should be drawn, followed by A K Q of Clubs. If the suit breaks, the last Trump is played. If the Clubs do not break, there is the additional chance that the player who is out of Clubs does not have the remaining Trump and that the 5 of Clubs can be ruffed in the dummy.

NORTH
♠ A 9 7 5
♡ Q 10 9
◇ 10 8 3
♣ 7 6 2

WEST
♠ K Q J 10
♡ 6 3 2
◇ Q 5
♣ J 9 4 3

EAST
♠ 8 6 4 2
♡ 8 5
◇ A K 9 7 2
♣ 10 8

SOUTH
♠ 3
♡ A K J 7 4
◇ J 6 4
♣ A K Q 5

25.   The squeeze

IN CONSIDERING the use of the squeeze play, look first at this
hand. You are South, the declarer at an ambitious contract of 7
Diamonds. West leads the King of Spades. Is there any way to make
this hand?

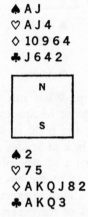

♠ A J
♡ A J 4
◊ 10 9 6 4
♣ J 6 4 2

♠ 2
♡ 7 5
◊ A K Q J 8 2
♣ A K Q 3

Prospects are not bright, because a Heart loser seems to be inevitable, and it appears that you have bid one trick beyond your capacity.
Suppose we show you the complete hand:

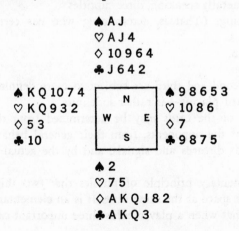

♠ A J
♡ A J 4
◊ 10 9 6 4
♣ J 6 4 2

♠ K Q 10 7 4
♡ K Q 9 3 2
◊ 5 3
♣ 10

♠ 9 8 6 5 3
♡ 10 8 6
◊ 7
♣ 9 8 7 5

♠ 2
♡ 7 5
◊ A K Q J 8 2
♣ A K Q 3

Can you make it now? You naturally win with the Ace of Spades and lead out all your top cards but one, and the position becomes:

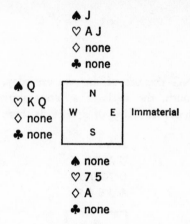

```
                  ♠ J
                  ♡ A J
                  ◇ none
                  ♣ none

        ♠ Q       ┌─────────┐
        ♡ K Q     │    N    │
        ◇ none    │ W     E │   Immaterial
        ♣ none    │    S    │
                  └─────────┘

                  ♠ none
                  ♡ 7 5
                  ◇ A
                  ♣ none
```

Now lead the last trump. What can West do? The answer is, nothing. If he tosses the Queen of Spades, you will throw the Jack of Hearts and dummy becomes high. If West lets go the Queen of Hearts, you will throw the Jack of Spades and the two Hearts will be high. You have just executed a squeeze play.

By far the most fascinating of the advanced plays is the squeeze. From time immemorial the ability to execute this play seems to have been the distinguishing mark of the expert.

While the operation of this play is at times very complex, nevertheless certain of the principles which govern its execution may be reduced to simple terms, and that is my purpose in this chapter.

There are, generally speaking, three subtitles:

1. Card Placing. (That is, determining who has certain pivotal cards.)

2. Preparation.

3. Completion.

While the second and third are subject to more definite rules, the first—that is, card placing—is rather indefinite.

The position of the cards may be determined from the bidding, from the lead of the opponents, from their general behavior during the play, such as discards and signals, and by the actual fall of the cards.

It is an elementary principle of physics that two things cannot occupy the same space at the same time. It is an elementary principle of the squeeze that when a player holds three important cards he will be compelled to let one go when it is necessary for him to reduce his hand to two cards. The squeeze, therefore, is a play which will turn a low card into a winner because the opposition has been compelled to discard the card that beats yours.

In the next example, Clubs are trumps, and the opponents hold against you the King and Queen of Spades and the Queen of Hearts. Can you win all the tricks?

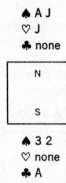

♠ A J
♡ J
♣ none

N

S

♠ 3 2
♡ none
♣ A

On the surface, no, but if West has all three cards, you will be able to do so by merely leading out the last trump.

Again Clubs are trumps. South leads the Ace. West, it will be seen, has three indispensable cards, and he is obliged to reduce his hand to two cards. He must therefore throw one of the indispensables. If he elects to throw a Heart, dummy will throw a Spade and will be good. If he elects to throw a Spade, dummy will throw a Heart and will similarly be good.

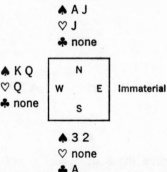

♠ A J
♡ J
♣ none

♠ K Q   N
♡ Q   W   E   Immaterial
♣ none   S

♠ 3 2
♡ none
♣ A

It will be seen that in the operation of a squeeze the essential feature is to force your adversary to select his discard before you are obliged to select yours.

The squeeze usually operates against one opponent who holds all the vital cards, but sometimes it operates against both. The procedure, then, is to knock out first one opponent and then work on the other. This will be demonstrated presently under "the three-suit squeeze" (double squeeze).

Threat cards

A losing card that may become a winner after the opponents' discard is known as a *threat card,* because it acts as a threat against a higher card that is outstanding.

In this diagram it will be seen that the dummy contains three winners, the Ace, King, and Queen:

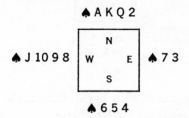

If West sometime later in the play is obliged to discard a Spade, the 2 will become a winner. It is, therefore, a threat card against West. There must be at least two threat cards in every squeeze, so that one or the other will eventually become good, because an opponent must make a choice of discards before you make your choice. A threat card is not really a threat card unless one opponent and only one must guard it.

For example:

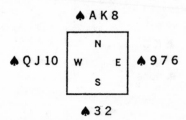

At the present time the 8 of Spades is not really a threat card, because either East or West can guard the 8 of Spades, but if East should let go the 6 of Spades, the 8 would now become a threat card against West, who is the only one who can guard Spades.

Similarly, if West should discard the 10 of Spades, then the 8 would become a threat card against East, who would have to keep all his Spades.

In the next diagram the 8 of Spades is the threat card against West, for he is the only one who can prevent it from becoming a winner:

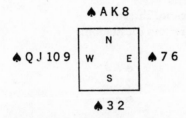

In each of the following illustrations East becomes immaterial to the play, inasmuch as he is unable to offer any protection:

In DIAGRAM A AND B the 2 of Spades is the threat against West.

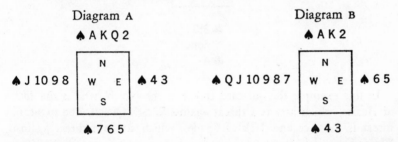

In DIAGRAM C the 10 of Spades is a threat against West, because if he should be obliged to let go a Spade, all of North's Spades will become good.

In DIAGRAM D dummy's Ace and Queen of Spades are winners, because the finesse succeeds and the 6 of Spades is a threat card against

West, who must hold at least three cards in the suit. If he is ever obliged to reduce his Spade holding to two cards, dummy's 6 will become a winner.

In order for a squeeze to operate, it has been pointed out that there must be at least two threat cards:

(a) A one-card threat.

(b) A two-or-more-card threat.

To refer back to a previous illustration:

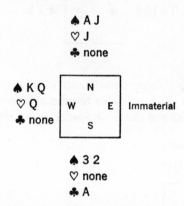

```
                ♠ A J
                ♡ J
                ♣ none

  ♠ K Q    ┌─────────┐
  ♡ Q      │    N    │
  ♣ none   │ W     E │   Immaterial
           │    S    │
           └─────────┘
                ♠ 3 2
                ♡ none
                ♣ A
```

In this example the one-card threat in the North hand is the Jack of Hearts, which acts as a threat against West's Queen. The two-card threat is the Ace and Jack of Spades, which act as a threat against West's King and Queen.

An essential principle is that no squeeze can be operated unless there is a connection between the two hands. In other words, no card in the dummy can act as a threat if there is no way to get to the dummy to use it after it becomes good.

An opponent is not subject to a squeeze until such time as his hand contains only essential cards, never before this. If a defender has as little as one non-essential card in his hand, the squeeze cannot operate.

Let us suppose that West is the player to be squeezed. The declarer must ask himself the question, "How many cards must West hold?" If the answer is five essential cards, then he cannot be squeezed until the ninth trick. In other words, at that time he will hold his five essential cards and must come down to four cards. No squeeze against him is possible at the eighth trick, because he will have one surplus card at that time which he is at liberty to throw off.

Let us see what is meant by the term "five essential cards":

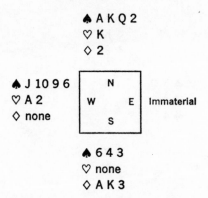

```
                    ♠ A K Q 2
                    ♡ K
                    ◊ 2

    ♠ J 10 9 6        N
    ♡ A 2          W     E      Immaterial
    ◊ none            S

                    ♠ 6 4 3
                    ♡ none
                    ◊ A K 3
```

The contract is No Trump, and South leads. West holds five essential cards. One is the Ace of Hearts, which is required to guard dummy's King. The other four are the Spades, every one of which is essential, because should West let go a Spade, North's deuce will be converted into a winner. Since West holds five essential cards, a squeeze cannot operate until the fifth trick from the end; that is, the ninth trick. At the eighth trick declarer will lead the Ace of Diamonds, and West is not in the squeeze, because he can discard the 2 of Hearts. He now comes down to his five essential cards, and on the next Diamond lead he is really squeezed and it is impossible for him to make a safe discard.

In the next example West holds three essential cards and cannot therefore be squeezed until the eleventh trick, at which trick he must come down to two cards. Since the diagram was made at the eleventh trick, the declarer is ready to operate the squeeze by leading the Ace of Diamonds:

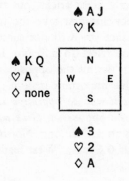

```
                    ♠ A J
                    ♡ K

    ♠ K Q             N
    ♡ A            W     E
    ◊ none            S

                    ♠ 3
                    ♡ 2
                    ◊ A
```

Let us change the diagram by adding a Club to each hand:

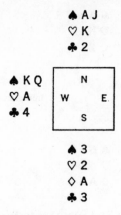

♠ A J
♡ K
♣ 2

♠ K Q
♡ A
♣ 4

♠ 3
♡ 2
◇ A
♣ 3

Here again West holds three essential cards, but the squeeze cannot be operated at this time, because it cannot work until the eleventh trick, and we have so far developed the hand only up to the tenth trick. If sometime during the play a Club trick had been given up, the squeeze might operate; but to repeat, when a defender has three essential cards, a squeeze cannot operate upon him at a time when he holds four cards.

We have been discussing in a general way the preparation for the squeeze. It will be seen, therefore, that in making your plans you must add up your winners—that is, the winners that are ready to be cashed —and they must come to exactly one less than the number of tricks you need to fulfill the contract.

Suppose your contract is 6 No Trump. You require twelve tricks. You must therefore immediately be able to cash eleven top-card tricks. Similarly, if your contract is 3 No Trump, you must have available to be run immediately exactly eight tricks, but that is not all. You must see to it that the opponents first take the tricks to which they are entitled. In a slam contract you will not succeed unless you first give the opponents their one trick. In a 3 No Trump contract you cannot succeed until you first permit the opposition to cash their four tricks, which brings us to this important maxim of squeezes: *Generally speaking, the squeeze will not be operative unless all inevitable losers are first conceded to the opponents. Give up your losers.*

West opens the bidding with 1 Diamond, North and East pass, and South subsequently arrives at 6 Spades. West leads the King of Diamonds.

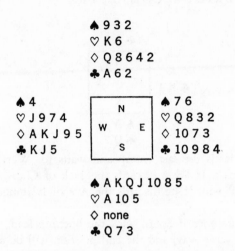

```
              ♠ 9 3 2
              ♡ K 6
              ◊ Q 8 6 4 2
              ♣ A 6 2

  ♠ 4          ┌─────────┐      ♠ 7 6
  ♡ J 9 7 4    │    N    │      ♡ Q 8 3 2
  ◊ A K J 9 5  │ W     E │      ◊ 10 7 3
  ♣ K J 5      │    S    │      ♣ 10 9 8 4
               └─────────┘
              ♠ A K Q J 10 8 5
              ♡ A 10 5
              ◊ none
              ♣ Q 7 3
```

Declarer's problem is to avoid the loss of two Club tricks, and since it is futile to hope that East has the King of Clubs, the only hope to fulfill the contract is a squeeze. The first step is card placing. The opening lead of the King of Diamonds shows that West held originally the Ace and King. The bidding corroborates this theory. The fact that East did not keep the bidding open indicates plainly that West also has the King of Clubs.

The next step is the preparation. Declarer counted his certain winners. There are seven Spade tricks, two Heart tricks, a Heart ruff in dummy, and the Ace of Clubs—a total of eleven tricks. This is one less than the twelve tricks required. However, at the present time declarer is not ready to operate the squeeze, because the opponents must be permitted to win their one trick first. At what point should the defenders be permitted to take the trick? The answer is, now. The declarer should refuse to ruff the King of Diamonds but discard the 3 of Clubs. No lead that West can make will embarrass declarer.

Let us assume that he leads a trump. The declarer draws two trumps then plays the Ace, King, and another Heart, ruffing in dummy, ruffs a Diamond and now runs down all his remaining trumps. West is obliged to keep three essential cards, one his Ace of Diamonds to guard the dummy's Queen, and the other two are the King and Jack of Clubs. The squeeze, therefore, will begin operating at such time that he must reduce his hand to two cards; namely, the eleventh trick. At the tenth trick the holding will be as follows:

◇ Q
♣ A 6

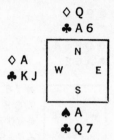

◇ A
♣ K J

♠ A
♣ Q 7

South now leads the last trump and waits for West to discard to the eleventh trick. If West discards the Jack of Clubs, both the Ace and Queen will win. If he discards the Ace of Diamonds, the Queen becomes high.

Note the difference if South wins the opening lead. The play will proceed in the same way, and the end position will be as follows:

◇ Q
♣ A 6 2

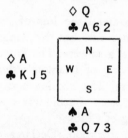

◇ A
♣ K J 5

♠ A
♣ Q 7 3

South will lead his last trump, and West, having one superfluous card in his hand, the 5 of Clubs, is able safely to discard it and still retain his three essential cards. Had West been permitted to hold the trick early in the play, he would now have no superfluous card to discard. To repeat: *In almost every squeeze the inevitable losers must be given up first.*

♠ A 9 7
♡ 10 6 4
◇ A K 10 9 2
♣ A Q

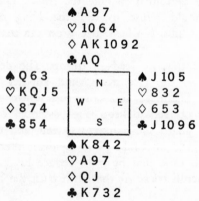

♠ Q 6 3
♡ K Q J 5
◇ 8 7 4
♣ 8 5 4

♠ J 10 5
♡ 8 3 2
◇ 6 5 3
♣ J 10 9 6

♠ K 8 4 2
♡ A 9 7
◇ Q J
♣ K 7 3 2

South is the declarer at a contract of 6 No Trump. West leads
the King of Hearts. Declarer can count five Diamonds, three Clubs,
two Spades, and one Heart—a total of eleven tricks. The only chance
for a twelfth is to be found in a squeeze. What should declarer do at
the first trick?

The answer is, he must allow the defenders to win their one trick
before the squeeze can operate. This is the best time to concede the
loser. The Queen of Hearts will be continued, which declarer wins.
West is now known to hold the Jack of Hearts, so that the 10 of
Hearts in dummy will be the threat card against West. The Ace and
Queen of Clubs are cashed and all the Diamonds are run. The position
at the eleventh trick will be as follows:

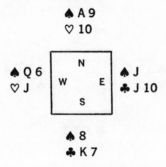

♠ A 9
♡ 10

♠ Q 6   N   ♠ J
♡ J   W   E   ♣ J 10
                   S

♠ 8
♣ K 7

The lead is in the South hand, and declarer plays the King of Clubs.
West will be obliged to discard the 6 of Spades, dummy discards the
10 of Hearts, and both Spades are good.

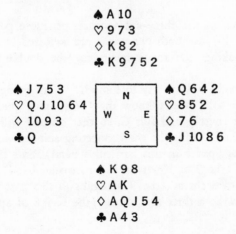

♠ A 10
♡ 9 7 3
♢ K 8 2
♣ K 9 7 5 2

♠ J 7 5 3   N   ♠ Q 6 4 2
♡ Q J 10 6 4   W   E   ♡ 8 5 2
♢ 10 9 3   ♢ 7 6
♣ Q   S   ♣ J 10 8 6

♠ K 9 8
♡ A K
♢ A Q J 5 4
♣ A 4 3

South is the declarer at a contract of 6 No Trump. West leads the Queen of Hearts. Declarer has eleven top tricks. If the Clubs break three–two, there will be no problem. In any event, one Club trick must be lost, so that the proper procedure is to give up the Club immediately.

West's Queen will win the trick, and the Heart will be continued. Now the Clubs are tried and they do not break. West is known to have the Hearts, East is known to have the Clubs, so that the 9 of Hearts will be the threat against West and the 9 of Clubs the threat against East, and neither one will be able to hold Spades. The end position will be as follows:

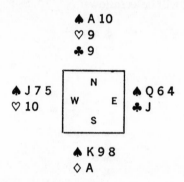

```
              ♠ A 10
              ♡ 9
              ♣ 9

                    N
  ♠ J 7 5                       ♠ Q 6 4
  ♡ 10         W       E        ♣ J
                    S

              ♠ K 9 8
              ◇ A
```

Declarer now leads the Ace of Diamonds, and West must discard the 5 of Spades. The 9 of Hearts in dummy now becomes useless and is discarded. East must retain the Jack of Clubs to guard dummy's 9 and, therefore, must discard a Spade. Declarer's three Spades now become good.

This is known as the three-suit squeeze, or, more popularly, the double squeeze, because both opponents are squeezed in turn.

Roughly speaking, the requirements for the double squeeze are as follows:

Declarer must be able to say to himself: "I am going to run suit A, which is my solid suit. I know that West must guard suit B. I know that East must guard suit C, so that no one will be able to guard suit D. Suit D must be the connecting suit between my hand and dummy (as Spades in this particular hand). Suit B must be a one-card threat (the 9 of Hearts in this particular hand), and suit C must be a one-card threat (the 9 of Clubs in this particular hand) and suit D must be a three-card threat (the K 9 8 of Spades in this case)."

Which opponent to squeeze

Where both of your threat cards are in the same hand, you can squeeze only the adversary immediately in front of your threat cards. For example:

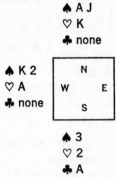

Both the threat cards (the Jack of Spades and the King of Hearts) are in the North hand. Therefore only West can be squeezed.

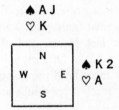

Both threat cards are in the North hand, so that only West can be squeezed. In this illustration, therefore, no squeeze is operative, because the dummy must discard before East and he waits to see what to do.

The double squeeze

South is the declarer at a contract of 4 Hearts doubled by West. West cashes the King and Queen of Spades and shifts to a Diamond. The Ace is played from dummy, and the Heart finesse loses to West's King. The Diamond is continued, and declarer ruffs. The defenders have cashed their three tricks, and the declarer has nine top tricks available, one less than his quota. The preparations for a squeeze, therefore, are completed.

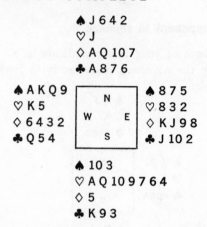

Now let us see if we have present the conditions for a double squeeze. Hearts is the suit declarer is to run. Let us call that suit A. West is known to hold the Ace of Spades. Let us call that suit B. It is virtually certain that East holds the King of Diamonds. Let us call that suit C. Therefore no one will be able to hold Clubs (suit D). Notice that the Jack of Spades is a one-card threat against West. The Queen of Diamonds is a one-card threat against East, and Clubs are a three-card threat against both, with a high card in each hand.

Declarer leads the last Heart, and West must hold the Ace of Spades, so he lets go a Club. Dummy's Jack of Spades is now useless and is discarded. East must hold the King of Diamonds, so he lets go a Club, and now declarer's three Clubs are good.

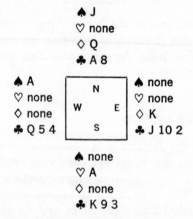

In the next hand, South is the declarer at a contract of 7 No Trump. West leads the King of Hearts. It need hardly be pointed out that this is no time to concede a loser. Declarer has twelve top-card tricks, with a chance for the thirteenth if the Diamonds break. He tries the suit and immediately learns that East stops Diamonds. Let us see if the conditions for a double squeeze are present.

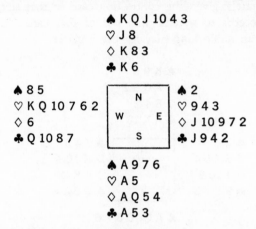

```
                    ♠ K Q J 10 4 3
                    ♡ J 8
                    ◊ K 8 3
                    ♣ K 6
♠ 8 5                    N                ♠ 2
♡ K Q 10 7 6 2      W         E           ♡ 9 4 3
◊ 6                                       ◊ J 10 9 7 2
♣ Q 10 8 7               S                ♣ J 9 4 2
                    ♠ A 9 7 6
                    ♡ A 5
                    ◊ A Q 5 4
                    ♣ A 5 3
```

The Jack of Hearts is a definite one-card threat against West. The 5 of Diamonds is a definite one-card threat against East. The Club suit provides a three-card threat with a high card in each hand. Declarer may recite to himself, "West must hold Hearts, East must hold Diamonds, no one can hold Clubs." The end position will be as follows:

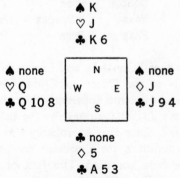

```
                    ♠ K
                    ♡ J
                    ♣ K 6
♠ none                   N                ♠ none
♡ Q                 W         E           ◊ J
♣ Q 10 8                                  ♣ J 9 4
                         S
                    ♣ none
                    ◊ 5
                    ♣ A 5 3
```

North now leads the last Spade, and East must discard a Club. South's 5 of Diamonds now becomes useless and is thrown. West is obliged to retain the Queen of Hearts to guard dummy's Jack and, therefore, lets go the 8 of Clubs. Declarer's three Clubs now are all good.

The Vienna Coup

The Vienna Coup is a preparation made for a squeeze play. The play is made by leading out a high card so that one of the opponents is deliberately given the controlling card in that suit. The declarer then proceeds to squeeze him out of that card. The Vienna Coup is really an unblocking play for the declarer:

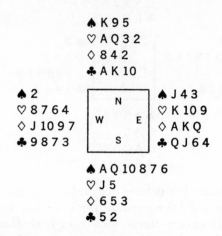

```
              ♠ K 9 5
              ♡ A Q 3 2
              ◊ 8 4 2
              ♣ A K 10
   ♠ 2                          ♠ J 4 3
   ♡ 8 7 6 4      N             ♡ K 10 9
   ◊ J 10 9 7   W   E           ◊ A K Q
   ♣ 9 8 7 3      S             ♣ Q J 6 4
              ♠ A Q 10 8 7 6
              ♡ J 5
              ◊ 6 5 3
              ♣ 5 2
```

The bidding:

NORTH	EAST	SOUTH	WEST
1 No Trump	Double	Pass	2 Clubs
Pass	Pass	3 Spades	Pass
4 Spades	Pass	Pass	Pass

West leads the Jack of Diamonds, and East cashes the Ace, King, and Queen and shifts to the Queen of Clubs. Declarer can count nine top-card tricks, and the tenth apparently depends upon the Heart finesse. However, East's double indicates that he holds that card and that the finesse will fail. Since East is probably also marked with the Jack of Clubs, the conditions for a squeeze are present. The three inevitable losers have been conceded. The Jack of Hearts will be a threat card against East's King. The 10 of Clubs will be a threat card against his Jack. The connection between declarer's hand and dummy's is the Club suit. If all the high cards are led out, East will be unable to discard safely. The only difference is that dummy will have to discard first, and if in the end the Queen of Hearts is thrown, East can safely unguard his King of Hearts, because while the Jack will

become good, declarer will be unable to reach it, since dummy will
be blocked.

The proper play, therefore, is to cash the Ace of Hearts first. This
is known as the Vienna Coup. Now all the trumps but one are led,
and the position is as follows:

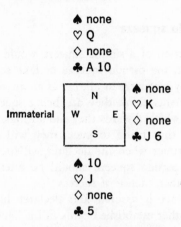

Declarer leads the last trump and discards the Queen of Hearts
from dummy. East finds it impossible to make a safe discard. Had the
Ace of Hearts not been cashed, the end position would have been as
follows:

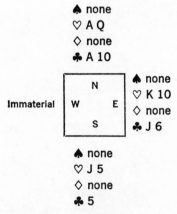

Now on the lead of the last trump, dummy would be obliged to
discard first, and East would merely follow dummy's discard. The
trouble here would be that both threat cards would be in the same
hand, in which case only the person who played before that hand

can be squeezed. Since East plays after dummy, and dummy has both threat cards, he could not be squeezed. The cashing of the Ace of Hearts first converts the Jack of Hearts into a threat card instead of the Queen of Hearts. Now we have a threat card in each hand and a connection (in Clubs) so that either opponent can be squeezed.

The pseudo squeeze

No description of a simple squeeze would be complete without its half brother, the pseudo squeeze or fake squeeze. The pseudo squeeze is not really a squeeze at all, but is an attempt by the declarer to make his opponents think they are being squeezed, so that they will have to guess which discards they should make. Sometimes when the opponents are thus made to guess they will fall into an error, and those are the times when the declarer will make his contract or an overtrick. The pseudo squeeze should be attempted when other means have no further chance of success.

When the contract is assured and declarer holds a number of good trumps and other established cards in his hand, it does no harm to play these out before conceding his low tricks. Frequently the opponents will not discard as well as they might and declarer will find himself presented with an entirely unexpected trick.

THIS IS frequently referred to as the strip play. It involves stripping an adversary of all the suits you do not wish him to lead and then throwing him in to compel the lead into your tenace or to compel the lead of a suit which will permit you to ruff in one hand and discard a loser from the other.

A few illustrations follow:

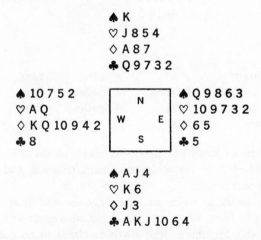

```
                      ♠ K
                      ♡ J 8 5 4
                      ◇ A 8 7
                      ♣ Q 9 7 3 2

  ♠ 10 7 5 2          ┌─────────┐          ♠ Q 9 8 6 3
  ♡ A Q               │    N    │          ♡ 10 9 7 3 2
  ◇ K Q 10 9 4 2      │ W     E │          ◇ 6 5
  ♣ 8                 │    S    │          ♣ 5
                      └─────────┘
                      ♠ A J 4
                      ♡ K 6
                      ◇ J 3
                      ♣ A K J 10 6 4
```

South is declarer at a contract of 5 Clubs. West leads the King of Diamonds, which is taken with the Ace. Declarer is faced with the danger of losing one Diamond and two Hearts unless at the proper time he can force West to lead Hearts. He must plan, therefore, to do so.

The King of Spades is cashed and the South hand entered with a trump. On the Ace of Spades a small Diamond is discarded from dummy. The Jack of Spades must be ruffed, and now the Diamond is played. The opening lead shows that West holds the Queen and must win the trick. If he continues with another Diamond, it will be trumped in dummy and a Heart discarded by declarer. If West leads a Spade, the same result is obtained. He is therefore obliged to lead the Ace of Hearts, which sets up declarer's King for the eleventh trick.

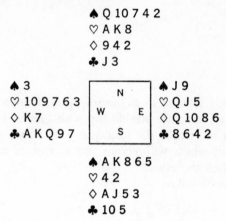

♠ Q 10 7 4 2
♡ A K 8
◇ 9 4 2
♣ J 3

♠ 3
♡ 10 9 7 6 3
◇ K 7
♣ A K Q 9 7

♠ J 9
♡ Q J 5
◇ Q 10 8 6
♣ 8 6 4 2

♠ A K 8 6 5
♡ 4 2
◇ A J 5 3
♣ 10 5

The bidding:

SOUTH	WEST	NORTH	EAST
1 Spade	2 Clubs	2 Spades	Pass
3 Spades	Pass	4 Spades	Pass
Pass	Pass		

West leads two rounds of Clubs and shifts to the 10 of Hearts. Declarer's problem is to lose only one Diamond trick, and his prospects do not appear bright.

The only hope is to force an advantageous lead from West. If declarer wishes to force West to make an advantageous lead, he must make it impossible for him to lead anything else. It is now impossible for West to lead Clubs safely. Two rounds of trumps will naturally make it impossible for West to lead trumps. The Ace and King of Hearts are cashed and a Heart ruffed by the closed hand. This makes it impossible for West to lead a Heart safely.

The bidding indicates the likelihood that West holds the King of Diamonds. The best chance appears to be that he holds exactly two Diamonds. Declarer, therefore, plays the Ace of Diamonds. If West plays low, another Diamond is led, which puts the opposition in a hopeless corner. Whether a Heart or a Club is returned, declarer ruffs in his own hand and discards the losing Diamond from dummy. If West drops the King of Diamonds under the Ace, dummy is entered with a trump and a low Diamond led toward the Jack.

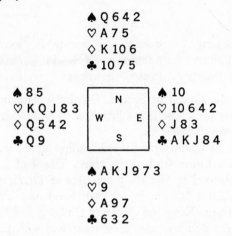

```
              ♠ Q 6 4 2
              ♡ A 7 5
              ◇ K 10 6
              ♣ 10 7 5

♠ 8 5                          ♠ 10
♡ K Q J 8 3        N           ♡ 10 6 4 2
◇ Q 5 4 2      W       E       ◇ J 8 3
♣ Q 9              S           ♣ A K J 8 4

              ♠ A K J 9 7 3
              ♡ 9
              ◇ A 9 7
              ♣ 6 3 2
```

South is declarer at a contract of 4 Spades. West leads the King of Hearts. On the surface it appears that declarer must lose three Club tricks and a Diamond, since he has no finesse in that suit. However, a finessing position can be created if the opposition is forced to lead Diamonds. Declarer must make it impossible for the opposition to lead anything else.

The Ace of Hearts is taken and another Heart ruffed immediately. Trumps are drawn and dummy's last Heart ruffed by declarer. He now gives up the lead with a Club. East can cash three Club tricks but is now obliged to lead a Diamond. If he leads the Jack, declarer wins with the Ace and finesses dummy's 10. If he leads the 3, West's Queen must be played to force out the King, and South now finesses the 9.

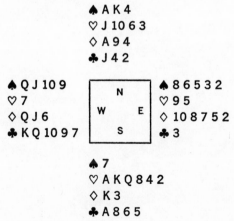

```
              ♠ A K 4
              ♡ J 10 6 3
              ◇ A 9 4
              ♣ J 4 2

♠ Q J 10 9                     ♠ 8 6 5 3 2
♡ 7                N           ♡ 9 5
◇ Q J 6        W       E       ◇ 10 8 7 5 2
♣ K Q 10 9 7       S           ♣ 3

              ♠ 7
              ♡ A K Q 8 4 2
              ◇ K 3
              ♣ A 8 6 5
```

The bidding:

SOUTH	WEST	NORTH	EAST
1 Heart	2 Clubs	3 Hearts	Pass
6 Hearts	Pass	Pass	Pass

West leads the Queen of Spades. On the surface it would appear that the declarer must lose two Clubs, but by proper manipulation he can hold his losses to one trick.

Two rounds of trumps are played, ending up in dummy. On the Ace of Spades a losing Club is discarded. The 4 of Spades is ruffed by declarer, followed by the King and Ace of Diamonds and a Diamond ruff. Declarer is now in his own hand and is confident that West holds both the King and Queen of Clubs. A low Club, therefore, is led toward the dummy, and West must win with the Queen. It is now impossible for him to make a safe lead. A Club return will permit the Jack to win. A Spade return permits declarer to ruff in one hand and discard a Club from the other.

27.   End plays

THE END PLAY is a term used to describe a number of different plays
that occur usually during the latter part of the hand, although the
principles involved may sometimes apply as early as the second trick.

The most frequently occurring type of end play is the throw-in,
which is just what its name implies. An opponent is thrown into the
lead and compelled to play the suit which you desire to have led up
to you. Let us take one or two simple illustrations:

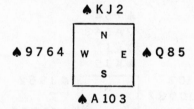

♠ K J 2

♠ 9 7 6 4   ♠ Q 8 5

♠ A 10 3

You are South, and your problem is to lose no Spade tricks. If you
can guess that East has the Queen, you can, of course, successfully
finesse the 10; but if you fear that you may make the wrong guess, it
may be possible at the end of the hand to throw one of the opponents
into the lead at a time when he has nothing left but Spades, in which
case he will perforce lead a Spade to you and a guess as to the location
of the Queen will be eliminated. Another illustration:

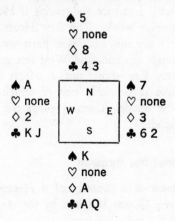

♠ 5
♡ none
◇ 8
♣ 4 3

♠ A   ♠ 7
♡ none   ♡ none
◇ 2   ◇ 3
♣ K J   ♣ 6 2

♠ K
♡ none
◇ A
♣ A Q

You are South playing a No Trump contract and these are your last four cards. The lead is in dummy, and you require three of the last four tricks. Apparently the Club finesse is the only hope, but you have reason to believe that West holds the King and that the finesse will fail. Your hope, therefore, is that you can force West to lead a Club to you. This can be accomplished by throwing him into the lead with a Spade. However, he will still have the deuce of Diamonds as an exit card, and you will be thrown back into the lead and be obliged to play from your Ace Queen of Clubs. Your plan, therefore, is to make it impossible for West to lead anything but Clubs. This is done by taking the Diamond out of his hand. Therefore you return to your own hand with the Ace of Diamonds and now lead the King of Spades. West is in and must lead a Club, surrendering both tricks. Let us take a complete hand:

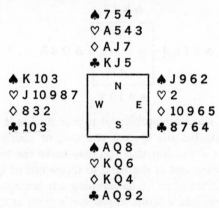

♠ 7 5 4
♡ A 5 4 3
◊ A J 7
♣ K J 5

♠ K 10 3
♡ J 10 9 8 7
◊ 8 3 2
♣ 10 3

♠ J 9 6 2
♡ 2
◊ 10 9 6 5
♣ 8 7 6 4

♠ A Q 8
♡ K Q 6
◊ K Q 4
♣ A Q 9 2

South plays 6 No Trump. West leads the Jack of Hearts. Declarer counts eleven tricks, with a chance for twelve if Hearts break three–three or the Spade finesse works. The first Heart is won with the Queen. Four Club tricks are run, and West parts with a Diamond and a Spade. Three Diamonds are run, and West lets go the 7 of Hearts. On the King of Hearts, East shows out. A Heart is led to the Ace. West is known to have three cards, one of which is the Heart 10. The other two must be Spades. Dummy plays the last Heart. West is in and must lead a Spade.

Defense against the throw-in

South is declarer at a contract of 4 Hearts. West leads the Jack of Spades, and the Queen is taken by the Ace. The Queen of

Diamonds is returned and permitted to hold. A Diamond is continued
and won with the Ace. Dummy is entered with the Jack of Hearts,
and on the King of Spades a Diamond is discarded. A Spade is ruffed
by declarer and dummy entered with the Queen of Hearts, exhausting
trumps. The remaining Diamond is ruffed by declarer, who now plays
the Ace of Clubs. If West plays low, he will be obliged to win the
next Club, and his lead of either a Diamond or a Spade will permit
declarer to ruff in dummy and discard a losing Club from his own
hand. West, therefore, must pray that his partner holds the Queen
and Jack of Clubs and should toss the King under the Ace, because
he cannot afford to win the lead. When the next Club is led, he plays
low, and East cashes the setting trick with the two high Clubs.

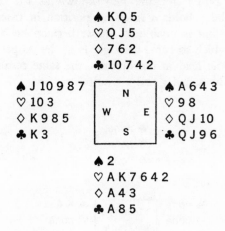

♠ K Q 5
♡ Q J 5
◇ 7 6 2
♣ 10 7 4 2

♠ J 10 9 8 7   ♠ A 6 4 3
♡ 10 3   ♡ 9 8
◇ K 9 8 5   ◇ Q J 10
♣ K 3   ♣ Q J 9 6

♠ 2
♡ A K 7 6 4 2
◇ A 4 3
♣ A 8 5

28.   Coups and grand coups

THE OPPORTUNITY for the play known as the Trump Coup occurs when declarer holds a finessing position in trumps over the right-hand player but is unable to finesse because he has no trump in dummy with which to come through. If at the proper time he can arrange to have the lead in the dummy, the same result can be obtained as though he actually had a trump.

To illustrate:

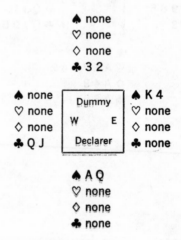

```
                    ♠ none
                    ♡ none
                    ◇ none
                    ♣ 3 2

    ♠ none      ┌─────────┐    ♠ K 4
    ♡ none      │ Dummy   │    ♡ none
    ◇ none      │ W     E │    ◇ none
    ♣ Q J       │ Declarer│    ♣ none
                └─────────┘
                    ♠ A Q
                    ♡ none
                    ◇ none
                    ♣ none
```

South is declarer at a Spade contract and desires to win both Spade tricks. If at this time the lead is in dummy, the same result is obtained as though a Spade were being led, because East will be obliged to trump a Club and South will overruff.

Note that if the lead were at the present time in declarer's hand this result could not be accomplished.

Let us take this illustration with the addition of one more card:

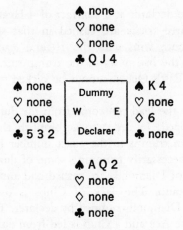

With this holding the play is not operative, because when dummy leads a Club, East will discard his Diamond and South is forced to ruff, placing the lead in his own hand.

It can be seen that the trump coup is not operative until such time as the declarer has precisely the same number of trumps as the player whom he is attempting to encircle. If early in the play the declarer had been able to use his deuce of Spades and found the lead in dummy at trick twelve, he would have succeeded. And that would be that rarest of all plays, a Grand Coup.

Let us illustrate with one or two complete hands:

Grand coup

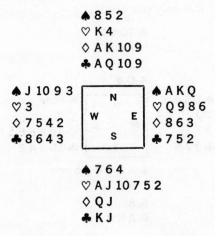

South is the declarer at a contract of 4 Hearts. West leads the Jack of Spades, three tricks are cashed in that suit, and the 6 of Hearts returned. South wins with the 10 and leads to the King of Hearts, finding out the bad news in the trump suit. On the surface it would appear that East's Queen cannot be picked up. However, there is a slight chance.

If at trick twelve the lead can come from the dummy, East's trump Queen can be trapped. In order to accomplish this result, declarer must reduce his own trumps to the exact number held by East. This can be done by unnecessarily trumping some of dummy's good cards. The Ace and King of Diamonds are cashed and another Diamond led and trumped by South. The Jack of Clubs is overtaken with the Queen and another Diamond trumped by declarer. The King of Clubs is overtaken with the Ace and a Club is led from dummy. If East ruffs with the 9, declarer will overruff. If East ruffs with the Queen, the same result is obtained.

And there you have the grand coup, which involves the ruffing of good tricks in order to reduce declarer's trumps to precisely the same number held by the adversary. An essential ingredient of the grand-coup technique is that the final lead must come through the hand that has the trump honor.

Outside trump play

South is the declarer at a contract of 6 Spades which has been doubled by West. The King of Diamonds was opened, and the first Spade lead revealed the unfortunate trump break. There is still hope for the declarer to lose only one Spade:

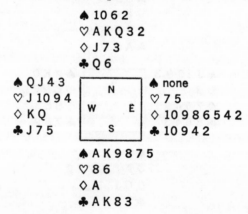

The technique to be employed in this hand is similar to that of the grand coup. The plan is for declarer to reduce his trumps to precisely the number held by his adversary and to relinquish the lead at trick eleven to force West to lead from his trump holding.

To trick three declarer leads a Heart, dummy wins with the Queen. A Diamond is ruffed by declarer, and the fall of the Queen makes it appear that West has no more of the suit. The King and Ace of Hearts are now cashed, declarer discarding a Club. West is now known to hold another Heart, so that the fourth Heart is trumped by declarer, who now holds exactly the same number of trumps as West. The Queen, King, and Ace of Clubs are cashed, and at trick eleven declarer leads a low Spade toward the 10. West is obliged to win with the Jack and is in a helpless position, since he must relinquish the last two tricks.

29.　　　　　　　　　　　　Miscellaneous plays

AT INFREQUENT INTERVALS you will meet with hands which require very special handling, with problems which can be solved only by the use of special plays. Suppose you held this hand:

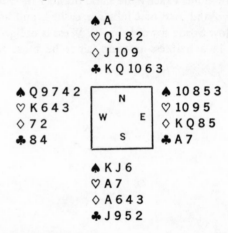

♠ A
♡ Q J 8 2
◇ J 10 9
♣ K Q 10 6 3

♠ Q 9 7 4 2
♡ K 6 4 3
◇ 7 2
♣ 8 4

N W E S

♠ 10 8 5 3
♡ 10 9 5
◇ K Q 8 5
♣ A 7

♠ K J 6
♡ A 7
◇ A 6 4 3
♣ J 9 5 2

South is declarer at a contract of 3 No Trump. West leads the 4 of Spades. What should be declarer's next play?

On the surface it would seem that the Ace of Clubs should be driven out, but this may result in East obtaining the lead and returning the Spade suit through the King Jack. Everything will now depend on the Heart finesse.

The proper technique is to make sure that East does not obtain the lead too soon. West can be given the lead with safety, since he cannot profitably lead Spades. The proper play, therefore, is the Queen of Hearts. If the finesse should win, the Ace of Clubs is immediately driven out and nine tricks are assured. If the finesse loses to West, he is unable to continue Spades without sacrificing a trick, and now declarer has time to drive out the Ace of Clubs and is assured of nine tricks.

South is declarer at a contract of 3 No Trump. West leads the 6 of Spades, and East's 10 is taken by declarer's King. Declarer has plenty of tricks available. The danger in the hand lies, however, in the fact that both finesses might lose and that West may cash three Spade tricks. If West has only a four-card suit, there is nothing to fear. If he has a five-card suit, an effort must be made to deprive him of any entry card he may have, so that he cannot possibly bring in the long Spades. The only available card of entry that West can hold is the King of Diamonds.

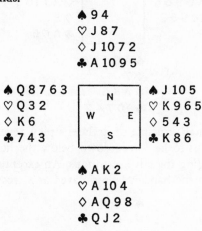

```
              ♠ 9 4
              ♡ J 8 7
              ◊ J 10 7 2
              ♣ A 10 9 5

♠ Q 8 7 6 3        N        ♠ J 10 5
♡ Q 3 2                     ♡ K 9 6 5
◊ K 6       W         E     ◊ 5 4 3
♣ 7 4 3            S        ♣ K 8 6

              ♠ A K 2
              ♡ A 10 4
              ◊ A Q 9 8
              ♣ Q J 2
```

The proper play, therefore, at trick two is the Ace and another Diamond. West will continue the Spades, and the Jack is permitted to win. Declarer wins the third Spade and may now take the Club finesse in perfect confidence. If it loses, East will have no more Spades to return. If he has a Spade, then only one more trick can be captured by the enemy.

Note how differently this hand develops if the Club finesse is taken first. It loses, and the Spades are cleared while West still has the King of Diamonds.

Postponing the drawing of trumps

South is the declarer at a contract of 4 Spades. West leads the King and another Heart, which South trumps. Declarer must not draw trumps at this point, since if the adverse trumps are divided four–two it will require every one of his trumps to get them out, and the Heart tricks will be cashed when the opponents get in with the Ace of Clubs.

The proper play is to lead a Club immediately. This trick will be taken by East and another Heart led, which declarer must refuse to ruff, discarding a good trick thereon.

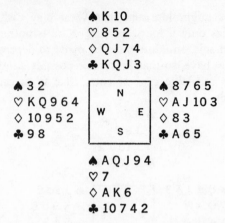

It is a fundamental principle of declarer's play never to permit the strong hand's trumps to be forced down below the number that will be required for pulling the adverse trumps. An exception to this principle is noted when the hand is being played at a crossruff.

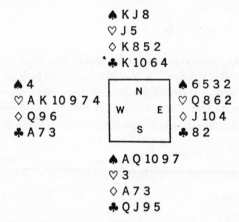

South is declarer at a contract of 4 Spades. West leads the King and Ace of Hearts. If declarer should make the mistake of ruffing this trick, the contract cannot be made, because if all the trumps are drawn, West will get in with the Ace of Clubs and cash the rest of the Hearts. If declarer draws only two trumps and leads Clubs, West will duck the first round but will give his partner a third-round ruff:

At trick two declarer should discard the 3 of Diamonds, which is a loser in any event. If West continues Hearts, that suit can be ruffed in dummy and trumps drawn, declarer retaining a trump, with time to drive out the Ace of Clubs.

Ducking

South is declarer at a contract of 4 Spades. West leads the King of Hearts and shifts to the Queen of Spades. It is declarer's play to this trick which determines the success or failure of the contract.

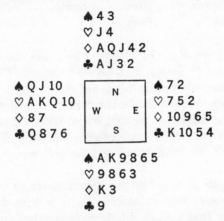

The proper play is to duck. One trump trick must be lost in any event, and this is the time to lose it.

If the Queen of Spades is taken and another trump drawn, declarer must attempt to take immediate Diamond discards. West will trump the third Diamond and cash the setting trick in Hearts. If, however, West is permitted to hold the Queen of Spades, trumps can be drawn and the Diamond suit run without interruption.

The principle of conceding an inevitable loser early in the play is illustrated in this extreme but interesting case:

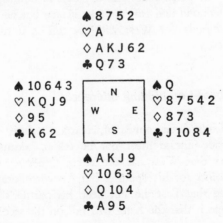

The bidding:

NORTH	EAST	SOUTH	WEST
1 Diamond	Pass	1 Spade	Pass
3 Spades	Pass	4 Clubs	Pass
4 Hearts	Pass	6 Spades	Pass
Pass	Pass		

West opened the King of Hearts, which was taken by dummy's lone Ace. A small Spade was then led from dummy. When the Queen came up, declarer was put on his guard that West held four Spades to the 10, which would provide him with a natural trump trick. If declarer thoughtlessly wins the first trump trick, the contract cannot be fulfilled, because while two Hearts could be ruffed in dummy, West would ruff the third round of Diamonds and prevent the run of that suit.

The proper play is to permit the Queen of Spades to hold. This is the most convenient time to concede the opponents their trick. East will presumably lead a Club, which declarer takes, ruffs a Heart in dummy, returns to his own hand with a trump, and ruffs the remaining Heart in dummy. He re-enters his own hand with the Queen of Diamonds, draws the two trumps, and discards his two losing Clubs on dummy's good Diamonds. In other words, he counted five Diamond tricks, one Heart trick, one Club trick, three Spade tricks in his own hand, and two ruffs in dummy, for a total of twelve tricks.

Observe into what complications declarer runs if he wins the Queen of Spades. He will presumably ruff a Heart in dummy, return to his hand with a Diamond and ruff another Heart, but he will be unable to run his Diamonds, for West will not ruff in until South has no more of the suit.

Plays based on bidding inferences

West leads three rounds of Hearts. Declarer ruffs the third round. The Spade finesse must not be taken, because the bidding plainly indicates that West has the King. Otherwise he would not have enough points for his opening bid. To corroborate this there is the circumstance that East did not keep his partner's bid alive. Declarer's only hope is that the King will fall on the second round:

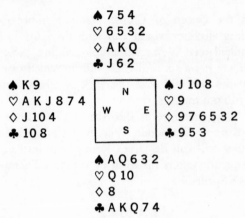

```
          ♠ 7 5 4
          ♡ 6 5 3 2
          ◇ A K Q
          ♣ J 6 2
♠ K 9                        ♠ J 10 8
♡ A K J 8 7 4                ♡ 9
◇ J 10 4                     ◇ 9 7 6 5 3 2
♣ 10 8                       ♣ 9 5 3
          ♠ A Q 6 3 2
          ♡ Q 10
          ◇ 8
          ♣ A K Q 7 4
```

The bidding:

WEST	NORTH	EAST	SOUTH
1 Heart	Pass	Pass	2 Spades
Pass	3 Spades	Pass	4 Spades
Pass	Pass	Pass	

The proper play, therefore, is the Ace of Trumps followed by a small one. When the King drops, declarer's contract is fulfilled.

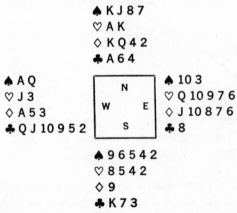

```
          ♠ K J 8 7
          ♡ A K
          ◇ K Q 4 2
          ♣ A 6 4
♠ A Q                        ♠ 10 3
♡ J 3                        ♡ Q 10 9 7 6
◇ A 5 3                      ◇ J 10 8 7 6
♣ Q J 10 9 5 2               ♣ 8
          ♠ 9 6 5 4 2
          ♡ 8 5 4 2
          ◇ 9
          ♣ K 7 3
```

The bidding:

WEST	NORTH	EAST	SOUTH
1 Club	Double	1 Heart	1 Spade
2 Clubs	4 Spades	Pass	Pass
Pass			

West leads the Queen of Clubs. Without information obtained from the bidding, declarer would win with the King in order to lead the trumps immediately. West's vulnerable bidding, however, indicates that he very likely has a six-card Club suit, in which case he will take the Ace of Spades and will lead the Jack of Clubs through dummy for partner to ruff out the Ace.

The proper play, therefore, is the Ace of Clubs from dummy, followed by the King of Diamonds. West will win, and if he continues with a Club, East will ruff declarer's losing Club instead of a winner. Declarer subsequently enters his hand by ruffing a Diamond and leads toward dummy's Spades.

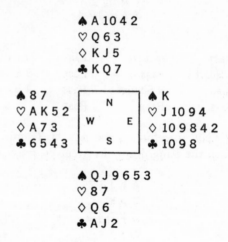

```
                    ♠ A 10 4 2
                    ♡ Q 6 3
                    ◇ K J 5
                    ♣ K Q 7

    ♠ 8 7                           ♠ K
    ♡ A K 5 2         N             ♡ J 10 9 4
    ◇ A 7 3        W     E          ◇ 10 9 8 4 2
    ♣ 6 5 4 3         S             ♣ 10 9 8

                    ♠ Q J 9 6 5 3
                    ♡ 8 7
                    ◇ Q 6
                    ♣ A J 2
```

The bidding:

WEST	NORTH	EAST	SOUTH
Pass	1 Club	Pass	1 Spade
Pass	2 Spades	Pass	4 Spades
Pass	Pass	Pass	

West led the King of Hearts and promptly shifted to a low Diamond, hoping to put the declarer to the guess if he did not hold the Queen.

Declarer played the King from dummy, which held. He then returned to his hand with the Jack of Clubs and led the Queen of Spades, intending to finesse (the proper percentage play with ten cards), and suddenly he referred back to the bidding. West is known to have had the Ace and King of Hearts and the Ace of Diamonds,

and yet he passed, as dealer. If he also held the guarded King of
Spades, he would have 14 high-card points and a pass would be
unthinkable. It was a moral certainty, therefore, that East held the
King of Spades and that the finesse could not succeed. The only hope,
therefore, was that the King was alone, and declarer went up with
the Ace, with pleasant effect.

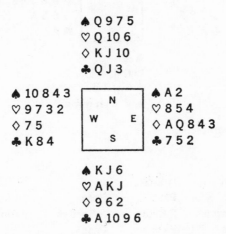

```
                    ♠ Q 9 7 5
                    ♡ Q 10 6
                    ◇ K J 10
                    ♣ Q J 3

   ♠ 10 8 4 3       ┌─────────┐      ♠ A 2
   ♡ 9 7 3 2        │    N    │      ♡ 8 5 4
   ◇ 7 5            │ W     E │      ◇ A Q 8 4 3
   ♣ K 8 4          │    S    │      ♣ 7 5 2
                    └─────────┘
                    ♠ K J 6
                    ♡ A K J
                    ◇ 9 6 2
                    ♣ A 10 9 6
```

The bidding:

SOUTH	WEST	NORTH	EAST
1 No Trump	Pass	3 No Trump	Pass
Pass	Pass		

Against the 3 No Trump contract West led the 3 of Spades, which
East won with the Ace. The return of the Spade offered very little
prospect for the defense. East reasoned that unless West had one of
the missing high cards the contract could not be defeated. If he had
either a high Club or a high Heart, there was a chance to defeat the
contract if the Diamond suit could be brought in.

He quite properly, therefore, returned the 4 of Diamonds. Since
nine tricks could not be cashed without the Club finesse, declarer
was obliged to try that play, and when West was in with the King
of Clubs a Diamond return defeated the contract two tricks.

Bidding inference

In the following hand West leads the King and Ace of
Spades and South ruffs the second lead:

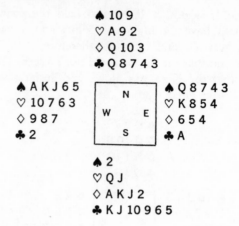

```
                    ♠ 10 9
                    ♡ A 9 2
                    ◊ Q 10 3
                    ♣ Q 8 7 4 3
♠ A K J 6 5                        ♠ Q 8 7 4 3
♡ 10 7 6 3          N             ♡ K 8 5 4
◊ 9 8 7         W       E         ◊ 6 5 4
♣ 2                 S             ♣ A
                    ♠ 2
                    ♡ Q J
                    ◊ A K J 2
                    ♣ K J 10 9 6 5
```

East-West vulnerable.

The bidding:

WEST	NORTH	EAST	SOUTH
Pass	Pass	Pass	1 Club
1 Spade	2 Clubs	2 Spades	5 Clubs
Pass	Pass	Pass	

The contract appears to depend upon the Heart finesse, but reference to the bidding will make it clear that the Heart finesse will fail, for if West had a good Spade suit headed by the Ace King, as indicated by a vulnerable overcall, and the King of Hearts, he would have opened the bidding originally instead of passing. By the same line of reasoning, East is marked with the Ace of Clubs. Declarer, therefore, hit upon a means of forcing East to lead a Heart. The success of the plan depended upon East having three Diamonds and the lone Ace of Clubs. Three rounds of Diamonds were cashed, and a Club presented East with the lead. Since a Spade would give declarer a ruff and discard, East led a Heart, hoping against hope that his partner held the Queen.

It will be noted that this contract could be defeated by proper defense. East should play the very discouraging 3 of Spades on the King of Spades, and a Heart shift, which would be indicated, would give declarer no chance to fulfill contract. In a position of this sort it is probably not necessary to resort to the suit-preference convention, suggesting the suit partner should shift to, since West's natural shift will be to a Heart. However, if East insists upon the employment of the suit-preference convention, he should make an unnatural discard, such as the Queen of Spades. This, being abnormal, would not be regarded as an ordinary signal and would ask West to shift to the higher-ranking suit.

Suit abandonment (by defender)

South is declarer at a contract of 3 No Trump. West leads the 4 of Clubs, and East's Jack holds the trick. The Queen is continued and West takes count. If West plays low, East will continue to establish the suit and West will hold two established Clubs, which are useless because they cannot be cashed. The Club suit, therefore, must be abandoned, since hope of future defense lies with the East hand. West, therefore, should overtake the Queen of Clubs with the King and shift to the only suit that offers any promise to develop tricks. The 10 of Spades is the proper play. This permits the defense to take two Clubs, two Spades, and the King of Diamonds:

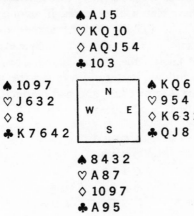

              ♠ A J 5
              ♡ K Q 10
              ♢ A Q J 5 4
              ♣ 10 3

♠ 10 9 7   ♠ K Q 6
♡ J 6 3 2   ♡ 9 5 4
♢ 8   ♢ K 6 3 2
♣ K 7 6 4 2   ♣ Q J 8

              ♠ 8 4 3 2
              ♡ A 8 7
              ♢ 10 9 7
              ♣ A 9 5

30.   Album of advanced plays

THIS CHAPTER will be made up of some unusual and difficult hands, all of which illustrate an advanced point of play.

The most unusual finesse in contract history

South is declarer at a contract of 6 Hearts. West leads the Jack of Hearts, declarer wins and draws the remaining two trumps, West discarding a Spade and a Club. The Ace and King of Diamonds are led, West discarding a Club on the second round. It now appears that two Diamond tricks must be lost, but there is one ray of hope. West is known to have eleven black cards. If among them are to be found the Ace of Clubs and the Jack of Spades, the hand can be made. Declarer, therefore, cashes the Ace of Spades, then leads the deuce of Spades and finesses the 10 in dummy. This holds the trick. The King of Clubs follows, declarer discarding the King of Spades. West was in with the Ace of Clubs and had nothing but black cards to lead to dummy's two good Queens, which took care of declarer's two losing Diamonds.

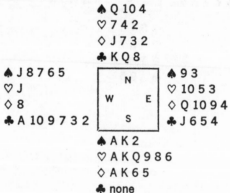

```
                    ♠ Q 10 4
                    ♡ 7 4 2
                    ◇ J 7 3 2
                    ♣ K Q 8
    ♠ J 8 7 6 5         ┌─────────┐       ♠ 9 3
    ♡ J                 │    N    │       ♡ 10 5 3
    ◇ 8               W │         │ E     ◇ Q 10 9 4
    ♣ A 10 9 7 3 2      │    S    │       ♣ J 6 5 4
                        └─────────┘
                    ♠ A K 2
                    ♡ A K Q 9 8 6
                    ◇ A K 6 5
                    ♣ none
```

A case of psychology

This hand exploits two fundamental principles of card playing. One is that a finesse should be looked upon not as an effort to encircle or capture a card, but as a means of gaining a trick. The other, that when you are trying to get away with something, do it early and do it quickly:

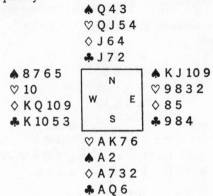

```
                        ♠ Q 4 3
                        ♡ Q J 5 4
                        ◇ J 6 4
                        ♣ J 7 2
        ♠ 8 7 6 5          N          ♠ K J 10 9
        ♡ 10                           ♡ 9 8 3 2
        ◇ K Q 10 9   W         E      ◇ 8 5
        ♣ K 10 5 3         S          ♣ 9 8 4
                        ♡ A K 7 6
                        ♠ A 2
                        ◇ A 7 3 2
                        ♣ A Q 6
```

The bidding:

WEST	NORTH	EAST	SOUTH
Pass	Pass	Pass	2 No Trump
Pass	3 No Trump	Pass	Pass
Pass			

South became declarer at a contract of 3 No Trump. West made the normal opening of the King of Diamonds, which went to South's Ace. This was a "break" for the declarer, inasmuch as it converted dummy's Jack into a certain winner after one lead.

Declarer was able to count four Heart tricks, two Diamond tricks, one Spade trick, and two in Clubs. The only difficulty lay in the fact that to realize these nine tricks declarer would have to relinquish the lead once in Diamonds and possibly once in Clubs. This would give the defense an opportunity to attack the Spade suit, which would be disastrous if East held the King of the suit.

On the surface it appears that dummy should be entered with a Heart and the Club finesse tried.

If it should fail, however, there is no doubt that West would shift to a Spade. If East has the King of Clubs, the finesse need not be taken, because it is perfectly safe to give him the trick, since a Spade lead by him cannot be damaging.

The proper play at trick two was selected by the declarer. It was the 6 of Clubs. At this early stage in the play West was not alert to the necessity of rushing in to make the Spade shift, and the Jack held the trick. From here in it was smooth sailing.

The trump squeeze

The trump squeeze is a very rare type of squeeze. It consists of leading out all the trumps but one and forcing the adversaries to discard in such a manner that a good trick can be established by ruffing. For example:

```
                    ♠ K 9 5
                    ♡ K 8 6
                    ◇ K 10 9
                    ♣ A K 10 5
    ♠ 8 6           ┌─────────┐         ♠ 3 2
    ♡ 9 5 3 2       │    N    │         ♡ 7 4
    ◇ J 7 5 2       │ W     E │         ◇ A Q 8 6 4 3
    ♣ Q 7 6         │    S    │         ♣ J 9 8
                    └─────────┘
                    ♠ A Q J 10 7 4
                    ♡ A Q J 10
                    ◇ none
                    ♣ 4 3 2
```

South is the declarer at a contract of 7 Spades, North having opened the bidding with 1 Club and East having overcalled with 1 Diamond. West leads the deuce of Diamonds, the fourth best of his partner's suit. The 10 was played from dummy, and the Queen was ruffed by declarer. Unless there is false-carding, which there is no reason to suspect in a situation of this sort, West's original holding is the Jack and three other Diamonds. Apparently declarer's only hope is for West to have both the Queen and Jack of Clubs. This appears to be asking for a little too much, and another line of play is sought. All the trumps but two are led, and then all the Hearts. The last five cards are:

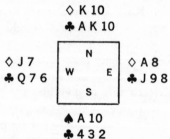

```
                    ◇ K 10
                    ♣ A K 10
    ◇ J 7           ┌─────────┐         ◇ A 8
    ♣ Q 7 6         │    N    │         ♣ J 9 8
                    │ W     E │
                    │    S    │
                    └─────────┘
                    ♠ A 10
                    ♣ 4 3 2
```

South then leads one more trump. West must make a discard. Let us assume that he throws a Club. North throws the 10 of Clubs.

Now East must make a discard. If he should drop a Club, the Ace and King of that suit are cashed in dummy, establishing the 4 of Clubs as a winner. If East should discard the 8 of Diamonds, dummy is now entered with the King of Clubs and the 10 of Diamonds led, forcing East's Ace. Declarer ruffs and dummy is high. If West, instead of discarding a Club, throws the 7 of Diamonds and permits East to discard a Club, declarer will enter dummy with the King of Clubs and lead the King of Diamonds. This will drop the Ace and Jack on the same trick and establish dummy's 10.

I do not think you will have much occasion to use this play, but it is fun when it does occur.

The squeeze coup

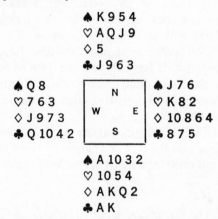

                          ♠ K 9 5 4
                          ♡ A Q J 9
                          ◊ 5
                          ♣ J 9 6 3

    ♠ Q 8   ♠ J 7 6
    ♡ 7 6 3   N   ♡ K 8 2
    ◊ J 9 7 3   W   E   ◊ 10 8 6 4
    ♣ Q 10 4 2   S   ♣ 8 7 5

                          ♠ A 10 3 2
                          ♡ 10 5 4
                          ◊ A K Q 2
                          ♣ A K

South is declarer at a contract of 6 Spades. The interesting feature is the accomplishment of the apparently impossible feat of losing no trump tricks with the above combination. This can be done by a very unusual line of play.

The 3 of Diamonds was opened, and East's 10 fell to the Queen. At the start it appears that a trump trick must be lost unless the Queen Jack are doubleton, so that apparently the success of the contract depends upon the Heart finesse. The Ace and King of Clubs were led and nothing happened. Then the deuce of Diamonds was ruffed in dummy and the 9 of Clubs ruffed in the closed hand. The 4 of Hearts was led to dummy's Queen, East winning with the King and returning a Heart. This was won with the 10, and declarer cashed the King of Diamonds, discarding the Jack of Hearts from dummy. This left the following situation:

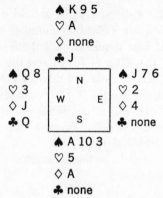

♠ K 9 5
♡ A
◇ none
♣ J

♠ Q 8   ♠ J 7 6
♡ 3   ♡ 2
◇ J   ◇ 4
♣ Q   ♣ none

♠ A 10 3
♡ 5
◇ A
♣ none

Now the declarer made a dramatic play which was not actually essential. He led the Ace of Diamonds and discarded the Ace of Hearts. The important consideration is that the Jack of Clubs must not be discarded, as will be seen in a moment. The low Heart is ruffed with the 5 of Spades in dummy and the Jack of Clubs put through. East is helpless. If he ruffs with the Jack of Spades, declarer will win with the Ace and finesse dummy's 9. If he ruffs with a small trump, declarer wins with the 10 and takes the last two tricks with the Ace and King of trumps.

The same result will be obtained if the declarer, instead of discarding the Ace of Hearts on the Ace of Diamonds, elects to ruff the Diamond in dummy and cashes the Heart before leading the Jack of Clubs.

Smother play

Is it possible for West's King of Spades to be captured, assuming that he refuses to cover on the Spade leads? On the surface it appears not, but the application of the smother-play technique makes this possible:

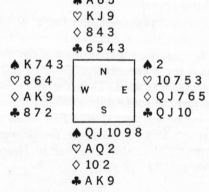

♠ A 6 5
♡ K J 9
◇ 8 4 3
♣ 6 5 4 3

♠ K 7 4 3   ♠ 2
♡ 8 6 4   ♡ 10 7 5 3
◇ A K 9   ◇ Q J 7 6 5
♣ 8 7 2   ♣ Q J 10

♠ Q J 10 9 8
♡ A Q 2
◇ 10 2
♣ A K 9

The bidding:

SOUTH	WEST	NORTH	EAST
1 Spade	Pass	1 No Trump	Pass
2 No Trump	Pass	3 Spades	Pass
4 Spades	Pass	Pass	Pass

In the play West opened the King of Diamonds and followed with the Ace and 9, which South ruffed. South then led the Queen of Spades followed by the Jack, which West, of course, refused to cover. East showed out on the second lead. Three rounds of Hearts were cashed, followed by the Ace, King and another Club, and East was compelled to win the trick. The cards remaining at this time are shown in the following diagram.

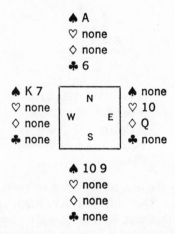

East was obliged to lead a red card, and South trumped with the 9 of Spades. West was helpless. If he covered, the Ace and 10 would take the last two tricks. If he ducked, the 6 of Clubs would be discarded from dummy. The success of the play required the great fortune of finding the Hearts and Clubs evenly divided and so distributed that East must win the third Club trick.

Bumping

The bidding is given as it actually occurred. West opened the Ace of Clubs and, despite the appearance of dummy, continued with the deuce. This made it quite clear that he held a high-low originally. Declarer was immediately faced with the problem of entering his hand in order to lead toward the King of Spades. The only apparent way to do this was to ruff a Club, but West's defense indicated that he held a doubleton and that the declarer, therefore, would be over-ruffed.

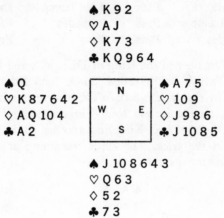

```
              ♠ K 9 2
              ♡ A J
              ◇ K 7 3
              ♣ K Q 9 6 4

♠ Q                          ♠ A 7 5
♡ K 8 7 6 4 2     N          ♡ 10 9
◇ A Q 10 4     W     E       ◇ J 9 8 6
♣ A 2             S          ♣ J 10 8 5

              ♠ J 10 8 6 4 3
              ♡ Q 6 3
              ◇ 5 2
              ♣ 7 3
```

The bidding:

SOUTH	WEST	NORTH	EAST
Pass	1 Heart	Double	Pass
1 Spade	2 Hearts	2 Spades	Pass
3 Spades	Pass	4 Spades	Pass
Pass	Pass		

Declarer hit upon the one combination of cards that would permit him to fulfill contract. The odds were very much against it, but it was the only hope, and that was for the Queen of Spades to be alone in either hand. He therefore boldly played the King out of dummy and was rewarded when the Ace and Queen fell on the same trick.

Note that the declarer did not play for the Ace to be singleton, because if that were the case there would be no way to avoid losing a trick to the Queen.

Safety play

South is declarer at a contract of 4 Spades. The Jack of Clubs was opened. Declarer won and drew three rounds of trumps. He then tried to break the Heart suit three–three. When they failed to break, he was obliged to lose two Clubs and two Hearts. The four–two split of the Heart suit was normal.

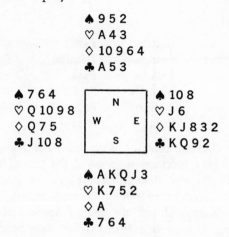

```
                    ♠ 9 5 2
                    ♡ A 4 3
                    ◊ 10 9 6 4
                    ♣ A 5 3

♠ 7 6 4                            ♠ 10 8
♡ Q 10 9 8          N             ♡ J 6
◊ Q 7 5        W         E        ◊ K J 8 3 2
♣ J 10 8            S             ♣ K Q 9 2

                    ♠ A K Q J 3
                    ♡ K 7 5 2
                    ◊ A
                    ♣ 7 6 4
```

Declarer could have given himself an additional chance. He should not have led more than one trump. The correct technique is then to lead a low Heart and duck. If the Hearts are three–three, the thirteenth card of that suit will automatically become good. If they are four–two, there is a slight chance that the player who has the doubleton Heart also has the doubleton trump. When the declarer next obtains the lead, he plays one more trump, then plays the Ace of Hearts and another Heart to the King. If the suit breaks, the remaining trump is drawn and the hand spread. If the suit does not break, there is the chance that the King of Hearts will go through and the thirteenth Heart can be trumped with the 9 of Spades.

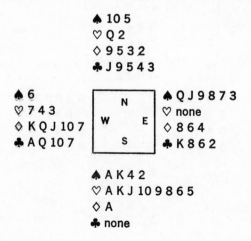

```
                    ♠ 10 5
                    ♡ Q 2
                    ◊ 9 5 3 2
                    ♣ J 9 5 4 3

♠ 6                               ♠ Q J 9 8 7 3
♡ 7 4 3             N             ♡ none
◊ K Q J 10 7   W         E        ◊ 8 6 4
♣ A Q 10 7          S             ♣ K 8 6 2

                    ♠ A K 4 2
                    ♡ A K J 10 9 8 6 5
                    ◊ A
                    ♣ none
```

The bidding:

WEST	NORTH	EAST	SOUTH
1 Diamond	Pass	1 Spade	2 Spades
Pass	3 Clubs	Pass	3 Hearts
Pass	4 Hearts	Pass	5 Diamonds
Pass	5 Hearts	Pass	6 Hearts
Pass	Pass	Pass	

Against the 6 Heart contract West leads the King of Diamonds. Obviously declarer's problem is to avoid the loss of more than one Spade trick. If declarer thoughtlessly plays the Ace and King of Spades with the intention of ruffing the third round, he will lose the hand, because West will ruff the second Spade and lead a trump. This will permit declarer to ruff one of his little Spades and he will be obliged to concede another at the end.

When the Ace of Spades goes through, declarer has a 100 per cent safety play which guarantees the fulfillment of the contract. He must concede a Spade trick immediately, without cashing the King. When this Spade is won, if the opponent is able to return a trump, it is taken in the closed hand and the remaining small Spade ruffed with the Queen of Trumps. The closed hand is re-entered, trumps are drawn, and the hand is spread.

Deschapelles coup

South is declarer at a contract of 3 No Trump. West leads the 3 of Spades, which East wins with the Ace. What card should be returned?

♠ 7 4
♡ A 6
◇ K Q 10 8 7 2
♣ 9 3 2

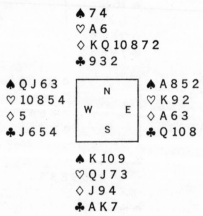

♠ Q J 6 3
♡ 10 8 5 4
◇ 5
♣ J 6 5 4

♠ A 8 5 2
♡ K 9 2
◇ A 6 3
♣ Q 10 8

♠ K 10 9
♡ Q J 7 3
◇ J 9 4
♣ A K 7

If he blindly returns his partner's suit, declarer will win the trick and drive out the Ace of Diamonds, taking in all five Diamonds, two Clubs, a Spade, and a Heart.

East should realize that the defense's only hope is to prevent the run of the Diamond suit. East himself can hold up with the Ace until the third round, but that will serve no purpose if dummy retains the Ace of Hearts.

The proper play at trick two is the King of Hearts, although it sacrifices a sure trick. Though declarer wins this trick, the best he can do is take two Clubs, two Diamonds, three Hearts, and one Spade, falling one short of contract.

Leading up to strength

South is declarer at a contract of 4 Spades. West opened the 6 of Clubs, which East won, declarer dropping the 9. All evidence pointed to the declarer holding a singleton.

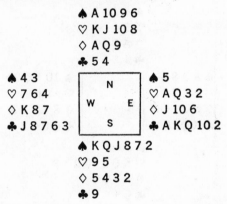

```
              ♠ A 10 9 6
              ♡ K J 10 8
              ◇ A Q 9
              ♣ 5 4
  ♠ 4 3                          ♠ 5
  ♡ 7 6 4            N           ♡ A Q 3 2
  ◇ K 8 7      W          E      ◇ J 10 6
  ♣ J 8 7 6 3        S           ♣ A K Q 10 2
              ♠ K Q J 8 7 2
              ♡ 9 5
              ◇ 5 4 3 2
              ♣ 9
```

The bidding:

EAST	SOUTH	WEST	NORTH
1 Club	1 Spade	2 Clubs	4 Spades
Double	Pass	Pass	Pass

In order to defeat the contract, therefore, it was essential to build up a Diamond trick before dummy's Hearts could be established. In order to do so, West would have to hold the King of Diamonds, which was very likely when his raise is considered. East, therefore, quite properly returned the Jack of Diamonds. This was won with the Queen, trumps drawn, and the 9 of Hearts finessed to East's Queen. Another Diamond lead established the setting trick.

Had East continued with a Club at trick two, it would have been to late to defeat the contract.

A play based on bidding inferenecs

In the following hand South was playing 4 Hearts. West chose to lead the King of Clubs (an original opening of the singleton Diamond would have been a happier choice), and East signaled with the 8. West now shifted to the singleton Diamond. Declarer can see that West intends to take the lead with the Ace of Hearts and put partner in with the Ace of Clubs in order to get a Diamond ruff. Before drawing trumps, declarer's plan is to break the communication between the East and West hands. This he does by winning the trick in dummy and leading the King of Spades. The bidding indicates that West very probably holds the Ace. Declarer discards his remaining Club on the King of Spades. West wins but is unable to give partner the lead for the Diamond ruff.

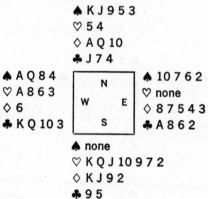

```
              ♠ K J 9 5 3
              ♡ 5 4
              ◇ A Q 10
              ♣ J 7 4
  ♠ A Q 8 4      N        ♠ 10 7 6 2
  ♡ A 8 6 3               ♡ none
  ◇ 6        W       E    ◇ 8 7 5 4 3
  ♣ K Q 10 3     S        ♣ A 8 6 2
              ♠ none
              ♡ K Q J 10 9 7 2
              ◇ K J 9 2
              ♣ 9 5
```

The bidding:

WEST	NORTH	EAST	SOUTH
1 Club	1 Spade	2 Clubs	4 Hearts
Double	Pass	Pass	Pass

Psychology

South was declarer at a contract of 3 No Trump. West elected to lead the 9 of Hearts. East started his deception tactics by playing the 10 on partner's 9. Declarer permitted the trick to hold, and the Queen was returned and won in dummy. The 10 of Diamonds was led. West won with the Ace and continued with the third round of

Hearts, East playing the Jack (successfully concealing the fact that he held the 5). The second round of Diamonds was played, and East won with the King. The natural instinct is to cash the 5 of Hearts at this point, but this will not be sufficient to defeat the contract. Declarer surely has the Ace of Spades and may be able to guess the location of the Queen, but if East fails to cash the Heart, declarer would naturally place that card with West and might be induced to take the Spade finesse the wrong way. East chose to exit with a Diamond. Declarer won and played the Ace of Spades, followed by a small Spade to the Jack, being confident that, even if the finesse lost, he was not in danger, since the thirteenth Heart was apparently with West. When the Queen of Spades held, the setting trick was naturally taken with the 5 of Hearts.

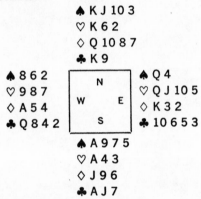

It will be observed that if East cashed the thirteenth Heart, declarer's proper play would be the Ace and King of Spades first, on the odd chance that the Queen might drop, after which he would still have a fifty-fifty chance of a Club finesse.

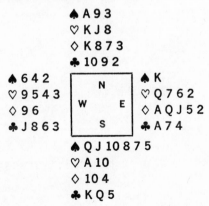

South was declarer at a contract of 4 Spades, East having bid Diamonds. West opened the 9 of Diamonds, East won with the Jack, and South followed with the 4. Declarer, therefore, is known to hold the 10 of Diamonds. East knows that his Ace of Diamonds will live. There is a temptation to cash his three tricks and then continue with the Diamond, in the hope that West can overruff, but it is very likely that declarer will play a high enough trump to beat anything that West can produce, and when he learns that West does not have the King he will naturally refuse the Spade finesse. East, therefore, cashed the Ace of Diamonds and the Ace of Clubs and continued with another Club. Declarer fell into the trap and took the Spade finesse. Whether or not a sharp declarer should have divined East's plan, I leave to the reader.

THE INTERNATIONAL CODE

THE LAWS OF CONTRACT BRIDGE

1963

The Scope of the Laws

The Laws are designed to define correct procedure and to provide an adequate remedy whenever a player accidentally, carelessly or inadvertently disturbs the proper course of the game, or gains an unintentional but nevertheless unfair advantage. An offending player should be ready to pay a prescribed penalty graciously.

The Laws are not designed to prevent dishonorable practices and there are no penalties to cover intentional violations. In the absence of penalty, moral obligations are strongest. Ostracism is the ultimate remedy for intentional offenses.

The object of the Proprieties is twofold: to familiarize players with the customs and etiquette of the game, generally accepted over a long period of years; and to enlighten those who might otherwise fail to appreciate when or how they are improperly conveying information to their partners—often a far more reprehensible offense than a violation of a law.

When these principles are appreciated, arguments are avoided and the pleasure which the game offers is materially enhanced.

Part 1   Definitions

Auction — 1. The process of determining the contract by means of successive calls. 2. The aggregate of calls made. 3. The period during which calls are made.

Bid — An undertaking to win at least a specified number of odd tricks in a specified denomination.

Call — Any bid, double, redouble, or pass.

Contract — The undertaking by declarer's side to win, at the denomination named, the number of odd tricks specified in the final bid, whether undoubled, doubled, or redoubled.

Convention — Any call or play which, by agreement or understanding between partners, serves to convey a meaning other than would be attributed to it by the opponents in the absence of an explanation.

Deal — 1. The distribution of the pack to form the hands of the four players. 2. The cards so distributed considered as a unit, including the auction and play thereof.

Declarer — The player who, for the side that makes the final bid, first bid the denomination named in that bid. He becomes declarer when the auction is closed.

Defective Trick — A trick that contains fewer or more than four legally played cards.

Defender — An opponent of declarer.

Denomination — The suit or no-trump specified in a bid.

Double — A call that increases the scoring values of odd tricks or undertricks at an opponent's bid.

Dummy — Declarer's partner. He becomes dummy when the auction is closed.

Follow Suit — To play a card of the suit that has been led.

Game — A unit in scoring denoting the accumulation of 100 or more trick points.

Hand — The cards originally dealt to a player or the remaining portion thereof.

Honor — Any Ace, King, Queen, Jack, or ten.

Irregularity — A deviation from the correct procedures set forth in the Laws and Proprieties.

Lead — The first card played to a trick.

Odd Trick — Each trick won by declarer's side in excess of six.

Opening Lead — The card led to the first trick.

Opponent — A player of the other side; a member of the partnership to which one is opposed.

Overtrick — Each trick won by declarer's side in excess of the contract.

Pack — The 52 playing cards with which the game of Contract Bridge is played.

Partial Designation — Incomplete specification by declarer of the rank or suit of a card to be played from dummy's hand (see Law 46).

Partner — The player with whom one plays as a side against the other two players.

Part Score — A unit in scoring denoting fulfillment of a contract of which the value is less than 100 trick points.

Pass — A call specifying that a player does not, at that turn, elect to bid, double, or redouble.

Penalty — An obligation or restriction imposed upon a side for violation of these Laws.

Penalty Card — A card that has been prematurely exposed by a defender and must be left face up on the table until legally played or permitted to be picked up.

Play — 1. The contribution of a card from one's hand to a trick, including the first card, which is the lead. 2. The aggregate of plays made. 3. The period during which the cards are played.

Premium Points — Any points earned other than trick points (see Law 75).

Rectification — Adjustment made to permit the auction or play to proceed as normally as possible after an irregularity has occurred.

Redeal — A second or subsequent deal by the same dealer to replace his first deal.

Redouble — A call that increases the scoring value of odd tricks or undertricks at a bid of one's own side that an opponent has doubled.

Revoke — The play of a card of another suit by a player who is able to follow suit.

Rotation — The order in which the right to deal, to call or to play progresses, which is clockwise.

Rubber — A unit in scoring denoting the winning of two games by a side.

Side — Two players who constitute a partnership against the other two players.

Slam — A contract to win twelve tricks, six odd tricks (called SMALL SLAM), or to win all thirteen tricks, seven odd tricks (called GRAND SLAM) ; also, the fulfillment of such a contract.

Specified Suit — Any suit that a player, in exacting a penalty, requires to be led or not to be led.

Suit — One of four groups of cards in the pack, each group comprising thirteen cards and having a characteristic symbol: spades (♠), hearts (♡), diamonds (♢), clubs (♣).

Trick — The unit by which the outcome of the contract is determined, regularly consisting of four cards, one contributed by each player in rotation, beginning with the lead.

Trick Points — Points earned by declarer's side by fulfilling the contract (see Law 75).

Trump — Each card of the suit, if any, named in the contract.

Turn — The correct time when a player may deal, call, or play.

Undertrick — Each trick by which declarer's side fails to fulfill the contract.

Vulnerability — The condition of being exposed to greater undertrick penalties and entitled to greater premiums, through having won one game toward the rubber (see Law 84).

Part 2   Preliminaries to the Rubber

1. *The players — The pack*

Contract Bridge is played by four players with a pack of 52 cards of identical back design and color, consisting of 13 cards in each of four suits. Two packs should be used, of which only one is in play at any time; and each pack should be clearly distinguishable from the other in back design or color.

2. *Rank of cards*

The cards of each suit rank in descending order: Ace, King, Queen, Jack, 10, 9, 8, 7, 6, 5, 4, 3, 2.

3. *The draw*

Before every rubber, each player draws a card from a pack shuffled and spread face down on the table. A card should not be exposed until all the players have drawn.

The two players who draw the highest cards play as partners against the two other players. When cards of the same rank are drawn, the rank of suits determines which is higher—spades (highest), hearts, diamonds, clubs.

The player with the highest card deals first and has the right to choose his seat and the pack with which he will deal. He may consult his partner but, having announced his decision, must abide by it. His partner sits opposite him. The opponents then occupy the two remaining seats as they wish and, having made their selection, must abide by it.

A player must draw again if he draws one of the four cards at either end of the pack, or a card adjoining one drawn by another player, or a card from the other pack; or if, in drawing, he exposes more than one card.

Part 3   The Deal

4. *The shuffle*

Before the cards are dealt they must be shuffled thoroughly, without exposure of the face of any card. The shuffle must be performed in full view of the players and to their satisfaction.

The pack to be used in each deal is prepared by the left-hand opponent of the player who will deal it. Preparation of the pack includes collecting

s

the cards, shuffling them, and placing the shuffled pack face down at the left of the next dealer.

A pack properly prepared should not be disturbed until the dealer picks it up for his deal, at which time he is entitled to the final shuffle.

No player other than the dealer and the player designated to prepare the pack may shuffle.

5. *The cut*

The pack must always be cut immediately before it is dealt. The dealer presents the pack to his right-hand opponent, who lifts off a portion and places it on the table toward the dealer. Each portion must contain at least four cards. The dealer completes the cut by placing what was originally the bottom portion upon the other portion.

No player other than the dealer's right-hand opponent may cut the pack.

6. *New cut — New shuffle*

There must be a new cut if any player demands one before the first card is dealt. In this case the dealer's right-hand opponent cuts again.

There must be a new shuffle, followed by a cut:

A. If any player demands one before the dealer has picked up the pack for his deal. In this case the player designated to prepare the pack shuffles again.

B. If any player demands one after the dealer has picked up the pack but before the first card is dealt. In this case only the dealer shuffles.

C. If a card is turned face up in shuffling. In this case the player who was shuffling shuffles again.

D. If a card is turned face up in cutting. In this case only the dealer shuffles.

E. If there is a redeal (see Law 10).

7. *Change of pack*

The two packs are used alternately, unless there is a redeal.

A pack containing a card so damaged or marked that it may be identified from its back must be replaced if attention is drawn to the imperfection before the first card of the current deal is dealt.

A pack originally belonging to a side must be restored on demand of any player before the last card of the current deal has been dealt.

8. *The deal*

The dealer distributes the cards face down, one at a time in rotation into four separate hands of thirteen cards each, the first card to the player on his left and the last card to himself. If he deals two cards simultaneously or consecutively to the same player, or fails to deal a card to a player, he may rectify the error, provided he does so immediately and to the satisfaction of the other players.

The dealer must not allow the face of any card to be seen while he is dealing. Until the deal is completed, no player but the dealer may touch any card except to correct or prevent an irregularity.

9. Rotation of the turn to deal

The turn to deal passes in rotation, unless there is a redeal. If a player deals out of turn, and attention is not drawn to the error before the last card has been dealt, the deal stands as though it had been in turn, the player who dealt the cards is the dealer, and the player who has missed his turn to deal has no redress; and the rotation continues as though the deal had been in turn, unless a redeal is required under Law 10.

10. Redeal

When there is a redeal, the current deal is canceled; the same dealer deals again, unless he was dealing out of turn; the same pack is used, unless it has been replaced as provided in Law 7; and the cards are shuffled and cut anew as provided in Laws 4 and 5.

There must be a redeal:

A. If, before the last card has been dealt, it is discovered that

i] a card has been turned face up in dealing or is face up in the pack or elsewhere;

ii] the cards have not been dealt correctly;

iii] a player is dealing out of turn or is dealing with a pack that was not shuffled or not cut, provided any player demands a redeal.

B. If, before the first call has been made, it is discovered that a player has picked up another player's hand and has seen a card in it.

C. If, before play has been completed, it is discovered that

i] the pack did not conform in every respect to the requirements of Law 1, including any case in which a missing card cannot be found after due search;

ii] one player has picked up too many cards, another too few;

iii] two or more players on opposing sides have allowed any cards from their hands to be mixed together, following a claim that a redeal is in order.

11. Missing card

When a player has too few cards and a redeal is not required by Law 10 C, the deal stands as correct, and:

A. If he has played more than one card to a previous trick, Law 68 applies;

B.   If a missing card is found elsewhere than in a previous trick, that card is deemed to have belonged continuously to the deficient hand and must be restored to that hand; it may become a penalty card, as provided in Law 23 or 49, and failure to have played it may constitute a revoke.

12.   *Surplus card*

When a player has too many cards and a redeal is not required by Law 10 C, the deal stands as correct, and:

A.   If the offender has omitted to play to a trick, Law 68 applies.

B.   If the offender has picked up a surplus card from a previous trick, or from dummy's hand, or from the other pack, or elsewhere, such surplus card must be restored to its proper place; and

> *i*] If the surplus card is in the offender's hand when it is discovered, there is no penalty.

> ii] If the surplus card has been led or played, the offender must substitute for it a card from his hand that he can legally play to the trick and if possible a card of the same suit as the surplus card, and the offense is subject to the rectification and penalty provisions of Laws 62 to 65.

Part 4   General Laws Governing Irregularities

13.   *Procedure following an irregularity*

When an irregularity has been committed, any player—except dummy as restricted by Law 43—may draw attention to it and give or obtain information as to the law applicable to it. The fact that a player draws attention to an irregularity committed by his side does not affect the rights of the opponents.

After attention has been drawn to an irregularity, no player should call or play until all questions in regard to rectification and to the assessment of a penalty have been determined. Premature correction of an irregularity on the part of the offender may subject him to a further penalty (see Law 26).

14.   *Assessment of a penalty*

A penalty may not be imposed until the nature of the irregularity to be penalized has been determined and the applicable penalty has been clearly stated; but a penalty once paid, or any decision agreed and acted upon by the players, stands, even though at some later time it be adjudged incorrect.

With the exception of dummy, either member of the nonoffending side may impose a penalty, but without consulting his partner.

15. *Waiver or forfeiture of penalty*

The right to penalize an offense is forfeited if a member of the nonoffending side

A.   waives the penalty;

B.   consults with his partner as to the imposition of a penalty before a penalty has been imposed;

C.   calls (Law 34) or plays (Law 60) after an irregularity committed by the opponent at his right.

Rectification or validation proceeds as provided in the law applicable to the specific irregularity.

16. *Unauthorized information*

Any player except declarer may be subject to penalty if he conveys information to his partner other than by a legal call or play.

Information conveyed by an illegal call, play or exposure of a card is subject to the applicable law in Part V or VI.

If any player except declarer conveys information to his partner by means of a remark or an unmistakable gesture or mannerism that suggests a call,* lead, play, or plan of play; and if attention is drawn to the offense and the penalty is assessed forthwith, as provided in Laws 13 and 14:

A.   If the offense occurs before the auction closes, (penalty) either member of the nonoffending side may require both members of the offender's side to pass during the remainder of the auction; and if the offender becomes a defender, then when first it is the turn of the offender's partner to lead, including the opening lead, declarer may either

 i] require the offender's partner to lead a specified suit, or

 ii] prohibit the offender's partner from leading a specified suit; this prohibition continues for as long as the offender's partner retains the lead.

B.   If the offense occurs after the auction closes, (penalty) declarer or either defender, as the case may be, may prohibit the offender's partner from making:

 i] a lead improperly suggested; this prohibition applies to any one lead, including the opening lead, and continues for as long as the offender's partner retains the lead; or

 ii] a play improperly suggested; this prohibition may be applied to only one play.

---

* After a deal has been completed, a player should not draw attention to the score, except to correct an error in recording. See Proprieties II G.

The rights of the nonoffending side are not affected by an intervening call or play by the offending side. If the offender's partner has called after the offense, but before a member of the nonoffending side has subsequently called, his call may be canceled. If the offender's partner has led or played after the offense, and before a member of the nonoffending side has subsequently played, he may be required to withdraw his card and to substitute a card that does not conform to the improper suggestion, and a defender's card so withdrawn becomes a penalty card.

Part 5   The Auction

Correct Procedure

17. *Duration of the auction*

The auction begins when the last card of a correct deal has been placed on the table. The dealer makes the first call, and thereafter each player calls in rotation. When three passes in rotation have followed any call, the auction is closed.

18. *Bids*

Each bid must name a number of odd tricks, from one to seven, and a denomination. A bid supersedes the previous bid if it names either a greater number of odd tricks, or the same number of odd tricks in a higher denomination. A bid that fulfills these requirements is sufficient; one that does not, is insufficient. The denominations rank in descending order: no-trump, spades, hearts, diamonds, clubs.

19. *Doubles and redoubles*

A player may double only the last preceding bid, and then only if it was made by an opponent and no call other than a pass has intervened.

A player may redouble only the last preceding double, and then only if it was made by an opponent and no call other than a pass has intervened.

A player should not, in doubling or redoubling, state the number of tricks or the denomination; but, if he states either or both incorrectly, he is deemed to have doubled or redoubled the bid as it was made.

All doubles and redoubles are superseded by a subsequent legal bid. If there is no subsequent bid, scoring values are increased as provided in Law 84.

20. *Review of the auction*

A player who does not hear a call distinctly may forthwith require that it be repeated.

Before the auction closes, a player is entitled to have all previous calls restated when it is his turn to call, unless he is required by law to pass.

After the auction closes, declarer or either defender may require previous calls to be restated. A defender's right to such a review terminates when a member of his side has led or played to the first trick; declarer's right terminates when he has played to the first trick or dummy has spread any part of his hand.

A request to have calls restated should be responded to only by an opponent. Dummy or a player required by law to pass may review the auction at an opponent's request. Any player, including dummy or a player required by law to pass, may and should promptly correct an error in restatement.

21. *Call based on misinformation*

A player has no recourse if he has made a call on the basis of his own misunderstanding.

A player may, without penalty, change any call he may have made as a result of misinformation given him by an opponent, provided his partner has not subsequently called. If he elects to correct his call, his left-hand opponent may then, in turn and without penalty, change any subsequent call he may have made.

22. *Procedure after the auction is closed*

After the auction is closed:

A.   If no player has bid, the hands are abandoned and the turn to deal passes in rotation.

B.   If any player has bid, the final bid becomes the contract and play begins.

Irregularities

23. *Card exposed or led during the auction*

Whenever, during the auction, a player faces a card on the table or holds a card so that it is possible for his partner to see its face, every such card must be left face up on the table until the auction closes; and:

A.   If it is a single card below the rank of an honor and not prematurely led, there is no penalty, and when the auction closes the card may be picked up.

B.   If it is a single card of honor rank, or any card prematurely led, or if more than one card is so exposed, (penalty) the offender's partner must pass when next it is his turn to call; and if the offender subsequently becomes a defender, declarer may treat every such card as a penalty card (Law 50).

24.   Immediate correction of a call

A player may substitute his intended call for an inadvertent call, but only if he does so without pause. If legal, his last call stands without penalty; if illegal, it is subject to the applicable law.

25.   Change of call

A call substituted for a call made previously at the same turn, when it is too late for correction as provided in Law 24, is canceled; and:

A.   If the first call was illegal, the offender is subject to the applicable law.

B.   If the first call was a legal one, the offender must either

i] allow his first call to stand and (penalty) his partner must pass when next it is his turn to call; or

ii] make any legal call and (penalty) his partner must pass whenever it is his turn to call.

The offender's partner may also be subject to a lead penalty as provided in Law 26.

26.   Unauthorized information given by change of call

When a player names a denomination not selected as his final call at that turn (as in changing a call* or in making or correcting an illegal call), then if he becomes a defender:

A.   If such denomination was a suit, (penalty) declarer may prohibit the offender's partner from leading that suit the first time the offender's partner has the lead, including the opening lead, and for as long as he retains the lead.

B.   If such denomination was no-trump, and if the offender's partner is to make the opening lead, (penalty) declarer may require the offender's partner to make the opening lead in a specified suit.

When a player has substituted another call for a double or redouble, the penalties provided in Law 27 (C) apply.

27.   Insufficient bid

An insufficient bid made in rotation must be corrected, if either opponent draws attention to it, by substituting either a sufficient bid or a

---

* Except as permitted under Law 24.

pass.* A double or redouble may not be substituted. If the call substituted is

A.   the lowest sufficient bid in the same denomination, the auction proceeds as though the irregularity had not occurred.

B.   any other sufficient bid, (penalty) the offender's partner must pass whenever it is his turn to call.

C.   a pass, (penalty) the offender's partner must pass whenever it is his turn to call; and if the offender's partner is to make the opening lead, declarer may either

> *i*] require the offender's partner to lead a specified suit, or
>
> *ii*] prohibit the offender's partner from leading a specified suit; this prohibition continues for as long as the offender's partner retains the lead.

If the offender attempts to substitute a double or redouble, it is canceled; he must pass and the offense is subject to the penalty provided in subsection C above.

If a player makes an insufficient bid out of rotation, Law 31 applies.

Call Out of Rotation

28.   *Calls considered to be in rotation*

A call is considered to be in rotation

A.   when it is made without waiting for the right-hand opponent to pass, if that opponent is required by law to pass.

B.   when it is made by the player whose turn it was to call, before a penalty has been imposed for a call out of rotation by an opponent; it waives any penalty for the call out of rotation and the auction proceeds as though that opponent had not called at that turn.

29.   *Procedure after a call out of rotation*

A call out of rotation is canceled if either opponent draws attention to it. The auction reverts to the player whose turn it was to call. The offender may make any legal call in proper turn but may be subject to penalty under Law 30, 31 or 32.

30.   *Pass out of rotation*

When a player has passed out of rotation

A.   before any player has bid, or when it was the turn of the opponent on his right to call, (penalty) the offender must pass when next it is his turn to call.

---

* The offender is entitled to select his final call at that turn after the applicable penalties have been stated, and any call he has previously attempted to substitute is canceled, but Law 26 may apply.

S*

B.   after any player has bid and when it was the turn of the offender's partner to call, (penalty) the offender must pass whenever it is his turn to call; the offender's partner may make a sufficient bid or may pass, but may not double or redouble at that turn; and if the offender's partner passes and subsequently is to make the opening lead, declarer may either

> *i*] require the offender's partner to lead a specified suit, or
>
> *ii*] prohibit the offender's partner from leading a specified suit; this prohibition continues for as long as the offender's partner retains the lead.

31.   Bid out of rotation
When a player has bid out of rotation

A.   before any player has called, (penalty) his partner must pass whenever it is his turn to call.

B.   after any player has called and when it was the turn of the offender's partner to call, (penalty) the offender's partner must pass whenever it is his turn to call; and if the offender's partner is to make the opening lead, declarer may either

> *i*] require the offender's partner to lead a specified suit, or
>
> *ii*] prohibit the offender's partner from leading a specified suit; this prohibition continues for as long as the offender's partner retains the lead.

C.   after any player has called and when it was the turn of the opponent on the offender's right* to call:

> *i*] If that opponent passes, the bid out of rotation, if sufficient, must be repeated and there is no penalty. If the bid out of rotation was insufficient it must be corrected as provided in Law 27.
>
> *ii*] If that opponent makes a legal bid, double, or redouble,† the offender may in turn make any legal call and (penalty) the offender's partner must pass when next it is his turn to call, and Law 26 may apply.

32.   Double or redouble out of rotation
When a player has doubled or redoubled out of rotation, and Law 36 or 37 does not apply:

A.   If it was the offender's partner's turn to call, (penalty) the offender's partner must pass whenever it is his turn to call; the offender may

---

* A call made after any player has called and when it is the turn of the opponent on the offender's left to call is treated as a change of call and Law 25 applies.

† An illegal call by that opponent may be penalized in the usual way, after which this subsection c (*ii*) applies.

not thereafter, in turn, double or redouble the same bid he doubled or redoubled out of turn; and if the offender's partner is to make the opening lead, declarer may either

> *i*] require the offender's partner to lead a specified suit, or
>
> *ii*] prohibit the offender's partner from leading a specified suit; this prohibition continues for as long as the offender's partner retains the lead.

B.   If it was the turn of the opponent on the offender's right to call:

> *i*] If the opponent on the offender's right passes, the double or redouble out of rotation must be repeated and there is no penalty.
>
> *ii*] If the opponent on the offender's right bids, the offender may in turn make any legal call, and (penalty) the offender's partner must pass when it is his turn to call, and Law 26 may apply.

33. *Simultaneous calls*

A call made simultaneously with one made by the player whose turn it was to call is deemed to be a subsequent call.

34. *Call in rotation after an illegal call*

A call by a member of the nonoffending side after an illegal call by the opponent on his right, and before a penalty has been assessed, forfeits the right to penalize that offense. The illegal call is treated as though it were legal, except that an inadmissible double or redouble or a bid of more than seven is treated as a pass; and Law 35 or 37 may apply.

35. *Retention of the right to call*

A player may not be deprived of any turn to call by one or more passes following a pass out of rotation, when there has been no subsequent bid. All such passes are canceled, the bidding reverts to the player who has missed his turn, and the auction continues as though there had been no irregularity.

Inadmissible Calls

36. *Inadmissible double or redouble*

Any double or redouble not permitted by Law 19 is canceled; and:

A.   If the offender has doubled or redoubled a bid that his side has already doubled or redoubled:

i] The offender may substitute a legal bid, and (penalty) his partner must pass whenever it is his turn to call, and if the offender's partner is to make the opening lead, declarer may prohibit the lead of the suit illegally doubled or redoubled, for as long as the offender's partner retains the lead; or

ii] The offender may substitute a pass, and (penalty) his partner must pass whenever it is his turn to call, either member of the nonoffending side may cancel all previous doubles or redoubles, and if the offender's partner is to make the opening lead, declarer may require the offender's partner to lead a specified suit, or prohibit the offender's partner from leading a specified suit; this prohibition continues for as long as the offender's partner retains the lead.

B.   If the offender has doubled a bid made by his side, redoubled an undoubled bid, or doubled or redoubled when there has been no bid, the offender in turn must make any legal call, and (penalty) his partner must pass when next it is his turn to call.

If the right of the nonoffending side to penalize is waived or forfeited, as provided in Law 15, the offender is deemed to have passed and the auction proceeds as though there had been no irregularity.

37.   *Bid, double or redouble in violation of the obligation to pass*

A bid, double or redouble by a player who is required by law to pass is canceled, and (penalty) both members of the offending side must pass during the remainder of the auction, and if the offender's partner is to make the opening lead, declarer may either

A.   require the offender's partner to lead a specified suit, or

B.   prohibit the offender's partner from leading a specified suit; this prohibition continues for as long as the offender's partner retains the lead.

If the right of the nonoffending side to penalize is waived or forfeited, as provided in Law 15, the offender's bid, double or redouble, if otherwise legal, stands at that turn; but if the offender was required to pass for the remainder of the auction he must still pass at subsequent turns.

38.   *Bid of more than seven*

A bid of more than seven by any player is canceled, and (penalty) both members of the offending side must pass during the remainder of the auction, and if the offender's partner is to make the opening lead, declarer may either

A.   require the offender's partner to lead a specified suit, or

B.   prohibit the offender's partner from leading a specified suit; this prohibition continues for as long as the offender's partner retains the lead.

If the right of the nonoffending side to penalize is waived or forfeited, as provided in Law 15, the offender must substitute a pass; any call that may have been made subsequently is canceled; and the auction proceeds as though there had been no irregularity. No play or score at a contract of more than seven is ever permissible.

39. *Call after the auction is closed*

A call after the auction is closed is canceled, and:

A.   If it is a pass by a defender or any call by declarer or dummy, there is no penalty.

B.   If it is a bid, double or redouble by a defender, (penalty) declarer may either

> *i*] require the offender's partner, when first it is his turn to lead, to lead a specified suit; or
>
> *ii*] prohibit the offender's partner, when first it is his turn to lead, from leading a specified suit; this prohibition continues for as long as the offender's partner retains the lead.

Part 6   The Play

Correct Procedure

40. *Commencement of play*

After the auction closes, the defender on declarer's left makes the opening lead. After the opening lead, dummy spreads his hand in front of him on the table, face up and grouped in suits with the trumps on his right. Declarer plays both his hand and that of dummy.

41. *Information as to contract*

After it is too late to have previous calls restated, as provided in Law 20, declarer or either defender is entitled to be informed what the contract is and whether, but not by whom, it was doubled or redoubled.

42. *Dummy's rights and limitations*

Dummy is entitled to give or obtain information as to fact or law; and provided he has not forfeited his rights (see Law 43) he may also:

A.   question players regarding revokes as provided in Law 61;

B.   draw attention to an irregularity, or try to prevent one.*

Except as provided in this law, dummy may not, on his own initiative, participate in the play, or make any comment on the bidding or play of

---

* He may, for example, warn declarer against leading from the wrong hand.

the current deal, or draw attention to the score, and if he does so, Law 16 may apply. If dummy consults with declarer as to the imposition of a penalty, the right to penalize is forfeited as provided in Law 15.

43. Forfeiture of dummy's rights

Dummy forfeits the rights provided in A and B of Law 42 if he exchanges hands with declarer, leaves his seat to watch declarer play, or, on his own initiative, looks at the face of a card in either defender's hand; and if, thereafter,

A. He is the first to draw attention to a defender's irregularity, declarer may not enforce any penalty for the offense.

B. He warns declarer not to lead from the wrong hand, (penalty) either defender may choose the hand from which declarer shall lead.

C. He is the first to ask declarer if a play from declarer's hand constitutes a revoke or failure to comply with a penalty, declarer must substitute a correct card if his play was illegal, and the penalty provisions of Law 64 apply.

44. Sequence and procedure of play

The player who leads to a trick may play any card in his hand.* After the lead, each other player in turn plays a card and the four cards so played constitute a trick.

In playing to a trick, each player must if possible follow suit. This obligation takes precedence over all other requirements of these Laws. If unable to follow suit, a player may play any card.*

A trick containing a trump is won by the player who has contributed to it the highest trump. A trick that does not contain a trump is won by the player who has contributed to it the highest card of the suit led. The player who has won the trick leads to the next trick.

45. Card played

Each player except dummy plays a card by detaching it from his hand and facing it near the middle of the table. Declarer plays a card from dummy's hand by moving the card toward the center of the table. If instructed by declarer to do so, dummy may play from his hand a card named or designated by declarer. In addition, a card must be played:

A. If it is a defender's card held so that it is possible for his partner to see its face.

B. If it is a card from declarer's hand that declarer holds face up in front of him and that is touching or near the table.

C. If it is a card in dummy touched by declarer except for the purpose of arranging dummy's cards or of reaching a card above or below the card or cards touched.

---

* Unless he is subject to restriction after an irregularity committed by his side.

D.   If the player who holds the card names or otherwise designates it as the card he proposes to play. A player may, without penalty, change an inadvertent designation if he does so without pause; but if an opponent has, in turn, played a card that was legal before the change of designation, that opponent may without penalty withdraw any card so played and substitute another.

E.   If it is a penalty card, subject to Law 50.

F.   If it is a card in dummy's hand that dummy has illegally suggested as a play, unless either defender forbids the play of such card, or an equal of it, or a card of the same suit, as provided in Law 16.

A card played may not be withdrawn except as provided in Law 47.

46.   *Partial designation of a card to be played from dummy's hand*

When declarer instructs dummy to play a card from dummy's hand, as permitted by Law 45, but names only a suit or only the rank of a card, or the equivalent, without fully specifying the card to be played, declarer must complete his partial designation. Dummy must not play a card before declarer has completed his partial designation, and if dummy prematurely plays a card, Law 16 applies on that trick only, unless a defender has subsequently played.

47.   *Retraction of a card played*

A card once played may be withdrawn only:

A.   to comply with a penalty, or to correct an illegal play;

B.   after a change of designation as permitted by Law 45 D;

C.   after an opponent's change of play, to substitute a card for one played.

Penalty Card

48.   *Exposure of declarer's cards*

Declarer is not subject to penalty for exposing a card, and no card of declarer's or dummy's ever becomes a penalty card. Declarer is not required to play any card dropped accidentally.

When declarer faces his cards after an opening lead out of turn, Law 54 applies.* When declarer faces his cards at any other time, he is deemed to have made a claim or concession of tricks and Law 71 applies.

49.   *Exposure of a defender's cards*

Whenever a defender faces a card on the table, holds a card so that it is possible for his partner to see its face, or names a card as being in his hand, before he is entitled to do so in the normal course of play or

---

* Declarer should, as a matter of propriety, refrain from spreading his hand.

application of the law, (penalty) each such card becomes a penalty card (Law 50).

50. *Disposition of a penalty card*

A penalty card must be left face up on the table until it is played or is permitted to be picked up. When a penalty card is permitted to be picked up, it ceases to be a penalty card.

A penalty card must be played at the first legal opportunity, whether in leading, following suit, discarding, or trumping. If a defender has two or more penalty cards that can legally be played, declarer may designate which is to be played. The obligation to follow suit, or to comply with a lead or play penalty, takes precedence over the obligation to play a penalty card, but the penalty card must still be left face up on the table and played at the next legal opportunity.

When a defender has or first obtains the lead while his partner has a penalty card, declarer may require him to lead the suit of the penalty card or prohibit him from leading that suit for as long as he retains the lead. If declarer exercises this option, the penalty card may be picked up. If declarer does not exercise this option, the defender may lead any card; but the penalty card remains a penalty card. The defender may not lead until declarer has indicated his choice.

If a defender has two or more penalty cards in one suit, and declarer requires the defender's partner to lead that suit, the defender may pick up every penalty card in that suit and may make any legal play to the trick.

If a defender has penalty cards in more than one suit, declarer may prohibit the defender's partner from leading every such suit; but the defender may then pick up every penalty card in every suit prohibited by declarer and may make any legal play to the trick.

51. *Penalty card illegally picked up*

When a defender attempts illegally to restore a penalty card to his unfaced hand, such card must be replaced face up on the table on demand of declarer; but if in the meantime that defender has played another card and declarer has thereafter played from either his hand or dummy, the card illegally picked up ceases to be a penalty card and need not be replaced on the table.

52. *Failure to lead or play a penalty card*

When a defender fails to lead or play a penalty card as required by Law 50, he may not, on his own initiative, withdraw any other card he may have played.

If a defender leads or plays another card when he could legally have led or played a penalty card,

A.   declarer may accept the defender's lead or play, and declarer must accept such lead or play if he has thereafter played from his or dummy's hand, but the unplayed penalty card remains a penalty card; or

B.   declarer may require the defender to substitute the penalty card
for the card illegally led or played. Every card illegally led or played by
the defender in the course of committing the irregularity becomes a penalty card.

Lead Out of Turn

53.   Lead out of turn accepted

Any lead out of turn may be treated as a correct lead. It becomes
a correct lead if declarer or either defender, as the case may be, accepts
it or plays a card before attention is drawn to the irregularity. A card so
played by declarer from either hand may not be withdrawn unless its play
constituted a revoke. Law 57 applies if such card is played by the defender
at the right of the player from whose hand the lead out of turn was made.

54.   Opening lead out of turn

When a defender makes the opening lead out of turn:

A.   If declarer accepts the lead as provided in Law 53, dummy's hand
is spread in accordance with Law 40 and the second card to the trick is
played from declarer's hand; but if declarer first plays to the trick from
dummy's hand, dummy's card may not be withdrawn except to correct a
revoke.

B.   If declarer may have seen any of dummy's cards (except cards that
dummy may have exposed during the auction and that were subject to
Law 23) he must accept the lead.

C.   If declarer begins to spread his hand as though he were dummy,*
and in so doing exposes one or more cards, and if subsection B above
does not apply, the lead must be accepted, declarer must spread his entire.
hand, and dummy becomes declarer.

When declarer requires the defender to retract his opening lead out of
turn, Law 56 applies.

55.   Declarer's lead out of turn

When declarer leads out of turn from his or dummy's hand and
either defender requires him to retract such lead:

A.   If it was a defender's turn to lead, declarer restores the card led
in error to his or dummy's hand without penalty.

B.   If declarer has led from the wrong hand when it was his turn to
lead from his or dummy's hand, he withdraws the card led in error; he
must lead from the correct hand, and, (penalty) if able to do so, a card
of the same suit. Failure to observe this obligation in playing from his
own hand may subject him to penalty under Law 65.

---

* Declarer should, as a matter of propriety, refrain from spreading his hand.

Either defender's drawing attention to declarer's lead out of turn is equivalent to requiring its retraction. Dummy's drawing attention to declarer's lead from the wrong hand does not affect the rights of the opponents.

56. Defender's lead out of turn

When declarer requires a defender to retract his lead out of turn:

A.   Declarer may treat the card illegally led as a penalty card and apply the provisions of Law 50; or

B.   Declarer may allow the card illegally led to be picked up; and if the offense occurred

> *i*] on the opening lead, or on a subsequent lead when it was the other defender's turn to lead, (penalty) declarer may require the offender's partner to lead the suit of the card led out of turn, or prohibit him from leading that suit for as long as he retains the lead.
>
> *ii*] when it was declarer's or dummy's turn to lead, declarer leads from the correct hand and (penalty) when first it is the turn of the offender's partner to lead, declarer may require him to lead the suit of the card led out of turn, or prohibit him from leading that suit for as long as he retains the lead.

Irregular Leads and Plays

57. Premature lead or play by a defender

When a defender leads to the next trick before his partner has played to the current trick, or plays out of turn before his partner has played, (penalty) declarer may require the offender's partner to play:

A.   his highest card of the suit led; or

B.   his lowest card of the suit led; or

C.   a card of another suit, specified by declarer.

Declarer must select one of these options, and if the offender's partner cannot comply with the penalty selected he may play any card, as provided in Law 59.

When, as a result of the application of the penalty, the offender's partner wins the current trick, he leads to the next trick; and any card led or played out of turn by the other defender becomes a penalty card (Law 50).

A defender is not subject to penalty for playing before his partner if declarer has played from both hands; but a singleton or one of two or more equal cards in dummy is not considered automatically played unless dummy has played the card or has illegally suggested that it be played (see Law 45).

58. *Simultaneous leads or plays*

A lead or play made simultaneously with another player's legal lead or play is deemed to be subsequent to it.

If a defender leads or plays two or more cards simultaneously, and if only one such card is visible, he must play that card; if more than one card is exposed, he must designate the card he proposes to play and each other card exposed becomes a penalty card (Law 50).

If declarer leads or plays two or more cards simultaneously from either hand, he must designate the card he proposes to play and must restore any other card to the correct hand. A defender who has played to the only visible card played by declarer may, without penalty, withdraw the card played and substitute another.

If the error remains undiscovered until both sides have played to the next trick, Law 68 applies.

59. *Inability to lead or play as required*

A player may play any correct card if he is unable to lead or play as required to comply with a penalty, either because he has no card of the required suit, or because he has only cards of a suit he is prohibited from leading, or because of his obligation to follow suit. The penalty is deemed to have been paid, except that the obligation to play a penalty card at the first legal opportunity continues.

60. *Play after an illegal play*

A play by a member of the nonoffending side after the opponent on his right has led or played out of turn or prematurely, and before a penalty has been assessed, forfeits the right to penalize that offense. The illegal play is treated as though it were legal, unless it constitutes a revoke. If the offending side had a previous obligation to play a penalty card or to comply with a lead or play penalty, the obligation remains at future turns (see Laws 52 and 65).

When a defender plays after declarer has been required to retract his lead out of turn from either hand, but before declarer has led from the correct hand, the defender's card becomes a penalty card (Law 50).

A play by a member of the offending side before a penalty has been assessed does not affect the rights of the opponents and may itself be subject to penalty.

The Revoke

61. *Failure to follow suit — Inquiries concerning a revoke*

Failure to follow suit in accordance with Law 44 constitutes a revoke. Any player, including dummy,* may ask a player who has failed

---

* Subject to Law 43. A claim of revoke does not warrant inspection of quitted tricks except as permitted in Law 67.

to follow suit whether he has a card of the suit led, and may demand that an opponent correct his revoke.

62. *Correction of a revoke*

A player must correct his revoke if he becomes aware of the occurrence of the revoke before it becomes established. To correct a revoke, the offender withdraws the card he played in revoking and follows suit with any card. A card so withdrawn becomes a penalty card (Law 50) if it was played from a defender's unfaced hand. The card may be replaced without penalty if it was played from declarer's or dummy's hand* or if it was a defender's faced card. Each member of the nonoffending side may, without penalty, withdraw any card he may have played after the revoke but before attention was drawn to it. The partner of the offender may not withdraw his card unless it too constituted a revoke.†

A revoke on the twelfth trick never becomes established, but it must be corrected if discovered before the cards have been mixed together, and declarer or either defender, as the case may be, may then require the offender's partner to play to the twelfth trick either of two cards he could legally have played to that trick.

63. *Establishment of a revoke*

A revoke in any of the first eleven tricks becomes established when the offender or his partner leads or plays to the following trick,‡ or names or otherwise designates a card to be so played, or makes a claim or concession of tricks orally or by facing his hand. The revoke may then no longer be corrected, and the trick on which the revoke occurred stands as played.

64. *Procedure after establishment of a revoke*

When a revoke has become established, (penalty) after play ceases, two tricks are transferred to the nonoffending side, if the side that has revoked has won two or more tricks after the revoke.§ Only one trick is transferred if the side that has revoked has won only one trick after the revoke. The trick on which the revoke occurred is counted as having been won after the revoke.§§ There is no penalty for an established revoke:

A.   If the side that revoked did not win either the trick on which the revoke occurred or any subsequent trick.

B.   If the revoke was a subsequent revoke in the same suit by the same player.

---

* Subject to Law 43. A claim of revoke does not warrant inspection of quitted tricks except as permitted in Law 67.

† In such case the card withdrawn becomes a penalty card if it was played from a defender's unfaced hand.

‡ Any such play, legal or illegal, establishes the revoke.

§ Failure to lead or play a card or suit specified by an opponent in accordance with an agreed penalty is not a revoke but may be subject to the same penalties (see Law 65).

§§ For the scoring of tricks transferred see Law 80.

c.   If the revoke was made in failing to play any card faced on the table or belonging to a hand faced on the table including a card from dummy's hand.

D.   If attention is first drawn to it after all players have abandoned their hands and permitted the cards to be mixed together.

65.   *Failure to comply with a lead or play penalty*

When a player is able to lead or play from an unfaced hand a card or suit required by law or specified by an opponent in accordance with an agreed penalty, but instead plays an incorrect card:

A.   The offender must correct his error if he becomes aware of it before he or his partner plays another card. Any card played in rotation by a member of the nonoffending side may be withdrawn, without penalty, if it was played after the error and before its correction. An incorrect card played from a defender's unfaced hand becomes a penalty card (Law 50).

B.   The offender may not withdraw any incorrect card he may have played if he or his partner has led or played to the following trick; and (penalty) the offense is subject to the penalty provisions of Law 64.

There is no penalty for failure to lead or play a faced card, including a penalty card* or a card from dummy's hand, but a member of the nonoffending side (except dummy) may demand rectification at any time before a member of his side has thereafter played a card.

Tricks

66.   *Collection and arrangement of tricks*

The cards constituting each completed trick are collected by a member of the side that won the trick and are then turned face down on the table. Each trick should be identifiable as such, and all tricks taken by a side should be arranged in sequence in front of declarer or of one defender, as the case may be, in such manner that each side can determine the number of tricks it has won and the order in which they were taken.

67.   *Inspection of tricks*

Declarer or either defender may, until a member of his side has led or played to the following trick, inspect a trick and inquire what card each player has played to it. Thereafter, until play ceases, quitted tricks may be inspected only to account for a missing or surplus card. After play ceases, the tricks and unplayed cards may be inspected to settle a claim of a revoke, of honors, or of the number of tricks won or lost. If, after a claim has been made, a player on one side mixes the cards in such way that the facts can no longer be ascertained, the issue must be decided in favor of the other side.

* A card played instead of the penalty card may be subject to penalty—see Law 52.

68. *Defective trick*

When a player has omitted to play to a trick, or has played too many cards to a trick, the error must be rectified if attention is drawn to the irregularity before a player on each side has played to the following trick. To rectify omission to play to a trick, the offender supplies a card he can legally play. To rectify the error of playing too many cards, the offender withdraws all but one card, leaving a card he can legally play. Each card so withdrawn becomes a penalty card (Law 50) if it was played from a defender's unfaced hand. After a card has been so withdrawn, each member of the nonoffending side may, without penalty, withdraw any card he played after the irregularity but before attention was drawn to it.

When attention is drawn to a defective trick after a player on each side has played to the following trick, the defective trick stands as played and:

A. A player with too few cards plays the remainder of his hand with fewer cards than the other players; he does not play to the final trick (or tricks) ; and if he wins a trick with his last card, the lead passes in rotation.

B. A player with too many cards forthwith faces and adds a card to the defective trick, and if possible one he could legally have played to it. A card so contributed does not change the ownership of the trick.

69. *Trick appropriated in error*

A trick appropriated by the wrong side must, upon demand, be restored to the side that has in fact won the trick by contributing the winning card to it. The scoring value of the trick must be credited to that side, subject to Law 81.

Claims and Concessions

70. *Declarer's claim or concession of tricks*

Declarer makes a claim whenever he announces that he will win or lose one or more of the remaining tricks, or suggests that play may be curtailed, or faces his hand. Declarer should not make a claim if there is any doubt as to the number of tricks to be won or lost.

71. *Procedure following declarer's claim*

When declarer has made a claim, play is temporarily suspended and declarer must place and leave his hand face up on the table and forthwith make a comprehensive statement as to his proposed plan of play, including the order in which he will play his remaining cards; and:

1] Either defender may, at any time thereafter, demand that declarer clarify or amplify his statement in any particular.

2] At any time after declarer's claim, either defender may face his hand for inspection by his partner and declarer may not impose a penalty for any irregularity committed by a defender whose hand is so faced.

3] Either defender may require that play continue as provided in Law 72.

Declarer's claim must be allowed if both defenders agree to it, or if either defender has allowed any of his remaining cards to be mixed with another player's cards.

72. Continuation of play after declarer's claim

Whenever either defender requires that play continue after declarer's claim, declarer must play on, leaving his hand face up on the table. Declarer may make no play inconsistent with any statement he may have made; and if he did not make an appropriate announcement at the time he made his claim, he may not exercise freedom of choice in making any play the success of which depends on finding either opponent with or without a particular unplayed card; and unless an opponent failed to follow to the suit of that card before the claim was made, declarer must play as directed by either defender. If declarer attempts to make a play prohibited under this law, either defender may accept the play or require declarer to withdraw the card so played and to substitute another that conforms to his obligations, provided neither defender has subsequently played. Any question not specifically dealt with should be resolved in favor of the defenders.*

73. Defender's claim or concession of tricks

When a defender makes a claim or concession of tricks he may do so by showing any or all of his cards to declarer only, but this does not necessarily exempt the defender from penalty under Law 16. If in the course of making a claim or concession a defender faces his hand, names a card as being in his hand, or makes it possible for his partner to see one or more of his remaining cards, his cards do not become penalty cards but declarer may treat the remaining cards of the other defender as penalty cards.

74. Concession withdrawn

A concession may be withdrawn:

A. If any player concedes a trick his side has, in fact, won; or if declarer concedes defeat of a contract he has already fulfilled; or if a defender concedes fulfillment of a contract his side has already defeated. If the score has been entered, it may be corrected, subject to Law 81.

B. If a trick that has been conceded cannot be lost by any sequence of play of the remaining cards, however improbable, and if attention is drawn to that fact before the cards have been mixed together.

C. If a defender concedes one or more tricks and his partner immediately objects, but Law 16 may apply.

---

* Example: Declarer may be required to draw, or not to draw, an outstanding trump that he may have overlooked and that is a possible winner.

Part 7   The Score

75. *Points earned*

The result of each deal played is recorded in points, which fall into two classes:

1.   *Trick points.* Only declarer's side can earn trick points, and only by winning at least the number of odd tricks specified in the contract. Only the value of odd tricks named in the contract may be scored as trick points. (See Law 84.) Trick points mark the progression of the rubber toward its completion.

2.   *Premium points.* Either side or both sides may earn premium points. Declarer's side earns premium points by winning one or more over-tricks; by fulfilling a doubled or redoubled contract; by bidding and making a slam; by holding scorable honors in declarer's or dummy's hand; or by winning the final game of a rubber.* The defenders earn premium points by defeating the contract (undertrick penalty) or by holding scorable honors in either of their hands. (See Law 84.)

Each side's premium points are added to its trick points at the conclusion of the rubber.

76. *Part score — game*

The basic units of trick scores are part score and game. A part score is recorded for declarer's side whenever declarer fulfills a contract for which the trick score is less than 100 points. Game is won by that side which is the first to have scored 100 or more trick points either in a single deal or by addition of two or more part scores made separately. No part score made in the course of one game is carried forward into the next game.

77. *The rubber*

A rubber ends when a side has won two games. At the conclusion of the rubber, the winners of two games are credited in their premium score with 500 points if the other side has won one game, or with 700 points if the other side has not won a game. The trick and premium points scored by each side in the course of the rubber are then added. The side with the larger combined total wins the rubber, and the difference between the two totals represents the margin of victory computed in points.

78. *Method of scoring*

The score of each deal must be recorded and preferably a member of each side should keep score.

---

* For incomplete rubber see Law 83.

Scores are entered in two adjacent columns separated by a vertical line. Each scorer enters points earned by his side in the left-hand column, and points earned by his opponents in the right-hand column.

Each side has a trick score and a premium score, separated by a horizontal line intersecting the vertical line. All trick points are entered, as they are earned, in descending order below the horizontal line; all premium points in ascending order above that line.

Whenever a game is won, another horizontal line is drawn under all trick scores recorded for either side, in order to mark completion of the game. Subsequent trick scores are entered below the line so drawn. Any line prematurely drawn must be erased, and a line incorrectly omitted must be drawn upon discovery of the error.

79. Responsibility for the score

When play ceases, all four players are equally responsible for ascertaining that the number of tricks won by each side is correctly determined and that all scores are promptly and correctly entered.

80. Transferred tricks

A transferred trick is reckoned for all scoring purposes as though it had been won in play by the side to which it has been awarded.

81. Correction of the score

Any scoring error conceded by both sides may be corrected at any time before the score of the rubber is agreed upon; except that an error made by each scorer in recording a trick score, or failing to enter one, may not be corrected after the last card of the second succeeding correct deal has been dealt, unless the majority of the players consent. In case of disagreement among two or more scores kept, the recollection of the majority of the players as to the facts governs.

82. Deals played with an incorrect pack

Scores recorded for deals played with an incorrect pack are not subject to change by reason of the discovery of the imperfection after the cards have been mixed together.

83. Incomplete rubber

When, for any reason, a rubber is not finished, the score is computed as follows:

If only one game has been completed, the winners of that game are credited with 300 points; if only one side has a part score or scores in a game not completed, that side is credited with 50 points; the trick and premium points of each side are then added, and the side with the greater number of points wins the difference between the two totals.

84. *Scoring table*

	Odd Tricks Bid and Won in	Undoubled	Doubled
TRICK POINTS FOR CONTRACTORS	Clubs or Diamonds, each	20	40
	Hearts or Spades, each	30	60
	No Trump {first	40	80
	{each subsequent	30	60

Redoubling doubles the doubled points for Odd Tricks.
Vulnerability does not affect points for Odd Tricks.
100 Trick Points constitute a game.

		Not Vulnerable	Vulnerable
PREMIUM POINTS FOR CONTRACTORS	*Overtricks*		
	Undoubled, each	Trick Value	Trick Value
	Doubled, each	100	200
	Making Doubled or Redoubled Contract	50	50
DEFENDERS	*Undertricks*		
	Undoubled, each	50	100
	Doubled {first	100	200
	{each subsequent	200	300

Redoubling doubles the doubled points for Overtricks and Undertricks,
but does not affect the points for making Doubled Contracts.

PREMIUM POINTS FOR CONTRACTORS/HOLDERS	*Honors in One Hand* {	4 Trump Honors	100
		5 Trump Honors or 4 Aces at No-Trump	150
	Slams Bid and Won {	Small, not vulnerable 500,　vulnerable	750
		Grand, "　　"　1000,　　"	1500
	Rubber Points {	Two game	700
		Three game	500

Unfinished Rubber—Winners of one game score 300 points. If but one
side has a part score in an unfinished game, it scores 50 points.
Doubling and Redoubling do not affect Honor, Slam, or Rubber points.
Vulnerability does not affect points for Honors.

Proprieties

I.   *General principles*

Communication between partners during the auction and play periods should be effected only by means of the calls and plays themselves, not the manner in which they are made. Calls should be made in a uniform tone without special emphasis or inflection, and without undue haste or hesitation. Plays should be made without emphasis, gesture or mannerism, and so far as possible at a uniform rate.

Intentional infringement of a law is a serious breach of ethics, even if there is a prescribed penalty which one is prepared to pay. The offense may be the more serious when no penalty is prescribed.*

A player should carefully avoid taking any advantage which might accrue from an impropriety committed by his side. While one should not allow partner's hesitation, remark or mannerism to influence one's call, lead or play, it is not improper to draw inferences from an opponent's gratuitous hesitation, remark or mannerism, but such inferences are drawn at one's own risk.

There is no obligation to draw attention to an inadvertent infringement of law by one's own side; however, a player should not attempt to conceal such an infringement, as by committing a second revoke, concealing a card involved in a revoke, or mixing the cards prematurely.

It is proper to warn partner against infringing a law of the game, for example, against revoking, or against calling, leading or playing out of turn.

II.   *Violations of ethical conduct*

The following acts should be carefully avoided and are considered breaches of ethics when committed intentionally. (a) A remark, question, gesture or mannerism which might convey information to partner or might mislead an opponent. (b) A call made with special emphasis, inflection, haste or undue hesitation. (c) A play made with emphasis, undue haste, or unreasonable delay, when the act might convey information to partner or might mislead an opponent. (d) Any indication of approval or disapproval of partner's call, or of satisfaction with an opponent's call. (e) Indication of expectation or intention of winning or losing a trick before the trick has been completed. (f) Mixing the cards before the result of the deal has been agreed upon. (g) A comment or act during the auction or play period, calling attention to an incident thereof, the state of the score, or the number of tricks already taken or still required.

---

* See the Scope of the Laws.

III. *Observance of proper etiquette*

A player should maintain at all times a courteous attitude toward his partner and opponents. He should carefully avoid any remark or action which might cause annoyance or embarrassment to another player or interfere with the enjoyment of the game.

Every player should follow uniformly correct procedure in calling and playing, since any departure from correct standards may interfere with the orderly progress of the game.

A player should refrain from: (a) The use of different designations for the same call. (b) Frequent review of the auction or play due to his own inattention. (c) Volunteering information that should be given only in response to a question. (d) Looking intently at any other player during the auction or play periods, or at another player's hand as for the purpose of observing the place from which he draws a card. (e) Making gratuitous comments during the play period as to the auction or the adequacy of the contract. (f) Exchanging hands with his partner, or letting his partner see his hand, whether or not a penalty may be incurred. (g) Detaching a card from his hand before it is his turn to lead or play. (h) Disorderly arrangement of completed tricks, which may make it difficult to determine the sequence of plays. (i) Making a claim or concession of tricks if there is any doubt as to the outcome of the deal.

IV. *Use of conventions*

It is improper to use, in calling or playing, any convention the meaning of which may not be understood by the opponents. Conventional calls or plays should be explained to the opponents before any player has looked at his cards. Advance notice may be given of the intention to use certain conventions of which full explanation may be deferred until the occasion arises. The explanation may be given only by the player whose partner made the conventional call or play. At any time this player must reply to an inquiry by an opponent as to the significance of a call or play that may be conventional, and should supply any information that may have been withheld.

Any sponsoring organization, club or tournament committee, or group of persons playing Contract Bridge, may restrict the use of conventions in games under its jurisdiction.

V. *Spectators*

A spectator, or a member of a table who is not playing, should refrain from gratuitous remarks or mannerisms of any kind. He should not call attention to any irregularity or mistake, or speak on any question of fact or law except by request of a member of each side.

WRITING a postscript to one's own book would seem a relatively simple and, to my mind, almost superfluous procedure. Yet, when all is said and done, it usually isn't.

This is to some extent a learner's book, though it might serve well as a refresher course for advanced players. For this reason, I have added not only the latest and current conventions, but also an entirely new set of quiz tests, my favorite method of teaching, to test you in all phases of bidding and playing the hand. Let's hope that the book fulfilled your expectations and justified the effort I put into this new, my latest, offering.

I am grateful to my many amateur bridge-playing friends who have unwittingly served as guinea pigs to test the book's theories. One of them said: "It's so direct and clear, there must be more to it."

Chas H Goren